PLAYFAIR
CRICKET ANNUAL 2015
68th edition
EDITED BY IAN MARSHALL
All statistics by the Editor unless otherwise stated

FOREWORD

The last twelve months or so will not be a period that England cricket fans will look back on with any great fondness. The aftermath of England's Ashes collapse in 2013-14 – and the removal of Kevin Pietersen from the side – still continues to reverberate. The story lingers on, the flames fanned by his many supporters, an autobiography that can have won him few new supporters, and now newspaper reports this weekend that he is going to try to return to the England fold, possibly sacrificing his (reduced) IPL contract for the chance to have another crack at the Australians. However, Pietersen will be 35 this summer, and has not played a first-class innings since January 2014. To think that he is the solution to any problems England might have at Test level, or indeed that he is what England need as they rebuild for the 2019 World Cup, seems doubtful, to put it mildly.

In Ballance, Bell, Root and Ali, England have the makings of an excellent top order, but for this summer's Ashes series they will need a strong opening pair in front of them. Alastair Cook may have been disappointed to lose his role as England's 50-over captain – a decision that was taken either too late or too early – but one hopes that a fresh mind and body will help him return to top form against Australia. No one has yet tied down the role as his opening partner since the retirement of Andrew Strauss. The Australian attack looks menacing, and has far more pace than England's, but we hope that England's bowlers will be able to utilise home conditions to maximum advantage.

Before the Ashes, however, England fly out to the Caribbean for three Tests and will then welcome New Zealand for two Tests. The latter appear to be one of the most-improved sides in world cricket, and England will have their work cut out to beat them if they perform at anything below their best.

England's cricket fans will be hoping for a better experience this summer than during the World Cup, when the side appeared formulaic and constrained by comparison with many other nations. Before any individuals are singled out for blame, it should be noted that England's track record in the World Cup since 1992 has been very poor. The problems are not new. The tournament (which has just reached the knockout stage at the time of writing) has been enlivened by the performance of the minnows, and it has been a joy to watch Ireland and Afghanistan in particular. The ICC, unlike every other world sports governing body, in its wisdom believes that the best way to advance the cause of the sport is to *reduce* the number of participants at the next World Cup. This decision has to be wrong, and I hope sense will prevail. A sixteen-team event, with four groups of four, will reduce the time taken before we get to the knockout stage, and give more countries an opportunity to show what they can do.

Cricket politics and activity on the field took a back seat in the most tragic of circumstances during the year, when Phillip Hughes was struck by a ball during a match in November and died from the resulting injuries. The moving way in which the game came together to recognise one of its own, and the powerful eulogy given by Australia's captain Michael Clarke, spoke volumes for why we love cricket so much.

This year's cover star is Joe Root, an honour he fully deserves, having been one of the brightest lights for England during the last year, as well as playing a small part in Yorkshire's triumph in the LV= County Championship. At the age of twenty-four, he is already being spoken of as a future England captain. If he can emulate the last Yorkshireman to hold the post, Michael Vaughan, he will do very well when his time does eventually arrive.

For those who want to keep up with all things *Playfair*-related, do please follow me on Twitter @IanPlayfair, where I will note as many individual and team landmarks as possible, while the website www.playfaircricket.co.uk will provide weekly reports during the summer, plus occasional updates to the register, so that you can have the latest information on any newcomers to the county scene.

Ian Marshall
Eastbourne, 15 March 2015

@IanPlayfair

ACKNOWLEDGEMENTS AND THANKS

As ever, this book could not have been compiled without the help of many people giving freely of their time and expertise, so I must thank the following for all they have done to help ensure this edition of *Playfair Cricket Annual* could be written:

At the counties, I would like to thank the following for their help over the last year: Derbyshire – Neil Bates and John Brown; Durham – Brian Hunt; Essex – Ashley Neave and Tony Choat; Glamorgan – Andrew Hignell; Gloucestershire – Lizzie Allen and Adrian Bull; Hampshire – Tim Tremlett and Kevin Baker; Kent – Thomas Brown and Lorne Hart; Lancashire – Diana Lloyd and Darrin White; Leicestershire – Jen Wilks and Paul Rogers; Middlesex – Rebecca Hart and Don Shelley; Northamptonshire – Tony Kingston; Nottinghamshire – Helen Palmer and Roger Marshall; Somerset – Spencer Bishop and Gerald Stickley; Surrey – Steve Howes and Keith Booth; Sussex – Colin Bowley and Mike Charman; Warwickshire – Keith Cook and Mel Smith; Worcestershire – Rhiannon Malbas and Dawn Pugh; Yorkshire – Janet Bairstow and John Potter.

Thanks to Alan Fordham for the Principal and Second XI Fixtures, and Philip August for the Minor Counties. Philip Bailey once again provided the first-class and List A career records, having done so since 1992, and he continues to be a vital help in compiling the book.

At Headline, my thanks once more go to Jonathan Taylor for his calm support and encouragement; Louise Rothwell remained serene as the deadlines approached and ensured the book was printed in no time at all; Sam Habib administers the *Playfair* website with great enthusiasm and passion for the game, so the latest news on new records set is available as soon as possible. John Skermer did his usual superb job on checking the proofs, yet again turning things round in no time at all. At Letterpart, the *Playfair* typesetter since 1994, Chris Leggett, Caroline Leggett and the whole team ensured the book was laid out superbly. Their latest offices now overlook a cricket ground, which seems appropriate.

Finally, as ever, I have to thank my daughters, Kiri and Sophia, who have learned that they will always find me in the office as deadline day approaches; they keep on threatening to take up cricket in the summer, so I hope the presence of more women's cricket in the Annual will inspire them. And finally, of course, my biggest thanks go to my wife, Sugra, whose help and support ensures the book happens at all.

GUIDE TO USING PLAYFAIR

The basic layout of *Playfair* has again remained the same for this edition. The Annual is divided into five sections, as follows: Test match cricket, county cricket, international limited-overs cricket (including Twenty20), other cricket (universities, IPL and Champions League and women's international cricket), and fixtures for the coming season. Each section, where applicable begins with a preview of forthcoming events, followed by events during the previous year, then come the player records, and finally the records section.

Within the players' register, I have added two new features to the biographies. After several requests, I have added in the squad numbers (where known at the time of going to press) given by the counties, which I hope will ease identification of players on the field. Given the increasing importance of major T20 competitions – with the IPL and Big Bash both televised in the UK – I have listed where players have appeared in these competitions. Players' Second XI Championship debuts and their England Under-19 Test appearances are given for players under the age of 25.

In the county limited-overs records in the Register, those records denoted by '50ov' cover any limited-overs game of 50 or more overs – in the early days, each team could have as many as 65 overs per innings. The '40ov' section refers to games of 40 or 45 overs per innings.

For the first time in *Playfair*'s history, records are provided for all three formats of the women's game – Test, limited-overs and T20. Also for the first time, I have included an England women's register. All this reflects the growing profile and professionalism of the women's game.

ENGLAND v NEW ZEALAND
SERIES RECORDS
1928 to 2013

HIGHEST INNINGS TOTALS

England	in England	567-8d	Nottingham	1994
	in New Zealand	593-6d	Auckland	1974-75
New Zealand	in England	551-9d	Lord's	1973
	in New Zealand	537	Wellington	1983-84

LOWEST INNINGS TOTALS

England	in England	126	Birmingham	1999
	in New Zealand	64	Wellington	1977-78
New Zealand	in England	47	Lord's	1958
	in New Zealand	26	Auckland	1954-55

HIGHEST MATCH AGGREGATE 1445 for 33 wickets Lord's 2004
LOWEST MATCH AGGREGATE 390 for 30 wickets Lord's 1958

HIGHEST INDIVIDUAL INNINGS

England	in England	310*	J.H.Edrich	Leeds	1965
	in New Zealand	336*	W.R.Hammond	Auckland	1932-33
New Zealand	in England	206	M.P.Donnelly	Lord's	1949
	in New Zealand	222	N.J.Astle	Christchurch	2001-02

HIGHEST AGGREGATE OF RUNS IN A SERIES

England	in England	469	(av 78.16)	L.Hutton	1949
	in New Zealand	563	(av 563.00)	W.R.Hammond	1932-33
New Zealand	in England	462	(av 77.00)	M.P.Donnelly	1949
	in New Zealand	347	(av 69..40)	P.G.Fulton	2012-13

RECORD WICKET PARTNERSHIPS – ENGLAND

1st	231	A.N.Cook (116)/N.R.D.Compton (117)	Dunedin	2012-13
2nd	369	J.H.Edrich (310*)/K.F.Barrington (163)	Leeds	1965
3rd	245	J.Hardstaff jr (114)/W.R.Hammond (140)	Lord's	1937
4th	266	M.H.Denness (181)/K.W.R.Fletcher (216)	Auckland	1974-75
5th	242	W.R.Hammond (227)/L.E.G.Ames (103)	Christchurch	1932-33
6th	281	G.P.Thorpe (200*)/A.Flintoff (137)	Christchurch	2001-02
7th	149	A.P.E.Knott (104)/P.Lever (64)	Auckland	1970-71
8th	246	L.E.G.Ames (137)/G.O.B.Allen (122)	Lord's	1931
9th	163*	M.C.Cowdrey (128*)/A.C.Smith (69*)	Wellington	1962-63
10th	59	A.P.E.Knott (49)/N.Gifford (25*)	Nottingham	1973

RECORD WICKET PARTNERSHIPS – NEW ZEALAND

1st	276	C.S.Dempster (136)/J.E.Mills (117)	Wellington	1929-30
2nd	241	J.G.Wright (116)/A.H.Jones (143)	Wellington	1991-92
3rd	210	B.A.Edgar (83)/M.D.Crowe (106)	Lord's	1986
4th	155	M.D.Crowe (143)/M.J.Greatbatch (68)	Wellington	1987-88
5th	180	M.D.Crowe (142)/S.A.Thomson (69)	Lord's	1994
6th	141	M.D.Crowe (115)/A.C.Parore (71)	Manchester	1994
7th	148	L.R.P.L.Taylor (120)/D.L.Vettori (88)	Hamilton	2007-08
8th	104	D.A.R.Moloney (64)/A.W.Roberts (66*)	Lord's	1937
9th	118	J.V.Coney (174*)/B.L.Cairns (64)	Wellington	1983-84
10th	118	N.J.Astle (222)/C.L.Cairns (23*)	Christchurch	2001-02

BEST INNINGS BOWLING ANALYSIS

England	in England	7- 32	D.L.Underwood	Lord's	1969
	in New Zealand	7- 47	P.C.R.Tufnell	Christchurch	1991-92
		7- 47	R.J.Sidebottom	Napier	2007-08
New Zealand	in England	7- 74	B.L.Cairns	Leeds	1983
	in New Zealand	7-143	B.L.Cairns	Wellington	1983-84

BEST MATCH BOWLING ANALYSIS

England	in England	12-101	D.L.Underwood	The Oval	1969
	in New Zealand	12- 97	D.L.Underwood	Christchurch	1970-71
New Zealand	in England	11-169	D.J.Nash	Lord's	1994
	in New Zealand	10-100	R.J.Hadlee	Wellington	1977-78

HIGHEST AGGREGATE OF WICKETS IN A SERIES

England	in England	34	(av 7.47)	G.A.R.Lock	1958
	in New Zealand	24	(av 17.08)	R.J.Sidebottom	2007-08
New Zealand	in England	21	(av 26.61)	R.J.Hadlee	1983
	in New Zealand	15	(av 19.53)	R.O.Collinge	1977-78
		15	(av 24.73)	R.J.Hadlee	1977-78

RESULTS SUMMARY: ENGLAND v NEW ZEALAND – IN ENGLAND

	Tests	Series E	Series NZ	Series D	Lord's E	Lord's NZ	Lord's D	The Oval E	The Oval NZ	The Oval D	Manchester E	Manchester NZ	Manchester D	Leeds E	Leeds NZ	Leeds D	Birmingham E	Birmingham NZ	Birmingham D	Nottingham E	Nottingham NZ	Nottingham D
1931	3	1	–	2	–	–	1	1	–	–	–	–	1	–	–	–	–	–	–	–	–	–
1937	3	1	–	2	–	–	1	–	–	1	–	–	1	–	–	–	–	–	–	–	–	–
1949	4	–	–	4	–	–	1	–	–	1	–	–	1	–	–	1	–	–	–	–	–	–
1958	5	4	–	1	1	–	–	1	–	–	1	–	1	–	–	–	1	–	–	–	–	–
1965	3	3	–	–	1	–	–	–	–	–	1	–	–	1	–	–	–	–	–	–	–	–
1969	3	2	–	1	1	–	–	1	–	–	–	–	–	–	–	–	–	–	–	–	–	1
1973	3	2	–	1	–	–	1	–	–	–	–	–	–	1	–	–	–	–	1	–	–	–
1978	3	3	–	–	1	–	–	1	–	–	–	–	–	–	–	–	1	–	–	–	–	–
1983	4	3	1	–	1	–	–	1	–	–	–	–	–	–	1	–	–	–	–	1	–	–
1986	3	–	1	2	–	–	1	–	–	1	–	–	–	–	–	–	–	–	–	–	1	–
1990	3	1	–	2	–	–	1	–	–	1	–	–	–	–	–	–	1	–	–	1	–	–
1994	3	1	–	2	–	–	1	–	–	1	–	–	–	–	1	–	–	–	–	1	–	–
1999	4	1	2	1	–	1	–	–	1	–	–	–	–	1	–	–	–	1	–	–	–	–
2004	3	3	–	–	1	–	–	–	–	–	1	–	–	1	–	–	–	–	–	–	–	–
2008	3	2	–	1	1	–	–	1	–	–	–	–	–	1	–	–	–	–	–	–	–	–
2013	2	2	–	–	1	–	–	–	–	–	–	–	–	1	–	–	–	–	–	–	–	–
	52	29	4	19	7	1	8	4	1	4	3	–	4	5	1	1	4	2	–	6	1	2

ENGLAND v NEW ZEALAND – IN NEW ZEALAND

	Tests	Series E	Series NZ	Series D	Christchurch E	Christchurch NZ	Christchurch D	Wellington E	Wellington NZ	Wellington D	Auckland E	Auckland NZ	Auckland D	Dunedin E	Dunedin NZ	Dunedin D	Hamilton E	Hamilton NZ	Hamilton D	Napier E	Napier NZ	Napier D
1929-30	4	1	–	3	1	–	–	–	–	1	–	–	2	–	–	–						
1932-33	2	–	–	2	–	1	–	–	–	1												
1946-47	1	–	–	1	–	–	1															
1950-51	2	1	–	1	–	1	1	1	–	–												
1954-55	2	2	–	–	–	–	1	–	1	–	1	–	–									
1958-59	2	1	–	1	1	–	–	–	–	1												
1962-63	3	3	–	–	1	–	–	1	–	–	1	–	–									
1965-66	3	–	–	3	–	–	1	–	–	1	–	–	1									
1970-71	2	1	–	1	1	–	–	–	–	1												
1974-75	2	1	–	1	1	–	–	–	–	1												
1977-78	3	1	1	1	–	1	–	1	–	–	–	–	1									
1983-84	3	–	1	2	–	1	–	–	1	–	–	–	1									
1987-88	3	–	–	3	–	1	–	–	–	1	–	–	1									
1991-92	3	2	–	1	–	–	1	1	–	–	1	–	–									
1996-97	3	2	–	1	1	–	–	–	–	1	–	1	–									
2001-02	3	1	1	1	1	–	–	–	1	–	–	–	1									
2007-08	3	2	1	–	–	–	–	–	1	–							1	–	–	1	–	–
2012-13	3	–	–	3	–	–	1	–	1	–	–	–	1									
	47	18	4	25	8	1	6	4	1	6	4	1	11	1	–	2	1	–	1	1	–	–
Totals	99	47	8	44																		

5

ENGLAND v AUSTRALIA

SERIES RECORDS

1876-77 to 2013-14

HIGHEST INNINGS TOTALS

England	in England	903-7d	The Oval	1938
	in Australia	644	Sydney	2010-11
Australia	in England	729-6d	Lord's	1930
	in Australia	659-8d	Sydney	1946-47

LOWEST INNINGS TOTALS

England	in England	52	The Oval	1948
	in Australia	45	Sydney	1886-87
Australia	in England	36	Birmingham	1902
	in Australia	42	Sydney	1887-88

HIGHEST MATCH AGGREGATE 1753 for 40 wickets Adelaide 1920-21
LOWEST MATCH AGGREGATE 291 for 40 wickets Lord's 1888

HIGHEST INDIVIDUAL INNINGS

England	in England	364	L.Hutton	The Oval	1938
	in Australia	287	R.E.Foster	Sydney	1903-04
Australia	in England	334	D.G.Bradman	Leeds	1930
	in Australia	307	R.M.Cowper	Melbourne	1965-66

HIGHEST AGGREGATE OF RUNS IN A SERIES

England	in England	732	(av 81.33)	D.I.Gower (6 Tests)	1985
	in Australia	905	(av 113.12)	W.R.Hammond	1928-29
Australia	in England	974	(av 139.14)	D.G.Bradman	1930
	in Australia	810	(av 90.00)	D.G.Bradman	1936-37

RECORD WICKET PARTNERSHIPS – ENGLAND

1st	323	J.B.Hobbs (178)/W.Rhodes (179)	Melbourne	1911-12
2nd	382	L.Hutton (364)/M.Leyland (187)	The Oval	1938
3rd	262	W.R.Hammond (177)/ D.R.Jardine (98)	Adelaide	1928-29
4th	310	P.D.Collingwood (206)/K.P.Pietersen (158)	Adelaide	2006-07
5th	206	E.Paynter (216*)/D.C.S.Compton (102)	Nottingham	1938
6th	215	L.Hutton (364)/J.Hardstaff jr (169*)	The Oval	1938
	215	G.Boycott (107)/A.P.E.Knott (135)	Nottingham	1977
7th	143	F.E.Woolley (133*)/J.Vine (36)	Sydney	1911-12
8th	124	E.H.Hendren (169)/H.Larwood (70)	Brisbane	1928-29
9th	151	W.H.Scotton (90)/W.W.Read (117)	The Oval	1884
10th	130	R.E.Foster (287)/W.Rhodes (40*)	Sydney	1903-04

RECORD WICKET PARTNERSHIPS – AUSTRALIA

1st	329	G.R.Marsh (138)/M.A.Taylor (219)	Nottingham	1989
2nd	451	W.H.Ponsford (266)/D.G.Bradman (244)	The Oval	1934
3rd	276	D.G.Bradman (187)/A.L.Hassett (128)	Brisbane	1946-47
4th	388	W.H.Ponsford (181)/D.G.Bradman (304)	Leeds	1934
5th	405	S.G.Barnes (234)/D.G.Bradman (234)	Sydney	1946-47
6th	346	J.H.W.Fingleton (136)/D.G.Bradman (270)	Melbourne	1936-37
7th	165	C.Hill (188)/H.Trumble (46)	Melbourne	1897-98
8th	243	R.J.Hartigan (116)/C.Hill (160)	Adelaide	1907-08
9th	154	S.E.Gregory (201)/J.M.Blackham (74)	Sydney	1894-95
10th	163	P.J.Hughes (81*)/A.C.Agar (98)	Nottingham	2013

BEST INNINGS BOWLING ANALYSIS

England	in England	10- 53	J.C.Laker	Manchester	1956
	in Australia	8- 35	G.A.Lohmann	Sydney	1886-87
Australia	in England	8- 31	F.Laver	Manchester	1909
	in Australia	9-121	A.A.Mailey	Melbourne	1920-21

BEST MATCH BOWLING ANALYSIS

England	in England	19- 90	J.C.Laker	Manchester	1956
	in Australia	15-124	W.Rhodes	Melbourne	1903-04
Australia	in England	16-137	R.A.L.Massie	Lord's	1972
	in Australia	13- 77	M.A.Noble	Melbourne	1901-02

HIGHEST AGGREGATE OF WICKETS IN A SERIES

England	in England	46	(av 9.60)	J.C.Laker	1956
	in Australia	38	(av 23.18)	M.W.Tate	1924-25
Australia	in England	42	(av 21.26)	T.M.Alderman (6 Tests)	1981
	in Australia	41	(av 12.85)	R.M.Hogg (6 Tests)	1978-79

RESULTS SUMMARY
ENGLAND v AUSTRALIA – IN ENGLAND

		Series			The Oval			Manchester			Lord's			Nottingham			Leeds			Birmingham			Sheffield			Cardiff		
Tests		E	A	D	E	A	D	E	A	D	E	A	D	E	A	D	E	A	D	E	A	D	E	A	D	E	A	D
1880	1	1	–	–	1																							
1882	1	–	1	–		1																						
1884	3	1	–	2			1			1	1																	
1886	3	3	–	–	1			1			1																	
1888	3	2	1	–	1			1				1																
1890	2	2	–	–	1						1																	
1893	3	1	–	2	1					1			1															
1896	3	2	1	–	1				1		1																	
1899	5	–	1	4			1			1		1				1			1									
1902	5	1	2	2	1				1				1									1		1				
1905	5	2	–	3			1	1					1	1					1									
1909	5	1	2	2			1			1		1						1		1								
1912	3	1	–	2	1					1			1															
1921	5	–	3	2			1			1		1			1			1										
1926	5	1	–	4	1					1			1			1			1									
1930	5	1	2	2		1				1		1		1					1									
1934	5	1	2	2		1				1	1				1				1									
1938	4	1	1	2	1								1			1		1										
1948	5	–	4	1		1				1		1			1			1										
1953	5	1	–	4	1					1			1			1			1									
1956	5	2	1	2			1	1				1				1	1											
1961	5	1	2	2			1		1			1					1					1						
1964	5	–	1	4			1			1			1			1		1										
1968	5	1	1	3	1				1				1						1			1						
1972	5	2	2	1		1		1				1				1	1											
1975	4	–	1	3			1						1						1		1							
1977	5	3	–	2			1	1					1	1			1											
1980	1	–	–	1									1															
1981	6	3	1	2			1	1					1		1		1			1								
1985	6	3	1	2	1					1		1				1	1			1								
1989	6	–	4	2			1		1			1			1			1				1						
1993	6	1	4	1	1				1			1				1		1			1							
1997	6	2	3	1	1				1				1		1			1		1								
2001	5	1	4	–		1						1			1		1				1							
2005	5	2	1	2			1			1		1		1						1								
2009	5	2	1	2	1						1							1				1						1
2013	5	3	–	2			1			1	1			1									1					
	161	48	47	66	16	6	14	7	7	15	7	14	14	5	7	9	7	9	8	5	3	5	1	1	–	–	–	1

(Sheffield column also used for Chester-le-St.)

ENGLAND v AUSTRALIA – IN AUSTRALIA

	Tests	Series			Melbourne			Sydney			Adelaide			Brisbane			Perth		
		E	A	D	E	A	D	E	A	D	E	A	D	E	A	D	E	A	D
1876-77	2	1	1	–	1	1	–												
1878-79	1	–	1	–	–	1	–												
1881-82	4	–	2	2	–	–	2	–	2	–									
1882-83	4	2	2	–	1	1	–	1	1	–									
1884-85	5	3	2	–	2	–	–	–	2	–	1	–	–						
1886-87	2	2	–	–				2	–	–									
1887-88	1	1	–	–				1	–	–									
1891-92	3	1	2	–	–	1	–	–	1	–	1	–	–						
1894-95	5	3	2	–	2	–	–	1	1	–	–	1	–						
1897-98	5	1	4	–	–	2	–	1	1	–	–	1	–						
1901-02	5	1	4	–	–	2	–	1	1	–	–	1	–						
1903-04	5	3	2	–	1	1	–	2	–	–	–	1	–						
1907-08	5	1	4	–	1	1	–	–	2	–	–	1	–						
1911-12	5	4	1	–	2	–	–	1	1	–	1	–	–						
1920-21	5	–	5	–	–	2	–	–	2	–	–	1	–						
1924-25	5	1	4	–	1	1	–	–	2	–	–	1	–						
1928-29	5	4	1	–	1	1	–	1	–	–	1	–	–	1	–	–			
1932-33	5	4	1	–	–	1	–	2	–	–	1	–	–	1	–	–			
1936-37	5	2	3	–	–	2	–	1	–	–	–	1	–	1	–	–			
1946-47	5	–	3	2	–	–	1	–	2	–	–	–	1	–	1	–			
1950-51	5	1	4	–	1	1	–	–	1	–	–	1	–	–	1	–			
1954-55	5	3	1	1	1	–	–	1	–	1	1	–	–	–	1	–			
1958-59	5	–	4	1	–	2	–	–	–	1	–	1	–	–	1	–			
1962-63	5	1	1	3	1	–	–	–	1	1	–	–	1	–	–	1			
1965-66	5	1	1	3	–	–	2	1	–	–	–	1	–	–	–	1			
1970-71	6	2	–	4	–	–	1	2	–	–	–	–	1	–	–	1	–	–	1
1974-75	6	1	4	1	1	–	1	–	1	–	–	1	–	–	1	–	–	1	–
1976-77	1	–	1	–	–	1	–												
1978-79	6	5	1	–	–	1	–	2	–	–	1	–	–	1	–	–	1	–	–
1979-80	3	–	3	–	–	1	–	–	1	–							–	1	–
1982-83	5	1	2	2	1	–	–	–	–	1	–	1	–	–	1	–	–	–	1
1986-87	5	2	1	2	1	–	–	–	1	–	–	–	1	1	–	–	–	–	1
1987-88	1	–	–	1				–	–	1									
1990-91	5	–	3	2	–	1	–	–	–	1	–	–	1	–	1	–	–	1	–
1994-95	5	1	3	1	–	1	–	–	–	1	1	–	–	–	1	–	–	1	–
1998-99	5	1	3	1	1	–	–	–	1	–	–	1	–	–	–	1	–	1	–
2002-03	5	1	4	–	–	1	–	1	–	–	–	1	–	–	1	–	–	1	–
2006-07	5	–	5	–	–	1	–	–	1	–	–	1	–	–	1	–	–	1	–
2010-11	5	3	1	1	1	–	–	1	–	–	1	–	–	–	–	1	–	1	–
2013-14	5	–	5	–	–	1	–	–	1	–	–	1	–	–	1	–	–	1	–
	175	57	91	27	20	28	7	22	26	7	9	17	5	5	11	5	1	9	3
Totals	336	105	138	93															

Matches abandoned without a ball bowled (Manchester 1890 and 1938, Melbourne 1970-71) are excluded from these tables.

2000 RUNS

	Tests	I	NO	HS	Runs	Avge	100	50
D.G.Bradman (A)	37	63	7	334	5028	89.78	19	12
J.B.Hobbs (E)	41	71	4	187	3636	54.26	12	15
A.R.Border (A)	47	82	19	200*	3548	56.31	8	21
D.I.Gower (E)	42	77	4	215	3269	44.78	9	12
S.R.Waugh (A)	46	73	18	177*	3200	58.18	10	14
G.Boycott (E)	38	71	9	191	2945	47.50	7	14
W.R.Hammond (E)	33	58	3	251	2852	51.85	9	7
H.Sutcliffe (E)	27	46	5	194	2741	66.85	8	16
C.Hill (A)	41	76	1	188	2660	35.46	4	16
J.H.Edrich (E)	32	57	3	175	2644	48.96	7	13
G.A.Gooch (E)	42	79	0	196	2632	33.31	4	16
G.S.Chappell (A)	35	65	8	144	2619	45.94	9	12
M.A.Taylor (A)	33	61	2	219	2496	42.30	6	15
R.T.Ponting (A)	35	58	2	196	2476	44.21	8	9
M.C.Cowdrey (E)	43	75	4	113	2433	34.26	5	11
L.Hutton (E)	27	49	6	364	2428	56.46	5	14
R.N.Harvey (A)	37	68	5	167	2416	38.34	6	12
V.T.Trumper (A)	40	74	5	185*	2263	32.79	6	9
D.C.Boon (A)	31	57	8	184*	2237	45.65	7	8
W.M.Lawry (A)	29	51	5	166	2233	48.54	7	13
M.E.Waugh (A)	29	51	7	140	2204	50.09	6	11
S.E.Gregory (A)	52	92	7	201	2193	25.80	4	8
W.W.Armstrong (A)	42	71	9	158	2172	35.03	4	6
K.P.Pietersen (E)	27	50	2	227	2158	44.95	4	13
I.M.Chappell (A)	30	56	4	192	2138	41.11	4	16
K.F.Barrington (E)	23	39	6	256	2111	63.96	5	13
M.J.Clarke (A)	30	53	6	187	2109	44.87	7	7
A.R.Morris (A)	24	43	2	206	2080	50.73	8	8

D.G.Bradman holds the unique record of scoring 2000 runs in both countries in this series (2674 runs in England and 2354 in Australia); J.B.Hobbs is the only other batsman to score 2000 runs in either country (2493 runs in Australia).

100 WICKETS

	Tests	Balls	Runs	Wkts	Avge	Best	5wI	10wM
S.K.Warne (A)	36	10757	4535	195	23.25	8- 71	11	4
D.K.Lillee (A)	29	8516	3507	167	21.00	7- 89	11	4
G.D.McGrath (A)	30	7280	3286	157	20.92	8- 38	10	–
I.T.Botham (E)	36	8479	4093	148	27.65	6- 78	9	2
H.Trumble (A)	31	7895	2945	141	20.88	8- 65	9	3
R.G.D.Willis (E)	35	7294	3346	128	26.14	8- 43	7	–
M.A.Noble (A)	39	6845	2860	115	24.86	7- 17	9	2
R.R.Lindwall (A)	29	6728	2559	114	22.44	7- 63	6	–
W.Rhodes (E)	41	5791	2616	109	24.00	8- 68	6	1
S.F.Barnes (E)	20	5749	2288	106	21.58	7- 60	12	1
C.V.Grimmett (A)	22	9224	3439	106	32.44	6- 37	11	2
D.L.Underwood (E)	29	8000	2770	105	26.38	7- 50	4	2
A.V.Bedser (E)	21	7065	2859	104	27.49	7- 44	7	2
G.Giffen (A)	31	6457	2791	103	27.09	7-117	7	1
W.J.O'Reilly (A)	19	7864	2587	102	25.36	7- 54	8	3
R.Peel (E)	20	5216	1715	101	16.98	7- 31	5	1
C.T.B.Turner (A)	17	5195	1670	101	16.53	7- 43	11	2
T.M.Alderman (A)	17	4717	2117	100	21.17	6- 47	11	1
J.R.Thomson (A)	21	4951	2418	100	24.18	6- 46	5	–

100 WICKET-KEEPING DISMISSALS

	Tests	Ct	St	Total
R.W.Marsh (A)	42	141	7	148
I.A.Healy (A)	33	123	12	135
A.P.E.Knott (E)	34	97	8	105

R.W.Marsh (141 catches) and W.A.S.Oldfield (A), (31 stumpings) hold the respective individual records in Anglo-Australian Tests.

9

TOURING TEAMS REGISTER 2015

Neither Australia nor New Zealand had selected their 2015 touring teams at the time of going to press. The following players, who had represented those teams in Test matches since 21 November 2013, were still available for selection:

AUSTRALIA

Full Names	Birthdate	Birthplace	Team	Type	F-C Debut
BAILEY, George John	07.09.82	Launceston	Tasmania	RHB/RM	2004-05
BIRD, Jackson Munro	11.12.86	Sydney	Tasmania	RHB/RFM	2011-12
BURNS, Joseph Anthony	06.09.89	Brisbane	Queensland	RHB/RM	2010-11
CLARKE, Michael John	02.04.81	Liverpool	NSW	RHB/SLA	1999-00
DOOLAN, Alexander James	29.11.85	Launceston	Tasmania	RHB/RMF	2008-09
HADDIN, Bradley James	23.10.77	Cowra	NSW	RHB/WK	1999-00
HARRIS, Ryan James	11.10.79	Sydney	Queensland	RHB/RF	2001-02
HAZLEWOOD, Josh Reginald	08.01.91	Tamworth	NSW	LHB/RFM	2008-09
JOHNSON, Mitchell Guy	02.11.81	Townsville	W Australia	LHB/LF	2001-02
LYON, Nathan Michael	20.11.87	Young	NSW	RHB/OB	2010-11
MARSH, Mitchell Ross	20.10.91	Perth	W Australia	RHB/RM	2009-10
MARSH, Shaun Edward	09.07.83	Narrogin	W Australia	LHB/SLA	2000-01
MAXWELL, Glenn James	14.10.88	Melbourne	Victoria	RHB/OB	2010-11
O'KEEFE, Stephen Norman John	09.12.84	Malaysia	NSW	RHB/SLA	2005-06
PATTINSON, James Lee	03.05.90	Melbourne	Victoria	LHB/RFM	2008-09
ROGERS, Christopher John Llewellyn	31.08.77	Sydney	Victoria	LHB/LBG	1998-99
SIDDLE, Peter Matthew	25.11.84	Traralgon	Victoria	RHB/RFM	2005-06
SMITH, Steven Peter Devereux	02.06.89	Sydney	NSW	RHB/LBG	2007-08
STARC, Mitchell Aaron	30.01.90	Sydney	NSW	LHB/LF	2008-09
WARNER, David Andrew	27.10.86	Paddington	NSW	LHB/LB	2008-09
WATSON, Shane Robert	17.06.81	Ipswich	NSW	RHB/RMF	2000-01

NEW ZEALAND

Full Names	Birthdate	Birthplace	Team	Type	F-C Debut
ANDERSON, Corey James	13.12.90	Christchurch	N Districts	LHB/LMF	2006-07
BOULT, Trent Alexander	22.07.89	Rotorua	N Districts	RHB/LFM	2008-09
BRACEWELL, Douglas Andrew John	28.09.90	Tauranga	C Districts	RHB/RMF	2008-09
CRAIG, Mark Donald	23.03.87	Auckland	Otago	LHB/OB	2010-11
FULTON, Peter Gordon	01.02.79	Christchurch	Canterbury	RHB/RM	2000-01
LATHAM, Thomas William Maxwell	02.04.92	Christchurch	Canterbury	LHB/RM	2010-11
McCULLUM, Brendon Barrie	27.09.81	Dunedin	Otago	RHB/WK	1999-00
NEESHAM, James Douglas Sheahan	17.09.90	Auckland	Otago	LHB/RMF	2009-10
REDMOND, Aaron James	23.09.79	Auckland	Otago	RHB/LB	1999-00
RUTHERFORD, Hamish Duncan	27.04.89	Dunedin	Otago	LHB	2008-09
SODHI, Inderbir Singh	31.10.92	Ludhiana, India	N Districts	RHB/LB	2012-13
SOUTHEE, Timothy Grant	11.12.88	Whangarei	N Districts	RHB/RMF	2006-07
TAYLOR, Luteru Ross Poutoa Lote	08.03.84	Lower Hutt	C Districts	RHB/OB	2002-03
VETTORI, Daniel Luca	27.01.79	Auckland	N Districts	LHB/SLA	1996-97
WAGNER, Neil	13.03.86	Pretoria, SA	Otago	LHB/LMF	2005-06
WATLING, Bradley-John	09.07.85	Durban, SA	N Districts	RHB/WK	2004-05
WILLIAMSON, Kane Stuart	08.08.90	Tauranga	N Districts	RHB/OB	2007-08

STATISTICAL HIGHLIGHTS IN 2014 TESTS

Including Tests from No. 2106 (Australia v England, 5th Test) and No. 2112 (Pakistan v Sri Lanka, 1st Test) to No. 2149 (Australia v India, 3rd Test), No. 2152 (South Africa v West Indies, 2nd Test), and No. 2154 (New Zealand v Sri Lanka, 1st Test).

† = National record

TEAM HIGHLIGHTS

HIGHEST INNINGS TOTALS

730-6d	Sri Lanka v Bangladesh	Mirpur
690	New Zealand v Pakistan	Sharjah
680-8d	New Zealand v India	Wellington

LOWEST INNINGS TOTALS

94	India v England	The Oval

HIGHEST MATCH AGGREGATE

1589-27	Sri Lanka (587 & 305-4d) v Bangladesh (426 & 271-3)	Chittagong

LARGE MARGINS OF VICTORY

Inns and 248 runs	Sri Lanka (730-6d) beat Bangladesh (232 & 250)	Mirpur
Inns and 244 runs	England (486) beat India (148 & 94)	The Oval
Inns and 220 runs	South Africa (552-5d) beat West Indies (201 & 131)	Centurion
356 runs†	Pakistan (570-6d & 293-3d) beat Australia (261 & 246)	Abu Dhabi

SIX FIFTIES IN AN INNINGS

New Zealand (690) v Pakistan	Sharjah
Sri Lanka (730-6d) v Bangladesh	Mirpur

BATTING HIGHLIGHTS

TRIPLE HUNDREDS

B.B.McCullum	302†	New Zealand v India	Wellington
K.C.Sangakkara	319	Sri Lanka v Bangladesh	Chittagong

DOUBLE HUNDREDS

H.M.Amla	208	South Africa v West Indies	Centurion
K.C.Brathwaite	212	West Indies v Bangladesh	Kingstown
D.P.M.D.Jayawardena	203*	Sri Lanka v Bangladesh	Mirpur
B.B.McCullum (2)	224	New Zealand v India	Auckland
	202	New Zealand v Pakistan	Sharjah
J.E.Root	200*	England v Sri Lanka	Lord's
K.C.Sangakkara	221	Sri Lanka v Pakistan	Galle
Younus Khan	213	Pakistan v Australia	Abu Dhabi

HUNDREDS IN THREE CONSECUTIVE INNINGS

Misbah-ul-Haq	101	101*	Pakistan v Australia	Abu Dhabi
		102*	Pakistan v New Zealand	Abu Dhabi
Younus Khan	106	103*	Pakistan v Australia	Dubai
		213	Pakistan v Australia	Abu Dhabi

11

HUNDRED IN EACH INNINGS OF A MATCH

Azhar Ali	109	100*	Pakistan v Australia	Abu Dhabi
V.Kohli	115	141	India v Australia	Adelaide
Misbah-ul-Haq	101	101*	Pakistan v Australia	Abu Dhabi

The first instance since I.M.Chappell and G.S.Chappell (v New Zealand, Wellington, 1973-74) that two batsmen on the same side have scored centuries in each innings of a match.

K.C.Sangakkara	319	105	Sri Lanka v Bangladesh	Chittagong

He became only the second batsman, after G.A.Gooch (v India, Lord's, 1990), to score a triple hundred and a century in a match in all first-class cricket.

D.A.Warner	135	145	Australia v South Africa	Cape Town
D.A.Warner	145	102	Australia v India	Adelaide
Younus Khan	106	103*	Pakistan v Australia	Dubai

FASTEST HUNDRED

Misbah-ul-Haq (101*) 56 balls Pakistan v Australia Abu Dhabi

Equalled I.V.A.Richards' record (v England, St John's, 1985-86) for the fastest Test century.

HUNDRED RUNS SCORED IN A SESSION

B.B.McCullum 0-102* New Zealand v Sri Lanka Christchurch

MOST SIXES IN AN INNINGS

11	B.B.McCullum (202)	New Zealand v Pakistan	Sharjah
11	B.B.McCullum (195)	New Zealand v Sri Lanka	Christchurch

150 RUNS OR MORE IN BOUNDARIES IN AN INNINGS

Runs	6s	4s			
176	8	32	K.C.Sangakkara	Sri Lanka v Bangladesh	Chittagong
152	4	32	B.B.McCullum	New Zealand v India	Wellington
150	11	21	B.B.McCullum	New Zealand v Pakistan	Sharjah

HUNDRED ON TEST DEBUT

J.D.S.Neesham (137*)	New Zealand v India	Wellington
S.van Zyl (101*)	South Africa v West Indies	Centurion

LONG INNINGS (Qualification: 600 mins and/or 400 balls)

Mins	Balls			
554	447	K.C.Brathwaite(212)	West Indies v Bangladesh	Kingstown
775	559	B.B.McCullum(302)	New Zealand v India	Wellington
551	482	K.C.Sangakkara(319)	Sri Lanka v Bangladesh	Chittagong
698	425	K.C.Sangakkara(221)	Sri Lanka v Pakistan	Galle

BATTING FOR AN HOUR OR MORE WITHOUT SCORING

Mins	Balls			
81	55	J.M.Anderson	England v Sri Lanka	Leeds

NOTABLE PARTNERSHIPS

Qualifications: 1st-4th wkts: 250 runs; 5th-6th: 225; 7th: 200; 8th: 175; 9th: 150; 10th: 100.

Second Wicket
297† B.B.McCullum/K.S.Williamson New Zealand v Pakistan Sharjah

Fourth Wicket

| 308† | H.M.Amla/A.B.de Villiers | South Africa v West Indies | Centurion |
| 262 | V.Kohli/A.M.Rahane | India v Australia | Melbourne |

Fifth Wicket

| 233 | S.E.Marsh/S.P.D.Smith | Australia v South Africa | Centurion |

Sixth Wicket

| 352† | B.B.McCullum/B.J.Watling | New Zealand v India | Wellington |

World record Test partnership for this wicket.

Tenth Wicket

| 198† | J.E.Root/J.M.Anderson | England v India | Nottingham |

World record Test partnership for this wicket.

| 111 | B.Kumar/Mohammed Shami | India v England | Nottingham |

BOWLING HIGHLIGHTS
EIGHT WICKETS IN AN INNINGS

| H.M.R.K.B.Herath | 9-127 | Sri Lanka v Pakistan | Colombo (SSC) |
| Taijul Islam | 8- 39† | Bangladesh v Zimbabwe | Mirpur |

TEN WICKETS IN A MATCH

M.D.Craig	10-203	New Zealand v Pakistan	Sharjah
H.M.R.K.B.Herath	14-184	Sri Lanka v Pakistan	Colombo (SSC)
M.G.Johnson	12-127	Australia v South Africa	Centurion
N.M.Lyon	12-286	Australia v India	Adelaide
Shakib Al Hasan	10-124	Bangladesh v Zimbabwe	Khulna

FIVE WICKETS IN AN INNINGS ON DEBUT

| J.R.Hazlewood | 5-68 | Australia v India | Brisbane |

HAT-TRICKS

| S.C.J.Broad | | England v Sri Lanka | Leeds |

60 OVERS IN AN INNINGS

| H.M.R.K.B.Herath | 60-12-148-1 | Sri Lanka v South Africa | Galle |

MOST RUNS CONCEDED IN AN INNINGS

| Yasir Shah | 44.1-4-193-4 | Pakistan v New Zealand | Sharjah |

ALL-ROUND RECORDS
MATCH DOUBLE (CENTURY AND TEN WICKETS IN A MATCH)

Shakib Al Hasan (137, 5-80, 5-44)   Bangladesh v Zimbabwe   Khulna

Shakib became only the third player in Test history, after I.T.Botham (v India, Bombay, 1979-80) and Imran Khan (v India, Faisalabad, 1982-83), to achieve this feat.

WICKET-KEEPING HIGHLIGHTS
SIX WICKET-KEEPING DISMISSALS IN AN INNINGS

| B.J.Haddin | 6ct | Australia v India | Brisbane |
| B.J.Watling | 6ct | New Zealand v India | Auckland |

NINE OR MORE WICKET-KEEPING DISMISSALS IN A MATCH

Q.de Kock	8ct,1st	South Africa v Sri Lanka	Galle
M.S.Dhoni	8ct,1st	India v Australia	Melbourne
B.J.Haddin	9ct	Australia v India	Brisbane
H.A.P.W.Jayawardena	9ct	Sri Lanka v Pakistan	Dubai
B.J.Watling	9ct	New Zealand v India	Auckland

FIELDING HIGHLIGHTS
FIVE CATCHES IN AN INNINGS IN THE FIELD

D.M.Bravo   5ct   West Indies v Bangladesh   Kingstown

SIX CATCHES IN A MATCH IN THE FIELD

D.M.Bravo   6ct   West Indies v Bangladesh   Kingstown

LEADING TEST AGGREGATES IN 2014
1000 RUNS IN 2014

	M	I	NO	HS	Runs	Avge	100	50
K.C.Sangakkara (SL)	12	22	1	319	**1493**	71.09	4	9
A.D.Mathews (SL)	12	21	6	160	**1317**	87.80	3	8
Younus Khan (P)	10	20	3	213	**1213**	71.35	6	2
B.B.McCullum (NZ)	9	16	–	302	**1164**	72.75	4	–
S.P.D.Smith (A)	9	17	3	192	**1146**	81.85	5	4
D.A.Warner (A)	9	18	–	145	**1136**	63.11	6	3
D.P.M.D.Jayawardena (SL)	11	19	1	203*	**1003**	55.72	3	5

RECORD CALENDAR YEAR RUNS AGGREGATE

	M	I	NO	HS	Runs	Avge	100	50
M.Yousuf (P) (2006)	11	19	1	202	**1788**	99.33	9	3

RECORD CALENDAR YEAR RUNS AVERAGE

	M	I	NO	HS	Runs	Avge	100	50
G.St A.Sobers (WI) (1958)	7	12	3	365*	**1193**	132.55	5	3

1000 RUNS IN DEBUT CALENDAR YEAR

	M	I	NO	HS	Runs	Avge	100	50
M.A.Taylor (A) (1989)	11	20	1	219	**1219**	64.15	4	5
A.N.Cook (E) (2006)	13	24	2	127	**1013**	46.04	4	3

50 WICKETS IN 2014

	M	O	R	W	Avge	Best	5wI	10wM
H.M.R.K.B.Herath (SL)	10	610.2	1647	60	27.45	9-127	5	1

RECORD CALENDAR YEAR WICKETS AGGREGATE

	M	O	R	W	Avge	Best	5wI	10wM
M.Muralitharan (SL) (2006)	11	588.4	1521	90	16.90	8-70	9	5
S.K.Warne (A) (2005)	14	691.4	2043	90	22.70	6-46	6	2

MOST WICKET-KEEPING DISMISSALS IN 2014

	M	Dis	Ct	St
B.J.Watling (NZ)	9	40	38	2

RECORD CALENDAR YEAR DISMISSALS AGGREGATE

	M	Dis	Ct	St
I.A.Healy (A) (1993)	16	67	58	9
M.V.Boucher (SA) (1998)	13	67	65	2

MOST CATCHES BY FIELDERS IN 2014

	M	Ct
A.N.Cook (E)	8	15
L.R.P.L.Taylor (NZ)	8	15

RECORD CALENDAR YEAR FIELDER'S AGGREGATE

	M	Ct
G.C.Smith (SA) (2008)	15	30

TEST MATCH SCORES
WEST INDIES v NEW ZEALAND (1st Test)

At Sabina Park, Kingston, Jamaica, on 8, 9, 10, 11 June 2014.
Toss: New Zealand. Result: **NEW ZEALAND** won by 186 runs.
Debut: New Zealand – M.D.Craig.

‡ K.C.Brathwaite

NEW ZEALAND

T.W.M.Latham	c and b Shillingford	83	(2) c Gayle b Roach		73
P.G.Fulton	c Ramdin b Taylor	1	(1) c Ramdin b Taylor		0
K.S.Williamson	b Benn	113	b Roach		2
L.R.P.L.Taylor	c Edwards b Shillingford	55	(5) lbw b Taylor		0
*B.B.McCullum	c Gayle b Benn	7	(6) b Shillingford		17
J.D.S.Neesham	c Ramdin b Benn	107	(7) c sub‡ b Shillingford		20
†B.J.Watling	c Powell b Shillingford	89	(8) not out		22
T.G.Southee	not out	21	(9) c Bravo b Benn		3
I.S.Sodhi			(4) lbw b Taylor		4
M.D.Craig			not out		7
T.A.Boult					
Extras	(B 19, LB 6, W 5, NB 2)	32	(LB 8)		8
Total	(7 wkts dec; 174.3 overs; 667 mins)	**508**	(8 wkts dec; 60.5 overs; 251 mins)		**156**

WEST INDIES

C.H.Gayle	c Watling b Southee	64	c Watling b Southee		10
K.O.A.Powell	lbw b Craig	28	c Latham b Southee		0
K.A.Edwards	c Taylor b Craig	0	c Neesham b Craig		14
D.M.Bravo	c and b Sodhi	0	c Watling b Craig		12
S.Chanderpaul	not out	84	lbw b Sodhi		24
M.N.Samuels	lbw b Southee	0	c Latham b Craig		0
*†D.Ramdin	c Watling b Southee	39	b Sodhi		34
K.A.J.Roach	c Fulton b Craig	4	c Watling b Craig		19
J.E.Taylor	c McCullum b Boult	7	c Watling b Sodhi		18
S.J.Benn	b Craig	17	c Watling b Williamson		25
S.Shillingford	c Watling b Southee	14	not out		53
Extras	(LB 2, W 1, NB 2)	5	(B 4, LB 2, W 1)		7
Total	(81.2 overs; 350 mins)	**262**	(47.4 overs; 206 mins)		**216**

WEST INDIES	O	M	R	W		O	M	R	W		FALL OF WICKETS			
Taylor	26	11	37	1		12	4	28	3			NZ	WI	NZ	WI
Roach	29	6	85	0		12	6	12	2		Wkt	1st	1st	2nd	2nd
Bravo	1	0	2	0							1st	9	60	0	8
Benn	52	14	142	3	(3)	17.5	3	47	1		2nd	174	60	7	11
Samuels	15	1	55	0		6	1	22	0		3rd	259	61	14	30
Shillingford	46.3	7	145	3	(4)	13	0	39	2		4th	277	104	14	54
Gayle	5	0	17	0							5th	279	104	55	54
											6th	480	176	118	76
NEW ZEALAND											7th	508	185	143	115
Boult	19	3	67	1		10	3	29	0		8th	–	194	146	121
Southee	16.2	9	19	4		9	2	32	2		9th	–	223	–	134
Craig	24	3	91	4		15	2	97	4		10th	–	262	–	216
Neesham	6	1	14	0		2	0	9	0						
Sodhi	16	1	69	1		11	1	42	3						
Williamson						0.4	0	1	1						

Umpires: R.K.Illingworth (*England*) (8) and R.J.Tucker (*Australia*) (30).
Referee: B.C.Broad (*England*) (61).   Test No. 2122/43 (WI495/NZ392)

WEST INDIES v NEW ZEALAND (2nd Test)

At Queen's Park Oval, Port of Spain, Trinidad, on 16, 17, 18, 19, 20 June 2014.
Toss: New Zealand. Result: **WEST INDIES** won by ten wickets.
Debut: West Indies – J.Blackwood.

NEW ZEALAND

T.W.M.Latham	c Benn b Roach	82	c Brathwaite b Benn		36
H.D.Rutherford	c Gayle b Taylor	3	(7) lbw b Taylor		13
K.S.Williamson	c sub (J.O.Holder) b Gabriel	42	c Ramdin b Roach		52
L.R.P.L.Taylor	not out	45	c Ramdin b Gabriel		36
*B.B.McCullum	lbw b Benn	4	(2) lbw b Taylor		3
J.D.S.Neesham	c Gayle b Taylor	15	(5) c and b Benn		7
†B.J.Watling	c Ramdin b Taylor	0	(6) not out		66
I.S.Sodhi	c Gayle b Taylor	0	c Ramdin b Roach		14
T.G.Southee	lbw b Benn	10	c Edwards b Roach		15
M.D.Craig	c Bravo b Gabriel	4	c Ramdin b Roach		67
T.A.Boult	lbw b Benn	1	c Ramdin b Gabriel		8
Extras	(B 4, LB 6, W 2, NB 3)	15	(B 9, LB 2, W 1, NB 2)		14
Total	**(74.4 overs; 349 mins)**	**221**	**(152.2 overs; 654 mins)**		**331**

WEST INDIES

C.H.Gayle	b Boult	1	not out	80
K.C.Brathwaite	c and b Boult	129	not out	14
S.J.Benn	b Southee	4		
K.A.Edwards	c Watling b Sodhi	55		
D.M.Bravo	c Craig b Williamson	109		
S.Chanderpaul	lbw b Sodhi	47		
K.A.J.Roach	c Neesham b Boult	6		
J.Blackwood	c Taylor b Sodhi	63		
*†D.Ramdin	c Taylor b Neesham	32		
J.E.Taylor	c Craig b Sodhi	4		
S.T.Gabriel	not out	0		
Extras	(LB 6, W 3, NB 1)	10	(LB 1)	1
Total	**(137.1 overs; 592 mins)**	**460**	**(0 wkts; 13.2 overs; 52 mins)**	**95**

WEST INDIES	O	M	R	W		O	M	R	W
Taylor	17	5	34	4		30	9	73	2
Roach	17	1	61	1		28	6	74	4
Gabriel	12	2	43	2		23.2	3	66	2
Benn	28.4	6	73	3		58	20	78	2
Gayle						13	3	29	0

NEW ZEALAND	O	M	R	W		O	M	R	W
Boult	30	6	75	3	(2)	3	0	27	0
Southee	30	9	69	1	(1)	4	1	21	0
Craig	29	4	111	0	(4)	3	0	17	0
Neesham	15	1	68	1					
Sodhi	19.1	2	96	4	(3)	2	0	21	0
Williamson	14	2	35	1	(5)	1.2	0	8	0

FALL OF WICKETS

	NZ	WI	NZ	WI
Wkt	1st	1st	2nd	2nd
1st	16	4	9	–
2nd	120	16	84	–
3rd	146	109	108	–
4th	161	291	121	–
5th	192	310	153	–
6th	198	333	176	–
7th	199	380	193	–
8th	210	456	212	–
9th	215	460	311	–
10th	221	460	331	–

Umpires: I.J.Gould (*England*) (38) and R.J.Tucker (*Australia*) (31).
Referee: B.C.Broad (*England*) (62).   **Test No. 2123/44 (WI496/NZ393)**

R.K.Illingworth (*England*) replaced R.J.Tucker as umpire after first drinks break on fourth day.

16

WEST INDIES v NEW ZEALAND (3rd Test)

At Kensington Oval, Bridgetown, Barbados, on 26, 27, 28, 29, 30 June 2014.
Toss: New Zealand. Result: **NEW ZEALAND** won by 53 runs.
Debut: West Indies – J.O.Holder.

NEW ZEALAND

T.W.M.Latham	lbw b Roach	14	c Shillingford b Roach		0
H.D.Rutherford	c Chanderpaul b Roach	4	c Ramdin b Roach		19
K.S.Williamson	c Bravo b Benn	43	not out		161
L.R.P.L.Taylor	c Benn b Roach	45	c Bravo b Holder		6
*B.B.McCullum	c Bravo b Benn	31	lbw b Roach		25
J.D.S.Neesham	run out	78	c Brathwaite b Holder		51
†B.J.Watling	c Gayle b Benn	1	c Holder b Roach		29
T.G.Southee	b Benn	6	c and b Taylor		7
M.D.Craig	not out	46	not out		4
N.Wagner	c Ramdin b Roach	2			
T.A.Boult	st Ramdin b Benn	12			
Extras	(B 5, LB 2, W 1, NB 3)	11	(B 20, LB 1, W 7, NB 1)		29
Total	(78.2 overs; 334 mins)	293	(7 wkts dec; 89.1 overs)		331

WEST INDIES

C.H.Gayle	c Rutherford b Craig	42	b Southee		11
K.C.Brathwaite	c Southee b Wagner	68	b Boult		6
K.A.Edwards	c Rutherford b Southee	58	c Taylor b Boult		10
D.M.Bravo	c Williamson b Wagner	24	(5) c Williamson b Southee		40
S.Chanderpaul	c Watling b Wagner	15	(4) st Watling b Craig		25
*†D.Ramdin	lbw b Boult	45	c Taylor b Southee		29
J.O.Holder	c Watling b Neesham	38	b Craig		52
K.A.J.Roach	c Watling b Boult	0	c Latham b Craig		7
S.Shillingford	not out	10	not out		30
S.J.Benn	b Wagner	1	c Southee b Wagner		10
J.E.Taylor	b Neesham	1	lbw b Boult		12
Extras	(B 2, LB 4, W 7, NB 2)	15	(B 4, LB 15, W 1, NB 2)		22
Total	(97.1 overs)	317	(82.2 overs)		254

WEST INDIES	O	M	R	W	O	M	R	W		FALL OF WICKETS			
										NZ	WI	NZ	WI
Taylor	11	2	55	0	16	4	54	1	Wkt	1st	1st	2nd	2nd
Roach	18	2	61	4	19.1	4	55	4	1st	17	79	1	7
Holder	10	4	24	0	(4) 10	2	26	2	2nd	28	153	56	23
Benn	26.2	1	93	5	(3) 26	1	94	0	3rd	102	197	68	31
Shillingford	13	0	53	0	18	2	81	0	4th	114	205	135	81
									5th	168	240	226	122
NEW ZEALAND									6th	172	277	305	129
Boult	23	5	71	2	16.2	1	48	3	7th	194	277	327	144
Southee	21	8	63	1	16	4	28	3	8th	258	313	–	221
Craig	18	2	90	1	28	7	84	3	9th	277	316	–	232
Wagner	27	7	64	4	16	3	50	1	10th	293	317	–	254
Williamson	2	0	11	0	(6) 3	0	16	0					
Neesham	6.1	1	12	2	(5) 3	1	9	0					

Umpires: I.J.Gould (*England*) (39) and R.K.Illingworth (*England*) (9).
Referee: J.Srinath (*India*) (33).   Test No. 2124/45 (WI497/NZ394)

ENGLAND v SRI LANKA (1st Test)

At Lord's, London, on 12, 13, 14, 15, 16 June 2014.
Toss: Sri Lanka. Result: **MATCH DRAWN**.
Debuts: England – M.M.Ali, C.J.Jordan, S.D.Robson.

ENGLAND

*A.N.Cook	b Kulasekara	17	(2) c H.A.P.W.Jayawardena b Eranga		28
S.D.Robson	c H.A.P.W.Jayawardena b Fernando	1	(1) b Eranga		19
G.S.Ballance	c H.A.P.W.Jayawardena b Fernando	23	not out		104
I.R.Bell	lbw b Eranga	56	b Eranga		9
J.E.Root	not out	200	lbw b Herath		15
M.M.Ali	c D.P.M.D.Jayawardena b Herath	48	b Herath		4
†M.J.Prior	c Silva b Eranga	86	c Thirimanne b Kulasekara		16
C.J.Jordan	c H.A.P.W.Jayawardena b Eranga	19	c Sangakkara b Herath		35
S.C.J.Broad	c Karunaratne b Fernando	47	c and b Herath		24
L.E.Plunkett	c Silva b Fernando	39	not out		2
J.M.Anderson	not out	9			
Extras	(B 12, LB 12, NB 6)	30	(B 3, LB 4, W 2, NB 2)		11
Total	**(9 wkts dec; 130.3 overs; 593 mins)**	**575**	**(8 wkts dec; 69 overs; 309 mins)**		**267**

SRI LANKA

F.D.M.Karunaratne	c Prior b Jordan	38	c Robson b Broad	16
J.K.Silva	c Prior b Anderson	63	c Prior b Jordan	57
K.C.Sangakkara	c Prior b Ali	147	b Anderson	61
D.P.M.D.Jayawardena	lbw b Broad	55	c Prior b Anderson	18
H.D.R.L.Thirimanne	c Robson b Anderson	2	c Jordan b Anderson	2
*A.D.Mathews	lbw b Plunkett	102	c Cook b Anderson	18
†H.A.P.W.Jayawardena	c Bell b Plunkett	6	lbw b Jordan	8
K.M.D.N.Kulasekara	c Prior b Jordan	9	lbw b Broad	1
H.M.R.K.B.Herath	b Anderson	2	c Prior b Broad	1
R.M.S.Eranga	not out	5	not out	0
A.N.P.R.Fernando	hit wkt b Jordan	4	not out	0
Extras	(B 7, LB 5, W 6, NB 2)	20	(B 11, LB 7, NB 1)	19
Total	**(138.4 overs; 631 mins)**	**453**	**(9 wkts; 90 overs; 405 mins)**	**201**

SRI LANKA	O	M	R	W		O	M	R	W		FALL OF WICKETS				
Kulasekara	22	3	83	1		15	2	65	1			E	SL	E	SL
Fernando	29	2	123	4		13	3	37	0		Wkt	1st	1st	2nd	2nd
Eranga	30	3	163	3		18	7	63	3		1st	14	54	46	25
Mathews	11	2	39	0							2nd	22	151	51	123
Herath	37.3	2	136	1	(4)	23	2	95	4		3rd	74	277	69	159
Thirimanne	1	0	7	0							4th	120	289	98	169
											5th	209	385	102	170
ENGLAND											6th	380	400	121	194
Anderson	31	7	93	3		19	10	25	4		7th	402	413	199	199
Broad	29	8	67	1		21	9	43	3		8th	466	430	256	201
Jordan	27.4	4	102	3		18	10	34	2		9th	547	442	–	201
Plunkett	32	2	116	2		16	5	39	0		10th	–	453	–	–
Ali	16	2	56	1		12	2	35	0						
Root	3	1	7	0		4	3	4	0						

Umpires: B.F.Bowden (*New Zealand*) (77) and P.R.Reiffel (*Australia*) (10).
Referee: A.J.Pycroft (*Zimbabwe*) (27).
Test No. 2125/27 (**E946/SL228**)

ENGLAND v SRI LANKA (2nd Test)

At Headingley, Leeds, on 20, 21, 22, 23, 24 June 2014.
Toss: England. Result: **SRI LANKA** won by 100 runs.
Debuts: None.

SRI LANKA

F.D.M.Karunaratne	b Plunkett	28	c Prior b Plunkett		45
J.K.Silva	c Prior b Anderson	13	c Prior b Plunkett		13
K.C.Sangakkara	c Bell b Broad	79	lbw b Ali		55
D.P.M.D.Jayawardena	c Jordan b Plunkett	22	c Prior b Anderson		79
H.D.R.L.Thirimanne	c Robson b Plunkett	0	b Ali		0
*A.D.Mathews	c Ballance b Anderson	26	c Ali b Anderson		160
†L.D.Chandimal	c Cook b Broad	45	c Ballance b Plunkett		7
K.T.G.D.Prasad	c Prior b Plunkett	0	c Root b Plunkett		0
H.M.R.K.B.Herath	not out	14	run out		48
R.M.S.Eranga	c Prior b Broad	0	not out		20
A.N.P.R.Fernando	c Prior b Plunkett	13	b Anderson		0
Extras	(B 8, LB 7, W 2)	17	(B 5, LB 10, W 10, NB 5)		30
Total	**(69.5 overs; 314 mins)**	**257**	**(132.5 overs; 579 mins)**		**457**

ENGLAND

*A.N.Cook	c Sangakkara b Prasad	17	(2) b Prasad		16
S.D.Robson	b Fernando	127	(1) c Jayawardena b Prasad		24
G.S.Ballance	c Chandimal b Mathews	74	lbw b Prasad		0
I.R.Bell	c Chandimal b Eranga	64	b Prasad		8
J.E.Root	c Chandimal b Mathews	13	c Thirimanne b Fernando		31
M.M.Ali	c Chandimal b Eranga	2	(7) not out		108
†M.J.Prior	not out	27	(8) c Silva b Prasad		10
C.J.Jordan	c Jayawardena b Eranga	17	(9) lbw b Herath		21
S.C.J.Broad	c Thirimanne b Mathews	4	(10) lbw b Herath		0
L.E.Plunkett	b Mathews	2	(6) c Fernando b Herath		0
J.M.Anderson	c and b Eranga	0	c Herath b Eranga		0
Extras	(LB 2, W 3, NB 13)	18	(B 11, LB 7, W 4, NB 9)		31
Total	**(115.5 overs; 517 mins)**	**365**	**(116.5 overs; 500 mins)**		**249**

ENGLAND	O	M	R	W		O	M	R	W
Anderson	19	5	49	2		25.5	5	91	3
Broad	15	3	46	3		29	6	86	0
Jordan	16	4	58	0		28	8	79	0
Plunkett	15.5	2	64	5		29	2	112	4
Ali	3	0	16	0		21	0	74	2
Root	1	0	9	0					

SRI LANKA	O	M	R	W		O	M	R	W
Fernando	22	3	90	1		13	2	55	1
Eranga	32.5	10	93	4		23.5	10	38	1
Herath	25	3	61	0		42	16	59	3
Prasad	20	3	75	1	(5)	22	5	50	5
Mathews	16	4	44	4	(4)	10	3	16	0
Jayawardena						6	2	13	0

FALL OF WICKETS				
	SL	E	SL	E
Wkt	1st	1st	2nd	2nd
1st	37	49	40	39
2nd	56	191	93	39
3rd	108	278	172	50
4th	108	311	176	52
5th	161	311	268	57
6th	228	313	277	124
7th	229	338	277	160
8th	229	344	426	212
9th	229	350	437	228
10th	257	365	457	249

Umpires: B.F.Bowden (*New Zealand*) (78) and S.J.Davis (*Australia*) (53).
Referee: A.J.Pycroft (*Zimbabwe*) (28).   **Test No. 2126/28 (E947/SL229)**

ENGLAND v INDIA (1st Test)

At Trent Bridge, Nottingham, on 9, 10, 11, 12, 13 July 2014.
Toss: India. Result: **MATCH DRAWN**.
Debut: India – S.T.R.Binny.

INDIA

M.Vijay	lbw b Anderson	146		c Prior b Ali		52
S.Dhawan	c Prior b Anderson	12		c and b Ali		29
C.A.Pujara	c Bell b Anderson	38		c Stokes b Plunkett		55
V.Kohli	c Bell b Broad	1		lbw b Broad		8
A.M.Rahane	c Cook b Plunkett	32		c Prior b Broad		24
*†M.S.Dhoni	run out	82		b Plunkett		11
R.A.Jadeja	c Prior b Stokes	25		c Prior b Anderson		31
S.T.R.Binny	c Root b Stokes	1		lbw b Ali		78
B.Kumar	c Root b Ali	58		not out		63
I.Sharma	b Broad	1		c Prior b Cook		13
Mohammed Shami	not out	51		not out		4
Extras	(B 1, LB 8, W 1)	10		(B 9, LB 7, NB 7)		23
Total	**(161 overs; 676 mins)**	**457**		**(9 wkts dec; 123 overs; 501 mins)**		**391**

ENGLAND

*A.N.Cook	b Shami	5
S.D.Robson	lbw b Sharma	59
G.S.Ballance	lbw b Sharma	71
I.R.Bell	c Dhoni b Sharma	25
J.E.Root	not out	154
M.M.Ali	c Dhawan b Shami	14
†M.J.Prior	c Dhoni b Kumar	5
B.A.Stokes	c Dhoni b Kumar	0
S.C.J.Broad	lbw b Kumar	47
L.E.Plunkett	b Kumar	7
J.M.Anderson	c Dhawan b Kumar	81
Extras	(B 6, LB 5, W 4, NB 13)	28
Total	**(144.5 overs; 632 mins)**	**496**

ENGLAND	O	M	R	W		O	M	R	W		FALL OF WICKETS		
												I	E	I
Anderson	38	10	123	3		21	8	47	1					
Broad	33	13	53	2		21	7	50	2		Wkt	1st	1st	2nd
Stokes	34	6	81	2	(5)	18	3	60	0		1st	33	9	49
Plunkett	37	8	88	1	(3)	20	1	85	2		2nd	106	134	140
Ali	18	0	97	1	(4)	28	4	105	3		3rd	107	154	140
Root	1	0	6	0		12	4	22	0		4th	178	172	168
Cook						2	0	6	1		5th	304	197	173
Ballance						1	1	0	0		6th	344	202	184
											7th	345	202	249
INDIA											8th	345	280	340
Kumar	30.5	8	82	5							9th	346	298	387
Mohammed Shami	29	3	128	2							10th	457	496	–
Sharma	38	3	150	3										
Jadeja	35	5	80	0										
Binny	10	0	37	0										
Vijay	2	0	8	0										

Umpires: H.D.P.K.Dharmasena (*Sri Lanka*) (24) and B.N.J.Oxenford (*Australia*) (18).
Referee: D.C.Boon (*Australia*) (22).   **Test No. 2127/108 (E948/I479)**

ENGLAND v INDIA (2nd Test)

At Lord's, London, on 17, 18, 19, 20, 21 July 2014.
Toss: England. Result: **INDIA** won by 95 runs.
Debuts: None.

INDIA

M.Vijay	c Ballance b Plunkett	24	c Prior b Anderson		95
S.Dhawan	c Ballance b Anderson	7	c Root b Stokes		31
C.A.Pujara	b Stokes	28	c Prior b Plunkett		43
V.Kohli	c Prior b Anderson	25	b Plunkett		0
A.M.Rahane	c and b Anderson	103	c Prior b Broad		5
*†M.S.Dhoni	c Prior b Broad	1	c Bell b Plunkett		19
R.A.Jadeja	lbw b Ali	3	(8) c Cook b Stokes		68
S.T.R.Binny	lbw b Anderson	9	(7) c Cook b Ali		0
B.Kumar	b Broad	36	c Bell b Stokes		52
Mohammed Shami	c Cook b Stokes	19	c Prior b Ali		0
I.Sharma	not out	12	not out		0
Extras	(B 17, LB 10, NB 1)	28	(B 19, LB 9, NB 1)		29
Total	**(91.4 overs; 396 mins)**	**295**	**(103.1 overs; 485 mins)**		**342**

ENGLAND

*A.N.Cook	c Dhoni b Kumar	10	(2) c Dhoni b Sharma		22
S.D.Robson	c Dhoni b Kumar	17	(1) lbw b Jadeja		7
G.S.Ballance	c Dhoni b Kumar	110	c Dhoni b Shami		27
I.R.Bell	c Jadeja b Kumar	16	b Sharma		1
J.E.Root	lbw b Jadeja	13	c Binny b Sharma		66
M.M.Ali	lbw b Vijay	32	c Pujara b Sharma		39
L.E.Plunkett	not out	55	(10) not out		7
†M.J.Prior	c Dhawan b Shami	23	(7) c Vijay b Sharma		12
B.A.Stokes	b Kumar	0	(8) c Pujara b Sharma		0
S.C.J.Broad	c Dhawan b Kumar	4	(9) c Dhoni b Sharma		8
J.M.Anderson	c Rahane b Jadeja	19	run out		2
Extras	(B 5, LB 10, W 2, NB 3)	20	(B 13, LB 16, W 1, NB 2)		32
Total	**(105.5 overs; 445 mins)**	**319**	**(88.2 overs; 369 mins)**		**223**

ENGLAND	O	M	R	W		O	M	R	W		FALL OF WICKETS				
Anderson	23	7	60	4		29	11	77	1			I	E	I	E
Broad	22	5	79	2		23	6	93	1	Wkt	1st	1st	2nd	2nd
Plunkett	15	5	51	1	(4)	22	6	65	3	1st	11	22	40	12
Stokes	17.4	5	40	2	(3)	18.1	2	51	3	2nd	48	31	118	70
Ali	14	2	38	1		11	3	28	2	3rd	86	70	118	71
										4th	113	113	123	72
INDIA										5th	123	211	202	173
Kumar	31	10	82	6		16	7	21	0	6th	128	214	203	198
Mohammed Shami	19	5	58	1		11	3	33	1	7th	145	265	235	201
Sharma	24	5	61	0		23	6	74	7	8th	235	276	334	201
Binny	10	0	45	0						9th	275	280	338	216
Jadeja	18.5	1	46	2	(4)	32.2	7	53	1	10th	295	319	342	223
Vijay	3	0	12	1	(5)	4	1	11	0					
Dhawan					(6)	2	0	2	0					

Umpires: H.D.P.K.Dharmasena (*Sri Lanka*) (25) and B.N.J.Oxenford (*Australia*) (19).
Referee: D.C.Boon (*Australia*) (23).   Test No. 2128/109 (E949/I480)

ENGLAND v INDIA (3rd Test)

At Rose Bowl, Southampton, on 27, 28, 29, 30, 31 July 2014.
Toss: England. Result: **ENGLAND** won by 266 runs.
Debuts: England – J.C.Buttler; India – Pankaj Singh.

ENGLAND

*A.N.Cook	c Dhoni b Jadeja	95	(2) not out		70
S.D.Robson	c Jadeja b Shami	26	(1) c Dhawan b Kumar		13
G.S.Ballance	c Dhoni b Sharma	156	c Pujara b Jadeja		38
I.R.Bell	c Pankaj b Kumar	167	b Jadeja		23
J.E.Root	c Dhoni b Kumar	3	b Jadeja		56
M.M.Ali	c Rahane b Kumar	12			
†J.C.Buttler	b Jadeja	85			
C.R.Woakes	not out	7			
C.J.Jordan					
S.C.J.Broad					
J.M.Anderson					
Extras	(B 5, LB 11, W 2)	18	(B 4, W 1)		5
Total	(7 wkts dec; 163.4 overs; 668 mins)	569	(4 wkts dec; 40.4 overs; 182 mins)		205

INDIA

M.Vijay	b Broad	35	run out		12
S.Dhawan	c Cook b Anderson	6	c Jordan b Root		37
C.A.Pujara	c Buttler b Broad	24	c Jordan b Ali		2
V.Kohli	c Cook b Anderson	39	c Buttler b Ali		28
A.M.Rahane	c sub (S.P.Terry) b Ali	54	not out		52
R.G.Sharma	c Broad b Ali	28	c Buttler b Anderson		6
*†M.S.Dhoni	c Buttler b Anderson	50	c Buttler b Anderson		6
R.A.Jadeja	lbw b Anderson	31	b Ali		15
B.Kumar	c Ballance b Broad	19	c Anderson b Ali		0
Mohammed Shami	c Buttler b Anderson	5	b Ali		0
Pankaj Singh	not out	1	b Ali		9
Extras	(B 16, LB 14, W 8)	38	(B 4, LB 6, W 1)		11
Total	(106.1 overs; 479 mins)	330	(66.4 overs; 282 mins)		178

INDIA	O	M	R	W		O	M	R	W
Kumar	37	10	101	3		10	0	59	1
Mohammed Shami	33	4	123	1	(3)	4	0	24	0
Pankaj Singh	37	8	146	0	(2)	10	4	33	0
Sharma	9	0	26	1		5	0	32	0
Jadeja	45.4	10	153	2		10.4	1	52	3
Dhawan	2	0	4	0					
Vijay					(6)	1	0	1	0

ENGLAND	O	M	R	W		O	M	R	W
Anderson	26.1	10	53	5		14	5	24	2
Broad	25	7	66	3		13	6	22	0
Jordan	17	4	59	0	(5)	5	0	22	0
Woakes	20	8	60	0	(3)	11	3	23	0
Ali	18	0	62	2	(4)	20.4	4	67	6
Root						2	0	5	1
Ballance						1	0	5	0

FALL OF WICKETS				
	E	I	E	I
Wkt	1st	1st	2nd	2nd
1st	55	17	22	26
2nd	213	56	80	29
3rd	355	88	106	80
4th	378	136	205	89
5th	420	210	–	112
6th	526	217	–	120
7th	569	275	–	152
8th	–	313	–	152
9th	–	329	–	154
10th	–	330	–	178

Umpires: M.Erasmus (*South Africa*) (24) and R.J.Tucker (*Australia*) (32).
Referee: D.C.Boon (*Australia*) (24).   **Test No. 2129/110 (E950/I481)**

ENGLAND v INDIA (4th Test)

At Old Trafford, Manchester, on 7, 8, 9 August 2014.
Toss: India. Result: **ENGLAND** won by an innings and 54 runs.
Debuts: None.

INDIA

M.Vijay	c Cook b Anderson	0	lbw b Woakes		18
G.Gambhir	c Root b Broad	4	c Buttler b Anderson		18
C.A.Pujara	c Jordan b Broad	0	lbw b Ali		17
V.Kohli	c Cook b Anderson	0	c Bell b Anderson		7
A.M.Rahane	c Bell b Jordan	24	c and b Ali		1
*†M.S.Dhoni	c Jordan b Broad	71	c Ballance b Ali		27
R.A.Jadeja	lbw b Anderson	0	c Jordan b Ali		4
R.Ashwin	c Robson b Broad	40	not out		46
B.Kumar	b Broad	0	run out		10
V.R.Aaron	not out	1	c Buttler b Jordan		9
Pankaj Singh	b Broad	0	b Jordan		0
Extras	(B 10, LB 1, W 1)	12	(B 1, LB 1, W 1, NB 1)		4
Total	**(46.4 overs; 232 mins)**	**152**	**(43 overs; 202 mins)**		**161**

ENGLAND

*A.N.Cook	c Pankaj b Aaron	17
S.D.Robson	b Kumar	6
G.S.Ballance	lbw b Aaron	37
I.R.Bell	c Dhoni b Kumar	58
C.J.Jordan	c Aaron b Kumar	13
J.E.Root	c Dhoni b Pankaj	77
M.M.Ali	b Aaron	13
†J.C.Buttler	c Pujara b Pankaj	70
C.R.Woakes	not out	26
S.C.J.Broad	retired hurt	12
J.M.Anderson	lbw b Jadeja	1
Extras	(B 5, LB 12, W 6, NB 6)	29
Total	**(105.3 overs; 478 mins)**	**367**

ENGLAND	O	M	R	W		O	M	R	W	FALL OF WICKETS
Anderson	14	3	46	3		9	4	18	2	

	O	M	R	W		O	M	R	W		I	E	I
Anderson	14	3	46	3		9	4	18	2	Wkt	1st	1st	2nd
Broad	13.4	6	25	6						1st	8	21	26
Woakes	10	1	43	0	(2)	9	2	37	1	2nd	8	36	53
Jordan	9	4	27	1	(3)	12	1	65	2	3rd	8	113	53
Ali					(4)	13	3	39	4	4th	8	136	61
										5th	62	140	61
INDIA										6th	63	170	66
Kumar	24	7	75	3						7th	129	304	105
Pankaj Singh	28	5	113	2						8th	137	325	133
Aaron	26	4	97	3						9th	152	367	161
Ashwin	14	1	29	0						10th	152	–	161
Jadeja	13.3	1	36	1									

Umpires: M.Erasmus (*South Africa*) (25) and R.J.Tucker (*Australia*) (33).
Referee: R.S.Madugalle (*Sri Lanka*) (149).   **Test No. 2130/111 (E951/I482)**
S.C.J.Broad retired hurt at 338-8.

ENGLAND v INDIA (5th Test)

At The Oval, London, on 15, 16, 17 August 2014.
Toss: India. Result: **ENGLAND** won by an innings and 244 runs.
Debuts: None.

INDIA

M.Vijay	c Root b Woakes	18	lbw b Anderson		2
G.Gambhir	c Buttler b Anderson	0	run out		3
C.A.Pujara	b Broad	4	c Buttler b Anderson		11
V.Kohli	lbw b Jordan	6	c Cook b Jordan		20
A.M.Rahane	c and b Jordan	0	c Ballance b Broad		4
*†M.S.Dhoni	c Woakes b Broad	82	c Robson b Woakes		0
S.T.R.Binny	c Cook b Anderson	5	not out		25
R.Ashwin	c Root b Woakes	13	c Bell b Jordan		7
B.Kumar	c Buttler b Broad	5	c Bell b Jordan		4
V.R.Aaron	c and b Woakes	1	run out		1
I.Sharma	not out	7	c Ali b Jordan		2
Extras	(B 6, LB 1)	7	(B 8, LB 6, W 1)		15
Total	**(61.1 overs; 289 mins)**	**148**	**(29.2 overs; 143 mins)**		**94**

ENGLAND

*A.N.Cook	c Vijay b Aaron	79
S.D.Robson	b Aaron	37
G.S.Ballance	c Pujara b Ashwin	64
I.R.Bell	c Dhoni b Sharma	7
J.E.Root	not out	149
M.M.Ali	b Ashwin	14
†J.C.Buttler	c Ashwin b Sharma	45
C.R.Woakes	c Dhoni b Kumar	0
C.J.Jordan	c Dhoni b Sharma	20
S.C.J.Broad	c Kohli b Sharma	37
J.M.Anderson	lbw b Ashwin	1
Extras	(B 18, LB 3, W 1, NB 11)	33
Total	**(116.3 overs; 535 mins)**	**486**

ENGLAND	O	M	R	W		O	M	R	W		FALL OF WICKETS		
Anderson	17	4	51	2		8	3	16	2			I	E	I
Broad	15.1	4	27	2		10	2	22	1		*Wkt*	*1st*	*1st*	*2nd*
Jordan	14	7	32	3	(4)	4.2	0	18	4		1st	3	66	6
Woakes	14	7	30	3	(3)	7	0	24	1		2nd	10	191	9
Ali	1	0	1	0							3rd	26	201	30
											4th	28	204	45
INDIA											5th	36	229	46
Kumar	24	3	86	1							6th	44	309	62
Sharma	30	8	96	4							7th	68	318	70
Aaron	29	1	153	2							8th	79	400	74
Binny	12	0	58	0							9th	90	463	84
Ashwin	21.3	2	72	3							10th	148	486	94

Umpires: H.D.P.K.Dharmasena (*Sri Lanka*) (26) and P.R.Reiffel (*Australia*) (11).
Referee: R.S.Madugalle (*Sri Lanka*) (150).   **Test No. 2131/112 (E952/I483)**

SRI LANKA v SOUTH AFRICA (1st Test)

At Galle International Stadium, on 16, 17, 18, 19, 20 July 2014.
Toss: South Africa. Result: **SOUTH AFRICA** won by 153 runs.
Debuts: None.

SOUTH AFRICA

A.N.Petersen	lbw b Perera	34	(2) c Chandimal b Perera		32
D.Elgar	c Chandimal b Lakmal	103	(1) c Chandimal b Herath		12
F.du Plessis	c Silva b Perera	80	b Herath		37
*H.M.Amla	c Perera b Herath	11	c Tharanga b Perera		22
A.B.de Villiers	b Lakmal	21	b Perera		51
†Q.de Kock	c Jayawardena b Perera	51	c and b Perera		36
D.W.Steyn	b Lakmal	3			
J.P.Duminy	not out	100	(7) not out		8
V.D.Philander	lbw b Mathews	27			
M.Morkel	b Perera	22			
Imran Tahir					
Extras	(LB 2, NB 1)	3	(B 4, LB 4)		8
Total	**(9 wkts dec; 166.2 overs; 665 mins)**	**455**	**(6 wkts dec; 50.2 overs; 205 mins)**		**206**

SRI LANKA

J.K.Silva	c Philander b Steyn	8	(2) c de Kock b Steyn		38
W.U.Tharanga	st de Kock b Duminy	83	(1) c de Kock b Steyn		14
K.C.Sangakkara	b Morkel	24	c Amla b Duminy		76
D.P.M.D.Jayawardena	lbw b Steyn	3	c de Kock b Morkel		10
H.D.R.L.Thirimanne	c de Kock b Steyn	38	c de Villiers b Steyn		12
*A.D.Mathews	b Tahir	89	not out		27
†L.D.Chandimal	c Petersen b Steyn	6	c de Kock b Morkel		1
M.D.K.Perera	c de Kock b Steyn	0	c de Kock b Steyn		0
H.M.R.K.B.Herath	c de Villiers b Morkel	19	c de Villiers b Duminy		20
R.A.S.Lakmal	c de Kock b Morkel	6	c Tahir b Morkel		12
R.M.S.Eranga	not out	1	c Elgar b Morkel		0
Extras	(B 4, LB 7, W 3, NB 1)	15	(LB 5, NB 1)		6
Total	**(104.5 overs; 465 mins)**	**292**	**(71.3 overs; 332 mins)**		**216**

SRI LANKA	O	M	R	W		O	M	R	W
Lakmal	33	12	75	3		9	0	35	0
Eranga	9	4	32	0					
Herath	60	12	148	1	(2)	22	2	84	2
Mathews	11	1	36	1					
Perera	53.2	8	162	4	(3)	19.2	1	79	4

SOUTH AFRICA	O	M	R	W		O	M	R	W
Steyn	23	8	54	5		17	4	45	4
Philander	15	6	31	0		11	4	34	0
Morkel	18.5	8	49	3		13.3	6	29	4
Imran Tahir	26	5	75	1		19	3	64	0
Duminy	15	4	47	1		10	4	38	2
Elgar	7	1	25	0		1	0	1	0

FALL OF WICKETS

	SA	SL	SA	SL
Wkt	1st	1st	2nd	2nd
1st	70	39	33	14
2nd	195	98	54	118
3rd	220	104	88	138
4th	246	136	131	149
5th	266	190	193	153
6th	290	200	206	158
7th	314	201	–	161
8th	389	272	–	190
9th	455	283	–	216
10th	–	292	–	216

Umpires: B.F.Bowden (*New Zealand*) (79) and R.A.Kettleborough (*England*) (21).
Referee: J.J.Crowe (*New Zealand*) (66). Test No. 2132/21 (SL230/SA385)

SRI LANKA v SOUTH AFRICA (2nd Test)

At Sinhalese Sports Club, Colombo, on 24, 25, 26, 27, 28 July 2014.
Toss: Sri Lanka. Result: **MATCH DRAWN**.
Debut: Sri Lanka – D.P.D.N.Dickwella.

SRI LANKA

W.U.Tharanga	c de Kock b Steyn	11	c de Kock b Steyn		30
J.K.Silva	c de Villiers b Duminy	44	c Philander b Morkel		26
K.C.Sangakkara	c Tahir b Steyn	0	c de Kock b Morkel		72
D.P.M.D.Jayawardena	run out	165	c Elgar b Tahir		0
*A.D.Mathews	c de Kock b Duminy	63	not out		63
K.D.K.Vithanage	c de Villiers b Morkel	13	c du Plessis b Morkel		7
†D.P.D.N.Dickwella	run out	72	c de Villiers b Steyn		16
M.D.K.Perera	c Amla b Tahir	12	b Tahir		7
H.M.R.K.B.Herath	not out	7	c de Villiers b Morkel		4
B.A.W.Mendis	c de Kock b Philander	2			
R.A.S.Lakmal	c de Kock b Philander	4			
Extras	(B 11, LB 14, NB 3)	28	(B 1, LB 2, NB 1)		4
Total	(121.4 overs; 562 mins)	421	(8 wkts dec; 53.4 overs; 242 mins)		229

SOUTH AFRICA

A.N.Petersen	c and b Herath	2	c Vithanage b Herath		0
D.Elgar	c Silva b Perera	1	b Perera		13
F.du Plessis	c Dickwella b Lakmal	36	c Jayawardena b Herath		10
*H.M.Amla	not out	139	(6) c Jayawardena b Perera		25
A.B.de Villiers	lbw b Perera	37	b Herath		12
†Q.de Kock	b Perera	0	(3) c Vithanage b Perera		37
J.P.Duminy	st Dickwella b Herath	3	lbw b Perera		3
V.D.Philander	b Perera	9	not out		27
D.W.Steyn	c Sangakkara b Herath	30	c Dickwella b Herath		6
Imran Tahir	c Tharanga b Herath	15	not out		4
M.Morkel	c Silva b Perera	0			
Extras	(LB 3, W 1, NB 6)	10	(B 5, LB 14, NB 3)		22
Total	(134.5 overs; 522 mins)	282	(8 wkts; 111 overs; 359 mins)		159

SOUTH AFRICA	O	M	R	W		O	M	R	W
Steyn	22	5	69	2		13	1	59	2
Philander	21.4	7	52	2		11	3	35	0
Morkel	26	6	69	1	(4)	9.4	1	45	4
Imran Tahir	33	4	121	1	(3)	18	0	76	2
Duminy	18	1	80	2	(6)	1	0	2	0
Elgar	1	0	5	0	(5)	1	0	9	0
SRI LANKA									
Lakmal	23	7	54	1	(4)	4	1	11	0
Herath	45	17	71	4	(1)	45	30	40	5
Perera	41.5	11	69	5	(2)	44	24	60	3
Mendis	21	1	68	0	(3)	13	8	17	0
Vithanage	4	0	17	0		5	1	12	0

FALL OF WICKETS

	SL	SA	SL	SA
Wkt	1st	1st	2nd	2nd
1st	16	3	38	4
2nd	16	13	82	47
3rd	115	71	83	68
4th	246	150	164	93
5th	285	150	174	105
6th	385	175	203	110
7th	404	204	214	130
8th	409	251	229	148
9th	415	279	–	–
10th	421	282	–	–

Umpires: R.A.Kettleborough (*England*) (22) and N.J.Llong (*England*) (25).
Referee: J.J.Crowe (*New Zealand*) (67). Test No. 2133/22 (SL231/SA386)

SRI LANKA v PAKISTAN (1st Test)

At Galle International Stadium, on 6, 7, 8, 9, 10 August 2014.
Toss: Pakistan. Result: **SRI LANKA** won by seven wickets.
Debuts: None.

PAKISTAN

Khurram Manzoor	lbw b Prasad	3	c Dickwella b Herath		3
Ahmed Shehzad	b Prasad	4	lbw b Perera		16
Azhar Ali	b Herath	30	(4) c Dickwella b Herath		41
Younus Khan	c Vithanage b Perera	177	(5) b Herath		13
*Misbah-ul-Haq	c Dickwella b Herath	31	(6) lbw b Perera		28
Asad Shafiq	lbw b Herath	75	(7) lbw b Herath		8
†Sarfraz Ahmed	c Mathews b Perera	55	(8) not out		52
Abdur Rehman	c Sangakkara b Perera	50	(9) c Dickwella b Eranga		1
Saeed Ajmal	c Jayawardena b Perera	12	(3) c Dickwella b Prasad		4
Mohammad Talha	not out	9	c Dickwella b Herath		4
Junaid Khan	c Jayawardena b Perera	0	lbw b Herath		0
Extras	(LB 4, NB 1)	5	(B 7, LB 3)		10
Total	**(140.5 overs; 622 mins)**	**451**	**(80.2 overs; 334 mins)**		**180**

SRI LANKA

W.U.Tharanga	lbw b Junaid	19	b Junaid		12
J.K.Silva	c Sarfraz b Talha	64			
K.C.Sangakkara	st Sarfraz b Rehman	221	c Manzoor b Talha		21
D.P.M.D.Jayawardena	lbw b Junaid	59	(2) b Junaid		26
*A.D.Mathews	c Younus b Ajmal	91	(4) not out		25
K.D.K.Vithanage	c Shafiq b Ajmal	5	(5) not out		11
†P.D.N.Dickwella	c Shafiq b Ajmal	5			
M.D.K.Perera	c Junaid b Ajmal	5			
K.T.G.D.Prasad	st Sarfraz b Ajmal	31			
H.M.R.K.B.Herath	not out	6			
R.M.S.Eranga					
Extras	(B 5, LB 11, W 7, NB 4)	27	(LB 3, W 1)		4
Total	**(9 wkts dec; 163.1 overs; 745 mins)**	**533**	**(3 wkts; 16.2 overs; 87 mins)**		**99**

SRI LANKA	O	M	R	W		O	M	R	W		FALL OF WICKETS				
Eranga	31	13	78	0	(2)	14	5	44	1			P	SL	P	SL
Prasad	24	3	81	2	(4)	8	3	10	1		Wkt	1st	1st	2nd	2nd
Mathews	15	7	25	0							1st	4	24	3	28
Herath	38	9	116	3	(1)	30.2	11	48	6		2nd	19	144	11	59
Perera	31.5	1	137	5	(3)	28	6	68	2		3rd	56	257	39	73
Vithanage	1	0	10	0							4th	156	438	55	–
											5th	293	450	111	–
PAKISTAN											6th	359	458	111	–
Junaid Khan	33	9	104	2	(2)	8	0	55	2		7th	388	475	133	–
Mohammad Talha	27	4	104	1	(3)	2.2	0	12	1		8th	424	511	153	–
Saeed Ajmal	59.1	8	166	5	(1)	6	0	29	0		9th	451	533	178	–
Abdur Rehman	39	2	123	1							10th	451	–	180	–
Ahmed Shehzad	5	0	20	0											

Umpires: I.J.Gould (*England*) (40) and B.N.J.Oxenford (*Australia*) (20).
Referee: A.J.Pycroft (*Zimbabwe*) (29).   Test No. 2134/47 (SL232/P381)

SRI LANKA v PAKISTAN (2nd Test)

At Sinhalese Sports Club Ground, Colombo, on 14, 15, 16, 17, 18 August 2014.
Toss: Sri Lanka. Result: **SRI LANKA** won by 105 runs.
Debuts: None.

SRI LANKA

W.U.Tharanga	c Ali b Riaz	92	b Rehman		45
J.K.Silva	c Sarfraz b Junaid	41	c Younus b Rehman		17
K.C.Sangakkara	b Riaz	22	c Ali b Ajmal		59
D.P.M.D.Jayawardena	lbw b Ajmal	4	c Shehzad b Ajmal		54
*A.D.Mathews	c Sarfraz b Riaz	39	not out		43
H.D.R.L.Thirimanne	c Sarfraz b Junaid	20	b Ajmal		10
†D.P.D.N.Dickwella	lbw b Junaid	24	lbw b Riaz		21
M.D.K.Perera	lbw b Junaid	0	lbw b Riaz		0
K.T.G.D.Prasad	lbw b Junaid	13	run out		19
H.M.R.K.B.Herath	c Younus b Rehman	17	b Riaz		0
U.W.M.B.C.A.Welagedara	not out	27	run out		0
Extras	(B 8, LB 7, NB 6)	21	(B 10, LB 2, W 1, NB 1)		14
Total	**(99.3 overs; 461 mins)**	**320**	**(109 overs; 482 mins)**		**282**

PAKISTAN

Khurram Manzoor	c Dickwella b Herath	23	c Dickwella b Prasad		10
Ahmed Shehzad	c Dickwella b Perera	58	lbw b Prasad		8
Azhar Ali	c Mathews b Herath	32	c Jayawardena b Herath		10
Younus Khan	c Dickwella b Herath	13	lbw b Herath		8
*Misbah-ul-Haq	c Dickwella b Herath	5	c Jayawardena b Herath		3
Asad Shafiq	b Herath	42	st Dickwella b Herath		32
†Sarfraz Ahmed	c Dickwella b Herath	103	c Sangakkara b Welagedara		55
Abdur Rehman	c Jayawardena b Herath	16	lbw b Perera		5
Wahab Riaz	c Welagedara b Herath	17	c Silva b Herath		17
Saeed Ajmal	b Herath	4	not out		3
Junaid Khan	not out	13	absent hurt		
Extras	(LB 3, NB 3)	6	(B 4, LB 7, NB 3)		14
Total	**(93.1 overs; 427 mins)**	**332**	**(52.1 overs; 231 mins)**		**165**

PAKISTAN	O	M	R	W		O	M	R	W	FALL OF WICKETS
Junaid Khan	27	6	87	5						
Wahab Riaz	20	3	88	3	(1)	25	3	76	3	
Abdur Rehman	19.3	4	53	1	(2)	35	3	97	2	
Saeed Ajmal	33	5	77	1	(3)	46	10	89	3	
Ahmed Shehzad					(4)	3	0	8	0	

		SL	P	SL	P
Wkt	1st	1st	2nd	2nd	
1st	79	47	54	17	
2nd	144	110	79	21	
3rd	167	122	186	31	
4th	177	131	189	39	
5th	215	140	212	50	
6th	249	233	247	105	
7th	249	273	247	122	
8th	261	301	278	151	
9th	284	315	282	165	
10th	320	332	282	–	

SRI LANKA	O	M	R	W		O	M	R	W	
Prasad	16	4	53	0	(2)	8	0	29	2	
Welagedara	18	2	65	0	(1)	9	4	22	1	
Herath	33.1	3	127	9		22.1	2	57	5	
Mathews	9	1	21	0						
Perera	17	1	63	1	(4)	13	1	46	1	

Umpires: I.J.Gould (*England*) (41) and R.K.Illingworth (*England*) (10).
Referee: A.J.Pycroft (*Zimbabwe*) (30).　　　　　**Test No. 2135/48 (SL233/P382)**

28

ZIMBABWE v SOUTH AFRICA (Only Test)

At Harare Sports Club, on 9, 10, 11, 12 August 2014.
Toss: Zimbabwe. Result: **SOUTH AFRICA** won by nine wickets.
Debuts: Zimbabwe – J.C.Nyumbu, D.T.Tiripano; South Africa – D.L.Piedt.

ZIMBABWE

Batsman		Runs			Runs
V.Sibanda	c Petersen b Steyn	0	(2)	c and b Piedt	45
H.Masakadza	b Piedt	45	(1)	c de Villiers b Morkel	19
M.A.Vermeulen	lbw b Piedt	14	(4)	lbw b Steyn	21
*B.R.M.Taylor	c Duminy b Piedt	93	(5)	c Elgar b Piedt	5
R.W.Chakabva	c Amla b Piedt	0	(6)	b Morkel	15
S.C.Williams	c de Kock b Steyn	24	(7)	c Duminy b Morkel	3
†R.Mutumbami	lbw b Steyn	21	(8)	c de Kock b Steyn	43
T.Panyangara	c de Kock b Philander	12	(11)	b Steyn	2
D.T.Tiripano	not out	15	(3)	b Piedt	5
T.L.Chatara	c de Kock b Steyn	22		not out	0
J.C.Nyumbu	c de Kock b Steyn	2	(9)	c and b Piedt	13
Extras	(LB 4, W 2, NB 2)	8		(B 2, LB 7, NB 1)	10
Total	**(92.4 overs, 403 mins)**	**256**		**(76.2 overs, 338 mins)**	**181**

SOUTH AFRICA

Batsman		Runs		Runs
D.Elgar	c Mutumbami b Tiripano	61	b Chatara	21
A.N.Petersen	c Mutumbami b Nyumbu	32	not out	17
F.du Plessis	c Chakabva b Nyumbu	98	not out	5
*H.M.Amla	c Sibanda b Chatara	4		
A.B.de Villiers	c Sibanda b Nyumbu	7		
†Q.de Kock	c Sibanda b Williams	81		
J.P.Duminy	c Taylor b Nyumbu	55		
V.D.Philander	b Williams	17		
D.W.Steyn	c Tiripano b Nyumbu	19		
D.L.Piedt	lbw b Tiripano	13		
M.Morkel	not out	2		
Extras	(B 3, LB 4, NB 1)	8	(LB 1)	1
Total	**(158.3 overs, 639 mins)**	**397**	**(1 wkt; 10.4 overs; 40 mins)**	**44**

SOUTH AFRICA	O	M	R	W		O	M	R	W
Steyn	22.4	11	46	5		21.2	9	38	3
Philander	18	5	51	1		10	3	25	0
Morkel	19	3	39	0		15	9	15	3
Piedt	24	1	90	4		25	3	62	4
Duminy	9	0	26	0		2	1	12	0
Elgar						3	0	20	0
ZIMBABWE									
Panyangara	30	12	39	0	(2)	3	1	5	0
Tiripano	26	8	65	2					
Nyumbu	49.3	7	157	5	(1)	4	0	24	0
Chatara	27	12	34	1	(3)	2	1	5	1
Williams	26	2	95	2	(4)	1.4	0	9	0

FALL OF WICKETS

	Z	SA	Z	SA
Wkt	1st	1st	2nd	2nd
1st	0	57	25	39
2nd	33	132	58	–
3rd	90	146	98	–
4th	90	157	98	–
5th	120	276	113	–
6th	179	292	121	–
7th	204	334	124	–
8th	220	367	178	–
9th	246	395	178	–
10th	256	397	181	–

Umpires: Alim Dar (*Pakistan*) (90) and C.B.Gaffaney (*New Zealand*) (1).
Referee: R.S.Mahanama (*Sri Lanka*) (52). **Test No. 2136/8 (Z94/SA387)**

WEST INDIES v BANGLADESH (1st Test)

At Arnos Vale Ground, Kingstown, St Vincent, on 5, 6, 7, 8, 9 September 2014.
Toss: Bangladesh. Result: **WEST INDIES** won by ten wickets.
Debuts: Bangladesh – Shuvugata Hom, Taijul Islam.

WEST INDIES

C.H.Gayle	lbw b Shuvagata	64	not out	9
K.C.Brathwaite	c Mominul b Taijul	212	not out	4
K.A.Edwards	c Mominul b Taijul	10		
D.M.Bravo	c Mahmudullah b Taijul	62		
S.Chanderpaul	not out	85		
J.Blackwood	lbw b Rubel	10		
*†D.Ramdin	c Rubel b Taijul	5		
J.E.Taylor	c Shuvagata b Taijul	10		
K.A.J.Roach	not out	2		
S.J.Benn				
S.T.Gabriel				
Extras	(B 5, LB 18, NB 1)	24		
Total	**(7 wkts dec; 160 overs)**	**484**	**(0 wkts; 2.4 overs; 9 mins)**	**13**

BANGLADESH

Tamim Iqbal	c Bravo b Roach	1	b Benn	53
Shamsur Rahman	c Bravo b Benn	35	c Ramdin b Roach	4
Imrul Kayes	c Bravo b Taylor	9	c Edwards b Gayle	25
Mominul Haque	c Ramdin b Gabriel	51	c Ramdin b Benn	12
Mahmudullah	lbw b Blackwood	7	c Ramdin b Roach	66
*†Mushfiqur Rahim	not out	48	c Bravo b Taylor	116
Nasir Hossain	c Benn b Blackwood	2	c Gabriel b Roach	19
Shuvagata Hom	c and b Benn	16	lbw b Roach	0
Taijul Islam	c Bravo b Benn	2	b Gabriel	0
Rubel Hossain	c Ramdin b Benn	1	b Gabriel	0
Al-Amin Hossain	c Bravo b Benn	5	not out	0
Extras	(LB 2, W 2, NB 1)	5	(B 12, LB 4, W 2, NB 1)	19
Total	**(71.4 overs)**	**182**	**(113.3 overs)**	**314**

BANGLADESH	O	M	R	W	O	M	R	W
Al-Amin Hossain	22	12	43	0	1.4	0	9	0
Rubel Hossain	30	1	110	1				
Mahmudullah	19	0	64	0				
Shuvagata Hom	37	6	104	1				
Taijul Islam	47	9	135	5	(2) 1	0	4	0
Nasir Hossain	4	1	4	0				
Mominul Haque	1	0	1	0				

WEST INDIES	O	M	R	W	O	M	R	W
Taylor	15	4	46	1	17.3	3	64	1
Roach	13	4	31	1	22	6	64	4
Gabriel	13	2	50	1	17	9	25	2
Benn	24.4	8	39	5	(5) 28	8	44	2
Blackwood	6	1	14	2	(4) 12	1	51	0
Gayle					17	3	50	1

FALL OF WICKETS

	WI	B	B	WI
Wkt	1st	1st	2nd	2nd
1st	116	1	11	–
2nd	133	18	81	–
3rd	261	80	104	–
4th	422	105	107	–
5th	451	110	237	–
6th	466	118	279	–
7th	479	147	291	–
8th	–	155	292	–
9th	–	166	292	–
10th	–	182	314	–

Umpires: M.Erasmus (*South Africa*) (26) and R.K.Illingworth (*England*) (11).
Referee: R.S.Mahanama (*India*) (53). **Test No. 2137/11 (WI498/B84)**

WEST INDIES v BANGLADESH (2nd Test)

At Beausejour Stadium, Gros Islet, St Lucia, on 13, 14 15, 16 September 2014.
Toss: Bangladesh. Result: **WEST INDIES** won by 296 runs.
Debut: West Indies – L.R.Johnson.

WEST INDIES

K.C.Brathwaite	c Taijul b Shafiul	63	c Shamsur b Mahmudullah		45
L.R.Johnson	lbw b Taijul	66	b Taijul		41
K.A.Edwards	c Shamsur b Mahmudullah	16	c Shamsur b Shafiul		2
D.M.Bravo	c Mushfiqur b Robiul	46	b Mahmudullah		7
S.Chanderpaul	not out	84	not out		101
J.Blackwood	c Anamul b Al-Amin	8	not out		66
*†D.Ramdin	c Mushfiqur b Al-Amin	0			
K.A.J.Roach	c Mushfiqur b Shafiul	0			
J.E.Taylor	c Mahmudullah b Taijul	40			
S.J.Benn	c Shafiul b Al-Amin	25			
S.T.Gabriel	b Robiul	4			
Extras	(B 8, LB 4, W 10, NB 6)	28	(LB 5, W 2)		7
Total	**(124 overs)**	**380**	**(4 wkts dec; 77 overs)**		**269**

BANGLADESH

Tamim Iqbal	c Ramdin b Roach	48	c Gabriel b Benn		64
Shamsur Rahman	c Ramdin b Roach	1	c Edwards b Taylor		39
Anamul Haque	c Bravo b Roach	9	c Ramdin b Benn		0
Mominul Haque	c Blackwood b Taylor	3	c Gabriel b Benn		56
*†Mushfiqur Rahim	b Taylor	4	(6) b Taylor		11
Mahmudullah	c Ramdin b Benn	53	(5) lbw b Gabriel		0
Nasir Hossain	c Ramdin b Roach	1	lbw b Benn		2
Taijul Islam	c Gabriel b Roach	12	c and b Benn		4
Shafiul Islam	c Ramdin b Gabriel	10	b Roach		14
Robiul Islam	lbw b Benn	0	lbw b Taylor		0
Al-Amin Hossain	not out	7	not out		0
Extras	(LB 10, W 1, NB 2)	13	(LB 1, W 1)		2
Total	**(62.3 overs)**	**161**	**(77.4 overs)**		**192**

BANGLADESH	O	M	R	W		O	M	R	W
Al-Amin Hossain	31	6	80	3	(2)	4	0	18	0
Shafiul Islam	27	7	80	2	(4)	13	1	42	1
Robiul Islam	26	7	63	2		12	3	42	0
Taijul Islam	22	4	89	2	(1)	28	5	81	1
Mahmudullah	16	2	49	1		16	2	64	2
Nasir Hossain	2	0	7	0					
Mominul Haque					(6)	4	0	17	0
WEST INDIES									
Taylor	19	5	41	2		13	4	39	3
Roach	20	5	42	5		15.4	1	43	1
Gabriel	15	1	49	1	(5)	11	2	24	1
Benn	8.3	2	19	2	(3)	32	6	72	5
Blackwood					(4)	2	0	4	0
Johnson						4	0	9	0

FALL OF WICKETS

	WI	B	WI	B
Wkt	1st	1st	2nd	2nd
1st	143	14	76	47
2nd	145	43	81	48
3rd	185	62	97	158
4th	251	65	100	160
5th	268	68	–	160
6th	268	69	–	167
7th	269	89	–	173
8th	323	134	–	188
9th	375	154	–	188
10th	380	161	–	192

Umpires: S.J.Davis (*Australia*) (54) and R.K.Illingworth (*England*) (12).
Referee: R.S.Mahanama (*India*) (54).   **Test No. 2138/12 (WI499/B85)**

PAKISTAN v AUSTRALIA (1st Test)

At Dubai Sports City Stadium, on 22, 23, 24, 25, 26 October 2014.
Toss: Pakistan. Result: **PAKISTAN** won by 221 runs.
Debuts: Pakistan – Imran Khan, Yasir Shah; Australia – M.R.Marsh, S.N.J.O'Keefe.

PAKISTAN

Ahmed Shehzad	b Siddle	3		lbw b O'Keefe	131
Mohammad Hafeez	lbw b Johnson	0			
Azhar Ali	c Doolan b Johnson	53	(2)	c Haddin b O'Keefe	30
Younus Khan	lbw b Johnson	106	(3)	not out	103
*Misbah-ul-Haq	c Johnson b Smith	69			
Asad Shafiq	c Marsh b O'Keefe	89			
†Sarfraz Ahmed	st Haddin b Lyon	109	(4)	not out	15
Yasir Shah	c Rogers b O'Keefe	2			
Zulfiqar Babar	retired hurt	7			
Rahat Ali	c Rogers b Lyon	0			
Imran Khan	not out	0			
Extras	(B 2, LB 14)	16		(B 2, LB 3, W 2)	7
Total	**(145 overs)**	**454**		**(2 wkts dec; 78 overs)**	**286**

AUSTRALIA

C.J.L.Rogers	b Rahat	38		b Imran	43
D.A.Warner	b Shah	133		st Sarfraz b Babar	29
A.J.Doolan	run out	5		lbw b Babar	0
*M.J.Clarke	c Azhar b Babar	2		lbw b Shah	3
S.P.D.Smith	c Hafeez b Shah	22	(6)	c Shafiq b Shah	55
M.R.Marsh	lbw b Shah	27	(7)	c Azhar b Babar	3
†B.J.Haddin	b Imran	22	(8)	b Babar	0
M.G.Johnson	c sub (Shan Masood) b Rahat	37	(9)	st Sarfraz b Shah	61
P.M.Siddle	lbw b Hafeez	0	(10)	c Azhar b Babar	15
S.N.J.O'Keefe	c Misbah b Shah	6	(11)	not out	0
N.M.Lyon	not out	4	(5)	lbw b Shah	0
Extras	(B 4, LB 2, NB 1)	7		(B 4, LB 1, NB 2)	7
Total	**(103.1 overs)**	**303**		**(91.1 overs)**	**216**

AUSTRALIA	O	M	R	W		O	M	R	W	FALL OF WICKETS				
Johnson	31	18	39	3		12	2	34	0		P	A	P	A
Siddle	24	11	50	1		14	5	44	0	Wkt	1st	1st	2nd	2nd
O'Keefe	30	3	107	2	(4)	27	3	112	2	1st	1	128	71	44
Marsh	17	4	44	0	(5)	7	1	19	0	2nd	7	151	239	44
Lyon	37	4	148	2	(3)	18	0	72	0	3rd	115	158	–	49
Smith	6	0	50	1						4th	198	206	–	49
PAKISTAN										5th	291	207	–	92
Rahat Ali	19	0	55	2	(2)	13	4	36	0	6th	415	249	–	101
Mohammad Hafeez	25.4	5	54	1	(3)	15	4	29	0	7th	442	262	–	105
Imran Khan	15	3	41	1	(1)	7	2	22	1	8th	454	267	–	170
Zulfiqar Babar	27	2	81	2		31.1	7	74	5	9th	454	299	–	213
Yasir Shah	16.3	1	66	3		25	6	50	4	10th	–	303	–	216

Umpires: M.Erasmus (*South Africa*) (27) and R.A.Kettleborough (*England*) (23).
Referee: R.S.Madugalle (*Sri Lanka*) (151).   **Test No. 2139/58 (P383/A767)**
Zulfiqar Babar retired not out at 454-8.

PAKISTAN v AUSTRALIA (2nd Test)

At Sheikh Zayed Stadium, Abu Dhabi, on 30, 31 October, 1, 2, 3 November 2014.
Toss: Pakistan. Result: **PAKISTAN** won by 356 runs.
Debuts: None.

PAKISTAN

Ahmed Shehzad	lbw b Lyon	35	b Johnson	14
Mohammad Hafeez	c Haddin b Johnson	45	c Starc b Johnson	3
Azhar Ali	c Warner b Starc	109	not out	100
Younus Khan	b Siddle	213	lbw b Smith	46
*Misbah-ul-Haq	c and b Smith	101	not out	101
Asad Shafiq	b Starc	21		
†Sarfraz Ahmed	not out	19		
Yasir Shah	not out	1		
Zulfiqar Babar				
Rahat Ali				
Imran Khan				
Extras	(B 10, LB 11, W 1, NB 4)	26	(B 23, LB 4, W 1, NB 1)	29
Total	**(6 wkts dec; 164 overs)**	**570**	**(3 wkts dec; 60.4 overs)**	**293**

AUSTRALIA

D.A.Warner	c Shah b Rahat	19	(2) c Shah b Hafeez	58
C.J.L.Rogers	c Sarfraz b Imran	5	(1) c Shafiq b Babar	2
N.M.Lyon	b Rahat	15	(11) c Azhar b Babar	0
G.J.Maxwell	b Babar	37	(3) lbw b Babar	4
*M.J.Clarke	b Imran	47	(4) b Babar	5
S.P.D.Smith	lbw b Babar	0	(5) lbw b Shah	97
M.R.Marsh	c Rahat b Imran	87	(6) c Shafiq b Hafeez	47
†B.J.Haddin	b Shah	10	(7) b Babar	13
M.G.Johnson	c Hafeez b Shah	0	(8) b Shah	0
P.M.Siddle	c Shah b Hafeez	28	(9) not out	4
M.A.Starc	not out	0	(10) b Shah	2
Extras	(LB 6, NB 7)	13	(B 5, LB 1, NB 3, Pen 5)	14
Total	**(67.2 overs)**	**261**	**(88.3 overs)**	**246**

AUSTRALIA	O	M	R	W		O	M	R	W		FALL OF WICKETS			
Johnson	25	7	59	1		7	1	45	2			P	A	P	A
Starc	27	3	86	2	(3)	11.4	2	56	0		Wkt	1st	1st	2nd	2nd
Siddle	31	8	75	1	(4)	14	4	48	0		1st	57	21	14	19
Lyon	37	1	154	1	(2)	18	3	48	0		2nd	96	34	21	31
Marsh	12	2	32	0	(6)	4	1	15	0		3rd	332	75	152	43
Maxwell	16	2	78	0							4th	513	97	–	101
Clarke	6	0	24	0							5th	537	100	–	208
Smith	10	0	41	1	(5)	6	0	54	1		6th	561	164	–	238
											7th	–	193	–	238
PAKISTAN											8th	–	199	–	238
Imran Khan	14	1	60	3	(2)	8	1	29	0		9th	–	261	–	245
Mohammad Hafeez	5.2	0	13	1	(3)	17	4	38	2		10th	–	261	–	246
Zulfiqar Babar	25	5	94	2	(4)	32.3	2	120	5						
Rahat Ali	9	0	41	2	(1)	8	6	3	0						
Yasir Shah	14	2	47	2		22	4	44	3						
Azhar Ali						1	0	1	0						

Umpires: R.A.Kettleborough (*England*) (24) and N.J.Llong (*England*) (26).
Referee: R.S.Madugalle (*Sri Lanka*) (152).   **Test No. 2140/59 (P384/A768)**

BANGLADESH v ZIMBABWE (1st Test)

At Shere Bangla National Stadium, Mirpur, on 25, 26, 27 October 2014.
Toss: Zimbabwe. Result: **BANGLADESH** won by three wickets.
Debuts: Bangladesh – Jubair Hossain; Zimbabwe – T.Kamungozi.

ZIMBABWE

V.Sibanda	c Mushfiqur b Shahadat	6		c Mushfiqur b Taijul	14
Sikandar Raza	c Mahmudullah b Jubair	51	(4)	c Shakib b Taijul	25
M.Masakadza	c Jubair b Shakib	13		b Shahadat	5
*B.R.M.Taylor	c Taijul b Jubair	28	(5)	not out	45
E.Chigumbura	c Mominul b Shakib	29	(6)	c Shuvagata b Taijul	0
C.R.Ervine	c Mominul b Taijul	34	(7)	lbw b Taijul	10
†R.W.Chakabva	c Shamsur b Shakib	25	(2)	c Shamsur b Taijul	10
J.C.Nyumbu	lbw b Shakib	14		c Mushfiqur b Shakib	1
T.Panyangara	c sub (Marshall Ayub) b Shakib	0		c Shamsur b Taijul	0
T.L.Chatara	not out	14		lbw b Taijul	4
T.Kamungozi	c Shamsur b Shakib	5		c Mushfiqur b Taijul	0
Extras	(B 12, NB 1)	13			
Total	(75.5 overs)	240		(35.5 overs)	114

BANGLADESH

Tamim Iqbal	c Masakadza b Panyangara	5		c Taylor b Chigumbura	0
Shamsur Rahman	c Chigumbura b Panyangara	8		b Panyangara	0
Mominul Haque	run out	53		c and b Chigumbura	0
Mahmudullah	lbw b Raza	63		b Chigumbura	28
Shakib Al Hasan	run out	5		c Nyumbu b Chatara	15
*†Mushfiqur Rahim	c Ervine b Panyangara	64		not out	23
Shuvagata Hom	c Chigumbura b Kamungozi	14		c Chakabva b Chigumbura	0
Taijul Islam	b Panyangara	19	(9)	not out	15
Shahadat Hossain	run out	0	(8)	c Taylor b Panyangara	11
Jubair Hossain	not out	7			
Al-Amin Hossain	b Panyangara	9			
Extras	(LB 6, W 1)	7		(B 4, W 5)	9
Total	(98 overs)	254		(7 wkts; 33.3 overs)	101

BANGLADESH	O	M	R	W		O	M	R	W
Shahadat Hossain	14	1	45	1		8	2	25	1
Al-Amin Hossain	8	2	22	0					
Shakib Al Hasan	24.5	5	59	6	(2)	10	2	44	1
Taijul Islam	13	3	42	1	(3)	16.5	7	39	8
Jubair Hossain	15	1	58	2	(4)	1	0	6	0
Mahmudullah	1	0	2	0					
ZIMBABWE									
Panyangara	23	5	59	5	(2)	8	2	30	2
Chatara	22	11	27	0	(3)	8	2	34	1
Chigumbura	14	6	34	0	(1)	10.3	4	21	4
Nyumbu	15	1	65	0	(6)	1	0	4	0
Kamungozi	21	5	51	1	(4)	5	1	7	0
Sikandar Raza	3	0	12	1	(5)	1	0	1	0

FALL OF WICKETS

	Z	B	Z	B
Wkt	1st	1st	2nd	2nd
1st	6	10	19	0
2nd	31	29	24	0
3rd	83	92	53	0
4th	128	114	58	46
5th	142	178	58	62
6th	192	209	92	62
7th	200	226	93	82
8th	221	226	104	—
9th	230	244	114	—
10th	240	254	114	—

Umpires: H.D.P.K.Dharmasena (*Sri Lanka*) (27) and S.Ravi (*India*) (4).
Referee: B.C.Broad (*England*) (63). **Test No. 2141/12 (B86/Z95)**

BANGLADESH v ZIMBABWE (2nd Test)

At Sheikh Abu Naser Stadium, Khulna, on 3, 4, 5, 6, 7 November 2014.
Toss: Bangladesh. Result: **BANGLADESH** won by 162 runs.
Debuts: Zimbabwe – B.B.Chari, N.M'shangwe.

BANGLADESH

Batsman	1st innings		2nd innings	
Tamim Iqbal	c Ervine b Masakadza	109	c and b Panyangara	20
Shamsur Rahman	lbw b Chigumbura	2	c Taylor b Waller	23
Mominul Haque	c and b Panyangara	35	c Chakabva b Waller	54
Mahmudullah	lbw b Panyangara	56	c Masakadza b M'shangwe	71
Shakib Al Hasan	b Waller	137	lbw b Waller	6
*†Mushfiqur Rahim	run out	11	c Chakabva b Waller	0
Shuvagata Hom	c Chari b Waller	15	c Masakadza b M'shangwe	50
Taijul Islam	c Masakadza b Chatara	32	c Panyangara b M'shangwe	1
Shahadat Hossain	c M'shangwe b Chatara	18	c Masakadza b M'shangwe	3
Jubair Hossain	lbw b M'shangwe	1		
Rubel Hossain	not out	0	(10) not out	8
Extras	(B 6, LB 6, W 2, NB 3)	17	(B 4, LB 4, W 3, NB 1)	12
Total	(158.5 overs; 646 mins)	433	(9 wkts dec; 83.5 overs; 338 mins)	248

ZIMBABWE

Batsman	1st innings		2nd innings	
Sikandar Raza	lbw b Taijul	11	c Mominul b Shakib	9
B.B.Chari	c Tamim b Taijul	25	c and b Taijul	4
H.Masakadza	b Shakib	158	c Mominul b Shakib	61
*B.R.M.Taylor	c Mominul b Shakib	37	c Shuvagata b Shakib	0
C.R.Ervine	c Mushfiqur b Shakib	17	(6) st Mushfiqur b Jubair	21
E.Chigumbura	c Mominul b Shakib	1	(7) c Mahmudullah b Shakib	12
†R.W.Chakabva	lbw b Taijul	101	(5) c Mahmudullah b Jubair	27
M.N.Waller	c Mushfiqur b Shakib	6	b Taijul	4
T.L.Chatara	c and b Rubel	0	(11) lbw b Taijul	1
N.M'shangwe	c Mushfiqur b Rubel	0	c Mushfiqur b Shakib	0
T.Panyangara	not out	1	(9) not out	8
Extras	(B 2, LB 7, W 1, NB 1)	11	(B 4)	4
Total	(135.1 overs; 537 mins)	368	(51.1 overs; 190 mins)	151

ZIMBABWE	O	M	R	W		O	M	R	W
Panyangara	29	10	49	2	(2)	12	3	45	1
Chigumbura	22	5	60	1	(1)	6	2	13	0
Chatara	27	7	61	2		7	3	19	0
M'shangwe	40.5	7	127	1	(6)	25.5	2	82	4
Waller	23	4	65	2	(4)	27	4	59	4
Sikandar Raza	11	2	31	0	(5)	6	0	22	0
Masakadza	6	1	28	1					

BANGLADESH	O	M	R	W		O	M	R	W
Shahadat Hossain	11	2	24	0					
Taijul Islam	32.1	6	96	3	(1)	15.1	3	44	3
Shakib Al Hasan	41	11	80	5	(2)	18	5	44	5
Jubair Hossain	19	2	64	0	(5)	10	0	42	2
Rubel Hossain	22	6	55	2	(4)	4	2	8	0
Shuvagata Hom	7	0	27	0	(3)	4	2	9	0
Mominul Haque	1	1	0	0					
Mahmudullah	2	0	13	0					

FALL OF WICKETS

	B	Z	B	Z
Wkt	1st	1st	2nd	2nd
1st	6	17	28	11
2nd	78	84	75	13
3rd	173	151	131	15
4th	305	181	145	85
5th	322	189	145	117
6th	376	336	220	137
7th	383	350	222	142
8th	426	354	236	142
9th	433	351	248	142
10th	433	368	–	151

Umpires: Alim Dar (*Pakistan*) (91) and B.F.Bowden (*New Zealand*) (80).
Referee: B.C.Broad (*England*) (64).   **Test No. 2142/13 (B87/Z96)**

BANGLADESH v ZIMBABWE (3rd Test)

At Zahur Ahmed Chowdhury Stadium, Chittagong, on 12, 13, 14, 15, 16 November 2014.
Toss: Bangladesh. Result: **BANGLADESH** won by 186 runs.
Debuts: None.

‡ (V.Sibanda)

BANGLADESH

Batsman	First innings		Second innings	
Tamim Iqbal	c H.Masakadza b Raza	109	b M'shangwe	65
Imrul Kayes	c sub‡ b H.Masakadza	130	c Mutumbami b Panyangara	15
Mominul Haque	c Taylor b Panyangara	48	not out	131
Mahmudullah	lbw b S.W.Masakadza	16	c Mutumbami b Panyangara	30
Shakib Al Hasan	c Ervine b Raza	71	c Ervine b M'shangwe	17
*†Mushfiqur Rahim	b H.Masakadza	15	c M'shangwe b Raza	46
Shuvagata Hom	run out	35	not out	3
Taijul Islam	c Mutumbami b S.W.Masakadza	1		
Shafiul Islam	c Ervine b Raza	10		
Rubel Hossain	not out	45		
Jubair Hossain	b Panyangara	5		
Extras	(B 2, LB 10, W 6)	18	(B 8, LB 3, W 1)	12
Total	(153.4 overs; 627 mins)	503	(5 wkts dec; 78 overs; 326 mins)	319

ZIMBABWE

Batsman	First innings		Second innings	
Sikandar Raza	c Mahmudullah b Jubair	82	c Taijul b Shuvagata	65
B.B.Chari	c Mushfiqur b Rubel	0	lbw b Rubel	0
H.Masakadza	lbw b Shafiul	81	c Mushfiqur b Shuvagata	38
*B.R.M.Taylor	c Taijul b Jubair	1	c Shakib b Jubair	24
R.W.Chakabva	lbw b Shafiul	65	not out	89
C.R.Ervine	b Jubair	14	(7) lbw b Mahmudullah	16
E.Chigumbura	c Imrul b Jubair	88	(6) c Imrul b Jubair	5
†R.Mutumbami	lbw b Shakib	20	lbw b Taijul	2
S.W.Masakadza	c Mahmudullah b Taijul	0	(10) b Shafiul	0
T.Panyangara	not out	6	(9) lbw b Rubel	0
N.M'shangwe	c Mahmudullah b Jubair	8	lbw b Shafiul	0
Extras	(B 6, LB 1, NB 2)	9	(B 14, LB 6, W 1)	21
Total	(106 overs; 416 mins)	374	(85 overs; 318 mins)	262

ZIMBABWE	O	M	R	W		O	M	R	W
Panyangara	20.4	2	70	2	(2)	12	3	31	2
Chigumbura	14	4	40	0	(5)	9	2	19	0
S.W.Masakadza	25	5	77	2	(1)	7	0	28	0
M'shangwe	47	5	149	0		18	2	77	2
Sikandar Raza	36	2	123	3	(3)	25	0	114	1
Chari	2	0	9	0					
H.Masakadza	9	1	23	2	(6)	7	1	39	0

BANGLADESH	O	M	R	W		O	M	R	W
Shafiul Islam	18	5	50	2		9	1	17	2
Rubel Hossain	9	1	46	1		4	2	16	2
Taijul Islam	30	2	100	1		22	4	48	1
Shakib Al Hasan	25	4	67	1	(5)	11	2	35	0
Jubair Hossain	20	1	96	5	(4)	19	3	56	2
Shuvagata Hom	3	1	0	1		16	1	66	2
Mahmudullah	3	0	7	0		4	1	4	1

FALL OF WICKETS

	B	Z	B	Z
Wkt	1st	1st	2nd	2nd
1st	224	9	36	4
2nd	272	169	149	97
3rd	312	172	204	116
4th	339	172	237	165
5th	378	209	308	179
6th	428	322	–	228
7th	429	356	–	237
8th	451	357	–	261
9th	452	360	–	262
10th	503	374	–	262

Umpires: Alim Dar (*Pakistan*) (92) and C.B.Gaffaney (*New Zealand*) (2).
Referee: B.C.Broad (*England*) (65).

Test No. 2143/14 (B88/Z97)

PAKISTAN v NEW ZEALAND (1st Test)

At Sheikh Zayed Stadium, Abu Dhabi, on 9, 10, 11, 12, 13 November 2014.
Toss: Pakistan. Result: **PAKISTAN** won by 248 runs.
Debuts: None.

PAKISTAN

Mohammad Hafeez	c and b Anderson	96		not out	101
Ahmed Shehzad	hit wkt b Anderson	176			
Azhar Ali	b Sodhi	87	(2)	lbw b Sodhi	23
Younus Khan	not out	100	(3)	lbw b Sodhi	28
*Misbah-ul-Haq	not out	102			
Asad Shafiq					
†Sarfraz Ahmed			(4)	not out	13
Yasir Shah					
Zulfiqar Babar					
Rahat Ali					
Imran Khan					
Extras	(B 2, LB 2, NB 1)	5		(B 6, LB 2, W 2)	10
Total	(3 wkts dec; 170.5 overs; 678 mins)	566		(2 wkts dec; 39.2 overs; 172 mins)	175

NEW ZEALAND

T.W.M.Latham	lbw b Rahat	103		c Shah b Babar	20
*B.B.McCullum	c Younus b Babar	18		lbw b Shah	39
K.S.Williamson	b Rahat	3		st Sarfraz b Hafeez	23
L.R.P.L.Taylor	c Shafiq b Babar	0		lbw b Shah	8
C.J.Anderson	b Rahat	48		lbw b Imran	23
J.D.S.Neesham	st Sarfraz b Hafeez	11		c Sarfraz b Rahat	0
†B.J.Watling	lbw b Babar	42		b Rahat	0
M.D.Craig	run out	1		b Shah	28
T.G.Southee	c Sarfraz b Rahat	0		b Babar	5
I.S.Sodhi	b Shah	25		lbw b Imran	63
T.A.Boult	not out	0		not out	19
Extras	(LB 7, NB 4)	11		(B 1, LB 2)	3
Total	(87.3 overs; 380 mins)	262		(70.3 overs; 299 mins)	231

NEW ZEALAND	O	M	R	W		O	M	R	W
Boult	26	7	62	0		7	2	25	0
Southee	23	5	62	0		9	0	33	0
Craig	33	1	126	0	(5)	5	0	29	0
Sodhi	43	6	162	1	(3)	13	1	66	2
Anderson	19	3	68	2	(4)	5	1	11	0
Neesham	16	0	50	0					
McCullum	10.5	1	32	0	(6)	0.2	0	3	0

PAKISTAN	O	M	R	W		O	M	R	W
Rahat Ali	17	10	22	4		11	1	48	2
Imran Khan	11	2	29	0		10.3	1	37	2
Zulfiqar Babar	27.3	5	79	3		24	6	48	2
Mohammad Hafeez	15	1	60	1	(5)	7	0	21	1
Yasir Shah	17	1	65	1	(4)	18	1	74	3

FALL OF WICKETS				
	P	NZ	P	NZ
Wkt	1st	1st	2nd	2nd
1st	178	33	69	57
2nd	347	38	139	61
3rd	373	47	–	69
4th	–	130	–	111
5th	–	150	–	112
6th	–	215	–	112
7th	–	219	–	121
8th	–	219	–	138
9th	–	262	–	177
10th	–	262	–	231

Umpires: R.E.J.Martinesz (*Sri Lanka*) (5) and R.J.Tucker (*Australia*) (34).
Referee: A.J.Pycroft (*Zimbabwe*) (31).

Test No. 2144/51 (P385/NZ395)

PAKISTAN v NEW ZEALAND (2nd Test)

At Dubai Sports City Stadium, on 17, 18, 19, 20, 21 November 2014.
Toss: New Zealand. Result: **MATCH DRAWN**.
Debuts: None.

NEW ZEALAND

T.W.M.Latham	c Sarfraz b Rahat	137	c Shafiq b Shah		9
*B.B.McCullum	c Masood b Adil	43	lbw b Babar		45
K.S.Williamson	b Babar	32	c Umar b Babar		11
L.R.P.L.Taylor	c Masood b Shah	23	st Sarfraz b Shah		104
C.J.Anderson	c Azhar b Adil	9	b Shah		0
J.D.S.Neesham	c Misbah b Shah	17	b Babar		11
†B.J.Watling	c sub (Haris Sohail) b Azhar	39	c Shafiq b Shah		11
M.D.Craig	lbw b Babar	43	c Rahat b Shah		34
T.G.Southee	b Babar	17	c Azhar b Babar		20
I.S.Sodhi	not out	32	not out		2
T.A.Boult	c Rahat b Babar	2			
Extras	(LB 9)	9	(LB 3)		3
Total	**(156 overs)**	**403**	**(9 wkts dec; 64.5 overs; 298 mins)**		**250**

PAKISTAN

Shan Masood	b Sodhi	13	lbw b Boult		40
Taufiq Umar	st Watling b Craig	16	c Watling b Southee		4
Azhar Ali	b Sodhi	75	c Neesham b Craig		24
Younus Khan	c Craig b Neesham	72	c Taylor b Craig		44
*Misbah-ul-Haq	c Taylor b Boult	28	c Watling b Boult		0
Asad Shafiq	c Taylor b Southee	44	not out		41
†Sarfraz Ahmed	c and b McCullum	112	not out		24
Yasir Shah	c Watling b Southee	2			
Ehsan Adil	lbw b Southee	0			
Zulfiqar Babar	c Watling b Boult	5			
Rahat Ali	not out	16			
Extras	(B 7, LB 2, NB 1)	10	(B 15, LB 2, W 1, NB 1)		19
Total	**(147 overs)**	**393**	**(5 wkts; 67 overs; 261 mins)**		**196**

PAKISTAN	O	M	R	W	O	M	R	W
Rahat Ali	32	8	69	1	8	0	39	0
Ehsan Adil	29	9	73	2	8	1	33	0
Zulfiqar Babar	45	8	137	4	27.5	5	96	4
Yasir Shah	41	7	92	2	21	1	79	5
Azhar Ali	9	1	23	1				

NEW ZEALAND	O	M	R	W	O	M	R	W
Boult	30	8	69	2	10	6	12	2
Southee	30	5	67	3	11	3	21	1
Craig	28	5	117	1	17	3	66	2
Sodhi	39	9	92	2	21	5	63	0
Anderson	7	0	26	0	3	1	4	0
Neesham	11	2	12	1	2	1	1	0
McCullum	2	1	1	1	3	0	12	0

FALL OF WICKETS

	NZ	P	NZ	P
Wkt	1st	1st	2nd	2nd
1st	77	28	42	8
2nd	153	32	63	70
3rd	226	145	78	73
4th	245	195	79	75
5th	245	220	125	149
6th	278	279	166	–
7th	346	285	226	–
8th	348	287	228	–
9th	387	312	250	–
10th	403	393	–	–

Umpires: R.E.J.Martinesz (*Sri Lanka*) (6) and P.R.Reiffel (*Australia*) (12).
Referee: A.J.Pycroft (*Zimbabwe*) (32).   **Test No. 2145/52 (P386/NZ396)**

PAKISTAN v NEW ZEALAND (3rd Test)

At Sharjah Cricket Association Stadium, on 26, 27 (*no play*), 28, 29, 30 November 2014.
Toss: Pakistan. Result: **NEW ZEALAND** won by an innings and 80 runs.
Debuts: None.

PAKISTAN

Mohammad Hafeez	c Boult b Sodhi	197	c and b Craig		24
Shan Masood	b Craig	12	c Southee b Boult		4
Azhar Ali	c Taylor b Craig	39	b Boult		6
Younus Khan	lbw b Vettori	5	lbw b Boult		0
*Misbah-ul-Haq	c Watling b Southee	38	c Watling b Craig		12
Asad Shafiq	c Sodhi b Craig	11	c Craig b Boult		137
†Sarfraz Ahmed	c Watling b Craig	15	c Taylor b Sodhi		37
Yasir Shah	c Taylor b Craig	25	lbw b Sodhi		10
Mohammad Talha	c Latham b Craig	0	lbw b Vettori		19
Rahat Ali	c Taylor b Craig	0	c McCullum b Craig		6
Zulfiqar Babar	not out	0	not out		0
Extras	(LB 4, W 4, NB 1)	9	(LB 2, W 1, NB 1)		4
Total	**(125.4 overs)**	**351**	**(63.3 overs)**		**259**

NEW ZEALAND

T.W.M.Latham	c Sarfraz b Rahat	13
*B.B.McCullum	b Shah	202
K.S.Williamson	c Younus b Rahat	192
L.R.P.L.Taylor	c Younus b Shah	50
C.J.Anderson	c Shah b Rahat	50
D.L.Vettori	lbw b Rahat	15
†B.J.Watling	lbw b Hafeez	8
M.D.Craig	c and b Hafeez	65
T.G.Southee	c Talha b Shah	50
I.S.Sodhi	c Younus b Shah	22
T.A.Boult	not out	0
Extras	(B 2, LB 7, W 8, NB 6)	23
Total	**(143.1 overs)**	**690**

NEW ZEALAND	O	M	R	W		O	M	R	W
Boult	21	6	54	0		15	6	38	4
Southee	24	4	54	1		11	3	20	0
Vettori	19	5	41	1	(4)	5	2	8	1
Anderson	12	4	28	0					
Craig	27.4	5	94	7	(3)	20.3	2	109	3
Sodhi	22	3	76	1	(5)	12	0	82	2

PAKISTAN	O	M	R	W
Mohammad Talha	22	2	136	0
Rahat Ali	29	2	99	4
Zulfiqar Babar	23	1	135	0
Yasir Shah	44.1	4	193	4
Mohammad Hafeez	23	2	110	2
Azhar Ali	2	0	8	0

FALL OF WICKETS

	P	NZ	P
Wkt	1st	1st	2nd
1st	44	51	13
2nd	131	348	20
3rd	160	464	24
4th	285	488	36
5th	311	528	63
6th	313	537	136
7th	336	546	146
8th	336	637	180
9th	346	682	258
10th	351	690	259

Umpires: P.R.Reiffel (*Australia*) (13) and R.J.Tucker (*Australia*) (35).
Referee: A.J.Pycroft (*Zimbabwe*) (33). **Test No. 2146/53 (P387/NZ397)**

AUSTRALIA v INDIA (1st Test)

At Adelaide Oval, on 9, 10, 11, 12, 13 December 2014.
Toss: Australia. Result: **AUSTRALIA** won by 48 runs.
Debut: India – K.V.Sharma.

AUSTRALIA

C.J.L.Rogers	c Dhawan b I.Sharma	9	c R.G.Sharma b K.V.Sharma		21
D.A.Warner	c I.Sharma b K.V.Sharma	145	b K.V.Sharma		102
S.R.Watson	c Dhawan b Aaron	14	b Shami		33
*M.J.Clarke	c Pujara b K.V.Sharma	128	c Saha b Aaron		7
S.P.D.Smith	not out	162	not out		52
M.R.Marsh	c Kohli b Aaron	41	c Vijay b R.G.Sharma		40
N.M.Lyon	b Shami	3			
†B.J.Haddin	c Saha b Shami	0	(7) not out		14
M.G.Johnson	not out	0			
P.M.Siddle					
R.J.Harris					
Extras	(LB 4, W 9, NB 2)	15	(B 1, LB 6, W 5, NB 9)		21
Total	**(7 wkts dec; 120 overs)**	**517**	**(5 wkts dec; 69 overs)**		**290**

INDIA

M.Vijay	c Haddin b Johnson	53	lbw b Lyon		99
S.Dhawan	b Harris	25	c Haddin b Johnson		9
C.A.Pujara	b Lyon	73	c Haddin b Lyon		21
*V.Kohli	c Harris b Johnson	115	c Marsh b Lyon		141
A.M.Rahane	c Watson b Lyon	62	c Rogers b Lyon		0
R.G.Sharma	c and b Lyon	43	c Warner b Lyon		6
†W.P.Saha	c Watson b Lyon	25	b Lyon		13
K.V.Sharma	b Siddle	4	not out		4
Mohammed Shami	c Watson b Siddle	34	c Johnson b Harris		5
I.Sharma	c Smith b Lyon	0	(11) st Haddin b Lyon		1
V.R.Aaron	not out	3	(10) lbw b Johnson		1
Extras	(LB 4, W 1, NB 2)	7	(B 5, LB 8, W 2)		15
Total	**(116.4 overs)**	**444**	**(87.1 overs)**		**315**

INDIA	O	M	R	W	O	M	R	W
Mohammed Shami	24	2	120	2	11	2	42	1
Aaron	23	1	136	2	(6) 10	0	43	1
I.Sharma	27	5	85	1	(2) 14	3	41	0
K.V.Sharma	33	1	143	2	(3) 16	2	95	2
Vijay	13	3	29	0	(4) 6	0	27	0
R.G.Sharma					(5) 12	2	35	1

AUSTRALIA	O	M	R	W	O	M	R	W
Johnson	22	6	102	2	16	2	45	2
Harris	21	6	55	1	19	6	49	2
Lyon	36	4	134	5	34.1	5	152	7
Siddle	18.4	2	88	2	9	3	21	0
Marsh	11	4	29	0	(7) 4	1	11	0
Watson	5	1	13	0	(5) 2	0	6	0
Smith	3	0	19	0	(6) 3	0	18	0

FALL OF WICKETS				
	A	I	A	I
Wkt	1st	1st	2nd	2nd
1st	50	30	38	16
2nd	88	111	140	57
3rd	258	192	168	242
4th	345	293	213	242
5th	352	367	266	277
6th	354	399	–	299
7th	517	406	–	304
8th	–	422	–	309
9th	–	422	–	314
10th	–	444	–	315

Umpires: M.Erasmus (*South Africa*) (28) and I.J.Gould (*England*) (42).
Referee: J.J.Crowe (*New Zealand*) (68). **Test No. 2147/87 (A769/I484)**
M.J.Clarke (60*) retired not out at 206-2 and resumed at 354-6.

AUSTRALIA v INDIA (2nd Test)

At Woolloongabba, Brisbane, on 17, 18, 19, 20 December 2014.
Toss: India. Result: **AUSTRALIA** won by four wickets.
Debut: Australia – J.R.Hazlewood.

INDIA

M.Vijay	c Haddin b Lyon	144	b Starc		27
S.Dhawan	c Haddin b M.R.Marsh	24	lbw b Lyon		81
C.A.Pujara	c Haddin b Hazlewood	18	c Lyon b Hazlewood		43
V.Kohli	c Haddin b Hazlewood	19	b Johnson		1
A.M.Rahane	c Haddin b Hazlewood	81	c Lyon b Johnson		10
R.G.Sharma	c Smith b Watson	32	c Haddin b Johnson		0
*†M.S.Dhoni	c Haddin b Hazlewood	33	lbw b Hazlewood		0
R.Ashwin	c Watson b Hazlewood	35	c Haddin b Starc		19
U.T.Yadav	c Rogers b Lyon	9	c Haddin b Johnson		30
V.R.Aaron	c sub (M.Labuschagne) b Lyon	4	c Hazlewood b Lyon		3
I.Sharma	not out	1	not out		1
Extras	(B 4, LB 1, W 2, NB 1)	8	(LB 2, W 5, NB 2)		9
Total	**(109.4 overs; 521 mins)**	**408**	**(64.3 overs; 303 mins)**		**224**

AUSTRALIA

C.J.L.Rogers	c Dhoni b Yadav	55	c Dhawan b I.Sharma		55
D.A.Warner	c Ashwin b Yadav	29	c Dhoni b I.Sharma		6
S.R.Watson	c Dhawan b Ashwin	25	c Dhoni b I.Sharma		0
*S.P.D.Smith	b I.Sharma	133	run out		28
S.E.Marsh	c Ashwin b Yadav	32	c Dhoni b Yadav		17
M.R.Marsh	b I.Sharma	11	(7) not out		6
†B.J.Haddin	c Pujara b Aaron	6	(6) c Kohli b Yadav		1
M.G.Johnson	c Dhoni b I.Sharma	88	not out		2
M.A.Starc	b Ashwin	52			
N.M.Lyon	c R.G.Sharma b Aaron	23			
J.R.Hazlewood	not out	32			
Extras	(LB 4, W 5, NB 10)	19	(B 4, LB 4, W 1, NB 6)		15
Total	**(109.4 overs; 502 mins)**	**505**	**(6 wkts; 23.1 overs; 120 mins)**		**130**

AUSTRALIA	O	M	R	W		O	M	R	W	FALL OF WICKETS				
											I	A	I	A
Johnson	21	4	81	0		17.3	4	61	4	*Wkt*	*1st*	*1st*	*2nd*	*2nd*
Hazlewood	23.2	6	68	5		16	0	74	2	1st	56	47	41	18
Starc	17	1	83	0		8	1	27	2	2nd	100	98	76	22
M.R.Marsh	6	1	14	1						3rd	137	121	86	85
Lyon	25.4	2	105	3		10	1	33	2	4th	261	208	86	114
Watson	14.4	6	39	1	(4)	13	6	27	0	5th	321	232	87	122
Warner	1	0	9	0						6th	328	247	117	122
Smith	1	0	4	0						7th	385	395	143	–
										8th	394	398	203	–
INDIA										9th	407	454	211	–
I.Sharma	23	2	117	3		9	2	38	3	10th	408	505	224	–
Aaron	26	1	145	2	(3)	5.1	0	38	0					
Yadav	25	4	101	3	(2)	9	0	46	2					
Ashwin	33.4	4	128	2										
R.G.Sharma	2	0	10	0										

Umpires: M.Erasmus (*South Africa*) (29) and I.J.Gould (*England*) (43).
Referee: J.J.Crowe (*New Zealand*) (69).   **Test No. 2148/88 (A770/I485)**
S.Dhawan (26*) retired not out at 71-1 and resumed at 117-6.

AUSTRALIA v INDIA (3rd Test)

At Melbourne Cricket Ground, on 26, 27, 28, 29, 30 December 2014.
Toss: Australia. Result: **MATCH DRAWN**.
Debuts: Australia – J.A.Burns; India – K.L.Rahul.

AUSTRALIA

C.J.L.Rogers	c Dhoni b Shami	57	(2)	b Ashwin	69
D.A.Warner	c Dhawan b Yadav	0	(1)	lbw b Ashwin	40
S.R.Watson	lbw b Ashwin	52		c Dhoni b Sharma	17
*S.P.D.Smith	b Yadav	192		c Rahane b Yadav	14
S.E.Marsh	c Dhoni b Shami	32		run out	99
J.A.Burns	c Dhoni b Yadav	13		c Dhoni b Sharma	9
†B.J.Haddin	c Dhoni b Shami	55		c Dhoni b Yadav	13
M.G.Johnson	st Dhoni b Ashwin	28		c Rahane b Shami	15
R.J.Harris	lbw b Ashwin	74		c Dhoni b Shami	21
N.M.Lyon	b Shami	11		not out	1
J.R.Hazlewood	not out	0		not out	0
Extras	(B 1, LB 9, W 1, NB 5)	16		(LB 13, W 2, NB 5)	20
Total	(142.3 overs)	530		(9 wkts dec; 98 overs)	318

INDIA

M.Vijay	c Marsh b Watson	68		lbw b Hazlewood	11
S.Dhawan	c Smith b Harris	28		lbw b Harris	0
C.A.Pujara	c Haddin b Harris	25	(6)	b Johnson	21
V.Kohli	c Haddin b Johnson	169		c Burns b Harris	54
A.M.Rahane	lbw b Lyon	147		c Marsh b Hazlewood	48
K.L.Rahul	c Hazlewood b Lyon	3	(3)	c Watson b Johnson	1
*†M.S.Dhoni	c Haddin b Harris	11		not out	24
R.Ashwin	c and b Harris	0		not out	8
Mohammed Shami	c Smith b Johnson	12			
U.T.Yadav	c Haddin b Johnson	0			
I.Sharma	not out	0			
Extras	(LB 1, W 1)	2		(LB 6, NB 1)	7
Total	(128.5 overs)	465		(6 wkts; 66 overs)	174

INDIA	O	M	R	W		O	M	R	W
Sharma	32	7	104	0	(3)	20	5	49	2
Yadav	32.3	3	130	3	(1)	22	3	89	2
Mohammed Shami	29	4	138	4	(2)	28	4	92	2
Ashwin	44	9	134	3		28	4	75	2
Vijay	5	0	14	0					

AUSTRALIA	O	M	R	W		O	M	R	W
Johnson	30.5	6	135	3		15	3	38	2
Harris	26	7	70	4		16	8	30	2
Hazlewood	25	6	75	0		15	3	40	2
Watson	16	3	65	1	(5)	6	1	14	0
Lyon	29	3	108	2	(4)	12	0	36	0
Smith	2	0	11	0		2	0	10	0

FALL OF WICKETS

Wkt	A 1st	I 1st	A 2nd	I 2nd
1st	0	55	57	2
2nd	115	108	98	5
3rd	115	147	131	19
4th	184	409	164	104
5th	216	415	176	141
6th	326	430	202	142
7th	376	434	234	–
8th	482	462	303	–
9th	530	462	317	–
10th	530	465	–	–

Umpires: H.D.P.K.Dharmasena (*Sri Lanka*) (28) and R.A.Kettleborough (*England*) (25).
Referee: R.S.Mahanama (*Sri Lanka*) (55).   **Test No. 2149/89 (A771/I486)**

AUSTRALIA v INDIA (4th Test)

At Sydney Cricket Ground, on 6, 7, 8, 9, 10 January 2015.
Toss: Australia. Result: **MATCH DRAWN**.
Debuts: None.

AUSTRALIA

C.J.L.Rogers	b Shami	95	c Raina b Kumar		56
D.A.Warner	c Vijay b Ashwin	101	c Vijay b Ashwin		4
S.R.Watson	c Ashwin b Shami	81	b Ashwin		16
*S.P.D.Smith	c Saha b Yadav	117	lbw b Shami		71
S.E.Marsh	c Saha b Shami	73	c Vijay b Ashwin		1
J.A.Burns	c Rahul b Shami	58	c Yadav b Ashwin		66
†B.J.Haddin	not out	9	not out		31
R.J.Harris	c Ashwin b Shami	25	not out		0
M.A.Starc					
N.M.Lyon					
J.R.Hazlewood					
Extras	(LB 6, W 7)	13	(B 2, LB 2, NB 2)		6
Total	**(7 wkts dec; 152.3 overs)**	**572**	**(6 wkts dec; 40 overs)**		**251**

INDIA

M.Vijay	c Haddin b Starc	0	c Haddin b Hazlewood		80
K.L.Rahul	c and b Starc	110	c Warner b Lyon		16
R.G.Sharma	b Lyon	53	c Smith b Watson		39
*V.Kohli	c Rogers b Harris	147	c Watson b Starc		46
A.M.Rahane	lbw b Watson	13	not out		38
S.K.Raina	c Haddin b Watson	0	lbw b Starc		0
†W.P.Saha	c Smith b Hazlewood	35	lbw b Lyon		0
R.Ashwin	c Haddin b Starc	50	lbw b Hazlewood		1
B.Kumar	c Watson b Lyon	30	not out		20
Mohammed Shami	not out	16			
U.T.Yadav	c Haddin b Harris	4			
Extras	(B 4, LB 7, W 1, NB 5)	17	(B 4, LB 8)		12
Total	**(162 overs)**	**475**	**(7 wkts; 89.5 overs)**		**252**

INDIA	O	M	R	W		O	M	R	W
Kumar	34	5	122	0		8	0	46	1
Yadav	27	5	137	1	(4)	3	0	45	0
Mohammed Shami	28.3	3	112	5		6	0	33	1
Ashwin	47	8	142	1	(2)	19	2	105	4
Raina	16	3	53	0		4	0	18	0

AUSTRALIA	O	M	R	W		O	M	R	W
Starc	32	7	106	3		19	7	36	2
Harris	31	7	96	2		13	3	34	0
Hazlewood	29	8	64	1	(4)	17	7	31	2
Lyon	46	11	123	2	(3)	30.5	5	110	2
Watson	20	4	58	2	(6)	8	2	22	1
Smith	4	0	17	0	(5)	2	0	7	0

FALL OF WICKETS				
	A	I	A	I
Wkt	1st	1st	2nd	2nd
1st	200	0	6	48
2nd	204	97	46	104
3rd	400	238	126	178
4th	415	292	139	201
5th	529	292	165	203
6th	546	352	251	208
7th	572	383	–	217
8th	–	448	–	–
9th	–	456	–	–
10th	–	475	–	–

Umpires: H.D.P.K.Dharmasena (*Sri Lanka*) (29) and R.A.Kettleborough (*England*) (26).
Referee: R.S.Mahanama (*Sri Lanka*) (56).   **Test No. 2150/90 (A772/1487)**

SOUTH AFRICA v WEST INDIES (1st Test)

At SuperSport Park, Centurion, on 17, 18, 19, 20 December 2014.
Toss: West Indies. Result: **SOUTH AFRICA** won by an innings and 220 runs.
Debut: South Africa – S.van Zyl.

SOUTH AFRICA

A.N.Petersen	c Smith b Roach	27
D.Elgar	c Samuels b Cottrell	28
F.du Plessis	c Ramdin b Roach	0
*H.M.Amla	c Taylor b Benn	208
A.B.de Villiers	c Blackwood b Benn	152
S.van Zyl	not out	101
†Q.de Kock	not out	18
V.D.Philander		
D.W.Steyn		
M.Morkel		
K.J.Abbott		
Extras	(B 8, LB 6, W 2, NB 2)	18
Total	**(5 wkts dec; 140.3 overs; 552 563 mins)**	**552**

WEST INDIES

K.C.Brathwaite	c Amla b Philander	34	c Petersen b Morkel		20
D.S.Smith	c de Villiers b Philander	35	c sub (T.Bavuma) b Philander		5
L.R.Johnson	c sub (R.J.Peterson) b Abbott	31	c de Villiers b Steyn		39
M.N.Samuels	b Morkel	33	c Elgar b Steyn		17
S.Chanderpaul	c Petersen b Philander	21	c de Villiers b Steyn		4
J.Blackwood	c Petersen b Philander	12	c sub (T.Bavuma) b Morkel		15
*†D.Ramdin	c van Zyl b Elgar	14	c de Villiers b Steyn		4
J.E.Taylor	c and b Morkel	4	c Amla b Steyn		9
S.J.Benn	not out	6	not out		6
S.S.Cottrell	b Morkel	2	c Abbott b Steyn		4
K.A.J.Roach	absent hurt	–	absent hurt		–
Extras	(LB 6, W 3)	9	(LB 3, W 4, NB 1)		8
Total	**(60.2 overs; 293 mins)**	**201**	**(42.3 overs; 194 mins)**		**131**

WEST INDIES	O	M	R	W		O	M	R	W
Taylor	26.1	5	108	0					
Cottrell	28	1	124	1					
Roach	15.5	4	52	2					
Benn	46	7	148	2					
Samuels	20	0	89	0					
Brathwaite	1	0	2	0					
Blackwood	3.3	0	15	0					

SOUTH AFRICA	O	M	R	W		O	M	R	W
Steyn	14	3	53	0		8.2	2	34	6
Philander	15	6	29	4	(3)	7	4	6	1
Abbott	14	3	50	1	(4)	3	0	11	0
Morkel	15.2	4	55	3	(2)	11.1	1	43	2
Elgar	2	0	8	1	(6)	3	0	12	0
Van Zyl					(5)	10	2	22	0

FALL OF WICKETS

	SA	WI	WI
Wkt	1st	1st	2nd
1st	57	72	8
2nd	57	73	52
3rd	57	117	87
4th	365	162	91
5th	520	169	101
6th	–	184	105
7th	–	193	117
8th	–	193	121
9th	–	201	131
10th	–	–	–

Umpires: Alim Dar (*Pakistan*) (93) and B.F.Bowden (*New Zealand*) (81).
Referee: R.S.Madugalle (*Sri Lanka*) (153).　　　　**Test No. 2151/26 (SA388/WI501)**

SOUTH AFRICA v WEST INDIES (2nd Test)

At St George's Park, Port Elizabeth, on 26, 27, 28, 29, 30 (*no play*) December 2014.
Toss: West Indies. Result: **MATCH DRAWN**.
Debuts: South Africa – T.Bavuma; West Indies – K.K.Peters.

SOUTH AFRICA

D.Elgar	c Ramdin b Peters	121
A.N.Petersen	c Johnson b Gabriel	17
F.du Plessis	c Ramdin b Taylor	103
*H.M.Amla	lbw b Holder	33
†A.B.de Villiers	b Taylor	10
T.Bavuma	c Ramdin b Gabriel	10
S.van Zyl	c Ramdin b Peters	29
V.D.Philander	not out	13
D.W.Steyn	c Holder b Benn	58
M.Morkel		
Imran Tahir		
Extras	(B 4, LB 5, W 6, NB 8)	23
Total	**(8 wkts dec; 122 overs; 562 mins)**	**417**

WEST INDIES

K.C.Brathwaite	c Petersen b Morkel	106
D.S.Smith	c Amla b Morkel	22
L.R.Johnson	c du Plessis b Morkel	0
M.N.Samuels	lbw b Philander	101
S.Chanderpaul	b Tahir	7
*†D.Ramdin	lbw b Tahir	20
J.O.Holder	c de Villiers b Morkel	1
J.E.Taylor	not out	10
S.J.Benn	c Petersen b Tahir	4
K.K.Peters	run out	0
S.T.Gabriel		
Extras	(LB 4)	4
Total	**(9 wkts; 79 overs; 349 mins)**	**275**

WEST INDIES	O	M	R	W
Taylor	30	7	114	2
Peters	20	7	69	2
Holder	22	7	43	1
Gabriel	21	0	80	2
Benn	28	4	102	1
Samuels	1	1	0	0

SOUTH AFRICA	O	M	R	W
Steyn	14	3	48	0
Philander	18	4	41	1
Morkel	20	2	69	4
Imran Tahir	26	2	108	3
Elgar	1	0	5	0

FALL OF WICKETS		
	SA	WI
Wkt	1st	1st
1st	47	55
2nd	226	55
3rd	274	231
4th	300	233
5th	304	260
6th	325	261
7th	348	265
8th	417	270
9th	–	275
10th	–	–

Umpires: B.F.Bowden (*New Zealand*) (82) and P.R.Reiffel (*Australia*) (14).
Referee: R.S.Madugalle (*Sri Lanka*) (154). **Test No. 2152/27 (SA389/WI502)**

SOUTH AFRICA v WEST INDIES (3rd Test)

At Newlands, Cape Town, on 2, 3, 4, 5, 6 January 2015.
Toss: West Indies. Result: **SOUTH AFRICA** won by eight wickets.
Debut: South Africa – S.R.Harmer.

WEST INDIES

Batsman	First innings		Second innings	
K.C.Brathwaite	c Elgar b Steyn	7	b Harmer	16
D.S.Smith	b Harmer	47	c de Villiers b Morkel	7
L.R.Johnson	lbw b Harmer	54	c Amla b Morkel	44
M.N.Samuels	c du Plessis b van Zyl	43	c Elgar b Harmer	74
S.Chanderpaul	st de Villiers b Harmer	9	run out	50
J.Blackwood	lbw b Steyn	56	b Steyn	13
*†D.Ramdin	c and b Steyn	53	c Harmer b Steyn	0
J.O.Holder	c van Zyl b Steyn	23	c Amla b Harmer	2
J.E.Taylor	c Steyn b Morkel	13	c Elgar b Harmer	0
S.J.Benn	c Bavuma b Morkel	5	c de Villiers b Steyn	0
S.T.Gabriel	not out	4	not out	2
Extras	(LB 15, W 8, NB 2)	15	(B 4, LB 3)	7
Total	**(99.5 overs; 424 mins)**	**329**	**(79.5 overs; 355 mins)**	**215**

SOUTH AFRICA

Batsman	First innings		Second innings	
A.N.Petersen	run out	42	(2) b Benn	0
D.Elgar	lbw b Holder	8	(1) not out	60
F.du Plessis	st Ramdin b Benn	68	c Blackwood b Benn	14
*H.M.Amla	c Ramdin b Holder	64	not out	38
†A.B.de Villiers	c Gabriel b Samuels	148		
T.Bavuma	b Gabriel	15		
S.van Zyl	lbw b Samuels	33		
V.D.Philander	run out	0		
S.R.Harmer	lbw b Taylor	10		
D.W.Steyn	run out	0		
M.Morkel	not out	0		
Extras	(LB 7, W 13, NB 10)	30	(B 8, LB 2, NB 2)	12
Total	**(122.4 overs; 521 mins)**	**421**	**(2 wkts; 37.4 overs; 148 mins)**	**124**

SOUTH AFRICA	O	M	R	W		O	M	R	W
Steyn	25	6	78	4		23.5	3	75	3
Philander	19	2	73	0		16	4	27	0
Morkel	19.5	1	83	2		14	7	18	2
Harmer	26	5	71	3		24	7	82	4
Van Zyl	8	2	13	1		2	0	6	0
Elgar	2	0	6	0					

WEST INDIES	O	M	R	W		O	M	R	W
Taylor	20	2	80	1		7	3	20	0
Gabriel	17	2	64	1	(5)	5	1	27	0
Holder	24	4	87	2	(4)	5	0	19	0
Samuels	16.4	0	68	2	(2)	3.4	0	24	0
Benn	45	9	115	1	(3)	17	8	24	2

FALL OF WICKETS

Wkt	WI 1st	SA 1st	WI 2nd	SA 2nd
1st	30	48	23	9
2nd	80	104	27	51
3rd	131	157	95	–
4th	162	254	182	–
5th	172	288	202	–
6th	266	384	204	–
7th	299	389	213	–
8th	316	404	213	–
9th	319	408	213	–
10th	329	421	215	–

Umpires: Alim Dar (*Pakistan*) (94) and P.R.Reiffel (*Australia*) (15).
Referee: R.S.Madugalle (*Sri Lanka*) (155). **Test No. 2153/28 (SA390/WI503)**

NEW ZEALAND v SRI LANKA (1st Test)

At Hagley Oval, Christchurch, on 26, 27, 28, 29 December 2014.
Toss: Sri Lanka. Result: **NEW ZEALAND** won by eight wickets.
Debut: Sri Lanka – P.H.T.Kaushal.

NEW ZEALAND

T.W.M.Latham	c Kaushal b Eranga	27	c Mathews b Kaushal		17
H.D.Rutherford	b Lakmal	18	c Dickwella b Eranga		10
K.S.Williamson	b Prasad	54	not out		31
L.R.P.L.Taylor	run out	7	not out		39
*B.B.McCullum	c Karunaratne b Kaushal	195			
J.D.S.Neesham	c Sangakkara b Mathews	85			
†B.J.Watling	lbw b Mathews	26			
M.D.Craig	not out	12			
T.G.Southee	c Thirimanne b Mathews	0			
N.Wagner	c Kaushal b Lakmal	4			
T.A.Boult	c Jayawardena b Lakmal	0			
Extras	(LB 4, W 2, NB 7)	13	(LB 6, W 2, NB 2)		10
Total	**(85.5 overs; 413 mins)**	**441**	**(2 wkts; 30.4 overs; 137 mins)**		**107**

SRI LANKA

F.D.M.Karunaratne	lbw b Boult	0	b Boult		152
J.K.Silva	lbw b Boult	4	c Watling b Southee		33
K.C.Sangakkara	c Southee b Boult	6	c Watling b Boult		1
H.D.R.L.Thirimanne	c Craig b Southee	24	c Watling b Neesham		25
*A.D.Mathews	c Latham b Wagner	50	c Watling b Southee		66
D.P.D.N.Dickwella	c McCullum b Southee	2	c Neesham b Boult		4
†H.A.P.W.Jayawardena	c Williamson b Wagner	10	(8) c Southee b Craig		23
K.T.G.D.Prasad	c McCullum b Neesham	18	(9) c Taylor b Southee		4
P.H.T.Kaushal	c Williamson b Wagner	6	(7) c Craig b Southee		12
R.M.S.Eranga	not out	10	not out		45
R.A.S.Lakmal	c McCullum b Neesham	2	c Southee b Boult		16
Extras	(LB 3, W 2, NB 1)	6	(B 4, LB 20, W 1, NB 1)		26
Total	**(42.4 overs; 204 mins)**	**138**	**(154 overs; 655 mins)**		**407**

SRI LANKA	O	M	R	W		O	M	R	W
Lakmal	19.5	3	90	3		6	2	16	0
Eranga	18	1	82	1	(3)	7	2	20	1
Mathews	12	2	39	3					
Prasad	12	2	62	1		4.4	1	17	0
Kaushal	22	0	159	1	(2)	13	0	48	1
Thirimanne	2	0	5	0					

NEW ZEALAND	O	M	R	W		O	M	R	W
Boult	11	4	25	3		39	8	100	4
Southee	12	4	17	2		37	8	91	4
Neesham	6.4	1	28	2	(5)	8	2	29	1
Wagner	11	0	60	3	(3)	30	6	76	0
Craig	2	0	5	0	(4)	38	10	83	1
McCullum						1	0	3	0
Williamson						1	0	5	0

FALL OF WICKETS				
	NZ	SL	SL	NZ
Wkt	1st	1st	2nd	2nd
1st	37	0	85	23
2nd	60	8	94	43
3rd	88	15	181	–
4th	214	58	277	–
5th	367	60	287	–
6th	420	88	307	–
7th	429	105	320	–
8th	431	118	325	–
9th	440	128	348	–
10th	441	138	407	–

Umpires: R.K.Illingworth (*England*) (13) and B.N.J.Oxenford (*Australia*) (21).
Referee: B.C.Broad (*England*) (66).   **Test No. 2154/29 (NZ398/SL234)**

NEW ZEALAND v SRI LANKA (2nd Test)

At Basin Reserve, Wellington, on 3, 4, 5, 6, 7 January 2015.
Toss: Sri Lanka. Result: **NEW ZEALAND** won by 193 runs.
Debuts: None.

NEW ZEALAND

T.W.M.Latham	c Jayawardena b Lakmal	6	c Jayawardena b Fernando	35
H.D.Rutherford	c Jayawardena b Fernando	37	c Chandimal b Fernando	40
K.S.Williamson	b Prasad	69	not out	242
L.R.P.L.Taylor	b Fernando	35	b Herath	0
*B.B.McCullum	b Lakmal	0	lbw b Prasad	22
J.D.S.Neesham	c Jayawardena b Fernando	15	lbw b Fernando	19
†B.J.Watling	c Chandimal b Mathews	11	not out	142
M.D.Craig	c Mathews b Lakmal	7		
D.A.J.Bracewell	b Prasad	16		
T.G.Southee	c Sangakkara b Fernando	0		
T.A.Boult	not out	16		
Extras	(LB 1, W 3, NB 5)	9	(B 7, LB 7, W 4, NB 6)	24
Total	(55.1 overs; 269 mins)	221	(5 wkts dec; 172 overs; 742 mins)	524

SRI LANKA

F.D.M.Karunaratne	c Neesham b Boult	16	c Rutherford b Craig	17
J.K.Silva	b Bracewell	5	c Craig b Bracewell	50
K.C.Sangakkara	c Boult b Neesham	203	(4) c Watling b Boult	5
H.D.R.L.Thirimanne	c McCullum b Bracewell	0	(5) not out	62
*A.D.Mathews	c Watling b Southee	15	(6) c Williamson b Bracewell	8
†H.A.P.W.Jayawardena	c Neesham b Bracewell	6	(7) c Williamson b Craig	10
L.D.Chandimal	c Watling b Neesham	67	(8) c Watling b Craig	13
K.T.G.D.Prasad	c Watling b Neesham	11	(3) c Neesham b Boult	6
H.M.R.K.B.Herath	c Watling b Boult	15	lbw b Craig	0
R.A.S.Lakmal	st Watling b Craig	5	run out	6
A.N.P.R.Fernando	not out	0	b Southee	1
Extras	(LB 4, W 6, NB 3)	13	(B 12, LB 2, W 3, NB 1)	18
Total	(102.1 overs; 448 mins)	356	(72.4 overs; 314 mins)	196

SRI LANKA	O	M	R	W		O	M	R	W
Lakmal	17	2	71	3		32	4	89	0
Fernando	16	0	63	4		37	4	117	3
Prasad	11.1	1	50	2	(4)	28	1	102	1
Mathews	9	3	29	1	(5)	11	3	29	0
Herath	2	0	7	0	(3)	56	8	154	1
Thirimanne						8	1	19	0

NEW ZEALAND	O	M	R	W		O	M	R	W
Boult	24	3	75	2		21	2	55	2
Southee	26	3	87	1		17.4	6	41	1
Bracewell	24	2	93	3		13	3	25	2
Neesham	11	0	42	3					
Craig	17.1	3	55	1	(4)	18	8	53	4
Rutherford					(5)	1	0	2	0
Williamson					(6)	2	0	6	0

FALL OF WICKETS

	NZ	SL	NZ	SL
Wkt	1st	1st	2nd	2nd
1st	31	18	75	42
2nd	62	25	78	51
3rd	141	29	79	61
4th	142	58	122	94
5th	162	78	159	110
6th	181	208	–	133
7th	182	242	–	156
8th	184	289	–	156
9th	195	356	–	189
10th	221	356	–	196

Umpires: S.J.Davis (*Australia*) (55) and R.K.Illingworth (*England*) (14).
Referee: B.C.Broad (*England*) (67).   **Test No. 2155/30 (NZ399/SL235)**

INTERNATIONAL UMPIRES AND REFEREES
2015

ELITE PANEL OF UMPIRES 2015

The Elite Panel of ICC Umpires and Referees was introduced in April 2002 to raise standards and guarantee impartial adjudication. Two umpires from this panel stand in Test matches while one officiates with a home umpire from the Supplementary International Panel in limited-overs internationals.

Full Names	Birthdate	Birthplace	Tests	Debut	LOI	Debut
ALIM Sarwar DAR	06.06.68	Jhang, Pakistan	94	2003-04	165	1999-00
BOWDEN, Brent 'Billy' Fraser	11.04.63	Henderson, New Zealand	82	1999-00	192	1994-95
DAVIS, Stephen James	09.04.52	London, England	55	1997-98	130	1992-93
DHARMASENA, H.D.P.Kumar	24.04.71	Colombo, Sri Lanka	29	2010-11	57	2008-09
ERASMUS, Marais	27.02.64	George, South Africa	29	2009-10	56	2007-08
GOULD, Ian James	19.08.57	Taplow, England	43	2008-09	96	2006
ILLINGWORTH, Richard Keith	23.08.63	Bradford, England	14	2012-13	33	2010
KETTLEBOROUGH, Richard Allan	15.03.73	Sheffield, England	26	2010-11	48	2009
LLONG, Nigel James	11.02.69	Ashford, England	26	2007-08	86	2006
OXENFORD, Bruce Nicholas James	05.03.60	Southport, Australia	21	2010-11	63	2007-08
REIFFEL, Paul Ronald	19.04.66	Box Hill, Australia	15	2012	37	2008-09
TUCKER, Rodney James	28.08.64	Sydney, Australia	35	2009-10	51	2008-09

ELITE PANEL OF REFEREES 2015

Full Names	Birthdate	Birthplace	Tests	Debut	LOI	Debut
BOON, David Clarence	29.12.60	Launceston, Australia	24	2011	59	2011
BROAD, Brian Christopher	29.09.57	Bristol, England	67	2003-04	253	2003-04
CROWE, Jeffrey John	14.09.58	Auckland, New Zealand	69	2004-05	207	2003-04
MADUGALLE, Ranjan Senerath	22.04.59	Kandy, Sri Lanka	155	1993-94	288	1993-94
MAHANAMA, Roshan Siriwardena	31.05.66	Colombo, Sri Lanka	56	2004	207	2004
PYCROFT, Andrew John	06.06.56	Harare, Zimbabwe	33	2009	112	2009
SRINATH, Javagal	31.08.69	Mysore, India	33	2006	156	2006-07

INTERNATIONAL UMPIRES PANEL 2015

Nominated by their respective cricket boards, members from this panel officiate in home LOIs and supplement the Elite panel for Test matches. Specialist third umpires have been selected to undertake adjudication involving television replays. The number of Test matches/LOI in which they have stood is shown in brackets.

			Third Umpire
Australia	J.D.Ward (-/6)	S.D.Fry (-/17)	M.D.Martell (-/3)
			P.Wilson (-/3)
Bangladesh	Enamul Haque (1/49)	Sharfuddoula (-/16)	Anisur Rahman (-/3)
England	R.J.Bailey (-/9)	M.A.Gough (-/11)	R.T.Robinson (-/4)
India	S.Ravi (4/21)	V.A.Kulkarni (-/17)	C.Shamshuddin (-/1)
			A.K.Chaudhary (-/1)
New Zealand	D.J.Walker (-/5)	C.B.Gaffaney (2/38)	G.A.V.Baxter (-/38)
Pakistan	Shozab Raza (-/10)	Ahsan Raza (-/17)	Ahmed Shahab (-/4)
South Africa	J.D.Cloete (-/47)	S.George (-/11)	A.T.Holdstock (-/4)
Sri Lanka	R.E.J.Martinesz (6/30)	R.S.A.Palliyaguruge (-/23)	R.R.Wimalasiri (-/3)
West Indies	P.J.Nero (-/22)	J.S.Wilson (-/18)	G.O.Brathwaite (-/13)
			N.Duguid (-/-)
Zimbabwe	R.B.Tiffin (44/136)	O.Chirombe (-/16)	T.J.Matibiri (-/7)

Test Match and LOI statistics to 13 February 2015.

49

TEST MATCH CAREER RECORDS

These records, complete to 12 April 2015, contain all players registered for county cricket in 2015 at the time of going to press, plus those who have played Test cricket since 21 November 2013 (Test No. 2102). Records are for performances for the country shown, and do not include figures for multi-national teams.

ENGLAND – BATTING AND FIELDING

	M	I	NO	HS	Runs	Avge	100	50	Ct/St
M.M.Ali	7	10	1	108*	286	31.77	1	–	4
T.R.Ambrose	11	16	1	102	447	29.80	1	3	31
J.M.Anderson	99	135	48	81	949	10.90	–	1	57
J.M.Bairstow	14	24	2	95	593	26.95	–	4	16
G.S.Ballance	8	13	1	156	729	60.75	3	3	7
G.J.Batty	7	8	1	38	144	20.57	–	–	3
I.R.Bell	105	181	22	235	7156	45.00	21	42	88
R.S.Bopara	13	19	1	143	575	31.94	3	–	6
S.G.Borthwick	1	2	–	4	5	2.50	–	–	2
T.T.Bresnan	23	26	4	91	575	26.13	–	3	8
S.C.J.Broad	74	104	13	169	2193	24.09	1	10	21
J.C.Buttler	3	3	–	85	200	66.66	–	2	11
M.A.Carberry	6	12	–	60	345	28.75	–	1	7
R.Clarke	2	3	–	55	96	32.00	–	1	1
P.D.Collingwood	68	115	10	206	4259	40.56	10	20	96
N.R.D.Compton	9	17	2	117	479	31.93	2	1	4
A.N.Cook	109	194	11	294	8423	46.02	25	38	108
S.T.Finn	23	29	14	56	169	11.26	–	1	6
A.Flintoff	78	128	9	167	3795	31.89	5	26	52
J.S.Foster	7	12	3	48	226	25.11	–	–	17/1
G.O.Jones	34	53	4	100	1172	23.91	1	6	128/5
C.J.Jordan	5	6	–	35	125	20.83	–	–	8
S.C.Kerrigan	1	1	1	1*	1	–	–	–	–
R.W.T.Key	15	26	1	221	775	31.00	1	3	11
E.J.G.Morgan	16	24	1	130	700	30.43	2	3	11
G.Onions	9	10	7	17*	30	10.00	–	–	–
M.S.Panesar	50	68	23	26	220	4.88	–	–	10
S.R.Patel	5	7	–	33	109	15.57	–	–	2
K.P.Pietersen	104	181	8	227	8181	47.28	23	35	62
L.E.Plunkett	13	20	5	55*	238	15.86	–	1	3
M.J.Prior	79	123	21	131*	4099	40.18	7	28	243/13
W.B.Rankin	1	2	–	13	13	6.50	–	–	–
C.M.W.Read	15	23	4	55	360	18.94	–	1	48/6
S.D.Robson	7	11	–	127	336	30.54	1	1	5
J.E.Root	22	40	6	200*	1732	50.94	5	7	15
O.A.Shah	6	10	–	88	269	26.90	–	2	2
A.Shahzad	1	1	–	5	5	5.00	–	–	2
R.J.Sidebottom	22	31	11	31	313	15.65	–	–	5
B.A.Stokes	6	11	–	120	279	25.36	1	–	2
J.W.A.Taylor	2	3	–	34	48	16.00	–	–	2
J.C.Tredwell	1	1	–	37	37	37.00	–	–	1
C.T.Tremlett	12	15	4	25*	113	10.27	–	–	4
M.E.Trescothick	76	143	10	219	5825	43.79	14	29	95
I.J.L.Trott	49	87	6	226	3763	46.45	9	18	29
C.R.Woakes	4	5	3	26*	75	37.50	–	–	2

ENGLAND – BOWLING

	O	M	R	W	Avge	Best	5wI	10wM
M.M.Ali	175.4	20	618	22	28.09	6- 67	1	–
J.M.Anderson	3685.4	880	11295	380	29.72	7- 43	16	2
G.S.Ballance	2	1	5	0	–	–	–	–
G.J.Batty	232.2	34	733	11	66.63	3- 55	–	–
I.R.Bell	18	3	76	1	76.00	1- 33	–	–
R.S.Bopara	72.2	10	290	1	290.00	1- 39	–	–
S.G.Borthwick	13	0	82	4	20.50	3- 33	–	–
T.T.Bresnan	779	185	2357	72	32.73	5- 48	1	–
S.C.J.Broad	2585.5	559	7894	264	29.90	7- 44	12	2
R.Clarke	29	11	60	4	15.00	2- 7	–	–
P.D.Collingwood	317.3	51	1018	17	59.88	3- 23	–	–
A.N.Cook	3	0	7	1	7.00	1- 6	–	–
S.T.Finn	724.4	135	2646	90	29.40	6-125	4	–
A.Flintoff	2457.5	502	7303	219	33.34	5- 58	3	–
C.J.Jordan	151	42	496	15	33.06	4- 18	–	–
S.C.Kerrigan	8	0	53	0	–	–	–	–
G.Onions	267.4	50	957	32	29.90	5- 38	1	–
M.S.Panesar	2079.1	469	5797	167	34.71	6- 37	12	2
S.R.Patel	101	19	257	4	64.25	2- 27	–	–
K.P.Pietersen	218.3	15	886	10	88.60	3- 52	–	–
L.E.Plunkett	443.1	71	1536	41	37.46	5- 64	1	–
W.B.Rankin	20.5	0	81	1	81.00	1- 47	–	–
J.E.Root	85	21	225	4	56.25	2- 9	–	–
O.A.Shah	5	0	31	0	–	–	–	–
A.Shahzad	17	4	63	4	15.75	3- 45	–	–
R.J.Sidebottom	802	188	2231	79	28.24	7- 47	5	1
B.A.Stokes	204.4	30	724	22	32.90	6- 99	1	–
J.C.Tredwell	65	13	181	6	30.16	4- 82	–	–
C.T.Tremlett	483.4	114	1431	53	27.00	6- 48	2	–
M.E.Trescothick	50	6	155	1	155.00	1- 34	–	–
I.J.L.Trott	117	11	398	5	79.60	1- 5	–	–
C.R.Woakes	95	28	313	6	52.16	3- 30	–	–

TEST

AUSTRALIA – BATTING AND FIELDING

	M	I	NO	HS	Runs	Avge	100	50	Ct/St
G.J.Bailey	5	8	1	53	183	26.14	–	1	10
J.M.Bird	3	4	3	6*	7	7.00	–	–	1
J.A.Burns	2	4	–	66	146	36.50	–	2	1
M.J.Clarke	108	186	20	329*	8432	50.79	28	27	125
A.J.Doolan	4	8	–	89	191	23.87	–	1	4
B.J.Haddin	63	108	13	169	3207	33.75	4	18	251/7
R.J.Harris	27	39	11	74	603	21.53	–	3	13
J.W.Hastings	1	2	–	32	52	26.00	–	–	1
J.R.Hazlewood	3	3	3	32*	32	–	–	–	2
B.W.Hilfenhaus	27	38	12	56*	355	13.65	–	1	7
M.G.Johnson	64	97	16	123*	1868	23.06	1	10	24
N.M.Lyon	39	49	23	40*	380	14.61	–	–	17
C.J.McKay	1	1	–	10	10	10.00	–	–	1
M.R.Marsh	4	8	1	87	262	37.42	–	1	2
S.E.Marsh	12	21	–	148	747	35.57	2	3	8
G.J.Maxwell	3	6	–	37	80	13.33	–	–	2
S.N.J.O'Keefe	1	2	1	6	6	6.00	–	–	–
J.L.Pattinson	13	18	7	42	331	30.09	–	–	1
C.J.L.Rogers	20	39	–	119	1535	39.35	4	11	14
P.M.Siddle	56	80	12	51	973	14.30	–	2	16
S.P.D.Smith	26	50	6	192	2304	52.36	8	10	23
M.A.Starc	15	23	7	99	485	30.31	–	4	6
S.W.Tait	3	5	2	8	20	6.66	–	–	1
D.A.Warner	36	68	3	180	3133	48.20	12	13	27
S.R.Watson	56	105	3	176	3646	35.74	4	24	42

AUSTRALIA – BOWLING

	O	M	R	W	Avge	Best	5wI	10wM
J.M.Bird	105.3	36	303	13	23.30	4- 41	–	–
M.J.Clarke	403.5	62	1176	31	37.93	6- 9	2	–
R.J.Harris	956	258	2658	113	23.52	7-117	5	–
J.W.Hastings	39	3	153	1	153.00	1- 51	–	–
J.R.Hazlewood	125.2	30	352	12	29.33	5- 68	1	–
B.W.Hilfenhaus	1013	258	2822	99	28.50	5- 75	2	–
M.G.Johnson	2401.5	464	7879	283	27.84	8- 61	12	3
N.M.Lyon	1558.5	299	4918	138	35.63	7- 94	7	1
C.J.McKay	28	5	101	1	101.00	1- 56	–	–
M.R.Marsh	61	14	164	1	164.00	1- 14	–	–
G.J.Maxwell	57	4	271	7	38.71	4-127	–	–
S.N.J.O'Keefe	57	6	219	4	54.75	2-107	–	–
J.L.Pattinson	425	96	1381	51	27.07	5- 27	3	–
P.M.Siddle	1981.1	519	5848	192	30.45	6- 54	8	–
S.P.D.Smith	176	18	758	14	54.14	3- 18	–	–
M.A.Starc	523	95	1772	50	35.44	6-154	2	–
S.W.Tait	69	6	302	5	60.40	3- 97	–	–
D.A.Warner	50	1	227	4	56.75	2- 45	–	–
S.R.Watson	886.5	234	2449	74	33.09	6- 33	3	–

TEST   **SOUTH AFRICA – BATTING AND FIELDING**

	M	I	NO	HS	Runs	Avge	100	50	Ct/St
K.J.Abbott	3	3	–	13	23	7.66	–	–	2
H.M.Amla	82	141	13	311*	6757	52.78	23	28	68
T.Bavuma	2	2	–	15	25	12.50	–	–	1
Q.de Kock	5	8	1	81	264	37.71	–	2	19/1
A.B.de Villiers	98	162	16	278*	7606	52.09	21	36	184/4
F.du Plessis	20	32	4	137	1447	51.67	4	7	12
J.P.Duminy	27	43	8	166	1280	36.57	4	6	19
D.Elgar	15	23	3	121	753	37.65	3	3	14
S.R.Harmer	1	1	–	10	10	10.00	–	–	1
Imran Tahir	16	16	7	29*	109	12.11	–	–	7
J.H.Kallis	165	278	39	224	13206	55.25	45	58	196
R.K.Kleinveldt	4	5	2	17*	27	9.00	–	–	4
R.McLaren	2	3	1	33*	47	23.50	–	–	–
M.Morkel	62	71	12	40	710	12.03	–	–	15
W.D.Parnell	4	3	–	22	44	14.66	–	–	1
A.N.Petersen	36	64	4	182	2093	34.88	5	8	31
R.J.Peterson	15	20	3	84	464	27.29	–	3	9
V.D.Philander	29	36	10	74	697	26.80	–	4	8
D.L.Piedt	1	1	–	13	13	13.00	–	–	2
A.G.Prince	66	104	16	162*	3665	41.64	11	11	47
J.A.Rudolph	48	83	9	222*	2622	35.43	6	11	29
G.C.Smith	116	203	13	277	9253	48.70	27	38	166
D.W.Steyn	78	97	21	76	1114	14.65	–	2	21
S.van Zyl	3	3	1	101*	163	81.50	1	–	2

SOUTH AFRICA – BOWLING

	O	M	R	W	Avge	Best	5wI	10wM
K.J.Abbott	87.4	27	258	13	19.84	7- 29	1	–
H.M.Amla	9	0	37	0	–	–	–	–
A.B.de Villiers	34	6	104	2	52.00	2- 49	–	–
F.du Plessis	13	0	69	0	–	–	–	–
J.P.Duminy	353	38	1259	32	39.34	4- 73	–	–
D.Elgar	59.1	1	254	4	63.50	1- 3	–	–
S.R.Harmer	50	12	153	7	21.85	4- 82	–	–
Imran Tahir	559.1	73	1995	43	46.39	5- 32	1	–
J.H.Kallis	3372	848	9535	292	32.65	6- 54	5	–
R.K.Kleinveldt	111.1	21	422	10	42.20	3- 65	–	–
R.McLaren	44	8	162	3	54.00	2- 72	–	–
M.Morkel	2010.2	428	6369	217	29.35	6- 23	6	–
W.D.Parnell	59.3	7	258	7	36.85	2- 17	–	–
A.N.Petersen	19	1	62	1	62.00	1- 2	–	–
R.J.Peterson	419.1	85	1416	38	37.26	5- 33	1	–
V.D.Philander	952.5	233	2657	121	21.95	6- 44	9	2
D.L.Piedt	49	4	152	8	19.00	4- 62	–	–
A.G.Prince	16	1	47	1	47.00	1- 2	–	–
J.A.Rudolph	110.4	13	432	4	108.00	1- 1	–	–
G.C.Smith	236.2	28	885	8	110.62	2-145	–	–
D.W.Steyn	2747.4	591	8932	396	22.55	7- 51	25	5
S.van Zyl	20	4	41	1	41.00	1- 13	–	–

TEST

WEST INDIES – BATTING AND FIELDING

	M	I	NO	HS	Runs	Avge	100	50	Ct/St
S.J.Benn	25	38	5	42	484	14.66	–	–	13
T.L.Best	25	38	6	95	401	12.53	–	1	6
J.Blackwood	5	8	1	66*	243	34.71	–	3	3
K.C.Brathwaite	17	32	2	212	1139	37.96	3	6	7
D.M.Bravo	32	57	4	218	2311	43.60	6	9	31
S.Chanderpaul	161	274	49	203*	11775	52.33	30	66	65
S.S.Cottrell	2	4	–	5	11	2.75	–	–	–
N.Deonarine	18	30	2	82	725	25.89	–	5	16
K.A.Edwards	17	32	1	121	986	31.80	2	8	15
S.T.Gabriel	11	13	5	13	24	3.00	–	–	8
C.H.Gayle	103	182	11	333	7214	42.18	15	37	96
J.O.Holder	3	5	–	52	116	23.20	–	1	2
L.R.Johnson	4	7	–	66	275	39.28	–	2	1
S.P.Narine	6	7	2	22*	40	8.00	–	–	2
B.P.Nash	21	33	–	114	1103	33.42	2	8	6
V.Permaul	4	6	–	20	57	9.50	–	–	1
K.K.Peters	1	1	–	0	0	0.00	–	–	–
K.O.A.Powell	21	40	1	134	1072	27.48	3	2	19
D.Ramdin	64	107	13	166	2510	26.70	4	12	184/7
K.A.J.Roach	29	44	8	41	329	9.13	–	–	8
D.J.G.Sammy	38	63	2	106	1323	21.68	1	5	65
M.N.Samuels	55	97	6	260	3251	35.72	6	21	24
S.Shillingford	16	26	6	53*	266	13.30	–	1	9
D.S.Smith	36	63	2	108	1500	24.59	1	5	29
J.E.Taylor	37	58	7	106	757	14.84	1	1	7

WEST INDIES – BOWLING

	O	M	R	W	Avge	Best	5wI	10wM
S.J.Benn	1168.1	223	3202	85	37.67	6-81	6	–
T.L.Best	619.2	80	2291	57	40.19	6-40	2	–
J.Blackwood	23.3	2	84	2	42.00	2-14	–	–
K.C.Brathwaite	8.4	0	52	1	52.00	1-43	–	–
D.M.Bravo	1	0	2	0	–	–	–	–
S.Chanderpaul	290	50	883	9	98.11	1- 2	–	–
S.S.Cottrell	46	4	196	2	98.00	1-72	–	–
N.Deonarine	250.3	49	713	24	29.70	4-37	–	–
K.A.Edwards	4	0	19	0	–	–	–	–
S.T.Gabriel	267.3	49	933	25	37.32	3-10	–	–
C.H.Gayle	1184.5	230	3120	73	42.73	5-34	2	–
J.O.Holder	71	17	199	5	39.80	2-26	–	–
L.R.Johnson	4	0	9	0	–	–	–	–
S.P.Narine	275	60	851	21	40.52	6-91	2	–
B.P.Nash	82	13	247	2	123.50	1-21	–	–
V.Permaul	141.4	20	452	12	37.66	3-32	–	–
K.K.Peters	20	7	69	2	34.50	2-69	–	–
K.A.J.Roach	939.5	188	2936	113	25.98	6-48	6	1
D.J.G.Sammy	1035.5	216	3007	84	35.79	7-66	4	–
M.N.Samuels	592.5	62	2031	36	56.41	4-13	–	–
S.Shillingford	782.2	122	2419	70	34.55	6-49	6	2
D.S.Smith	1	0	3	0	–	–	–	–
J.E.Taylor	1082.1	217	3716	103	36.07	5-11	3	–

TEST   **NEW ZEALAND – BATTING AND FIELDING**

	M	I	NO	HS	Runs	Avge	100	50	Ct/St
A.R.Adams	1	2	–	11	18	9.00	–	–	1
C.J.Anderson	10	16	1	116	457	30.46	1	2	5
T.A.Boult	30	40	21	52*	322	16.94	–	1	11
D.A.J.Bracewell	19	34	2	43	353	11.03	–	–	5
M.D.Craig	8	12	4	67	318	39.75	–	2	8
G.D.Elliott	5	9	1	25	86	10.75	–	–	2
J.E.C.Franklin	31	46	7	122*	808	20.71	1	2	12
P.G.Fulton	23	39	1	136	967	25.44	2	5	25
M.J.Guptill	31	59	1	189	1718	29.62	2	12	33
T.W.M.Latham	9	17	–	137	684	40.23	2	3	5
B.B.McCullum	92	159	8	302	5870	38.87	11	28	190/11
H.J.H.Marshall	13	19	2	160	652	38.35	2	2	1
C.Munro	1	2	–	15	15	7.50	–	–	–
J.D.S.Neesham	8	15	1	137*	606	43.28	2	3	7
J.S.Patel	19	30	7	27*	276	12.00	–	–	12
A.J.Redmond	8	16	1	83	325	21.66	–	2	5
H.D.Rutherford	16	29	1	171	755	26.96	1	1	11
J.D.Ryder	18	33	2	201	1269	40.93	3	6	12
I.S.Sodhi	11	16	3	63	337	25.92	–	2	4
T.G.Southee	39	63	6	77*	1009	17.70	–	3	23
L.R.P.L.Taylor	62	113	11	217*	4631	45.40	12	23	103
D.L.Vettori	112	172	22	140	4523	30.15	6	23	58
N.Wagner	16	23	6	37	200	11.76	–	–	4
B.J.Watling	29	49	7	142*	1578	37.57	4	8	93/3
K.S.Williamson	39	71	5	242*	3034	45.96	9	15	34

NEW ZEALAND – BOWLING

	O	M	R	W	Avge	Best	5wI	10wM
A.R.Adams	31.4	5	105	6	17.50	3- 44	–	–
C.J.Anderson	166	31	473	13	36.38	3- 47	–	–
T.A.Boult	1049.4	242	3013	110	27.39	6- 40	3	1
D.A.J.Bracewell	567.4	95	1931	55	35.10	6- 40	2	–
M.D.Craig	323.2	55	1227	31	39.58	7- 94	1	1
G.D.Elliott	47	9	140	4	35.00	2- 8	–	–
J.E.C.Franklin	794.3	143	2786	82	33.97	6-119	3	–
M.J.Guptill	55.2	3	258	5	51.60	3- 37	–	–
B.B.McCullum	23.1	3	69	1	69.00	1- 1	–	–
H.J.H.Marshall	1	0	4	0	–	–	–	–
C.Munro	18	4	40	2	20.00	2- 40	–	–
J.D.S.Neesham	109.5	12	361	11	32.81	3- 42	–	–
J.S.Patel	787.1	164	2520	52	48.46	5-110	1	–
A.J.Redmond	17.3	3	80	3	26.66	2- 47	–	–
H.D.Rutherford	1	0	2	0	–	–	–	–
J.D.Ryder	82	23	280	5	56.00	2- 7	–	–
I.S.Sodhi	375.4	49	1426	27	52.81	4- 96	–	–
T.G.Southee	1384.5	295	4163	136	30.61	7- 64	4	1
L.R.P.L.Taylor	16	3	48	2	24.00	2- 4	–	–
D.L.Vettori	4775.2	1194	12330	361	34.15	7- 87	20	3
N.Wagner	586.4	114	2000	58	34.48	5- 64	1	–
K.S.Williamson	293.1	42	983	24	40.95	4- 44	–	–

TEST

INDIA – BATTING AND FIELDING

	M	I	NO	HS	Runs	Avge	100	50	Ct/St
V.R.Aaron	5	10	3	9	29	4.14	–	–	1
R.Ashwin	24	36	8	124	1007	35.96	2	4	11
S.T.R.Binny	3	6	1	78	118	23.60	–	1	1
S.Dhawan	13	23	–	187	823	35.78	2	2	13
M.S.Dhoni	90	144	16	224	4876	38.09	6	33	256/38
G.Gambhir	56	100	5	206	4046	42.58	9	21	38
R.A.Jadeja	12	19	2	68	364	21.41	–	1	11
Z.Khan	92	127	24	75	1231	11.95	–	3	19
V.Kohli	33	59	4	169	2547	46.30	10	10	30
B.Kumar	12	18	3	63*	393	26.20	–	3	4
Mohammed Shami	12	19	6	51*	166	12.76	–	1	1
Pankaj Singh	2	4	1	9	10	3.33	–	–	2
C.A.Pujara	27	48	4	206*	2073	47.11	6	6	20
A.M.Rahane	14	27	3	147	1077	44.87	3	6	7
K.L.Rahul	2	4	–	110	130	32.50	1	–	1
S.K.Raina	18	31	2	120	768	26.48	1	7	23
W.P.Saha	4	8	–	36	147	18.37	–	–	6
I.Sharma	61	92	34	31*	527	9.08	–	–	13
K.V.Sharma	1	2	1	4*	8	8.00	–	–	–
R.G.Sharma	10	18	2	177	662	41.37	2	2	10
M.Vijay	31	55	–	167	2188	39.78	5	10	28
U.T.Yadav	12	15	5	30	79	7.90	–	–	3

INDIA – BOWLING

	O	M	R	W	Avge	Best	5wI	10wM
V.R.Aaron	151.1	11	741	13	57.00	3- 97	–	–
R.Ashwin	1226.4	236	3650	119	30.67	7-103	9	2
S.T.R.Binny	32	0	140	0	–	–	–	–
S.Dhawan	5	0	9	0	–	–	–	–
M.S.Dhoni	16	1	67	0	–	–	–	–
G.Gambhir	2	0	4	0	–	–	–	–
R.A.Jadeja	570.4	144	1367	45	30.37	6-138	2	–
Z.Khan	3130.5	624	10247	311	32.94	7- 87	11	1
V.Kohli	24	1	70	0	–	–	–	–
B.Kumar	318.5	68	1015	29	35.00	6- 82	2	–
Mohammed Shami	446.3	62	1699	47	36.14	5- 47	2	–
Pankaj Singh	75	17	292	2	146.00	2-113	–	–
S.K.Raina	173.3	22	603	13	46.38	2- 1	–	–
I.Sharma	2077.3	387	6976	187	37.30	7- 74	6	1
K.V.Sharma	49	3	238	4	59.50	2- 95	–	–
R.G.Sharma	54.4	3	197	2	98.50	1- 26	–	–
M.Vijay	35	4	105	1	105.00	1- 12	–	–
U.T.Yadav	366	42	1588	43	36.93	5- 93	1	–

TEST

PAKISTAN – BATTING AND FIELDING

	M	I	NO	HS	Runs	Avge	100	50	Ct/St
Abdur Rehman	22	31	3	60	395	14.10	–	2	8
Adnan Akmal	21	29	5	64	591	24.62	–	3	66/11
Ahmed Shehzad	8	15	–	176	718	47.86	3	2	3
Asad Shafiq	33	52	5	137	1891	40.23	5	10	30
Azhar Ali	39	74	5	157	2851	41.31	7	18	35
Azhar Mahmood	21	34	4	136	900	30.00	3	1	14
Bilawal Bhatti	2	3	1	32	70	35.00	–	–	–
Ehsan Adil	2	3	–	12	21	7.00	–	–	–
Imran Khan	3	1	1	0*	0	–	–	–	–
Junaid Khan	18	24	8	17	111	6.93	–	–	4
Khurram Manzoor	16	30	1	146	817	28.17	1	7	8
Misbah-ul-Haq	53	92	16	161*	3736	49.15	8	26	39
Mohammad Hafeez	40	77	7	197	2640	37.71	7	10	29
Mohammad Talha	4	5	1	19	34	8.50	–	–	1
Rahat Ali	11	15	6	35*	92	10.22	–	–	7
Saeed Ajmal	35	53	12	50	451	11.00	–	1	11
Sarfraz Ahmed	13	24	5	112	832	43.78	3	4	23/7
Shahid Afridi	27	48	1	156	1716	36.51	5	8	10
Shan Masood	4	8	–	75	165	20.62	–	1	4
Sohail Tanvir	2	3	–	13	17	5.66	–	–	2
Taufiq Umar	44	83	5	236	2963	37.98	7	14	48
Wahab Riaz	8	11	3	27	91	11.37	–	–	1
Yasir Arafat	3	3	1	50*	94	47.00	–	1	–
Yasir Shah	5	5	1	25	40	10.00	–	–	5
Younus Khan	96	172	16	313	8327	53.37	28	29	105
Zulfiqar Babar	7	6	4	25*	39	19.50	–	–	–

PAKISTAN – BOWLING

	O	M	R	W	Avge	Best	5wI	10wM
Abdur Rehman	1148.4	256	2910	99	29.39	6- 25	2	–
Ahmed Shehzad	8	0	28	0	–	–	–	–
Azhar Ali	37	3	132	2	66.00	1- 4	–	–
Azhar Mahmood	502.3	111	1402	39	35.94	4- 50	–	–
Bilawal Bhatti	73	12	291	6	48.50	3- 65	–	–
Ehsan Adil	49.1	12	160	4	40.00	2- 54	–	–
Imran Khan	65.3	10	218	7	31.14	3- 60	–	–
Junaid Khan	657.4	136	1874	65	28.83	5- 38	5	–
Mohammad Hafeez	579.5	102	1515	43	35.23	4- 16	–	–
Mohammad Talha	123.2	11	504	9	56.00	3- 65	–	–
Rahat Ali	373.4	68	1137	31	36.67	6-127	2	–
Saeed Ajmal	1932	386	5003	178	28.10	7- 55	10	4
Shahid Afridi	532.2	69	1709	48	35.60	5- 52	1	–
Sohail Tanvir	84	15	316	5	63.20	3- 83	–	–
Taufiq Umar	13	2	44	0	–	–	–	–
Wahab Riaz	209.2	33	744	23	32.34	5- 63	1	–
Yasir Arafat	104.3	12	438	9	48.66	5-161	1	–
Yasir Shah	218.4	27	710	27	26.29	5- 79	1	–
Younus Khan	134	18	491	9	54.55	2- 23	–	–
Zulfiqar Babar	345.2	51	1128	33	34.18	5- 74	1	–

TEST **SRI LANKA – BATTING AND FIELDING**

	M	I	NO	HS	Runs	Avge	100	50	Ct/St
L.D.Chandimal	15	26	3	116*	1014	44.08	3	6	24/4
D.P.D.N.Dickwella	4	7	–	72	144	20.57	–	1	15/2
R.M.S.Eranga	16	21	10	45*	186	16.90	–	–	5
A.N.P.R.Fernando	9	14	4	17*	53	5.30	–	–	1
H.M.R.K.B.Herath	58	83	18	80*	866	13.32	–	1	15
D.P.M.D.Jayawardena	149	252	15	374	11814	49.84	34	50	205
H.A.P.W.Jayawardena	58	83	11	154*	2124	29.50	4	5	124/32
F.D.M.Karunaratne	15	29	2	152	886	32.81	1	4	11
P.H.T.Kaushal	1	2	–	12	18	9.00	–	–	2
K.M.D.N.Kulasekara	21	28	1	64	391	14.48	–	1	8
R.A.S.Lakmal	23	32	11	18	144	6.85	–	–	4
A.D.Mathews	46	78	16	160	3193	51.50	4	20	24
B.A.W.Mendis	19	19	6	78	213	16.38	–	1	2
M.D.K.Perera	7	10	–	95	128	12.80	–	1	5
K.T.G.D.Prasad	17	25	1	47	377	15.70	–	–	5
K.C.Sangakkara	130	225	17	319	12203	58.66	38	51	178/20
S.M.S.M.Senanayake	1	1	–	5	5	5.00	–	–	1
J.K.Silva	16	30	–	139	1046	34.86	1	7	20/1
W.U.Tharanga	19	34	1	165	1019	30.87	1	5	13
H.D.R.L.Thirimanne	16	32	5	155*	721	26.70	1	3	8
K.D.K.Vithanage	6	8	2	103*	245	40.83	1	1	5
U.W.M.B.C.A.Welegedara	21	30	6	48	218	9.08	–	–	5

SRI LANKA – BOWLING

	O	M	R	W	Avge	Best	5wI	10wM
R.M.S.Eranga	561.5	115	1814	52	34.88	4- 49	–	–
A.N.P.R.Fernando	297.4	33	1199	21	57.09	4- 63	–	–
H.M.R.K.B.Herath	2803.2	548	7717	261	29.56	9-127	21	4
D.P.M.D.Jayawardena	98.1	20	310	6	51.66	2- 32	–	–
F.D.M.Karunaratne	2	0	5	0	–	–	–	–
P.H.T.Kaushal	35	0	207	2	103.50	1- 48	–	–
K.M.D.N.Kulasekara	594.3	120	1794	48	37.37	4- 21	–	–
R.A.S.Lakmal	705.2	132	2366	49	48.28	4- 78	–	–
A.D.Mathews	426	84	1271	23	55.26	4- 44	–	–
B.A.W.Mendis	788.2	118	2434	70	34.77	6- 99	4	1
M.D.K.Perera	363.1	67	1083	36	30.08	5- 69	3	–
K.T.G.D.Prasad	457.1	49	1827	37	49.37	5- 50	1	–
K.C.Sangakkara	14	0	49	0	–	–	–	–
S.M.S.M.Senanayake	23	2	96	0	–	–	–	–
H.D.R.L.Thirimanne	14	1	51	0	–	–	–	–
K.D.K.Vithanage	26	1	112	1	112.00	1- 73	–	–
U.W.M.B.C.A.Welegedara	633.1	114	2273	55	41.32	5- 52	2	–

A.N.P.R.Fernando is also known as N.Pradeep.

TEST ZIMBABWE – BATTING AND FIELDING

	M	I	NO	HS	Runs	Avge	100	50	Ct/St
R.W.Chakabva	8	16	1	101	495	33.00	1	3	9
B.B.Chari	2	4	–	25	29	7.25	–	–	1
T.L.Chatara	7	14	2	22	82	6.83	–	–	–
E.Chigumbura	14	27	–	88	569	21.07	–	4	6
C.R.Ervine	7	14	2	49	286	23.83	–	–	8
S.M.Ervine	5	8	–	86	261	32.62	–	3	7
K.M.Jarvis	8	14	6	25*	58	7.25	–	–	3
T.Kamungozi	1	2	–	5	5	2.50	–	–	–
H.Masakadza	29	58	2	158	1712	30.57	4	6	18
S.W.Masakadza	5	9	1	24	88	11.00	–	–	2
N.M'shangwe	2	4	–	8	8	2.00	–	–	2
R.Mutumbami	6	12	1	43	217	19.72	–	–	17/2
J.C.Nyumbu	2	4	–	14	30	7.50	–	–	1
T.Panyangara	9	18	6	40*	201	16.75	–	–	3
V.Sibanda	14	28	–	93	591	21.10	–	2	16
Sikandar Raza	4	8	–	82	327	40.87	–	4	–
B.R.M.Taylor	23	46	3	171	1493	34.72	4	7	23
D.T.Tiripano	1	2	1	15*	20	20.00	–	–	1
M.A.Vermeulen	9	18	–	118	449	24.94	1	2	6
M.N.Waller	9	18	1	72*	396	23.29	–	3	6
S.C.Williams	2	4	–	31	64	16.00	–	–	1

ZIMBABWE – BOWLING

	O	M	R	W	Avge	Best	5wI	10wM
B.B.Chari	2	0	9	0	–		–	–
T.L.Chatara	241.1	70	585	20	29.25	5- 61	1	–
E.Chigumbura	301	61	966	21	46.00	5- 54	1	–
S.M.Ervine	95	18	388	9	43.11	4-116	–	–
K.M.Jarvis	261.3	47	952	30	31.73	5- 54	2	–
T.Kamungozi	26	6	58	1	58.00	1- 51	–	–
H.Masakadza	149	38	360	13	27.69	3- 24	–	–
S.W.Masakadza	176.1	34	515	16	32.18	4- 32	–	–
N.M'shangwe	131.4	16	435	7	62.14	4- 82	–	–
J.C.Nyumbu	69.3	8	250	5	50.00	5-157	1	–
T.Panyangara	314.5	87	813	31	26.22	5- 59	1	–
Sikandar Raza	82	4	303	5	60.60	3-123	–	–
B.R.M.Taylor	7	0	38	0	–		–	–
D.T.Tiripano	26	8	65	2	32.50	2- 65	–	–
M.A.Vermeulen	1	0	5	0	–		–	–
M.N.Waller	53	8	132	6	22.00	4- 59	–	–
S.C.Williams	28.4	2	113	2	56.50	2-104	–	–

TEST

BANGLADESH – BATTING AND FIELDING

	M	I	NO	HS	Runs	Avge	100	50	Ct/St
Abdur Razzak	12	20	6	43	245	17.50	–	–	4
Al-Amin Hossain	6	9	6	32*	68	22.66	–	–	–
Anamul Haque	4	8	–	22	73	9.12	–	–	2
Imrul Kayes	19	38	–	130	868	22.84	2	1	19
Jubair Hossain	3	3	1	7*	13	6.50	–	–	1
Mahmudullah	23	44	2	115	1285	30.59	1	11	24
Marshall Ayub	3	6	–	41	125	20.83	–	–	2
Mominul Haque	12	23	4	181	1198	63.05	4	7	12
Mushfiqur Rahim	43	81	6	200	2511	33.48	3	14	73/11
Nasir Hossain	16	27	1	100	958	36.84	1	6	10
Robiul Islam	9	17	6	33	99	9.00	–	–	5
Rubel Hossain	22	38	17	45*	195	9.28	–	–	10
Shafiul Islam	8	15	1	53	183	13.07	–	1	2
Shahadat Hossain	37	69	17	40	521	10.01	–	–	8
Shakib Al Hasan	37	71	5	144	2529	38.31	3	17	16
Shamsur Rahman	6	12	–	106	305	25.41	1	–	7
Shuvagata Hom	4	8	1	50	133	19.00	–	1	3
Sohag Gazi	10	16	1	101*	325	21.66	1	–	5
Taijul Islam	5	9	1	32	86	10.75	–	–	5
Tamim Iqbal	37	72	–	151	2743	38.09	6	17	10

BANGLADESH – BOWLING

	O	M	R	W	Avge	Best	5wI	10wM
Abdur Razzak	469.3	65	1550	23	67.39	3- 93	–	–
Al-Amin Hossain	146.4	32	460	6	76.66	3- 80	–	–
Imrul Kayes	2	0	8	0	–	–	–	–
Jubair Hossain	84	7	322	11	29.27	5- 96	1	–
Mahmudullah	479.2	49	1621	35	46.31	5- 51	1	–
Marshall Ayub	10	0	53	0	–	–	–	–
Mominul Haque	45.1	1	167	1	167.00	1- 10	–	–
Nasir Hossain	143.3	22	413	8	51.62	3- 52	–	–
Robiul Islam	310	55	992	25	39.68	6- 71	2	–
Rubel Hossain	600	61	2347	32	73.34	5-166	1	–
Shafiul Islam	233	37	758	15	50.53	3- 86	–	–
Shahadat Hossain	896.2	92	3727	72	51.76	6- 27	4	–
Shakib Al Hasan	1511.5	297	4403	140	31.45	7- 36	14	1
Shamsur Rahman	1	0	5	0	–	–	–	–
Shuvagata Hom	65	9	207	3	69.00	2- 66	–	–
Sohag Gazi	525.1	66	1599	38	42.07	6- 74	2	–
Taijul Islam	227.1	43	678	25	27.12	8- 39	2	–
Tamim Iqbal	5	0	20	0	–	–	–	–

INTERNATIONAL TEST MATCH RESULTS

Complete to 12 April 2015.

	Opponents	Tests	Won by										Tied	Drawn
			E	A	SA	WI	NZ	I	P	SL	Z	B		
England	Australia	336	105	138	–	–	–	–	–	–	–	–	–	93
	South Africa	141	56	–	31	–	–	–	–	–	–	–	–	54
	West Indies	148	45	–	–	53	–	–	–	–	–	–	–	50
	New Zealand	99	47	–	–	–	8	–	–	–	–	–	–	44
	India	112	43	–	–	–	–	21	–	–	–	–	–	48
	Pakistan	74	22	–	–	–	–	–	16	–	–	–	–	36
	Sri Lanka	28	10	–	–	–	–	–	–	8	–	–	–	10
	Zimbabwe	6	3	–	–	–	–	–	–	–	0	–	–	3
	Bangladesh	8	8	–	–	–	–	–	–	–	–	0	–	0
Australia	South Africa	91	–	50	21	–	–	–	–	–	–	–	–	20
	West Indies	111	–	54	–	32	–	–	–	–	–	–	1	24
	New Zealand	52	–	27	–	–	8	–	–	–	–	–	–	17
	India	90	–	40	–	–	–	24	–	–	–	–	1	25
	Pakistan	59	–	28	–	–	–	–	14	–	–	–	–	17
	Sri Lanka	26	–	17	–	–	–	–	–	1	–	–	–	8
	Zimbabwe	3	–	3	–	–	–	–	–	–	0	–	–	0
	Bangladesh	4	–	4	–	–	–	–	–	–	–	0	–	0
South Africa	West Indies	28	–	–	18	3	–	–	–	–	–	–	–	7
	New Zealand	40	–	–	23	–	4	–	–	–	–	–	–	13
	India	29	–	–	13	–	–	7	–	–	–	–	–	9
	Pakistan	23	–	–	12	–	–	–	4	–	–	–	–	7
	Sri Lanka	22	–	–	11	–	–	–	–	5	–	–	–	6
	Zimbabwe	8	–	–	7	–	–	–	–	–	0	–	–	1
	Bangladesh	8	–	–	8	–	–	–	–	–	–	0	–	0
West Indies	New Zealand	45	–	–	–	13	13	–	–	–	–	–	–	19
	India	90	–	–	–	30	–	16	–	–	–	–	–	44
	Pakistan	46	–	–	–	15	–	–	16	–	–	–	–	15
	Sri Lanka	15	–	–	–	3	–	–	–	6	–	–	–	6
	Zimbabwe	8	–	–	–	6	–	–	–	–	0	–	–	2
	Bangladesh	12	–	–	–	8	–	–	–	–	–	2	–	2
New Zealand	India	54	–	–	–	–	10	18	–	–	–	–	–	26
	Pakistan	53	–	–	–	–	8	–	24	–	–	–	–	21
	Sri Lanka	30	–	–	–	–	12	–	–	8	–	–	–	10
	Zimbabwe	15	–	–	–	–	9	–	–	–	0	–	–	6
	Bangladesh	11	–	–	–	–	8	–	–	–	–	0	–	3
India	Pakistan	59	–	–	–	–	–	9	12	–	–	–	–	38
	Sri Lanka	35	–	–	–	–	–	14	–	6	–	–	–	15
	Zimbabwe	11	–	–	–	–	–	7	–	–	2	–	–	2
	Bangladesh	7	–	–	–	–	–	6	–	–	–	0	–	1
Pakistan	Sri Lanka	48	–	–	–	–	–	–	17	13	–	–	–	18
	Zimbabwe	17	–	–	–	–	–	–	10	–	3	–	–	4
	Bangladesh	8	–	–	–	–	–	–	8	–	–	0	–	0
Sri Lanka	Zimbabwe	15	–	–	–	–	–	–	–	10	0	–	–	5
	Bangladesh	16	–	–	–	–	–	–	–	14	–	0	–	2
Zimbabwe	Bangladesh	14	–	–	–	–	–	–	–	–	6	5	–	3
		2155	339	361	144	163	80	122	121	71	11	7	2	734

	Tests	Won	Lost	Drawn	Tied	Toss Won
England	945	339	275	338	–	458
Australia	773†	362†	205	204	2	391†
South Africa	390	144	129	117	–	187
West Indies	503	163	170	169	1	262
New Zealand	399	80	160	159	–	201
India	487	122	156	208	1	246
Pakistan	387	121	110	156	–	181
Sri Lanka	235	71	84	80	–	129
Zimbabwe	97	11	60	26	–	55
Bangladesh	88	7	70	11	–	46

† total includes Australia's victory against the ICC World XI.

INTERNATIONAL TEST CRICKET RECORDS

(To 12 April 2015)
TEAM RECORDS
HIGHEST INNINGS TOTALS

952-6d	Sri Lanka v India	Colombo (RPS)	1997-98
903-7d	England v Australia	The Oval	1938
849	England v West Indies	Kingston	1929-30
790-3d	West Indies v Pakistan	Kingston	1957-58
765-6d	Pakistan v Sri Lanka	Karachi	2008-09
760-7d	Sri Lanka v India	Ahmedabad	2009-10
758-8d	Australia v West Indies	Kingston	1954-55
756-5d	Sri Lanka v South Africa	Colombo (SSC)	2006
751-5d	West Indies v England	St John's	2003-04
749-9d	West Indies v England	Bridgetown	2008-09
747	West Indies v South Africa	St John's	2004-05
735-6d	Australia v Zimbabwe	Perth	2003-04
730-6d	Sri Lanka v Bangladesh	Dhaka	2013-14
729-6d	Australia v England	Lord's	1930
726-9d	India v Sri Lanka	Mumbai	2009-10
713-3d	Sri Lanka v Zimbabwe	Bulawayo	2003-04
710-7d	England v India	Birmingham	2011
708	Pakistan v England	The Oval	1987
707	India v Sri Lanka	Colombo (SSC)	2010
705-7d	India v Australia	Sydney	2003-04
701	Australia v England	The Oval	1934
699-5	Pakistan v India	Lahore	1989-90
695	Australia v England	The Oval	1930
692-8d	West Indies v England	The Oval	1995
690	New Zealand v Pakistan	Sharjah	2014-15
687-8d	West Indies v England	The Oval	1976
682-6d	South Africa v England	Lord's	2003
681-8d	West Indies v England	Port-of-Spain	1953-54
680-8d	New Zealand v India	Wellington	2013-14
679-7d	Pakistan v India	Lahore	2005-06
676-7	India v Sri Lanka	Kanpur	1986-87

675-5d	India v Pakistan	Multan	2003-04
674	Australia v India	Adelaide	1947-48
674-6	Pakistan v India	Faisalabad	1984-85
674-6d	Australia v England	Cardiff	2009
671-4	New Zealand v Sri Lanka	Wellington	1990-91
668	Australia v West Indies	Bridgetown	1954-55
664	India v England	The Oval	2007
660-5d	West Indies v New Zealand	Wellington	1994-95
659-8d	Australia v England	Sydney	1946-47
659-4d	Australia v India	Sydney	2011-12
658-8d	England v Australia	Nottingham	1938
658-9d	South Africa v West Indies	Durban	2003-04
657-8d	Pakistan v West Indies	Bridgetown	1957-58
657-7d	India v Australia	Calcutta	2000-01
656-8d	Australia v England	Manchester	1964
654-5	England v South Africa	Durban	1938-39
653-4d	England v India	Lord's	1990
653-4d	Australia v England	Leeds	1993
652-8d	West Indies v England	Lord's	1973
652	Pakistan v India	Faisalabad	1982-83
652-7d	England v India	Madras	1984-85
652-7d	Australia v South Africa	Johannesburg	2001-02
651	South Africa v Australia	Cape Town	2008-09
650-6d	Australia v West Indies	Bridgetown	1964-65

The highest for Zimbabwe is 563-9d (v WI, Harare, 2001), and for Bangladesh 638 (v SL, Galle, 2012-13).

LOWEST INNINGS TOTALS

† One batsman absent

26	New Zealand v England	Auckland	1954-55
30	South Africa v England	Port Elizabeth	1895-96
30	South Africa v England	Birmingham	1924
35	South Africa v England	Cape Town	1898-99
36	Australia v England	Birmingham	1902
36	South Africa v Australia	Melbourne	1931-32
42	Australia v England	Sydney	1887-88
42	New Zealand v Australia	Wellington	1945-46
42†	India v England	Lord's	1974
43	South Africa v England	Cape Town	1888-89
44	Australia v England	The Oval	1896
45	England v Australia	Sydney	1886-87
45	South Africa v Australia	Melbourne	1931-32
45	New Zealand v South Africa	Cape Town	2012-13
46	England v West Indies	Port-of-Spain	1993-94
47	South Africa v England	Cape Town	1888-89
47	New Zealand v England	Lord's	1958
47	West Indies v England	Kingston	2003-04
47	Australia v South Africa	Cape Town	2011-12
49	Pakistan v South Africa	Johannesburg	2012-13

The lowest for Sri Lanka is 71 (v P, Kandy, 1994-95), for Zimbabwe 51 (v NZ, Napier, 2011-12), and for Bangladesh 62 (v SL, Colombo PPS, 2006-07).

BATTING RECORDS
5000 RUNS IN TESTS

Runs			M	I	NO	HS	Avge	100	50
15921	S.R.Tendulkar	I	200	329	33	248*	53.78	51	68
13378	R.T.Ponting	A	168	287	29	257	51.85	41	62
13289	J.H.Kallis	SA/ICC	166	280	40	224	55.37	45	58
13288	R.S.Dravid	I/ICC	164	286	32	270	52.31	36	63
12203	K.C.Sangakkara	SL	130	225	17	319	58.66	38	51
11953	B.C.Lara	WI/ICC	131	232	6	400*	52.88	34	48
11814	D.P.M.D.Jayawardena	SL	149	252	15	374	49.84	34	50
11775	S.Chanderpaul	WI	161	274	49	203*	52.33	30	66
11174	A.R.Border	A	156	265	44	205	50.56	27	63
10927	S.R.Waugh	A	168	260	46	200	51.06	32	50
10122	S.M.Gavaskar	I	125	214	16	236*	51.12	34	45
9265	G.C.Smith	SA/ICC	117	205	13	277	48.25	27	38
8900	G.A.Gooch	E	118	215	6	333	42.58	20	46
8832	Javed Miandad	P	124	189	21	280*	52.57	23	43
8830	Inzamam-ul-Haq	P/ICC	120	200	22	329	49.60	25	46
8781	V.V.S.Laxman	I	134	225	34	281	45.97	17	56
8625	M.L.Hayden	A	103	184	14	380	50.73	30	29
8586	V.Sehwag	I/ICC	104	180	6	319	49.34	23	32
8540	I.V.A.Richards	WI	121	182	12	291	50.23	24	45
8463	A.J.Stewart	E	133	235	21	190	39.54	15	45
8432	M.J.Clarke	A	108	186	20	329*	50.79	28	27
8423	A.N.Cook	E	109	194	11	294	46.02	25	38
8327	Younus Khan	P	96	172	16	313	53.37	28	29
8231	D.I.Gower	E	117	204	18	215	44.25	18	39
8181	K.P.Pietersen	E	104	181	8	227	47.28	23	35
8114	G.Boycott	E	108	193	23	246*	47.72	22	42
8032	G.St A.Sobers	WI	93	160	21	365*	57.78	26	30
8029	M.E.Waugh	A	128	209	17	153*	41.81	20	47
7728	M.A.Atherton	E	115	212	7	185*	37.70	16	46
7696	J.L.Langer	A	105	182	12	250	45.27	23	30
7624	M.C.Cowdrey	E	114	188	15	182	44.06	22	38
7606	A.B.de Villiers	SA	98	162	16	278*	52.09	21	36
7558	C.G.Greenidge	WI	108	185	16	226	44.72	19	34
7530	Mohammad Yousuf	P	90	156	12	223	52.29	24	33
7525	M.A.Taylor	A	104	186	13	334*	43.49	19	40
7515	C.H.Lloyd	WI	110	175	14	242*	46.67	19	39
7487	D.L.Haynes	WI	116	202	25	184	42.29	18	39
7422	D.C.Boon	A	107	190	20	200	43.65	21	32
7289	G.Kirsten	SA	101	176	15	275	45.27	21	34
7249	W.R.Hammond	E	85	140	16	336*	58.45	22	24
7214	C.H.Gayle	WI	103	182	11	333	42.18	15	37
7212	S.C.Ganguly	I	113	188	17	239	42.17	16	35
7172	S.P.Fleming	NZ	111	189	10	274*	40.06	9	46
7156	I.R.Bell	E	105	181	22	235	45.00	21	42
7110	G.S.Chappell	A	87	151	19	247*	53.86	24	31
7037	A.J.Strauss	E	100	178	6	177	40.91	21	27
6996	D.G.Bradman	A	52	80	10	334	99.94	29	13
6973	S.T.Jayasuriya	SL	110	188	14	340	40.07	14	31
6971	L.Hutton	E	79	138	15	364	56.67	19	33
6868	D.B.Vengsarkar	I	116	185	22	166	42.13	17	35
6806	K.F.Barrington	E	82	131	15	256	58.67	20	35
6757	H.M.Amla	SA	82	141	13	311*	52.78	23	28
6744	G.P.Thorpe	E	100	179	28	200*	44.66	16	39
6361	P.A.de Silva	SL	93	159	11	267	42.97	20	22

64

Runs			M	I	NO	HS	Avge	100	50
6235	M.E.K.Hussey	A	79	137	16	195	51.52	19	29
6227	R.B.Kanhai	WI	79	137	6	256	47.53	15	28
6215	M.Azharuddin	I	99	147	9	199	45.03	22	21
6167	H.H.Gibbs	SA	90	154	7	228	41.95	14	26
6149	R.N.Harvey	A	79	137	10	205	48.41	21	24
6080	G.R.Viswanath	I	91	155	10	222	41.93	14	35
5949	R.B.Richardson	WI	86	146	12	194	44.39	16	27
5870	B.B.McCullum	NZ	92	159	8	302	38.87	11	28
5842	R.R.Sarwan	WI	87	154	8	291	40.01	15	31
5825	M.E.Trescothick	E	76	143	10	219	43.79	14	29
5807	D.C.S.Compton	E	78	131	15	278	50.06	17	28
5768	Salim Malik	P	103	154	22	237	43.69	15	29
5764	N.Hussain	E	96	171	16	207	37.19	14	33
5762	C.L.Hooper	WI	102	173	15	233	36.46	13	27
5719	M.P.Vaughan	E	82	147	9	197	41.44	18	18
5570	A.C.Gilchrist	A	96	137	20	204*	47.60	17	26
5515	M.V.Boucher	SA/ICC	147	206	24	125	30.30	5	35
5502	M.S.Atapattu	SL	90	156	15	249	39.02	16	17
5492	T.M.Dilshan	SL	87	145	11	193	40.98	16	23
5462	T.T.Samaraweera	SL	81	132	20	231	48.76	14	30
5444	M.D.Crowe	NZ	77	131	11	299	45.36	17	18
5410	J.B.Hobbs	E	61	102	7	211	56.94	15	28
5357	K.D.Walters	A	74	125	14	250	48.26	15	33
5345	I.M.Chappell	A	75	136	10	196	42.42	14	26
5334	J.G.Wright	NZ	82	148	7	185	37.82	12	23
5312	M.J.Slater	A	74	131	7	219	42.84	14	21
5248	Kapil Dev	I	131	184	15	163	31.05	8	27
5234	W.M.Lawry	A	67	123	12	210	47.15	13	27
5200	I.T.Botham	E	102	161	6	208	33.54	14	22
5138	J.H.Edrich	E	77	127	9	310*	43.54	12	24
5105	A.Ranatunga	SL	93	155	12	135*	35.69	4	38
5062	Zaheer Abbas	P	78	124	11	274	44.79	12	20

The most for Zimbabwe is 4794 (112 innings) by A.Flower, and for Bangladesh 3026 by Habibul Bashar (99 innings).

750 RUNS IN A SERIES

Runs		Series		M	I	NO	HS	Avge	100	50
974	D.G.Bradman	A v E	1930	5	7	–	334	139.14	4	–
905	W.R.Hammond	E v A	1928-29	5	9	1	251	113.12	4	–
839	M.A.Taylor	A v E	1989	6	11	1	219	83.90	2	5
834	R.N.Harvey	A v SA	1952-53	5	9	–	205	92.66	4	3
829	I.V.A.Richards	WI v E	1976	4	7	–	291	118.42	3	2
827	C.L.Walcott	WI v A	1954-55	5	10	–	155	82.70	5	2
824	G.St A.Sobers	WI v P	1957-58	5	8	2	365*	137.33	3	3
810	D.G.Bradman	A v E	1936-37	5	9	–	270	90.00	3	1
806	D.G.Bradman	A v SA	1931-32	5	5	1	299*	201.50	4	–
798	B.C.Lara	WI v E	1993-94	5	8	–	375	99.75	2	2
779	E.de C.Weekes	WI v I	1948-49	5	7	–	194	111.28	4	2
774	S.M.Gavaskar	I v WI	1970-71	4	8	3	220	154.80	4	3
769	S.P.D.Smith	A v I	2014-15	4	8	2	192	128.16	4	2
766	A.N.Cook	E v A	2010-11	5	7	1	235*	127.66	3	2
765	B.C.Lara	WI v E	1995	6	10	1	179	85.00	3	3
761	Mudassar Nazar	P v I	1982-83	6	8	2	231	126.83	4	1
758	D.G.Bradman	A v E	1934	5	8	–	304	94.75	2	1
753	D.C.S.Compton	E v SA	1947	5	8	–	208	94.12	4	2
752	G.A.Gooch	E v I	1990	3	6	–	333	125.33	3	2

65

HIGHEST INDIVIDUAL INNINGS

400*	B.C.Lara	WI v E	St John's	2003-04
380	M.L.Hayden	A v Z	Perth	2003-04
375	B.C.Lara	WI v E	St John's	1993-94
374	D.P.M.D.Jayawardena	SL v SA	Colombo (SSC)	2006
365*	G.St A.Sobers	WI v P	Kingston	1957-58
364	L.Hutton	E v A	The Oval	1938
340	S.T.Jayasuriya	SL v I	Colombo (RPS)	1997-98
337	Hanif Mohammed	P v WI	Bridgetown	1957-58
336*	W.R.Hammond	E v NZ	Auckland	1932-33
334*	M.A.Taylor	A v P	Peshawar	1998-99
334	D.G.Bradman	A v E	Leeds	1930
333	G.A.Gooch	E v I	Lord's	1990
333	C.H.Gayle	WI v SL	Galle	2010-11
329*	M.J.Clarke	A v I	Sydney	2011-12
329	Inzamam-ul-Haq	P v NZ	Lahore	2001-02
325	A.Sandham	E v WI	Kingston	1929-30
319	V.Sehwag	I v SA	Chennai	2007-08
319	K.C.Sangakkara	SL v B	Chittagong	2013-14
317	C.H.Gayle	WI v SA	St John's	2004-05
313	Younus Khan	P v SL	Karachi	2008-09
311*	H.M.Amla	SA v E	The Oval	2012
311	R.B.Simpson	A v E	Manchester	1964
310*	J.H.Edrich	E v NZ	Leeds	1965
309	V.Sehwag	I v P	Multan	2003-04
307	R.M.Cowper	A v E	Melbourne	1965-66
304	D.G.Bradman	A v E	Leeds	1934
302	L.G.Rowe	WI v E	Bridgetown	1973-74
302	B.B.McCullum	NZ v I	Wellington	2013-14
299*	D.G.Bradman	A v SA	Adelaide	1931-32
299	M.D.Crowe	NZ v SL	Wellington	1990-91
294	A.N.Cook	E v I	Birmingham	2011
293	V.Sehwag	I v SL	Mumbai	2009-10
291	I.V.A.Richards	WI v E	The Oval	1976
291	R.R.Sarwan	WI v E	Bridgetown	2008-09
287	R.E.Foster	E v A	Sydney	1903-04
287	K.C.Sangakkara	SL v SA	Colombo (SSC)	2006
285*	P.B.H.May	E v WI	Birmingham	1957
281	V.V.S.Laxman	I v A	Calcutta	2000-01
280*	Javed Miandad	P v I	Hyderabad	1982-83
278*	A.B.de Villiers	SA v P	Abu Dhabi	2010-11
278	D.C.S.Compton	E v P	Nottingham	1954
277	B.C.Lara	WI v A	Sydney	1992-93
277	G.C.Smith	SA v E	Birmingham	2003
275*	D.J.Cullinan	SA v NZ	Auckland	1998-99
275	G.Kirsten	SA v E	Durban	1999-00
275	D.P.M.D.Jayawardena	SL v I	Ahmedabad	2009-10
274*	S.P.Fleming	NZ v SL	Colombo (SSC)	2002-03
274	R.G.Pollock	SA v A	Durban	1969-70
274	Zaheer Abbas	P v E	Birmingham	1971
271	Javed Miandad	P v NZ	Auckland	1988-89
270*	G.A.Headley	WI v E	Kingston	1934-35
270	D.G.Bradman	A v E	Melbourne	1936-37
270	R.S.Dravid	I v P	Rawalpindi	2003-04
270	K.C.Sangakkara	SL v Z	Bulawayo	2004
268	G.N.Yallop	A v P	Melbourne	1983-84

267*	B.A.Young	NZ v SL	Dunedin	1996-97
267	P.A.de Silva	SL v NZ	Wellington	1990-91
267	Younus Khan	P v I	Bangalore	2004-05
266	W.H.Ponsford	A v E	The Oval	1934
266	D.L.Houghton	Z v SL	Bulawayo	1994-95
262*	D.L.Amiss	E v WI	Kingston	1973-74
262	S.P.Fleming	NZ v SA	Cape Town	2005-06
261*	R.R.Sarwan	WI v B	Kingston	2004
261	F.M.M.Worrell	WI v E	Nottingham	1950
260	C.C.Hunte	WI v P	Kingston	1957-58
260	Javed Miandad	P v E	The Oval	1987
260	M.N.Samuels	WI v B	Khulna	2012-13
259*	M.J.Clarke	A v SA	Brisbane	2012-13
259	G.M.Turner	NZ v WI	Georgetown	1971-72
259	G.C.Smith	SA v E	Lord's	2003
258	T.W.Graveney	E v WI	Nottingham	1957
258	S.M.Nurse	WI v NZ	Christchurch	1968-69
257*	Wasim Akram	P v Z	Sheikhupura	1996-97
257	R.T.Ponting	A v I	Melbourne	2003-04
256	R.B.Kanhai	WI v I	Calcutta	1958-59
256	K.F.Barrington	E v A	Manchester	1964
255*	D.J.McGlew	SA v NZ	Wellington	1952-53
254	D.G.Bradman	A v E	Lord's	1930
254	V.Sehwag	I v P	Lahore	2005-06
253*	H.M.Amla	SA v I	Nagpur	2009-10
253	S.T.Jayasuriya	SL v P	Faisalabad	2004-05
251	W.R.Hammond	E v A	Sydney	1928-29
250	K.D.Walters	A v NZ	Christchurch	1976-77
250	S.F.A.F.Bacchus	WI v I	Kanpur	1978-79
250	J.L.Langer	A v E	Melbourne	2002-03

The highest for Bangladesh is 200 by Mushfiqur Rahim (v SL, Galle, 2012-13).

20 HUNDREDS

			200	Inn	Opponents									
					E	A	SA	WI	NZ	I	P	SL	Z	B
51	S.R.Tendulkar	I	6	329	7	11	7	3	4	–	2	9	3	5
45	J.H.Kallis	SA	2	280	8	5	–	8	6	7	6	1	3	1
41	R.T.Ponting	A	6	287	8	–	8	7	2	8	5	1	1	1
38	K.C.Sangakkara	SL	11	225	3	1	3	3	4	5	10	–	2	7
36	R.S.Dravid	I	5	286	7	2	2	5	6	–	5	3	3	3
34	S.M.Gavaskar	I	4	214	4	8	–	13	2	–	5	2	–	–
34	B.C.Lara	WI	9	232	7	9	4	–	1	2	4	5	1	1
34	D.P.M.D.Jayawardena	SL	7	252	8	2	6	1	3	6	2	–	1	5
32	S.R.Waugh	A	1	260	10	–	3	2	2	2	3	3	1	2
30	M.L.Hayden †	A	2	184	5	–	6	5	1	6	1	3	2	–
30	S.Chanderpaul	WI	2	274	5	5	5	–	2	7	1	–	1	4
29	D.G.Bradman	A	12	80	19	–	4	2	–	4	–	–	–	–
28	Younus Khan	P	5	172	2	3	4	2	2	5	–	7	1	2
28	M.J.Clarke	A	2	186	7	–	5	1	4	7	1	3	–	–
27	G.C.Smith	SA	5	205	5	3	–	7	2	–	4	–	1	3
27	A.R.Border	A	2	265	8	–	–	3	5	4	6	1	–	–
26	G.St A.Sobers	WI	2	160	10	4	–	–	1	8	3	–	–	–
25	A.N.Cook	E	2	194	–	4	2	4	2	5	3	3	–	2
25	Inzamam-ul-Haq	P	2	200	5	1	–	4	3	3	–	5	2	2
24	G.S.Chappell	A	4	151	9	–	–	5	3	1	6	–	–	–
24	Mohammad Yousuf	P	4	156	6	1	–	7	1	4	–	1	2	2

		200	Inn	E	A	SA	WI	NZ	I	P	SL	Z	B
								Opponents					
24	I.V.A.Richards	WI	3	182	8	5	–	–	1	8	2	–	–
23	H.M.Amla	SA	3	141	4	5	–	1	4	5	2	1	–	1
23	V.Sehwag	I	6	180	2	3	5	2	2	–	4	5	–	–
23	K.P.Pietersen	E	3	181	–	4	3	3	2	6	2	3	–	–
23	J.L.Langer	A	3	182	5	–	2	3	4	3	4	2	–	–
23	Javed Miandad	P	6	189	2	6	–	2	7	5	–	1	–	–
22	W.R.Hammond	E	7	140	–	9	6	1	4	2	–	–	–	–
22	M.Azharuddin	I	–	147	6	2	4	–	2	–	3	5	–	–
22	M.C.Cowdrey	E	–	188	–	5	3	6	2	3	3	–	–	–
22	G.Boycott	E	1	193	–	7	1	5	2	4	3	–	–	–
21	R.N.Harvey	A	2	137	6	–	8	3	–	4	–	–	–	–
21	A.B.de Villiers	SA	2	162	2	5	–	6	–	3	4	1	–	–
21	G.Kirsten	SA	3	176	5	2	–	3	2	3	2	1	1	2
21	A.J.Strauss	E	–	178	–	4	3	6	3	3	2	–	–	–
21	I.R.Bell	E	1	181	–	4	2	1	1	4	4	2	–	3
21	D.C.Boon	A	1	190	7	–	–	3	3	6	1	1	–	–
20	K.F.Barrington	E	1	131	–	5	2	3	3	4	2	–	–	–
20	P.A.de Silva	SL	2	159	2	1	–	2	5	8	–	1	1
20	M.E.Waugh	A	–	209	6	–	4	4	1	1	3	1	–
20	G.A.Gooch	E	2	215	–	4	5	4	5	1	1	–	–

† Includes century scored for Australia v ICC in 2005-06.

The most for New Zealand is 17 by M.D.Crowe (131 innings), for Zimbabwe 12 by A.Flower (112), and for Bangladesh 6 by Mohammad Ashraful (119 innings) and 6 by Tamim Iqbal (72 innings).

The most double hundreds by batsmen not included above are 6 by M.S.Atapattu (16 hundreds for Sri Lanka), 4 by L.Hutton (19 for England), 4 by C.G.Greenidge (19 for West Indies), 4 by Zaheer Abbas (12 for Pakistan), and 4 by B.B.McCullum (11 for New Zealand).

HIGHEST PARTNERSHIP FOR EACH WICKET

1st	415	N.D.McKenzie/G.C.Smith	SA v B	Chittagong	2007-08
2nd	576	S.T.Jayasuriya/R.S.Mahanama	SL v I	Colombo (RPS)	1997-98
3rd	624	K.C.Sangakkara/D.P.M.D.Jayawardena	SL v SA	Colombo (SSC)	2006
4th	437	D.P.M.D.Jayawardena/T.T.Samaraweera	SL v P	Karachi	2008-09
5th	405	S.G.Barnes/D.G.Bradman	A v E	Sydney	1946-47
6th	365*	K.S.Williamson/B.J.Watling	NZ v SL	Wellington	2014-15
7th	347	D.St E.Atkinson/C.C.Depeiza	WI v A	Bridgetown	1954-55
8th	332	I.J.L.Trott/S.C.J.Broad	E v P	Lord's	2010
9th	195	M.V.Boucher/P.L.Symcox	SA v P	Johannesburg	1997-98
10th	198	J.E.Root/J.M.Anderson	E v I	Nottingham	2014

BOWLING RECORDS
200 WICKETS IN TESTS

Wkts			M	Balls	Runs	Avge	5 wI	10 wM
800	M.Muralitharan	SL/ICC	133	44039	18180	22.72	67	22
708	S.K.Warne	A	145	40705	17995	25.41	37	10
619	A.Kumble	I	132	40850	18355	29.65	35	8
563	G.D.McGrath	A	124	29248	12186	21.64	29	3
519	C.A.Walsh	WI	132	30019	12688	24.44	22	3
434	Kapil Dev	I	131	27740	12867	29.64	23	2
431	R.J.Hadlee	NZ	86	21918	9612	22.30	36	9
421	S.M.Pollock	SA	108	24453	9733	23.11	16	1
414	Wasim Akram	P	104	22627	9779	23.62	25	5

Wkts			M	Balls	Runs	Avge	5 wI	10 wM
413	Harbhajan Singh	I	101	28293	13372	32.37	25	5
405	C.E.L.Ambrose	WI	98	22104	8500	20.98	22	3
396	D.W.Steyn	SA	78	16486	8932	22.55	25	5
390	M.Ntini	SA	101	20834	11242	28.82	18	4
383	I.T.Botham	E	102	21815	10878	28.40	27	4
380	J.M.Anderson	E	99	22114	11295	29.72	16	2
376	M.D.Marshall	WI	81	17584	7876	20.94	22	4
373	Waqar Younis	P	87	16224	8788	23.56	22	5
362	Imran Khan	P	88	19458	8258	22.81	23	6
362	D.L.Vettori	NZ/ICC	113	28814	12441	34.36	20	3
355	D.K.Lillee	A	70	18467	8493	23.92	23	7
355	W.P.J.U.C.Vaas	SL	111	23438	10501	29.58	12	2
330	A.A.Donald	SA	72	15519	7344	22.25	20	3
325	R.G.D.Willis	E	90	17357	8190	25.20	16	–
311	Z.Khan	I	92	18785	10247	32.94	11	1
310	B.Lee	A	76	16531	9554	30.81	10	–
309	L.R.Gibbs	WI	79	27115	8989	29.09	18	2
307	F.S.Trueman	E	67	15178	6625	21.57	17	3
297	D.L.Underwood	E	86	21862	7674	25.83	17	6
292	J.H.Kallis	SA/ICC	166	20232	9535	32.65	5	–
291	C.J.McDermott	A	71	16586	8332	28.63	14	2
283	M.G.Johnson	A	64	14411	7879	27.84	12	3
266	B.S.Bedi	I	67	21364	7637	28.71	14	1
264	S.C.J.Broad	E	74	15515	7894	29.90	12	2
261	H.M.R.K.B.Herath	SL	58	16820	7717	29.56	21	4
261	Danish Kaneria	P	61	17697	9082	34.79	15	2
259	J.Garner	WI	58	13169	5433	20.97	7	–
259	J.N.Gillespie	A	71	14234	6770	26.13	8	–
255	G.P.Swann	E	60	15349	7642	29.96	17	3
252	J.B.Statham	E	70	16056	6261	24.84	9	1
249	M.A.Holding	WI	60	12680	5898	23.68	13	2
248	R.Benaud	A	63	19108	6704	27.03	16	1
248	M.J.Hoggard	E	67	13909	7564	30.50	7	1
246	G.D.McKenzie	A	60	17681	7328	29.78	16	3
242	B.S.Chandrasekhar	I	58	15963	7199	29.74	16	2
236	A.V.Bedser	E	51	15918	5876	24.89	15	5
236	J.Srinath	I	67	15104	7196	30.49	10	1
236	Abdul Qadir	P	67	17126	7742	32.80	15	5
235	G.St A.Sobers	WI	93	21599	7999	34.03	6	–
234	A.R.Caddick	E	62	13558	6999	29.91	13	1
233	C.S.Martin	NZ	71	14026	7878	33.81	10	1
229	D.Gough	E	58	11821	6503	28.39	9	–
228	R.R.Lindwall	A	61	13650	5251	23.03	12	–
226	S.J.Harmison	E/ICC	63	13375	7192	31.82	8	1
226	A.Flintoff	E/ICC	79	14951	7410	32.78	3	–
218	C.L.Cairns	NZ	62	11698	6410	29.40	13	1
217	M.Morkel	SA	62	12062	6369	29.35	6	–
216	C.V.Grimmett	A	37	14513	5231	24.21	21	7
216	H.H.Streak	Z	65	13559	6079	28.14	7	–
212	M.G.Hughes	A	53	12285	6017	28.38	7	1
208	S.C.G.MacGill	A	44	11237	6038	29.02	12	2
208	Saqlain Mushtaq	P	49	14070	6206	29.83	13	3
202	A.M.E.Roberts	WI	47	11136	5174	25.61	11	2
202	J.A.Snow	E	49	12021	5387	26.66	8	1
200	J.R.Thomson	A	51	10535	5601	28.00	8	–

The most for Bangladesh is 140 in 37 Tests by Shakib Al Hasan.

35 OR MORE WICKETS IN A SERIES

Wkts			Series	M	Balls	Runs	Avge	5 wI	10 wM
49	S.F.Barnes	E v SA	1913-14	4	1356	536	10.93	7	3
46	J.C.Laker	E v A	1956	5	1703	442	9.60	4	2
44	C.V.Grimmett	A v SA	1935-36	5	2077	642	14.59	5	3
42	T.M.Alderman	A v E	1981	6	1950	893	21.26	4	–
41	R.M.Hogg	A v E	1978-79	6	1740	527	12.85	5	2
41	T.M.Alderman	A v E	1989	6	1616	712	17.36	6	1
40	Imran Khan	P v I	1982-83	6	1339	558	13.95	4	2
40	S.K.Warne	A v E	2005	5	1517	797	19.92	3	2
39	A.V.Bedser	E v A	1953	5	1591	682	17.48	5	1
39	D.K.Lillee	A v E	1981	6	1870	870	22.30	2	1
38	M.W.Tate	E v A	1924-25	5	2528	881	23.18	5	1
37	W.J.Whitty	A v SA	1910-11	5	1395	632	17.08	2	–
37	H.J.Tayfield	SA v E	1956-57	5	2280	636	17.18	4	1
37	M.G.Johnson	A v E	2013-14	5	1132	517	13.97	3	–
36	A.E.E.Vogler	SA v E	1909-10	5	1349	783	21.75	4	1
36	A.A.Mailey	A v E	1920-21	5	1465	946	26.27	4	2
36	G.D.McGrath	A v E	1997	6	1499	701	19.47	2	–
35	G.A.Lohmann	E v SA	1895-96	3	520	203	5.80	4	2
35	B.S.Chandrasekhar	I v E	1972-73	5	1747	662	18.91	4	–
35	M.D.Marshall	WI v E	1988	5	1219	443	12.65	3	1

The most for New Zealand is 33 by R.J.Hadlee (3 Tests v A, 1985-86), for Sri Lanka 30 by M.Muralitharan (3 Tests v Z, 2001-02), for Zimbabwe 22 by H.H.Streak (3 Tests v P, 1994-95), and for Bangladesh 18 by Enamul Haque II (2 Tests v Z, 2004-05) and 18 by Shakib Al Hasan (3 Tests v Z, 2014-15).

15 OR MORE WICKETS IN A TEST († *On debut*)

19- 90	J.C.Laker	E v A	Manchester	1956
17-159	S.F.Barnes	E v SA	Johannesburg	1913-14
16-136†	N.D.Hirwani	I v WI	Madras	1987-88
16-137†	R.A.L.Massie	A v E	Lord's	1972
16-220	M.Muralitharan	SL v E	The Oval	1998
15- 28	J.Briggs	E v SA	Cape Town	1888-89
15- 45	G.A.Lohmann	E v SA	Port Elizabeth	1895-96
15- 99	C.Blythe	E v SA	Leeds	1907
15-104	H.Verity	E v A	Lord's	1934
15-123	R.J.Hadlee	NZ v A	Brisbane	1985-86
15-124	W.Rhodes	E v A	Melbourne	1903-04
15-217	Harbhajan Singh	I v A	Madras	2000-01

The best analysis for South Africa is 13-132 by M.Ntini (v WI, Port-of-Spain, 2004-05), for West Indies 14-149 by M.A.Holding (v E, The Oval, 1976), for Pakistan 14-116 by Imran Khan (v SL, Lahore, 1981-82), for Zimbabwe 11-257 by A.G.Huckle (v NZ, Bulawayo, 1997-98), and for Bangladesh 12-200 by Enamul Haque II (v Z, Dhaka, 2004-05).

NINE OR MORE WICKETS IN AN INNINGS

10-53	J.C.Laker	E v A	Manchester	1956
10-74	A.Kumble	I v P	Delhi	1998-99
9-28	G.A.Lohmann	E v SA	Johannesburg	1895-96
9-37	J.C.Laker	E v A	Manchester	1956
9-51	M.Muralitharan	SL v Z	Kandy	2001-02
9-52	R.J.Hadlee	NZ v A	Brisbane	1985-86
9-56	Abdul Qadir	P v E	Lahore	1987-88
9-57	D.E.Malcolm	E v SA	The Oval	1994

9- 65	M.Muralitharan	SL v E	The Oval	1998
9- 69	J.M.Patel	I v A	Kanpur	1959-60
9- 83	Kapil Dev	I v WI	Ahmedabad	1983-84
9- 86	Sarfraz Nawaz	P v A	Melbourne	1978-79
9- 95	J.M.Noreiga	WI v I	Port-of-Spain	1970-71
9-102	S.P.Gupte	I v WI	Kanpur	1958-59
9-103	S.F.Barnes	E v SA	Johannesburg	1913-14
9-113	H.J.Tayfield	SA v E	Johannesburg	1956-57
9-121	A.A.Mailey	A v E	Melbourne	1920-21
9-127	H.M.R.K.B.Herath	SL v P	Colombo (SSC)	2014

The best analysis for Zimbabwe is 8-109 by P.A.Strang (v NZ, Bulawayo, 2000-01), and for Bangladesh 8-39 by Taijul Islam (v Z, Dhaka, 2014-15).

HAT-TRICKS

F.R.Spofforth	Australia v England	Melbourne	1878-79
W.Bates[7]	England v Australia	Melbourne	1882-83
J.Briggs[7]	England v Australia	Sydney	1891-92
G.A.Lohmann	England v South Africa	Port Elizabeth	1895-96
J.T.Hearne	England v Australia	Leeds	1899
H.Trumble	Australia v England	Melbourne	1901-02
H.Trumble	Australia v England	Melbourne	1903-04
T.J.Matthews (2)[2]	Australia v South Africa	Manchester	1912
M.J.C.Allom[1]	England v New Zealand	Christchurch	1929-30
T.W.J.Goddard	England v South Africa	Johannesburg	1938-39
P.J.Loader	England v West Indies	Leeds	1957
L.F.Kline	Australia v South Africa	Cape Town	1957-58
W.W.Hall	West Indies v Pakistan	Lahore	1958-59
G.M.Griffin[7]	South Africa v England	Lord's	1960
L.R.Gibbs	West Indies v Australia	Adelaide	1960-61
P.J.Petherick[1/7]	New Zealand v Pakistan	Lahore	1976-77
C.A.Walsh[3]	West Indies v Australia	Brisbane	1988-89
M.G.Hughes[3/7]	Australia v West Indies	Perth	1988-89
D.W.Fleming[1]	Australia v Pakistan	Rawalpindi	1994-95
S.K.Warne	Australia v England	Melbourne	1994-95
D.G.Cork	England v West Indies	Manchester	1995
D.Gough[7]	England v Australia	Sydney	1998-99
Wasim Akram[4]	Pakistan v Sri Lanka	Lahore	1998-99
Wasim Akram[4]	Pakistan v Sri Lanka	Dhaka	1998-99
D.N.T.Zoysa[3]	Sri Lanka v Zimbabwe	Harare	1999-00
Abdul Razzaq	Pakistan v Sri Lanka	Galle	2000-01
G.D.McGrath	Australia v West Indies	Perth	2000-01
Harbhajan Singh	India v Australia	Calcutta	2000-01
Mohammad Sami[7]	Pakistan v Sri Lanka	Lahore	2001-02
J.J.C.Lawson[7]	West Indies v Australia	Bridgetown	2002-03
Alok Kapali[7]	Bangladesh v Pakistan	Peshawar	2003
A.M.Blignaut	Zimbabwe v Bangladesh	Harare	2003-04
M.J.Hoggard	England v West Indies	Bridgetown	2003-04
J.E.C.Franklin	New Zealand v Bangladesh	Dhaka	2004-05
I.K.Pathan[6/7]	India v Pakistan	Karachi	2005-06
R.J.Sidebottom[7]	England v New Zealand	Hamilton	2007-08
P.M.Siddle	Australia v England	Brisbane	2010-11
S.C.J.Broad	England v India	Nottingham	2011
Sohag Gazi[7]	Bangladesh v New Zealand	Chittagong	2013-14
S.C.J.Broad[7]	England v Sri Lanka	Leeds	2014

[1] On debut. [2] Hat-trick in each innings. [3] Involving both innings. [4] In successive Tests. [5] His first 3 balls (second over of the match). [6] The fourth, fifth and sixth balls of the match. [7] On losing side.

WICKET-KEEPING RECORDS
100 DISMISSALS IN TESTS†

Total			Tests	Ct	St
555	M.V.Boucher	South Africa/ICC	147	532	23
416	A.C.Gilchrist	Australia	96	379	37
395	I.A.Healy	Australia	119	366	29
355	R.W.Marsh	Australia	96	343	12
294	M.S.Dhoni	India	90	256	38
270†	P.J.L.Dujon	West Indies	79	265	5
269	A.P.E.Knott	England	95	250	19
258	B.J.Haddin	Australia	63	251	7
256	M.J.Prior	England	79	243	13
241†	A.J.Stewart	England	82	227	14
228	Wasim Bari	Pakistan	81	201	27
219	R.D.Jacobs	West Indies	65	207	12
219	T.G.Evans	England	91	173	46
206	Kamran Akmal	Pakistan	53	184	22
201†	A.C.Parore	New Zealand	67	194	7
198	S.M.H.Kirmani	India	88	160	38
191	D.Ramdin	West Indies	64	184	7
189	D.L.Murray	West Indies	62	181	8
187	A.T.W.Grout	Australia	51	163	24
178†	B.B.McCullum	New Zealand	52	167	11
176	I.D.S.Smith	New Zealand	63	168	8
174	R.W.Taylor	England	57	167	7
165	R.C.Russell	England	54	153	12
156	H.A.P.W.Jayawardena	Sri Lanka	58	124	32
152	D.J.Richardson	South Africa	42	150	2
151†	K.C.Sangakkara	Sri Lanka	48	131	20
151†	A.Flower	Zimbabwe	55	142	9
147†	Moin Khan	Pakistan	66	127	20
141	J.H.B.Waite	South Africa	49	124	17
133	G.O.Jones	England	34	128	5
130	Rashid Latif	Pakistan	37	119	11
130	K.S.More	India	49	110	20
130	W.A.S.Oldfield	Australia	54	78	52
119	R.S.Kaluwitharana	Sri Lanka	49	93	26
112†	J.M.Parks	England	43	101	11
107	N.R.Mongia	India	44	99	8
104	Salim Yousuf	Pakistan	32	91	13
101†	J.R.Murray	West Indies	31	98	3

The most for Bangladesh is 87 (78 ct, 9 st) by Khaled Masud in 44 Tests.

† *Excluding catches taken in the field*

25 OR MORE DISMISSALS IN A SERIES

29	B.J.Haddin	Australia v England	2013
28	R.W.Marsh	Australia v England	1982-83
27 (inc 2st)	R.C.Russell	England v South Africa	1995-96
27 (inc 2st)	I.A.Healy	Australia v England (6 Tests)	1997
26 (inc 3st)	J.H.B.Waite	South Africa v New Zealand	1961-62
26	R.W.Marsh	Australia v West Indies (6 Tests)	1975-76
26 (inc 5st)	I.A.Healy	Australia v England (6 Tests)	1993
26 (inc 1st)	M.V.Boucher	South Africa v England	1998
26 (inc 2st)	A.C.Gilchrist	Australia v England	2001
26 (inc 2st)	A.C.Gilchrist	Australia v England	2006-07
25 (inc 2st)	I.A.Healy	Australia v England	1994-95
25 (inc 2st)	A.C.Gilchrist	Australia v England	2002-03
25	A.C.Gilchrist	Australia v India	2007-08

TEN OR MORE DISMISSALS IN A TEST

11	R.C.Russell	England v South Africa	Johannesburg	1995-96
11	A.B.de Villiers	South Africa v Pakistan	Johannesburg	2012-13
10	R.W.Taylor	England v India	Bombay	1979-80
10	A.C.Gilchrist	Australia v New Zealand	Hamilton	1999-00

SEVEN DISMISSALS IN AN INNINGS

7	Wasim Bari	Pakistan v New Zealand	Auckland	1978-79
7	R.W.Taylor	England v India	Bombay	1979-80
7	I.D.S.Smith	New Zealand v Sri Lanka	Hamilton	1990-91
7	R.D.Jacobs	West Indies v Australia	Melbourne	2000-01

FIVE STUMPINGS IN AN INNINGS

5	K.S.More	India v West Indies	Madras	1987-88

FIELDING RECORDS
100 CATCHES IN TESTS

Total			Tests	Total			Tests
210	R.S.Dravid	India/ICC	164	120	I.T.Botham	England	102
205	D.P.M.D.Jayawardena	Sri Lanka	149	120	M.C.Cowdrey	England	114
200	J.H.Kallis	South Africa/ICC	166	115	C.L.Hooper	West Indies	102
196	R.T.Ponting	Australia	168	115	S.R.Tendulkar	India	200
181	M.E.Waugh	Australia	128	112	S.R.Waugh	Australia	168
171	S.P.Fleming	New Zealand	111	110	R.B.Simpson	Australia	62
169	G.C.Smith	South Africa/ICC	117	110	W.R.Hammond	England	85
164	B.C.Lara	West Indies/ICC	131	109	G.St A.Sobers	West Indies	93
157	M.A.Taylor	Australia	104	108	A.N.Cook	England	109
156	A.R.Border	Australia	156	108	S.M.Gavaskar	India	125
135	V.V.S.Laxman	India	134	105	I.M.Chappell	Australia	75
128	M.L.Hayden	Australia	103	105	Younus Khan	Pakistan	96
125	M.J.Clarke	Australia	108	105	M.Azharuddin	India	99
125	S.K.Warne	Australia	145	105	G.P.Thorpe	England	100
122	G.S.Chappell	Australia	87	103	L.R.P.L.Taylor	New Zealand	62
122	I.V.A.Richards	West Indies	121	103	G.A.Gooch	England	118
121	A.J.Strauss	England	100				

The most for Zimbabwe is 60 by A.D.R.Campbell (60) and for Bangladesh 25 by Mohammad Ashraful (61).

15 CATCHES IN A SERIES

15	J.M.Gregory	Australia v England	1920-21

SEVEN CATCHES IN A TEST

7	G.S.Chappell	Australia v England	Perth	1974-75
7	Yajurvindra Singh	India v England	Bangalore	1976-77
7	H.P.Tillekeratne	Sri Lanka v New Zealand	Colombo (SSC)	1992-93
7	S.P.Fleming	New Zealand v Zimbabwe	Harare	1997-98
7	M.L.Hayden	Australia v Sri Lanka	Galle	2003-04

FIVE CATCHES IN AN INNINGS

5	V.Y.Richardson	Australia v South Africa	Durban	1935-36
5	Yajurvindra Singh	India v England	Bangalore	1976-77
5	M.Azharuddin	India v Pakistan	Karachi	1989-90
5	K.Srikkanth	India v Australia	Perth	1991-92
5	S.P.Fleming	New Zealand v Zimbabwe	Harare	1997-98

			E	A	SA	WI	NZ	I	P	SL	Z	B
5	G.C.Smith	South Africa v Australia							Perth			2012-13
5	D.J.G.Sammy	West Indies v India							Mumbai			2013-14
5	D.M.Bravo	West Indies v Bangladesh							Kingstown			2014

APPEARANCE RECORDS
100 TEST MATCH APPEARANCES
Opponents

			E	A	SA	WI	NZ	I	P	SL	Z	B
200	S.R.Tendulkar	India	32	39	25	21	24	–	18	25	9	7
168	S.R.Waugh	Australia	46	–	16	32	23	18	20	8	3	2
168†	R.T.Ponting	Australia	35	–	26	24	17	29	15	14	3	4
166†	J.H.Kallis	South Africa/ICC	31	28	–	24	18	19	19	15	6	6
164†	R.S.Dravid	India/ICC	21	32	21	23	15	–	15	20	9	7
161	S.Chanderpaul	West Indies	32	20	24	–	21	25	14	7	8	10
156	A.R.Border	Australia	47	–	6	31	23	20	22	7	–	–
149	D.P.M.D.Jayawardena	Sri Lanka	23	16	18	11	13	18	29	–	8	13
147†	M.V.Boucher	South Africa/ICC	25	20	–	24	17	14	15	17	6	8
145†	S.K.Warne	Australia	36	–	24	19	20	14	15	13	1	2
134	V.V.S.Laxman	India	17	29	19	22	10	–	15	13	6	3
133	A.J.Stewart	England	–	33	23	24	16	9	13	9	6	–
133†	M.Muralitharan	Sri Lanka/ICC	16	12	15	12	14	22	16	–	14	11
132	A.Kumble	India	19	20	21	17	11	–	15	18	7	4
132	C.A.Walsh	West Indies	36	38	10	–	10	15	18	3	2	–
131	Kapil Dev	India	27	20	4	25	10	–	29	14	2	–
131†	B.C.Lara	West Indies/ICC	30	30	18	–	11	17	12	8	2	2
130	K.C.Sangakkara	Sri Lanka	22	11	17	12	12	15	21	–	5	15
128	M.E.Waugh	Australia	29	–	18	28	14	14	15	9	1	–
125	S.M.Gavaskar	India	38	20	–	27	9	–	24	7	–	–
124†	G.D.McGrath	Australia	30	–	17	23	14	11	17	8	1	2
124	Javed Miandad	Pakistan	22	24	–	17	18	28	–	12	3	–
121	I.V.A.Richards	West Indies	36	34	–	–	7	28	16	–	–	–
120†	Inzamam-ul-Haq	Pakistan/ICC	19	13	13	15	12	10	–	20	11	6
119	I.A.Healy	Australia	33	–	12	28	11	9	14	11	1	–
118	G.A.Gooch	England	–	42	3	26	15	19	10	3	–	–
117	D.I.Gower	England	–	42	–	19	13	24	17	2	–	–
117†	G.C.Smith	South Africa/ICC	21	21	–	14	13	15	16	7	2	8
116	D.L.Haynes	West Indies	36	33	1	–	10	19	16	1	–	–
116	D.B.Vengsarkar	India	26	24	–	25	11	–	22	8	–	–
115	M.A.Atherton	England	–	33	18	27	11	7	11	4	4	–
114	M.C.Cowdrey	England	–	43	14	21	18	8	10	–	–	–
113	S.C.Ganguly	India	12	24	17	12	8	–	12	14	9	5
113†	D.L.Vettori	New Zealand/ICC	17	18	14	10	–	15	9	11	9	9
111	S.P.Fleming	New Zealand	19	14	15	11	–	13	9	13	11	6
111	W.P.J.U.C.Vaas	Sri Lanka	15	12	11	9	10	14	18	–	15	7
110	S.T.Jayasuriya	Sri Lanka	13	13	15	10	13	10	17	–	13	5
110	C.H.Lloyd	West Indies	34	29	–	–	8	28	11	–	–	–
109	A.N.Cook	England	–	25	11	14	11	20	11	13	–	4
108	G.Boycott	England	–	38	7	29	15	13	6	–	–	–
108†	M.J.Clarke	Australia	30	–	14	10	11	22	10	8	–	2
108	C.G.Greenidge	West Indies	29	32	–	–	10	23	14	–	–	–
108	S.M.Pollock	South Africa	23	13	–	16	11	12	12	13	5	3
107	D.C.Boon	Australia	31	–	6	22	17	11	11	9	–	–
105	I.R.Bell	England	–	28	11	9	10	20	10	10	–	6
105†	J.L.Langer	Australia	21	–	11	18	14	14	13	8	3	2
104	K.P.Pietersen	England	–	27	10	14	8	16	14	11	–	4
104†	V.Sehwag	India/ICC	17	23	15	10	12	–	9	11	3	4

			E	A	SA	WI	NZ	I	P	SL	Z	B
104	M.A.Taylor	Australia	33	–	11	20	11	9	12	8	–	–
104	Wasim Akram	Pakistan	18	13	4	17	9	12	–	19	10	2
103	C.H.Gayle	West Indies	20	8	16	–	12	14	8	10	8	7
103†	M.L.Hayden	Australia	20	–	19	15	11	18	6	7	2	4
103	Salim Malik	Pakistan	19	15	1	7	18	22	–	15	6	–
102	I.T.Botham	England	–	36	–	20	15	14	14	3	–	–
102	C.L.Hooper	West Indies	24	25	10	–	2	19	14	6	2	–
101	Harbhajan Singh	India	14	18	11	11	13	–	9	15	7	3
101	G.Kirsten	South Africa	22	18	–	13	13	10	11	93	2	
101	M.Ntini	South Africa	18	15	–	15	11	10	9	12	3	8
100	G.P.Thorpe	England	–	16	16	27	13	5	8	9	2	4
100	A.J.Strauss	England	–	20	16	18	9	12	13	8	–	4

† Includes appearance in the Australia v ICC 'Test' in 2005-06. The most for Zimbabwe is 67 by G.W.Flower, and for Bangladesh 61 by Mohammad Ashraful.

100 CONSECUTIVE TEST APPEARANCES

153	A.R.Border	Australia	March 1979 to March 1994
107	A.N.Cook	England	May 2006 to August 2014
107	M.E.Waugh	Australia	June 1993 to October 2002
106	S.M.Gavaskar	India	January 1975 to February 1987

50 TESTS AS CAPTAIN

			Won	Lost	Drawn	Tied
109	G.C.Smith	South Africa	53	29	27	–
93	A.R.Border	Australia	32	22	38	1
80	S.P.Fleming	New Zealand	28	27	25	–
77	R.T.Ponting	Australia	48	16	13	–
74	C.H.Lloyd	West Indies	36	12	26	–
60	M.S.Dhoni	India	27	18	15	–
57	S.R.Waugh	Australia	41	9	7	–
56	A.Ranatunga	Sri Lanka	12	19	25	–
54	M.A.Atherton	England	13	21	20	–
53	W.J.Cronje	South Africa	27	11	15	–
51	M.P.Vaughan	England	26	11	14	–
50	I.V.A.Richards	West Indies	27	8	15	–
50	M.A.Taylor	Australia	26	13	11	–
50	A.J.Strauss	England	24	11	15	–

The most for Pakistan is 48 by Imran Khan, for Zimbabwe 21 by A.D.R.Campbell and H.H.Streak, and for Bangladesh 18 by Habibul Bashar.

50 TEST UMPIRING APPEARANCES

128	S.A.Bucknor	(West Indies)	28.04.1989 to 22.03.2009
108	R.E.Koertzen	(South Africa)	26.12.1992 to 24.07.2010
95	D.J.Harper	(Australia)	28.11.1998 to 23.06.2011
94	Alim Dar	(Pakistan)	21.10.2003 to 06.01.2015
92	D.R.Shepherd	(England)	01.08.1985 to 07.06.2005
82	B.F.Bowden	(New Zealand)	11.03.2000 to 30.12.2014
78	D.B.Hair	(Australia)	25.01.1992 to 08.06.2008
74	S.J.A.Taufel	(Australia)	26.12.2000 to 20.08.2012
73	S.Venkataraghavan	(India)	29.01.1993 to 20.01.2004
66	H.D.Bird	(England)	05.07.1973 to 24.06.1996
55	S.J.Davis	(Australia)	27.11.1997 to 07.01.2015

THE FIRST-CLASS COUNTIES
REGISTER, RECORDS AND 2014 AVERAGES

All statistics are to 15 March 2015.

ABBREVIATIONS – General

*	not out/unbroken partnership	IT20	International Twenty20
b	born	l-o	limited-overs
BB	Best innings bowling analysis	LOI	Limited-Overs Internationals
Cap	Awarded 1st XI County Cap	Tests	International Test Matches
f-c	first-class	F-c Tours	Overseas tours involving first-class
HS	Highest Score		appearances

Awards

PCA 2014	Professional Cricketers' Association Player of 2014
Wisden 2013	One of *Wisden Cricketers' Almanack*'s Five Cricketers of 2013
YC 2014	Cricket Writers' Club Young Cricketer of 2014

ECB Competitions

BHC	Benson & Hedges Cup (1972-2002)	CD	Central Districts
CB40	Clydesdale Bank 40 (2010-12)	CSK	Chennai Super Kings
CC	LV= County Championship	DC	Deccan Chargers
CGT	Cheltenham & Gloucester Trophy (2001-06)	DD	Delhi Daredevils
FPT	Friends Provident Trophy (2007-09)	EL	England Lions
NL	National League (1999-2005)	EP	Eastern Province
NWT	NatWest Trophy (1981-2000)	HB	Habib Bank Limited
P40	NatWest PRO 40 League (2006-09)	HH	Hobart Hurricanes
RLC	Royal London One-Day Cup	KKC	Kalabagan Krira Chakra
SL	Sunday League (1969-98)	KKR	Kolkata Knight Riders
T20	Twenty20 Competition	KRL	Khan Research Laboratories
Y40	Yorkshire Bank 40 (2013)	KXIP	Kings XI Punjab

Education

		KZN	KwaZulu-Natal Inland
Ac	Academy	ME	Mashonaland Eagles
BHS	Boys' High School	MI	Mumbai Indians
C	College	MR	Melbourne Renegades
CFE	College of Further Education	MS	Melbourne Stars
CHE	College of Higher Education	MT	Matabeleland Tuskers
CS	Comprehensive School	MWR	Mid West Rhinos
GS	Grammar School	NBP	National Bank of Pakistan
HS	High School	ND	Northern Districts
I	Institute	NSW	New South Wales
S	School	NT	Northern Transvaal
SFC	Sixth Form College	NW	North West
SS	Secondary School	(O)FS	(Orange) Free State
TC	Technical College	PDSC	Prime Doleshwar Sporting Club
U	University	PIA	Pakistan International Airlines
UWIC	University of Wales Institute, Cardiff	PS	Perth Scorchers

Playing Categories

		PTC	Pakistan Telecommunication Co
LBG	Bowls right-arm leg-breaks and googlies	PW	Pune Warriors
LF	Bowls left-arm fast	Q	Queensland
LFM	Bowls left-arm fast-medium	RCB	Royal Challengers Bangalore
LHB	Bats left-handed	RR	Rajasthan Royals
LM	Bowls left-arm medium pace	REDCO	Really Efficient Development Co
LMF	Bowls left-arm medium fast	SH	Sunrisers Hyderabad
OB	Bowls right-arm off-breaks	SJD	Sheikh Jamal Dhanmondi
RF	Bowls right-arm fast	SNGPL	Sui Northern Gas Pipelines Limited
RFM	Bowls right-arm fast-medium	SR	Southern Rocks
RHB	Bats right-handed	SS	Sydney Sixers
RM	Bowls right-arm medium pace	SSGC	Sui Southern Gas Corporation
RMF	Bowls right-arm medium-fast	ST	Sydney Thunder
SLA	Bowls left-arm leg-breaks	Tas	Tasmania
SLC	Bowls left-arm 'Chinamen'	T&T	Trinidad & Tobago
WK	Wicket-keeper	Vic	Victoria
Teams (see also p 217)		WA	Western Australia
AS	Adelaide Strikers	WAPDA	Water & Power Development Authority.
BH	Brisbane Heat	WP	Western Province
CC&C	Combined Campuses & Colleges	ZTB	Zarai Taraqiati Bank Limited

DERBYSHIRE

18 70
Cricket
DERBYSHIRE

Formation of Present Club: 4 November 1870
Inaugural First-Class Match: 1871
Colours: Chocolate, Amber and Pale Blue
Badge: Rose and Crown
County Champions: (1) 1936
NatWest Trophy Winners: (1) 1981
Benson and Hedges Cup Winners: (1) 1993
Sunday League Winners: (1) 1990
Twenty20 Cup Winners: (0) best – Quarter-Finalist 2005

Chief Executive: Simon Storey, Derbyshire County Cricket Club, The 3aaa County Ground, Nottingham Road, Derby, DE21 6DA • Tel: 01332 388101 • Fax: 0844 500 8322 • Email: info@derbyshireccc.com • Web: www. derbyshireccc.com • Twitter: @DerbyshireCCC (14,350 followers)

Elite Performance Director: Graeme Welch. **Captain**: W.L.Madsen. **Vice-Captain**: None. **Overseas Player**: M.J.Guptill. **2015 Beneficiary**: None. **Head Groundsman**: Neil Godrich. **Scorer**: John Brown. ‡ New registration. NQ Not qualified for England.

CLARE, Jonathan Luke (St Theodore's HS), b Burnley, Lancs 14 Jun 1986. 6'4". RHB, RMF. Squad No 13. Debut (Derbyshire) 2007, taking 5-90 v Notts (Chesterfield); cap 2012. HS 130 v Glamorgan (Derby) 2011. BB 7-74 v Northants (Northampton) 2008. LO HS 57 v Warwks (Derby) 2012 (CB40). LO BB 3-39 v Scotland (Derby) 2008 (FPT). T20 HS 35*. T20 BB 2-20.

CORK, Gregory Teodor Gerald (Denstone C), b Derby 29 Sep 1994. Son of D.G.Cork (Derbyshire, Lancashire, Hampshire and England 1990-2011). 6'2". RHB, LMF. Squad No 14. Derbyshire 2nd XI debut 2011. Awaiting f-c debut. T20 HS 13*. T20 BB 2-36.

COTTON, Benjamin David (Clayton Hall C; Stoke-on-Trent SFC), b Stoke-on-Trent, Staffs 13 Sep 1993. 6'4". RHB, RMF. Squad No 36. Debut (Derbyshire) 2014. Derbyshire 2nd XI debut 2011. HS 21 and BB 4-20 v Leics (Derby) 2014. LO HS 18* v Yorks (Scarborough) 2014 (RLC). LO BB 2-42 v Northants (Northampton) 2014 (RLC). T20 HS – . T20 BB 1-49.

DAVIS, William Samuel (Stafford GS), b 6 Mar 1996. 6'1". RHB, RFM. Squad No 44. Derbyshire 2nd XI debut 2013. Awaiting 1st XI debut.

DURSTON, Wesley John (Millfield S; University C, Worcester), b Taunton, Somerset 6 Oct 1980. 5'10". RHB, OB. Squad No 3. Somerset 2002-09. Derbyshire debut 2010; cap 2012. Unicorns 2010 (l-o only). 1000 runs (1): 1138 (2011). HS 151 v Glos (Derby) 2011. BB 5-19 v Worcs (Derby) 2014. LO HS 134 v Hants (Derby) 2014 (RLC). LO BB 3-7 v Worcs (Derby) 2011 (CB40). T20 HS 111 v Notts (Nottingham) 2010 – De record. T20 BB 3-25.

ELSTONE, Scott Liam (Friary Grange C), b Burton-on-Trent, Staffs 10 Jun 1990. 5'8". RHB, OB. Squad No 10. Debut (Derbyshire) 2014. Nottinghamshire 2nd XI debut 2006, aged 16y 81d. Unicorns (l-o only) 2013. HS 63 v Glos (Derby) 2014. BB 2-8 v Leics (Leicester) 2014. LO HS 75* Uni v Somerset (Taunton) 2013 (Y40). LO BB 1-22 Nt v Scotland (Nottingham) 2010 (CB40). T20 HS 24*. T20 BB – .

FOOTITT, Mark Harold Alan (Carlton le Willows S; West Notts C), b Nottingham 25 Nov 1985. 6'2". RHB, LFM. Squad No 4. Nottinghamshire 2005-09. MCC 2006. No f-c appearances in 2008. Derbyshire debut 2010; cap 2014. HS 30 v Surrey (Oval) 2010. 50 wkts (1): 84 (2014). BB 6-48 v Glamorgan (Derby) 2014. LO HS 11* v Notts (Nottingham) 2014 (RLC). LO BB 5-28 v Scotland (Edinburgh) 2013 (Y40). T20 HS 2*. T20 BB 3-22.

GODLEMAN, Billy Ashley (Islington Green S), b Islington, London 11 Feb 1989. 6'3". LHB, LB. Squad No 1. Middlesex 2005-09. Essex 2010-12. Derbyshire debut 2013. HS 130 Ex v Leics (Leicester) 2011 and 130 Ex v Glos (Cheltenham) 2012. De HS 104* v Surrey (Oval) 2014. BB – . LO HS 96 v Glos (Derby) 2014 (RLC). T20 HS 69.

NQ**GUPTILL, Martin** James (Avondale C), b Auckland, New Zealand 30 Sep 1986. 6'3". RHB, OB. Squad No 31. Auckland 2005-06 to date. Derbyshire debut 2011; cap 2012. Big Bash: ST 2012-13. **Tests** (NZ): 31 (2008-09 to 2013); HS 189 v B (Hamilton) 2009-10; BB 3-37 v P (Napier) 2009-10. **LOI** (NZ): 105 (2008-09 to 2014-15); HS 189* v E (Southampton) 2013; BB 2-7 v B (Napier) 2009-10. **IT20** (NZ): 48 (2008-90 to 2014-15); HS 101* v SA (East London) 2012-13; BB – . F-c Tours (NZ): E 2013; A 2011-12; SA 2012-13; WI 2012; I 2008-09 (NZ A), 2010-11, 2012; SL 2009, 2012-13; Z 2010-11 (NZ A), 2011-12. HS 195* Auck v Canterbury (Rangiora) 2011-12. De HS 143 v Glos (Derby) 2011. BB 3-37 (see Tests). De BB – . LO HS 189* (see LOI). LO BB 2-7 (see LOI). T20 HS 120*. T20 BB – .

HOSEIN, Harvey Richard (Denstone C), b Chesterfield 12 Aug 1996. 5'10". RHB, WK. Squad No 16. Debut (Derbyshire) 2014, taking seven catches in an innings and UK record-equalling 11 in match v Surrey (The Oval). Derbyshire 2nd XI debut 2010, aged 13y 287d. HS 13 v Leics (Derby) 2014.

HUGHES, Alex Lloyd (Ounsdale HS, Wolverhampton), b Wordsley, Staffs 29 Sep 1991. 5'10". RHB, RM. Squad No 18. Debut (Derbyshire) 2013. Derbyshire 2nd XI debut 2009. HS 82 v Kent (Canterbury) 2014. BB 4-46 v Glamorgan (Derby) 2014. LO HS 59* and LO BB 3-56 v Essex (Leek) 2013 (Y40). T20 HS 43*. T20 BB 3-32.

NQ**HUGHES, Chesney** Francis (Albena Lake Hodge CS, Anguilla), b Anguilla 20 January 1991. 6'2". LHB, SLA. Squad No 22. British passport. Debut (Derbyshire) 2010. Derbyshire 2nd XI debut 2009. Leeward Is 2009-10 to 2011-12 (l-o only). HS 270* v Yorks (Leeds) 2013. BB 2-9 v Middx (Derby) 2011. LO HS 81 Leeward Is v Windward Is (Kingston) 2010-11. LO BB 5-29 v Unicorns (Wormsley) 2012 (CB40). T20 HS 65. T20 BB 4-23.

KNIGHT, Thomas Craig ('**Tom**') (Eckington C), b Sheffield, Yorks 28 Jun 1993. 6'0½". RHB, SLA. Squad No 27. Debut (Derbyshire) 2011. No f-c appearances 2012-14. HS 14 v Surrey (Oval) 2011. BB 2-32 v Glamorgan (Cardiff) 2011. LO HS 10 v Hants (Derby) 2013 (Y40). LO BB 3-36 v Durham (Derby) 2013 (Y40). T20 HS 44*. T20 BB 3-16.

NQ**MADSEN, Wayne** Lee (Kearsney C, Durban; U of South Africa), b Durban, South Africa 2 Jan 1984. Nephew of M.B.Madsen (Natal 1967-68 to 1978-79), T.R.Madsen (Natal 1976-77 to 1989-90) and H.R.Fotheringham (Natal, Transvaal 1971-72 to 1989-90), cousin of G.S.Fotheringham (KwaZulu-Natal 2008-09 to 2009-10). 5'11". RHB, OB. Squad No 77. KwaZulu-Natal 2003-04 to 2007-08. Dolphins 2006-07 to 2007-08. Derbyshire debut 2009, scoring 170 v Glos (Cheltenham); cap 2011; captain 2012 to date. Qualified for England by residence in February 2015. 1000 runs (2); most – 1239 (2013). HS 231* v Northants (Northampton) 2012. BB 3-45 KZN v EP (Pt Elizabeth) 2007-08. De BB 2-9 v Sussex (Hove) 2013. LO HS 138 v Hants (Derby) 2014 (RLC). LO BB 3-27 v Durham (Derby) 2013 (Y40). T20 HS 65.

PALLADINO, Antonio Paul (Cardinal Pole SS; Anglia Polytechnic U), b Tower Hamlets, London 29 Jun 1983. 6'0''. RHB, RMF. Squad No 28. Cambridge UCCE 2003-05. Essex 2003-10. Namibia 2009-10. Derbyshire debut 2011; cap 2012. HS 106 v Australia A (Derby) 2012. CC HS 68 v Warwks (Birmingham) 2013. 50 wkts (2); most – 56 (2012). BB 7-53 v Kent (Derby) 2012. Hat-trick v Leics (Leicester) 2012. LO HS 31 Namibia v Boland (Windhoek) 2009-10. LO BB 5-49 v Lancs (Derby) 2014 (RLC). T20 HS 14*. T20 BB 4-21.

POYNTON, Thomas (John Taylor HS, Barton-under-Needwood; Repton S), b Burton upon Trent, Staffs 25 Nov 1989. 5'10''. RHB, WK. Squad No 23. Debut (Derbyshire) 2007. No f-c appearances in 2009 and 2011. Missed entire 2014 season after suffering serious injury in a car crash. HS 106 v Northants (Northampton) 2012. BB 2-96 v Glamorgan (Cardiff) 2010. LO HS 40 v Middx (Chesterfield) 2011 (CB40). T20 HS 19.

SLATER, Benjamin Thomas (Netherthorpe S; Leeds Met U), b Chesterfield 26 Aug 1991. 5'10''. LHB, LB. Squad No 26. Debut (Leeds/Bradford MCCU) 2012. Southern Rocks 2012-13. Derbyshire 2nd XI debut 2009. HS 199 v Leics (Derby) 2014, also scored 104 in same match. BB – . LO HS 46 SR v MWR (Masvingo) 2012-13. T20 HS 57.

TAYLOR, Thomas Alex Ian (Trentham HS, Stoke-on-Trent), b Stoke-on-Trent, Staffs 21 Dec 1994. 6'2''. RHB, RMF. Squad No 15. Debut (Derbyshire) 2014. Derbyshire 2nd XI debut 2011. HS 40 v Leics (Leicester) 2014. BB 5-58 v Glos (Cheltenham) 2014. LO HS – . LO BB 3-48 v Worcs (Worcester) 2014 (RLC).

‡**THAKOR, Shiv**sinh Jaysinh (Loughborough GS; Uppingham S), b Leicester 22 Oct 1993. 6'1''. RHB, RM. Squad No 57. Leicestershire 2011-13. No f-c appearances in 2014. Leicestershire 2nd XI debut 2008, aged 14y 218d. England U19s 2010-11. HS 134 Le v Loughborough MCCU (Leicester) 2011 – on debut. CC HS 114 Le v Kent (Leicester) 2013. BB 3-57 Le v Surrey (Leicester) 2011. LO HS 83* Le v Lancs (Leicester) 2012 (CB40). LO BB Le 4-49 v Worcs (Leicester) 2014 (RLC). T20 HS 42. T20 BB 3-30.

WAINWRIGHT, David John (Hemsworth HS and SFC; Loughborough U); b Pontefract, Yorks 21 Mar 1985. 5'9''. LHB, SLA. Squad No 21. Yorkshire 2004-11; cap 2010. Derbyshire debut/cap 2012. Loughborough UCCE 2005-06. British U 2006. Police Sports Club 2011-12. HS 109 v Leics (Leicester) 2014. 50 wkts (1): 50 (2012). BB 6-33 v Northants (Derby) 2012. LO HS 41 v Notts (Nottingham) 2014 (RLC). LO BB 4-11 v Durham (Derby) 2013 (Y40). T20 HS 20*. T20 BB 3-6.

WHEATCROFT, Adam Thomas (Belper S), b Belper 10 Oct 1994. 6'0''. RHB, RMF. Squad No 32. Derbyshire 2nd XI debut 2014. Awaiting 1st XI debut.

WHITE, Harry John (John Port S, Etwall; Repton S), b Derby 19 Feb 1995. 6'4''. RHB, LM. Squad No 19. Derbyshire 2nd XI debut 2012. Awaiting 1st XI debut.

WHITE, Wayne Andrew (John Port S, Etwall; Nottingham Trent U), b Derby 22 Apr 1985. 6'2''. RHB, RMF. Squad No 11. Derbyshire 2005-08, 2014 to date. Leicestershire 2009-12; cap 2012. Lancashire 2013-14. HS 101* Le v Derbys (Derby) 2010. De HS 38 v Glamorgan (Cardiff) 2014. BB 5-54 Le v Derbys (Derby) 2012. De BB 5-87 v Northants (Northampton) 2007. LO HS 46* Le v Glamorgan (Leicester) 2009 (P40). LO BB 6-29 Le v Notts (Leics) 2010 (CB40). T20 HS 26. T20 BB 3-27.

(Having made a 1st XI appearance in 2014)

BORRINGTON, Paul Michael (Repton S; Chellarton S; Loughborough U), b Nottingham 24 May 1988. Son of A.J.Borrington (Derbyshire 1971-80). 5'10". RHB, OB. Debut Derbyshire 2005-14. Loughborough UCCE 2008-09. HS 105 LU v Hants (Southampton) 2009. De HS 98 v Northants (Derby) 2012. BB – . LO HS 72 v Surrey (Oval) 2013 (Y40).

NQCHANDERPAUL, Shivnarine (Cove and John SS, Unity Village), b Unity Village, Demerara, Guyana 16 Aug 1974. 5'6". LHB, LB. Guyana 1991-92 to date. Durham 2007-09. Lancashire 2010; cap 2010. Warwickshire 2011. Derbyshire debut 2013; cap 2014. IPL: RCB 2007-08. *Wisden* 2007. **Tests** (WI): 161 (1993-94 to 2014-15, 14 as captain); HS 203* v SA (Georgetown) 2004-05; BB 1-2 v A (Adelaide) 1996-97. **LOI** (WI): 268 (1994-95 to 2010-11, 16 as captain); HS 150 v SA (E London) 1998-99; BB 3-18 v I (Sharjah) 1997-98. **IT20** (WI): 22 (2005-06 to 2010); HS 41 v E (Oval) 2007. F-c Tours (WI) (C=Captain): E 1995, 2000, 2004, 2007, 2009, 2012; A 1995-96, 1996-97, 2000-01, 2005-06C, 2009-10; SA 1998-99, 2003-04, 2007-08, 2014-15; NZ 1994-95, 1999-00, 2005-06C, 2008-09, 2013-14; I 1994-95, 2002-03, 2011-12, 2013-14; P 1997-98, 2001-02 (Sharjah), 2006-07; SL 2005C, 2010-11; Z 2001, 2003-04; B 1999-00, 2002-03, 2011-12, 2012-13; K 2001. 1000 runs (1+1); most – 1107 (2004-05). HS 303* Guyana v Jamaica (Kingston) 1995-96. CC HS 201* Du v Worcs (Worcester) 2009. De HS 129 v Surrey (Derby) 2013. BB 4-48 Guyana v Leeward Is (Basseterre) 1992-93. De BB 2-32 v Somerset (Taunton) 2013. LO HS 150 (*see LOI*). LO BB 4-22 Guyana v Trinidad (Hampton Court) 1995-96. T20 HS 87*.

CROSS, Gareth David (Moorside S; Eccles C), b Bury, Lancs 20 Jun 1984. 5'9". RHB, WK, occ RMF. Lancashire 2005-13. No f-c appearances in 2009. Derbyshire 2014. HS 125 La v Sussex (Hove) 2011. De HS 30 v Glamorgan (Cardiff) 2014. LO HS 76 La v Warwks (Birmingham) 2007 (P40). LO BB 2-26 La v Durham (Chester-le-St) 2008 (FPT). T20 HS 65*.

GROENEWALD, T.D. – *see SOMERSET*.

HIGGINBOTTOM, Matthew (New Mills SFC; Leeds Met U), b Stockport, Cheshire 20 Oct 1990. 6'2". LHB, RMF. Debut (Leeds/Bradford MCCU) 2012. Derbyshire 2013. Bradford/Leeds MCCU 2009-12. Derbyshire 2nd XI debut 2009. HS 31* LBU v Yorks (Leeds) 2012. De HS 9 (twice) (2013). BB 3-59 v Middx (Derby) 2013. LO HS and LO BB –. T20 HS – . T20 BB 1-34.

JOHNSON, Richard Matthew (Solihull S), b Solihull, Warwicks 1 Sep 1988. 5'10". RHB, WK. Warwickshire 2008-12. Derbyshire 2012-14. Herefordshire 2006. HS 72 Wa v Cambridge UCCE (Cambridge) 2008 (on debut) and 72 v Surrey (Derby) 2013. LO HS 79 v Yorks (Chesterfield) 2012 (CB40). T20 HS 14.

MOORE, Stephen Colin (St Stithian's C, Johannesburg; Exeter U), b Johannesburg, South Africa 4 Nov 1980. 6'1". RHB, RM. Worcestershire 2003-09. Lancashire 2010-13; cap 2011. Derbyshire 2014. MCC 2009, 2011. F-c Tour (Eng A): NZ 2008-09. 1000 runs (4); most – 1451 (2008). HS 246 Wo v Derbys (Worcester) 2005. De HS 128 v Hants (Derby) 2014. BB 1-13 Wo v Lancs (Worcester) 2004. LO HS 118 La v Surrey (Croydon) 2010 (CB40). LO BB 1-1 Wo v Scotland (Worcester) 2004 (NL). T20 HS 83*.

RELEASED/RETIRED continued on p 93

DERBYSHIRE 2014

RESULTS SUMMARY

		Place	Won	Lost	Tied	Drew	NR
LV= County Championship	(2nd Division)	4th	6	5		5	
All First-Class Matches			6	5		6	
Royal London One-Day Cup	(Group A)	QF	4	3			2
NatWest t20 Blast	(North Division)	9th	1	12			1

LV= COUNTY CHAMPIONSHIP AVERAGES
BATTING AND FIELDING

Cap		M	I	NO	HS	Runs	Avge	100	50	Ct/St
	C.A.Pujara	3	6	2	100*	219	54.75	1	1	1
2014	S.Chanderpaul	7	12	2	92	496	49.60	–	6	–
	B.T.Slater	7	14	–	119	646	46.14	2	3	6
2011	W.L.Madsen	16	29	2	111*	1046	38.74	1	8	20
2012	W.J.Durston	10	18	4	74*	525	37.50	–	5	11
	S.C.Moore	9	16	1	128	474	31.60	1	3	6
2012	D.J.Wainwright	14	22	5	109	467	27.47	1	3	4
	A.L.Hughes	13	21	4	82	448	26.35	–	3	5
	B.A.Godleman	9	17	1	104*	418	26.12	1	3	7
2011	T.D.Groenewald	6	9	2	56*	180	25.71	–	2	2
	P.M.Borrington	7	13	2	86*	281	25.54	–	1	9
	S.L.Elstone	6	9	–	63	199	22.11	–	1	2
2012	A.P.Palladino	14	21	4	60*	334	19.64	–	1	4
	M.J.North	5	8	–	44	148	18.50	–	–	3
	T.A.I.Taylor	6	9	2	40	115	16.42	–	–	1
2014	M.H.A.Footitt	16	22	8	26*	154	11.00	–	–	4
	G.D.Cross	11	17	–	30	175	10.29	–	–	30/4
	C.F.Hughes	4	7	–	24	70	10.00	–	–	3
	W.A.White	4	6	–	38	56	9.33	–	–	–

Also batted: B.D.Cotton (2 matches) 15, 21; D.M.Hodgson (1) 0, 1 (1 ct); H.R.Hosein (2) 4, 13 (15 ct); R.M.Johnson (2) 2, 21, 1 (4 ct); M.L.Turner (2) 0, 6, 0 (1 ct).

BOWLING

	O	M	R	W	Avge	Best	5wI	10wM
M.H.A.Footitt	468.2	96	1568	82	19.12	6-48	6	–
W.A.White	79	17	229	11	20.81	4-27	–	–
A.P.Palladino	409.4	126	991	39	25.41	5-62	1	–
W.J.Durston	166.5	17	578	20	28.90	5-19	1	–
T.D.Groenewald	152	40	464	16	29.00	5-44	1	–
T.A.I.Taylor	142	31	451	15	30.06	5-58	1	–
D.J.Wainwright	334.1	59	1119	27	41.44	5-54	1	–
A.L.Hughes	144.4	33	440	10	44.00	4-46	–	–
Also bowled:								
B.D.Cotton	39.1	10	111	8	13.87	4-20	–	–
S.L.Elstone	30.1	4	124	6	20.66	2- 8	–	–

C.F.Hughes 19.4-0-74-2; W.L.Madsen 9.5-2-36-0; M.J.North 53.3-7-142-2; C.A.Pujara 1-0-6-0; M.L.Turner 65-10-230-1.

The First-Class Averages (pp 217–233) give the records of Derbyshire players in all first-class county matches (Derbyshire's other opponents being Durham MCCU), with the exception of C.A.Pujara and W.A.White, whose first-class figures for Derbyshire are as above, and:
T.D.Groenewald 7-10-3-56*-186-26.57-0-2-2ct. 174-47-513-22-23.31-5/27-2-0.

DERBYSHIRE RECORDS

FIRST-CLASS CRICKET

Highest Total	For 801-8d		v	Somerset	Taunton	2007
	V 677-7d		by	Yorkshire	Leeds	2013
Lowest Total	For 16		v	Notts	Nottingham	1879
	V 23		by	Hampshire	Burton upon T	1958
Highest Innings	For 274	G.A.Davidson	v	Lancashire	Manchester	1896
	V 343*	P.A.Perrin	for	Essex	Chesterfield	1904

Highest Partnership for each Wicket

1st	322	H.Storer/J.Bowden	v	Essex	Derby	1929
2nd	417	K.J.Barnett/T.A.Tweats	v	Yorkshire	Derby	1997
3rd	316*	A.S.Rollins/K.J.Barnett	v	Leics	Leicester	1997
4th	328	P.Vaulkhard/D.Smith	v	Notts	Nottingham	1946
5th	302*†	J.E.Morris/D.G.Cork	v	Glos	Cheltenham	1993
6th	212	G.M.Lee/T.S.Worthington	v	Essex	Chesterfield	1932
7th	258	M.P.Dowman/D.G.Cork	v	Durham	Derby	2000
8th	198	K.M.Krikken/D.G.Cork	v	Lancashire	Manchester	1996
9th	283	A.Warren/J.Chapman	v	Warwicks	Blackwell	1910
10th	132	A.Hill/M.Jean-Jacques	v	Yorkshire	Sheffield	1986

† 346 runs were added for this wicket in two separate partnerships

Best Bowling	For 10- 40	W.Bestwick	v	Glamorgan	Cardiff	1921
(Innings)	V 10- 45	R.L.Johnson	for	Middlesex	Derby	1994
Best Bowling	For 17-103	W.Mycroft	v	Hampshire	Southampton	1876
(Match)	V 16-101	G.Giffen	for	Australians	Derby	1886

Most Runs – Season	2165	D.B.Carr	(av 48.11)		1959
Most Runs – Career	23854	K.J.Barnett	(av 41.12)		1979-98
Most 100s – Season	8	P.N.Kirsten			1982
Most 100s – Career	53	K.J.Barnett			1979-98
Most Wkts – Season	168	T.B.Mitchell	(av 19.55)		1935
Most Wkts – Career	1670	H.L.Jackson	(av 17.11)		1947-63
Most Career W-K Dismissals	1304	R.W.Taylor	(1157 ct; 147 st)		1961-84
Most Career Catches in the Field	563	D.C.Morgan			1950-69

LIMITED-OVERS CRICKET

Highest Total	50ov	366-4		v	Comb Univs	Oxford	1991
	40ov	321-5		v	Essex	Leek	2013
	T20	222-5		v	Yorkshire	Leeds	2010
Lowest Total	50ov	73		v	Lancashire	Derby	1993
	40ov	60		v	Kent	Canterbury	2008
	T20	72		v	Leics	Derby	2013
Highest Innings	50ov	173*	M.J.Di Venuto	v	Derbys CB	Derby	2000
	40ov	141*	C.J.Adams	v	Kent	Chesterfield	1992
	T20	111	W.J.Durston	v	Notts	Nottingham	2010
Best Bowling	50ov	8-21	M.A.Holding	v	Sussex	Hove	1988
	40ov	6- 7	M.Hendrick	v	Notts	Nottingham	1972
	T20	5-27	T.Lungley	v	Leics	Leicester	2009

DURHAM

Formation of Present Club: 23 May 1882
Inaugural First-Class Match: 1992
Colours: Navy Blue, Yellow and Maroon
Badge: Coat of Arms of the County of Durham
County Champions: (3) 2008, 2009, 2013
Friends Provident Trophy Winners: (1) 2007
Royal London One-Day Cup Winners: (1) 2014
Twenty20 Cup Winners: (0); best – Semi-Finalist 2008

Chief Executive: David Harker, Emirates Durham International Cricket Ground, Chester-le-Street, Co Durham DH3 3QR • Tel: 0191 387 1717 • Fax: 0191 387 1616 • Email: marketing@durhamccc.co.uk • Web: www.durhamccc.co.uk • Twitter: @DurhamCricket (21,815 followers)

Director of Cricket: Geoff Cook. **First Team Coach**: Jon Lewis. **Bowling Coach**: Alan Walker. **Captain**: P.D.Collingwood (f-c) and M.D.Stoneman (l-o). **Vice-Captain**: None. **Overseas Player**: J.W.Hastings. **2015 Beneficiary**: G.Onions. **Head Groundsman**: tbc. **Scorer**: Brian Hunt. ‡ New registration. ^{NQ} Not qualified for England.

Durham initially awarded caps immediately after their players joined the staff but revised this policy in 1998, again capping players on merit, past 'awards' having been nullified. Durham abolished both their capping and 'awards' systems after the 2005 season.

ARSHAD, Usman (Beckfoot GS, Bingley), b Bradford, Yorks 9 Jan 1993. 5'11". RHB, RMF. Squad No 78. Debut (Durham) 2013. Northumberland 2011. HS 83 v Sussex (Hove) 2013. BB 4-78 v Northants (Northampton) 2014. LO HS and BB – . T20 HS 10. T20 BB 2-21.

BORTHWICK, Scott George (Farringdon Community Sports C, Sunderland), b Sunderland 19 Apr 1990. 5'9". LHB, LBG. Squad No 16. Debut (Durham) 2009. **Tests**: 1 (2013-14); HS 4 and BB 3-33 v A (Sydney) 2013-14. **LOI**: 2 (2011 to 2011-12); HS 15 v Ireland (Dublin) 2011; BB – . **IT20**: 1 (2011); HS 14 and BB 1-15 v WI (Oval) 2011. F-c Tours: A 2013-14; SL 2013-14 (EL). 1000 runs (3); most – 1187 (2014). HS 216 v Middx (Chester-le-St) 2014, sharing Du record 2nd wkt partnership of 274 with M.D.Stoneman. BB 6-70 v Surrey (Oval) 2013. LO HS 80 v Hants (Chester-le-St) 2013 (Y40). LO BB 4-51 v Hants (Southampton) 2012 (CB40). T20 HS 62. T20 BB 3-19.

BUCKLEY, Ryan Sean (Hummersknott Ac, Darlington; Darlington Queen Elizabeth SFC), b Darlington 2 Apr 1994. 5'10". RHB, OB. Squad No 4. Debut (Durham) 2013, taking 5-86 v Surrey (Oval). Durham 2nd XI debut 2011. Development contract 2015. HS 9 v Lancs (Manchester) 2014. BB 5-86 (*see above*).

CHASE, Peter Karl David (Malahide Community S), b Dublin, Ireland 9 Oct 1993. 6'4". RHB, RMF. Debut (Durham) 2014, taking 5-64 v Notts (Chester-le-St). Durham 2nd XI debut 2011. Development contract 2015. **LOI** (Ire): 1 (2014-15); HS – . HS 4* v Middx (Lord's) 2014. BB 5-64 (*see above*). LO HS 22* and LO BB 1-60 Ire v Sri Lanka A (Belfast) 2014.

CLARK, Graham (St Benedict's Catholic HS, Whitehaven), b Whitehaven, Cumbria 16 Mar 1993. Younger brother of J.Clark (*see LANCASHIRE*). 6'1". RHB, LB. Durham 2nd XI debut 2011. MCC YC 2013. Development contract 2015. Awaiting 1st XI debut.

83

COLLINGWOOD, Paul David (Blackfyne CS; Derwentside C), b Shotley Bridge 26 May 1976. 5'11". RHB, RM. Squad No 5. Debut (Durham) 1996 v Northants (Chester-le-St) taking wicket of D.J.Capel with his first ball before scoring 91 and 16; cap 1998; benefit 2007; captain 2012 (*part*) to date. IPL: DD 2009-10. MBE 2005. *Wisden* 2007. **Tests:** 68 (2003-04 to 2010-11); HS 206 v A (Adelaide) 2006-07; BB 3-23 v NZ (Wellington) 2007-08. **LOI:** 197 (2001 to 2010-11, 25 as captain); HS 120* v A (Melbourne) 2006-07; BB 6-31 v B (Nottingham) 2005 – record analysis for E, and first to score a hundred (112*) and take six wickets in same LOI. **IT20:** 35 (2005 to 2010-11, 30 as captain); HS 79 v WI (Oval) 2007; BB 4-22 v SL (Southampton) 2006. F-c Tours: A 2006-07, 2010-11; SA 2009-10; WI 2003-04, 2008-09; NZ 2007-08; I 2005-06, 2008-09; P 2005-06; SL 2003-04, 2007-08; B 2009-10. 1000 runs (2); most – 1120 (2005), inc six hundreds (Du record). HS 206 (*see Tests*). Du HS 190 v SL (Chester-le-St) 2002 and 190 v Derbys (Derby) 2005, sharing Du record 4th wkt partnership of 250 with D.M.Benkenstein. BB 5-52 v Somerset (Stockton) 2005. LO HS 120* (*see LOI*). LO BB 6-31 (*see LOI*). T20 HS 79. T20 BB 5-6 v Northants (Chester-le-St) 2011 – Du record.

COUGHLIN, Paul (St Robert of Newminster Catholic CS, Washington), b Sunderland 23 Oct 1992. 6'3". RHB, RM. Squad No 29. Debut (Durham) 2012. Northumberland 2011. No 1st XI appearances in 2013. Development contract 2015. HS 85 and BB 3-42 v Lancs (Chester-le-St) 2014, sharing Du record 9th wkt partnership of 150 with P.Mustard. LO HS 2* v Yorks (Leeds) 2014 (RLC). LO BB 1-34 v Surrey (Chester-le-St) 2014 (RLC). T20 HS – . T20 BB 1-30.

HARRISON, Jamie (Sedburgh S), b Whiston, Lancs 19 Nov 1990. 6'0". RHB, LMF. Squad No 13. Debut (Durham) 2012. Durham 2nd XI debut 2009. Gloucestershire 2nd XI 2008. HS 65 v Northants (Northampton) 2014. BB 5-31 v Surrey (Chester-le-St) 2013. LO HS 7* and LO BB 2-51 v Somerset (Chester-le-St) 2012 (CB40).

^{NQ}**HASTINGS, John** Wayne, b Penrith, NSW, Australia 4 Nov 1985. 6'6". RHB, RFM. Victoria 2007-08 to date. Durham debut 2014. IPL: CSK 2014. Big Bash: MS 2012-13 to date. **Tests** (A): 1 (2012-13); HS 32 and BB 1-51 v SA (Perth) 2012-13. **LOI** (A): 11 (2010-11 to 2011); HS 21* v B (Dhaka) 2011; BB 2-35 v E (Brisbane) 2010-11. **IT20** (A): 3 (2010-11 to 2011); HS 15 v SL (Perth) 2010-11; BB 3-14 v SL (Pallekele) 2011. HS 93 Vic v Tas (Hobart) 2009-10. Du HS 83 v Lancs (Manchester) 2014. BB 5-30 Vic v WA (Perth) 2012-13. Du BB 5-94 v Warwks (Chester-le-St) 2014. LO HS 69* Vic v S Australia (Adelaide) 2012-13. LO BB 5-46 v Warwks (Gosforth) 2014 (RLC). T20 HS 80*. T20 BB 4-26.

JENNINGS, Keaton Kent (King Edward VII S, Johannesburg), b Johannesburg, South Africa 19 June 1992. Son of R.V.Jennings (Transvaal 1973-74 to 1992-93), brother of D.Jennings (Gauteng and Easterns 1999 to 2003-04), nephew of K.E.Jennings (Northern Transvaal 1981-82 to 1982-83). 6'4". LHB, RMF. Squad No 1. Debut (Gauteng) 2011-12. Durham debut 2012. HS 127 v Sussex (Hove) 2013. BB 2-8 Gauteng v WP (Cape Town) 2011-12. Du BB 1-4 v Northants (Northampton) 2014. LO HS 71* Gauteng v KZN (Johannesburg) 2011-12. LO BB 1-9 v Surrey (Chester-le-St) 2014 (RLC). T20 HS 0*. T20 BB 2-23.

McCARTHY, Barry John (St Michael's C, Dublin; Dublin U), b Dublin, Ireland 13 Sep 1992. 5'11". RHB, RMF. Durham 2nd XI debut 2014. Awaiting 1st XI debut. Development contract 2015.

MacLEOD, Calum Scott (Hillpark S, Glasgow), b Glasgow, Scotland 15 Nov 1988. 6'0". RHB, RMF. Squad No 14. Scotland 2007 to date. Warwickshire 2008-09. Durham debut 2014. **LOI** (Scot): 33 (2008 to 2014-15); HS 175 v Canada (Christchurch) 2013-14; BB 2-26 v Kenya (Aberdeen) 2013. **IT20** (Scot): 15 (2009 to 2013-14); HS 57 v Netherlands (Dubai) 2011-12; BB 2-17 v Kenya (Aberdeen) 2013. F-c Tours (Scot): UAE 2011-12, 2012-13; Namibia 2011-12. HS 84 v Lancs (Manchester) 2014. BB 4-66 Sc v Canada (Aberdeen) 2009. LO HS 175 (*see LOI*). LO BB 3-37 Sc v UAE (Queenstown) 2013-14. T20 HS 104*. T20 BB 2-17.

MAIN, Gavin Thomas, b Lanark, Scotland 28 Feb 1995. 6'2". RHB, RMF. Squad No 20. Debut (Durham) 2014. Durham 2nd XI debut 2013. Academy contract 2015. HS – . BB 3-72 v Notts (Nottingham) 2014 – only 1st XI appearance.

MUCHALL, Gordon James (Durham S), b Newcastle upon Tyne, Northumb 2 Nov 1982. 6'0". RHB, RM. Squad No 24. Northumberland 1999. Older brother of P.B.Muchall (Gloucestershire 2012). Debut (Durham) 2002; cap 2005; benefit 2014. No f-c appearances in 2013. F-c Tour: SL 2002-03 (ECB Acad). HS 219 v Kent (Canterbury) 2006, sharing Du record 6th wkt partnership of 249 with P.Mustard (*see below*). BB 3-26 v Yorks (Leeds) 2003. LO HS 101* v Yorks (Leeds) 2005 (NL). LO BB 1-15 v Sussex (Hove) 2003 (NL). T20 HS 66*. T20 BB 1-8.

MUSTARD, Philip (Usworth CS), b Sunderland 8 Oct 1982. Cousin of C.Rushworth (*see below*). 5'11". LHB, WK. Squad No 19. Debut (Durham) 2002; captain 2010 (*part*) to 2012 (*part*). Mountaineers 2011-12. Auckland 2012-13. **LOI**: 10 (2007-08); HS 83 v NZ (Napier) 2007-08. **IT20**: 2 (2007-08); HS 40 v NZ (Christchurch) 2007-08. HS 130 v Kent (Canterbury) 2006. LO HS 143 v Surrey (Chester-le-St) 2012 (CB40). T20 HS 97*.

ONIONS, Graham (St Thomas More RC S, Blaydon), b Gateshead 9 Sep 1982. 6'1". RHB, RFM. Squad No 9. Debut (Durham) 2004; benefit 2015. Dolphins 2013-14. MCC 2007-08. *Wisden* 2009. Missed entire 2010 season through back injury. **Tests**: 9 (2009 to 2012); HS 17* v A (Lord's) 2009; BB 5-38 v WI (Lord's) 2009 – on debut. **LOI**: 4 (2009 to 2009-10); HS 1 v A (Centurion) 2009-10; BB 2-58 v SL (Johannesburg) 2009-10. F-c Tours: SA 2009-10; NZ 2012-13; I 2007-08 (EL), 2012-13; SL 2013-14; B 2006-07 (Eng A); UAE 2011-12 (*part*). HS 41 v Yorks (Leeds) 2007. 50 wkts (5); most – 73 (2013). BB 9-67 v Notts (Nottingham) 2012. LO HS 19 v Derbys (Derby) 2008 (FPT). LO BB 4-45 v Lancs (Chester-le-St) 2013 (Y40). T20 HS 31. T20 BB 3-15.

POYNTER, Stuart William (Teddington S), b Hammersmith, London 18 Oct 1990. Younger brother of A.D.Poynter (Middlesex and Ireland 2005 to date). 5'9". RHB, WK. Squad No 90. Middlesex 2010. Ireland 2011 to date. Warwickshire 2013. Middlesex 2nd XI debut 2007. **LOI** (Ire): 3 (2014); HS 8 v Scotland (Dublin) 2014. HS 63 Ire v Australia A (Belfast) 2013. CC HS 0. LO HS 109 Ire v Sri Lanka A (Belfast) 2014.

PRINGLE, Ryan David (Durham SFC), b Sunderland 17 Apr 1992. RHB, OB. Squad No 17. Debut (Durham) 2014. Durham 2nd XI debut 2009. Northumberland 2011-12. HS 63* v Warwks (Birmingham) 2014. BB 2-94 v Somerset (Taunton) 2014. LO HS 26 v Hants (Southampton) 2013 (Y40). LO BB 1-12 v Derbys (Derby) 2013 (Y40). T20 HS 17. T20 BB 2-13.

RICHARDSON, Michael John (Rondebosch HS; Stonyhurst C, Nottingham U), b Pt Elizabeth, South Africa 4 Oct 1986. Son of D.J.Richardson (South Africa, EP and NT 1977-78 to 1997-98), grandson of J.H.Richardson (NE Transvaal and Transvaal B 1952-53 to 1960-61), nephew of R.P.Richardson (WP 1984-85 to 1988-89). 5'10". RHB, WK. Squad No 18. Debut (Durham) 2010. Colombo CC 2014-15. MCC YC 2008-09. HS 148 v Yorks (Chester-le-St) 2014. LO HS 45 v Glamorgan (Colwyn Bay) 2012 (CB40). T20 HS 19.

RUSHWORTH, Christopher (Castle View CS, Sunderland), b Sunderland 11 Jul 1986. Cousin of P.Mustard (*see above*). 6'2". RHB, RMF. Squad No 22. Debut (Durham) 2010. MCC 2013. Northumberland 2004-05. HS 46 v Somerset (Taunton) 2014. 50 wkts (2); most – 65 (2014). BB 9-52 (15-95 match) v Northants (Chester-le-St) 2014. LO HS 12* v Northants (Chester-le-St) 2011 (CB40). LO BB 5-31 v Notts (Chester-le-St) 2010 (CB40). T20 HS 5. T20 BB 3-19.

STOKES, Benjamin Andrew (Cockermouth S), b Christchurch, Canterbury, New Zealand 4 Jun 1991. 6'1". LHB, RFM. Squad No 38. Debut (Durham) 2010. Durham 2nd XI debut 2007, aged 16y 99d. England U19s 2009 to 2009-10. Big Bash: MR 2014-15. YC 2013. **ECB Central Contract 2014-15. Tests**: 6 (2013-14 to 2014); HS 120 v A (Perth) 2013-14; BB 6-99 v A (Sydney) 2013-14. **LOI**: 24 (2011 to 2014-15); HS 70 v A (Perth) 2013-14; BB 5-61 v A (Southampton) 2013. **IT20**: 7 (2011 to 2013-14); HS 31 v WI (Oval) 2011; BB – . F-c Tours: A 2013-14; WI 2010-11 (EL). HS 185 v Lancs (Chester-le-St) 2014. BB 7-67 (10-121 match) v Sussex (Chester-le-St) 2014. LO HS 164 v Notts (Chester-le-St) 2014 (RLC) – Du record. LO BB 5-61 (*see LOI*). T20 HS 77. T20 BB 2-14.

STONEMAN, Mark Daniel (Whickham CS), b Newcastle upon Tyne, Northumb 26 Jun 1987. 5'11". LHB, RM. Squad No 23. Debut (Durham) 2007; captain (l-o only) 2015. 1000 runs (2); most – 1068 (2013). HS 187 v Middx (Chester-le-St) 2014, sharing Du record 2nd wkt partnership of 274 with S.G.Borthwick. BB – . LO HS 136* v Scotland (Chester-le-St) 2012 (CB40). T20 HS 51.

WOOD, Mark Andrew (Ashington HS; Newcastle C), b Ashington 11 Jan 1990. 5'11". RHB, RMF. Squad No 33. Debut (Durham) 2011. Northumberland 2008-10. F-c Tours (EL): SA 2014-15; SL 2013-14. HS 58* v Notts (Nottingham) 2013. BB 5-32 EL v Sri Lanka A (Colombo, RPS) 2013-14. Du BB 5-37 v Somerset (Taunton) 2014. LO HS 15* v Lancs (Chester-le-St) 2013 (Y40). LO BB 3-23 v Scotland (Chester-le-St) 2013 (Y40). T20 HS 12. T20 BB 1-9.

RELEASED/RETIRED

(Having made a 1st XI appearance in 2014)

AARON, Varun Raymond (Loyola S, Jamshedpur; Jain C, Bangalore), b Jamshedpur, Bihar 29 Oct 1989. RHB, RFM. Jharkhand 2008-09 to date. Durham 2014. IPL: DD 2011-12. RCB 2014. **Tests** (I): 5 (2011-12 to 2014-15); HS 9 and BB 3-97 v E (Manchester) 2014. **LOI** (I): 9 (2011-12 to 2014-15); HS 6* v WI (Cuttack) 2011-12; BB 3-24 v E (Mumbai) 2011-12. F-c Tours (I): E 2014; A 2014-15. HS 72 Jharkhand v Goa (Porvorim) 2010-11. Du HS 13 v Northants (Chester-le-St) 2014. BB 5-17 Jharkhand v Tripura (Agartala) 2010-11. BB 2-81 v Warwks (Birmingham) 2014. LO HS 34 v Jharkhand v Gujarat (Indore) 2010-11. LO BB 5-47 East Zone v West Zone (Jaipur) 2010-11. T20 HS 17*. T20 BB 3-16.

BREESE, Gareth Rohan (Wolmer's BHS, Kingston; Kingston U of Technology, Jamaica), b Montego Bay, Jamaica 9 Jan 1976. 5'7". RHB, OB. Jamaica 1995-96 to 2005-06; captain/ overseas player 2003-04 to 2005-06. British passport (Welsh father). Durham 2004-14; cap 2005; benefit 2014. **Tests** (WI): 1 (2002-03); HS 5 and BB 2-108 v I (Madras) 2002-03. F-c Tours (WI): E 2002 (WI A); I 2002-03. HS 165* v Somerset (Taunton) 2004. BB 7-60 Jamaica v Barbados (Bridgetown) 2000-01. Du BB 5-41 (10-151 match) v Yorks (Scarborough) 2004 – scored 35 and 68 to complete match double. LO HS 68* v Notts (Chester-le-St) 2007 (FPT). LO BB 5-41 v Derbys (Chester-le-St) 2008 (FPT). T20 HS 37. T20 BB 4-14.

SANGAKKARA, K.C. – *see SURREY*.

M.G.Morley and Ramanpreet Singh left the staff without making a 1st XI appearance in 2014.

DURHAM 2014

RESULTS SUMMARY

	Place	Won	Lost	Tied	Drew	NR
LV= County Championship (1st Division)	5th	5	4		7	
All First-Class Matches		5	4		8	
Royal London One-Day Cup (Group B)	Winners	7	3			1
NatWest t20 Blast (North Division)	6th	5	7			2

LV= COUNTY CHAMPIONSHIP AVERAGES

BATTING AND FIELDING

Cap		M	I	NO	HS	Runs	Avge	100	50	Ct/St
	S.G.Borthwick	15	27	1	216	1137	43.73	3	4	30
	J.Harrison	4	7	3	65	173	43.25	–	1	–
	R.D.Pringle	2	4	1	63*	126	42.00	–	1	–
1998	P.D.Collingwood	16	28	5	101	864	37.56	2	5	9
2005	G.J.Muchall	11	19	4	158*	550	36.66	1	2	11
	M.D.Stoneman	16	28	–	187	1004	35.85	3	4	5
	M.J.Richardson	16	28	–	148	957	34.17	2	4	16
	P.Coughlin	5	7	1	85	191	31.83	–	1	3
	G.R.Breese	4	6	–	62	174	29.00	–	1	8
	B.A.Stokes	7	11	–	85	314	28.54	–	2	1
	C.S.MacLeod	3	5	–	84	142	28.40	–	1	4
	J.W.Hastings	8	14	1	83	337	25.92	–	3	2
	K.K.Jennings	16	28	1	103	693	25.66	1	4	5
	P.Mustard	13	21	2	91	414	21.78	–	3	42/1
	U.Arshad	4	5	1	38*	81	20.25	–	–	–
	G.Onions	5	7	2	23*	71	14.20	–	–	–
	M.A.Wood	7	11	2	20*	127	14.11	–	–	–
	C.Rushworth	16	22	5	46	219	12.88	–	–	6
	P.K.D.Chase	3	5	3	4*	7	3.50	–	–	1

Also played: V.R.Aaron (2 matches) 13, 2, 4*; R.S.Buckley (1) 2*, 9; G.T.Main (1) did
not bat (1 ct); K.C.Sangakkara (2) 0, 14, 159 (3 ct).

BOWLING

	O	M	R	W	Avge	Best	5wI	10wM
P.K.D.Chase	46.2	5	173	11	15.72	5-64	1	–
J.W.Hastings	272	69	812	37	21.94	5-94	1	–
C.Rushworth	488.1	99	1578	64	24.65	9-52	3	1
B.A.Stokes	187.4	23	756	30	25.20	7-67	1	1
U.Arshad	82.1	18	309	12	25.75	4-78	–	–
M.A.Wood	173.1	28	615	18	34.16	5-37	2	–
G.Onions	151.2	28	504	12	42.00	4-65	–	–
S.G.Borthwick	183.2	13	762	13	58.61	3-70	–	–
Also bowled:								
P.D.Collingwood	85	19	306	9	34.00	3-26	–	–
P.Coughlin	80	21	306	9	34.00	3-42	–	–
J.Harrison	102	16	379	8	47.37	3-83	–	–

V.R.Aaron 32.3-7-108-3; G.R.Breese 45-12-141-0; R.S.Buckley 2-0-9-0; K.K.Jennings
37-4-125-2; G.T.Main 13-2-72-3; R.D.Pringle 21.3-1-108-2; M.D.Stoneman 21-0-82-0.

The First-Class Averages (pp 217–233) give the records of Durham players in all first-class
county matches (Durham's other opponents being Durham MCCU), with the exception of
V.R.Aaron, K.C.Sangakkara and B.A.Stokes, whose first-class figures for Durham are as
above.

DURHAM RECORDS

FIRST-CLASS CRICKET

Highest Total	For 648-5d		v	Notts	Chester-le-St[2]	2009
	V 810-4d		by	Warwicks	Birmingham	1994
Lowest Total	For 67		v	Middlesex	Lord's	1996
	V 18		by	Durham MCCU	Chester-le-St[2]	2012
Highest Innings	For 273	M.L.Love	v	Hampshire	Chester-le-St[2]	2003
	V 501*	B.C.Lara	for	Warwicks	Birmingham	1994

Highest Partnership for each Wicket

1st	334*	S.Hutton/M.A.Roseberry	v	Oxford U	Oxford	1996
2nd	274	M.D.Stoneman/S.G.Borthwick	v	Middlesex	Chester-le-St[2]	2014
3rd	212	M.J.Di Venuto/D.M.Benkenstein	v	Essex	Chester-le-St[2]	2010
4th	331	B.A.Stokes/D.M.Benkenstein	v	Lancashire	Chester-le-St[2]	2011
5th	247	G.J.Muchall/I.D.Blackwell	v	Worcs	Worcester	2011
6th	249	G.J.Muchall/P.Mustard	v	Kent	Canterbury	2006
7th	315	D.M.Benkenstein/O.D.Gibson	v	Yorkshire	Leeds	2006
8th	147	P.Mustard/L.E.Plunkett	v	Yorkshire	Leeds	2009
9th	150	P.Mustard/P.Coughlin	v	Lancashire	Chester-le-St[2]	2014
10th	103	M.M.Betts/D.M.Cox	v	Sussex	Hove	1996

Best Bowling	For 10- 47	O.D.Gibson	v	Hampshire	Chester-le-St[2]	2007
(Innings)	V 9- 36	M.S.Kasprowicz	for	Glamorgan	Cardiff	2003
Best Bowling	For 14-177	A.Walker	v	Essex	Chelmsford	1995
(Match)	V 13-110	M.S.Kasprowicz	for	Glamorgan	Chester-le-St[2]	2003

Most Runs – Season	1654	M.J.Di Venuto	(av 78.76)	2009
Most Runs – Career	9242	P.D.Collingwood	(av 34.23)	1996-2014
Most 100s – Season	6	P.D.Collingwood		2005
	6	M.J.Di Venuto		2009
Most 100s – Career	21	D.M.Benkenstein		2005-11
Most Wkts – Season	80	O.D.Gibson	(av 20.75)	2007
Most Wkts – Career	518	S.J.E.Brown	(av 28.30)	1992-2002
Most Career W-K Dismissals	617	P.Mustard	(598 ct; 19 st)	2002-14
Most Career Catches in the Field	175	P.D.Collingwood		1996-2014

LIMITED-OVERS CRICKET

Highest Total	50ov	353-8		v	Notts	Chester-le-St[2]	2014
	40ov	325-9		v	Surrey	The Oval	2011
	T20	225-2		v	Leics	Chester-le-St[2]	2010
Lowest Total	50ov	82		v	Worcs	Chester-le-St[1]	1968
	40ov	72		v	Warwicks	Birmingham	2002
	T20	93		v	Kent	Canterbury	2009
Highest Innings	50ov	164	B.A.Stokes	v	Notts	Chester-le-St[2]	2014
	40ov	150*	B.A.Stokes	v	Warwicks	Birmingham	2011
	T20	91	P.Mustard	v	Yorkshire	Chester-le-St[2]	2013
Best Bowling	50ov	7-32	S.P.Davis	v	Lancashire	Chester-le-St[1]	1983
	40ov	6-31	N.Killeen	v	Derbyshire	Derby	2000
	T20	5- 6	P.D.Collingwood	v	Northants	Chester-le-St[2]	2011

[1] Chester-le-Street CC (Ropery Lane) [2] Emirates Durham International Cricket Ground

ESSEX

Formation of Present Club: 14 January 1876
Inaugural First-Class Match: 1894
Colours: Blue, Gold and Red
Badge: Three Seaxes above Scroll bearing 'Essex'
County Champions: (6) 1979, 1983, 1984, 1986, 1991, 1992
NatWest/Friends Prov Trophy Winners: (3) 1985, 1997, 2008
Benson and Hedges Cup Winners: (2) 1979, 1998
Pro 40/National League (Div 1) Winners: (2) 2005, 2006
Sunday League Winners: (3) 1981, 1984, 1985
Twenty20 Cup Winners: (0); best – Semi-Finalist 2006, 2008, 2010

Chief Executive: Derek Bowden, The Ford County Ground, New Writtle Street, Chelmsford CM2 0PG • Tel: 01245 252420 • Fax: 01245 254030 • Email: administration@essexcricket.org.uk • Web: www.essexcricket.org.uk • Twitter: @EssexCricket (25,956 followers)

Head Coach: Paul Grayson. **Assistant Head Coach**: Chris Silverwood. **Captain**: J.S.Foster (f-c) and R.N.ten Doeschate (l-o). **Vice-Captain**: None. **Overseas Players**: J.D.Ryder and S.W.Tait (T20 only). **2015 Beneficiary**: R.S.Bopara. **Head Groundsman**: Stuart Kerrison. **Scorer**: Tony Choat. ‡ New registration. NQ Not qualified for England.

BOPARA, Ravinder Singh (Brampton Manor S; Barking Abbey Sports C), b Newham, London 4 May 1985. 5'8". RHB, RM. Squad No 25. Debut (Essex) 2002; cap 2005; benefit 2015. Auckland 2009-10. Dolphins 2010-11. IPL: KXIP 2009-10. MCC 2006, 2008. YC 2008. **Tests**: 13 (2007-08 to 2012); HS 143 v WI (Lord's) 2009; BB 1-39 v SL (Galle) 2007-08. **LOI**: 120 (2006-07 to 2014-15); HS 101* v Ireland (Dublin) 2013; BB 4-38 v B (Birmingham) 2010. **IT20**: 38 (2008 to 2014); HS 65* v A (Hobart) 2013-14; BB 4-10 v WI (Oval) 2011 – England record. F-c Tours: WI 2008-09, 2010-11 (EL); SL 2007-08, 2011-12. 1000 runs (1): 1256 (2008). HS 229 v Northants (Chelmsford) 2007. BB 5-75 v Surrey (Chelmsford) 2006. LO HS 201* v Leics (Leicester) 2008 (FPT) – Ex l-o record. LO BB 5-63 Dolphins v Warriors (Pietermaritzburg) 2010-11. T20 HS 105*. T20 BB 4-10.

BROWNE, Nicholas Lawrence Joseph (Trinity Catholic HS, Woodford Green), b Leytonstone 24 Mar 1991. 6'3½". LHB, LB. Debut (Essex) 2013. Essex 2nd XI debut 2007. HS 132* v Derbys (Chesterfield) 2014, also scored 100* in the same match. BB –

COOK, Alastair Nathan (Bedford S), b Gloucester 25 Dec 1984. 6'3". LHB, OB. Squad No 26. Debut (Essex) 2003; cap 2005; benefit 2014. MCC 2004-07. YC 2005. *Wisden* 2011. ECB central contract 2014-15. **Tests**: 109 (2005-06 to 2014, 28 as captain); HS 294 v I (Birmingham) 2011. Scored 60 and 104* v I (Nagpur) 2005-06 on debut. Third, after D.G.Bradman and S.R.Tendulkar, to score seven Test hundreds before his 23rd birthday. Second, after M.A.Taylor, to score 1000 runs in the calendar year of his debut. BB –. **LOI**: 92 (2006 to 2014-15, 69 as captain); HS 137 v P (Abu Dhabi) 2011-12. **IT20**: 4 (2007 to 2009-10); HS 26 v SA (Centurion) 2009-10. F-c Tours (C=Captain): A 2006-07, 2010-11, 2013-14C; SA 2009-10; WI 2005-06 (Eng A), 2008-09; NZ 2007-08, 2012-13C; I 2005-06, 2008-09, 2012-13C; SL 2004-05 (Eng A), 2007-08, 2011-12; B 2009-10C; UAE 2011-12 (v P). 1000 runs (5+1); most – 1466 (2005). HS 294 (*see Tests*). CC HS 195 v Northants (Northampton) 2005. BB 3-13 v Northants (Chelmsford) 2005. LO HS 137 (*see LOI*). BB –. T20 HS 100*.

FOSTER, James Savin (Forest S, Snaresbrook; Collingwood C, Durham U), b Whipps Cross 15 Apr 1980. 6'0". RHB, WK. Squad No 7. British U 2000-01. Essex debut 2000; cap 2001; captain 2010 (*part*) to date; benefit 2011. Durham UCCE 2001. MCC 2004, 2008-10. **Tests**: 7 (2001-02 to 2002-03); HS 48 v I (Bangalore) 2001-02. **LOI**: 11 (2001-02); HS 13 v I (Bombay) 2001-02. **IT20**: 5 (2009); HS 14* v P (Oval) 2009. F-c Tours: A 2002-03; WI 2000-01 (Eng A); NZ 2001-02; I 2001-02, 2007-08 (Eng A). 1000 runs (1): 1037 (2004). HS 212 v Leics (Chelmsford) 2004. BB 1-122 v Northants (Northampton) 2008 – in contrived circumstances. LO HS 83* v Durham, inc 5 sixes in 5 balls off S.G.Borthwick (Chester-le-St) 2009 (P40). T20 HS 65*.

GOUGH, Liam James (Stowe S), b Dewsbury, Yorks 24 Nov 1994. Son of D.Gough (Yorkshire, Essex & England 1989-2008). RHB, OB. Essex 2nd XI debut 2014. Awaiting 1st XI debut. Short-term contract until end May.

IMTIAZ, Safwaan M. (Chigwell S), b London 16 Mar 1996. RHB, WK. Essex 2nd XI debut 2013. Awaiting 1st XI debut. Short-term contract until end May.

LAWRENCE, Daniel William (Trinity Catholic HS, Woodford Green), b Whipps Cross 12 Jul 1997. 6'2". RHB, LB. Essex 2nd XI debut 2013, aged 15y 321d. Awaiting 1st XI debut.

MASTERS, David Daniel (Fort Luton HS; Mid Kent CHE), b Chatham, Kent 22 Apr 1978. Son of K.D.Masters (Kent 1983-84), elder brother of D.Masters (Leicestershire 2009-10). 6'4". RHB, RMF. Squad No 9. Kent 2000-02. Leicestershire 2003-07; cap 2007. Essex debut/cap 2008; benefit 2013. HS 119 Le v Sussex (Hove) 2003. Ex HS 67 v Leics (Chelmsford) 2009. 50 wkts (4); most – 93 (2011). BB 8-10 v Leics (Southend) 2011. LO HS 39 Le v Glos (Cheltenham) 2006 (P40). LO BB 5-17 v Surrey (Oval) 2008 (FPT). T20 HS 14. T20 BB 3-7.

MICKLEBURGH, Jaik Charles (Bungay HS), b Norwich, Norfolk 30 Mar 1990. 5'10". RHB, RM. Squad No 32. Debut (Essex) 2008; cap 2013. Mid West Rhinos 2012-13. Essex 2nd XI debut 2006, aged 16y 160d. Norfolk 2007. England U19s 2009. HS 243 v Leics (Chelmsford) 2013. BB – . LO HS 73 MWR v ME (Kwekwe) 2012-13. T20 HS 47*.

MOORE, Thomas Cambridge (St Martin's S, Brentwood; Brentwood S), b Basildon 29 Mar 1992. 6'5". RHB, RMF. Debut (Essex) 2014. Essex 2nd XI debut 2011. HS 17 and BB 4-78 v Glamorgan (Chelmsford) 2014. T20 HS – .

NAPIER, Graham Richard (The Gilberd S, Colchester), b Colchester 6 Jan 1980. 5'9½". RHB, RM. Squad No 17. Debut (Essex) 1997; cap 2003; benefit 2012. Wellington 2008-09. IPL: MI 2009. MCC 2004. F-c Tour (Eng A): I 2003-04. HS 196 v Surrey (Croydon) 2011, hitting a world record-equalling 16 sixes and being dismissed just 28 balls after reaching his century. Won 2008 Walter Lawrence Trophy with 44-ball hundred v Sussex (Chelmsford). Won 2012 Walter Lawrence Trophy with 48-ball hundred v Cambridge MCCU (Cambridge). 50 wkts (2); most – 52 (2014). BB 7-21 v Cambridge MCCU (Cambridge) 2014. CC BB 7-90 v Leics (Leicester) 2013. LO HS 79 Essex CB v Lancs CB (Chelmsford) 2000 (NWT). LO BB 7-32 v Surrey (Chelmsford) 2013 (Y40). T20 HS 152* v Sussex (Chelmsford) 2008 – Ex record; 5th highest score in all T20. T20 BB 4-10.

NIJJAR, Aron Stuart Singh (Ilford County HS), b Goodmayes 24 Sep 1994. LHB, SLA. Essex 2nd XI debut 2013. Suffolk 2014. Awaiting 1st XI debut. Short-term contract until end May.

PANESAR, Mudhsuden Singh ('**Monty**') (Stopsley HS; Bedford Modern S; Loughborough U), b Luton, Beds 25 Apr 1982. 6'0". LHB, SLA. Squad No 77. Northamptonshire 2001-09; cap 2006. British U 2002-05. Loughborough UCCE 2004. Lions 2009-10. Sussex 2010-13; cap 2010. Essex debut 2013 (on loan). MCC 2006, 2014. Bedfordshire 1998-99. *Wisden* 2007. **Tests**: 50 (2005-06 to 2013-14); HS 26 v SL (Nottingham) 2006; BB 6-37 v NZ (Manchester) 2008. **LOI**: 26 (2006-07 to 2007-08); HS 13 v WI (Nottingham) 2007; BB 3-25 v B (Bridgetown) 2006-07. **IT20**: 1 (2006-07); HS 1 and BB 2-40 v A (Sydney) 2006-07. F-c Tours: A 2006-07, 2010-11, 2013-14; WI 2008-09; NZ 2007-08, 2012-13; I 2005-06, 2008-09, 2012-13; SL 2002-03 (ECB Acad), 2007-08, 2011-12; UAE 2011-12 (v P). HS 46* Sx v Middx (Hove) 2010. Ex HS 38 v Worcs (Chelmsford) 2014. 50 wkts (6); most – 71 (2006). BB 7-60 (13-137 match) Sx v Somerset (Taunton) 2012. Ex BB 6-111 v Leics (Chelmsford) 2014. LO HS 17* Nh v Leics (Northampton) 2008 (FPT). LO BB 5-20 ECB Acad v SL Acad XI (Colombo) 2002-03. T20 HS 3*. T20 BB 3-14.

PETTINI, Mark Lewis (Comberton Village C; Hills Road SFC, Cambridge; Cardiff U), b Brighton, Sussex 7 Aug 1983. 5'10". RHB, RM. Debut (Essex) 2001; cap 2006; captain 2007 (*part*) to 2010 (*part*). Mountaineers 2011-12 to date. MCC 2005. 1000 runs (1): 1218 (2006). HS 209 Mountaineers v MT (Bulawayo) 2013-14. Ex HS 208* v Derbys (Chelmsford) 2006. BB 1-72 v Leics (Leicester) 2012 – in contrived circumstances. LO HS 144 v Surrey (Oval) 2007 (FPT). T20 HS 95*.

PORTER, James Alexander (Oak Park HS, Newbury Park; Epping Forest C), b Leytonstone 25 May 1993. 5'11½". RHB, RMF. Debut (Essex) 2014. MCC YCs 2011-13. Essex 2nd XI debut 2014. HS 5 v Worcs (Chelmsford) 2014. BB 3-26 v Leics (Leicester) 2014.

NQRYDER, Jesse Daniel (Napier BHS), b Masterton, Wairarapa, New Zealand 6 Aug 1984. LHB, RM. C Districts 2002-03 to 2003-04. Wellington 2004-05 to 2012-13. Otago 2013-14 to date. Essex debut/cap 2014. IPL: RCB 2009. PW 2011-12. **Tests** (NZ): 18 (2008-09 to 2011-12); HS 201 v I (Napier) 2008-09; BB 2-7 v A (Brisbane) 2008-09. **LOI** (NZ): 48 (2007-08 to 2013-14); HS 107 v P (Auckland) 2010-11; BB 3-29 v I (Auckland) 2008-09. **IT20** (NZ): 22 (2007-08 to 2013-14); HS 62 v WI (Hamilton) 2008-09; BB 1-2 v E (Auckland) 2007-08. F-c Tours (NZ): A 2008-09, 2011-12; I 2010-11; SL 2005-06 (NZ A), 2009; B 2008-09. HS 236 Wellington v CD (Palmerston N) 2004-05. Ex HS 133 v Glos (Chelmsford) 2014. BB 5-24 v Worcs (Chelmsford) 2014. LO HS 115 Otago v ND (Hamilton) 2013-14. LO BB 4-39 Wellington v ND (Wellington) 2005-06. T20 HS 90*. T20 BB 5-27.

SALISBURY, Matthew Edward Thomas (Shenfield HS; Anglia Ruskin U), b Chelmsford 18 Apr 1993. 6'0½". RHB, RMF. Cambridge MCCU 2012-13. Essex debut 2014. Essex 2nd XI debut 2011. HS 19 and BB 4-50 v Worcs (Worcester) 2014. LO HS 5* v Leics (Chelmsford) 2014 (RLC). LO BB 4-55 v Lancs (Chelmsford) 2014 (RLC). T20 HS 1*. T20 BB 2-19.

NQSMITH, Gregory Marc (St Stithins C), b Johannesburg, South Africa 20 Apr 1983. 5'9". RHB, RM/OB. Squad No 83. Debut (SA Academy) 2003-04. Griqualand West 2003-04. Derbyshire 2006-11 (Kolpak registration); cap 2009; captain 2010 (*part*). Mountaineers 2010-11. Essex debut 2012. HS 177 v Glos (Bristol) 2013. BB 5-42 v Leics (Chelmsford) 2013. LO HS 89 Abahani v KKC (Savar) 2013-14. LO BB 4-53 De v Lancs (Derby) 2009 (P40). T20 HS 100*. T20 BB 5-17.

^{NQ}**TAIT, Shaun** William (Oakwood Area State S, S Aus), b Bedford Park, Adelaide, S Australia 22 Feb 1983. 6'4". RHB, RF. S Aus 2002-03 to 2008-09. Durham 2004. Rejoins Essex in 2015 for T20 only. IPL: RR 2009-13. Big Bash: MR 2011-12. AS 2012-13 to date. **Tests** (A): 3 (2005 to 2007-08); HS 8 v I (Perth) 2007-08; BB 3-97 v E (Nottingham) 2005. **LOI** (A): 35 (2006-07 to 2010-11); HS 11 v E (Sydney) 2006-07; BB 4-39 v SA (Gros Islet) 2006-07. **IT20** (A): 19 (2007-08 to 2010-11); HS 6 v P (Birmingham) 2010; BB 3-13 v P (Melbourne) 2009-10. F-c Tour (A): E 2005. HS 68 S Aus v Vic (Adelaide) 2005-06. CC HS 4. BB 7-29 (10-98 match) S Aus v Q (Brisbane) 2007-08. CC BB – . LO HS 22* Aus A v Z (Perth) 2003-04. LO BB 8-43 inc hat-trick S Aus v Tas (Adelaide) 2003-04, 8th best analysis in all l-o cricket. T20 HS 26. T20 BB 5-32.

TAYLOR, Callum John, b Norwich, Norfolk 26 Jun 1997. RHB, RM. Essex 2nd XI debut 2013. Norfolk 2014. Awaiting 1st XI debut.

^{NQ}**Ten DOESCHATE, Ryan** Neil (Fairbairn C; Cape Town U), b Port Elizabeth, South Africa 30 Jun 1980. 5'10½". RHB, RMF. Squad No 27. Debut (Essex) 2003; cap 2006; captain (l-o) 2014 to date. EU passport – Dutch ancestry. Netherlands 2005 to 2009-10. Otago 2012-13. IPL: KKR 2011-14. Big Bash: AS 2014-15. **LOI** (Ne): 33 (2006 to 2010-11); HS 119 v E (Nagpur) 2010-11; BB 4-31 v Canada (Nairobi) 2006-07. **IT20** (Ne): 9 (2008 to 2009-10); HS 56 v Kenya (Belfast) 2008; BB 3-23 v Scotland (Belfast) 2008. F-c Tours (Ne): SA 2006-07, 2007-08; K 2005-06, 2009-10; Ireland 2005. HS 259* and BB 6-20 (9-112 match) Netherlands v Canada (Pretoria) 2006. Ex HS 164 v Sri Lankans (Chelmsford) 2011. CC HS 159* v Surrey (Guildford) 2009. Ex BB 6-57 v NZ (Chelmsford) 2008. CC BB 5-13 v Hants (Chelmsford) 2010. LO HS 180 v Scotland (Chelmsford) 2013 (Y40) – Ex 40-over record, inc 15 sixes. LO BB 5-50 v Glos (Bristol) 2007 (FPT). T20 HS 121*. T20 BB 4-24.

TOPLEY, Reece James William (Royal Hospital S, Ipswich), b Ipswich, Suffolk 21 February 1994. Son of T.D.Topley (Surrey, Essex, GW 1985-94) and nephew of P.A.Topley (Kent 1972-75). 6'7". RHB, LMF. Squad No 6. Debut (Essex) 2011; cap 2013. Took 5-46 on CC debut. Essex 2nd XI debut 2010, aged 16y 156d. England U19s 2012-13. F-c Tour (EL): SL 2013-14. HS 12 v Hants (Southampton) 2014. BB 6-29 (11-85 match) v Worcs (Chelmsford) 2013. LO HS 19 v Somerset (Taunton) 2011 (CB40). LO BB 4-26 v Derbys (Colchester) 2013 (Y40). T20 HS 4*. T20 BB 4-26.

VELANI, Kishen Shailesh (Brentwood S), b Newham, London 2 Sep 1994. 5'10". RHB, RM. Debut (Essex) 2013. Essex 2nd XI debut 2012. England U19s 2012-13. HS 29 v Kent (Chelmsford) 2014. BB – . LO HS 27 v Northants (Northampton) 2014 (RLC). T20 HS 34.

WESTLEY, Thomas (Linton Village C; Hills Road SFC), b Cambridge 13 March 1989. 6'2". RHB, OB. Squad No 21. Debut (Essex) 2007; cap 2013. MCC 2007, 2009. Durham MCCU 2010-11. Cambridgeshire 2005. HS 185 v Glamorgan (Colchester) 2012. BB 4-55 DU v Durham (Durham) 2010. CC BB 3-5 v Kent (Chelmsford) 2012. LO HS 111* v Yorks (Scarborough) 2014 (RLC). LO BB 4-60 v Northants (Northampton) 2014 (RLC). T20 HS 109*. T20 BB 1-7.

RELEASED/RETIRED

(Having made a 1st XI appearance in 2014)

CRADDOCK, Thomas Richard (Holmfirth HS; Huddersfield New C; Leeds Met U), b Huddersfield, Yorks 13 Jul 1989. 5'10". RHB, LB. Essex 2011-14. Leeds/Bradford MCCU (not f-c) 2010-11. HS 21 v Leics (Southend) 2011. BB 5-96 v Derbys (Chelmsford) 2012. LO HS 5* and LO BB 2-38 v Somerset (Taunton) 2011 (CB40). T20 HS – . T20 BB – .

FOAKES, B.T. – see SURREY.

MAHMOOD, Sajid Iqbal (North C, Bolton), b Bolton, Lancs 21 Dec 1981. 6'4". RHB, RFM. Lancashire 2002-12; cap 2007. Somerset 2012 (on loan). Essex 2013-14. MCC 2005, 2009. **Tests**: 8 (2006 to 2006-07); HS 34 and BB 4-22 v P (Leeds) 2006. **LOI**: 26 (2004 to 2009-10); HS 22* v P (Birmingham) 2006; BB 4-50 v SL (North Shore, Antigua) 2006-07. **IT20**: 4 (2006 to 2009-10); HS 1* v SA (Centurion) 2009-10; BB 1-31 v SA (Johannesburg) 2009-10. F-c Tours (Eng A): A 2006-07 (Eng); WI 2005-06; NZ 2008-09; I 2003-04; SL 2004-05. HS 94 La v Sussex (Manchester) 2004. Ex HS 54 v Worcs (Worcester) 2013. BB 6-30 La v Durham (Chester-le-St) 2009. Ex BB 3-54 v Hants (Colchester) 2014. LO HS 29 La v Staffs (Stone) 2004 (CGT). LO BB 5-16 La v Sri Lanka A (Liverpool) 2007. T20 HS 34. T20 BB 4-21.

MILLS, T.S. – *see SUSSEX*.

PHILLIPS, Timothy James (Felsted S; St Hild & St Bede C, Durham U), b Cambridge 13 Mar 1981. 6'1". LHB, SLA. Essex 1999-2014; cap 2006. Durham UCCE 2001-02. HS 89 v Worcs (Worcester) 2005. BB 5-41 v Derbys (Chelmsford) 2006. LO HS 58* v Glos (Cheltenham) 2011 (CB40). LO BB 5-28 v Unicorns (Bury St Edmunds) 2011 (CB40). T20 HS 57*. T20 BB 4-22.

^{NQ}TANVEER SIKANDAR, b Islamabad, Pakistan 6 Feb 1987. RHB, RM. SNGPL 2013-14. Essex 2014. Hertfordshire 2014. HS 5 SNGPL v NBP (Islamabad) 2013-14. HS 5 and BB 2-90 v Leics (Chelmsford) 2014. LO HS – . LO BB 1-30 SNGPL v Pakistan TV (Rawalpindi) 2013-14. T20 HS 4*. T20 BB – .

DERBYSHIRE RELEASED/RETIRED (continued from p 80)

^{NQ}**NORTH, Marcus** James (Kent Street Sr HS), b Pakenham, Melbourne, Australia 28 Jul 1979. 6'1". LHB, OB. Debut (Aus Academy in Zim) 1998-99. W Australia 1999-00 to 2013-14. Durham 2004. Lancashire 2005. Derbyshire 2006, 2014. Gloucestershire 2007-08; cap 2007. Hampshire 2009 (one match only). Glamorgan 2012-13; l-o captain in 2013. **Tests** (A): 21 (2008-09 to 2010-11); scored 117 v SA (Johannesburg) 2008-09 – on debut; HS 128 v I (Bangalore) 2010-11; BB 6-55 v P (Lord's) 2010. **LOI** (A): 2 (2009); HS 5 v P (Abu Dhabi) 2009; BB – . **IT20** (A): 1 (2009); HS 20 v P (Dubai) 2009. F-c Tours (Aus): E 2009, 2010 (v P); SA 2008-09; NZ 2009-10; I 2010-11; P 2005-06 (Aus A); Z 1998-99 (Aus Acad). 1000 runs (0+1): 1074 (2003-04). HS 239* WA v Vic (Perth) 2006-07. UK HS 219 Du v Glamorgan (Cardiff) 2004. De HS 161 v Worcs (Chesterfield) 2006. Won Walter Lawrence Trophy 2007 for 73-ball hundred v Leics (Bristol). BB 6-55 (*see Tests*). CC BB 5-30 Gm v Hants (Cardiff) 2013. De BB 1-25 v Surrey (Derby) 2014. LO HS 137* v Middx (Lord's) 2013 (Y40). LO BB 4-26 Durham CB v Bucks (Beaconsfield) 2001 (CGT). T20 HS 90. T20 BB 2-19.

^{NQ}**PUJARA, Cheteshwar** Arvindbhai, b Rajkot, India 25 Jan 1988. RHB, LB. Son of A.S.Pujara (Saurashtra 1976-77 to 1979-80), nephew of B.S.Pujara (Saurashtra 1983-84 to 1996-97). Saurashtra 2005-06 to date. Derbyshire 2014. IPL: KKR 2009-10. RCB 2011-13. KXIP 2014. **Tests** (I): 27 (2010-11 to 2014-15); HS 206* v E (Ahmedabad) 2012-13. **LOI** (I): 5 (2013 to 2014); HS 27 v B (Dhaka) 2014. F-c Tours (I): E 2010 (I A), 2014; A 2006 (I A), 2014-15; SA 2010-11, 2013 (I A), 2013-14; WI 2012 (I A); NZ 2013-14; Z/Ken 2007-08 (I A). 1000 runs (0+2): most – 1585 (2012-13). HS 352 Saur v Karnataka (Rajkot) 2012-13. De HS 100* v Leics (Derby) 2014. BB 2-4 Saur v Rajasthan (Jaipur) 2007-08. LO HS 158* Ind B v India A (Rajkot) 2012-13. T20 HS 62.

TURNER, Mark Leif (Thornhill CS), b Sunderland, Co Durham 23 Oct 1984. 5'11". RHB, RMF. Durham 2005-06. Somerset 2007-09, no f-c appearances in 2010. Derbyshire 2011-14. HS 57 Sm v Derbys (Taunton) 2007. De HS 27* v Glamorgan (Derby) 2011. BB 5-32 v Northants (Northampton) 2011. LO HS 15* Sm v Essex (Taunton) 2009 (P40). LO BB 4-36 Sm v Worcs (Bath) 2010 (CB40). T20 HS 11*. T20 BB 4-35.

P.I.Burgoyne and J.Marsden left the staff without making a 1st XI appearance for Derbyshire in 2014.

ESSEX 2014

RESULTS SUMMARY

	Place	Won	Lost	Tied	Drew	NR
LV= County Championship (2nd Division)	3rd	7	2		7	
All First-Class Matches		8	2		7	
Royal London One-Day Cup (Group A)	QF	5	2			2
NatWest t20 Blast (South Division)	QF	10	5			

LV= COUNTY CHAMPIONSHIP AVERAGES
BATTING AND FIELDING

Cap		M	I	NO	HS	Runs	Avge	100	50	Ct/St
2005	A.N.Cook	3	5	–	181	386	77.20	2	–	5
	N.L.J.Browne	9	15	3	132*	650	54.16	3	2	9
2001	J.S.Foster	16	23	2	132	949	45.19	2	5	53/3
2005	R.S.Bopara	12	18	1	162	759	44.64	2	1	2
2014	J.D.Ryder	12	18	1	133	630	37.05	2	2	13
2006	R.N.ten Doeschate	6	10	2	104*	283	35.37	1	1	3
	T.Westley	16	27	3	116	705	29.37	1	4	20
	B.T.Foakes	10	16	3	132*	341	26.23	1	1	4
2006	M.L.Pettini	4	7	–	71	181	25.85	–	2	6
	K.S.Velani	4	5	1	29	98	24.50	–	–	–
2013	J.C.Mickleburgh	9	14	1	67	312	24.00	–	1	8
	G.M.Smith	11	17	1	85	348	21.75	–	2	7
	T.S.Mills	6	7	4	30	64	21.33	–	–	–
	T.C.Moore	4	4	2	17	27	13.50	–	–	–
2003	G.R.Napier	11	15	–	62	195	13.00	–	1	4
	M.E.T.Salisbury	4	6	1	19	50	10.00	–	–	–
	S.I.Mahmood	2	4	1	17	30	10.00	–	–	1
2013	R.J.W.Topley	4	5	3	12	18	9.00	–	–	–
2008	D.D.Masters	9	11	–	26	92	8.36	–	–	2
	M.S.Panesar	14	17	2	38	101	6.73	–	–	3

Also batted: T.R.Craddock (1 match) 0; O.J.Newby (2) 4, 0, 0* (1 ct); T.J.Phillips (2 – cap 2006) 4, 12, 1 (3 ct); J.A.Porter (3) 0*, 0*, 5 (1 ct); Tanveer Sikandar (2) 5, 0.

BOWLING

	O	M	R	W	Avge	Best	5wI	10wM
J.D.Ryder	289.5	76	796	44	18.09	5- 24	4	1
G.R.Napier	235.4	43	781	43	18.16	5- 54	1	–
D.D.Masters	282.3	87	712	37	19.24	6- 46	2	–
R.J.W.Topley	150.2	30	502	25	20.08	6- 41	2	1
M.S.Panesar	392.2	111	1111	42	26.45	6-111	4	1
T.S.Mills	134	27	442	13	34.00	4- 45	–	–
G.M.Smith	136.1	23	374	10	37.40	4- 46	–	–
Also bowled:								
J.A.Porter	31.1	4	116	6	19.33	3- 26	–	–
T.Westley	72.2	8	218	6	36.33	3- 35	–	–
T.C.Moore	98	19	328	8	41.00	4- 78	–	–
R.S.Bopara	80	13	268	6	44.66	3- 14	–	–
M.E.T.Salisbury	81	12	296	5	59.20	4- 50	–	–

N.L.J.Browne 22-4-94-0; T.R.Craddock 11-1-53-1; B.T.Foakes 1-0-6-0; S.I.Mahmood 17-0-76-3; O.J.Newby 52.1-18-179-3; T.J.Phillips 31-1-119-4; Tanveer Sikandar 38-6-117-3; R.N.ten Doeschate 33.2-1-176-4; K.S.Velani 4.3-0-13-0.

The First-Class Averages (pp 217–233) give the records of Essex players in all first-class county matches (Essex's other opponents being Cambridge MCCU), with the exception of: A.N.Cook 4-7-0-181-485-69.28-2-1-6ct.

ESSEX RECORDS

FIRST-CLASS CRICKET

Highest Total	For 761-6d		v	Leics	Chelmsford	1990
	V 803-4d		by	Kent	Brentwood	1934
Lowest Total	For 20		v	Lancashire	Chelmsford	2013
	V 14		by	Surrey	Chelmsford	1983
Highest Innings	For 343*	P.A.Perrin	v	Derbyshire	Chesterfield	1904
	V 332	W.H.Ashdown	for	Kent	Brentwood	1934

Highest Partnership for each Wicket

1st	316	G.A.Gooch/P.J.Prichard	v	Kent	Chelmsford	1994
2nd	403	G.A.Gooch/P.J.Prichard	v	Leics	Chelmsford	1990
3rd	347*	M.E.Waugh/N.Hussain	v	Lancashire	Ilford	1992
4th	314	Salim Malik/N.Hussain	v	Surrey	The Oval	1991
5th	339	J.C.Mickleburgh/J.S.Foster	v	Durham	Chester-le-St[2]	2010
6th	253	A.J.A.Wheater/J.S.Foster	v	Northants	Chelmsford	2011
7th	261	J.W.H.T.Douglas/J.Freeman	v	Lancashire	Leyton	1914
8th	263	D.R.Wilcox/R.M.Taylor	v	Warwicks	Southend	1946
9th	251	J.W.H.T.Douglas/S.N.Hare	v	Derbyshire	Leyton	1921
10th	218	F.H.Vigar/T.P.B.Smith	v	Derbyshire	Chesterfield	1947

Best Bowling	For 10- 32	H.Pickett	v	Leics	Leyton	1895
(Innings)	V 10- 40	E.G.Dennett	for	Glos	Bristol	1906
Best Bowling	For 17-119	W.Mead	v	Hampshire	Southampton	1895
(Match)	V 17- 56	C.W.L.Parker	for	Glos	Gloucester	1925

Most Runs – Season	2559	G.A.Gooch	(av 67.34)	1984
Most Runs – Career	30701	G.A.Gooch	(av 51.77)	1973-97
Most 100s – Season	9	J.O'Connor		1929, 1934
	9	D.J.Insole		1955
Most 100s – Career	94	G.A.Gooch		1973-97
Most Wkts – Season	172	T.P.B Smith	(av 27.13)	1947
Most Wkts – Career	1610	T.P.B.Smith	(av 26.68)	1929-51
Most Career W-K Dismissals	1231	B.Taylor	(1040 ct; 191 st)	1949-73
Most Career Catches in the Field	519	K.W.R.Fletcher		1962-88

LIMITED-OVERS CRICKET

Highest Total	50ov	391-5		v	Surrey	The Oval	2008
	40ov	368-7		v	Scotland	Chelmsford	2013
	T20	242-3		v	Sussex	Chelmsford	2008
Lowest Total	50ov	57		v	Lancashire	Lord's	1996
	40ov	69		v	Derbyshire	Chesterfield	1974
	T20	74		v	Middlesex	Chelmsford	2013
Highest Innings	50ov	201*	R.S.Bopara	v	Leics	Leicester	2008
	40ov	180	R.N.ten Doeschate	v	Scotland	Chelmsford	2013
	T20	152*	G.R.Napier	v	Sussex	Chelmsford	2008
Best Bowling	50ov	5- 8	J.K.Lever	v	Middlesex	Westcliff	1972
		5- 8	G.A.Gooch	v	Cheshire	Chester	1995
	40ov	8-26	K.D.Boyce	v	Lancashire	Manchester	1971
	T20	6-16	T.G.Southee	v	Glamorgan	Chelmsford	2011

GLAMORGAN

Formation of Present Club: 6 July 1888
Inaugural First-Class Match: 1921
Colours: Blue and Gold
Badge: Gold Daffodil
County Champions: (3) 1948, 1969, 1997
Pro 40/National League (Div 1) Winners: (2) 2002, 2004
Sunday League Winners: (1) 1993
Twenty20 Cup Winners: (0); best – Semi-Finalist 2004

GLAMORGAN

Chief Executive: Hugh Morris, SWALEC Stadium, Cardiff, CF11 9XR • Tel: 02920 409380 • Fax: 02920 419389 • email: info@glamorgancricket.co.uk • Web: www.glamorgancricket.com • Twitter: @GlamCricket (15,810 followers)

Head Coach: Toby Radford. **Assistant Coach**: Robert Croft. **2nd XI Coach**: Steve Watkin. **Player Development Manager**: Richard Almond. **Captain**: J.A.Rudolph. **Vice-Captain**: M.A.Wallace. **Overseas Players**: C.A.Ingram and J.A.Rudolph. **2015 Beneficiary**: None. **Head Groundsman**: Keith Exton. **Scorer**: Andrew K.Hignell. ‡ New registration. NQ Not qualified for England.

BRAGG, William David (Rougemont S, Newport; UWIC), b Newport, Monmouthshire 24 Oct 1986. 5'9". LHB, RM. Squad No 22. Debut (Glamorgan) 2007. No f-c appearances in 2008. Wales MC 2004-09. 1000 runs (2); most – 1033 (2011). HS 110 v Leics (Colwyn Bay) 2011. BB 2-10 v Worcs (Cardiff) 2013. LO HS 88 v Surrey (Guildford) 2014 (RLC). LO BB 1-11 v Glos (Cardiff) 2013 (Y40). T20 HS 15.

BULL, Kieran Andrew (Q Elizabeth HS, Haverfordwest), b Haverfordwest 5 Apr 1995. 6'2". RHB, OB. Squad No 11. Debut (Glamorgan) 2014. Wales MC 2012-13. HS 12 and BB 4-62 v Kent (Canterbury) 2014.

COOKE, Christopher Barry (Bishops S, Cape Town; U of Cape Town), b Johannesburg, South Africa 30 May 1986. 5'11". RHB, WK. Squad No 46. W Province 2009-10. Glamorgan debut 2013. Glamorgan 2nd XI debut 2010. HS 171 v Kent (Canterbury) 2014. LO HS 137* v Somerset (Taunton) 2012 (CB40). T20 HS 65*.

COSKER, Dean Andrew (Millfield S), b Weymouth, Dorset 7 Jan 1978. 5'11". RHB, SLA. Squad No 23. Debut (Glamorgan) 1996; cap 2000; benefit 2010. MCC 2010. F-c Tours (Eng A): SA 1998-99; SL 1997-98; Z 1998-99; K 1997-98. HS 52 v Glos (Bristol) 2005. 50 wkts (1): 51 (2010). BB 6-91 (11-126 match) v Essex (Cardiff) 2009. LO HS 50* v Northants (Northampton) 2009 (FPT). LO BB 5-54 v Essex (Chelmsford) 2003 (NL). T20 HS 21*. T20 BB 3-11.

DONALD, Aneurin Henry Thomas (Pontarddulais CS), b Swansea 20 Dec 1996. RHB, OB. Squad No 12. Debut (Glamorgan) 2014. Glamorgan 2nd XI debut 2012, aged 15y 189d. Wales MC 2012. HS 59 v Hants (Cardiff) 2014 – only 1st XI appearance.

HOGAN, Michael Garry, b Newcastle, New South Wales, Australia 31 May 1981. British passport. 6'5". RHB, RFM. Squad No 31. W Australia 2009-10 to date. Glamorgan debut/cap 2013. Big Bash: HH 2011-13. HS 51 and BB 7-92 v Glos (Bristol) 2013. 50 wkts (2); most – 67 (2013). LO HS 27 WA v Vic (Melbourne) 2011-12. LO BB 5-44 WA v Vic (Melbourne) 2010-11. T20 HS 5*. T20 BB 4-26.

‡^{NQ}**INGRAM, Colin** Alexander, b Port Elizabeth, South Africa 3 Jul 1985. LHB, LB. Squad No 41. Free State 2004-05 to 2005-06. Eastern Province 2005-06 to 2008-09. Warriors 2006-07 to date. Somerset 2014. Joins Glamorgan as a Kolpak signing in 2015. IPL: DD 2011. **LOI** (SA): 31 (2010-11 to 2013-14); HS 124 v Z (Bloemfontein) 2010-11 – on debut; BB – . **IT20** (SA): 9 (2010-11 to 2011-12); HS 78 v I (Johannesburg) 2011-12. HS 190 EP v KZN (Port Elizabeth) 2008-09. CC HS 37 Sm v Northants (Northampton) 2014. BB 4-16 EP v Boland (Port Elizabeth) 2005-06. LO HS 127 SA A v Bangladesh A (Mirpur) 2010. LO BB 2-13 EP v Boland (Port Elizabeth) 2005-06. T20 HS 84. T20 BB 1-16.

‡**KETTLEBOROUGH, James** Michael (Bedford S), b Huntingdon 22 Oct 1992. 5'11". RHB, OB. Squad No 3. Northamptonshire 2014. Northamptonshire 2nd XI debut 2012. Middlesex 2nd XI 2011-12. Bedfordshire 2009-13. HS 73 Nh v Middx (Lord's) 2014. LO HS 26 Nh v Lancs (Manchester) 2014 (RLC).

LAWLOR, Jeremy Lloyd (Radyr CS; Cardiff Met U), b Cardiff 4 Nov 1995. Son of P.J.Lawlor (Glamorgan 1981). 6'0". RHB, OB. Squad No 6. Glamorgan 2nd XI debut 2012. Wales MC 2013. Awaiting 1st XI debut.

LLOYD, David Liam (Darland HS; Shrewsbury S), b St Asaph, Denbighs 15 May 1992. 5'9". RHB, OB. Squad No 14. Debut (Glamorgan) 2012. Glamorgan 2nd XI debut 2008. Wales MC 2010-11. HS 41 v Kent (Canterbury) 2014. BB 2-22 v Derbys (Cardiff) 2014. LO HS 32 v Surrey (Guildford) 2014 (RLC). BB 4-10 v Durham (Cardiff) 2014 (RLC). T20 HS 3.

‡**MESCHEDE, Craig** Anthony Joseph (King's C, Taunton), b Johannesburg, South Africa 21 Nov 1991. 6'1". RHB, RMF. Squad No 44. Somerset 2011-14. Somerset 2nd XI debut 2008, aged 16y 244d. Joins Glamorgan in 2015 for season-long loan. HS 62 Sm v Durham (Chester-le-St) 2012. BB 4-43 Sm v Surrey (Taunton) 2013. LO HS 40* Sm v Glamorgan (Taunton) 2013 (Y40). LO BB 4-5 Sm v Leics (Taunton) 2013 (Y40). T20 HS 53. T20 BB 3-9.

MURPHY, Jack Roger (Greenhill S, Tenby), b Haverfordwest 15 Jul 1995. LHB, LFM. Squad No 7. Glamorgan 2nd XI debut 2011. Wales MC 2011-13. Awaiting 1st XI debut.

OWEN, William Thomas (Prestatyn HS; UWIC), b St Asaph, Flintshire 2 Sep 1988. 6'0". RHB, RMF. Squad No 34. Debut (Glamorgan) 2007. Wales MC 2007-10. HS 69 v Derbys (Derby) 2011. BB 5-124 v Middx (Cardiff) 2011. LO HS 13* v Leics (Leicester) 2013 (Y40). LO BB 5-49 v Unicorns (Bournemouth) 2010 (CB40). T20 HS 8. T20 BB 3-21.

PENRHYN JONES, Dewi (Ellesmere S), b Wrexham, Denbighs 9 Sep 1994. 6'1". RHB, RFM. Squad No 30. Glamorgan 2nd XI debut 2013. Wales MC 2012-14. Awaiting f-c debut. LO HS – and LO BB 1-22 v Middx (Cardiff) 2014 (RLC) – only 1st XI appearance.

^{NQ}**RUDOLPH, Jacobus** Andries ('**Jacques**') (Afrikaanse Hoer Seunskool), b Springs, Transvaal, South Africa 4 May 1981. Elder brother of G.J.Rudolph (Limpopo and Namibia 2006-07 to 2012-13). 5'11". LHB, LBG. Squad No 4. Northerns 1997-98 to 2003-04. Titans 2004-05 to date. Eagles 2005-06 to 2007-08. Yorkshire 2007-11 (Kolpak registration); scored 122 v Surrey (Oval) on debut; cap 2007. Surrey 2012. Glamorgan debut/cap 2014; captain 2015. **Tests** (SA): 48 (2003 to 2012-13); HS 222* v B (Chittagong) 2003 – on debut; BB 1-1 v E (Leeds) 2003. **LOI** (SA): 45 (2003 to 2005-06); HS 81 v B (Dhaka) 2003. **IT20** (SA): 1 (2005-06); HS 6* v A (Brisbane) 2005-06. F-c Tours (SA): E 2003, 2012; A 2001-02, 2005-06, 2012-13; WI 2004-05; NZ 2003-04, 2011-12; I 2004-05; SL 2004, 2005-06, 2006; B 2003. 1000 runs (4+1); most – 1375 (2010). HS 228* Y v Durham (Leeds) 2010. Gm HS 139 and Gm BB 1-25 v Glos (Bristol) 2014. BB 5-80 Eagles v Cape Cobras (Cape Town) 2007-08. CC BB 1-13 Y v Somerset (Scarborough) 2008. LO HS 169* v Sussex (Hove) 2014 – Gm record. LO BB 4-41 SA A v New Zealand A (Colombo) 2005-06. T20 HS 83*. T20 BB 3-16.

SALTER, Andrew Graham (Milford Haven SFC; Cardiff Met U), b Haverfordwest 1 Jun 1993. 5'9". RHB, OB. Squad No 21. Cardiff MCCU 2012-14. Glamorgan debut 2013. Glamorgan 2nd XI debut 2010. Wales MC 2010-11. HS 25* v Worcs (Worcester) 2014. BB 3-66 v Leics (Swansea) 2013. LO HS 36* v Notts (Cardiff) 2014 (RLC). LO BB 2-41 v Notts (Nottingham) 2012 (CB40) and 2-41 v Notts (Lord's) 2013 (Y40). T20 HS 10. T20 BB 2-19.

SMITH, Ruaidhri Alexander James (Llandaff Cathedral S; Shrewsbury S; Bristol U), b Glasgow, Scotland 5 Aug 1994. 6'1". RHB, RM. Squad No 20. Debut (Glamorgan) 2013. Wales MC 2010-11. Glamorgan 2nd XI debut 2011. Scotland (l-o only) 2013. HS 57* v Glos (Bristol) 2014. BB 3-38 v Hants (Southampton) 2014. LO HS 7 Scot v Hants (Glasgow) 2013 (Y40). LO BB 3-48 Scot v Surrey (Oval) 2013 (Y40). T20 HS 2.

WAGG, Graham Grant (Ashlawn S, Rugby), b Rugby, Warwks 28 Apr 1983. 6'0". RHB, LM. Squad No 8. Warwickshire 2002-04. Derbyshire 2006-10; cap 2007. Glamorgan debut 2011; cap 2013. F-c Tour (Eng A): I 2003-04. HS 116* v Kent (Canterbury) 2014. 50 wkts (2); most – 59 (2008). BB 6-29 v Surrey (Oval) 2014. LO HS 54 v Glos (Cardiff) 2013 (Y40). LO BB 4-35 De v Durham (Derby) 2008 (FPT). T20 HS 62. T20 BB 5-14 v Worcs (Worcester) 2013 – Gm record.

WALLACE, Mark Alexander (Crickhowell HS), b Abergavenny, Monmouthshire 19 Nov 1981. 5'9". LHB, WK. Squad No 18. Debut (Glamorgan) 1999; cap 2003; captain 2012-14; benefit 2013. F-c Tour (ECB Acad): SL 2002-03. 1000 runs (1): 1020 (2011). HS 139 v Surrey (Oval) 2009, sharing Gm record 6th wkt partnership of 240 with J.Allenby. LO HS 118* v Glos (Cardiff) 2013 (Y40). T20 HS 69*.

WRIGHT, Ben James (Cowbridge CS), b Preston, Lancs 5 Dec 1987. 5'9". RHB, RM. Squad No 29. Debut (Glamorgan) 2006; cap 2011. No f-c appearances in 2008. HS 172 v Glos (Cardiff) 2010. BB 1-14 v Essex (Chelmsford) 2007. LO HS 79 v Lancs (Colwyn Bay) 2010 (CB40). LO BB 1-19 v Derbys (Derby) 2009 (FPT). T20 HS 55*. T20 BB 1-16.

RELEASED/RETIRED

(Having made a 1st XI appearance in 2014)

ALLENBY, J. – *see SOMERSET*.

GLOVER, John Charles (Llantarnam CS; St Aidan's C, Durham U), b Cardiff 29 Aug 1989. 6'4". RHB, RMF. Durham MCCU 2008-10. Glamorgan 2011-14. Wales MC 2008-11. HS 55 v Kent (Cardiff) 2012. BB 5-38 DU v Durham (Durham) 2009. Gm BB 4-49 v Kent (Canterbury) 2011. LO HS 10 v Hants (Cardiff) 2012 (CB40). LO BB 3-34 v Scotland (Cardiff) 2012 (CB40).

[NQ]**GOODWIN, Murray** William (Newton Moore HS, Bunbury, WA), b Salisbury, Rhodesia 11 Dec 1972. Younger brother of D.G.Goodwin (Zimbabwe 1986-87 to 1989-90). Migrated to Australia in Nov 1986 and gained Australian citizenship in Sep 1997. 5'9". RHB, LB. WA 1994-95 to 2005-06. Mashonaland 1997-98 to 1998-99. Sussex 2001-12; cap 2001. Warriors 2006-07. Glamorgan 2013-14. Netherlands 1997. **Tests** (Z): 19 (1997-98 to 2000); HS 166* v P (Bulawayo) 1997-98. **LOI** (Z): 71 (1997-98 to 2000); HS 112* v WI (Chester-le-St) 2000; BB 1-12 v SL (Sharjah) 1998-99. F-c Tours (Z): E 2000, SA 1999-00; WI 1999-00; NZ 1997-98; P 1998-99; SL 1997-98. 1000 runs (10+1); most – 1654 (2001). HS 344* Sx v Somerset (Taunton) 2009 (Sx record), sharing record Sx 4th wkt partnership of 363 with C.D.Hopkinson. Gm HS 194 v Lancs (Manchester) 2013. BB 2-23 Z v Lahore City (Lahore) 1998-99. UK BB – . LO HS 167 WA v NSW (Perth) 2000-01. LO BB 1-9 Mashonaland v Eng A (Harare) 1998-99. T20 HS 102*.

LANCEFIELD, Thomas John (Whitgift S), b Epsom, Surrey 8 Oct 1990. 5'9". LHB, LM. Surrey 2010-11. Tamil Union 2010-11. Glamorgan 2014. HS 74 Sy v Worcs (Worcester) 2010. Gm HS 19 v Leics (Cardiff) 2014. BB 1-12 Tamil Union v Colts (Colombo, CCC) 2010-11. CC BB – . LO HS 80 Unicorns v Somerset (Truro) 2013 (Y40). T20 HS 27.

REES, Gareth Peter (Coedcae CS; Bath U), b Swansea 8 Apr 1985. 6'1". LHB, OB. Wales MC 2003-05. Glamorgan 2006-14; cap 2009. MCC 2012. 1000 runs (2); most – 1088 (2008). HS 154 v Surrey (Oval) 2008. BB 1-6 v Hants (Southampton) 2014. LO HS 123* v Essex (Chelmsford) 2009 (FPT). T20 HS 38.

SAMMY, D.J.G – *see NOTTINGHAMSHIRE*.

NQ**WALTERS, Stewart** Jonathan (Guildford GS, Perth, WA), b Mornington, Victoria, Australia 25 Jun 1983. 6'1". RHB, RM. Surrey 2006-10. Glamorgan 2011-14. HS 188 Sy v Leics (Oval) 2009. Gm HS 159 v Essex (Colchester) 2012. BB 1-4 Sy v Durham (Chester-le-St) 2007. LO HS 91 Sy v Northants (Oval) 2008 (P40). LO BB 1-12 Sy v Yorks (Scarborough) 2007 (P40). T20 HS 53*. T20 BB 1-9:

M.T.Reed and H.T.Waters left the staff without making a 1st XI appearance for Glamorgan in 2014.

COUNTY CAPS AWARDED IN 2014

Derbyshire	S.Chanderpaul, M.H.A.Footitt
Durham	–
Essex	J.D.Ryder
Glamorgan	J.A.Rudolph
Gloucestershire	M.D.Craig, P.J.Grieshaber, G.O.Jones, A.P.Rouse, W.A.Tavaré
Hampshire	–
Kent	–
Lancashire	–
Leicestershire	–
Middlesex	–
Northamptonshire	–
Nottinghamshire	L.J.Fletcher, J.E.C.Franklin, P.A.Jaques, P.M.Siddle
Somerset	–
Surrey	Z.S.Ansari, R.J.Burns, J.J.Roy, V.S.Solanki, C.T.Tremlett, G.C.Wilson
Sussex	B.C.Brown, C.J.Jordan
Warwickshire	W.T.S.Porterfield
Worcestershire (colours)	A.D.Hales, T.Kohler-Cadmore, M.J.McClenaghan, C.A.J.Morris, R.K.Oliver
Yorkshire	A.Z.Lees

Durham abolished their capping system after 2005. Gloucestershire award caps on first-class debut. Worcestershire award club colours on Championship debut. Glamorgan's capping system is now based on a player's number of appearances and not on his performances.

GLAMORGAN 2014

RESULTS SUMMARY

	Place	Won	Lost	Tied	Drew	NR
LV= County Championship (2nd Division)	8th	3	6	7		
All First-Class Matches		3	6	8		
Royal London One-Day Cup (Group B)	5th	4	4			
NatWest t20 Blast (South Division)	QF	6	6		1	2

LV= COUNTY CHAMPIONSHIP AVERAGES

BATTING AND FIELDING

Cap		M	I	NO	HS	Runs	Avge	100	50	Ct/St
	C.B.Cooke	12	20	1	171	807	42.47	1	7	3
2013	G.G.Wagg	12	21	5	116*	572	35.75	1	5	4
2010	J.Allenby	16	28	1	100	923	34.18	1	5	15
	W.D.Bragg	16	29	2	93	899	33.29	–	6	6
2014	J.A.Rudolph	15	27	–	139	857	31.74	2	5	13
	S.J.Walters	5	9	1	57*	213	26.62	–	1	9
2003	M.A.Wallace	16	28	2	82	647	24.88	–	4	65/3
2009	G.P.Rees	7	14	1	81	313	24.07	–	3	1
	W.T.Owen	5	7	3	37*	93	23.25	–	–	1
	M.W.Goodwin	8	15	–	50	347	23.13	–	1	6
2011	B.J.Wright	7	11	–	123	254	23.09	1	–	3
2000	D.A.Cosker	16	27	7	45	279	13.95	–	–	11
	D.L.Lloyd	3	6	–	41	82	13.66	–	–	2
	A.G.Salter	4	6	1	25*	67	13.40	–	–	2
2013	M.G.Hogan	13	21	7	36	183	13.07	–	–	6
	J.A.R.Harris	2	4	–	22	51	12.75	–	–	1
	R.A.J.Smith	7	11	1	57*	105	10.50	–	1	2
	T.G.Helm	4	5	2	17	25	8.33	–	–	1
	K.A.Bull	3	6	2	12	31	7.75	–	–	–
	T.J.Lancefield	3	5	–	19	24	4.80	–	–	1

Also batted: A.H.T.Donald (1 match) 4, 59 (1 ct); J.C.Glover (1) 6, 19*.

BOWLING

	O	M	R	W	Avge	Best	5wI	10wM
M.G.Hogan	444.5	106	1232	63	19.55	5-58	3	1
J.Allenby	442.4	119	1107	52	21.28	6-54	2	1
D.A.Cosker	414.1	108	1175	40	29.37	5-39	3	–
G.G.Wagg	367.4	77	1258	41	30.68	6-29	1	–
R.A.J.Smith	157.4	21	630	12	52.50	3-38	–	–
Also bowled:								
K.A.Bull	44.3	6	168	7	24.00	4-62	–	–
J.A.R.Harris	47	10	138	5	27.60	2-34	–	–
T.G.Helm	84	15	276	7	39.42	2- 9	–	–
W.T.Owen	113	18	495	8	61.87	3-42	–	–

W.D.Bragg 19.3-2-76-0; J.C.Glover 17-1-82-1; T.J.Lancefield 1-0-6-0; D.L.Lloyd 29-1-110-3; G.P.Rees 1-0-6-1; J.A.Rudolph 14.3-2-54-1; A.G.Salter 83-14-332-4.

The First-Class Averages (pp 217–233) give the records of Glamorgan players in all first-class county matches (Glamorgan's other opponents being Cardiff MCCU), with the exception of J.A.R.Harris, T.G.Helm and A.G.Salter, whose first-class figures for Glamorgan are as above.

GLAMORGAN RECORDS

FIRST-CLASS CRICKET

Highest Total	For 718-3d		v	Sussex	Colwyn Bay	2000
	V 712		by	Northants	Northampton	1998
Lowest Total	For 22		v	Lancashire	Liverpool	1924
	V 33		by	Leics	Ebbw Vale	1965
Highest Innings	For 309*	S.P.James	v	Sussex	Colwyn Bay	2000
	V 322*	M.B.Loye	for	Northants	Northampton	1998

Highest Partnership for each Wicket

1st	374	M.T.G.Elliott/S.P.James	v	Sussex	Colwyn Bay	2000
2nd	252	M.P.Maynard/D.L.Hemp	v	Northants	Cardiff	2002
3rd	313	D.E.Davies/W.E.Jones	v	Essex	Brentwood	1948
4th	425*	A.Dale/I.V.A.Richards	v	Middlesex	Cardiff	1993
5th	264	M.Robinson/S.W.Montgomery	v	Hampshire	Bournemouth	1949
6th	240	J.Allenby/M.A.Wallace	v	Surrey	The Oval	2009
7th	211	P.A.Cottey/O.D.Gibson	v	Leics	Swansea	1996
8th	202	D.Davies/J.J.Hills	v	Sussex	Eastbourne	1928
9th	203*	J.J.Hills/J.C.Clay	v	Worcs	Swansea	1929
10th	143	T.Davies/S.A.B.Daniels	v	Glos	Swansea	1982

Best Bowling	For 10- 51	J.Mercer	v	Worcs	Worcester	1936
(Innings)	V 10- 18	G.Geary	for	Leics	Pontypridd	1929
Best Bowling	For 17-212	J.C.Clay	v	Worcs	Swansea	1937
(Match)	V 16- 96	G.Geary	for	Leics	Pontypridd	1929

Most Runs – Season	2276	H.Morris	(av 55.51)	1990
Most Runs – Career	34056	A.Jones	(av 33.03)	1957-83
Most 100s – Season	10	H.Morris		1990
Most 100s – Career	54	M.P.Maynard		1985-2005
Most Wkts – Season	176	J.C.Clay	(av 17.34)	1937
Most Wkts – Career	2174	D.J.Shepherd	(av 20.95)	1950-72
Most Career W-K Dismissals	933	E.W.Jones	(840 ct; 93 st)	1961-83
Most Career Catches in the Field	656	P.M.Walker		1956-72

LIMITED-OVERS CRICKET

Highest Total	50ov	429		v	Surrey	The Oval	2002
	40ov	328-4		v	Lancashire	Colwyn Bay	2011
	T20	206-6		v	Somerset	Taunton	2006
Lowest Total	50ov	68		v	Lancashire	Manchester	1973
	40ov	42		v	Derbyshire	Swansea	1979
	T20	94-9		v	Essex	Cardiff	2010
Highest Innings	50ov	169*	J.A.Rudolph	v	Sussex	Hove	2014
	40ov	155*	J.H.Kallis	v	Surrey	Pontypridd	1999
	T20	116*	I.J.Thomas	v	Somerset	Taunton	2004
Best Bowling	50ov	6-20	S.D.Thomas	v	Comb Univs	Cardiff	1995
	40ov	7-16	S.D.Thomas	v	Surrey	Swansea	1998
	T20	5-14	G.G.Wagg	v	Worcs	Worcester	2013

GLOUCESTERSHIRE

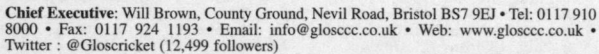

Formation of Present Club: 1871
Inaugural First-Class Match: 1870
Colours: Blue, Gold, Brown, Silver, Green and Red
Badge: Coat of Arms of the City and County of Bristol
County Champions (since 1890): (0); best – 2nd 1930, 1931, 1947, 1959, 1969, 1986
Gillette/NatWest/C&G Trophy Winners: (5) 1973, 1999, 2000, 2003, 2004
Benson and Hedges Cup Winners: (3) 1977, 1999, 2000
Pro 40/National League (Div 1) Winners: (1) 2000
Twenty20 Cup Winners: (0); best – Finalist 2007

Chief Executive: Will Brown, County Ground, Nevil Road, Bristol BS7 9EJ • Tel: 0117 910 8000 • Fax: 0117 924 1193 • Email: info@gloscc.co.uk • Web: www.gloscc.co.uk • Twitter : @Gloscricket (12,499 followers)

Head Coach: Richard Dawson. **Asst Head Coach:** Ian Harvey. **Bowling Coach:** Mark Thorburn. **Captains:** G.O.Jones (f-c) and M.Klinger (l-o). **Overseas Players:** P.S.P.Handscomb and M.Klinger. **2015 Beneficiary:** H.J.H.Marshall. **Head Groundsman:** Sean Williams. **Scorer:** Adrian Bull. ‡ New registration. NQ Not qualified for England.

Gloucestershire revised their capping policy in 2004 and now award players with their County Caps when they make their first-class debut.

COCKBAIN, Ian Andrew (Maghull HS), b Bootle, Liverpool 17 Feb 1987. Son of I.Cockbain (Lancs and Minor Cos 1979-94). 6'0". RHB, RM. Squad No 28. Debut (Gloucestershire) 2011; cap 2011. MCC YC 2008-10. HS 151* v Surrey (Bristol) 2014. LO HS 98* v Worcs (Worcester) 2014 (RLC). T20 HS 84.

DENT, Christopher David James (Backwell CS; Alton C), b Bristol 20 Jan 1991. 5'9". LHB, WK, occ SLA. Squad No 15. Debut (Gloucestershire) 2010; cap 2010. Gloucestershire 2nd XI debut 2007, aged 16y 80d. England U19s 2009-10. 1000 runs (1): 1128 (2013). HS 203* v Cardiff MCCU (Bristol) 2014. CC HS 153 v Kent (Cheltenham) 2013. BB 1-12 v Hants (Bristol) 2013. LO HS 151* v Glamorgan (Cardiff) 2013 (Y40). LO BB 4-43 v Leics (Bristol) 2012 (CB40). T20 HS 63*. T20 BB 1-4.

NQ FULLER, James Kerr (Otago U, NZ), b Cape Town, South Africa 24 Jan 1990. British passport. 6'3". RHB, RFM. Squad No 26. Otago 2009-10 to 2012-13. Gloucestershire debut/cap 2011. HS 57 v Leics (Cheltenham) 2012. BB 6-24 (10-79 match) Otago v Wellington (Dunedin) 2012-13. Gs BB 6-47 v Surrey (Oval) 2014. Hat-trick v Worcs (Cheltenham) 2013. LO HS 43 v Lancs (Bristol) 2012 (CB40). LO BB 6-35 v Netherlands (Amstelveen) 2012 (CB40). T20 HS 36. T20 BB 4-24.

GRIESHABER, Patrick James (Sheldon S, Chippenham), b Bath, Somerset 24 Nov 1996. 5'9". RHB, WK. Debut (Gloucestershire) 2014; cap 2014. Gloucestershire 2nd XI debut 2012, aged 15y 180d. HS 10 v Glamorgan (Bristol) 2014 – only 1st XI appearance.

HAMMOND, Miles Arthur Halhead (St Edward's S, Oxford), b Cheltenham 11 Jan 1996. 5'11". LHB, OB. Squad No 88. Debut (Gloucestershire) 2013; cap 2013. England U19s 2012-13. Gloucestershire 2nd XI debut 2010, aged 14y 120d. HS 4 v Worcs (Cheltenham) 2013. BB 1-96 v Glamorgan (Bristol) 2013. LO HS – . LO BB 2-29 v Yorks (Bristol) 2013 (Y40). T20 HS and BB – .

HAMPTON, Thomas Robert Garth (John Hampden S, High Wycombe), b Kingston-upon-Thames, Surrey 5 Oct 1990. RHB, RMF. Squad No 16. Middlesex 2010. HS 1* and BB 1-15 M v Oxford MCCU (Oxford) 2010. Middlesex 2nd XI 2008-10. MCC YCs 2011-12. Buckinghamshire 2014.

‡NQ**HANDSCOMB, Peter** Stephen Patrick (Mt Waverley SC; Deakin U, Melbourne), b Melbourne, Australia 26 Apr 1991. RHB, WK. British passport (English parents). Victoria 2011-12 to date. Leicestershire 2nd XI 2011. Big Bash: MS 2012-13 to date. HS 134 Vic v S Aus (Adelaide) 2014-15. LO HS 72 Vic v Q (Sydney) 2014-15. T20 HS 103*.

HERRING, Cameron Lee (Tredegar CS), b Abergavenny, Monmouthshire 15 July 1994. 5'6". RHB, WK. Squad No 29. Debut (Gloucestershire) 2013; cap 2013. Gloucestershire 2nd XI debut 2011. HS 114* v Cardiff MCCU (Bristol) 2014. CC HS 43 v Northants (Bristol) 2013. T20 HS 23*.

HOWELL, Benny Alexander Cameron (The Oratory S), b Bordeaux, France 5 Oct 1988. Son of J.B.Howell (Warwickshire 2nd XI 1978). 5'11". RHB, RM. Squad No 13. Hampshire 2011. Gloucestershire debut/cap 2012. Berkshire 2007. HS 83* v Yorks (Scarborough) 2012. BB 5-57 v Leics (Leicester) 2013. LO HS 122 v Surrey (Croydon) 2011 (CB40). LO BB 2-26 v Leics (Leicester) 2012 (CB40). T20 HS 55*. T20 BB 4-26.

JONES, Geraint Owen (Harristown State HS, Toowoomba and MacGregor State HS, Brisbane, Australia), b Kundiawa, Papua New Guinea 14 Jul 1976. Welsh parents. 5'10". RHB, WK. Squad No 8. Kent 2001-13; cap 2003; benefit 2012. Gloucestershire debut/cap 2014; captain 2015. MBE 2005. Papua New Guinea (l-o and T20). **Tests**: 34 (2003-04 to 2006-07); HS 100 v NZ (Leeds) 2004. **LOI** (E/PNG): 51 (49 for E 2004 to 2006; 2 for PNG 2014-15); HS 80 v Z (Bulawayo) 2004-05. **IT20**: 2 (2005 to 2006); HS 19 v A (Southampton) 2005. F-c Tours: A 2006-07; SA 2004-05; WI 2003-04; I 2005-06; P 2005-06; SL 2003-04. 1000 runs (2); most – 1345 (2009). HS 178 K v Somerset (Canterbury) 2010. Gs HS 93 v Leics (Leicester) 2014. LO HS 86 v Surrey (Oval) 2008 (FPT). T20 HS 56.

NQ**KLINGER, Michael** (Scopus Memorial C, Kew), b Kew, Melbourne, Australia 4 Jul 1980. 5'10½". RHB. Squad No 2. Victoria 1999-00 to 2007-08. S Australia 2008-09 to 2013-14. Worcestershire 2012; cap 2012. Gloucestershire debut/cap 2013; captain 2013 to date. W Australia 2014-15. Big Bash: AS 2011-12 to 2013-14. PS 2014-15. 1000 runs (1+1); most – 1203 (2008-09). HS 255 S Aus v WA (Adelaide) 2008-09. Gs HS 163 v Hants (Bristol) 2013. LO HS 140* S Aus v Tas (Sydney) 2013-14. T20 HS 108*.

MARSHALL, Hamish John Hamilton (Mahurangi C, Warkworth; King C, Auckland), b Warkworth, New Zealand 15 Feb 1979. Twin brother of J.A.H.Marshall (ND and NZ 1997-98 to 2011-12). Irish passport, qualified to play in April 2011. 5'9". RHB, RM. Squad No 9. N Districts 1998-99 to 2011-12. Gloucestershire debut 2006 (scoring 102 v Worcs on UK debut); cap 2006; benefit 2015. MCC 2012. Buckinghamshire 2003. **Tests** (NZ): 13 (2000-01 to 2005-06); HS 160 v SL (Napier) 2004-05. **LOI** (NZ): 66 (2003-04 to 2006-07); HS 101* v P (Faisalabad) 2003-04. **IT20** (NZ): 3 (2004-05 to 2005-06); HS 8 v A (Auckland) 2004-05. F-c Tours (NZ): A 2004-05; SA 2000-01, 2005-06; Z 2005; B 2004-05. 1000 runs (2); most – 1218 (2006). HS 170 ND v Canterbury (Rangiora) 2009-10. Gs HS 168 v Leics (Cheltenham) 2006. BB 4-24 v Leics (Leicester) 2009. LO HS 122 v Sussex (Hove) 2007 (P40). LO BB 2-21 v Hants (Southampton) 2009 (P40). T20 HS 102.

MILES, Craig Neil (Bradon Forest S, Swindon; Filton C, Bristol), b Swindon, Wilts 20 July 1994. Brother of A.J.Miles (Cardiff MCCU 2012). 6'4". RHB, RMF. Squad No 34. Debut (Gloucestershire) 2011; cap 2011. Gloucestershire 2nd XI debut 2009, aged 14y 318d. HS 62* v Worcs (Cheltenham) 2014. BB 6-88 v Lancs (Liverpool) 2013. LO HS 12 v Northants (Cheltenham) 2014 (RLC). LO BB 3-48 v Kent (Canterbury) 2014 (RLC). T20 HS 2. T20 BB – .

MONTGOMERY, Robbie Jay (Mindarie Senior C, Perth, WA), b Taunton, Somerset 22 Sep 1994. 6'2". RHB, RFM. Squad No 20. Somerset 2nd XI 2011-14. Gloucestershire 2nd XI debut 2014. T20 HS 8*. T20 BB – .

‡^{NQ}**NOEMA-BARNETT, Kieran**, b Dunedin, New Zealand 4 Jun 1987. LHB, RM. Squad No 11. Central Districts 2008-09 to date. HS 107 CD v Auckland (Auckland) 2011-12. BB 4-20 CD v Otago (Dunedin) 2010-11. LO HS 67 CD v Wellington (Wellington) 2012-13. LO BB 3-42 CD v Auckland (Auckland) 2013-14. T20 HS 57*. T20 BB 2-13.

NORWELL, Liam Connor (Redruth SS), b Bournemouth, Dorset 27 Dec 1991. 6'3". RHB, RMF. Squad No 24. Debut (Gloucestershire) 2011; cap 2011. Gloucestershire 2nd XI debut 2009. HS 78 v Worcs (Cheltenham) 2014. BB 6-46 v Derbys (Bristol) 2011 – on debut. LO HS 1* v Middx (Cheltenham) 2012 (CB40). LO BB 6-52 v Leics (Leicester) 2012 (CB40). T20 HS 1*. T20 BB 3-27.

PAYNE, David Alan (Lytchett Minster S), b Poole, Dorset, 15 Feb 1991. 6'2". RHB, LMF. Squad No 14. Debut (Gloucestershire) 2011; cap 2011. Gloucestershire 2nd XI debut 2008. Dorset 2009. England U19s 2010. HS 62 v Glamorgan (Bristol) 2011. BB 6-26 v Leics (Bristol) 2011. LO HS 18 v Leics (Leicester) 2013 (Y40). LO BB 7-29 v Essex (Chelmsford) 2010 (CB40), inc 4 wkts in 4 balls and 6 wkts in 9 balls – Gs l-o record. T20 HS 10. T20 BB 3-17.

^{NQ}**RODERICK, Gareth** Hugh (Maritzburg C), b Durban, South Africa 29 Aug 1991. 6'0". RHB, WK. Squad No 27. British passport. KZN 2010-11 to 2011-12. Gloucestershire debut/cap 2013. Gloucestershire 2nd XI debut 2012. Northamptonshire 2nd XI 2011. HS 171 v Leics (Bristol) 2014. LO HS 63 v Yorks (Leeds) 2013 (Y40). T20 HS 32.

SMITH, Thomas Michael John (Seaford Head Community C; Sussex Downs C), b Eastbourne, Sussex 29 Aug 1987. 5'9". RHB, SLA. Squad No 6. Sussex 2007-09. No f-c appearances in 2008. Surrey 2009 (l-o only). Middlesex 2010-13. Gloucestershire debut/cap 2013. HS 80 v Surrey (Bristol) 2014. BB 4-35 v Kent (Canterbury) 2014. LO HS 65 Sy v Leics (Leicester) 2009 (P40). LO BB 3-26 M v Derbys (Lord's) 2010 (CB40). T20 HS 36*. T20 BB 5-24.

TAVARÉ, William Andrew (Bristol GS; Loughborough U), b Bristol 1 Jan 1990. Nephew of C.J.Tavaré (Kent, Somerset & England 1974-93). 6'0". RHB, RM. Squad No 4. Loughborough MCCU 2010-12. Gloucestershire debut/cap 2014. Gloucestershire 2nd XI debut 2006. 1000 runs (1): 1014 (2014). HS 139 v Hants (Bristol) 2014 – on CC debut. LO HS 77 v Hants (Bristol) 2014 (RLC) – on l-o debut.

TAYLOR, Jack Martin Robert (Chipping Norton S), b Banbury, Oxfordshire 12 Nov 1991. Elder brother of M.D.Taylor (*see below*). 5'11". RHB, OB. Squad No 10. Debut (Gloucestershire) 2010; cap 2010. Gloucestershire 2nd XI debut 2007, aged 15y 191d. Oxfordshire 2009-11. HS 63 v Glamorgan (Swansea) 2012. BB 4-125 v Essex (Chelmsford) 2014. LO HS 53 v Derbys (Derby) 2014 (RLC). LO BB 4-38 v Hants (Bristol) 2014 (RLC). T20 HS 38. T20 BB 4-16.

TAYLOR, Matthew David (Chipping Norton S), b Banbury, Oxfordshire 8 Jul 1994. Younger brother of J.M.R.Taylor (*see above*). 6'0". RHB, LM. Squad No 36. Debut (Gloucestershire) 2013; cap 2013. Gloucestershire 2nd XI debut 2011. Oxfordshire 2011-12. HS 32* v Essex (Chelmsford) 2014. BB 5-75 v Hants (Bristol) 2014. LO HS 7* and LO BB 2-43 v Notts (Cheltenham) 2011 (CB40).

RELEASED/RETIRED

(Having made a 1st XI appearance in 2014)

NQCRAIG, **Mark** Donald, b Auckland, New Zealand 23 Mar 1987. LHB, OB. Otago 2010-11 to date. Gloucestershire 2014; cap 2014. **Tests** (NZ): 8 (2014 to 2014-15); HS 67 v WI (Port of Spain) 2014; BB 7-94 v P (Sharjah) 2014. F-c Tour (NZ): E 2014 (NZ A); WI 2014; UAE 2014-15 (v P). HS 93 Otago v ND (Dunedin) 2014-15. Gs HS 7 and Gs BB 2-85 v Worcs (Worcester) 2014. BB 7-94 (*see Tests*). LO HS 44* Otago v CD (New Plymouth) 2014-15. LO BB 3-6 NZ A v Kent (Canterbury) 2014. T20 HS 7. T20 BB 3-29.

GIDMAN, A.P.R. – *see WORCESTERSHIRE.*

GIDMAN, W.R.S. – *see NOTTINGHAMSHIRE.*

HOUSEGO, Daniel Mark (Oratory S, Reading), b Windsor, Berkshire 12 Oct 1988. 5'8". RHB, LB. Middlesex 2008-11. Glamorgan 2012-14; cap 2012. Mountaineers 2013-14. Berkshire 2006. HS 217* and BB 1-5 Mt v SR (Masvingo) 2013-14. Gs HS 150 v Essex (Chelmsford) 2013. Gs BB – . LO HS 132 v S Africans (Bristol) 2012. LO BB 1-16 Mt v SR (Masvingo) 2013-14. T20 HS 59*.

McCARTER, Graeme John (Foyle and Londonderry C), b Londonderry, N.Ireland 10 Oct 1992. 6'2". RHB, RFM. Ireland 2011 to date. Gloucestershire 2012-14; cap 2012. Gloucestershire 2nd XI debut 2008, aged 15y 292d. **LOI** (Ire): 1 (2014); HS 1* and BB – v Scotland (Dublin) 2014. HS 29* v Yorks (Bristol) 2012. BB 4-95 v Lancs (Liverpool) 2013. LO HS 18* v Leics (Leicester) 2013 (Y40). LO BB 3-15 v Leics (Bristol) 2012 (CB40). T20 HS 16*. T20 BB 5-35 v Sussex (Hove) 2014 – Gs record.

ROUSE, Adam Paul (Perrins Community Sports C; Peter Symonds C, Winchester), b Harare, Zimbabwe 30 Jun 1992. 5'8". RHB, WK. Hampshire 2013. Gloucestershire 2014; cap 2014. Hampshire 2nd XI debut 2008, aged 15y 331d. England U19s 2010. HS 49 v Essex (Chelmsford) 2014. LO HS 7 H v Bangladesh A (Southampton) 2013. T20 HS 35*.

SAXELBY, Ian David (Oakham S), b Nottingham 22 May 1989. Nephew of K.Saxelby (Nottinghamshire 1978-90) and M.Saxelby (Notts, Durham and Derbys 1989-2000). 6'2". RHB, RMF. Gloucestershire 2008-14; cap 2008. No 1st XI appearances in 2010 and in 2013 due to injuries. England U19s 2008. HS 60* v Northants (Northampton) 2009. BB 6-48 v Leics (Cheltenham) 2012. LO HS 7* and BB 4-31 v Surrey (Bristol) 2009 (FPT). T20 HS 7*. T20 BB 4-16.

T.W.Shrewsbury left the staff without making a 1st XI appearance for Gloucestershire in 2014.

GLOUCESTERSHIRE 2014

RESULTS SUMMARY

	Place	Won	Lost	Tied	Drew	NR
LV= County Championship (2nd Division)	7th	4	5		7	
All First-Class Matches		4	5		8	
Royal London One-Day Cup (Group A)	QF	4	3			2
NatWest t20 Blast (South Division)	8th	5	7			2

LV= COUNTY CHAMPIONSHIP AVERAGES
BATTING AND FIELDING

Cap		M	I	NO	HS	Runs	Avge	100	50	Ct/St
2013	G.H.Roderick	4	8	–	171	470	58.75	1	3	14
2011	W.R.S.Gidman	13	20	5	125	826	55.06	3	3	5
2004	A.P.R.Gidman	16	29	2	264	1277	47.29	4	3	14
2014	G.O.Jones	3	4	1	93	136	45.33	–	1	6
2014	W.A.Tavaré	15	26	1	139	953	38.12	4	3	11
2006	H.J.H.Marshall	16	27	3	118	821	34.20	2	3	2
2011	D.A.Payne	7	10	4	54*	189	31.50	–	1	3
2013	T.M.J.Smith	13	19	4	80	453	30.20	–	1	5
2011	I.A.Cockbain	9	16	1	151*	443	29.53	1	2	7
2013	M.Klinger	10	18	1	129*	490	28.82	2	1	11
2011	C.N.Miles	4	7	1	62*	170	28.33	–	1	2
2012	B.A.C.Howell	11	17	3	78*	360	25.71	–	2	8
2011	L.C.Norwell	10	12	5	78	173	24.71	–	1	1
2010	C.D.J.Dent	13	22	–	61	436	19.81	–	4	9
2014	A.P.Rouse	4	7	–	49	124	17.71	–	–	13/2
2013	M.D.Taylor	9	12	5	32*	118	16.85	–	–	2
2011	J.K.Fuller	6	7	1	28	88	14.66	–	–	1
2010	J.M.R.Taylor	2	4	–	40	57	14.25	–	–	
2013	C.L.Herring	4	6	–	22	46	7.66	–	–	17/1

Also batted: M.D.Craig (1 match – cap 2014) 7; P.J.Grieshaber (1 – cap 2014) 10; D.M.Housego (1 – cap 2012) 0, 27; G.J.McCarter (2 – cap 2012) 3, 1, 20 (1 ct); I.D.Saxelby (2 – cap 2008) 1, 3, 20.

BOWLING

	O	M	R	W	Avge	Best	5wI	10wM
C.N.Miles	93	16	358	18	19.88	5- 90	1	–
W.R.S.Gidman	357.3	97	943	39	24.17	6- 50	2	–
B.A.C.Howell	250.2	59	714	23	31.04	4- 60	–	–
J.K.Fuller	159.4	27	581	18	32.27	6- 47	1	–
L.C.Norwell	304.4	51	1166	29	40.20	4- 69	–	–
T.M.J.Smith	388.3	60	1294	32	40.43	4- 35	–	–
M.D.Taylor	216.2	35	905	21	43.09	5- 75	1	–
D.A.Payne	185	41	594	11	54.00	3- 29	–	–

Also bowled:

G.J.McCarter	43.3	7	144	6	24.00	3- 64		
J.M.R.Taylor	70.1	9	267	7	38.14	4-125		

M.D.Craig   25-3-105-2;   C.D.J.Dent   35.3-2-165-1;   D.M.Housego   6-0-25-0;
H.J.H.Marshall 25-6-66-2; I.D.Saxelby 20.1-5-71-3.

The First-Class Averages (pp 217–233) give the records of Gloucestershire players in all first-class county matches (Gloucestershire's other opponents being Cardiff MCCU), with the exception of M.D.Craig, whose first-class figures for Gloucestershire are as above.

† Gloucestershire revised their capping policy in 2004 and now award players with their County Caps when they make their first-class debut.

GLOUCESTERSHIRE RECORDS

FIRST-CLASS CRICKET

Highest Total	For	695-9d		v	Middlesex	Gloucester	2004
	V	774-7d		by	Australians	Bristol	1948
Lowest Total	For	17		v	Australians	Cheltenham	1896
	V	12		by	Northants	Gloucester	1907
Highest Innings	For	341	C.M.Spearman	v	Middlesex	Gloucester	2004
	V	319	C.J.L.Rogers	for	Northants	Northampton	2006

Highest Partnership for each Wicket

1st	395	D.M.Young/R.B.Nicholls	v	Oxford U	Oxford	1962
2nd	256	C.T.M.Pugh/T.W.Graveney	v	Derbyshire	Chesterfield	1960
3rd	392	G.H.Roderick/A.P.R.Gidman	v	Leics	Bristol	2014
4th	321	W.R.Hammond/W.L.Neale	v	Leics	Gloucester	1937
5th	261	W.G.Grace/W.O.Moberley	v	Yorkshire	Cheltenham	1876
6th	320	G.L.Jessop/J.H.Board	v	Sussex	Hove	1903
7th	248	W.G.Grace/E.L.Thomas	v	Sussex	Hove	1896
8th	239	W.R.Hammond/A.E.Wilson	v	Lancashire	Bristol	1938
9th	193	W.G.Grace/S.A.P.Kitcat	v	Sussex	Bristol	1896
10th	137	C.N.Miles/L.C.Norwell	v	Worcs	Cheltenham	2014

Best Bowling	For	10-40	E.G.Dennett	v	Essex	Bristol	1906
(Innings)	V	10-66	A.A.Mailey	for	Australians	Cheltenham	1921
		10-66	K.Smales	for	Notts	Stroud	1956
Best Bowling	For	17-56	C.W.L.Parker	v	Essex	Gloucester	1925
(Match)	V	15-87	A.J.Conway	for	Worcs	Moreton-in-M	1914

Most Runs – Season	2860	W.R.Hammond	(av 69.75)		1933
Most Runs – Career	33664	W.R.Hammond	(av 57.05)		1920-51
Most 100s – Season	13	W.R.Hammond			1938
Most 100s – Career	113	W.R.Hammond			1920-51
Most Wkts – Season	222	T.W.J.Goddard	(av 16.80)		1937
	222	T.W.J.Goddard	(av 16.37)		1947
Most Wkts – Career	3170	C.W.L.Parker	(av 19.43)		1903-35
Most Career W-K Dismissals	1054	R.C.Russell	(950 ct; 104 st)		1981-2004
Most Career Catches in the Field	719	C.A.Milton			1948-74

LIMITED-OVERS CRICKET

Highest Total	50ov	401-7		v	Bucks	Wing	2003
	40ov	344-6		v	Northants	Cheltenham	2001
	T20	254-3		v	Middlesex	Uxbridge	2011
Lowest Total	50ov	82		v	Notts	Bristol	1987
	40ov	49		v	Middlesex	Bristol	1978
	T20	68		v	Hampshire	Bristol	2010
Highest Innings	50ov	177	A.J.Wright	v	Scotland	Bristol	1997
	40ov	153	C.M.Spearman	v	Warwicks	Gloucester	2003
	T20	119	K.J.O'Brien	v	Middlesex	Uxbridge	2011
Best Bowling	50ov	6-13	M.J.Procter	v	Hampshire	Southampton	1977
	40ov	7-29	D.A.Payne	v	Essex	Chelmsford	2010
	T20	5-35	G.J.McCarter	v	Sussex	Hove	2014

HAMPSHIRE

HAMPSHIRE
CRICKET

Formation of Present Club: 12 August 1863
Inaugural First-Class Match: 1864
Colours: Blue, Gold and White
Badge: Tudor Rose and Crown
County Champions: (2) 1961, 1973
NatWest/C&G/FP Trophy Winners: (3) 1991, 2005, 2009
Benson and Hedges Cup Winners: (2) 1988, 1992
Sunday League Winners: (3) 1975, 1978, 1986
Clydesdale Bank Winners: (1) 2012
Twenty20 Cup Winners: (2) 2010, 2012

Chairman: Rod Bransgrove, The Ageas Bowl, Botley Road, West End, Southampton SO30 3XH • Tel: 023 8047 2002 • Fax: 023 8047 2122 • Email: enquiries@ageasbowl.com • Web: www.ageasbowl.com Twitter:@hantscricket (20,642 followers)

CEO: David Mann. **Cricket Operations Manager**: Tim Tremlett. **Director of Cricket**: Giles White. **1st XI Coach**: Dale Benkenstein. **Batting Coach**: Tony Middleton. **Assistant Coach**: Craig White. **Captain**: J.H.K.Adams. **Vice-Captain and T20 Captain**: J.M.Vince. **Overseas Players**: J.M.Bird and Yasir Arafat (T20 only). **2015 Beneficiary**: J.H.K.Adams. **Head Groundsman**: Nigel Gray. Scorer: Kevin Baker. ‡ New registration. [NQ] Not qualified for England.

‡[NQ]**ADAMS, Andre** Ryan (Westlake BHS, Auckland), b Mangere, Auckland, New Zealand 17 Jul 1975. 5'9". RHB, RMF. Squad No 41. Auckland 1997-98 to 2011-12. Essex 2004-06, scoring 124 on debut (*see below*); cap 2004. Nottinghamshire 2007-14; cap 2007 (Kolpak registration). MCC 2014. Herefordshire 2001. **Tests** (NZ): 1 (2001-02); HS 11 and BB 3-44 v E (Auckland) 2001-02. **LOI** (NZ): 42 (2000-01 to 2006-07); HS 45 v P (Rawalpindi) 2001-02; BB 5-22 v I (Queenstown) 2002-03. **IT20** (NZ): 4 (2004-05 to 2005-06); HS 7 v A (Auckland) 2004-05; BB 2-20 v SL (Auckland) 2006-07. HS 124 Ex v Leics (Leicester) 2004 (91 balls, 7 sixes, 13 fours; 100 off 80 balls) on UK debut. 50 wkts (3); most – 68 (2010). BB 7-32 (10-50 match) Nt v Lancs (Manchester) 2012. Hat-trick Ex v Somerset (Taunton) 2005. LO HS 90* North Is Selection XI v Sri Lankans (New Plymouth) 2000-01. LO BB 5-7 Auckland v ND (Auckland) 1999-00. T20 HS 54*. T20 BB 5-20.

ADAMS, James Henry Kenneth (Sherborne S; University C, London; Loughborough U), b Winchester 23 Sep 1980. 6'2". LHB, LM. Squad No 4. British U 2002-04. Hampshire debut 2002; cap 2006; captain 2012 to date; benefit 2015. Loughborough UCCE 2003-04 – scoring 107 v Somerset (Taunton) on debut. MCC 2013. Dorset 1998. F-c Tour (EL): WI 2010-11. 1000 runs (5); most – 1351 (2009). HS 262* v Notts (Nottingham) 2006. BB 2-16 v Durham (Chester-le-St) 2004. LO HS 131 v Warwks (Birmingham) 2010 (CB40). LO BB 1-34 v Essex (Chelmsford) 2007 (FPT). T20 HS 101*. T20 BB – .

AKRAM, Basil Mohammad Ramzan (Brentwood S; Loughborough U), b Walthamstow 23 Feb 1993. 6'1". RHB, RFM. Squad No 46. Loughborough MCCU 2014. Essex 2nd XI 2010. Northamptonshire 2nd XI 2011-13. Hampshire 2nd XI debut 2014. Development contract in 2015. HS 36 and BB 2-82 LU v Sussex (Hove) 2014 – only f-c appearance. LO HS 1 and BB – v Yorks (Southampton) 2014 (RLC) – only 1st XI appearance.

ALSOP, Thomas Philip (Lavington S), b High Wycombe, Bucks 26 Nov 1995. Younger brother of O.J.Alsop (Wiltshire 2010-12). 5'11". LHB, WK. Squad No 9. Debut (Hampshire) 2014. Hampshire 2nd XI debut 2013. England U19 2014. Development contract 2015. HS 33 v Kent (Southampton) 2014. LO HS 0.

BARBER, Thomas Edward (Bournemouth GS), b Poole, Dorset 31 May 1994. 6'3". RHB, LFM. Squad No 20. Hampshire 2nd XI debut 2013. Awaiting f-c debut. Development contract 2015. LO HS 0. LO BB 2-22 v Yorks (Southampton) 2014 (RLC).

‡**BERG, Gareth** Kyle (South African College S), b Cape Town, South Africa 18 Jan 1981. 6'0". RHB, RMF. Squad No 13. England qualified through residency. Middlesex 2008-14; cap 2010. Italy (T20 only) 2011-12 to date. HS 130* M v Leics (Leicester) 2011, sharing M record 9th wkt partnership of 172 with T.J.Murtagh. BB 6-58 M v Glamorgan (Cardiff) 2011. LO HS 75 M v Glamorgan (Lord's) 2013 (Y40). LO BB 4-24 M v Worcs (Worcester) 2011 (CB40). T20 HS 90. T20 BB 4-20.

‡[NQ]**BIRD, Jackson** Munro (St Pius C, Sydney; St Ignatius C, Riverview), b Paddington, Sydney, Australia 11 Dec 1986. RHB, RFM. Squad No 22. Tasmania 2011-12 to date. Big Bash: MS 2011-12 to date. **Tests** (A): 3 (2012-13 to 2013); HS 6* and BB 4-41 v SL (Sydney) 2012-13. F-c Tours (A): E 2012 (Aus A), 2013, 2013 (Aus A). HS 26 and BB 6-25 Tas v WA (Hobart) 2012-13. LO HS 5* Tas v Q (Hobart) 2012-13. LO BB 3-39 Tas v S Aus (Adelaide) 2011-12. T20 HS 3. T20 BB 4-31.

BRIGGS, Danny Richard (Isle of Wight C), b Newport, IoW, 30 Apr 1991. 6'2". RHB, SLA. Squad No 19. Debut (Hampshire) 2009; cap 2012. Hampshire 2nd XI debut 2007, aged 16y 120d. **LOI**: 1 (2011-12); HS – ; BB 2-39 v P (Dubai) 2011-12. **IT20**: 7 (2012 to 2013-14); HS 0*; BB 2-25 v A (Chester-le-St) 2013. F-c Tour (EL): WI 2010-11. HS 54 v Glos (Bristol) 2013. BB 6-45 EL v Windward Is (Roseau) 2010-11. CC BB 6-65 v Notts (Southampton) 2011. LO HS 25 and LO BB 4-32 v Glamorgan (Cardiff) 2012 (CB40). T20 HS 10. T20 BB 5-19.

CARBERRY, Michael Alexander (St John Rigby Catholic C), b Croydon, Surrey 29 Sep 1980. 6'0". LHB, OB. Squad No 15. Surrey 2001-02. Kent 2003-05. Hampshire debut/cap 2006. MCC 2008. Big Bash: PS 2014-15. **Tests**: 6 (2009-10 to 2013-14); HS 60 v A (Adelaide) 2013-14. **LOI**: 6 (2013 to 2014); HS 63 v A (Cardiff) 2013. **IT20**: 1 (2014); HS 7 v SL (Oval) 2014. F-c Tours: A 2013-14; B 2006-07 (Eng A), 2009-10. 1000 runs (3); most – 1251 (2009). HS 300* v Yorks (Southampton) 2011, sharing in UK 3rd highest and UK record 3rd-wkt partnership of 523 with N.D.McKenzie. BB 2-85 v Durham (Chester-le-St) 2006. LO HS 150* v Lancs (Southampton) 2013 (Y40). LO BB 3-37 v Derbys (Derby) 2013 (Y40). T20 HS 100*. T20 BB 1-16.

DAWSON, Liam Andrew (John Bentley S, Calne), b Swindon, Wilts 1 Mar 1990. 5'8". RHB, SLA. Squad No 8. Debut (Hampshire) 2007; cap 2013. Mountaineers 2011-12. Wiltshire 2006-07. HS 169 v Somerset (Southampton) 2011. BB 7-51 Mountaineers v ME (Mutare) 2011-12 (also scored 110* in same match). BB 5-29 v Leics (Southampton) 2012. LO HS 113* SJD v Kalabagan (Savar) 2014-15. LO BB 4-45 v Middx (Lord's) 2008 (P40). T20 HS 30. T20 BB 4-19.

ERVINE, Sean Michael (Lomagundi C, Chinhoyi), b Harare, Zimbabwe 6 Dec 1982. Elder brother of C.R.Ervine (Midlands, SR 2003-04 to date); son of R.M.Ervine (Rhodesia 1977-78); grandson of M.A.Den (Rhodesia 1935-36); nephew of N.B.Ervine (Rhodesia 1977-78) and G.M.Den (Rhodesia and Eastern Province 1963-64 to 1969-70). 6'2". LHB, RM. Squad No 7. CFX Academy 2000-01 to 2001. Midlands 2001-02 to 2003-04. Hampshire debut/cap 2005; qualified for England in 2013 season. W Australia 2006-07 to 2007-08. Southern Rocks 2009-10. Matabeleland Tuskers 2011-12 to 2012-13. **Tests** (Z): 5 (2003 to 2003-04); HS 86 v B (Harare) 2003-04; BB 4-146 v A (Perth) 2003-04. **LOI** (Z): 42 (2001-02 to 2003-04); HS 100 v I (Adelaide) 2003-04; BB 3-29 v P (Sharjah) 2001-02. F-c Tours (Z): E 2003; A 2003-04. HS 237* v Somerset (Southampton) 2010. BB 6-82 Midlands v Mashonaland (Kwekwe) 2002-03. H BB 5-60 v Glamorgan (Cardiff) 2005. LO HS 167* v Ireland (Southampton) 2009 (FPT). LO BB 5-50 v Glamorgan (Cardiff) 2005 (CGT). T20 HS 82. T20 BB 4-12.

FOLEY, Jake Matthew (Felsted S; Southampton Solent U), b Colchester, Essex 21 Sep 1994. 6'2''. LHB, SLA. Hampshire 2nd XI debut 2014. LO debut v Sri Lanka (Southampton) without batting or bowling.

GATTING, Joe Stephen (Cardinal Newman C; Brighton C), b Brighton 25 Nov 1987. Son of S.P.Gatting (Middlesex 2nd XI, football for Arsenal, Brighton & Hove Albion, Charlton Athletic), nephew of M.W.Gatting (Middlesex and England 1975-98). 6'0''. RHB, OB. Squad No 6. Sussex 2009-13, scoring 152 v Cambridge UCCE (Cambridge) on debut. Hampshire debut 2014. HS 152 (*see above*). CC HS 116* Sx v Worcs (Worcester) 2011. H HS 67 v Derbys (Derby) 2014. BB 1-8 Sx v Notts (Nottingham) 2011. H BB - . LO HS 122 Sx v Worcs (Horsham) 2011 (CB40). LO BB - . T20 HS 45*. LO BB 1-12.

KING, Matthew John (Fort Hill Community S), b Basingstoke 25 Feb 1994. 6'1''. RHB, RFM. Hampshire 2nd XI debut 2012. Awaiting f-c debut. LO HS 8 v Bangladesh A (Southampton) 2013. LO BB - .

McMANUS, Lewis David (Clayesmore S, Bournemouth), b Poole, Dorset 9 Oct 1994. 5'10''. RHB, WK. Squad No 18. Hampshire 2nd XI debut 2011. Dorset 2011-13. Awaiting 1st XI debut. Development contract 2015.

NUGENT, Thomas Michael (Loughborough U), b Bath, Somerset 11 Jul 1994. RHB, RFM. Hampshire 2nd XI debut 2012. Berkshire 2012-14. LO HS - and LO BB 1-15 v Sri Lanka A (Southampton) 2014. Awaiting f-c debut.

PORTER, Michael James (Poole GS; Brockenhurst C), b Poole, Dorset 21 Apr 1995. 6'0''. RHB, LB. Hampshire 2nd XI debut 2013. Dorset 2013-14. LO HS - . Awaiting f-c debut.

SHAH, Owais Alam (Isleworth & Syon S), b Karachi, Pakistan 22 Oct 1978. 6'0''. RHB, OB. Middlesex 1996-2010; cap 2000; captain 2004 (*part*); benefit 2008. Cape Cobras 2010-11. Essex 2011-13; cap 2011. MCC 2002-08. YC 2001. Hampshire T20 only in 2014. **Tests**: 6 (2005-06 to 2008-09); HS 88 v I (Bombay) 2005-06; BB - . **LOI**: 71 (2001 to 2009-10); HS 107* v I (Oval) 2007; BB 3-15 v Ire (Belfast) 2009. **IT20**: 17 (2007 to 2009); HS 55* v WI (Oval) 2007. F-c Tours (Eng A): A 1996-97; WI 2005-06 (*part*), 2008-09 (Eng); I 2005-06 (Eng – *part*); SL 1997-98, 2004-05, 2007-08 (Eng). 1000 runs (8); most – 1728 (2005). HS 203 M v Derbys (Southgate) 2001. BB 3-33 M v Glos (Bristol) 1999. LO HS 134 M v Sussex (Arundel) 1999 (NL). LO BB 4-11 M v Leics (Lord's) 2009 (P40). T20 HS 84. T20 BB 2-26.

SMITH, William Rew (Bedford S; Collingwood C, Durham U), b Luton, Beds 28 Sep 1982. 5'9''. RHB, OB. Squad No 2. Nottinghamshire 2002-06. Durham UCCE 2003-05; captain 2004-05. British U 2004. Durham 2007-13; captain 2009-10 (*part*). Hampshire debut 2014. Bedfordshire 1999-2002. 1000 runs (1): 1187 (2014). HS 201* Du v Surrey (Guildford) 2008. H HS 151* v Essex (Southampton) 2014. BB 3-34 DU v Leics (Leicester) 2005. H BB 2-27 v Kent (Southampton) 2014. LO HS 120* Du v Surrey (Chester-le-St) 2013 (Y40). LO BB 2-19 Du v Derbys (Derby) 2013 (Y40). T20 HS 55. T20 BB 3-15.

TAYLOR, Bradley Jacob, b Winchester 14 Mar 1997. 5'11''. RHB, OB. Squad No 93. Debut (Hampshire) 2013. Hampshire 2nd XI debut 2013. England 1st XI debut 2013. Development contract 2015. HS 20 and BB 4-64 v Lancs (Southport) 2013. LO HS 2* and LO BB 2-23 v Bangladesh A (Southampton) 2013. T20 HS - .

TERRY, Sean Paul (Aquinas C, Perth; Notre Dame U, Perth, Australia), b Southampton 1 Aug 1991. Son of V.P.Terry (Hampshire and England 1978-96). 5'11''. RHB, OB. Squad No 10. Debut (Hampshire) 2012. Hampshire 2nd XI debut 2011. Development contract 2015. HS 59* v Loughborough MCCU (Southampton) 2012 – on debut. CC HS 58 v Worcs (Worcester) 2013. LO HS 63 v Leics (Southampton) 2014 (RLC).

TOMLINSON, James Andrew (Harrow Way S, Andover; Cardiff U), b Winchester 12 Jun 1982. 6'1''. LHB, LMF. Squad No 21. British U 2002-03. Hampshire debut 2002; cap 2008. Wiltshire 2001. HS 51 v Glos (Southampton) 2014. 50 wkts (2); most – 67 (2008). BB 8-46 (10-194 match) v Somerset (Taunton) 2008. LO HS 14 v Durham (Chester-le-St) 2010 (CB40). LO BB 4-47 v Glamorgan (Southampton) 2006 (CGT). T20 HS 5. T20 BB 1-20.

VINCE, James Michael (Warminster S), b Cuckfield, Sussex 14 Mar 1991. 6'2''. RHB, RM. Squad No 14. Debut (Hampshire) 2009; cap 2013. Hampshire 2nd XI debut 2006. Wiltshire 2007-08. F-c Tours (EL): SA 2014-15; SL 2013-14. 1000 runs (2); most – 1525 (2014). HS 240 v Essex (Southampton) 2014. BB 5-41 v Loughborough MCCU (Southampton) 2013. CC BB 2-2 v Lancs (Southport) 2013. LO HS 131 v Scotland (Southampton) 2011 (CB40). LO BB 1-18 EL v Australia A (Sydney) 2012-13. T20 HS 93*. T20 BB 1-5.

‡**WHEAL, Bradley** Thomas James (Clifton C), b Durban, South Africa 28 Aug 1996. 5'9''. RHB, RM. Squad No 43. Joins from KZN U19.

WHEATER, Adam Jack Aubrey (Millfield S), b Whipps Cross, Essex 13 Feb 1990. 5'6''. RHB, WK. Squad No 31. Essex 2008-12. Cambridge MCCU 2010. Matabeleland Tuskers 2010-11 to 2012-13. Badureliya Sports Club 2011-12. Northern Districts 2012-13. Hampshire debut 2013. HS 164 Ex v Northants (Chelmsford) 2011, sharing Ex record 6th wkt partnership of 253 with J.S.Foster. H HS 140 v Lancs (Southport) 2013. BB 1-86 Ex v Leics (Leicester) 2012 – in contrived circumstances. LO HS 135 v Essex (Chelmsford) 2014 (RLC). T20 HS 34.

WOOD, Christopher Philip (Alton C), b Basingstoke 27 June 1990. 6'2''. RHB, LM. Squad No 25. Debut (Hampshire) 2010. Hampshire 2nd XI debut 2007. England U19s 2009. HS 105* v Leics (Leicester) 2012. BB 5-39 v Kent (Canterbury) 2014. LO HS 41 v Essex (Southampton) 2013 (Y40). LO BB 5-22 v Glamorgan (Cardiff) 2012 (CB40). T20 HS 27. T20 BB 4-24.

‡[NQ]**YASIR ARAFAT** Satti (Gordon C, Rawalpindi), b Rawalpindi, Pakistan 12 Mar 1982. 5'9½''. RHB, RFM. Squad No 99. Rawalpindi 1997-98 to 2012-13. Pakistan Reserves 1999-00. KRL 2000-01 to date. NBP 2005-06. Sussex 2006-10; cap 2006. Kent 2007-08; cap 2007. Federal Areas 2007-08 to 2008-09. Surrey 2011. Big Bash: PS 2013 to date. **Tests** (P): 3 (2007-08 to 2008-09); HS 50* v SL (Karachi) 2008-09; BB 5-161 v I (Bangalore) 2007-08 – on debut. **LOI** (P): 11 (1999-00 to 2009); HS 27 v SA (Chandigarh) 2006-07; BB 1-28 v SL (Karachi) 1999-00. **IT20** (P): 13 (2007-08 to 2012-13); HS 17 v Scotland (Durban) 2007-08; BB 3-18 v SL (Hambantota) 2012. F-c Tours (P): WI 2010-11 (Pak A); I 2007-08; SL 2001 (Pak A), 2004-05 (Pak A). HS 170 KRL v Multan (Multan) 2011-12. CC HS 122 K v Sussex (Canterbury) 2007. 50 wkts (0+4); most – 91 (2001-02). BB 9-35 KRL v SSGC (Rawalpindi) 2008-09. CC BB 6-86 K v Hants (Canterbury) 2008. LO HS 110* Otago v Auckland (Oamaru) 2009-10. LO BB 6-24 Pakistan A v England A (Colombo) 2004-05. T20 HS 49. T20 BB 4-5.

RELEASED/RETIRED

(Having made a 1st XI appearance in 2014)

[NQ]**ABBOTT, Kyle** John, b Empangeni, South Africa 18 Jun 1987. RHB, RFM. KwaZulu-Natal 2008-09 to 2009-10. Dolphins 2008-09 to date. Hampshire 2014. **Tests** (SA): 3 (2012-13 to 2014-15); HS 13 and BB 7-29 v P (Centurion) 2012-13. **LOI** (SA): 14 (2012-13 to 2014-15); HS 23 v Z (Bulawayo) 2014; BB 4-21 v Ireland (Canberra) 2014-15. **IT20** (SA): 8 (2012-13 to 2014-15); HS 2* v A (Melbourne) 2014-15; BB 3-21 v A (Adelaide) 2014-15. HS 80 Dolphins v Titans (Benoni) 2010-11. H HS 40 v Leics (Leicester) 2014. BB 8-45 (12-96 match) Dolphins v Cobras (Cape Town) 2012-13. H BB 5-44 v Essex (Southampton) 2014. LO HS 45* Dolphins v Titans (Durban) 2013-14. LO BB 4-21 (*see LOI*). T20 HS 16. T20 BB 3-13.

BALCOMBE, D.J. – *see SURREY.*

BATES, Michael David (Lord Wandsworth C, Hook), b Frimley, Surrey 10 Oct 1990. 5'10". RHB, WK. Hampshire 2010-14. Hampshire 2nd XI debut 2007. Berkshire 2009. England U19s 2009-10. HS 103 v Yorks (Leeds) 2012. LO HS 24* v Warwks (Birmingham) 2011 (CB40). T20 HS 15.

BRATHWAITE, Ruel Marlon Ricardo (Queen's C, Barbados; Dulwich C; Loughborough U; Queens' C, Cambridge), b Bridgetown, Barbados 6 Sep 1985. 6'2". RHB, RFM. British passport. Loughborough UCCE 2006-08. British U 2006. MCC 2007. Cambridge U 2009 (blue). Durham 2010-12. Hampshire 2013. HS 76* LU v Worcs (Worcester) 2007. H HS 17 v Essex (Southampton) 2013. BB 5-54 CU v Oxford U (Cambridge) 2009. CC BB 5-56 Du v Sussex (Chester-le-St) 2011. H BB 3-112 v Northants (Southampton) 2013. LO HS – . LO BB 1-19 WI v EL (Worcester) 2007. T20 HS 0. T20 BB 1-33.

COLES, M.T. – *see KENT.*

^{NQ}**IMRAN TAHIR,** Mohammad (Government Pakistan Angels HS and MAO College, Lahore), b Lahore, Pakistan 4 Jun 1979. 5'11". RHB, LB. Lahore City 1996-97 to 1997-98. WAPDA 1998-99. REDCO 1999-00. Lahore Whites 2000-01. SNGPL 2001-02 to 2003-04. Sialkot 2002-03. Middlesex 2003. Lahore Blues 2004-05. PIA 2004-05 to 2006-07. Lahore Ravi 2005-06. Yorkshire (1 match) 2007. Titans 2007-08 to 2009-10. Hampshire 2008-14; cap 2009. Easterns 2008-09 to 2009-10. Warwickshire 2010; cap 2010. Dolphins 2010-11 to date. Lions 2012-13 to 2013-14. Staffordshire 2004-05. Qualified for SA on 1 Apr 2009. IPL: DD 2014. **Tests** (SA): 16 (2011-12 to 2014-15); HS 29* v SL (Centurion) 2011-12; BB 5-32 v P (Dubai) 2013-14. **LOI** (SA): 36 (2010-11 to 2014-15); HS 23* v Z (Harare) 2014; LO BB 5-45 v WI (Sydney) 2014-15. **IT20** (SA): 16 (2013 to 2014-15); HS 9* and BB 4-21 v Netherlands (Chittagong) 2013-14. F-c Tours (SA): E 2012; A 2012-13; NZ 2011-12; SL 2004-05 (Pak A), 2014; UAE 2013-14 (v P). HS 77* v Somerset (Southampton) 2009. 50 wkts (2+2); most – 74 (2004-05). BB 8-76 REDCO v Karachi Blues (Lahore) 1999-00. UK BB 7-66 (12-189 match) v Lancs (Manchester) 2008 – on H debut. LO HS 41* Staffs v Lancs (Stone) 2004 (CGT). LO BB 5-27 v Sussex (Southampton) 2008 (P40). T20 HS 17*. T20 BB 4-21 (see *IT20*).

MAXWELL, G.J. – *see YORKSHIRE.*

^{NQ}**RIMMINGTON, Nathan** John, b Redcliffe, Queensland, Australia 11 Nov 1982. 5'10". RHB, RFM. Queensland 2005-06 to 2010-11. W Australia 2011-12 to date. Hampshire 2014. HS 102* WA v NSW (Sydney) 2011-12. H HS 65* and H BB 2-51 v Essex (Colchester) 2014. BB 5-27 WA v Q (Perth) 2014-15. LO HS 55 WA v Tas (Sydney) 2014-15. LO BB 4-40 Q v Vic (Melbourne) 2008-09. T20 HS 24*. T20 BB 5-27.

HAMPSHIRE 2014

RESULTS SUMMARY

		Place	Won	Lost	Tied	Drew	NR
LV= County Championship (2nd Division)		1st	7	1		8	
All First-Class Matches			7	1		8	
Royal London One-Day Cup (Group A)		9th	1	5			2
NatWest t20 Blast (South Division)		QF	9	6			

LV= COUNTY CHAMPIONSHIP AVERAGES

BATTING AND FIELDING

Cap		M	I	NO	HS	Runs	Avge	100	50	Ct/St
2013	J.M.Vince	16	28	3	240	1525	61.00	4	7	22
	W.R.Smith	16	27	4	151*	1187	51.60	2	6	12
2013	D.J.Balcombe	4	4	2	65*	91	45.50	–	1	–
2005	S.M.Ervine	16	23	4	121	856	45.05	2	4	13
2006	J.H.K.Adams	16	29	1	231	1215	43.39	1	8	7
2006	M.A.Carberry	12	21	1	125	847	42.35	3	3	5
	A.J.A.Wheater	12	20	1	107	610	32.10	1	3	19/2
	C.P.Wood	4	6	1	61	132	26.40	–	1	1
	M.D.Bates	7	10	3	50	181	25.85	–	1	16/2
2008	J.A.Tomlinson	16	16	10	51	135	22.50	–	1	2
	Imran Tahir	2	4	2	22*	44	22.00	–	–	3
2013	L.A.Dawson	10	18	1	64	354	20.82	–	1	15
2012	D.R.Briggs	8	10	4	38*	116	19.33	–	–	2
	J.S.Gatting	8	12	1	67	191	17.36	–	1	2
	K.J.Abbott	9	10	1	40	127	14.11	–	–	–
	M.T.Coles	15	18	–	83	251	13.94	–	1	6
	T.P.Alsop	2	4	–	33	50	12.50	–	–	2

Also batted: G.J.Maxwell (1 match) 24, 85; N.J.Rimmington (1) 65*, 0; B.J.Taylor (1) 1 (1 ct).

BOWLING

	O	M	R	W	Avge	Best	5wI	10wM
C.P.Wood	83	22	252	15	16.80	5- 39	1	–
K.J.Abbott	251	77	732	36	20.33	5- 44	2	–
J.A.Tomlinson	416.5	103	1215	47	25.85	6- 48	1	–
D.R.Briggs	250.1	73	705	27	26.11	5- 50	1	–
M.T.Coles	353.3	80	1165	41	28.41	4- 84	–	–
L.A.Dawson	175.3	40	529	17	31.11	4- 58	–	–
S.M.Ervine	217	41	686	19	36.10	3- 22	–	–
Also bowled:								
W.R.Smith	33.5	6	114	5	22.80	2- 27	–	–
Imran Tahir	49.4	8	180	6	30.00	3-140	–	–
D.J.Balcombe	63	10	244	5	48.80	3- 53	–	–

M.A.Carberry 5-0-31-0; J.S.Gatting 3-0-22-0; G.J.Maxwell 6-0-33-2; N.J.Rimmington 16-4-51-2; B.J.Taylor 19-3-74-1; J.M.Vince 57-7-190-2.

Hampshire played no first-class fixtures outside the County Championship in 2014. The First-Class Averages (pp 217–233) give the records of Hampshire players in all first-class county matches.

HAMPSHIRE RECORDS

FIRST-CLASS CRICKET

Highest Total	For 714-5d		v	Notts	Southampton	2005
	V 742		by	Surrey	The Oval	1909
Lowest Total	For 15		v	Warwicks	Birmingham	1922
	V 23		by	Yorkshire	Middlesbrough	1965
Highest Innings	For 316	R.H.Moore	v	Warwicks	Bournemouth	1937
	V 303*	G.A.Hick	for	Worcs	Southampton	1997

Highest Partnership for each Wicket

1st	347	V.P.Terry/C.L.Smith	v	Warwicks	Birmingham	1987
2nd	373	J.H.K.Adams/M.A.Carberry	v	Somerset	Taunton	2011
3rd	523	M.A.Carberry/N.D.McKenzie	v	Yorkshire	Southampton	2011
4th	278	J.H.K.Adams/J.M.Vince	v	Yorkshire	Scarborough	2010
5th	235	G.Hill/D.F.Walker	v	Sussex	Portsmouth	1937
6th	411	R.M.Poore/E.G.Wynyard	v	Somerset	Taunton	1899
7th	325	G.Brown/C.H.Abercrombie	v	Essex	Leyton	1913
8th	257	N.Pothas/A.J.Bichel	v	Glos	Cheltenham	2005
9th	230	D.A.Livingstone/A.T.Castell	v	Surrey	Southampton	1962
10th	192	H.A.W.Bowell/W.H.Livsey	v	Worcs	Bournemouth	1921

Best Bowling	For 9- 25	R.M.H.Cottam	v	Lancashire	Manchester	1965
(Innings)	V 10- 46	W.Hickton	for	Lancashire	Manchester	1870
Best Bowling	For 16- 88	J.A.Newman	v	Somerset	Weston-s-Mare	1927
(Match)	V 17-103	W.Mycroft	for	Derbyshire	Southampton	1876

Most Runs – Season	2854	C.P.Mead	(av 79.27)		1928
Most Runs – Career	48892	C.P.Mead	(av 48.84)		1905-36
Most 100s – Season	12	C.P.Mead			1928
Most 100s – Career	138	C.P.Mead			1905-36
Most Wkts – Season	190	A.S.Kennedy	(av 15.61)		1922
Most Wkts – Career	2669	D.Shackleton	(av 18.23)		1948-69
Most Career W-K Dismissals	700	R.J.Parks	(630 ct; 70 st)		1980-92
Most Career Catches in the Field	629	C.P.Mead			1905-36

LIMITED-OVERS CRICKET

Highest Total	50ov	371-4	v	Glamorgan	Southampton	1975
	40ov	353-8	v	Middlesex	Lord's	2005
	T20	225-2	v	Middlesex	Southampton	2006
Lowest Total	50ov	50	v	Yorkshire	Leeds	1991
	40ov	43	v	Essex	Basingstoke	1972
	T20	85	v	Sussex	Southampton	2008
Highest Innings	50ov	177	C.G.Greenidge	v	Glamorgan	Southampton	1975
	40ov	172	C.G.Greenidge	v	Surrey	Southampton	1987
	T20	124*	M.J.Lumb	v	Essex	Southampton	2009
Best Bowling	50ov	7-30	P.J.Sainsbury	v	Norfolk	Southampton	1965
	40ov	6-20	T.E.Jesty	v	Glamorgan	Cardiff	1975
	T20	5-14	A.D.Mascarenhas	v	Sussex	Hove	2004

KENT

Formation of Present Club: 1 March 1859
Substantial Reorganisation: 6 December 1870
Inaugural First-Class Match: 1864
Colours: Maroon and White
Badge: White Horse on a Red Ground
County Champions: (6) 1906, 1909, 1910, 1913, 1970, 1978
Joint Champions: (1) 1977
Gillette Cup Winners: (2) 1967, 1974
Benson and Hedges Cup Winners: (3) 1973, 1976, 1978
Pro 40/National League (Div 1) Winners: (1) 2001
Sunday League Winners: (4) 1972, 1973, 1976, 1995
Twenty20 Cup Winners: (1) 2007

Cricket Chief Executive: Jamie Clifford, The Spitfire Ground, Old Dover Road, Canterbury, CT1 3NZ • Tel: 01227 456886 • Fax: 01227 762168 • Email: feedback.kent@ecb.co.uk • Web: www.kentcricket.co.uk • Twitter : @kentcricket (19,226 followers)

Head Coach: Jimmy Adams. **High Performance Director**: Simon Willis. **Assistant Coach**: Matt Walker. **Captain**: R.W.T.Key. **Vice-Captain**: S.A.Northeast. **Overseas Player**: None. **2015 Beneficiary**: None. **Head Groundsman**: Simon Williamson. **Scorer**: Lorne Hart. ‡ New registration. NQ Not qualified for England.

BALL, Adam James (Beths GS, Bexley) b Greenwich, London 1 March 1993. 6'1". RHB, LFM. Squad No 24. Debut (Kent) 2011. No f-c appearances in 2012. Kent 2nd XI debut 2009, aged 16y 117d. England U19s 2010 to 2010-11. HS 69 v Lancs (Canterbury) 2013. BB 3-36 v Leics (Leicester) 2011. LO HS 28 v Warwks (Birmingham) 2013 (Y40). LO BB 3-36 v Sussex (Horsham) 2013 (Y40). T20 HS 18. T20 BB 2-18.

BELL-DRUMMOND, Daniel James (Millfield S), b Lewisham, London 4 Aug 1993. 6'0". RHB, RMF. Squad No 23. Debut (Kent) 2011. MCC 2014. Kent 2nd XI debut 2009, aged 16y 21d. England U19s 2010 to 2010-11. 1000 runs (1): 1058 (2014). HS 153 v Hants (Southampton) 2014. BB – . LO HS 83 v Sussex (Canterbury) 2014 (RLC). T20 HS 59.

BILLINGS, Samuel William (Haileybury S; Loughborough U), b Pembury 15 Jun 1991. 5'11". RHB, WK. Squad No 20. Loughborough MCCU 2011, scoring 131 v Northants (Loughborough) on f-c debut. Kent debut 2011. Kent 2nd XI debut 2007, aged 15y 349d. HS 131 (*see above*). K HS 92 v Hants (Southampton) 2014. LO HS 143 v Derbys (Canterbury) 2012 (CB40). T20 HS 59.

BLAKE, Alexander James (Hayes SS; Leeds Met U), b Farnborough 25 Jan 1989. 6'1". LHB, RMF. Squad No 10. Debut (Kent) 2008. Leeds/Bradford UCCE 2009-11 (not f-c). HS 105* v Yorks (Leeds) 2010. BB 2-9 v Pakistanis (Canterbury) 2010. CC BB 1-60 v Hants (Southampton) 2010. LO HS 81* v Scotland (Canterbury) 2010 (CB40). LO BB 2-13 v Yorks (Leeds) 2011 (CB40). T20 HS 58*.

CLAYDON, Mitchell Eric (Westfield Sports HS, Sydney), b Fairfield, NSW, Australia 25 Nov 1982. 6'4". LHB, RFM. Squad No 8. Yorkshire 2005-06. Durham 2007-13. Canterbury 2010-11. Kent debut 2013 (on loan). HS 77 v Leics (Leicester) 2014. 50 wkts (1): 59 (2014). BB 6-104 Du v Somerset (Taunton) 2011. K BB 5-61 v Glos (Canterbury) 2014. LO HS 19 Du v Glos (Bristol) 2009 (FPT). LO BB 4-39 Cant v Otago (Timaru) 2010-11. T20 HS 19. T20 BB 5-26.

COLES, Matthew Thomas (Maplesden Noakes S; Mid-Kent C), b Maidstone 26 May 1990. 6'3". LHB, RMF. Squad No 26. Debut (Kent) 2009; cap 2012. Hampshire 2013-14. HS 103* v Yorks (Leeds) 2012. 50 wkts (1): 59 (2012). BB 6-51 v Northants (Northampton) 2012. LO HS 47 v Yorks (Leeds) 2011 (CB40). LO BB 6-32 v Yorks (Leeds) 2012 (CB40). T20 HS 54. T20 BB 3-14.

COWDREY, Fabian Kruuse (Tonbridge S), b Canterbury 30 Jan 1993. Son of C.S.Cowdrey (Kent, Glamorgan, England 1977-92), grandson of M.C.Cowdrey (Kent, Oxford U, England 1950-76), nephew of G.R.Cowdrey (Kent 1984-97). 6'0". RHB, SLA. Squad No 30. Cardiff MCCU 2013. Kent debut 2014. Kent 2nd XI debut 2009, aged 16y 207d. HS 62 CfU v Glamorgan (Cardiff) 2013. K HS 21 and BB 3-59 v Hants (Canterbury) 2014. LO HS 75 v Surrey (Oval) 2014 (RLC). LO BB 2-28 v Glos (Canterbury) 2014 (RLC. T20 HS 55. T20 BB 2-28.

DAVIES, Ryan Christopher (Sandwich TS), b Thanet 5 Nov 1996. 5'9". RHB, WK. Squad No 7. Kent 2nd XI debut 2013. Awaiting 1st XI debut.

DENLY, Joseph Liam (Chaucer TC), b Canterbury 16 Mar 1986. 6'0". RHB, LB. Squad No 6. Kent debut 2004; cap 2008. Middlesex 2012-14; cap 2012. MCC 2013. **LOI**: 9 (2009 to 2009-10); HS 67 v Ireland (Belfast) 2009 – on debut. **IT20**: 5 (2009 to 2009-10); HS 14 and BB 1-9 v SA (Centurion) 2009-10. F-c Tours (Eng A): NZ 2008-09; I 2007-08. 1000 runs (2); most – 1024 (2011). HS 199 v Derbys (Derby) 2011. BB 3-43 v Surrey (Oval) 2011. LO HS 115 v Warwks (Birmingham) 2009 (FPT). LO BB 3-19 Brothers v Abahani (Fatullah) 2014-15. T20 HS 100. T20 BB 1-9.

GRIFFITHS, David Andrew (Sandown HS, IoW), b Newport, IoW 10 Sep 1985. 6'1". LHB, RFM. Squad No 18. Hampshire 2006-13. Kent debut 2014. HS 31* H v Surrey (Southampton) 2007. K HS 12 and BB 6-63 v Glos (Canterbury) 2014. LO HS 12* v Warwks (Birmingham) 2014 (RLC). LO BB 4-29 H v Glos (Southampton) 2009 (P40). T20 HS 18*. T20 BB 4-2.

HAGGETT, Calum John (Millfield S), b Taunton, Somerset 30 Oct 1990. 6'3". LHB, RMF. Squad No 25. Debut (Kent) 2013. Somerset 2nd XI 2009-11. Kent 2nd XI debut 2012. England U19s 2009-10. HS 44* v Glos (Canterbury) 2013. BB 4-94 v Glamorgan (Canterbury) 2013. LO HS 36 and LO BB 2-54 v Durham (Canterbury) 2014 (RLC). T20 HS 2. T20 BB 1-15.

HARMISON, Ben William (Ashington HS), b Ashington, Northumb 9 Jan 1986. Younger brother of S.J.Harmison (Durham, Yorkshire and England 1996-2012). 6'5". LHB, RMF. Squad No 21. Durham 2006-10, scoring 110 v Oxford U (Oxford) on debut. Scored 105 in his second match (v West Indies A) to emulate A.Fairbairn (Middlesex 1947) in scoring hundreds in first two f-c matches, those matches being in England. Kent debut 2012. HS 125 v Glos (Bristol) 2014. BB 4-27 Du v Surrey (Guildford) 2008. K BB 2-26 v Essex (Canterbury) 2014. LO HS 67 Du v Notts (Chester-le-St) 2009 (P40). LO BB 3-40 v Glos (Canterbury) 2014 (RLC). T20 HS 24. T20 BB 3-20.

HARTLEY, Charles Frederick (Millfield S), b Redditch, Worcs 4 Jan 1994. 6'2". RHB, RMF. Squad No 22. Debut (Kent) 2014. Kent 2nd XI debut 2013. HS 2 and BB 2-40 v Leics (Leicester) 2014. LO HS 5 v Sri Lankans (Canterbury) 2014. LO BB 1-51 v New Zealand A (Canterbury) 2014.

HUNN, Matthew David (St Joseph's C, Ipswich), b Colchester, Essex 22 Mar 1994. 6'5". RHB, RMF. Squad No 14. Debut (Kent) 2013. Essex 2nd XI 2012. Kent 2nd XI debut 2013. Suffolk 2011-13. HS 0*. BB 2-51 v Lancs (Canterbury) 2013.

KEY, Robert William Trevor (Colfe's S), b East Dulwich, London 12 May 1979. 6'1". RHB, RM/OB. Squad No 4. Debut (Kent) 1998; cap 2001; captain 2006-12, 2014 to date; benefit 2011. MCC 2002-04, 2009. *Wisden* 2004. **Tests**: 15 (2002 to 2004-05); HS 221 v WI (Lord's) 2004. **LOI**: 5 (2003 to 2004); HS 19 v WI (Lord's) 2004. **IT20**: 1 (2009); HS 10* v Netherlands (Lord's) 2009. F-c Tours: A 2002-03; SA 1998-99 (Eng A), 2004-05; NZ 2008-09 (EL – captain); SL 2002-03 (ECB Acad); Z 1998-99 (Eng A). 1000 runs (7); most – 1896 (2004). HS 270* v Glamorgan (Cardiff) 2009. BB 2-31 v Somerset (Canterbury) 2010. LO HS 144* v Netherlands (Tunbridge W) 2013 (Y40). T20 HS 98*.

NQ**NASH, Brendan** Paul (St Joseph's C, Nudgee), b Attadale, Western Australia 14 Dec 1977. 5'8". LHB, LM. Squad No 40. Queensland 2000-01 to 2006-07. Jamaica 2007-08 to 2011-12. Kent debut 2012; cap 2013. Kolpak signing. **Tests** (WI): 21 (2008-09 to 2011); HS 114 v SA (Basseterre) 2010; BB 1-21 v SL (Galle) 2010-11. **LOI** (WI): 9 (2008 to 2008-09); HS 39* and BB 3-56 v Canada (King City) 2008. F-c Tours (WI): E 2009; A 2009-10; NZ 2008-09; SL 2010-11; B 2010 (WI A). 1000 runs (1): 1110 (2013). HS 207 Jamaica v T&T (St Augustine) 2010-11. K HS 199* v Glos (Cheltenham) 2013. BB 2-7 Jamaica v CC&C (Kingston) 2007-08. K BB 1-2 v Glamorgan (Canterbury) 2012. LO HS 98* v Warwks (Birmingham) 2013 (Y40). LO BB 4-20 Jamaica v Guyana (Bridgetown) 2007-08. T20 HS 26. T20 BB 1-32.

NORTHEAST, Sam Alexander (Harrow S), b Ashford 16 Oct 1989. 5'11". RHB, OB. Squad No 17. Debut (Kent) 2007; cap 2012. MCC 2013. England U19s 2009. HS 176 v Loughborough MCCU (Canterbury) 2011. CC HS 165 v Derbys (Canterbury) 2012. BB 1-60 v Glos (Cheltenham) 2013. LO HS 132 v Somerset (Taunton) 2014 (RLC). T20 HS 75.

QAYYUM, Imran (Villiers HS, Southall; Greenford SFC; City U), b Ealing, Middx 23 May 1993. 6'0". RHB, SLA. Squad No 11. Kent 2nd XI debut 2013. Northamptonshire 2nd XI 2013. Awaiting 1st XI debut.

RILEY, Adam Edward Nicholas (Beths GS, Bexley; Loughborough U), b Sidcup 23 Mar 1992. 6'2". RHB, OB. Squad No 33. Debut (Kent) 2011. Loughborough MCCU 2012-14. Kent 2nd XI debut 2010. F-c Tour (EL): SA 2014-15. HS 23* v Glamorgan (Cardiff) 2014. 50 wkts (1): 57 (2014). BB 7-150 v Hants (Southampton) 2013. LO HS 5* v New Zealand A (Canterbury) 2014. LO BB 2-32 v Sussex (Hove) 2011 (CB40). T20 HS 5*. T20 BB 4-22.

STEVENS, Darren Ian (Hinckley C), b Leicester 30 Apr 1976. 5'11". RHB, RM. Squad No 3. Leicestershire 1997-2004; cap 2002. MCC 2002. Kent debut/cap 2005. F-c Tour (ECB Acad): SL 2002-03. 1000 runs (3); most – 1304 (2013). HS 208 v Glamorgan (Canterbury) 2005 and 208 v Middx (Uxbridge) 2009. 50 wkts (1): 56 (2014). BB 7-21 (11-70 match) v Surrey (Canterbury) 2011. LO HS 133 Le v Northumb (Jesmond) 2000 (NWT). LO BB 5-32 v Scotland (Edinburgh) 2005 (NL). T20 HS 77. T20 BB 4-14.

THOMAS, Ivan Alfred Astley (John Roan S, Blackheath; Leeds U), b Greenwich, London 25 Sep 1991. 6'4". RHB, RMF. Squad No 5. Leeds/Bradford MCCU 2012-14. Kent debut 2012. Kent 2nd XI debut 2011. HS 11 LBU v Yorks (Leeds) 2012. BB 3-39 LBU v Somerset (Taunton) 2014. K HS 0* and K BB 2-29 v Essex (Chelmsford) 2012. LO HS 1 v New Zealand A (Canterbury) 2014. LO BB – .

TREDWELL, James Cullum (Southlands Community CS, New Romney), b Ashford 27 Feb 1982. 6'0". LHB, OB. Squad No 15. Debut (Kent) 2001; cap 2007; captain 2013. Sussex (on loan) 2014. MCC 2004, 2008. **Tests**: 1 (2009-10); HS 37 and BB 4-82 v B (Dhaka) 2009-10. **LOI**: 45 (2009-10 to 2014-15); HS 30 v I (Nottingham) 2014; BB 4-41 v Scotland (Aberdeen) 2014. **IT20**: 17 (2012-13 to 2014); HS 22 and BB 1-16 v WI (Bridgetown) 2013-14. F-c Tours: NZ 2012-13 (*part*); I 2003-04 (Eng A, captain); B 2009-10. HS 123* v New Zealanders (Canterbury) 2008. CC HS 116* v Yorks (Tunbridge W) 2007. 50 wkts (1): 69 (2009). BB 8-66 (11-120 match) v Glamorgan (Canterbury) 2009. LO HS 88 v Surrey (Oval) 2007 (FPT). LO BB 6-27 v Middx (Southgate) 2009 (FPT). T20 HS 34*. T20 BB 4-21.

WELLER, Sam David (Millfield S; Oxford Brookes U), b Chislehurst 21 Nov 1994. 6'2". RHB, RFM. Squad No 19. Oxford MCCU 2014. Kent 2nd XI debut 2011. Awaiting 1st XI debut. HS 18* and BB 3-66 OU v Warwicks (Oxford) 2014.

RELEASED/RETIRED

(Having made a 1st XI appearance in 2014)

NQ**BOLLINGER, Douglas** Erwin (Newman C, WA; Greystanes, NSW), b Baulkham Hills, Sydney, Australia 24 July 1981. 6'4" LHB, LFM. NSW 2002-03 to date. Worcestershire 2007; cap 2007. Kent 2014. IPL: CSK 2009-12. Big Bash: ST 2011-12. HH 2012-13 to date. SS 2014-15. **Tests** (A): 12 (2008-09 to 2010-11); HS 21 v P (Lord's) 2010; BB 5-28 v NZ (Wellington) 2009-10. **LOI** (A): 39 (2009 to 2011-12); HS 30 v E (Hobart) 2010-11; BB 5-35 v P (Abu Dhabi) 2009 and v I (Guwahati) 2009-10. **IT20** (A): 9 (2011-12 to 2014-15) HS 1* v I (Dhaka) 2013-14; BB 1-22 v SA (Adelaide) 2014-15. F-c Tours (A): E 2010; SA 2008-09; NZ 2009-10; I 2008-09 (Aus A), 2010-11; P 2007-08 (Aus A). HS 41* NSW v Tas (Hobart) 2014-15. K HS 33* v Hants (Canterbury) 2014. BB 6-47 NSW v S Aus (Sydney) 2008-09. K BB 5-29 v Derbys (Derby) 2014. LO HS 30 (*see LOI*). LO BB 5-35 (*see LOI*). T20 HS 17. T20 BB 4-13.

JONES, G.O. – *see GLOUCESTERSHIRE.*

JOSEPH, Robert ('Robbie') Hartman (Sutton Valence S; St Mary's C, Twickenham), b Antigua 20 Jan 1982. Resided in England since 1997. 6'1". RHB, RFM. Debut (First-Class Counties XI v NZ) 2000. Kent 2004-14. Leeward Is. Leicestershire 2012. F-c Tour (EL): NZ 2008-09. HS 36* v Sussex (Hove) 2007. 50 wkts (1): 55 (2008). BB 6-32 v Durham (Chester-le-St) 2008. LO HS 15 v Sussex (Canterbury) 2005 (NL). LO BB 5-13 v Derbys (Canterbury) 2008 (P40). T20 HS 1*. T20 BB 2-14.

M.Davies left the staff without making a 1st XI appearance in 2014.

KENT 2014

RESULTS SUMMARY

	Place	Won	Lost	Tied	Drew	NR
LV= County Championship (2nd Division)	6th	4	6		6	
All First-Class Matches		4	6		7	
Royal London One-Day Cup (Group B)	SF	5	2	1		2
NatWest t20 Blast (South Division)	6th	6	7	1		

LV= COUNTY CHAMPIONSHIP AVERAGES

BATTING AND FIELDING

Cap		M	I	NO	HS	Runs	Avge	100	50	Ct/St
	D.J.Bell-Drummond	16	28	3	153	955	38.20	2	6	5
2012	S.A.Northeast	14	24	1	128	872	37.91	4	4	5
2013	B.P.Nash	15	25	2	126	839	36.47	1	4	8
2005	D.I.Stevens	16	26	2	105	859	35.79	1	4	14
	S.W.Billings	16	24	2	92	755	34.31	–	7	50/6
	A.J.Ball	8	10	2	50	268	33.50	–	1	5
	B.W.Harmison	15	24	–	125	642	26.75	1	1	12
	D.E.Bollinger	8	9	5	33*	91	22.75	–	–	4
2001	R.W.T.Key	15	26	1	126	561	22.44	1	2	5
	C.J.Haggett	4	7	–	44	119	17.00	–	–	–
	M.E.Claydon	15	22	2	77	291	14.55	–	1	1
	R.H.Joseph	6	7	2	29*	70	14.00	–	–	2
	F.K.Cowdrey	4	7	–	21	85	12.14	–	–	1
	A.E.N.Riley	15	20	9	23*	132	12.00	–	–	10
2007	J.C.Tredwell	4	7	–	29	81	11.57	–	–	9

Also batted: D.A.Griffiths (1 match) 12, 6; C.F.Hartley (2) 2, 0, 0; M.D.Hunn (2) 0, 0*, 0* (1 ct).

BOWLING

	O	M	R	W	Avge	Best	5wI	10wM
D.E.Bollinger	241.4	54	713	27	26.40	5- 29	2	–
D.I.Stevens	515.4	121	1517	56	27.08	6- 64	6	–
M.E.Claydon	506.5	90	1711	55	31.10	5- 61	3	–
A.E.N.Riley	460.4	79	1564	48	32.58	5- 78	2	–
R.H.Joseph	142	30	464	12	38.66	3- 43	–	–
J.C.Tredwell	139	22	426	11	38.72	4-102	–	–
Also bowled:								
D.A.Griffiths	27.3	5	85	6	14.16	6- 63	1	–
C.F.Hartley	48	6	190	5	38.00	2- 40	–	–
A.J.Ball	82.2	8	335	5	67.00	1- 9	–	–
C.J.Haggett	94	9	353	5	70.60	2- 48	–	–

S.W.Billings 0.1-0-4-0; F.K.Cowdrey 12.4-1-59-3; B.W.Harmison 35.1-3-141-3; M.D.Hunn 36-6-155-3; R.W.T.Key 2-0-12-0; B.P.Nash 25-3-100-1; S.A.Northeast 1-0-4-0.

The First-Class Averages (pp 217–233) give the records of Kent players in all first-class county matches (Kent's other opponents being Loughborough MCCU), with the exception of A.E.N.Riley and J.C.Tredwell, whose first-class figures for Kent are as above.

KENT RECORDS
FIRST-CLASS CRICKET

Highest Total	For 803-4d		v	Essex	Brentwood	1934
	V 676		by	Australians	Canterbury	1921
Lowest Total	For 18		v	Sussex	Gravesend	1867
	V 16		by	Warwicks	Tonbridge	1913
Highest Innings	For 332	W.H.Ashdown	v	Essex	Brentwood	1934
	V 344	W.G.Grace	for	MCC	Canterbury	1876

Highest Partnership for each Wicket

1st	300	N.R.Taylor/M.R.Benson	v	Derbyshire	Canterbury	1991
2nd	366	S.G.Hinks/N.R.Taylor	v	Middlesex	Canterbury	1990
3rd	323	R.W.T.Key/M.van Jaarsveld	v	Surrey	Tunbridge Wells	2005
4th	368	P.A.de Silva/G.R.Cowdrey	v	Derbyshire	Maidstone	1995
5th	277	F.E.Woolley/L.E.G.Ames	v	N Zealanders	Canterbury	1931
6th	315	P.A.de Silva/M.A.Ealham	v	Notts	Nottingham	1995
7th	248	A.P.Day/E.Humphreys	v	Somerset	Taunton	1908
8th	177	G.O.Jones/Yasir Arafat	v	Warwicks	Canterbury	2007
9th	171	M.A.Ealham/P.A.Strang	v	Notts	Nottingham	1997
10th	235	F.E.Woolley/A.Fielder	v	Worcs	Stourbridge	1909

Best Bowling	For 10- 30	C.Blythe	v	Northants	Northampton	1907
(Innings)	V 10- 48	C.H.G.Bland	for	Sussex	Tonbridge	1899
Best Bowling	For 17- 48	C.Blythe	v	Northants	Northampton	1907
(Match)	V 17-106	T.W.J.Goddard	for	Glos	Bristol	1939

Most Runs – Season	2894	F.E.Woolley	(av 59.06)	1928
Most Runs – Career	47868	F.E.Woolley	(av 41.77)	1906-38
Most 100s – Season	10	F.E.Woolley		1928, 1934
Most 100s – Career	122	F.E.Woolley		1906-38
Most Wkts – Season	262	A.P.Freeman	(av 14.74)	1933
Most Wkts – Career	3340	A.P.Freeman	(av 17.64)	1914-36
Most Career W-K Dismissals	1253	F.H.Huish	(901 ct; 352 st)	1895-1914
Most Career Catches in the Field	773	F.E.Woolley		1906-38

LIMITED-OVERS CRICKET

Highest Total	50ov	384-6		v	Berkshire	Finchampstead	1994
	40ov	337-7		v	Sussex	Canterbury	2013
	T20	217		v	Glos	Gloucester	2010
Lowest Total	50ov	60		v	Somerset	Taunton	1979
	40ov	83		v	Middlesex	Lord's	1984
	T20	72		v	Hampshire	Southampton	2011
Highest Innings	50ov	143	C.J.Tavaré	v	Somerset	Taunton	1985
	40ov	146	A.Symonds	v	Lancashire	Tunbridge Wells	2004
	T20	112	A.Symonds	v	Middlesex	Maidstone	2004
Best Bowling	50ov	8-31	D.L.Underwood	v	Scotland	Edinburgh	1987
	40ov	6- 9	R.A.Woolmer	v	Derbyshire	Chesterfield	1979
	T20	5-17	Wahab Riaz	v	Glos	Beckenham	2011

LANCASHIRE

Formation of Present Club: 12 January 1864
Inaugural First-Class Match: 1865
Colours: Red, Green and Blue
Badge: Red Rose
County Champions (since 1890): (8) 1897, 1904, 1926,
1927,1928, 1930, 1934, 2011
Joint Champions: (1) 1950
Gillette/NatWest Trophy Winners: (7) 1970, 1971, 1972,
1975, 1990, 1996, 1998
Benson and Hedges Cup Winners: (4) 1984, 1990, 1995,
1996
Pro 40/National League (Div 1) Winners: (1) 1999.
Sunday League Winners: (4) 1969, 1970, 1989, 1998
Twenty20 Cup Winners: (0); best – Finalist 2005, 2014

Chief Executive: Daniel Gidney, Emirates Old Trafford, Talbot Road, Manchester M16
0PX • Tel: 0161 282 4000 • Fax: 0161 282 4100 • Email: enquiries@lccc.co.uk • Web:
www.lccc.co.uk • Twitter : @LancsCCC (33,093 followers)

Cricket Director/Head Coach: Ashley Giles. **Player/Coach**: Glen Chapple. **Assistant
Coach**: Gary Yates. **Captain**: T.C.Smith. **Vice-Captain**: S.J.Croft. **Overseas Player**:
P.M.Siddle. **2015 Beneficiary**: None. **Head Groundsman**: Matthew Merchant. **Scorer**:
Darrin White. ‡ New registration. [NQ] Not qualified for England.

ANDERSON, James Michael (St Theodore RC HS and SFC, Burnley), b Burnley 30 Jul
1982. 6'2". LHB, RFM. Squad No 9. Debut (Lancashire) 2002; cap 2003; benefit 2012. YC
2003. *Wisden* 2008. **ECB central contract 2014-15. Tests**: 99 (2003 to 2014); HS 81 v I
(Nottingham) 2014, sharing a world Test record 10th wkt partnership of 198 with J.E.Root;
BB 7-43 v NZ (Nottingham) 2008. **LOI**: 194 (2002-03 to 2014-15); HS 28 v NZ
(Southampton) 2013; BB 5-23 v SA (Port Elizabeth) 2009-10. Hat-trick v P (Oval) 2003 –
1st for E in 373 LOI. **IT20**: 19 (2006-07 to 2009-10); HS 1* v A (Sydney) 2006-07; BB
3-23 v Netherlands (Lord's) 2009. F-c Tours: A 2006-07, 2010-11, 2013-14; SA 2004-05,
2009-10; WI 2003-04, 2005-06 (Eng A) (*part*), 2008-09; NZ 2007-08, 2012-13; I 2005-06
(*part*), 2008-09, 2012-13; SL 2003-04, 2007-08, 2011-12; UAE 2011-12 (v P). HS 81 (*see
Tests*). La HS 37* v Durham (Manchester) 2005. 50 wkts (3); most – 60 (2005). BB 7-43
(*see Tests*). La BB 6-23 v Hants (Southampton) 2002. Hat-trick v Essex (Manchester) 2003.
LO HS 28 (*see LOI*). LO BB 5-23 (*see LOI*). T20 HS 16. T20 BB 3-23.

BAILEY, Thomas Ernest (Our Lady's Catholic HS, Preston), b Preston 21 Apr 1991. 6'4".
RHB, RMF. Squad No 8. Debut (Lancashire) 2012. Lancashire 2nd XI debut 2011. HS 25*
v Yorks (Manchester) 2014. BB 2-36 v Middx (Manchester) 2014. LO HS 4* v Worcs
(Worcester) 2014 (RLC). LO BB 3-41 v Derbys (Derby) 2014 (RLC).

BROWN, Karl Robert (Hesketh Fletcher HS, Atherton), b Bolton 17 May 1988. 5'10".
RHB, RMF. Squad No 14. Debut (Lancashire) 2006. Moors Sports Club 2011-12. HS 114 v
Sussex (Liverpool) 2011. BB 2-30 v Notts (Nottingham) 2009. LO HS 129 v Yorks
(Manchester) 2014 (RLC). T20 HS 67*.

‡**BUCK, Nathan** Liam (Newbridge HS; Ashby S), b Leicester 26 Apr 1991. 6'2" RHB, RMF. Squad No 11. Leicestershire 2009-14; cap 2011. Leicestershire 2nd XI debut 2008. England U19s 2009 to 2009-10. F-c Tour (EL): WI 2010-11. HS 29* Le v Worcs (Worcester) 2014. BB 5-76 Le v Essex (Chelmsford) 2014. LO HS 21 Le v Glamorgan (Leicester) 2009 (P40). LO BB 4-39 EL v Sri Lanka A (Dambulla) 2011-12. T20 HS 8*. T20 BB 3-16.

BUTTLER, Joseph Charles (King's C, Taunton), b Taunton, Somerset 8 Sep 1990. 6'0". RHB, WK. Squad No 6. Somerset 2009-13; cap 2013.Lancashire debut 2014. Big Bash: MR 2013-14. **ECB Central Contract 2014-15. Tests**: 3 (2014); HS 85 v I (Southampton) 2014. **LOI**: 55 (2011-12 to 2014-15); HS 121 v SL (Lord's) 2014. **IT20**: 37 (2011 to 2014); HS 67 v WI (Bridgetown) 2013-14. HS 144 Sm v Hants (Southampton) 2010. La HS 100* v Durham (Chester-le-St) 2014. BB – . LO HS 121 (*see LOI*). T20 HS 72*.

CHAPPLE, Glen (West Craven HS; Nelson & Colne C), b Skipton, Yorks 23 Jan 1974. 6'1". RHB, RMF. Squad No 3. Debut (Lancashire) 1992; cap 1994; benefit 2004; captain 2009-14. *Wisden* 2011. **LOI**: 1 (2006); HS 14 and BB – v Ireland (Belfast) 2006. F-c Tours (Eng A): A 1996-97; WI 1995-96 (La); I 1994-95. HS 155 v Somerset (Manchester) 2001. Scored 100 off 27 balls in contrived circumstances v Glamorgan (Manchester) 1993. 50 wkts (7); most – 57 (2011). BB 7-53 v Durham (Blackpool) 2007. LO HS 81* v Derbys (Manchester) 2002 (CGT). LO BB 6-18 v Essex (Lord's) 1996 (NWT) – La record. T20 HS 55*. T20 BB 3-36.

CLARK, Jordan (Sedbergh S), b Whitehaven, Cumbria 14 Oct 1990. 6'4". Elder brother of G.Clark (*see DURHAM*). RHB, RM, occ WK. Squad No 16. Awaiting f-c debut. Lancashire 2nd XI debut 2008. Cumberland 2007-08. LO HS 72 v Durham (Chester-le-St) 2013 (Y40). LO BB 2-41 v Derbys (Derby) 2014 (RLC). T20 HS 44. T20 BB 4-22.

CROFT, Steven John (Highfield HS, Blackpool; Myerscough C), b Blackpool 11 Oct 1984. 5'10". RHB, RMF. Squad No 15. Debut (Lancashire) 2005; cap 2010. Auckland 2008-09. HS 156 v Northants (Manchester) 2014. BB 6-41 v Worcs (Manchester) 2012. LO HS 107 v Somerset (Taunton) 2011 (CB40). LO BB 4-24 v Scotland (Manchester) 2008 (FPT). T20 HS 88. T20 BB 3-6.

DAVIES, Alexander Luke (Queen Elizabeth GS, Blackburn), b Darwen 23 Aug 1994. 5'7". RHB, WK. Squad No 17. Debut (Lancashire) 2012, without batting or bowling. Lancashire 2nd XI debut 2011. HS 62 v Somerset (Manchester) 2014. LO HS 53 v Derbys (Derby) 2014 (RLC). T20 HS 7.

‡**EDWARDS, George** Alexander (St Joseph C, Croydon), b King's College H, Camberwell, London 29 Jul 1992. 6'3". RHB, RFM. Squad No 22. Surrey 2011-13. Surrey 2nd XI debut 2009, aged 16y 322d. HS 19 Sy v Cambridge MCCU (Cambridge) 2011. CC HS 17 and BB 4-44 Sy v Worcs (Worcester) 2012. LO HS 8* Sy v Glamorgan (Guildford) 2014 (RLC). LO BB 1-29 Sy v Durham (Chester-le-St) 2014 (RLC). T20 BB – .

122

FLINTOFF, Andrew (Ribbleton Hall HS), b Preston 6 Dec 1977. 6'4". RHB, RFM. Squad No 26. Debut (Lancashire) 1995; cap 1998; benefit 2006. IPL: CSK 2009. Big Bash: BH 2014-15. YC 1998. *Wisden* 2003. PCA 2004, 2005. MBE 2005. BBC Sports Personality of 2005. **Tests**: 78 (1998 to 2009, 11 as captain); HS 167 v WI (Birmingham) 2004; BB 5-58 v WI (Bridgetown) 2003-04. Also played 'Test' for ICC v A. **LOI**: 138 (1998-99 to 2008-09, 14 as captain); HS 123 v WI (Lord's) 2004; BB 5-19 v WI (Gros Islet) 2008-09. Also played 3 LOIs for ICC v A. **IT20**: 7 (2005 to 2007-08); HS 31 v A (Cape Town) 2007-08; BB 2-23 v SA (Cape Town) 2007-08. F-c Tours (C=Captain): A 2002-03 (*part*), 2006-07C; SA 1998-99 (Eng A), 1999-00, 2004-05; WI 2003-04; SL 1998-99; NZ 2001-02; I 2001-02, 2005-06C, 2008-09; P 2000-01 (*part*), 2005-06; SL 1997-98 (Eng A), 2003-04; Z 1998-99 (Eng A); K 1997-98 (Eng A). HS 167 (*see Tests*). La HS 160 v Yorks (Manchester) 1999. BB 5-24 v Hants (Southampton) 1999. LO HS 143 (off 66 balls) v Essex (Chelmsford) 1999 (NL) – La record. LO BB 5-19 (*see LOI*). T20 HS 93. T20 BB 4-12.

GRIFFITHS, Gavin Timothy (St Mary's C, Crosby), b Ormskirk 19 Nov 1993. 6'2". RHB, RFM. Squad No 18. Lancashire 2nd XI debut 2011. Awaiting f-c debut. England U19s 2012-13. LO BB – .

HAMEED, Haseem (Bolton S), b Bolton 17 Jan 1997. 6'2". RHB, LB. Squad No 23. Lancashire 2nd XI debut 2013. Awaiting 1st XI debut.

HORTON, Paul James (St Margaret's HS, Liverpool), b Sydney, Australia 20 Sep 1982. 5'10". RHB, RM. Squad No 20. UK resident since 1997. Debut (Lancashire) 2003; cap 2007. Matabeleland Tuskers 2010-11 to 2011-12. 1000 runs (3); most – 1116 (2007). HS 209 MT v SR (Masvingo) 2010-11. La HS 173 v Somerset (Taunton) 2009. LO HS 111* v Derbys (Manchester) 2009 (FPT). T20 HS 71*.

[NQ]**JARVIS, Kyle** Malcolm (St John's C, Harare), b Harare, Zimbabwe 16 Feb 1989. Son of M.P.Jarvis (Zimbabwe 1979-80 to 1994-95). 6'4". RHB, RFM. Squad No 27. Mashonaland Eagles 2009-10 to 2012-13. C Districts 2011-12 to 2012-13. Lancashire debut 2013. **Tests** (Z): 8 (2011 to 2013); HS 25* v P (Bulawayo) 2011; BB 5-54 v WI (Bridgetown) 2012-13. **LOI** (Z): 24 (2009-10 to 2013); HS 13 v SA (Centurion) 2009-10; BB 3-36 v Kenya (Harare) 2009-10. **IT20** (Z): 9 (2011 to 2012-13); HS 9* v SA (Hambantota) 2012-13; BB 3-15 v P (Harare) 2011. F-c Tour (Z): WI 2012-13. HS 48 ME v MWR (Harare) 2012-13. La HS 3* and La BB 3-72 v Kent (Canterbury) 2013. BB 7-35 ME v MT (Bulawayo) 2012-13. LO HS 33 MWR v Mountaineers (Kwekwe) 2014-15. LO BB 4-35 ME v Mountaineers (Mutare) 2011-12. T20 HS 10. T20 BB 3-15.

KERRIGAN, Simon Christopher (Corpus Christi RC HS, Preston), b Preston 10 May 1989. 5'9". RHB, SLA. Squad No 10. Debut (Lancashire) 2010; cap 2013. MCC 2013. **Tests**: 1 (2013); HS 1* and BB – v A (Oval) 2013. F-c Tour (EL): SL 2013-14. HS 62* v Hants (Southport) 2013. 50 wkts (2); most – 58 (2013). BB 9-51 (12-192 match) v Hants (Liverpool) 2011. LO HS 10 v Middx (Lord's) 2012 (CB40). LO BB 3-21 EL v Sri Lanka A (Northampton) 2011. T20 HS 4*. T20 BB 3-17.

LILLEY, Arron Mark (Mossley Hollins HS; Ashton SFC), b Tameside 1 Apr 1991. 6'1". RHB, OB. Squad No 19. Debut (Lancashire) 2013. Lancashire 2nd XI debut 2010. HS 35* v Glamorgan (Manchester) 2013. BB 1-41 v Worcs (Worcester) 2013. LO HS 10 v Hants (Manchester) 2013 (Y40). LO BB 4-30 v Derbys (Manchester) 2013 (Y40). T20 HS 18. T20 BB 2-28.

LIVINGSTONE, Liam Stephen (Chetwynde S, Barrow-in-Furness), b Barrow-in-Furness, Cumberland 4 Aug 1993. 6'1". RHB, LB. Squad No 7. Lancashire 2nd XI debut 2012. Cumberland 2011. Awaiting 1st XI debut.

MAHMOOD, Saqib (Matthew Moss HS, Rochdale), b Birmingham 25 Feb 1997. 6'3''. RHB, RFM. Squad No 25. England U19s 2014. Awaiting 1st XI debut.

PARKINSON, Matthew William (Bolton S), b Bolton 24 Oct 1996. 6'0''. RHB, LB. Squad No 28. Lancashire 2nd XI debut. Staffordshire 2014. Awaiting 1st XI debut.

PARRY, Stephen David (Audenshaw HS), b Manchester 12 Jan 1986. 6'0''. RHB, SLA. Squad No 4. Debut (Lancashire) 2007, taking 5-23 v Durham U (Durham). No 1st XI appearances in 2008. Cumberland 2005-06. Big Bash: BH 2014-15. **LOI**: 2 (2013-14); HS – ; BB 3-32 v WI (North Sound) 2013-14. **IT20**: 3 (2013-14); HS 1 v Netherlands (Chittagong) 2013-14; BB – . HS 37 v Durham (Manchester) 2014. CC BB 3-51 v Kent (Canterbury) 2013. BB 5-23 (*see above*). LO HS 31 v Essex (Chelmsford) 2009 (FPT). LO BB 5-17 v Surrey (Manchester) 2013 (Y40). T20 HS 11. T20 BB 4-23.

‡^{NQ}**PETERSEN, Alviro** Nathan, b Port Elizabeth, South Africa 25 November 1980. RHB, RM/OB. Northerns 2000-01 to 2005-06. Titans 2004-05 to 2005-06. Lions 2005-06 to date. North West 2008-09. Glamorgan 2011; cap/captain 2011. Essex 2012. Somerset 2013-14; cap 2013. **Tests** (SA): 36 (2009-10 to 2014-15); HS 182 v E (Leeds) 2012; scored 100 v I (Kolkata) on debut; BB 1-2 v WI (Port of Spain) 2010. **LOI** (SA): 21 (2006-07 to 2013); HS 80 v Z (Potchefstroom) 2006-07; BB – . **IT20** (SA): 2 (2010); HS 8 v WI (North Sound) 2010. F-c Tours (SA): E 2012; A 2012-13; WI 2010; NZ 2011-12; I 2007-08 (SA A), 2009-10; SL 2014; Z 2007 (SA A), 2014; B 2010 (SA A); UAE (v P) 2010-11, 2013-14. 1000 runs (1+2); most – 1376 (2008-09). HS 210 Gm v Surrey (Oval) 2011. BB 3-58 Lions v Warriors (Port Elizabeth) 2013-14. CC BB 1-27 Sm v Sussex (Taunton) 2013. LO HS 145* Lions v Dolphins (Potchefstroom) 2011-12. LO BB 2-48 Lions v Cape Cobras (Johannesburg) 2011-12. T20 HS 84*. T20 BB 1-4.

^{NQ}**PRINCE, Ashwell** Gavin (St Thomas Senior SS, UPE), b Port Elizabeth, South Africa, 28 May 1977. 5'8''. LHB, OB. Squad No 5. E Province 1995-96 to 1997-98. W Province 1997-98 to 2003-04. W Province-Boland 2004-05. Cape Cobras 2005-06 to 2007-08. Nottinghamshire 2008. Warriors 2008-09 to 2013-14. Lancashire debut 2009; cap 2010. **Tests** (SA): 66 (2001-02 to 2011-12, 2 as captain); HS 162* v B (Centurion) 2008-09; BB 1-2 v NZ (Cape Town) 2006. **LOI** (SA): 52 (2002-03 to 2007); HS 89* v WI (Port of Spain) 2005; BB – . **IT20** (SA): 1 (2005-06); HS 5 v NZ (Johannesburg) 2005-06. F-c Tours (SA): E 2008; A 2005-06; WI 2000 (SA A), 2005, 2010; I 2007-08, 2009-10; P 2007-08; SL 2006; Z 2007 (SA A); B 2007-08; UAE 2010-11 (v P). 1000 runs (3+1): 1180 (2008-09). HS 257* v Northants (Manchester) 2014. BB 2-11 SA v Middx (Uxbridge) 2008. CC BB – . LO HS 128 Warriors v Dolphins (East London) 2009-10. LO BB – . T20 HS 74. T20 BB – .

PROCTER, Luke Anthony (Counthill S, Oldham), b Oldham 24 June 1988. 5'11''. LHB, RM. Squad No 2. Debut (Lancashire) 2010. Cumberland 2007. HS 106 v Glos (Bristol) 2013. BB 7-71 v Surrey (Liverpool) 2012. LO HS 97 v West Indies A (Manchester) 2010. LO BB 3-29 v Unicorns (Colwyn Bay) 2010 (CB40). T20 HS 25*. T20 BB 3-22.

REECE, Luis Michael (St Michael's HS, Chorley; Leeds Met U), b Taunton, Somerset 4 Aug 1990. 6'1''. LHB, LM. Squad No 21. Leeds/Bradford MCCU 2012-13. Lancashire debut 2013. MCC 2014. Lancashire 2nd XI debut 2008. Unicorns 2011-12. HS 114* and BB 4-28 LBU v Leics (Leicester) 2013. La HS 97 v Glos (Bristol) 2013. La BB 1-20 v Hants (Southport) 2013. LO HS 59 Unicorns v Derbys (Chesterfield) 2012 (CB40). LO BB 4-35 Unicorns v Glos (Exmouth) 2011 (CB40).

‡NQSIDDLE, Peter Matthew, b Traralgon, Victoria, Australia 25 Nov 1984. 6'1½". RHB, RFM. Victoria 2005-06 to date. Nottinghamshire 2014; cap 2014. Big Bash: MR 2013-14 to date. Tests (A): 56 (2008-09 to 2014-15); HS 51 v I (Delhi) 2012-13; BB 6-54 v E (Brisbane) 2010-11. LOI (A): 17 (2008-09 to 2010-11); HS 9* v SL (Sydney) 2010-11; BB 3-55 v E (Centurion) 2009-10. IT20 (A): 2 (2008-09 to 2010-11); HS 1* and BB 2-24 v NZ (Sydney) 2008-09. F-c Tours (A): E 2009, 2013; SA 2008-09, 2011-12, 2013-14; WI 2011-12; I 2008-09 (Aus A), 2008-09, 2012-13; SL 2011; Z 2011 (Aus A); UAE 2014-15 (v P). HS 103* Aus A v Scotland (Edinburgh) 2013. CC HS 48* Nt v Yorks (Leeds) 2014. 50 wkts (0+1): 54 (2011-12). BB 8-54 Vic v S Aus (Adelaide) 2014-15. CC BB 4-61 Nt v Northants (Nottingham) 2014. LO HS 25* Vic v Tas (Hobart) 2010-11. LO BB 4-27 Vic v Tas (Hobart) 2008-09. T20 HS 9*. T20 BB 4-29.

SMITH, Thomas Christopher (Parkland HS, Chorley; Runshaw C, Leyland), b Liverpool 26 Dec 1985. 6'3". LHB, RMF. Squad No 24. Debut (Lancashire) 2005; cap 2010; captain 2015. Leicestershire (on loan) 2008. F-c Tour (Eng A): B 2006-07. HS 128 v Hants (Southampton) 2010. 50 wkts (1): 54 (2014). BB 6-46 v Yorks (Manchester) 2009. LO HS 117 and LO BB 4-48 v Notts (Nottingham) 2011 (CB40). T20 HS 92*. T20 BB 3-12.

RELEASED/RETIRED

(Having made a 1st XI appearance in 2014)

AGATHANGELOU, Andrea Peter (Fields C, Rustenburg), b Rustenburg, South Africa 16 Nov 1989. 6'3". RHB, LB. North West 2007-08 to 2010-11. Lions 2008-09. Lancashire 2011-14. HS 158 NW v KZN (Potchefstroom) 2009-10. La HS 121 v Hants (Southampton) 2013. BB 2-18 v Glos (Liverpool) 2013. LO HS 94 NW v EP (Port Elizabeth) 2010-11. LO BB – . T20 HS 21.

ALI, Kabir (Moseley CS and SFC), b Moseley, Birmingham, Warwks 24 Nov 1980. 6'0". Cousin of A.K.Ali (Worcs, Glos 2000-10) and M.M.Ali (see WORCESTERSHIRE). RHB, RMF. Worcestershire 1999-2009. Rajasthan 2006-07. Hampshire 2010-12. Lancashire 2014. Tests: 1 (2003); HS 9 and BB 3-80 v SA (Leeds) 2003. LOI: 14 (2003 to 2006); HS 39* v P (Rawalpindi) 2005-06; BB 4-45 v I (Delhi) 2005-06. F-c Tours: WI 2005-06 (Eng A); SL 2002-03 (ECB Acad). HS 84* Wo v Durham (Stockton) 2003. La HS 26 v Durham (Chester-le-St) 2014. 50 wkts (5); most – 71 (2002). BB 8-50 Wo v Lancs (Manchester) 2007. Took 8-53 before lunch first day Wo v Yorks (Scarborough) 2003. La BB 3-17 v Northants (Northampton) 2014. LO HS 92 Wo v Essex (Worcester) 2003 (NL). LO BB 5-36 Wo v Yorks (Leeds) 2002 (NL). T20 HS 50. T20 BB 4-44.

HOGG, Kyle William (Saddleworth HS), b Birmingham, Warwks 2 Jul 1983. Son of W.Hogg (Lancashire, Warwickshire 1976-83); grandson of S.Ramadhin (Trinidad, Lancashire and West Indies 1949-50 to 1965). 6'4". LHB, RFM. Lancashire 2001-14; cap 2010. Otago 2006-07. Worcestershire 2007 (on loan). Nottinghamshire 2007 (on loan). MCC 2014. F-c Tour (ECB Acad): SL 2002-03. HS 88 v Yorks (Manchester) 2010. 50 wkts (2); most – 60 (2013). BB 7-27 v Northants (Manchester) 2013. LO HS 66* v Scotland (Manchester) 2008 (FPT). LO BB 4-20 v Hants (Southampton) 2002 (NL). T20 HS 44. T20 BB 2-10.

RELEASED/RETIRED continued on p 145

LANCASHIRE 2014

RESULTS SUMMARY

	Place	Won	Lost	Tied	Drew	NR
LV= County Championship (1st Division)	8th	3	6		7	
All First-Class Matches		3	6		7	
Royal London One-Day Cup (Group A)	8th	2	5			1
NatWest t20 Blast (North Division)	Finalist	12	3			2

LV= COUNTY CHAMPIONSHIP AVERAGES

BATTING AND FIELDING

Cap		M	I	NO	HS	Runs	Avge	100	50	Ct/St
2010	S.J.Croft	12	20	3	156	786	46.23	2	4	16
2010	A.G.Prince	16	28	1	257*	1160	42.96	3	3	11
	J.C.Buttler	10	18	1	100*	633	37.23	1	5	28
2010	T.C.Smith	15	27	4	79	773	33.60	–	7	10
2007	P.J.Horton	16	30	2	140	891	31.82	2	3	16
	U.T.Khawaja	7	13	–	117	413	31.76	1	3	8
	A.L.Davies	10	17	–	62	469	27.58	–	3	16/1
	T.E.Bailey	3	5	3	25*	55	27.50	–	–	2
	L.A.Procter	7	12	1	81*	273	24.81	–	1	2
1994	G.Chapple	15	23	4	45*	459	24.15	–	–	4
	S.D.Parry	3	5	–	37	98	19.60	–	–	1
2003	J.M.Anderson	4	8	3	28	93	18.60	–	–	3
	A.P.Agathangelou	6	12	1	48	185	16.81	–	–	7
	Kabir Ali	7	11	3	26	134	16.75	–	–	–
	L.M.Reece	9	17	1	53	262	16.37	–	1	4
	K.R.Brown	6	10	1	29	112	12.44	–	–	5
2010	K.W.Hogg	8	10	1	47*	98	10.88	–	–	–
2013	S.C.Kerrigan	16	24	6	33	156	8.66	–	–	5
	W.A.White	4	6	1	13	37	7.40	–	–	2

Also played: K.M.Jarvis (2 matches) 0, 1*, 0*; Junaid Khan (1) did not bat.

BOWLING

	O	M	R	W	Avge	Best	5wI	10wM
T.C.Smith	365.3	83	1105	54	20.46	5-42	4	–
J.M.Anderson	166.4	43	432	21	20.57	5-41	3	1
K.W.Hogg	212.4	59	563	21	26.80	6-70	1	–
Kabir Ali	146.4	31	517	17	30.41	3-17	–	–
S.C.Kerrigan	530	99	1556	44	35.36	4-38	–	–
G.Chapple	500.4	99	1415	39	36.28	5-51	1	–
Also bowled:								
L.A.Procter	59.3	10	205	5	41.00	4-50	–	–
W.A.White	87	12	331	8	41.37	2-41	–	–
S.J.Croft	113	10	357	8	44.62	3-25	–	–
T.E.Bailey	85	19	272	6	45.33	2-36	–	–

K.M.Jarvis 49-7-201-2; Junaid Khan 47-11-147-3; S.D.Parry 60-5-197-4; L.M.Reece 14-2-59-0.

Lancashire played no first-class fixtures outside the County Championship in 2014. The First-Class Averages (pp 217–233) give the records of their players in all first-class county matches, with the exception of J.M.Anderson, J.C.Buttler and W.A.White, whose first-class figures for Lancashire are as above.

LANCASHIRE RECORDS

FIRST-CLASS CRICKET

Highest Total	For 863		v	Surrey	The Oval	1990
	V 707-9d		by	Surrey	The Oval	1990
Lowest Total	For 25		v	Derbyshire	Manchester	1871
	V 20		by	Essex	Chelmsford	2013
Highest Innings	For 424	A.C.MacLaren	v	Somerset	Taunton	1895
	V 315*	T.W.Hayward	for	Surrey	The Oval	1898

Highest Partnership for each Wicket

1st	368	A.C.MacLaren/R.H.Spooner	v	Glos	Liverpool	1903
2nd	371	F.B.Watson/G.E.Tyldesley	v	Surrey	Manchester	1928
3rd	364	M.A.Atherton/N.H.Fairbrother	v	Surrey	The Oval	1990
4th	358	S.P.Titchard/G.D.Lloyd	v	Essex	Chelmsford	1996
5th	360	S.G.Law/C.L.Hooper	v	Warwicks	Birmingham	2003
6th	278	J.Iddon/H.R.W.Butterworth	v	Sussex	Manchester	1932
7th	248	G.D.Lloyd/I.D.Austin	v	Yorkshire	Leeds	1997
8th	158	J.Lyon/R.M.Ratcliffe	v	Warwicks	Manchester	1979
9th	142	L.O.S.Poidevin/A.Kermode	v	Sussex	Eastbourne	1907
10th	173	J.Briggs/R.Pilling	v	Surrey	Liverpool	1885

Best Bowling	For	10-46	W.Hickton	v	Hampshire	Manchester	1870
(Innings)	V	10-40	G.O.B.Allen	for	Middlesex	Lord's	1929
Best Bowling	For	17-91	H.Dean	v	Yorkshire	Liverpool	1913
(Match)	V	16-65	G.Giffen	for	Australians	Manchester	1886

Most Runs – Season	2633	J.T.Tyldesley	(av 56.02)	1901
Most Runs – Career	34222	G.E.Tyldesley	(av 45.20)	1909-36
Most 100s – Season	11	C.Hallows		1928
Most 100s – Career	90	G.E.Tyldesley		1909-36
Most Wkts – Season	198	E.A.McDonald	(av 18.55)	1925
Most Wkts – Career	1816	J.B.Statham	(av 15.12)	1950-68
Most Career W-K Dismissals	925	G.Duckworth	(635 ct; 290 st)	1923-38
Most Career Catches in the Field	556	K.J.Grieves		1949-64

LIMITED-OVERS CRICKET

Highest Total	50ov	381-3		v	Herts	Radlett	1999
	40ov	324-4		v	Worcs	Worcester	2012
	T20	229-4		v	Worcs	Worcester	2014
Lowest Total	50ov	59		v	Worcs	Worcester	1963
	40ov	68		v	Yorkshire	Leeds	2000
		68		v	Surrey	The Oval	2002
	T20	91		v	Derbyshire	Manchester	2003
Highest Innings	50ov	162*	A.R.Crook	v	Bucks	Wormsley	2005
	40ov	143	A.Flintoff	v	Essex	Chelmsford	1999
	T20	102*	L.Vincent	v	Derbyshire	Manchester	2008
Best Bowling	50ov	6-10	C.E.H.Croft	v	Scotland	Manchester	1982
	40ov	6-25	G.Chapple	v	Yorkshire	Leeds	1998
	T20	5-29	M.J.McClenaghan	v	Notts	Manchester	2013

LEICESTERSHIRE

Formation of Present Club: 25 March 1879
Inaugural First-Class Match: 1894
Colours: Dark Green and Scarlet
Badge: Gold Running Fox on Green Ground
County Champions: (3) 1975, 1996, 1998
Benson and Hedges Cup Winners: (3) 1972, 1975, 1985
Sunday League Champions: (2) 1974, 1977
Twenty20 Cup Winners: (3) 2004, 2006, 2011

Chief Executive: Wasim Khan, County Ground, Grace Road, Leicester LE2 8AD • Tel: 0871 282 1879 • Fax: 0871 282 1873 • Email: enquiries@leicestershireccc.co.uk • Web: www.leicestershireccc.co.uk • Twitter: @leicsccc (11,830 followers)

Head Coach: Andrew McDonald. **Senior Coach**: Ben Smith. **Captain**: M.J.Cosgrove. **Vice-Captain**: E.J.H.Eckersley. **Overseas Players**: M.J.Cosgrove, G.D.Elliott (T20 only) and C.J.McKay. **2015 Beneficiary**: None. **Head Groundsman**: Andy Ward. **Scorer**: Paul Rogers. ‡ New registration. NQ Not qualified for England.

ALI, Aadil Masud (Lancaster S, Leicester; Q Elizabeth C), b Leicester 29 Dec 1994. 5'11". RHB, OB. Squad No 14. Leicestershire 2nd XI debut 2013. Awaiting 1st XI debut.

BOYCE, Matthew Andrew Golding (Oakham S; Nottingham U), b Cheltenham, Glos 13 Aug 1985. 5'9". LHB, RM. Squad No 11. Debut (Leicestershire) 2006; cap 2013. HS 135 v Kent (Leicester) 2013. BB – . LO HS 80 v Hants (Leicester) 2009 (FPT). T20 HS 63*.

CHAPPELL, Zachariah John ('**Zak**') (Stamford S), b Grantham, Lincs 21 Aug 1996. 6'4". RHB, RFM. Squad No 32. Awaiting 1st XI debut.

‡COSGROVE, Mark James, b Elizabeth, Adelaide, Australia 14 Jun 1984. 5'9". LHB, RM. S Australia 2002-03 to date. Tasmania 2010-11 to 2013-14. Glamorgan 2006-210; cap 2006. Joins Leicestershire as captain for 2015 and 2016. Big Bash: HH 2011-12. ST 2012-13 to date. SS 2013-14. **LOI** (A): 3 (2006); HS 74 v B (Fatullah) 2006; BB 1-1 v WI (Kuala Lumpur) 2006. 1000 runs (1): 1187 (2010). HS 233 Gm v Derbys (Derby) 2006. BB 3-3 S Aus v Tas (Adelaide) 2006-07. CC BB 3-30 Gm v Derbys (Derby) 2009. LO HS 121 S Aus v WA (Perth) 2005-06. LO BB 2-21 S Aus v Q (Brisbane) 2005-06. T20 HS 89. T20 BB 2-11.

ECKERSLEY, Edmund John Holden ('**Ned**') (St Benedict's GS, Ealing), b Oxford 9 Aug 1989. 6'0". RHB, WK, occ OB. Squad No 33. Debut (Leicestershire) 2011; cap 2013. Mountaineers 2011-12. MCC 2013. Middlesex 2nd XI 2008. Northamptonshire 2nd XI 2010. 1000 runs (1): 1302 (2013). HS 147 v Essex (Chelmsford) 2013. BB 2-29 v Lancs (Manchester) 2013. LO HS 108 v Yorks (Leicester) 2013 (Y40). T20 HS 43.

‡NQELLIOTT, Grant David (St Stithians) b Johannesburg, South Africa 21 Mar 1979. 6'1". RHB, RMF. Debut Transvaal B 1996-97. Griqualand West 1999-00 to 2000-01. Gauteng 2001-02 to 2002-03. Wellington 2005-06 to date. Surrey 2009 (one f-c match). Qualified for NZ in 2007. **Tests** (NZ): 5 (2007-08 to 2009-10); HS 25 v P (Dunedin) 2009-10. BB 2-8 v P (Wellington) 2009-10. **LOI** (NZ): 64 (2008 to 2014-15); HS 115 v A (Sydney) 2008-09; BB 4-31 v E (Johannesburg) 2009-10. **IT20** (NZ): 3 (2008-09 to 2012-13); HS 23* and BB 1-11 v A (Sydney) 2008-09. F-c matches (NZ): 3. HS 196* Wellington v Auckland (Wellington) 2007-08. CC HS 22 Sy v Middx (Oval) 2009. BB 5-33 Wellington v ND (Whangarei) 2013-14. LO HS 115 (*see LOI*). LO BB 5-34 Wellington v Otago (Wellington) 2007-08. T20 HS 70. T20 BB 3-16.

FRECKINGHAM, Oliver Henry (K Edward S, Melton Mowbray), b Oakham, Rutland 12 Nov 1988. RHB, RMF. Squad No 24. Debut (Leicestershire) 2013. HS 30 v Glos (Bristol) 2013. BB 6-125 v Northants (Northampton) 2013. LO HS – . LO BB 2-38 v Worcs (Leicester) 2014 (RLC).

HILL, Lewis John (Hastings HS, Hinckley; John Cleveland C), b Leicester 5 Oct 1990. 5'7½". RHB, WK. Squad No 23. Leicestershire 2nd XI debut 2009. Unicorns 2012-13. Awaiting 1st XI debut. LO HS 35 Unicorns v Warwks (Wormsley) 2012 (CB40).

‡^{NQ} **McKAY, Clinton** James, b Melbourne, Australia 22 Feb 1983. 6'4". RHB, RFM. Victoria 2006-07 to date. IPL: MI 2012. Big Bash: MS 2011-12 to date. **Tests** (A): 1 (2009-10); HS 10 and BB 1-56 v WI (Perth) 2009-10. **LOI** (A): 59 (2009-10 to 2013-14); HS 30 v SL (Oval) 2013; BB 5-28 v SL (Adelaide) 2011-12. **IT20** (A): 6 (2010-11 to 2013-14); HS 7 and BB 2-24 v WI (Bridgetown) 2011-12. HS 65 Vic v WA (Melbourne) 2012-13. BB 6-40 Vic v Tas (Melbourne) 2011-12. LO HS 57 Vic v Tas (Brisbane) 2014-15. LO BB 5-28 (see LOI). T20 HS 21*. T20 BB 4-33.

NAIK, Jigar Kumar Hakumatrai (Rushey Mead SS; Gateway SFC; Nottingham Trent U; Loughborough U), b Leicester 10 Aug 1984. 6'2". RHB, OB. Squad No 22. Debut (Leicestershire) 2006; cap 2013. Loughborough UCCE 2007. Colombo CC 2010-11. HS 109* v Derbys (Leicester) 2009. BB 7-96 v Surrey (Oval) 2010. LO HS 36* v Derbys (Leicester) 2014 (RLC). LO BB 3-21 v Lancs (Leicester) 2009 (P40). T20 HS 16*. T20 BB 3-3.

O'BRIEN, Niall John (Marian C, Dublin), b Dublin, Ireland 8 Nov 1981. Son of B.A.O'Brien (Ireland 1966-81); elder brother of K.J.O'Brien (see SURREY). 5'6". LHB, WK. Squad No 81. Kent 2004-06. Ireland 2005-06 to date. Northamptonshire 2007-12; cap 2011. Leicestershire debut 2013. MCC 2012. **LOI** (Ire): 70 (2006 to 2014-15); HS 80* v Scotland (Dubai, DSC) 2014-15. **IT20** (Ire): 21 (2008 to 2013-14); HS 50 v Canada (Colombo, SSC) 2009-10. HS 182 Nh v Glamorgan (Cardiff) 2012. Le HS 133 v Glamorgan (Leicester) 2013. BB 1-4 K v Cambridge UCCE (Cambridge) 2006. LO HS 121 Nh v Hants (Southampton) 2011 (CB40). T20 HS 84.

PINNER, Neil Douglas (RGS Worcester), b Wordsley, Stourbridge, Worcs 29 Sep 1990. 5'11". RHB, OB. Squad No 9. Worcestershire 2011-13. Worcestershire 2nd XI debut 2008. Surrey 2nd XI 2013. Leicestershire 2nd XI 2014. HS 82 Wo v Lancs (Worcester) 2012. BB – . LO HS 37 Wo v Kent (Canterbury) 2011 (CB40). LO BB – .

RAINE, Benjamin Alexander (St Aidan's RC SS, Sunderland) b Sunderland, Co Durham 14 Sep 1991. 6'0". LHB, RM. Squad No 44. Durham 2011. Leicestershire debut 2013. Durham 2nd XI debut 2010. HS 72 v Lancs (Manchester) 2013. BB 4-98 v Glamorgan (Swansea) 2013. LO HS 43 v Yorks (Leicester) 2014 (RLC). LO BB 2-59 v Glamorgan (Swansea) 2013 (Y40). T20 HS 20*. T20 BB 3-12.

REDFERN, Daniel James (Adam's GS, Newport, Shropshire), b Shrewsbury, Shrops 18 Apr 1990. 5'9". LHB, OB. Squad No 6. Derbyshire 2007-13; cap 2012. Leicestershire debut 2014. HS 133 De v Hants (Southampton) 2012. Le HS 64 v Surrey (Leicester) 2014. BB 3-33 De v Durham (Chester-le-St) 2013. Le BB 2-20 v Worcs (Worcester) 2014. LO HS 57* De v Yorks (Derby) 2007 (P40). LO BB 2-10 De v Kent (Chesterfield) 2009 (P40). T20 HS 43. T20 BB 2-17.

ROBSON, Angus James (Marcellin C, Randwick; Australian C of PE), b Darlinghurst, Sydney, Australia 19 Feb 1992. Younger brother of S.D.Robson (see MIDDLESEX). 5'9". RHB, LB. Squad No 8. Debut (Leicestershire) 2013. Leicestershire 2nd XI debut 2012. 1000 runs (1): 1086 (2014). HS 115 v Hants (Southampton) 2014. BB – . LO HS 28 v Essex (Chelmsford) 2014 (RLC).

SAYER, Robert John (Ramsey Abbey C; Leeds Beckett U), b Huntingdon, Cambridgeshire 25 Jan 1995. 6'3". RHB, OB. Squad No 12. Leicestershire 2nd XI debut 2013. Cambridgeshire 2013. Summer contract to end of 2016. Awaiting 1st XI debut.

SHEIKH, Atif (Bluecoat S), b Nottingham 18 Feb 1991. 6'0". RHB, LMF. Squad No 3. Derbyshire 2010. Leicestershire debut 2014. England U19s 2010. Derbyshire 2nd XI debut 2008. Leicestershire 2nd XI debut 2012. HS 12 v Essex (Leicester) 2014. BB 4-97 v Glos (Bristol) 2014, inc hat-trick. T20 HS 14. T20 BB 2-11.

SHRECK, Charles Edward (Truro S), b Truro, Cornwall 6 Jan 1978. 6'7". RHB, RFM. Squad No 4. Nottinghamshire 2003-11; cap 2006. Wellington 2005-06 to 2007-08. Kent 2012-13. Leicestershire debut 2014. MCC 2008. Cornwall 1997-2002. HS 56 v Surrey (Oval) 2014.. 50 wkts (3); most – 61 (2006, 2008). BB 8-31 (12-129 match) Nt v Middx (Nottingham) 2006. Le BB 3-44 v Glos (Bristol) 2014. Hat-trick Nt v Middx (Lord's) 2006. LO HS 9* Wellington v CD (Palmerston N) 2005-06. LO BB 5-19 Cornwall v Worcs (Truro) 2002 (CGT). T20 HS 10. T20 BB 4-22.

SYKES, James Stuart (St Ives S, Huntingdon), b Hinchingbrooke, Cambs 26 Apr 1992. 6'2". LHB, SLA. Squad No 80. Debut (Leicestershire) 2013. Leicestershire 2nd XI debut 2009. Cambridgeshire 2010. HS 34 v Lancs (Manchester) 2013. BB 4-176 v Essex (Chelmsford) 2013 – on debut. LO HS 15 v Glos (Bristol) 2013 (Y40). LO BB 3-34 v Hants (Southampton) 2014 (RLC). T20 HS 2*. T20 BB 2-24.

TAYLOR, Robert Meadows Lombe (Harrow S; Loughborough U), b Northampton 21 Dec 1989. 6'3". LHB, LMF. Squad No 10. Loughborough MCCU 2010-12. Leicestershire debut 2011. Leicestershire 2nd XI debut 2008. Northamptonshire 2nd XI 2010. **LOI** (Scot): 14 (2012-13 to 2014-15); HS 46* v Kenya (Christchurch) 2013-14; BB 3-39 v Kenya (Aberdeen) 2013. **IT20** (Scot): 4 (2013-14); HS 41* and BB 1-16 v Netherlands (Dubai) 2013-14. HS 101* LU v Leics (Leicester) 2011. Le HS 98 v Kent (Leicester) 2014. BB 5-55 v Glos (Leicester) 2014. LO HS 48* v Yorks (Scarborough) 2013 (Y40). LO BB 3-39 (*see LOI*). T20 HS 41*. T20 BB 4-11.

WELLS, Thomas Joshua (Gartree HS; Beauchamp C, Leicester), b Grantham, Lincs 15 Mar 1993. Father, John Wells, played rugby for Leicester. 6'2". RHB, RMF. Debut (Leicestershire) 2013. Leicestershire 2nd XI debut 2010. HS 82 v Hants (Leicester) 2013. BB 1-36 v Lancs (Leicester) 2013. LO HS 32* v Glamorgan (Swansea) 2013 (Y40). LO BB – . T20 HS 4.

WYATT, Alexander Charles Frederick (Oakham S), b Roehampton 23 Jul 1990. 6'7". RHB, RMF. Debut (Leicestershire) 2009. Leicestershire 2nd XI debut 2007. HS 32 v Hants (Southampton) 2014. BB 3-35 v Hants (Leicester) 2012 and v Essex (Leicester) 2013. LO HS 9* v Netherlands (Leicester) 2012 (CB40). LO BB 2-36 v Durham (Leicester) 2011 (CB40). T20 HS 0*. T20 BB 3-14.

RELEASED/RETIRED

(Having made a 1st XI appearance in 2014)

BUCK, N.L. – *see LANCASHIRE*.

COBB, J.J. – see NORTHAMPTONSHIRE.

[NQ]**IRELAND, Anthony** John (Plumtree HS), b Masvingo, Zimbabwe 30 Aug 1984. 6'2". RHB, RM. Midlands 2002-03 to 2004-05. Gloucestershire 2007-10, 2012; cap 2007. Middlesex 2011. Leicestershire 2013-14. Kolpak registration. **LOI** (Z): 26 (2005-06 to 2006-07); HS 8* v Kenya (Bulawayo) 2005-06; BB 3-41 v B (Harare) (twice) – 2006 and 2006-07. **IT20** (Z): 1 (2006-07); HS 2* and BB 1-33 v B (Khulna) 2006-07. HS 52 v Kent (Canterbury) 2014. BB 7-36 Zimbabwe A v Bangladesh A (Mirpur) 2006-07. CC BB 6-31 Gs v Leics (Bristol) 2009. Le BB 3-81 v Glamorgan (Leicester) 2014. LO HS 27 v Somerset (Taunton) 2013 (Y40). LO BB 4-16 Zimbabwe A v Kenya (Harare) 2005-06. T20 HS 23. T20 BB 5-22.

[NQ]**SARWAN, Ramnaresh** Ronnie (North Gromuel S), b Wakenaam Island, Essequibo, Guyana 23 Jun 1980. 5'7½". RHB, LB. Guyana 1995-96 to 2013-14 (youngest to play f-c cricket in WI). Gloucestershire 2005; cap 2005. Leicestershire 2012-14; captain 2013-14. IPL: KXIP 2007-08. **Tests** (WI): 87 (2000 to 2011); HS 291 v E (Bridgetown) 2008-09; BB 4-37 v B (St Lucia) 2004. **LOI** (WI): 181 (2000 to 2013); HS 120* v Z (St George's) 2012-13; BB 3-31 v NZ (Lord's) 2004. **IT20** (WI): 18 (2007 to 2010); HS 59 v E (Port of Spain) 2008-09; BB 2-10 v B (Johannesburg) 2007. F-c Tours (WI): E 2000, 2004, 2007, 2009; A 2000-01, 2005-06, 2009-10; SA 2003-04; NZ 2005-06, 2008-09; I 2002-03; P 2006-07; SL 2001-02; Z 2001, 2003-04; B 2002-03. HS 291 (*see Tests*). CC HS 117 Gs v Sussex (Hove) 2005 and 117 v Essex (Leicester) 2012. BB 6-62 Guyana v Leeward Is (Antigua) 2000-01. CC BB 2-38 Gs v Glamorgan (Bristol) 2005. Le BB – . LO HS 120* (*see LOI*). LO BB 5-10 Guyana v Bermuda (Hampton Court) 1998-99. T20 HS 70. T20 BB 2-10.

SMITH, G.P. – *see NOTTINGHAMSHIRE.*

[NQ]**STYRIS, Scott** Bernard (Hamilton BHS), b Brisbane, Australia 10 Jul 1975. 5'10". RHB, RMF. N Districts 1994-95 to 2010-11. Middlesex 2005-06; cap 2006. Auckland 2005-06 to 2009-10. Durham 2007. Leicestershire 2014 (l-o and T20 only). IPL: DC 2007-09. CSK: 2011.Big Bash: HH 2012-13. **Tests** (NZ): 29 (2002-2007-08); HS 170 v SA (Auckland) 2003-04; BB 3-28 v I (Wellington) 2002-03. **LOI** (NZ): 188 (1999-00 to 2010-11); HS 141 v SL (Bloemfontein) 2002-03; BB 6-25 v WI (Port of Spain) 2002. **IT20** (NZ): 31 (2004-05 to 2010-11); HS 66 v A (Auckland) 2004-05; BB 3-5 v Z (Providence) 2009-10. F-c Tours (NZ): E 2000 (NZ A), 2004; A 2004-05; SA 2000-01, 2005-06, 2007-08; WI 2002; I 2003-04; SL 2002-03; Z 2005; B 2004-05. HS 212* ND v Otago (Hamilton) 2001-02. UK HS 133 and UK BB 6-71 M v Lancs (Lord's) 2006. LO HS 141 (*see LOI*). LO BB 6-25 (*see LOI*). T20 HS 106*. T20 BB 3-5.

THAKOR, S.J. – *see DERBYSHIRE.*

THORNELY, Michael Alistair (Brighton C), b Camden, London 19 Oct 1987. 6'1". RHB, RM. Sussex 2007-10. ME 2011-12. Leicestershire 2012-14, scoring 97 and 131 v Glamorgan (Cardiff) on debut. HS 131 (*see above*). BB 2-14 Sx v Worcs (Hove) 2010. Le BB 2-29 v Glos (Cheltenham) 2012. LO HS 105* Unicorns v Somerset (Taunton) 2011 (CB40). LO BB 1-20 v Australians (Leicester) 2012. T20 HS 20. T20 BB – .

LEICESTERSHIRE 2014

RESULTS SUMMARY

	Place	Won	Lost	Tied	Drew	NR
LV= County Championship (2nd Division)	9th		10		6	
All First-Class Matches			10		6	
Royal London One-Day Cup (Group A)	5th	3	4			1
NatWest t20 Blast (North Division)	8th	4	9			1

LV= COUNTY CHAMPIONSHIP AVERAGES
BATTING AND FIELDING

Cap		M	I	NO	HS	Runs	Avge	100	50	Ct/St
	N.J.O'Brien	15	28	3	133	971	38.84	2	5	43/4
	A.J.Robson	16	30	–	115	1086	36.20	1	9	12
	J.J.Cobb	14	26	3	137	803	34.91	1	7	8
	G.P.Smith	15	28	–	118	862	30.78	2	4	14
	D.J.Redfern	9	17	1	64	463	28.93	–	5	2
2013	E.J.H.Eckersley	16	30	–	119	818	27.26	2	1	12
2013	M.A.G.Boyce	5	9	–	68	209	23.22	–	1	4
	R.M.L.Taylor	15	27	1	98	567	21.80	–	4	7
	N.L.Buck	9	15	6	29*	192	21.33	–	–	2
2013	J.K.H.Naik	13	22	6	59*	338	21.12	–	1	11
	B.A.Raine	7	13	1	55	239	19.91	–	1	2
	C.E.Shreck	15	23	6	56	332	19.52	–	1	4
	R.R.Sarwan	5	10	–	60	184	18.40	–	1	3
	A.J.Ireland	6	10	2	52	111	13.87	–	1	–
	A.C.F.Wyatt	3	5	–	32	59	11.80	–	–	–
	J.S.Sykes	3	6	1	8*	35	7.00	–	–	2
	A.Sheikh	4	7	2	12	24	4.80	–	–	1
	O.H.Freckingham	3	4	1	6	12	4.00	–	–	–

Also batted: R.A.Jones (1 match) 3, 6; M.A.Thornely (1) 21; T.J.Wells 15, 13 (1 ct).

BOWLING

	O	M	R	W	Avge	Best	5wI	10wM
N.L.Buck	327.1	54	1290	42	30.71	5- 76	3	–
R.M.L.Taylor	349.3	66	1231	35	35.17	5- 55	2	–
B.A.Raine	196	42	656	18	36.44	3- 47	–	–
A.J.Ireland	176.1	24	600	15	40.00	3- 81	–	–
C.E.Shreck	560	135	1759	42	41.88	3- 44	–	–
J.K.H.Naik	445.2	81	1535	20	76.75	3- 76	–	–

Also bowled:

	O	M	R	W	Avge	Best	5wI	10wM
D.J.Redfern	62	10	251	8	31.37	2- 20	–	–
O.H.Freckingham	81.5	12	362	8	45.25	4-138	–	–
J.S.Sykes	110	13	381	8	47.62	3- 72	–	–

J.J.Cobb 22-1-84-0; E.J.H.Eckersley 3.3-0-16-0; R.A.Jones 28-6-93-2; A.J.Robson 16.3-1-84-0; M.A.Thornely 2-0-6-0; T.J.Wells 5-1-34-0; A.C.F.Wyatt 60-14-214-4.

Leicestershire played no first-class fixtures outside the County Championship in 2014. The First-Class Averages (pp 217–233) give the records of their players in all first-class county matches, with the exception of R.A.Jones, whose first-class figures for Leicestershire are as above.

LEICESTERSHIRE RECORDS

FIRST-CLASS CRICKET

Highest Total	For	701-4d		v	Worcs	Worcester	1906
	V	761-6d		by	Essex	Chelmsford	1990
Lowest Total	For	25		v	Kent	Leicester	1912
	V	24		by	Glamorgan	Leicester	1971
		24		by	Oxford U	Oxford	1985
Highest Innings	For	309*	H.D.Ackerman	v	Glamorgan	Cardiff	2006
	V	341	G.H.Hirst	for	Yorkshire	Leicester	1905

Highest Partnership for each Wicket

1st	390	B.Dudleston/J.F.Steele	v	Derbyshire	Leicester	1979
2nd	289*	J.C.Balderstone/D.I.Gower	v	Essex	Leicester	1981
3rd	436*	D.L.Maddy/B.J.Hodge	v	L'boro UCCE	Leicester	2003
4th	360*	J.W.A.Taylor/A.B.McDonald	v	Middlesex	Leicester	2010
5th	330	J.W.A.Taylor/S.J.Thakor	v	L'boro MCCU	Leicester	2011
6th	284	P.V.Simmons/P.A.Nixon	v	Durham	Chester-le-St[2]	1996
7th	219*	J.D.R.Benson/P.Whitticase	v	Hampshire	Bournemouth	1991
8th	195	J.W.A.Taylor/J.K.H.Naik	v	Derbyshire	Leicester	2009
9th	160	R.T.Crawford/ W.W.Odell	v	Worcs	Leicester	1902
10th	228	R.Illingworth/K.Higgs	v	Northants	Leicester	1977

Best Bowling	For	10- 18	G.Geary	v	Glamorgan	Pontypridd	1929
(Innings)	V	10- 32	H.Pickett	for	Essex	Leyton	1895
Best Bowling	For	16- 96	G.Geary	v	Glamorgan	Pontypridd	1929
(Match)	V	16-102	C.Blythe	for	Kent	Leicester	1909

Most Runs – Season	2446	L.G.Berry	(av 52.04)		1937
Most Runs – Career	30143	L.G.Berry	(av 30.32)		1924-51
Most 100s – Season	7	L.G.Berry			1937
	7	W.Watson			1959
	7	B.F.Davison			1982
Most 100s – Career	45	L.G.Berry			1924-51
Most Wkts – Season	170	J.E.Walsh	(av 18.96)		1948
Most Wkts – Career	2131	W.E.Astill	(av 23.18)		1906-39
Most Career W-K Dismissals	905	R.W.Tolchard	(794 ct; 111 st)		1965-83
Most Career Catches in the Field	426	M.R.Hallam			1950-70

LIMITED-OVERS CRICKET

Highest Total	50ov	406-5		v	Berkshire	Leicester	1996
	40ov	344-4		v	Durham	Chester-le-St[2]	1996
	T20	221-3		v	Yorkshire	Leeds	2004
Lowest Total	50ov	56		v	Northants	Leicester	1964
		56		v	Minor Cos	Wellington	1982
	40ov	36		v	Sussex	Leicester	1973
	T20	90		v	Notts	Nottingham	2014
Highest Innings	50ov	201	V.J.Wells	v	Berkshire	Leicester	1996
	40ov	154*	B.J.Hodge	v	Sussex	Horsham	2004
	T20	111	D.L.Maddy	v	Yorkshire	Leeds	2004
Best Bowling	50ov	6-16	C.M.Willoughby	v	Somerset	Leicester	2005
	40ov	6-17	K.Higgs	v	Glamorgan	Leicester	1973
	T20	5-13	A.B.McDonald	v	Notts	Nottingham	2010

MIDDLESEX

Formation of Present Club: 2 February 1864
Inaugural First-Class Match: 1864
Colours: Blue
Badge: Three Seaxes
County Champions (since 1890): (10) 1903, 1920, 1921, 1947, 1976, 1980, 1982, 1985, 1990, 1993
Joint Champions: (2) 1949, 1977
Gillette/NatWest Trophy Winners: (4) 1977, 1980, 1984, 1988
Benson and Hedges Cup Winners: (2) 1983, 1986
Sunday League Winners: (1) 1992
Twenty20 Cup Winners: (1) 2008

Chief Executive: Vincent Codrington, Lord's Cricket Ground, London NW8 8QN • Tel: 020 7289 1300 • Fax: 020 7289 5831 • Email: enquiries@middlesexccc.com • Web: www.middlesexccc.com • Twitter: @Middlesex_CCC (16,071 followers)

Managing Director of Cricket: Angus Fraser. **Head Coach**: Richard Scott. **Assistant Coach**: Richard Johnson. **Captains**: A.C.Voges (f-c) and E.J.G.Morgan (l-o). **Overseas Player**: A.C.Voges. **2015 Beneficiary**: T.J.Murtagh. **Head Groundsman**: Mick Hunt. **Scorer**: Don Shelley. ‡ New registration. NQ Not qualified for England.

NQ**BALBIRNIE, Andrew** (St Andrew's C, Dublin; UWIC), b Dublin, Ireland 28 Dec 1990. 6'2". RHB, OB. Squad No 15. Cardiff MCCU 2012-13. Ireland 2012. Middlesex debut 2012. Middlesex 2nd XI debut 2011. MCC YCs 2010. **LOI** (Ire): 17 (2010 to 2014-15); HS 97 v Z (Hobart) 2014-15; LO BB 1-26 v Afghanistan (Dubai, DSC) 2014-15. HS 38 Ire v Scotland (Dublin) 2013. M HS 14 v Surrey (Oval) 2012. BB 1-5 Ire v Netherlands (Deventer) 2013. LO HS 129 Ire v NZ A (Dubai, CA) 2014-15. LO BB 1-26 (*see LOI*). T20 HS 2.

COMPTON, Nicholas Richard Denis (Harrow S; Durham U), b Durban, South Africa 26 Jun 1983. Son of R.Compton (Natal 1978-79 to 1980-81); grandson of D.C.S.Compton (Middlesex, England, Holkar, Europeans, Commonwealth and Cavaliers 1936-64); great-nephew of L.H.Compton (Middlesex 1938-56). 6'1". RHB, OB. Squad No 3. Middlesex debut 2004; cap 2006. Somerset 2010-14; cap 2011. Mashonaland Eagles 2010-11. Worcestershire (1 game) 2013. MCC 2007. PCA 2012. *Wisden* 2012. **Tests**: 9 (2012-13 to 2013); HS 117 v NZ (Dunedin) 2012-13. F-c Tours: NZ 2012-13; I 2012-13; B 2006-07 (Eng A). 1000 runs (5); most – 1494 (2012). Scored 685 runs in April 2012 – a record for April. HS 254* Sm v Durham (Chester-le-St) 2011; M HS 190 v Durham (Lord's) 2006. BB 1-1 Sm v Hants (Southampton) 2010. M BB 1-94 v Sussex (Southgate) 2007. LO HS 131 v Kent (Canterbury) 2009 (FPT). LO BB 1-0 v Scotland (Lord's) 2009 (FPT). T20 HS 74.

DEXTER, Neil John (Northwood HS, Durban; Varsity C; U of South Africa), b Johannesburg, South Africa 21 Aug 1984. 6'0". RHB, RMF. Squad No 4. Kent 2005-08. Essex 2008. Middlesex debut 2009; cap 2010; captain 2010 (*part*) to 2013. Qualified for England in 2010. HS 163* v Northants (Northampton) 2014. BB 6-63 v Lancs (Lord's) 2014. LO HS 135* K v Glamorgan (Cardiff) 2006 (CGT). LO BB 3-17 K v Leics (Canterbury) 2006 (P40). T20 HS 73. T20 BB 4-21.

NQ**ESKINAZI, Stephen** Sean (Christ Church GS, Claremont; U of WA), b Johannesburg, South Africa 28 Mar 1994. 6'2". RHB, WK. Squad No 28. Middlesex 2nd XI debut 2013. Awaiting 1st XI debut. British passport.

FINN, Steven Thomas (Parmiter's S, Garston), b Watford, Herts 4 Apr 1989. 6'7½". RHB, RF. Squad No 9. Debut (Middlesex) 2005; cap 2009. Otago 2011-12. YC 2010. **ECB central contract 2014-15. Tests**: 23 (2009-10 to 2013); HS 56 v NZ (Dunedin) 2012-13; BB 6-125 v A (Brisbane) 2010-11. **LOI**: 56 (2010-11 to 2014-15); HS 35 v A (Brisbane) 2010-11; BB 5-33 v I (Brisbane) 2014-15. **IT20**: 19 (2011 to 2014); HS 8* v I (Colombo, RPS) 2012-13; BB 3-16 v NZ (Pallekele) 2012-13. F-c Tours: A 2010-11, 2013-14; NZ 2012-13; I 2012-13; SL 2011-12; B 2009-10; UAE 2011-12 (v P). HS 56 (*see Tests*). M HS 37* v Warwks (Birmingham) 2014. 50 wkts (2); most – 64 (2010). BB 9-37 (14-106 match) v Worcs (Worcester) 2010. LO HS 42* v Glamorgan (Cardiff) 2014 (RLC). LO BB 5-33 v Derbys (Lord's) 2011 (CB40). T20 HS 8*. T20 BB 3-16.

‡**[NQ]FRANKLIN, James** Edward Charles (Wellington C; Victoria U), Wellington, New Zealand 7 Nov 1980. 6'4½". LHB, LM. Squad No 74. Irish passport. Wellington 1998-99 to date. Gloucestershire 2004-10; cap 2004. Glamorgan 2006; cap 2006. Nottinghamshire 2014; cap 2014. IPL: MI 2011-12. Big Bash: AS 2011-12. **Tests** (NZ): 31 (2000-01 to 2012-13); HS 122* v SA (Cape Town) 2006-07; BB 6-119 v A (Auckland) 2004-05. Hat-trick v B (Dhaka) 2004-05. **LOI** (NZ): 110 (2000-01 to 2013); HS 98* v I (Bangalore) 2010-11; BB 5-42 v E (Chester-le-St) 2004. **IT20** (NZ): 38 (2005-06 to 2013); HS 60 v Z (Hamilton) 2011-12; BB 4-15 v E (Hamilton) 2012-13. F-c Tours (NZ): E 2004; A 2004-05; SA 2004-05 (NZ A), 2005-06, 2012-13; I 2012; SL 2012-13; Z 2005, 2010-11 (NZ A); B 2004-05. HS 219 Wellington v Auckland (Auckland) 2008-09. CC HS 109 Gs v Derbys (Cheltenham) 2009; became only the second man for Gs to score a hundred and take a hat-trick in the same match. BB 7-14 Gs v Derbys (Bristol) 2010. Hat-tricks (*see above*). LO HS 133* Gs v Derbys (Bristol) 2010 (CB40). LO BB 5-42 (*see LOI*). T20 HS 90. T20 BB 4-15.

GUBBINS, Nicholas Richard Trail (Radley C; Leeds U), b Richmond, Surrey 31 Dec 1993. 6'0½". LHB, LB. Squad No 18. Leeds/Bradford MCCU 2013-14. Middlesex debut 2014. Middlesex 2nd XI debut 2012. HS 95 v Somerset (Uxbridge) 2014. LO HS 38 v Glamorgan (Cardiff) 2014 (RLC).

HARRIS, James Alexander Russell (Pontardulais CS; Gorseinon C), b Morriston, Swansea, Glamorgan 16 May 1990. 6'0". RHB, RMF. Squad No 5. Glamorgan 2007-12, making debut aged 16y 351d – youngest Glamorgan player to take an f-c wicket; cap 2010. Middlesex debut 2013. Loaned to Glamorgan during 2014. Glamorgan 2nd XI debut 2005, aged 14y 353d. Wales MC 2005-08. England U19s 2007. F-c Tours (EL): WI 2010-11; SL 2013-14. HS 87* Gm v Notts (Swansea) 2007. M HS 43* v Cambridge MCCU (Cambridge) 2013. 50 wkts (1): 63 (2010). BB 7-66 (12-118 match) Gm v Glos (Bristol) 2007 – youngest (17y 3d) to take 10 wickets in any CC match. M BB 4-80 v Notts (Lord's) 2014. LO HS 29 EL v Sri Lanka A (Northampton) 2011. LO BB 4-48 Gm v Kent (Canterbury) 2008 (P40). T20 HS 18. T20 BB 4-23.

HELM, Thomas George (Misbourne S, Gt Missenden), b Stoke Mandeville Hospital, Bucks 7 May 1994. 6'4". RHB, RMF. Squad No 14. Debut (Middlesex) 2013. Glamorgan 2014 (on loan). Middlesex 2nd XI debut 2011. Buckinghamshire 2011. HS 18 and BB 3-46 v Yorks (Leeds) 2013. LO HS – . LO BB 3-27 v Unicorns (Southend) 2013 (Y40).

HIGGINS, Ryan Francis (Bradfield C), b Harare, Zimbabwe 6 Jan 1995. 5'10". RHB, OB. Squad No 11. Middlesex 2nd XI debut 2012. Awaiting f-c debut. LO HS 27 v Somerset (Lord's) 2014 (RLC). T20 HS 44*.

HOLDEN, Max David Edward (Sawston Village C; Hills Road SFC, Cambridge), b Cambridge 18 Dec 1997. 5'11". LHB, OB. Squad No 24. Middlesex 2nd XI debut 2013. Awaiting 1st XI debut.

MALAN, Dawid Johannes (Paarl HS), b Roehampton, Surrey 3 Sep 1987. Son of D.J.Malan (WP B and Transvaal B 1978-79 to 1981-82), elder brother of C.C.Malan (Loughborough MCCU 2009-10). 6'0". LHB, LB. Squad No 29. Boland 2005-06. MCC YC 2006-07. Middlesex debut 2008, scoring 132* v Northants (Uxbridge); cap 2010. MCC 2010-11, 2013. 1000 runs (2); most – 1137 runs (2014). HS 156* v Cambridge MCCU (Cambridge) 2013. CC HS 154* v Northants (Lord's) 2014. BB 5-61 v Lancs (Liverpool) 2012. LO HS 134 v Essex (Lord's) 2012 (CB40). LO BB 4-25 PDSC v Partex (Savar) 2014-15. T20 HS 103. T20 BB 2-10.

MORGAN, Eoin Joseph Gerard (Catholic University S), b Dublin, Ireland 10 Sep 1986. 6'0". LHB, RM. Squad No 7. British passport. Ireland 2004 to 2007-08. Middlesex debut 2006; cap 2008; l-o captain 2014 to date. *Wisden* 2010. **Tests**: 16 (2010 to 2011-12); HS 130 v P (Nottingham) 2010. **LOI** (E/Ire): 140 (23 for Ire 2006 to 2008-09; 117 for E 2009 to 2014-15, 19 as captain); HS 124* v Ireland (Dublin) 2013. **IT20**: 50 (2009 to 2014, 7 as captain); HS 85* v SA (Johannesburg) 2009-10. F-c Tours (Ire): A 2010-11 (E); NZ 2008-09 (Eng A); Namibia 2005-06; UAE 2006-07, 2007-08, 2011-12 (E v P). 1000 runs (1): 1085 (2008). HS 209* Ire v UAE (Abu Dhabi) 2006-07. M HS 191 v Notts (Nottingham) 2014. BB 2-24 v Notts (Lord's) 2007. LO HS 161 v Kent (Canterbury) 2009 (FPT). LO BB – . T20 HS 85*.

MURTAGH, Timothy James (John Fisher S; St Mary's C), b Lambeth, London 2 Aug 1981. Elder brother of C.P.Murtagh (Loughborough UCCE and Surrey 2005-09); nephew of A.J.Murtagh (Hampshire and EP 1973-77). 6'0". LHB, RFM. Squad No 34. British U 2000-03. Surrey 2001-06. Middlesex debut 2007; cap 2008; benefit 2015. MCC 2010. **LOI** (ire): 10 (2012 to 2014); HS 23* v Scotland (Belfast) 2013; BB 3-33 v E (Dublin) 2013. **IT20** (Ire): 7 (2012 to 2013-14); HS 3 v B (Belfast) 2012; BB 2-24 v Afghanistan (Abu Dhabi) 2013-14. HS 74* Sy v Middx (Oval) 2004 and 74* Sy v Warwks (Croydon) 2005. M HS 55 v Leics (Leicester) 2011, sharing M record 9th wkt partnership of 172 with G.K.Berg. 50 wkts (6); most – 85 (2011). BB 7-82 v Derbys (Derby) 2009. LO HS 35* v Surrey (Lord's) 2008 (FPT). LO BB 4-14 Sy v Derbys (Derby) 2005 (NL). T20 HS 40*. T20 BB 6-24 Sy v Middx (Lord's) 2005 – Sy record and 4th best UK figs.

PATEL, Ravi Hasmukh (Merchant Taylors' S, Northwood; Loughborough U), b Harrow 4 Aug 1991. 5'8". RHB, SLA. Squad No 36. Debut (Middlesex) 2010. No 1st XI appearances in 2011. Loughborough MCCU 2011. Middlesex 2nd XI debut 2008. HS 26* v Warwks (Uxbridge) 2013. BB 5-69 v Cambridge MCCU (Cambridge) 2013. CC BB 4-72 v Lancs (Lord's) 2012. LO HS 0*. LO BB 3-71 EL v Sri Lanka A (Taunton) 2014. T20 HS 1*. T20 BB 4-18.

PODMORE, Harry William (Twyford HS), b Hammersmith, London 23 Jul 1994. 6'3". RHB, RM. Squad No 23. Middlesex 2nd XI debut 2011. MCC YC 2013. Awaiting f-c debut. LO HS 1* v Notts (Lord's) 2014 (RLC). LO BB 2-46 v Somerset (Lord's) 2014 (RLC). T20 HS 7. T20 BB 3-13.

RAYNER, Oliver Philip (St Bede's S, Upper Dicker), b Fallingbostel, W Germany, 1 Nov 1985. 6'5". RHB, OB. Squad No 2. Sussex 2006-11, scoring 101 v Sri Lankans (Hove) – first hundred on debut for Sussex since 1920. Middlesex debut 2011. MCC 2014. F-c Tour (EL): SL 2013-14. HS 143* v Notts (Nottingham) 2012. BB 8-46 (15-118 match) v Surrey (Oval) 2013. LO HS 61 Sx v Lancs (Hove) 2006 (P40). LO BB 3-31 v Somerset (Lord's) 2013 (Y40). T20 HS 41*. T20 BB 5-18.

ROBSON, Sam David (Marcellin C, Randwick), b Paddington, Sydney, Australia 1 Jul 1989. Elder brother of A.J.Robson (*see LEICESTERSHIRE*). 6'0". RHB, LB. Squad No 12. Qualified for England in April 2013. Debut (Middlesex) 2009; cap 2013. **Tests**: 7 (2014); HS 127 v SL (Leeds) 2014. F-c Tours (EL): SA 2014-15; SL 2013-14. 1000 runs (2); most – 1180 (2013). HS 215* v Warwks (Birmingham) 2013. BB 1-4 EL v Sri Lanka A (Dambulla) 2013-14. M BB – . LO HS 65 v Sussex (Lord's) 2011 (CB40). T20 HS 28*.

ROLAND-JONES, Tobias Skelton ('**Toby**') (Hampton S; Leeds U), b Ashford 29 Jan 1988. 6'4". RHB, RMF. Squad No 21. Debut (Middlesex) 2010; cap 2012. MCC 2011. Leeds/Bradford UCCE 2009 (not f-c). HS 77 v Somerset (Taunton) 2014. 50 wkts (1): 64 (2012). BB 6-50 (12-105 match) v Northants (Northampton) 2014. Hat-trick v Derbys (Lord's) 2013. LO HS 29* EL v New Zealand A (Worcester) 2014. LO BB 4-42 v Sussex (Hove) 2014 (RLC). T20 HS 30. T20 BB 4-25.

SANDHU, Gurjit Singh (Isleworth & Syon S; Heathland S), b W Middlesex Hospital 24 Mar 1992. 6'4". RHB, LMF. Squad No 92. Debut (Middlesex) 2011. Middlesex 2nd XI debut 2008, aged 16y 85d. HS 8 v Sri Lankans (Uxbridge) 2011. CC HS 6* v Somerset (Taunton) 2014. BB 4-49 v Cambridge MCCU (Cambridge) 2013. CC BB 2-54 v Sussex (Hove) 2013. LO HS 0 and LO BB 3-28 v Essex (Lord's) 2012 (CB40). T20 HS 2*. T20 BB 2-15.

SCOTT, George Frederick Buchan (Beechwood Park S; St Albans S; Leeds U), b Hemel Hempstead, Herts 6 Nov 1995. Younger brother of J.E.B.Scott (Hertfordshire 2013 to date). 6'2". RHB, RM. Squad No 17. Middlesex 2nd XI debut 2013. Hertfordshire 2011-14. Awaiting 1st XI debut.

SIMPSON, John Andrew (St Gabriel's RC HS), b Bury, Lancs 13 Jul 1988. 5'10". LHB, WK. Squad No 20. Debut (Middlesex) 2009; cap 2011. Cumberland 2007. MCC YCs 2008. HS 143 v Surrey (Lord's) 2011. LO HS 82 v Glos (Cheltenham) 2010 (CB40). T20 HS 60*.

NQSTEEL, Cameron Tate (Scotch C, Perth, Australia; Durham U), b San Francisco, USA 13 Sep 1995. 5'10". RHB, LB. Squad No 22. Durham MCCU 2014. Middlesex 2nd XI debut 2013. Somerset 2nd XI 2013. Awaiting 1st XI debut. HS 68 and BB 1-39 DU v Durham (Chester-le-St) 2014.

NQSTIRLING, Paul Robert (Belfast HS), b Belfast, N Ireland 3 Sep 1990. Father Brian Stirling was an international rugby referee. 5'10". RHB, OB. Squad No 39. Ireland 2007-08 to date. Middlesex debut 2013. **LOI** (Ire): 57 (2008 to 2014-15); HS 177 v Canada (Toronto) 2010; BB 4-11 v Netherlands (Amstelveen) 2010. **IT20** (Ire): 26 (2009 to 2013-14); HS 79 v Afghanistan (Dubai, DSC) 2011-12; BB 3-21 v B (Belfast) 2012. F-c Tours (Ire): WI 2009-10; Kenya 2011-12; UAE 2013-14. HS 115 Ire v Australia A (Belfast) 2013. M HS 66* v Notts (Nottingham) 2013. BB 2-43 v Surrey (Lord's) 2013. LO HS 177 *(see LOI)*. LO BB 4-11 *(see LOI)*. T20 HS 82*. T20 BB 4-10.

NQVOGES, Adam Charles (Edith Cowan U, Perth), b Perth, Australia 4 Oct 1979. 6'0". RHB, SLA. Squad No 32. W Australia 2002-03 to date. Nottinghamshire 2008-12; cap 2008. Middlesex debut 2013; captain 2015. IPL: RR 2009-10. Big Bash: MS: 2011-12. PS 2012-13 to date. **LOI** (A): 31 (2006-07 to 2013-14); HS 112* v WI (Melbourne) 2012-13. BB 1-3 v E (Birmingham) 2013. **IT20** (A): 7 (2007-08 to 2013-14); HS 51 v WI (Brisbane) 2012-13; BB 2-5 v I (Melbourne) 2007-08. F-c Tours (Aus A): I 2008-09; P 2007-08. 1000 runs (0+1): 1132 (2014-15). HS 249 WA v S Aus (Adelaide) 2014-15. UK HS 165 Nt v Oxford MCCU (Oxford) 2011. M HS 150 v Warwks (Uxbridge) 2013. BB 4-92 WA v S Aus (Adelaide) 2006-07. UK BB 3-21 Nt v Durham (Nottingham) 2008. M BB 1-10 v Derbys (Derby) 2013. LO HS 112* *(see LOI)*. LO BB 3-25 Nt v Sussex (Hove) 2009 (P40). T20 HS 82*. T20 BB 2-4.

WHITE, Robert George (Harrow S; Loughborough U), b 15 Sep 1995. RHB, WK, occ RM. Squad No 14. Middlesex 2nd XI debut 2013. Awaiting 1st XI debut.

(Having made a County 1st XI appearance in 2014)

BERG, G.K. – *see HAMPSHIRE.*

NQ**CHRISTIAN, Daniel** Trevor, b Camperdown, NSW, Australia 4 May 1983. RHB, RFM. S Australia 2007-08 to 2012-13. Hampshire 2010. Gloucestershire 2013; cap 2013. Victoria 2013-14 to date. Middlesex 2014 (T20 only). IPL: DC 2011-12. RCB 2013. Big Bash: BH 2011-12 to date. **LOI** (A): 19 (2011-12 to 2013-14); HS 39 v I (Adelaide) 2011-12; BB 5-31 v SL (Melbourne) 2011-12. **IT20** (A): 15 (2009-10 to 2013-14); HS 6* v E (Hobart) 2013-14; BB 3-27 v WI (Gros Islet) 2011-12. HS 131* S Aus v NSW (Adelaide) 2011-12. CC HS 36 and CC BB 2-115 H v Somerset (Taunton) 2010. BB 5-24 (9-87 match) S Aus v WA (Perth) (2009-10). LO HS 117 Vic v NSW (Sydney) 2013-14. LO BB 6-48 S Aus v Vic (Geelong) 2010-11. T20 HS 129. T20 BB 5-26.

DENLY, J.L. – *see KENT.*

NQ**ROGERS, Christopher** John Llewellyn (Wesley C, Perth; Curtin U, Perth), b St George, Sydney, Australia 31 Aug 1977. Son of W.J.Rogers (NSW 1968-69 to 1969-70). 5'10". LHB, LBG. W Australia 1998-99 to 2007-08. Derbyshire 2004-10; cap 2008; captain 2008 (*part*) to 2010 (*part*). Leicestershire 2005. Northamptonshire 2006-07. Victoria 2008-09 to date. Middlesex 2011-14; cap 2011; captain 2013-14. MCC 2011. Big Bash: ST 2012-13. **Tests** (A): 20 (2007-08 to 2014-15); HS 119 v E (Sydney) 2013-14. F-c Tours (A): E 2013; SA 2013-14; P 2007-08 (Aus A); UAE 2014-15 (v P). 1000 runs (8+2); most – 1536 (2013). HS 319 Nh v Glos (Northampton) 2006. M HS 214 v Yorks (Lord's) 2014. BB 1-16 Nh v Leics (Northampton) 2006. LO HS 140 Vic v S Aus (Melbourne) 2009-10. LO BB 2-22 Nh v Durham (Northampton) 2006. T20 HS 58.

ROSSINGTON, A.M. – *see NORTHAMPTONSHIRE.*

O.Wilkin left the staff without making a County 1st XI appearance in 2014.

MIDDLESEX 2014

RESULTS SUMMARY

	Place	Won	Lost	Aband	Drew	NR
LV= County Championship (1st Division)	7th	4	5	1	6	
All First-Class Matches		4	5	1	6	
Royal London One-Day Cup (Group B)	7th	3	4			1
NatWest t20 Blast (South Division)	9th	2	11			1

LV= COUNTY CHAMPIONSHIP AVERAGES

BATTING AND FIELDING

Cap		M	I	NO	HS	Runs	Avge	100	50	Ct/St
2011	C.J.L.Rogers	15	28	4	241*	1333	55.54	4	4	10
2008	E.J.G.Morgan	11	20	1	191	871	45.84	2	4	7
2010	D.J.Malan	15	26	1	154*	1137	45.48	2	4	21
	P.R.Stirling	6	10	2	66*	351	43.87	–	4	1
2013	S.D.Robson	11	20	3	163	674	39.64	1	4	12
	N.R.T.Gubbins	4	7	–	95	240	34.28	–	3	–
2011	J.A.Simpson	15	23	3	110	669	33.45	2	4	36/3
2012	T.S.Roland-Jones	13	19	3	77	500	31.25	–	3	3
2010	N.J.Dexter	13	22	3	163*	535	28.15	1	3	3
2012	J.L.Denly	9	14	–	70	327	23.35	–	3	1
	O.P.Rayner	8	11	–	77	229	20.81	–	1	12
	J.A.R.Harris	7	9	3	41*	105	17.50	–	–	4
2008	T.J.Murtagh	14	17	3	42	231	16.50	–	–	3
	R.H.Patel	7	6	4	18	27	13.50	–	–	2
2009	S.T.Finn	11	15	5	37*	125	12.50	–	–	6
	A.M.Rossington	3	5	–	8	25	5.00	–	–	1

Also played: G.K.Berg (1 match – cap 2010) did not bat; T.G.Helm (1) 11*, 0 (1 ct); G.S.Sandhu (1) 6*.

BOWLING

	O	M	R	W	Avge	Best	5wI	10wM
T.J.Murtagh	527.4	116	1646	58	28.37	6- 60	5	1
S.T.Finn	393.1	58	1475	48	30.72	6- 80	2	–
T.S.Roland-Jones	406.1	87	1337	43	31.09	6- 50	3	1
N.J.Dexter	256	65	771	17	45.35	6- 63	1	–
J.A.R.Harris	198	49	666	12	55.50	4- 80	–	–
R.H.Patel	210.5	37	647	10	64.70	3- 49	–	–

Also bowled:
O.P.Rayner 219 36 596 5 119.20 2-101 – –

G.K.Berg 20-7-50-0; J.L.Denly 43.2-7-157-4; T.G.Helm 32-5-74-2; D.J.Malan 30.3-9-90-4; E.J.G.Morgan 0.5-0-7-0; S.D.Robson 1-0-6-0; C.J.L.Rogers 1-0-2-0; G.S.Sandhu 30-3-118-1; P.R.Stirling 14-2-49-1.

Middlesex played no first-class fixtures outside the County Championship in 2014. The First-Class Averages (pp 217–233) give the records of their players in all first-class county matches, with the exception of N.R.T.Gubbins, J.A.R.Harris, T.G.Helm, S.D.Robson and A.M.Rossington, whose first-class figures for Middlesex are as above.

MIDDLESEX RECORDS

FIRST-CLASS CRICKET

Highest Total	For	642-3d		v	Hampshire	Southampton	1923
	V	850-7d		by	Somerset	Taunton	2007
Lowest Total	For	20		v	MCC	Lord's	1864
	V	31		by	Glos	Bristol	1924
Highest Innings	For	331*	J.D.B.Robertson	v	Worcs	Worcester	1949
	V	341	C.M.Spearman	for	Glos	Gloucester	2004

Highest Partnership for each Wicket

1st	372	M.W.Gatting/J.L.Langer	v	Essex	Southgate	1998
2nd	380	F.A.Tarrant/J.W.Hearne	v	Lancashire	Lord's	1914
3rd	424*	W.J.Edrich/D.C.S.Compton	v	Somerset	Lord's	1948
4th	325	J.W.Hearne/E.H.Hendren	v	Hampshire	Lord's	1919
5th	338	R.S.Lucas/T.C.O'Brien	v	Sussex	Hove	1895
6th	270	J.D.Carr/P.N.Weekes	v	Glos	Lord's	1994
7th	271*	E.H.Hendren/F.T.Mann	v	Notts	Nottingham	1925
8th	182*	M.H.C.Doll/H.R.Murrell	v	Notts	Lord's	1913
9th	172	G.K.Berg/T.J.Murtagh	v	Leics	Leicester	2011
10th	230	R.W.Nicholls/W.Roche	v	Kent	Lord's	1899

Best Bowling	For	10- 40	G.O.B.Allen	v	Lancashire	Lord's	1929
(Innings)	V	9- 38	R.C.R.Glasgow†	for	Somerset	Lord's	1924
Best Bowling	For	16-114	G.Burton	v	Yorkshire	Sheffield	1888
(Match)		16-114	J.T.Hearne	v	Lancashire	Manchester	1898
	V	16-100	J.E.B.B.P.Q.C.Dwyer	for	Sussex	Hove	1906

Most Runs – Season	2669	E.H.Hendren	(av 83.41)		1923
Most Runs – Career	40302	E.H.Hendren	(av 48.81)		1907-37
Most 100s – Season	13	D.C.S.Compton			1947
Most 100s – Career	119	E.H.Hendren			1907-37
Most Wkts – Season	158	F.J.Titmus	(av 14.63)		1955
Most Wkts – Career	2361	F.J.Titmus	(av 21.27)		1949-82
Most Career W-K Dismissals	1223	J.T.Murray	(1024 ct; 199 st)		1952-75
Most Career Catches in the Field	561	E.H.Hendren			1907-37

LIMITED-OVERS CRICKET

Highest Total	50ov	341-7		v	Somerset	Lord's	2009
	40ov	350-6		v	Lancashire	Lord's	2012
	T20	213-4		v	Glamorgan	Richmond	2010
Lowest Total	50ov	41		v	Essex	Westcliff	1972
	40ov	23		v	Yorkshire	Leeds	1974
	T20	92		v	Surrey	Lords	2013
Highest Innings	50ov	163	A.J.Strauss	v	Surrey	The Oval	2008
	40ov	147*	M.R.Ramprakash	v	Worcs	Lord's	1990
	T20	129	D.T.Christian	v	Kent	Canterbury	2014
Best Bowling	50ov	7-12	W.W.Daniel	v	Minor Cos E	Ipswich	1978
	40ov	6- 6	R.W.Hooker	v	Surrey	Lord's	1969
	T20	5-13	M.Kartik	v	Essex	Lord's	2007

† R.C.Robertson-Glasgow

NORTHAMPTONSHIRE

Formation of Present Club: 31 July 1878
Inaugural First-Class Match: 1905
Colours: Maroon
Badge: Tudor Rose
County Champions: (0); best – 2nd 1912, 1957, 1965, 1976
Gillette/NatWest/C&G/FP Trophy Winners: (2) 1976, 1992
Benson and Hedges Cup Winners: (1) 1980
Twenty20 Cup Winners: (1) 2013

Acting Chief Executive: Ray Payne, County Ground, Abington Avenue, Northampton, NN1 4PR • Tel: 01604 514455 • Fax: 01604 609288 • Email: post@nccc.co.uk • Web: www.nccc.co.uk • Twitter: @NorthantsCCC (14,130 followers)

Head Coach: David Ripley. **Captain**: A.G.Wakely. **Vice-Captain**: D.J.Willey. **Overseas Players**: R.K.Kleinveldt and Shahid Afridi (T20 only). **2015 Beneficiary**: None. **Head Groundsman**: Paul Marshall. **Scorer**: Tony Kingston. ‡ New registration. ^NQ Not qualified for England.

AZHAR ULLAH, Mohammad (also known as AZHARULLAH), b Burewala, Punjab, Pakistan 25 Dec 1983. 5'7". RHB, RFM. Squad No 92. Multan 2004-05 to 2006-07. WAPDA 2004-05 to 2012-13. Quetta 2005-06. Baluchistan 2007-08 to 2008-09. Northamptonshire debut 2013. UK qualified through residency and British wife. HS 41 WAPDA v Karachi Whites (Karachi) 2007-08. Nh HS 28 v Lancs (Manchester) 2014. BB 7-74 Quetta v Lahore Ravi (Quetta) 2005-06. Nh BB 7-76 (10-158 match) v Sussex (Northampton) 2014. LO HS 9 (twice). LO BB 5-38 v Hants (Southampton) 2014 (RLC). T20 HS 5*. T20 BB 4-14.

BARRETT, Chad Anthony (King Edward VII S, Johannesburg), b Johannesburg, South Africa 22 May 1989. 6'2". RHB, RMF. Debut (Northamptonshire) 2014. Somerset 2nd XI 2009. Middlesex 2nd XI 2013. Gloucestershire 2nd XI 2013. HS 20* and BB – v Sri Lankans (Northampton) 2014 – only 1st XI appearance.

CHAMBERS, Maurice Anthony (Homerton TC; Sir George Monoux C), b Port Antonio, Portland, Jamaica 14 Sep 1987. 6'3". RHB, RFM. Squad No 29. Essex 2005-13. No f-c appearances 2006-07 – stress fracture of the back. Warwickshire 2013 (on loan). Northamptonshire debut 2014. MCC YC 2004. F-c Tour (EL): WI 2010-11. HS 58 Wa v Derbys (Derby) 2013. Nh HS 20 v Middx (Lord's) 2014. BB 6-68 (10-123 match) Ex v Notts (Chelmsford) 2010. Nh BB 2-23 v Yorks (Northampton) 2014. LO HS 2 Ex v Lancs (Chelmsford) 2012 (CB40). LO BB 3-29 v Lancs (Manchester) 2014 (RLC). T20 HS 10*. T20 BB 3-31.

‡COBB, Joshua James (Oakham S), b Leicester 17 Aug 1990. Son of R.A.Cobb (Leics and N Transvaal 1980-89). 5'11½". RHB, LB. Squad No 4. Leicestershire 2007-14; l-o captain 2014. Leicestershire 2nd XI debut 2006, aged 16y 5d. England U19s 2009. HS 148* Le v Middx (Lord's) 2008. BB 2-11 Le v Glos (Leicester) 2008. LO HS 137 Le v Lancs (Manchester) 2012 (CB40). LO BB 3-34 Le v Glos (Leicester) 2013 (Y40). T20 HS 70. T20 BB 4-22.

COETZER, Kyle James (Aberdeen GS), b Aberdeen, Scotland 14 Apr 1984. 5'11". RHB, RM. Squad No 30. Durham 2004-10. Northamptonshire debut 2011; cap 2013. Scotland 2004 to date. **LOI** (Scot): 25 (2008 to 2014-15); HS 156 v B (Nelson) 2014-15; BB 1-35 v Netherlands (Aberdeen) 2011. **IT20** (Scot): 20 (2008 to 2013-14); HS 62 v Ireland (Dubai, DSC) 2011-12; BB 3-25 v Afghanistan (Abu Dhabi) 2009-10. F-c Tour (Scot): Kenya 2009-10. HS 219 v Leics (Leicester) 2013. BB 2-16 Scot v Kenya (Nairobi) 2009-10. CC BB 1-9 v Glamorgan (Northampton) 2012. LO HS 156 (*see LOI*). LO BB 1-2 v Notts (Nottingham) 2013 (Y40). T20 HS 71*. T20 BB 3-25.

CROOK, Steven Paul (Rostrevor C; Magill U), b Modbury, S Australia 28 May 1983. Younger brother of A.R.Crook (S Australia, Aus Academy, Lancashire, Northamptonshire 1998-99 to 2008). 5'11". RHB, RFM. Squad No 25. British passport. Lancashire 2003-05. Northamptonshire debut 2005; cap 2013. Middlesex 2011-12. Aus Academy 2001-02. HS 131 v Middx (Lord's) 2014. BB 5-48 M v Lancs (Lord's) 2012. Nh BB 5-71 v Essex (Northampton) 2009. LO HS 100 SJD v PDSC (Savar) 2013-14. LO BB 5-36 v Warwks (Northampton) 2013 (Y40). T20 HS 63. T20 BB 3-19.

DUCKETT, Ben Matthew (Stowe S), b Farnborough, Kent 17 Oct 1994. LHB, WK, occ OB. Squad No 17. Debut (Northamptonshire) 2013. Northamptonshire 2nd XI debut 2011. England U19s 2012-13. HS 144* v Somerset (Taunton) 2014. LO HS 49 v Worcs (Milton Keynes) 2014 (RLC). T20 HS 39*.

KEOGH, Robert Ian (Queensbury S; Dunstable C), b Luton, Beds 21 Oct 1991. 5'11". RHB, OB. Squad No 14. Debut (Northamptonshire) 2012. Northamptonshire 2nd XI debut 2009. Bedfordshire 2009-10. HS 221 v Hants (Southampton) 2013. BB 2-46 v Sri Lankans (Northampton) 2014. CC BB 1-5 v Somerset (Taunton) 2014. LO HS 61 v Warwks (Birmingham) 2013 (Y40). LO BB – . T20 HS 28. T20 BB – .

‡ⁿᵒ**KLEINVELDT, Rory** Keith, b Cape Town, South Africa 15 Mar 1983. Cousin of M.C.Kleinveldt (W Province 2010-11 to date). Nephew of J.Kleinveldt (W Province and Transvaal 1979-80 to 1982-83). RHB, RMF. Squad No 6. W Province 2002-03 to 2005-06. Cape Cobras 2005-06 to date. Hampshire 2008 (1 game). **Tests** (SA): 4 (2012-13); HS 17* v A (Brisbane) 2012-13; BB 3-65 v A (Adelaide) 2012-13. **LOI** (SA): 10 (2012-13 to 2013); HS 43 v E (Oval) 2013; BB 4-22 v P (Bloemfontein) 2012-13. **IT20** (SA): 6 (2008-09 to 2012-13); HS 22 v P (Centurion) 2012-13; BB 3-18 v NZ (Durban) 2012-13. F-c Tours (SA A): A 2012-13 (SA); I 2007-08; SL 2010. HS 115* WP v KZN (Chatsworth) 2005-06. BB 8-47 Cobras v Warriors (Stellenbosch) 2005-06. LO HS 55 WP v KZN (Durban) 2010-11. LO BB 4-22 (*see LOI*). T20 HS 46. T20 BB 3-18 (*see IT20*).

ⁿᵒ**LEVI, Richard** Ernst, b Johannesburg, South Africa 14 Jan 1988. RHB, RM. Squad No 88. W Province 2006-07 to 2013-14. Cape Cobras 2008-09 to date. Northamptonshire debut 2014 (Kolpak signing in 2015). **IT20** (SA): 13 (2011-12 to 2012-13); HS 117* v NZ (Hamilton) 2011-12. HS 150* WP v EP (Cape Town) 2006-07. Nh HS 64 v Sri Lankans (Northampton) 2014. CC HS 59 v Lancs (Manchester) 2014. LO HS 166 Cobras v Titans (Paarl) 2012-13. T20 HS 117*.

MURPHY, David (Richard Hale S, Hertford; Loughborough U), b Welwyn Garden City, Herts 24 June 1989. 5'11". RHB, WK. Squad No 19. Loughborough MCCU 2009-11. Northamptonshire debut 2009. **LOI** (Scot): 8 (2012-13 to 2013); HS 20* v Ireland (Belfast) 2013. **IT20** (Scot): 4 (2012-13 to 2013-14); HS 81 v Hants (Northampton) 2013. LO HS 31* v Netherlands (Northampton) 2010 (CB40). T20 HS 20.

NEWTON, Robert Irving (Framlingham C), b Taunton, Somerset 18 Jan 1990. 5'8". RHB, OB. Squad No 21. Debut (Northamptonshire) 2010. HS 119* v Derbys (Northampton) 2012. BB – . LO HS 88* v Kent (Tunbridge W) 2013 (Y40). T20 HS 38.

PETERS, Stephen David (Coopers Coborn & Co S), b Harold Wood, Essex 10 Dec 1978. 5'11". RHB, occ LB. Squad No 11. Essex 1996-2001, scoring 110 and 12* v Cambridge U (Cambridge) on debut. Worcestershire 2002-05. Northamptonshire debut 2006; cap 2007; captain 2013-14. MCC 2011, 2012. 1000 runs (4); most – 1320 (2010). HS 222 v Glamorgan (Swansea) 2011. BB 1-19 Ex v Oxford U (Chelmsford) 1999. LO HS 107 v Yorks (Leeds) 2007 (FPT). T20 HS 61*.

ROSSINGTON, Adam Matthew (Mill Hill S), b Edgware 5 May 1993. 5'11". RHB, WK. Squad No 7. Middlesex 2010-14. Northamptonshire debut 2014. Middlesex 2nd XI debut 2010. England U19s 2010-11, scoring 113 v SL on debut. Summer contract. HS 103* v Cambridge MCCU (Cambridge) 2013, winning the Walter Lawrence Trophy with 55-ball century. Nh HS 103 v Notts (Northampton) 2014. LO HS 82 v Glos (Cheltenham) 2014 (RLC). T20 HS 74.

NQ**SHAHID** KHAN **AFRIDI**, Sahibzaha Mohammad (Ibrahim Alibhai S; Islamia Science C, Karachi) b Kohat, Pakistan, 1 Mar 1980. Brother of Tariq Afridi (Karachi 1999-00) and Ashfaq Afridi (Karachi Blues 2008-09). RHB, LBG. Squad No 10. Debut Combined XI v Eng A 1995-96. Karachi 1995-96 to 2003-04. HB 1997-98 to date. Leicestershire 2001; cap 2001. Derbyshire 2003. GW 2003-04. Sind 2007-08 to 2008-09. MCC 2001. Northamptonshire T20 contract for 2015. IPL: DC 2007-08. Big Bash: MR 2011-12. **Tests** (P): 27 (1998-99 to 2010, 1 as captain); HS 156 v I (Faisalabad) 2005-06; BB 5-52 v A (Karachi) 1998-99 – on debut. **LOI** (P): 396 (1996-97 to 2014-15, 38 as captain); HS 124 v B (Dambulla) 2010; BB 7-12 v WI (Providence) 2013, 2nd best analysis in all LOIs. Scored a 37-ball hundred which included the joint record 11 sixes v SL (Nairobi) 1996-97 in his first LOI innings. **IT20** (P): 77 (2006-07 to 2014-15, 22 as captain); HS 54* v SL (Lord's) 2009; BB 4-11 v Netherlands (Lord's) 2009. F-c Tours (P): E 2006, 2010; A 1996-97, 2004-05; WI 1999-00, 2005; I 1998-99, 2004-05; SL 2005-06; Z 2002-03; B 1998-99. HS 164 Le v Northants (Northampton) 2001. BB 6-101 HB v KRL (Rawalpindi) 1997-98. UK BB 5-84 Le v Essex (Chelmsford) 2001. LO HS 124 (*see LOI*). LO BB 7-12 (*see LOI*). T20 HS 80. T20 BB 5-20.

STONE, Oliver Peter (Thorpe St Andrew HS), b Norwich, Norfolk 9 Oct 1983. 6'1". RHB, RMF. Squad No 9. Debut (Northamptonshire) 2012. Northamptonshire 2nd XI debut 2010. Norfolk 2011. Captained England U19s 2012-13. HS 26* v Yorks (Northampton) 2012. BB 5-48 v Sussex (Northampton) 2014. LO HS 21 v Worcs (Milton Keynes) 2014 (RLC). LO BB 1-12 v Derbys (Northampton) 2012 (CB40). T20 HS 6*. T20 BB 2-18.

WAKELY, Alexander George (Bedford S), b Hammersmith, London 3 Nov 1988. 6'2". RHB, OB. Squad No 8. Debut (Northamptonshire) 2007; cap 2012; captain 2015. Missed entire 2014 season due to ruptured Achilles. Bedfordshire 2004-05. HS 113* v Glamorgan (Cardiff) 2009. BB 2-62 v Somerset (Taunton) 2007 – on debut. LO HS 102 v Kent (Tunbridge W) 2013 (Y40). LO BB 2-14 v Lancs (Northampton) 2007 (P40). T20 HS 62. T20 BB – .

WHITE, Graeme Geoffrey (Stowe S), b Milton Keynes, Bucks 18 Apr 1987. 5'11". RHB, SLA. Squad No 87. Debut (Northamptonshire) 2006. Nottinghamshire 2010-13. HS 65 Nh v Glamorgan (Colwyn Bay) 2007. BB 4-72 Nt v Durham (Nottingham) 2011. Nh BB 2-28 v Sri Lankans (Northampton) 2014. LO HS 39* v Somerset (Taunton) 2012 (CB40). LO BB 5-35 v Scotland (Edinburgh) 2010 (CB40). T20 HS 26*. T20 BB 5-22 Nt v Lancs (Nottingham) 2013 – Nt record.

WILLEY, David Jonathan (Northampton S), b Northampton 28 Feb 1990. Son of P.Willey (Northants, Leics and England 1966-91). 6'1". RHB, LHB, LFM. Squad No 15. Debut (Northamptonshire) 2009; cap 2013. Bedfordshire 2008. HS 81 v Glamorgan (Northampton) 2013. BB 5-29 (10-75 match) v Glos (Northampton) 2011. LO HS 167 v Warwks (Birmingham) 2013 (Y40). LO BB 5-62 EL v New Zealand A (Bristol) 2014. T20 HS 95. T20 BB 4-9.

ZAIB, Saif Ali (RGS High Wycombe), b High Wycombe, Bucks 22 May 1998. LHB, SLA. Squad No 5. Northamptonshire 2nd XI debut 2013, aged 15y 90d. Awaiting f-c debut. LO HS and BB – .

RELEASED/RETIRED

(Having made a County 1st XI appearance in 2014)

NOBUTLER, Ian Gareth (home educated), b Otahuhu, Auckland, New Zealand 24 Nov 1981. 6'3''. RHB, RFM. N Districts 2001-02 to 2004-05. Gloucestershire 2003. Kent 2004. Otago 2008-09 to 2013-14. Northamptonshire 2014. **Tests** (NZ): 8 (2001-02 to 2004-05); HS 26 v WI (Bridgetown) 2001-02; BB 6-46 v P (Wellington) 2003-04. **LOI** (NZ): 26 (2001-02 to 2009-10); HS 25 v SL (Colombo, RPS) 2009; BB 4-44 v P (Johannesburg) 2009-10. Dismissed M.E.Trescothick with his fifth ball in LOI. **IT20** (NZ): 19 (2008-09 to 2013); HS 2* v SL (Nottingham) 2009; BB 3-19 v Scotland (Oval) 2009 and v P (Bridgetown) 2010. F-c Tours (NZ): A 2004-05; WI 2001-02; I 2003-04; B 2004-05. HS 73* Otago v CD (Napier) 2012-13. CC HS 68 K v Surrey (Canterbury) 2004. Nh HS 48* v Middx (Northampton) 2014. BB 6-46 (see Tests). CC BB 4-41 v Yorks (Northampton) 2014. LO HS 53* Otago v Canterbury (Timaru) 2009-10. LO BB 5-33 Otago v ND (Dunedin) 2011-12. T20 HS 46*. T20 BB 6-28.

NOHALL, Andrew James (Alberton HS), b Alberton, Johannesburg, South Africa 31 Jul 1975. 6'0''. RHB, RFM. Transvaal/Gauteng 1995-96 to 2000-01. Easterns 2001-02 to 2003-04. Worcestershire 2003-04. Lions 2004-05 to 2005-06. Kent 2005-07; cap 2005. Northamptonshire 2008-14; cap 2009; captain 2010 (part) to 2012. Dolphins 2009-10. ME 2010-11. Durham CB 1999. Suffolk 2002. **Tests** (SA): 21 (2001-02 to 2006-07); HS 163 v I (Kanpur) 2004-05; BB 3-1 v SL (Johannesburg) 2002-03. **LOI** (SA): 88 (1998-99 to 2007); HS 81 v SL (Galle) 2000-01; BB 5-18 v E (Bridgetown) 2006-07. **IT20** (SA): 2 (2005-06); HS 11 v A (Brisbane) 2005-06; BB 3-22 v A Johannesburg) 2005-06. F-c Tours (SA): E 2003; WI 2004-05; I 2004-05; SL 2006; Z 1995-96 (Transvaal B), 2007-08 (SA A). 1000 runs (1): 1161 (2009). HS 163 (see Tests). UK HS 159 v Leics (Northampton) 2009. BB 6-77 (11-99 match) Easterns v WP (Pt Elizabeth) 2002-03. UK BB 5-29 v Essex (Northampton) 2009. LO HS 129* Gauteng v Border (E London) 1999-00. LO BB 5-18 (see LOI). T20 HS 66* and T20 BB 6-21 v Worcs (Northampton) 2008 (Nh record analysis, and 1st man in UK to score 50 and take 5 wkts in a game).

KETTLEBOROUGH, J.M. – see GLAMORGAN.

MIDDLEBROOK, James Daniel (Pudsey Crawshaw S), b Leeds, Yorks 13 May 1977. 6'1''. RHB, OB. Yorkshire 1998-2001. Essex 2002-09; cap 2003. Northamptonshire 2010-14, cap 2011. MCC 2010, 2013. HS 127 Ex v Middx (Lord's) 2007. Nh HS 121 v Glos (Northampton) 2012. 50 wkts (1): 56 (2003). BB 6-78 v Kent (Northampton) 2013. Took 4 wkts in 5 balls for Y v Hants (Southampton) 2000. Hat-trick Ex v Kent (Canterbury) 2003. LO HS 57* v Derbys (Derby) 2010 (CB40). LO BB 4-27 Ex v Somerset (Taunton) 2006 (CGT). T20 HS 43. T20 BB 3-13.

SALES, David John Grimwood (Caterham S; Cumnor House S), b Carshalton, Surrey 3 Dec 1977. 6'0''. RHB, RM. Northamptonshire 1996-2014, scoring 0 and 210* v Worcs (Kidderminster) on debut – record Championship score on f-c debut; youngest (18y 237d) to score 200 in a Championship match; cap 1999; captain 2004-07; benefit 2007. Missed entire 2009 season with knee injury. Wellington 2001-02. MCC 2010. F-c Tours (Eng A): NZ 1999-00; SL 1997-98; K 1997-98; B 1999-00. 1000 runs (6); most – 1384 (2007). HS 303* v Essex (Northampton) 1999 – youngest Englishman (21y 240d) to score a f-c 300. BB 4-25 v Sri Lanka A (Northampton) 1999. CC BB 2-7 v Yorks (Scarborough) 1999. LO HS 161 v Yorks (Northampton) 2006 (CGT) – Nh record. LO BB – . T20 HS 78*. T20 BB 1-10.

SPRIEGEL, Matthew Neil William (Whitgift S; Loughborough U), b Epsom, Surrey 4 Mar 1987. 6'3". LHB, OB. Loughborough UCCE 2007-08; captain 2007-08. Surrey 2008-12. Northamptonshire 2013-14. HS 108* Sy v Bangladeshis (Oval) 2010. CC HS 103 Sy v Northants (Oval) 2010. Nh HS 97 v Durham (Northampton) 2014. BB 3-26 v Middx (Lord's) 2014. LO HS 86 Sy v Durham (Oval) 2011 (CB40). LO BB 3-29 v Worcs (Worcester) 2013 (Y40). T20 HS 53*. T20 BB 4-33.

NQ**WAGNER, Neil**, b Pretoria, South Africa 13 Mar 1986. LHB, LMF. Northerns 2005-06 to 2007-08. Titans 2006-07 to 2007-08. Otago 2008-09 to date. Northamptonshire 2014. **Tests** (NZ): 16 (2012 to 2014-15); HS 37 v WI (Dunedin) 2013-14; BB 5-64 v B (Dhaka) 2013-14. F-c Tours (NZ): E 2013; SA 2012-13; WI 2012, 2014; Z 2007 (SA Acad); B 2013-14. HS 70 Otago v Wellington (Queenstown) 2009-10. Nh HS 18 v Warwks (Birmingham) 2014. 50 wkts (0+2); most – 51 (2010-11, 2012-13). BB 7-46 Otago v Wellington (Dunedin) 2011-12. Nh BB 5-104 v Durham (Chester-le-St) 2014. LO HS 42 Otago v CD (Dunedin) 2014-15. LO BB 5-34 Otago v Wellington (Wellington) 2008-09. T20 HS 14. T20 BB 4-33.

LANCASHIRE RELEASED/RETIRED (continued from p 125)

NQ**JUNAID KHAN**, Mohammad, b Matra, NW Frontier, Pakistan 24 Dec 1989. RHB, LMF. Abbottabad 2006-07 to 2011-12. NW Frontier Province 2008-09. KRL 2008-09. Lancashire 2011-14. WAPDA 2012-13. **Tests** (P): 18 (2011 to 2014); HS 17 v Z (Harare) 2013; BB 5-38 v SL (Abu Dhabi) 2011-12. **LOI** (P): 48 (2011 to 2014); HS 25 v SA (Benoni) 2012-13; BB 4-12 v Ireland (Belfast) 2011. **IT20** (P): 9 (2011 to 2013-14): HS 3* v WI (Gros Islet) 2011; BB 3-24 v Afghanistan (Sharjah) 2013-14. F-c Tours (P): SA 2012-13; WI 2010-11; SL 2010 (P A), 2012, 2014; Z 2011, 2013; UAE 2011-12 (v E), 2013-14 (v SA), 2013-14 (v SL). HS 71 Abbottabad v Rawalpindi (Abbottabad) 2007-08. La HS 16 v Durham (Liverpool) 2011. BB 7-46 (13-77 match) Abbottabad v Peshawar (Peshawar) 2007-08. La BB 3-84 v Middx (Manchester) 2014. LO HS 32 P A v South Africa A (Colombo, PSS) 2010. La LO BB 5-45 Fighters v Warriors (Karachi) 2014-15. T20 HS 17*. T20 BB 4-12.

NQ**KHAWAJA, Usman** Tariq (Westfield Sports HS; U of NSW), b Islamabad, Pakistan 18 Dec 1986. 5'9". LHB, RM. NSW 2007-08 to 2011-12. Derbyshire 2011-12. Queensland 2012-13 to date. Lancashire 2014. **Tests** (A): 9 (2010-11 to 2013); HS 65 v SA (Johannesburg) 2011-12. **LOI** (A): 3 (2012-13); HS 8* v WI (Perth) 2012-13. F-c Tours (A): E 2013; SA 2011-12; I 2012-13; SL 2011; Z 2011 (Aus A). HS 214 and BB 1-21 NSW v S Aus (Adelaide) 2010-11. CC HS 135 De v Kent (Canterbury) 2011. La HS 117 v Yorks (Manchester) 2014. CC BB – . LO HS 166 Q v Tas (Sydney) 2014-15. T20 HS 67.

NEWBY, Oliver James (Ribblesdale HS; Myerscough C), b Blackburn 26 Aug 1984. 6'5". RHB, RMF. Lancashire 2003-13. Nottinghamshire 2005 (on loan). Gloucestershire 2008 (on loan) 2008; cap 2008. No f-c appearances in 2010. Essex (on loan) 2014. HS 38* Nt v Kent (Nottingham) 2005 – on Notts debut. La HS 29* v Oxford MCCU (Oxford) 2011. BB 5-69 Gs v Northants (Bristol) 2008. La BB 4-21 v Durham MCCU (Durham) 2009. LO HS 36* v Glos (Bristol) 2012 (CB40). LO BB 5-35 v Essex (Chelmsford) 2012 (CB40). T20 HS 6*. T20 BB 2-34.

WHITE, W.A. – *see DERBYSHIRE*.

NORTHAMPTONSHIRE 2014

RESULTS SUMMARY

	Place	Won	Lost	Tied	Drew	NR
LV= County Championship (1st Division)	9th		12		4	
All First-Class Matches			12		5	
Royal London One-Day Cup (Group A)	6th	2	4			2
NatWest t20 Blast (North Division)	7th	4	7			3

LV= COUNTY CHAMPIONSHIP AVERAGES
BATTING AND FIELDING

Cap		M	I	NO	HS	Runs	Avge	100	50	Ct/St
	A.M.Rossington	6	10	–	103	440	44.00	1	2	13/3
	B.M.Duckett	13	23	1	144*	615	27.95	1	5	14/1
2011	J.D.Middlebrook	16	30	–	87	825	27.50	–	5	14
2009	A.J.Hall	16	29	3	75	693	26.65	–	4	15
2013	S.P.Crook	8	15	1	131	373	26.64	1	1	5
	J.M.Kettleborough	8	15	–	73	398	26.53	–	3	5
	R.I.Keogh	8	13	1	129	317	26.41	1	1	–
	I.G.Butler	2	4	1	48*	76	25.33	–	–	–
2007	S.D.Peters	13	25	1	88	594	24.75	–	3	4
	M.N.W.Spriegel	12	24	2	97	494	22.45	–	2	5
	R.I.Newton	12	24	2	114	473	21.50	1	–	6
	R.E.Levi	3	6	–	59	120	20.00	–	1	–
2013	K.J.Coetzer	9	17	–	54	323	19.00	–	2	3
1999	D.J.G.Sales	3	6	–	43	103	17.16	–	–	2
2013	D.J.Willey	8	15	–	53	241	16.06	–	2	1
	Azhar Ullah	14	25	15	28	137	13.70	–	–	–
	D.Murphy	5	10	3	23*	74	10.57	–	–	7/4
	M.A.Chambers	8	15	3	20	107	8.91	–	–	4
	O.P.Stone	5	9	2	15	46	6.57	–	–	2
	N.Wagner	5	8	–	18	52	6.50	–	–	1

Also batted: G.G.White (2 matches) 4, 6, 2.

BOWLING

	O	M	R	W	Avge	Best	5wI	10wM
O.P.Stone	154.3	36	503	19	26.47	5- 48	1	–
D.J.Willey	163.1	36	515	19	27.10	4- 46	–	–
Azhar Ullah	462.1	92	1504	46	32.69	7- 76	1	1
A.J.Hall	451.1	83	1481	35	42.31	4- 77	–	–
J.D.Middlebrook	414.3	93	1307	29	45.06	5- 62	2	–
M.A.Chambers	222.3	37	814	13	62.61	2- 23	–	–
S.P.Crook	210	22	833	13	64.07	3- 26	–	–
N.Wagner	182	26	728	10	72.80	5-104	1	–

Also bowled:

	O	M	R	W	Avge	Best	5wI	10wM
M.N.W.Spriegel	99	11	378	8	47.25	3- 26	–	–

I.G.Butler 51-11-179-4; K.J.Coetzer 22-2-77-1; R.I.Keogh 39-6-111-2; G.G.White 19-2-104-0.

The First-Class Averages (pp 217–233) give the records of Northamptonshire players in all first-class county matches (Northamptonshire's other opponents being the Sri Lankans), with the exception of A.M.Rossington, whose first-class figures for Northamptonshire are as above.

NORTHAMPTONSHIRE RECORDS

FIRST-CLASS CRICKET

Highest Total	For 781-7d		v	Notts	Northampton	1995
	V 673-8d		by	Yorkshire	Leeds	2003
Lowest Total	For 12		v	Glos	Gloucester	1907
	V 33		by	Lancashire	Northampton	1977
Highest Innings	For 331*	M.E.K.Hussey	v	Somerset	Taunton	2003
	V 333	K.S.Duleepsinhji	for	Sussex	Hove	1930

Highest Partnership for each Wicket

1st	375	R.A.White/M.J.Powell	v	Glos	Northampton	2002
2nd	344	G.Cook/R.J.Boyd-Moss	v	Lancashire	Northampton	1986
3rd	393	A.Fordham/A.J.Lamb	v	Yorkshire	Leeds	1990
4th	370	R.T.Virgin/P.Willey	v	Somerset	Northampton	1976
5th	401	M.B.Loye/D.Ripley	v	Glamorgan	Northampton	1998
6th	376	R.Subba Row/A.Lightfoot	v	Surrey	The Oval	1958
7th	293	D.J.G.Sales/D.Ripley	v	Essex	Northampton	1999
8th	179	A.J.Hall/J.D.Middlebrook	v	Surrey	The Oval	2011
9th	156	R.Subba Row/S.Starkie	v	Lancashire	Northampton	1955
10th	148	B.W.Bellamy/J.V.Murdin	v	Glamorgan	Northampton	1925

Best Bowling	For 10-127	V.W.C.Jupp	v	Kent	Tunbridge W	1932
(Innings)	V 10- 30	C.Blythe	for	Kent	Northampton	1907
Best Bowling	For 15- 31	G.E.Tribe	v	Yorkshire	Northampton	1958
(Match)	V 17- 48	C.Blythe	for	Kent	Northampton	1907

Most Runs – Season	2198	D.Brookes	(av 51.11)	1952
Most Runs – Career	28980	D.Brookes	(av 36.13)	1934-59
Most 100s – Season	8	R.A.Haywood		1921
Most 100s – Career	67	D.Brookes		1934-59
Most Wkts – Season	175	G.E.Tribe	(av 18.70)	1955
Most Wkts – Career	1102	E.W.Clark	(av 21.26)	1922-47
Most Career W-K Dismissals	810	K.V.Andrew	(653 ct; 157 st)	1953-66
Most Career Catches in the Field	469	D.S.Steele		1963-84

LIMITED-OVERS CRICKET

Highest Total	50ov	360-2		v	Staffs	Northampton	1990
	40ov	324-6		v	Warwicks	Birmingham	2013
	T20	224-5		v	Glos	Milton Keynes	2005
Lowest Total	50ov	62		v	Leics	Leicester	1974
	40ov	41		v	Middlesex	Northampton	1972
	T20	47		v	Durham	Chester-le-St[2]	2011
Highest Innings	50ov	161	D.J.G.Sales	v	Yorkshire	Northampton	2006
	40ov	172*	W.Larkins	v	Warwicks	Luton	1983
	T20	111*	L.Klusener	v	Worcs	Kidderminster	2007
Best Bowling	50ov	7-10	C.Pietersen	v	Denmark	Brondby	2005
	40ov	7-39	A.Hodgson	v	Somerset	Northampton	1976
	T20	6-21	A.J.Hall	v	Worcs	Northampton	2008

NOTTINGHAMSHIRE

Formation of Present Club: March/April 1841
Substantial Reorganisation: 11 December 1866
Inaugural First-Class Match: 1864
Colours: Green and Gold
Badge: Badge of City of Nottingham
County Champions (since 1890): (6) 1907, 1929, 1981, 1987, 2005, 2010
NatWest Trophy Winners: (1) 1987
Benson and Hedges Cup Winners: (1) 1989
Sunday League Winners: (1) 1991
Yorkshire Bank 40 Winners: (1) 2013
Twenty20 Cup Winners: (0); best – Finalist 2006

Chief Executive: Lisa Pursehouse, Trent Bridge, Nottingham NG2 6AG • Tel: 0115 982 3000 • Fax: 0115 982 3037 • Email: administration@nottsccc.co.uk • Webs: www.nottsccc.co.uk • www.trentbridge.co.uk • Twitter: @TrentBridge (21,803 followers)

Director of Cricket: Mick Newell. **Assistant Coach**: Wayne Noon. **Bowling Coach**: Andy Pick. **Captains**: C.M.W.Read (f-c) and J.W.A.Taylor (l-o). **Vice-Captain**: J.W.A.Taylor. **Overseas Players**: B.W.Hilfenhaus, V.D.Philander and D.J.G.Sammy (T20 only). **2015 Beneficiary**: None. **Head Groundsman**: Steve Birks. **Scorer**: Roger Marshall. ‡ New registration. ^{NQ} Not qualified for England.

BALL, Jacob Timothy (**'Jake'**) (Meden CS), b Mansfield 14 Mar 1991. Nephew of B.N.French (Notts and England 1976-95). 6'0". RHB, RM. Squad No 28. Debut (Nottinghamshire) 2011. Nottinghamshire 2nd XI debut 2008. England U19s 2010. HS 31 v Oxford MCCU (Oxford) 2014. CC HS 20 and CC BB 3-60 v Durham (Chester-le-St) 2014. BB 3-18 v Durham MCCU (Nottingham) 2013. LO HS 19* v Sri Lanka A (Nottingham) 2011. BB 4-25 v Somerset (Nottingham) 2013 (Y40). T20 HS 1*. T20 BB 3-38.

BROAD, Stuart Christopher John (Oakham S), b Nottingham 24 Jun 1986. 6'6". LHB, RFM. Squad No 16. Son of B.C.Broad (Glos, Notts, OFS and England 1979-94). Debut (Leicestershire) 2005; cap 2007. Nottinghamshire debut/cap 2008. YC 2006. *Wisden* 2009. **ECB central contract 2014-15. Tests**: 74 (2007-08 to 2014); HS 169 v P (Lord's) 2010, sharing in record Test and UK f-c 8th-wkt partnership of 332 with I.J.L.Trott; BB 7-44 v NZ (Lord's) 2013. Hat-tricks (2) v I (Nottingham) 2011, and v SL (Leeds) 2014. **LOI**: 119 (2006 to 2014-15, 3 as captain); HS 45* v I (Manchester) 2007; BB 5-23 v SA (Nottingham) 2008. **IT20**: 56 (2006 to 2013-14, 27 as captain); HS 18* v SA (Chester-le-St) 2012 and 18* v A (Melbourne) 2013-14; BB 4-24 v NZ (Auckland) 2012-13. F-c Tours: A 2010-11, 2013-14; SA 2009-10; WI 2005-06 (Eng A), 2008-09; NZ 2007-08, 2012-13; I 2008-09, 2012-13; SL 2007-08, 2011-12; B 2006-07 (Eng A), 2009-10; UAE 2011-12 (v P). HS 169 (*see Tests*). CC HS 91* Le v Derbys (Leicester) 2007. Nt HS 60 v Worcs (Nottingham) 2009. BB 8-52 (11-131 match) v Warwks (Birmingham) 2010. LO HS 45* (*see LOI*). LO BB 5-23 (*see LOI*). T20 HS 18*. T20 BB 4-24.

CARTER, Andrew (Lincoln C), b Lincoln 27 Aug 1988. 6'4". RHB, RM. Squad No 37. Debut (Nottinghamshire) 2009. Essex 2010 (on loan). Nottinghamshire 2nd XI debut 2006. Lincolnshire 2007-10. HS 17* v Sussex (Hove) 2012. BB 5-40 Ex v Kent (Canterbury) 2010. Nt BB 5-55 v Worcs (Worcester) 2014. LO HS 12 v Sussex (Hove) 2009 (P40). LO BB 4-45 v Durham (Nottingham) 2012 (CB40). T20 HS 5*. T20 BB 4-20.

FLETCHER, Luke Jack (Henry Mellish S, Nottingham), b Nottingham 18 Sep 1988. 6'6". RHB, RMF. Squad No 19. Debut (Nottinghamshire) 2008; cap 2014. HS 92 v Hants (Southampton) 2009. BB 5-52 v Warwks (Nottingham) 2013. LO HS 40* v Durham (Chester-le-St) 2009 (P40). LO BB 4-44 v Warwks (Nottingham) 2014 (RLC). T20 HS 8. T20 BB 4-30.

FRANKS, Paul John (Southwell Minster CS), b Mansfield 3 Feb 1979. 6'2". LHB, RMF. Squad No 8. Debut (Nottinghamshire) 1996; cap 1999; benefit 2007. Canterbury 2002-03. MWR 2010-11. YC 2000. **LOI**: 1 (2000); HS 4 v WI (Nottingham) 2000. F-c Tours (Eng A): SA 1998-99; WI 2000-01; NZ 1999-00; SL 2004-05; B 1999-00. HS 123* v Leics (Leicester) 2003. 50 wkts (2); most – 63 (1999). BB 7-56 v Middx (Lord's) 2000. Hat-trick v Warwks (Nottingham) 1997. LO HS 84* v Lincs (Lincoln) 2003 (CGT). LO BB 6-27 v Durham (Chester-le-St) 2000 (NL). T20 HS 29*. T20 BB 2-12.

‡**GIDMAN, William** Robert Simon (Wycliffe C; Berkshire C of Agriculture), b High Wycombe, Bucks 14 Feb 1985. Younger brother of A.P.R.Gidman (*see WORCESTERSHIRE*). 6'2". LHB, RM. Squad No 24. Durham 2007. No f-c appearances in 2008-10. Gloucesterhire 2011-14; cap 2011, becoming first player for Gs to score 1000 runs and take 50 wkts in debut season. MCC YC 2004-06. 1000 runs (1): 1006 (2011). HS 143 and BB 6-15 (10-43 match) Gs v Leics (Bristol) 2013 – only the fifth Gs player to score a century and take ten wkts in a match. 50 wkts (2); most – 55 (2013). LO HS 76 Gs v Worcs (Worcester) 2012 (CB40). LO BB 4-36 Du v Hants (Chester-le-St) 2010 (CB40). T20 HS 40*. T20 BB 2-23.

GURNEY, Harry Frederick (Garendon HS; Loughborough GS; Leeds U), b Nottingham 25 Oct 1986. 6'2". RHB, LFM. Squad No 11. Leicestershire 2007-11. Nottinghamshire debut 2012. MCC 2014. Bradford/Leeds UCCE 2006-07 (not f-c). **LOI**: 10 (2014 to 2014-15); HS 6* v SL (Colombo, RPS) 2014-15; BB 4-55 v SL (Lord's) 2014. HS 24* Le v Middx (Leicester) 2009. Nt HS 22* v Somerset (Taunton) 2013. BB 5-81 v Somerset (Nottingham) 2013. Hat-trick v Sussex (Hove) 2013. LO HS 13* v Durham (Chester-le-St) 2012 (CB40). LO BB 5-24 Le v Hants (Leicester) 2010 (CB40). T20 HS 5*. T20 BB 3-21.

HALES, Alexander Daniel (Chesham S), b Hillingdon, Middx 3 Jan 1989. 6'5". RHB, RM, occ WK. Squad No 10. Debut (Nottinghamshire) 2008; cap 2011. Worcestershire 2014 (1 game, on loan). Buckinghamshire 2006-07. MCC YCs 2006-07. Big Bash: MR 2012-13. AS 2013-14. HH 2014-15. **LOI**: 9 (2014 to 2014-15); HS 42 v I (Nottingham) 2014. **IT20**: 33 (2011 to 2014); HS 116* v SL (Chittagong) 2013-14, E record. 1000 runs (2); most – 1127 (2011). HS 184 v Somerset (Nottingham) 2011. BB 2-63 v Yorks (Nottingham) 2009. LO HS 150* v Worcs (Nottingham) 2009 (P40) – Nt record. T20 HS 116*.

‡**NQHILFENHAUS, Benjamin** William, b Ulverston, Tasmania, Australia 15 Mar 1983. 6'1". RHB, RFM. Squad No 20. Tasmania 2005-06 to date. IPL: CSK 2012-14. Big Bash: HH 2011-12 to date. **Tests** (A): 27 (2008-09 to 2012-13); HS 56* v P (Lord's) 2010; BB 5-75 v I (Melbourne) 2011-12. **LOI** (A): 25 (2006-07 to 2012); HS 16 v I (Nagpur) 2009-10; BB 5-33 v I (Brisbane) 2011-12. **IT20** (A): 7 (2006-07 to 2012); HS 2 v P (Dubai, DSC) 2009; BB 2-15 v SA (Melbourne) 2008-09. F-c Tours (A): E 2009, 2010 (v P); SA 2008-09; WI 2011-12; I 2010-11; Z 2013 (A A). HS 56* (*see Tests*). 50 wkts (1): 60 (2006-07). BB 7-58 (10-87 match) Tas v NSW (Hobart) 2005-06. LO HS 18* Tas v Q (Hobart) 2008-09. LO BB 5-33 (*see LOI*). T20 HS 38*. T20 BB 4-27.

HUTTON, Brett Alan (Worksop C), b Doncaster, Yorks 6 Feb 1993. 6'2". RHB, RM. Squad No 26. Debut (Nottinghamshire) 2011. Nottinghamshire 2nd XI debut 2010. No 1st XI appearances in 2014. HS 42 and BB 1-31 v Somerset (Nottingham) 2013. LO HS 17* and LO BB 1-60 v Sri Lanka A (Nottingham) 2011.

KEEDY, Gary (Garforth CS), b Wakefield, Yorks 27 Nov 1974. 6'0". LHB, SLA. Squad No 3. Yorkshire 1994 (one match). Lancashire 1995-2012; cap 2000; benefit 2009. Surrey 2013. Nottinghamshire debut 2014. MCC 2011. F-c Tour: WI 1995-96 (La). HS 64 La v Sussex (Hove) 2008. Nt HS 15* v Durham (Chester-le-St) 2014. 50 wkts (4); most – 72 (2004). BB 7-68 (10-128 match) La v Durham (Manchester) 2010. Nt BB 5-163 v Yorks (Nottingham) 2014. LO HS 33 La v Derbys (Derby) 2008. LO BB 5-30 La v Sussex (Manchester) 2000 (NL). T20 HS 9*. T20 BB 4-15.

LIBBY, Jacob ('Jake') Daniel (Plymouth C; UWIC), b Plymouth, Devon 3 Jan 1993. 5'9". RHB, OB. Squad No 2. Cardiff MCCU 2014. Nottinghamshire debut 2014. Cornwall 2011-14. HS 108 v Sussex (Nottingham) 2014 – on Nt debut. BB 1-18 CfU v Glamorgan (Cardiff) 2014.

LUMB, Michael John (St Stithians C, Johannesburg), b Johannesburg, South Africa 12 Feb 1980. Son of R.G.Lumb (Yorkshire 1970-84); nephew of A.J.S.Smith (SAU and Natal 1972-73 to 1983-84). 6'0". LHB, RM. Squad No 45. Yorkshire 2000-06; ECB qualified and CC debut 2001; cap 2003. Hampshire 2007-11; cap 2008. Nottinghamshire debut/cap 2012. IPL: RR 2009-10. DC 2011. Big Bash: SS 2011-12 to date. **LOI**: 3 (2013-14); HS 106 v WI (North Sound) 2013-14, becoming only the 2nd England player after D.L.Amiss to score a century on LOI debut. **IT20**: 27 (2009-10 to 2013-14); HS 63 v WI (Bridgetown) 2013-14. F-c Tour (Eng A): I 2003-04. 1000 runs (3); most – 1120 (2013). HS 221* v Derbys (Nottingham) 2013. BB 2-10 Y v Kent (Canterbury) 2001. LO HS 110 EL v Pakistan A (Dubai) 2009-10. LO BB – . T20 HS 124* H v Essex (Southampton) 2009 – H record. T20 BB 3-32.

MULLANEY, Steven John (St Mary's RC S, Astley), b Warrington, Cheshire 19 Nov 1986. 5'9". RHB, RM. Squad No 5. Lancashire 2006-08. No f-c appearances in 2009. Nottinghamshire debut 2010, scoring 100* v Hants (Southampton); cap 2013. HS 165* La v Durham UCCE (Durham) 2007. Nt HS 125 v Middx (Lord's) 2013. BB 4-31 v Essex (Nottingham) 2010. LO HS 63* v Glamorgan (Cardiff) 2014 (RLC). LO BB 4-29 v Kent (Nottingham) 2013 (Y40). T20 HS 53. T20 BB 4-19.

PATEL, Samit Rohit (Worksop C), b Leicester 30 Nov 1984. Elder brother of A.Patel (Derbyshire and Notts 2007-11). 5'8". RHB, SLA. Squad No 21. Debut (Nottinghamshire) 2002; cap 2008. MCC 2014. Nottinghamshire 2nd XI debut 1999, aged 14y 274d. **Tests**: 5 (2011-12 to 2012-13); HS 33 v I (Kolkata) 2012-13; BB 2-27 v SL (Galle) 2011-12. **LOI**: 36 (2008 to 2012-13); HS 70* v I (Mohali) 2011-12; BB 5-41 v SA (Oval) 2008. **IT20**: 18 (2011 to 2012-13); HS 67 v SL (Pallekele) 2012-13; BB 2-6 v Afghanistan (Colombo, RPS) 2012-13. F-c Tours: I 2012-13; SL 2011-12; NZ 2008-09 (Eng A). 1000 runs (1): 1125 (2014). HS 256 v Durham MCCU (Nottingham) 2013. CC HS 176 v Glos (Nottingham) 2007. BB 7-68 (11-111 match) v Hants (Southampton) 2011. LO HS 129* v Warwks (Nottingham) 2013 (Y40). LO BB 6-13 v Ireland (Dublin) 2009 (FPT). T20 HS 84*. T20 BB 3-11.

‡^{NQ}**PHILANDER, Vernon** Darryl, b Bellville, Cape Province, South Africa 24 Jun 1985. RHB, RMF. Squad No 25. Western Province 2003-04 to 2009-10. WP Boland 2004-05. Cape Cobras 2005-06 to date. Middlesex 2008. Somerset 2012. Kent 2013. Devon 2004. **Tests** (SA): 29 (2011-12 to 2014-15); HS 74 v P (Centurion) 2012-13; BB 6-44 (10-114 match) v NZ (Hamilton) 2011-12. **LOI** (SA): 27 (2007 to 2014-15); HS 23 v E (Leeds) 2008; BB 4-12 v Ireland (Belfast) 2007 – on debut. **IT20** (SA): 7 (2007-08); HS 6 v E (Cape Town) 2007-08; BB 2-23 v B (Cape Town) 2007-08. F-c Tours (SA): A 2012-13; NZ 2011-12; SL 2010 (SA A), 2014; Z 2014; B 2010 (SA A); UAE (v P) 2013-14. HS 168 WP v GW (Kimberley) 2004-05. UK HS 61 and UK BB 5-30 SA v E (Lord's) 2012. CC HS 38 Sm v Warwks (Birmingham) 2012. 50 wkts (0+2); most – 59 (2009-10). BB 7-61 Cobras v Knights (Cape Town) 2011-12. CC BB 5-43 Sm v Middx (Taunton) 2012. LO HS 79* SA A v Bangladesh A (East London) 2010-11. LO BB 4-12 (*see LOI*). T20 HS 56*. T20 BB 5-17.

READ, Christopher Mark Wells (Torquay GS; Bath U), b Paignton, Devon 10 Aug 1978. 5'8". RHB, WK. Squad No 7. Gloucestershire (l-o only) 1997. Debut 1997-98 for England A in Kenya. Nottinghamshire debut 1998; cap 1999; captain 2008 to date; benefit 2009. MCC 2002. Devon 1995-97. *Wisden* 2010. **Tests**: 15 (1999 to 2006-07); HS 55 v P (Leeds) 2006. Made six dismissals twice in successive innings 2006-07 to establish an Ashes record. **LOI**: 36 (1999-00 to 2006-07); HS 30* v SA (Manchester) 2003. **IT20**: 1 (2006); HS 13 v P (Bristol) 2006. F-c Tours: A 2006-07; SA 1998-99 (Eng A), 1999-00; WI 2000-01 (Eng A), 2003-04, 2005-06 (Eng A); SL 1997-98 (Eng A), 2002-03 (ECB Acad), 2003-04; Z 1998-99 (Eng A); B 2003-04; K 1997-98 (Eng A). 1000 runs (3); most – 1203 (2009). HS 240 v Essex (Chelmsford) 2007. T20 HS 58*. BB – . LO HS 135 v Durham (Nottingham) 2006 (CGT). T20 HS 58*.

‡ᴺᴼ**SAMMY, Darren** Julius Garvey, b Micoud, St Lucia, 20 Dec 1983. RHB, RM. Squad No 88. Windward 2002-03 to 2012-13. Glamorgan 2014 (T20 only). Joins Nottinghamshire for T20 only in 2015. IPL: SH 2013-14. Big Bash: HH 2014-15. **Tests** (WI): 38 (2007 to 2013-14, 30 as captain); HS 106 v E (Nottingham) 2012; BB 7-66 v E (Manchester) 2007. **LOI** (WI): 125 (2004 to 2014-15, 51 as captain); HS 89 v Ireland (Nelson) 2014-15; BB 4-26 v Z (Kingstown) 2009-10. **IT20** (WI): 58 (2007 to 2014-15, 39 as captain); HS 42* v P (Dhaka) 2013-14; BB 5-26 v Z (Port of Spain) 2009-10. F-c Tours (WI)(C=Captain): E 2006 (WI A), 2007, 2009, 2012C; A 2009-10; SA 2007-08; NZ 2013-14C; I 2011-12C, 2013-14C; SL 2005 (WI A), 2010-11C, 2012-13C. HS 121 Windward Is v Barbados (Bridgetown) 2008-09. BB 7-66 (*see Tests*). LO HS 89 (*see LOI*). LO BB 4-16 WI A v Sri Lanka A (Gros Islet) 2006-07. T20 HS 60. T20 BB 5-26.

‡**SMITH, Gregory** Philip (Oundle S; St Hild & St Bede C, Durham U), b Leicester 16 Nov 1988. 6'0". RHB, LBG. Squad No 22. Leicestershire 2008-14. Durham MCCU 2009-11. Badureliya 2013-14. Colombo CC 2014-15. HS 158* Le v Glos (Leicester) 2010. BB 1-64 Le v Glos (Leicester) 2008. LO HS 135* Le v Somerset (Leicester) 2013 (Y40). T20 HS 102.

‡ᴺᴼ**TAYLOR, Brendan** Ross Murray, b Harare, Zimbabwe 6 Feb 1986. RHB, WK, OB. Mashonaland 2001-02 to 2004-05. Northerns (Zim) 2007-08 to 2008-09. MRW 209-10 to 2013-14. **Tests** (Z): 23 (2004 to 2014-15, 13 as captain); HS 171 v B (Harare) 2013; BB – . **LOI** (Z): 167 (2004 to 2014-15, 34 as captain); HS 145* v SA (Bloemfontein) 2009; BB 3-54 v B (Dhaka) 2004-05. **IT20** (Z): 26 (2006-07 to 2013-14, 17 as captain); HS 75* v NZ (Hamilton) 2011-12; BB 1-16 v SA (Kimberley) 2010-11. F-c Tours (Z) (C = Captain): SA 2004-05, 2007-08; WI 2010, 2012-13C; NZ 2011-12C; I 2005-06; P 2004-05, 2007-08; B 2003-04 (ZA), 2004-05, 2014-15C. 1000 runs (0+1): 1058 (2009-10). HS 217 MWR v SR (Masvingo) 2009-10. BB Mashonaland v Manicaland (Mutare) 2003-04. LO HS 145* (see LOI). LO BB 5-28 Zim A v India A (Harare) 2004. T20 HS 101*. T20 BB 3-38.

TAYLOR, James William Arthur (Shrewsbury S), b Nottingham 6 Jan 1990. 5'6". RHB, LB. Squad No 4. Leicestershire 2008-11; cap 2009. Nottinghamshire debut/cap 2012; l-o captain 2014 to date. Sussex (1 game) 2013. MCC 2010. Shropshire 2007. YC 2009. **Tests**: 2 (2012); HS 34 v SA (Leeds) 2012. **LOI**: 17 (2011 to 2014-15); HS 98* v A (Melbourne) 2014-15. F-c Tours (EL): WI 2010-11, SL 2013-14. 1000 runs (4); most – 1602 (2011). HS 242 EL v Sri Lanka A (Dambulla) 2013-14. CC HS 207* Le v Surrey (Oval) 2009. Nt HS 204* v Sussex (Nottingham) 2013. BB – . LO HS 146* v Derbys (Nottingham) 2014 (RLC). LO BB 4-61 Le v Warwks (Leicester) 2010 (CB40). T20 HS 62*. T20 BB 1-10.

[NQ]**WESSELS, Mattheus Hendrik ('Riki')** (Woodridge C, Pt Elizabeth; Northampton U), b Marogudoore, Queensland, Australia 12 Nov 1985. Left Australia when 2 months old. Son of K.C.Wessels (OFS, Sussex, WP, NT, Q, EP, GW, Australia and South Africa 1973-74 to 1999-00). 5'11". RHB, WK. Squad No 9. MCC 2004. Northamptonshire 2005-09. Nondescripts 2007-08. MWR 2009-10 to 2011-12. Nottinghamshire debut 2011. Big Bash: SS 2014-15. 1000 runs (1): 1213 (2014). HS 199 v Sussex (Hove) 2012. BB 1-10 MWR v MT (Bulawayo) 2009-10. LO HS 100 Nh v Surrey (Oval) 2008 (P40). LO BB 1-0 MWR v MT (Bulawayo) 2009-10. T20 HS 95*.

WOOD, Luke (Portland CS, Worksop), b Sheffield, Yorks 2 Aug 1995. 5'9". LHB, LM. Squad No 14. Nottinghamshire 2nd XI debut 2012. England U19s 2014. HS 12 and BB 2-87 v Sussex (Nottingham) 2014 – only 1st XI game.

WOOD, Samuel Kenneth William (Colonel Frank Seely S, Nottingham), b Nottingham 3 Apr 1993. 5'11". LHB, OB. Squad No 23. Debut (Nottinghamshire) 2011. Nottinghamshire 2nd XI debut 2008, aged 15y 40d. England U19s 2010-11. HS 45 and BB 3-64 v Surrey (Oval) 2012. LO HS 32 v Bangladesh A (Nottingham) 2013. LO BB 2-24 v Lancs (Manchester) 2011 (CB40). T20 HS 13*. T20 BB 2-21.

RELEASED/RETIRED

(Having made a County 1st XI appearance in 2014)

ADAMS, A.R. – *see HAMPSHIRE*.

FRANKLIN, J.E.C. – *see MIDDLESEX*.

JAQUES, Philip Anthony (Fig Tree HS, Wollongong; Australian C of PE, Homebush), b Wollongong, NSW, Australia 3 May 1979. 6'1". LHB, SLC. British passport (English parents) and now UK qualified. NSW 2000-01 to 2011-12. Northamptonshire 2003; cap 2003. Yorkshire 2004-13; cap 2005. Worcestershire 2006-07, 2010. Nottinghamshire 2014; cap 2014. Big Bash: HH 2011-12. **Tests** (A): 11 (2005-06 to 2008); HS 150 v SL (Hobart) 2007-08. **LOI** (A): 6 (2005-06 to 2006-07); HS 94 v SA (Melbourne) 2005-06. F-c Tours (A): WI 2008; P 2005-06 (Aus A), 2007-08 (Aus A); B 2005-06. 1000 runs (4+2); most – 1409 (2003). HS 244 Wo v Essex (Chelmsford) 2006. Nt HS 150* v Somerset (Taunton) 2014. BB 1-75 Y v Sussex (Hove) 2013. LO HS 171* NSW v Q (Sydney) 2009-10. T20 HS 92.

KELSALL, Samuel (Trentham HS, Stoke), b Stoke-on-Trent, Staffs 14 Mar 1993. 5'7". RHB, RM. Nottinghamshire 2011-14. Nottinghamshire 2nd XI debut 2008, aged 15y 158d. No f-c appearances in 2013. Hs 57 V Oxford MCCU (Oxford) 2014. CC HS 35 v Warwks (Nottingham) 2012. LO HS 40 v Sri Lanka A (Nottingham) 2011.

SHAHZAD, A. – *see SUSSEX*.

SIDDLE, P.M. – *see LANCASHIRE*.

NOTTINGHAMSHIRE 2014

RESULTS SUMMARY

	Place	Won	Lost	Tied	Drew	NR
LV= County Championship (1st Division)	4th	6	6		4	
All First-Class Matches		6	6		5	
Royal London One-Day Cup (Group B)	SF	5	2	1		2
NatWest t20 Blast (North Division)	QF	9	4			2

LV= COUNTY CHAMPIONSHIP AVERAGES
BATTING AND FIELDING

Cap		M	I	NO	HS	Runs	Avge	100	50	Ct/St
2011	A.D.Hales	11	20	1	183	954	50.21	3	4	13
2014	P.A.Jaques	11	20	2	150*	894	49.66	2	6	3
	M.H.Wessels	16	29	4	158	1197	47.88	1	8	22
1999	C.M.W.Read	16	25	5	96	877	43.85	–	6	54/1
2012	J.W.A.Taylor	15	28	2	126	992	38.15	1	8	7
2008	S.R.Patel	16	30	–	156	1098	36.60	2	6	18
2013	A.Shahzad	8	12	5	68*	203	29.00	–	1	2
2012	M.J.Lumb	14	26	–	99	740	28.46	–	3	4
2014	P.M.Siddle	11	16	5	48*	250	22.72	–	–	5
2013	S.J.Mullaney	11	21	–	91	380	18.09	–	3	8
2014	L.J.Fletcher	11	19	–	49	240	12.63	–	–	4
	J.T.Ball	4	7	–	20	56	8.00	–	–	–
	G.Keedy	3	6	3	15*	19	6.33	–	–	2
	H.F.Gurney	10	17	8	15	51	5.66	–	–	1
2007	A.R.Adams	9	11	–	19	61	5.54	–	–	9
	A.Carter	5	7	1	11*	27	4.50	–	–	1

Also batted: S.C.J.Broad (2 matches – cap 2008) 0, 8; J.E.C.Franklin (1 – cap 2014) 24, 39; J.D.Libby (1) 108, 12 (1 ct); L.Wood (1) 5*, 12.

BOWLING

	O	M	R	W	Avge	Best	5wI	10wM
A.Carter	127.5	24	441	17	25.94	5- 55	1	–
L.J.Fletcher	338.5	79	1054	38	27.73	4- 76	–	–
A.R.Adams	294.5	47	1013	36	28.13	5- 65	1	–
P.M.Siddle	351.5	80	1165	37	31.48	4- 61	–	–
H.F.Gurney	335.3	58	1248	38	32.84	4- 22	–	–
G.Keedy	127	12	465	13	35.76	5-163	1	–
A.Shahzad	192.2	32	730	18	40.55	4- 46	–	–
S.R.Patel	278	49	979	22	44.50	3- 13	–	–
Also bowled:								
J.T.Ball	83	14	264	9	29.33	3- 60	–	–
S.J.Mullaney	93.2	15	286	9	31.77	2- 35	–	–
S.C.J.Broad	51	10	177	5	35.40	3- 78	–	–

J.E.C.Franklin 9-1-36-1; A.D.Hales 2-0-4-0; M.H.Wessels 5-0-19-0; L.Wood 39-4-180-3.

The First-Class Averages (pp 217–233) give the records of Nottinghamshire players in all first-class county matches (Nottinghamshire's other opponents being Oxford MCCU), with the exception of S.C.J.Broad, A.D.Hales and J.D.Libby, whose first-class figures for Nottinghamshire are as above, and:
J.W.A.Taylor 16-23-2-204*-956-45.52-2-5-8ct.
G.G.White 2-2-0-23-23-11.50-0-0-0ct. 39.4-9-100-3-33.33-2/24-0-0.

NOTTINGHAMSHIRE RECORDS

FIRST-CLASS CRICKET

Highest Total	For	791		v	Essex	Chelmsford	2007
	V	781-7d		by	Northants	Northampton	1995
Lowest Total	For	13		v	Yorkshire	Nottingham	1901
	V	16		by	Derbyshire	Nottingham	1879
		16		by	Surrey	The Oval	1880
Highest Innings	For	312*	W.W.Keeton	v	Middlesex	The Oval	1939
	V	345	C.G.Macartney	for	Australians	Nottingham	1921

Highest Partnership for each Wicket

1st	406*	D.J.Bicknell/G.E.Welton	v	Warwicks	Birmingham	2000
2nd	398	A.Shrewsbury/W.Gunn	v	Sussex	Nottingham	1890
3rd	367	W.Gunn/J.R.Gunn	v	Leics	Nottingham	1903
4th	361	A.O.Jones/J.R.Gunn	v	Essex	Leyton	1905
5th	359	D.J.Hussey/C.M.W.Read	v	Essex	Nottingham	2007
6th	372*	K.P.Pietersen/J.E.Morris	v	Derbyshire	Derby	2001
7th	301	C.C.Lewis/B.N.French	v	Durham	Chester-le-St[2]	1993
8th	220	G.F.H.Heane/R.Winrow	v	Somerset	Nottingham	1935
9th	170	J.C.Adams/K.P.Evans	v	Somerset	Taunton	1994
10th	152	E.B.Alletson/W.Riley	v	Sussex	Hove	1911
	152	U.Afzaal/A.J.Harris	v	Worcs	Nottingham	2000

Best Bowling	For	10-66	K.Smales	v	Glos	Stroud	1956
(Innings)	V	10-10	H.Verity	for	Yorkshire	Leeds	1932
Best Bowling	For	17-89	F.C.L.Matthews	v	Northants	Nottingham	1923
(Match)	V	17-89	W.G.Grace	for	Glos	Cheltenham	1877

Most Runs – Season	2620	W.W.Whysall	(av 53.46)	1929
Most Runs – Career	31592	G.Gunn	(av 35.69)	1902-32
Most 100s – Season	9	W.W.Whysall		1928
	9	M.J.Harris		1971
	9	B.C.Broad		1990
Most 100s – Career	65	J.Hardstaff jr		1930-55
Most Wkts – Season	181	B.Dooland	(av 14.96)	1954
Most Wkts – Career	1653	T.G.Wass	(av 20.34)	1896-1920
Most Career W-K Dismissals	957	T.W.Oates	(733 ct; 224 st)	1897-1925
Most Career Catches in the Field	466	A.O.Jones		1892-1914

LIMITED-OVERS CRICKET

Highest Total	50ov	368-2		v	Middlesex	Lord's	2014
	40ov	296-7		v	Somerset	Taunton	2002
	T20	220-4		v	Leics	Leicester	2014
Lowest Total	50ov	74		v	Leics	Leicester	1987
	40ov	57		v	Glos	Nottingham	2009
	T20	91		v	Lancashire	Manchester	2006
Highest Innings	50ov	167*	P.Johnson	v	Kent	Nottingham	1993
	40ov	150*	A.D.Hales	v	Worcs	Nottingham	2009
	T20	96	M.J.Lumb	v	Durham	Chester-le-St[2]	2004
Best Bowling	50ov	6-10	K.P.Evans	v	Northumb	Jesmond	1994
	40ov	6-12	R.J.Hadlee	v	Lancashire	Nottingham	1980
	T20	5-22	G.G.White	v	Lancashire	Nottingham	2013

SOMERSET

Formation of Present Club: 18 August 1875
Inaugural First-Class Match: 1882
Colours: Black, White and Maroon
Badge: Somerset Dragon
County Champions: (0); best – 2nd (Div 1) 2001, 2010, 2012
Gillette/NatWest/C&G Trophy Winners: (3) 1979, 1983, 2001
Benson and Hedges Cup Winners: (2) 1981, 1982
Sunday League Winners: (1) 1979
Twenty20 Cup Winners: (1) 2005

Chief Executive: Guy Lavender, County Ground, Taunton TA1 1JT • Tel: 0845 337 1875 • Fax: 01823 332395 • Email: enquiries@somersetcountycc.co.uk • Web: www.somerset-cricketclub.co.uk • Twitter: @SomersetCCC (25,032 followers)

Director of Cricket: Dave Nosworthy. **Assistant/Batting Coach**: Dave Houghton. **Assistant/Bowling Coach**: Jason Kerr. **Director of High Performance**: Andy Hurry. **Captain**: M.E.Trescothick. **Vice-Captain**: tbc. **Overseas Players**: Abdur Rehman, C.J.Anderson (T20 only) and Sohail Tanvir (T20 only). **2015 Beneficiary**: P.D.Trego. **Groundsman**: Simon Lee. **Scorer**: Gerald Stickley. ‡ New registration. NQ Not qualified for England.

ABELL, Thomas Benjamin (Taunton S; Exeter U), b Taunton 5 Mar 1994. 5'10". RHB, RM. Squad No 28. Debut (Somerset) 2014. Somerset 2nd XI debut 2010. HS 95 v Warwks (Taunton) 2014 – on debut. BB – .

NQ**ABDUR REHMAN**, b Sialkot, Pakistan 1 Mar 1980. LHB, SLA. Squad No 36. Gujranwala 1997-98 to 2001-02. HB 1999-00 to date. Sialkot 2003-04 to 2012-13. Somerset debut 2012. **Tests** (P): 22 (2007-08 to 2014); HS 60 v SA (Abu Dhabi) 2010-11; BB 6-25 v E (Abu Dhabi) 2011-12. **LOI** (P): 31 (2006-07 to 2013-14); HS 31 v SA (Multan) 2007-08; BB 4-48 v Ireland (Dublin) 2013. **IT20** (P): 8 (2006-07 to 2013-14); HS 7* v SA (Dubai, DSC) 2013-14; BB 2-7 v Kenya (Nairobi) 2007. F-c Tours (P): E 2010; A 2006 (Pak A), 2009 (Pak A); WI 2011; NZ 2010-11; SL 2009 (Pak A), 2012, 2014; Z 2013; B 2011-12; UAE 2010-11 (v SA), 2011-12 (v SL and E), 2011-12 (v SL). HS 96 HB v NBP (Multan) 2005-06. Sm HS 17 v Notts (Taunton) 2012. 50 wkts (1): 88 (2009-10). BB 9-65 (14-101 match) v Worcs (Taunton) 2012. LO HS 50 HB v KRL (Rawalpindi) 2007-08. LO BB 6-16 v Notts (Taunton) 2012 (CB40) – Sm record. T20 HS 21. T20 BB 3-17.

‡**ALLENBY, James** (Christ Church GS, Perth), b Perth, W Australia 12 Sep 1982. 6'0". RHB, RM. Squad No 6. Leicestershire 2006-09. Glamorgan 2009-14; cap 2010; captain (T20) 2014. 1000 runs (1): 1202 (2013). HS 138* Le v Bangladesh A (Leicester) 2008 and 138* Gm v Leics (Leicester) 2013. 50 wkts (1): 54 (2014). BB 6-54 (10-128 match) Gm v Hants (Cardiff) 2014. LO HS 91* Le v Middx (Lord's) 2007 (P40). LO BB 5-43 Le v Derbys (Leicester) 2007 (FPT). T20 HS 110. T20 BB 5-21 Le v Lancs (Manchester) 2008, inc 4 wkts in 4 balls.

‡NQ**ANDERSON, Corey** James, b Christchurch, New Zealand 13 Dec 1990. LHB, LMF. Canterbury 2006-07 to 2009-10. Northern Districts 2011-12 to date. IPL: MI 2014. **Tests** (NZ): 10 (2013-14 to 2014-15); HS 116 v B (Dhaka) 2013-14; BB 3-47 v WI (Hamilton) 2013-14. **LOI** (NZ): 32 (2013 to 2014-15); HS 131* v WI (Queenstown) 2013-14; BB 5-63 v I (Auckland) 2013-14. **IT20** (NZ): 15 (2012-13 to 2014-15); HS 48 v P (Dubai, DSC) 2014-15; BB 2-21 v B (Dhaka) 2013-14. F-c Tours (NZ): I 2013-14 (NZA); SL 2013-14 (NZA); B 2013-14; UAE 2014-15 (v P). HS 167 NB v Otago (Hamilton) 2012-13. HB 5-22 ND v Canterbury (Hamilton) 2009-10. LO HS 131* (see LOI). LO BB 5-26 ND v Canterbury (Hamilton) 2009-10. T20 HS 95*. T20 BB 2-18.

155

BARROW, Alexander William Rodgerson (King's C, Taunton), b Frome 6 May 1992. 5'7". RHB, RM/OB. Squad No 18. Debut (Somerset) 2011. Somerset 2nd XI debut 2009. HS 88 v Northants (Taunton) 2014. BB 1-4 v Hants (Southampton) 2011. LO HS 72 v Durham (Chester-le-St) 2012 (CB40).

‡NOCOOPER, Tom Lexley William, b Wollongong, NSW, Australia 26 Nov 1986. 6'1½". RHB, OB. Squad No 26. S Australia 2008-09 to date. Netherlands 2011-13. Big Bash: AS 2011-12. MR 2012-13 to date. **LOI** (Ne): 23 (2010 to 2013); HS 101 v Afghanistan (Hague) 2010; BB 3-11 v Afghanistan (Sharjah) 2011-12. **IT20** (Ne): 15 (2011-12 to 2013-14); HS 72* v Z (Sylhet) 2013-14; BB 2-18 v UAE (Sylhet) 2013-14. HS 203* S Aus v NSW (Sydney) 2011-12; BB 2-43 Neth v Ireland (Deventer) 2013. LO HS 126* Neth v Middx (Lord's) 2011(CB40). LO BB 3-11 (*see LOI*). T20 HS 74. T20 BB 2-7.

DAVEY, Joshua Henry (Culford S), b Aberdeen, Scotland 3 Aug 1990. RHB, RM. Squad No 38. Middlesex 2010-12. Scotland 2011-12 to date. Somerset 2nd XI debut 2013. Suffolk 2014. **LOI** (Scot): 23 (2010 to 2014-15); HS 64 v Afghanistan (Sharjah) 2012-13; BB 6-28 v Afghanistan (Abu Dhabi) 2014-15. **IT20** (Scot): 1 (2012); HS 7 and BB 3-23 v B (The Hague) 2012. HS 72 and BB 2-41 M v Oxford MCCU (Oxford) 2010 – on debut. CC HS 61 M v Glos (Bristol) 2010. CC BB – . LO HS 91 Scot v Warwks (Birmingham) 2011 (CB40). LO BB 6-28 (*see LOI*). T20 HS 18*. T20 BB 3-23.

DIBBLE, Adam John (Taunton S), b Exeter, Devon 9 Mar 1991. 6'4". RHB, RMF. Squad No 16. Debut (Somerset) 2011. No 1st XI appearances in 2014. Somerset 2nd XI debut 2009. Devon 2009. HS 43 and BB 3-42 v Warwks (Birmingham) 2012. LO HS 15 v Glamorgan (Cardiff) 2013 (Y40). LO BB 4-52 v Yorks (Taunton) 2013 (Y40). T20 HS – . T20 BB 1-20.

DOCKRELL, George Henry (Gonzaga C, Dublin), b Dublin, Ireland 22 Jul 1992. 6'3". RHB, SLA. Squad No 20. Ireland 2010 to date. Somerset debut 2011. **LOI** (Ire): 47 (2009-10 to 2014-15); HS 25 v SA (Canberra) 2014-15; BB 4-24 v Scotland (Belfast) 2013. **IT20** (Ire): 26 (2009-10 to 2013-14); HS 2* v Kenya (Mombasa) 2011-12; BB 4-20 v Netherlands (Dubai) 2009-10. HS 53 Ire v Namibia (Belfast) 2011. Sm HS 31 v Durham (Taunton) 2013. BB 6-27 v Middx (Taunton) 2012. LO HS 25 (*see LOI*). LO BB 4-24 (*see LOI*). T20 HS 2*. T20 BB 4-20.

GREGORY, Lewis (Hele's S, Plympton), b Plymouth, Devon 24 May 1992. 6'0". RHB, RMF. Squad No 24. Debut (Somerset) 2011. Somerset 2nd XI debut 2008, aged 16y 87d. Devon 2008. England U19s 2010 to 2010-11. HS 69 v Yorks (Taunton) 2014. BB 6-47 (11-122 match) v Northants (Northampton) 2014. LO HS 105* v Durham (Taunton) 2014 (RLC). LO BB 4-27 v Glos (Taunton) 2011 (CB40). T20 HS 22. T20 BB 4-15.

GROENEWALD, Timothy Duncan (Maritzburg C; South Africa U), b Pietermaritzburg, South Africa 10 Jan 1984. 6'0". RHB, RFM. Squad No 5. Debut Cambridge UCCE 2006. Warwickshire 2006-08. Derbyshire 2009-14; cap 2011. Somerset debut 2014. HS 78 Wa v Bangladesh A (Birmingham) 2008. CC HS 76 Wa v Durham (Chester-le-St) 2006. Sm HS 1 (three times). BB 6-50 De v Surrey (Croydon) 2009. Sm BB 2-56 v Yorks (Leeds) 2014. Hat-trick De v Essex (Chelmsford) 2014. LO HS 57 v Warwks (Birmingham) 2014 (RLC). LO BB 4-22 De v Worcs (Worcester) 2011 (CB40). T20 HS 41. T20 BB 4-21.

HILDRETH, James Charles (Millfield S), b Milton Keynes, Bucks 9 Sep 1984. 5'10", RHB, RMF. Squad No 25. Debut (Somerset) 2003; cap 2007. F-c Tour (EL): WI 2010-11. 1000 runs (4); most – 1440 (2010). HS 303* v Warwks (Taunton) 2009. BB 2-39 v Hants (Taunton) 2004. LO HS 151 v Scotland (Taunton) 2009 (FPT). LO BB 2-26 v Worcs (Worcester) 2008 (FPT). T20 HS 107*. T20 BB 3-24.

KIESWETTER, Craig (Diocesan C; Millfield S), b Johannesburg, South Africa 18 Nov 1987. 6'1". RHB, WK. Squad No 22. Debut (Somerset) 2007; cap 2009. Represented South Africa in U19 World Cup 2006. Qualified for England Feb 2010. Big Bash: BH 2013-14. **LOI**: 46 (2009-10 to 2012-13); HS 107 v B (Chittagong) 2009-10. **IT20**: 25 (2009-10 to 2012-13); HS 63 v A (Bridgetown) 2009-10. F-c Tour (EL): WI 2010-11. 1000 runs (1): 1242 (2009). HS 164 v Notts (Nottingham) 2011. BB 2-3 v Worcs (Worcester) 2012. LO HS 143 England XI v Bangladesh CB (Fatullah) 2009-10. T20 HS 89*.

LEACH, Matthew **Jack** (Bishop Fox's Community S, Taunton; Richard Huish C; UWIC), b Taunton 22 Jun 1991. 6'0". LHB, SLA. Squad No 17. Cardiff MCCU 2012. Somerset debut 2012. Somerset 2nd XI debut 2009. Dorset 2011. HS 43 v Yorks (Leeds) 2014. BB 5-63 v Warwks (Taunton) 2013. LO HS 18 v Surrey (Oval) 2014 (RLC). LO BB 3-53 v Kent (Taunton) 2014 (RLC).

[NQ]**MYBURGH, Johannes** Gerhardus (Pretoria BHS; U of SA), b Pretoria, South Africa 22 Oct 1980. 5'7". Elder brother of S.J.Myburgh (Northerns, KZN and Netherlands 2005-06 to date); brother-in-law of F.de Wet (Northerns, NW, Lions, Hampshire, Dolphins and South Africa 2001-02 to 2011-12). RHB, OB. Squad No 9. Northerns 1997-98 to 2006-07. Titans 2004-05. Canterbury 2007-08 to 2009-10. Hampshire 2011. Durham 2012. Somerset debut 2014. EU qualified through wife's visa. HS 203 Northerns B v Easterns (Pretoria) 1997-98. Sm HS 91 v Yorks (Taunton) 2014. BB 4-56 Canterbury v ND (Hamilton) 2008-09. Sm BB 2-13 v Middx (Taunton) 2011. LO HS 112 Canterbury v Auckland (Christchurch) 2009-10. LO BB 2-22 Canterbury v CD (Christchurch) 2009-10. T20 HS 88. T20 BB 3-16.

OVERTON, Craig (West Buckland S), b Barnstaple, Devon 10 Apr 1994. 6'5". RHB, RMF. Squad No 12. Debut (Somerset) 2012. Somerset 2nd XI debut 2011. Devon 2010-11. HS 99 v Lancs (Taunton) 2014. BB 5-63 v Durham (Taunton) 2014. LO HS 36 v Kent (Taunton) 2014 (RLC). LO BB 2-30 EL v Australia A (Melbourne) 2012-13. T20 HS 15. T20 BB 1-23.

OVERTON, Jamie (West Buckland S), b Barnstaple, Devon 10 Apr 1994. 6'5". RHB, RFM. Squad No 11. Debut (Somerset) 2012. Somerset 2nd XI debut 2011. Devon 2011. HS 56 v Warwks (Birmingham) 2014. BB 6-95 v Middx (Taunton) 2013. LO HS 14 v Glos (Bristol) 2013 (Y40). LO BB 4-42 v Durham (Chester-le-St) 2012 (CB40).

REGAN, James Alan (All Hallows Catholic S; Farnborough SFC), b Frimley, Surrey 30 May 1994. 5'10". RHB, WK. Squad No 19. Debut (Somerset) 2012, without batting or bowling. Somerset 2nd XI debut 2010, aged 16y 81d. No 1st XI appearances in 2013 and 2014.

‡[NQ]**SOHAIL TANVIR**, b Rawalpindi, Pakistan 12 Dec 1984. LHB, LMF. Rawalpindi 2004-05 to date. KRL 2007-08 to 2008-09. Federal Areas 2007-08 to 2011-12. ZTB 2009-10 to date. Hampshire 2013. IPL: RR 2007-09. **Tests** (P): 2 (2007-08); HS 13 and BB 3-83 v I (Delhi) 2007-08. **LOI** (P): 62 (2007-08 to 2014-15); HS 59 v Hong Kong (Karachi) 2008; BB 5-48 v SL (Karachi) 2008. **IT20** (P): 42 (2007 to 2014-15); HS 41 v SL (Dubai) 2013-14; BB 3-12 v SL (Hambantota) 2012. F-c Tour (P): I 2007-08. HS 163 ZTB v Lahore Lions (Lahore) 2014-15. CC HS 38 and CC BB 3-62 H v Glamorgan (Cardiff) 2013. BB 8-54 (15-174 match) KRL v PIA (Mirpur) 2008-09. LO HS 93 KRL v SSGC (Rawalpindi) 2008-09. LO BB 7-34 KRL v WAPDA (Lahore) 2007-08. T20 HS 60*. T20 BB 6-14.

NQTHOMAS, Alfonso Clive (Ravensmead SS; Parow HS), b Cape Town, South Africa 9 Feb 1977. 5'10". RHB, RFM. Squad No 8. W Province 1998-99. North West 2000-01 to 2002-03. Northerns 2003-04 to 2005-06. Titans 2004-05 to 2007-08. Warwickshire 2007. Somerset debut 2008; cap 2008 (Kolpak registration). **IT20** (SA): 1 (2006-07); HS – and BB 3-25 v P (Johannesburg) 2006-07. F-c Tour (SA A): Z 2004. HS 119* NW v Northerns (Pretoria) 2002-03. UK HS 94 v Hants (Taunton) 2011. 50 wkts (1): 57 (2014). BB 7-54 Titans v Cobras (Cape Town) 2005-06. UK BB 6-60 (10-88 match) v Sussex (Taunton) 2011 and 6-60 v Warwks (Taunton) 2012. LO HS 49* v Kent (Taunton) 2014 (RLC). LO BB 4-18 v Glos (Bristol) 2009 (P40). T20 HS 30*. T20 BB 5-24.

TREGO, Peter David (Wyvern CS, W-s-M), b Weston-super-Mare 12 Jun 1981. 6'0". RHB, RMF. Squad No 7. Somerset 2000-02, 2006 to date; cap 2007; benefit 2015. Kent 2003. Middlesex 2005. C Districts 2013-14. MCC 2013. Herefordshire 2005. HS 141 CD v Auckland (Napier) 2013-14. Sm HS 140 v West Indies A (Taunton) 2002. CC HS 135 v Derbys (Taunton) 2006. 50 wkts (1): 50 (2012). BB 7-84 (11-153 match) v Yorks (Leeds) 2014. LO HS 147 v Glamorgan (Taunton) 2010 (CB40). LO BB 5-40 EL v West Indies A (Worcester) 2010. T20 HS 94*. T20 BB 4-27.

TRESCOTHICK, Marcus Edward (Sir Bernard Lovell S), b Keynsham 25 Dec 1975. 6'2". LHB, RM, occ WK. Squad No 2. Debut (Somerset) 1993; cap 1999; joint captain 2002; benefit 2008; captain 2010 to date. PCA 2000, 2009, 2011. *Wisden* 2004. MBE 2005. **Tests**: 76 (2000 to 2006, 2 as captain); HS 219 v SA (Oval) 2003; BB 1-34 v P (Karachi) 2000-01. **LOI**: 123 (2000 to 2006, 10 as captain); HS 137 v P (Lord's) 2001; BB 2-7 v Z (Manchester) 2000. **IT20**: 3 (2005 to 2006); HS 72 v SL (Southampton) 2006. F-c Tours: A 2002-03; SA 2004-05; WI 1999-00 (Eng A), 2001-02; I 2001-02, 2005-06 (*part*); P 2000-01, 2005-06; SL 2000-01, 2003-04; B 1999-00 (Eng A), 2003-04. 1000 runs (6); most – 1817 (2009). HS 284 v Northants (Northampton) 2007. BB 4-36 (inc hat-trick) v Young A (Taunton) 1995. CC BB 4-82 v Yorks (Leeds) 1998. Hat-trick 1995 (*see above*). LO HS 184 v Glos (Taunton) 2008 (P40) – Sm l-o record. LO BB 4-50 v Northants (Northampton) 2000 (NL). T20 HS 108*.

WALLER, Maximilian Thomas Charles (Millfield S; Bournemouth U), b Salisbury, Wiltshire 3 March 1988. 6'0". RHB, LB. Squad No 10. Debut (Somerset) 2009. Dorset 2007-08. No f-c appearances in 2013 and 2014. HS 28 v Hants (Southampton) 2009. BB 3-33 v Cardiff MCCU (Taunton Vale) 2012. CC BB 2-27 v Sussex (Hove) 2009. LO HS 25* v Glamorgan (Taunton) 2013 (Y40). LO BB 3-39 v Middx (Taunton) 2010 (Y40). T20 HS 3. T20 BB 4-16.

RELEASED/RETIRED

(Having made a County 1st XI appearance in 2014)

BURKE, J.E. – *see SURREY*.

COMPTON, N.R.D. – *see MIDDLESEX*.

INGRAM, C.A. – *see GLAMORGAN*.

JONES, Chris Robert (Poole GS; Richard Huish C, Taunton; Grey C, Durham U), b Harold Wood, Essex 5 Nov 1990. 6'3". RHB, RM. Somerset 2010-14. Durham MCCU 2011-13. Somerset 2nd XI debut 2006, aged 15y 290d. Dorset 2008-11. HS 130 v Australians (Taunton) 2013. CC HS 87 v Northants (Northampton) 2014. BB 1-17 v Surrey (Taunton) 2012. LO HS 45* v Essex (Taunton) 2011 (CB40). T20 HS 53*.

RELEASED/RETIRED continued on p 166

158

SOMERSET 2014

RESULTS SUMMARY

	Place	Won	Lost	Tied	Drew	NR
LV= County Championship (1st Division)	6th	4	2		10	
All First-Class Matches		4	2		11	
Royal London One-Day Cup (Group B)	6th	3	4	1		
NatWest t20 Blast (South Division)	5th	6	7			1

LV= COUNTY CHAMPIONSHIP AVERAGES

BATTING AND FIELDING

Cap		M	I	NO	HS	Runs	Avge	100	50	Ct/St
2011	N.R.D.Compton	16	25	3	156	961	43.68	2	5	9
	A.W.R.Barrow	4	7	2	88	218	43.60	–	1	14
1999	M.E.Trescothick	16	25	–	133	1049	41.96	4	5	23
	T.B.Abell	4	7	–	95	292	41.71	–	3	4
2013	A.N.Petersen	11	16	1	155	605	40.33	1	4	8
2009	C.Kieswetter	13	17	3	78*	508	36.28	–	5	35/4
2007	P.D.Trego	15	20	1	107*	644	33.89	1	3	4
2007	J.C.Hildreth	15	24	1	182	763	33.17	1	4	19
	C.Overton	12	16	3	99	431	33.15	–	3	3
	J.G.Myburgh	12	17	1	91	521	32.56	–	3	3
	L.Gregory	9	11	1	69	296	29.60	–	1	5
	C.A.J.Meschede	5	6	1	59*	142	28.40	–	1	2
	C.R.Jones	8	12	–	87	339	28.25	–	3	8
	G.H.Dockrell	9	11	7	27	109	27.25	–	–	2
	J.Overton	7	8	3	56	133	26.60	–	2	–
2008	A.C.Thomas	14	17	5	54	193	16.08	–	1	–

Also batted: T.D.Groenewald (2 matches) 1, 1, 1 (2 ct); C.A.Ingram (1) 14, 37 (1 ct); M.J.Leach (3) 8*, 43, 8.

BOWLING

	O	M	R	W	Avge	Best	5wI	10wM
A.C.Thomas	469.3	124	1313	53	24.77	5- 40	3	–
L.Gregory	332	74	1121	43	26.06	6- 47	3	1
P.D.Trego	442.4	92	1391	49	28.38	7- 84	1	1
C.Overton	339.1	65	1181	40	29.52	5- 63	1	–
G.H.Dockrell	279.1	50	751	21	35.76	3- 44	–	–
J.G.Myburgh	212.1	39	581	11	52.81	2- 13	–	–
J.Overton	165	14	708	10	70.80	2- 35	–	–
Also bowled:								
M.J.Leach	121	34	286	8	35.75	3- 40	–	–
C.A.J.Meschede	101	19	387	7	55.28	3-105	–	–

T.B.Abell 2-0-11-0; N.R.D.Compton 1-0-8-0; T.D.Groenewald 64-10-205-2; J.C.Hildreth 14-1-48-1; A.N.Petersen 32-5-78-1.

The First-Class Averages (pp 217–233) give the records of Somerset players in all first-class county matches (Somerset's other opponents being Leeds/Bradford MCCU), with the exception of T.D.Groenewald, whose first-class figures for Somerset are as above.

SOMERSET RECORDS

FIRST-CLASS CRICKET

Highest Total	For 850-7d		v	Middlesex	Taunton	2007
	V 811		by	Surrey	The Oval	1899
Lowest Total	For 25		v	Glos	Bristol	1947
	V 22		by	Glos	Bristol	1920
Highest Innings	For 342	J.L.Langer	v	Surrey	Guildford	2006
	V 424	A.C.MacLaren	for	Lancashire	Taunton	1895

Highest Partnership for each Wicket

1st	346	L.C.H.Palairet/ H.T.Hewett	v	Yorkshire	Taunton	1892
2nd	450	N.R.D.Compton/J.C.Hildreth	v	Cardiff MCCU	Taunton Vale	2012
3rd	319	P.M.Roebuck/M.D.Crowe	v	Leics	Taunton	1984
4th	310	P.W.Denning/I.T.Botham	v	Glos	Taunton	1980
5th	320	J.D.Francis/I.D.Blackwell	v	Durham UCCE	Taunton	2005
6th	265	W.E.Alley/K.E.Palmer	v	Northants	Northampton	1961
7th	279	R.J.Harden/G.D.Rose	v	Sussex	Taunton	1997
8th	172	I.V.A.Richards/I.T.Botham	v	Leics	Leicester	1983
	172	A.R.K.Pierson/P.S.Jones	v	N Zealanders	Taunton	1999
9th	183	C.H.M.Greetham/H.W.Stephenson	v	Leics	Weston-s-Mare	1963
	183	C.J.Tavaré/N.A.Mallender	v	Sussex	Hove	1990
10th	163	I.D.Blackwell/N.A.M.McLean	v	Derbyshire	Taunton	2003

Best Bowling	For	10- 49	E.J.Tyler	v	Surrey	Taunton	1895
(Innings)	V	10- 35	A.Drake	for	Yorkshire	Weston-s-Mare	1914
Best Bowling	For	16- 83	J.C.White	v	Worcs	Bath	1919
(Match)	V	17-137	W.Brearley	for	Lancashire	Manchester	1905

Most Runs – Season	2761	W.E.Alley	(av 58.74)		1961
Most Runs – Career	21142	H.Gimblett	(av 36.96)		1935-54
Most 100s – Season	11	S.J.Cook			1991
Most 100s – Career	49	H.Gimblett			1935-54
Most Wkts – Season	169	A.W.Wellard	(av 19.24)		1938
Most Wkts – Career	2165	J.C.White	(av 18.03)		1909-37
Most Career W-K Dismissals	1007	H.W.Stephenson	(698 ct; 309 st)		1948-64
Most Career Catches in the Field	381	J.C.White			1909-37

LIMITED-OVERS CRICKET

Highest Total	50ov	413-4		v	Devon	Torquay	1990
	40ov	377-9		v	Sussex	Hove	2003
	T20	250-3		v	Glos	Taunton	2006
Lowest Total	50ov	58		v	Middlesex	Southgate	2000
	40ov	58		v	Essex	Chelmsford	1977
	T20	82		v	Kent	Taunton	2010
Highest Innings	50ov	177	S.J.Cook	v	Sussex	Hove	1990
	40ov	184	M.E.Trescothick	v	Glos	Taunton	2008
	T20	141*	C.L.White	v	Worcs	Worcester	2006
Best Bowling	50ov	8-66	S.R.G.Francis	v	Derbyshire	Derby	2004
	40ov	6-16	Abdur Rehman	v	Notts	Taunton	2012
	T20	6- 5	A.V.Suppiah	v	Glamorgan	Cardiff	2011

SURREY

Formation of Present Club: 22 August 1845
Inaugural First-Class Match: 1864
Colours: Chocolate
Badge: Prince of Wales' Feathers
County Champions (since 1890): (18) 1890, 1891, 1892, 1894, 1895, 1899, 1914, 1952, 1953, 1954, 1955, 1956, 1957, 1958, 1971, 1999, 2000, 2002
Joint Champions: (1) 1950
NatWest Trophy Winners: (1) 1982
Benson and Hedges Cup Winners: (3) 1974, 1997, 2001
Pro 40/National League (Div 1) Winners: (1) 2003
Sunday League Winners: (1) 1996
Clydesdale Bank 40 Winners: (1) 2011
Twenty20 Cup Winners: (1) 2003

Chief Executive: Richard Gould, The Kia Oval, London, SE11 5SS • Tel: 0844 376 1845 • Fax: 020 7820 5601 • E-mail: enquiries@surreycricket.com • Web: www.kiaoval.com • Twitter: @surreycricket (32,240 followers)

Head Coach: Graham Ford. **Captain**: G.J.Batty. **Vice-Captain**: tba. **Overseas Player**: K.C.Sangakkara. **2015 Beneficiary**: None. **Head Groundsman**: Lee Fortiss. **Scorer**: Keith Booth. ‡ New registration. NQ Not qualified for England.

ANSARI, Zafar Shahaan (Hampton S; Trinity Hall, Cambridge), b Ascot, Berks 10 Dec 1991. Younger brother of A.S.Ansari (Cambridge U 2008-13). 5'11". LHB, SLA. Squad No 22. Cambridge MCCU 2011-13. Surrey debut 2011; cap 2014. Surrey 2nd XI debut 2008, aged 16y 133d. 1000 runs (1): 1029 (2014). HS 112 v Glamorgan (Colwyn Bay) 2014. BB 5-33 CU v Surrey (Cambridge) 2011. Sy BB 5-93 v Leics (Oval) 2014. LO HS 62 v Hants (Southampton) 2013 (Y40). LO BB 4-42 v Scotland (Oval) 2013 (Y40). T20 HS 38*. T20 BB 3-27.

NQAZHAR MAHMOOD Sagar (F.G. No. 1 HS, Islamabad), b Rawalpindi, Pakistan 28 Feb 1975. 5'11". RHB, RFM. Islamabad 1993-94 to 2006-07. United Bank 1995-96 to 1996-97. Rawalpindi 1998-99 to 2004-05. PIA 2001-02. Surrey debut 2002; cap 2004. HB 2006-07 to 2010-11. Kent 2008-12, (British passport holder) scoring 116 v Notts (Canterbury) on debut; cap 2008. MCC 2001. Returns to Surrey in 2015 for l-o and T20 only. IPL: KXIP 2012-13. Big Bash: ST 2012-13. **Tests** (P): 21 (1997-98 to 2001); HS 136 v SA (Johannesburg) 1997-98; BB 4-50 v E (Lord's) 2001. Scored 128* and 50* v SA (Rawalpindi) 1997-98 on debut. **LOI** (P): 143 (1996-97 to 2006-07); HS 67 v I (Adelaide) 1999-00; BB 6-18 v WI (Sharjah) 1999-00. F-c Tours (P): E 1997 (Pak A), 2001; A 1999-00; SA 1997-98; I 1998-99; SL 2000; Z 1997-98. HS 204* v Middx (Oval) 2005. 50 wkts (0+1): 59 (1996-97). BB 8-61 v Lancs (Oval) 2002. LO HS 101* v Glamorgan (Oval) 2006 (CGT). LO BB 6-18 (*see LOI*). T20 HS 106*. T20 BB 5-24.

‡BALCOMBE, David John (St John's S, Leatherhead; St Hild & St Bede C, Durham), b City of London 24 Dec 1984. 6'4". RHB, RFM. Squad No 84. Durham UCCE 2005-07. British U 2006. Hampshire 2007-14; cap 2013. Kent 2011 (on loan). HS 73 DU v Leics (Leicester) 2005 and 73 H v Leics (Leicester) 2012. BB 8-71 (11-119 match) H v Glos (Southampton) 2012. LO HS 6 K v Netherlands (Rotterdam) 2011 (CB40). LO BB 4-38 H v Worcs (Worcester) 2011 (CB40). T20 HS 3. T20 BB 1-23.

BATTY, Gareth Jon (Bingley GS), b Bradford, Yorks 13 Oct 1977. Younger brother of J.D.Batty (Yorkshire and Somerset 1989-96). 5'11". RHB, OB. Squad No 13. Yorkshire 1997. Surrey 1999-2001, rejoined in 2010; cap 2011; captain 2015. Worcestershire 2002-09. MCC 2012. **Tests**: 7 (2003-04 to 2005); HS 38 v SL (Kandy) 2003-04; BB 3-55 v SL (Galle) 2003-04. Took wicket with his third ball in Test cricket. **LOI**: 10 (2002-03 to 2008-09); HS 17 v WI (Bridgetown) 2008-09; BB 2-40 v WI (Gros Islet, St Lucia) 2003-04. **IT20**: 1 (2008-09); HS 4 v WI (Port of Spain) 2008-09. F-c Tours: WI 2003-04, 2005-06; NZ 2008-09 (Eng A); SL 2002-03 (ECB Acad); SL 2003-04; B 2003-04. HS 133 Wo v Surrey (Oval) 2004. Sy HS 79 v Essex (Croydon) 2011. 50 wkts (2); most – 60 (2003). BB 8-68 v Essex (Chelmsford) 2014. LO HS 83* v Yorks (Oval) 2001 (NL). LO BB 5-35 Wo v Hants (Southampton) 2009 (FPT). T20 HS 87. T20 BB 4-13.

BEAVEN, Luke Edward (Highdown S; Reading U), b Reading, Berks 31 Aug 1989. 6'2". RHB, SLA. Debut (Surrey) 2014. Surrey 2nd XI debut 2006. MCC YCs 2007-09. Berkshire 2006-11. Unicorns (l-o only) 2011-13. HS 2 and BB 1-39 v New Zealand A (Oval) 2014 – only f-c game. LO HS 25* Unic v Warwicks (Wormsley) 2012 (CB40). LO BB 3-35 Unic v Glamorgan (Wormsley) 2011 (CB40).

‡**BURKE, James** Edward (Plymouth C), b Plymouth, Devon 25 Jan 1991. 6'3". RHB, RMF. Squad No 8. Somerset 2012. Somerset 2nd XI debut 2008. Devon 2008-13. HS – . BB 2-51 Sm v Cardiff MCCU (Taunton) 2012. T20 HS 4.

BURNS, Rory Joseph (City of London Freemen's S), b Epsom 26 Aug 1990. 5'9". LHB, WK, occ RM. Squad No 17. Debut (Surrey) 2011; cap 2014. Surrey 2nd XI debut 2009. MCC Univs 2010. 1000 runs (1): 1055 (2014). HS 199 v Glos (Bristol) 2014. BB 1-18 v Middx (Lord's) 2013. LO HS 87 v Glamorgan (Guildford) 2014 (RLC). T20 HS 28.

NQ**CURRAN, Thomas** Kevin (Hilton C, Durban), b Cape Town, South Africa 12 Mar 1995. Son of K.M.Curran (Glos, Natal, Northants, Boland and Zimbabwe 1980-81 to 1999); grandson of K.P.Curran (Rhodesia 1947-48 to 1954-55). 6'0". RHB, RFM. Squad No 59. Debut (Surrey) 2104. Surrey 2nd XI debut 2012. HS 9* and BB 5-51 v Derbys (Derby) 2014. LO HS 1* v Hants (Southampton) 2013 (Y40). LO BB 5-34 v Scotland (Oval) 2013 (Y40). T20 HS – . T20 BB 3-23.

DAVIES, Steven Michael (King Charles I S, Kidderminster), b Bromsgrove, Worcs 17 Jun 1986. 5'10". LHB, WK. Squad No 9. Worcestershire 2005-09. Surrey debut 2010; cap 2011. MCC 2006-07, 2011. **LOI**: 8 (2009-10 to 2010-11); HS 87 v P (Chester-le-St) 2010. **IT20**: 5 (2008-09 to 2010-11); HS 33 v P (Cardiff) 2010. F-c Tours: A 2010-11; B 2006-07 (Eng A); UAE 2011-12 (v P). 1000 runs (5); most – 1090 (2010). HS 192 Wo v Glos (Bristol) 2014. Sy HS 174 v Leics (Leicester) 2014. LO HS 127* v Hants (Oval) 2013 (Y40). T20 HS 99*.

DERNBACH, Jade Winston (St John the Baptist S), b Johannesburg, South Africa 3 Mar 1986. 6'1½". RHB, RFM. Squad No 16. Italian passport. UK resident since 1998. Debut (Surrey) 2003; cap 2011. **LOI**: 24 (2011 to 2013); HS 5 v SL (Leeds) 2011; BB 4-45 v P (Dubai) 2011-12. **IT20**: 34 (2011 to 2013-14); HS 12 v I (Colombo, RPS) 2012-13; BB 4-22 v I (Manchester) 2011. F-c Tour (EL): WI 2010-11. HS 56* v Northants (Northampton) 2010. 50 wkts (1): 51 (2010). BB 6-47 v Leics (Leicester) 2009. LO HS 31 v Somerset (Taunton) 2010 (CB40). LO BB 5-31 v Derbys (Chesterfield) 2008 (P40). T20 HS 24*. T20 BB 4-22.

DUNN, Matthew Peter (Bearwood C, Wokingham), b Egham 5 May 1992. 6'2". LHB, RFM. Squad No 4. Debut (Surrey) 2010. Surrey 2nd XI debut 2009. England U19s 2010. HS 31* v Kent (Guildford) 2014. BB 5-48 v Glos (Oval) 2014. LO HS – . LO BB 2-32 England Dev XI v Sri Lanka A (Manchester) 2011. T20 HS – . BB 3-8.

‡**FOAKES, Ben**jamin Thomas (Tendring TC), b Colchester, Essex 15 Feb 1993. 6'1''. RHB, WK. Squad No 7. Essex 2011-14. Essex 2nd XI debut 2008, aged 15y 172d. England U19s 2010-11. F-c Tour (EL): SL 2013-14. HS 132* Ex v Glos (Bristol) 2014. LO HS 56 EL v Australia A (Hobart) 2012-13. T20 HS 46.

HARINATH, Arun (Tiffin Boys GS; Loughborough U), b Sutton 26 Mar 1987. 5'11''. LHB, OB. Squad No 10. Loughborough UCCE 2007-09. Surrey debut 2009. MCC 2008. Buckinghamshire 2007-08. HS 154 v Derbys (Derby) 2013. BB 2-1 v Glamorgan (Colwyn Bay) 2014. LO HS 52 v Derbys (Oval) 2013 (Y40). LO BB – .

KAPIL, Aneesh (Denstone C), b Wolverhampton 3 Aug 1993. 5'8''. RHB, RFM. Squad No 47. Worcestershire 2011-13. Surrey debut 2014. Worcestershire 2nd XI debut 2008, aged 15y 10d. HS 104* v New Zealand A (Oval) 2014. CC HS 54 Wo v Sussex (Horsham) 2011 – on debut. BB 3-17 Wo v Notts (Worcester) 2012. Sy BB 2-23 v Kent (Canterbury) 2014. LO HS 59 v Somerset (Oval) 2014 (RLC). LO BB 1-18 Wo v Netherlands (Worcester) 2011 (CB40). T20 HS 13. T20 BB 3-9.

LINLEY, Timothy Edward (St Mary's RC CS, Menston; Notre Dame SFC; Oxford Brookes U), b Leeds, Yorks 23 Mar 1982. 6'2''. RHB, RFM. Squad No 12. Oxford UCCE 2003-05. British U 2004. Sussex 2006 (1 match). Surrey debut 2009. HS 42 OU v Derbys (Oxford) 2005. Sy HS 36 v Kent (Canterbury) 2009. 50 wkts (1): 73 (2011). BB 6-57 (9-79 match) v Leics (Leicester) 2011. LO HS 20* v Warwks (Oval) 2009 (P40). LO BB 3-50 v Hants (Croydon) 2011 (CB40). T20 HS 8. T20 BB 2-28.

MEAKER, Stuart Christopher (Cranleigh S), b Durban, South Africa 21 Jan 1989. Moved to UK in 2001. 6'1''. RHB, RFM. Squad No 18. Debut (Surrey) 2008; cap 2012. England U19s 2007 to 2008. **LOI**: 2 (2011-12); HS 1 and BB 1-45 v I (Mumbai) 2011-12. **IT20**: 2 (2012-13); HS – ; BB 1-28 v I (Pune) 2013-14. F-c Tour: I 2012-13. HS 94 v Bangladeshis (Oval) 2010. CC HS 72 v Essex (Colchester) 2009. 50 wkts (1): 51 (2012). BB 8-52 (11-167 match) v Somerset (Oval) 2010. LO HS 21* v Glamorgan (Oval) 2012 (CB40). LO BB 4-47 EL v Bangladesh A (Chittagong) 2011-12. T20 HS 17. T20 BB 4-30.

ROY, Jason Jonathan (Whitgift S), b Durban, South Africa 21 Jul 1990. 6'0''. RHB, RM. Squad No 20. Debut (Surrey) 2010; cap 2014. Surrey 2nd XI debut 2008. **IT20**: 1 (2014); HS 8 v I (Birmingham) 2014. 1000 runs (1): 1078 (2014). HS 121* and BB 3-9 v Glos (Bristol) 2014. LO HS 141 EL v SA A (Kimberley) 2014-15. LO BB – . T20 HS 101* v Kent (Beckenham) 2010 – Sy record. T20 BB 1-23.

‡**NOSANGAKKARA, Kumar** Chokshanada (Trinity C, Kandy; Colombo U), b Matale, Sri Lanka, 27 Oct 1977. 5'11''. LHB, WK, occ OB. Squad No 11. Nondescripts 1997-98 to date. Central Province 2003-04 to 2004-05. Warwickshire 2007; cap 2007. Durham 2014. IPL: KXIP 2007-10. DC 2011-12. SH 2013. *Wisden* 2011. **Tests** (SL): 130 (2000 to 2014-15, 15 as captain); HS 319 v B (Chittagong) 2013-14 (also scored 105 to become only the 2nd man, after G.A.Gooch, to score a treble century and a century in the same match). Scored 287 v SA (Colombo, SSC) 2006, sharing in world record f-c partnership for any wkt of 624 with D.P.M.D.Jayawardena; BB – . **LOI** (SL): 403 (2000 to 2014-15, 45 as captain); HS 169 v SA (Colombo, RPS) 2013. **IT20** (SL): 56 (2006 to 2013-14, 22 as captain); HS 78 v I (Nagpur) 2009-10. F-c Tours (SL) (C=Captain): E 2002, 2006, 2011, 2014; A 2004, 2007-08, 2012-13; SA 1999-00 (SL A), 2000-01, 2011-12; WI 2003, 2007-08; NZ 2004-05, 2006-07, 2014-15; I 2005-06, 2009-10C; P 2001-02, 2004-05, 2008-09; Z 2004, 2008-09; B 2005-06, 2008-09, 2013-14; UAE 2011-12 (v P), 2013-14 (v P). 1000 runs (0+1): 1191 (2003-04). HS 319 (*see Tests*). CC HS 159 Du v Sussex (Hove) 2014. BB 1-13 SL v Zim A (Harare) 2004. LO HS 169 (*see LOI*). T20 HS 94.

SIBLEY, Dominic Peter (Whitgift S, Croydon), b Epsom 5 Sep 1995. 6'3''. RHB, LB. Squad No 45. Debut (Surrey) 2013. Surrey 2nd XI debut 2011, aged 15y 302d. England U19s 2012-13 to 2014. HS 242 v Yorks (Oval) 2013. LO HS 37 v Durham (Chester-le-St) 2013 (Y40).

SOLANKI, Vikram Singh (Regis S, Wolverhampton), b Udaipur, India 1 Apr 1976. 6'0". RHB, OB, occ WK. Squad No 42. Worcestershire 1995-2012; cap 1998; captain 2005-10; benefit 2007. Rajasthan 2006-07. Surrey debut 2013; cap 2014. **LOI**: 51 (1999-00 to 2006); HS 106 v SA (Oval) 2003; BB 1-17 v SL (Leeds) 2006. **IT20**: 3 (2005 to 2007-08); HS 43 v I (Durban) 2007-08. F-c Tours (Eng A): SA 1998-99, 1999-00 (Eng – *part*); WI 2000-01, 2005-06 (Captain); NZ 1999-00; SL 2004-05; Z 1996-97 (Wo), 1998-99; B 1999-00. 1000 runs (6); most – 1339 (1999). HS 270 Wo v Glos (Cheltenham) 2008, sharing Wo 2nd wkt record partnership of 316 with S.C.Moore. Sy HS 162 v Warwks (Birmingham) 2013. Won Walter Lawrence Trophy in 2009 with 49-ball hundred v Glamorgan (Worcester). BB 5-40 Wo v Middx (Lord's) 2004. Sy BB 2-20 v Hants (Oval) 2014. LO HS 164* Wo v Worcs CB (Worcester) 2003 (CGT). LO BB 4-14 Wo v Somerset (Taunton) 2006 (P40). T20 HS 100. T20 BB 1-6.

TREMLETT, Christopher Timothy (Thornden S, Chandler's Ford; Taunton's C, Southampton), b Southampton, Hampshire 2 Sep 1981. Son of T.M.Tremlett (Hampshire 1976-91); grandson of M.F.Tremlett (Somerset, CD and England 1947-60). 6'7". RHB, RFM. Squad No 33. Hampshire 2000-09, taking wicket of M.H.Richardson (NZ A) with his first ball; cap 2004. Surrey debut 2010; cap 2014. **Tests**: 12 (2007 to 2013-14); HS 25* v I (Oval) 2007; BB 6-48 v SL (Southampton) 2011. **LOI**: 15 (2005 to 2010-11); HS 19* v I (Birmingham) 2007; BB 4-32 v B (Nottingham) 2005 – on debut (hat-trick ball hit stump without dislodging bails). **IT20**: 1 (2007-08); BB 2-45 v I (Durban) 2007-08. F-c Tours: A 2010-11, 2013-14; SL 2002-03 (ECB Acad); UAE 2011-12 (v P). HS 90 v Leics (Oval) 2014. BB 8-96 v Durham (Chester-le-St) 2013. Hat-trick: H v Notts (Nottingham) 2005. LO HS 38* H v Cheshire (Alderley Edge) 2004 (CGT). LO BB 4-25 H v Essex (Southend) 2002 (NL). T20 HS 13. T20 BB 4-16.

VAN DEN BERGH, Frederick Oliver Edward (Whitgift S, Croydon; Hatfield C, Durham U), b Farnborough, Kent 14 Jun 1992. 6'2". RHB, SLA. Squad No 5. Debut (Surrey) 2011. Durham MCCU 2013-14. Surrey 2nd XI debut, aged 16y 326d. Summer contract. HS 34 and BB 4-84 DU v Notts (Nottingham) 2013. Sy HS 16* v Leeds/Bradford MCCU (Oval) 2012. Sy BB 3-79 v Cambridge MCCU (Cambridge) 2011. LO HS 29* v Sussex (Oval) 2014 (RLC). LO BB – .

[NQ]**WILSON, Gary** Craig (Methodist C, Belfast; Manchester Met), b Dundonald, N Ireland 5 Feb 1986. 5'10". RHB, WK. Ireland 2005 to date. Surrey debut 2010; cap 2014. MCC YC 2005. **LOI** (Ire): 57 (2007 to 2014-15); HS 113 v Netherlands (Dublin) 2010. **IT20** (Ire): 34 (2008 to 2013-14); HS 41* v B (Belfast) 2012. HS 160* v Leics (Oval) 2014. BB – . LO HS 113 (*see LOI*). T20 HS 63*.

RELEASED/RETIRED

(Having made a County 1st XI appearance in 2014)

[NQ]**AMLA, Hashim** Mahomed, b Durban, South Africa 31 Mar 1983. Younger brother of A.M.Amla (Natal B, KZN, Dolphins 1997-98 to 2012-13). RHB, RM/OB. KZN 1999-00 to 2003-04. Dolphins 2004-05 to 2011-12. Essex 2009. Nottinghamshire 2010; cap 2010. Surrey 2013-14. *Wisden* 2012. **Tests** (SA): 82 (2004-05 to 2014-15, 6 as captain); HS 311* v E (Oval) 2012; BB – . **LOI** (SA): 113 (2007-08 to 2014-15, 6 as captain); HS 159 v Ireland (Canberra) 2014-15. **IT20** (SA): 26 (2008-09 to 2013-14, 2 as captain); HS 56 v E (Chittagong) 2013-14. F-c Tours (SA) (C=Captain): E 2008, 2012; A 2008-09, 2012-13; WI 2010; NZ 2011-12; I 2004-05, 2007-08 (SA A), 2007-08, 2009-10; P 2007-08; SL 2005-06 (SA A), 2006, 2014C; Z 2004 (SA A), 2007 (SA A), 2014C; UAE 2010-11, 2013-14 (v P). 1000 runs (0+2); most – 1126 (2005-06). HS 311* (*see Tests*). CC HS 181 Ex v Glamorgan (Chelmsford) 2009 – on debut. Sy HS 151 v Yorks (Oval) 2013. BB 1-10 SA A v India A (Kimberley) 2001-02. LO HS 159 (*see LOI*). T20 HS 88*.

NQDILSHAN, Tillakaratne Mudiyanselage, b Kalutara, Sri Lanka 14 Oct 1975. RHB, OB. Kulatara 1996-97. Singha SC 1997-98. Sebastianites 1998-99 to 1999-00. Bloomfield 2000-01 to 2008-09. Tamil Union 2012-13 to date. Surrey 2014. **Tests** (SL): 87 (1999-00 to 2012-13, 11 as captain); HS 193 v E (Lord's) 2011; BB 4-10 v B (Chittagong) 2008-09. **LOI** (SL): 313 (1999-00 to 2014-15, 26 as captain); HS 161* v B (Melbourne) 2014-15; BB 4-4 v Z (Pallekele) 2010-11. **IT20** (SL): 62 (2006 to 2014, 5 as captain); HS 104* v A (Pallekele) 2011; BB 2-4 v Kenya (Johannesburg) 2007. F-c Tours (SL)(C=Captain): E 1999 (SL A), 2006, 2011C; A 2004, 2012-13; SA 1999-00 (SL A), 2000-01, 2011-12C; WI 2003, 2007-08; NZ 2004-05; I 2001-02 (Bloomfield), 2005-06, 2009-10; P 1999-00, 2008-09; Z 1999-00 (SL A), 2004, 2007-08 (SL A); B 2005-06, 2008-09; UAE (v P) 2011-12C. 1000 runs (0+2); most – 1284. HS 200* NC Prov v Central Prov (Colombo) 2004-05. Sy HS 69 and Sy BB 2-29 v Hants (Oval) 2014. BB 5-49 Bloomfield v Sinhalese SC (Colombo) 2002-03. LO HS 188 Bloomfield v Colts (Colombo) 2007-08. LO BB 4-4 (*see LOI*). T20 HS 104*. T20 BB 3-16.

EDWARDS, G.A. – see LANCASHIRE.

NQO'BRIEN, Kevin Joseph (Marian C, Dublin; Tallaght I of T), b Dublin, Ireland 4 Mar 1984. RHB, RMF. Son of B.A.O'Brien (Ireland 1966-81) and younger brother of N.J.O'Brien (*see LEICESTERSHIRE*). Ireland 2006-07 to date. Nottinghamshire 2009. Surrey 2014. **LOI** (Ire): 89 (2006 to 2014-15); HS 142 v Kenya (Nairobi) 2006-07; BB 4-13 v Netherlands (Amstelveen) 2013. **IT20** (Ire): 37 (2008 to 2013-14); HS 42* v Netherlands (Sylhet) 2013-14; BB 3-35 v Scotland (Dubai) 2011-12. HS 171* Ire v Kenya (Nairobi) 2008-09. Sy HS 17 v Hants (Oval) 2014. BB 5-39 Ire v Canada (Toronto) 2010. LO HS 142 (*see LOI*). LO BB 4-31 (*see LOI*). T20 HS 119 Gs v Middx (Uxbridge) 2011 – Gs record. T20 BB 4-22.

NQPETERSON, Robin John, b Pt Elizabeth, South Africa 4 Aug 1979. LHB, SLA. E Province 1998-99 to 2003-04. Warriors 2004-05 to 2008-09. Cape Cobras 2009-10 to date. Derbyshire 2010 (Kolpak registration). Surrey 2014 (l-o and T20 only). IPL: MI 2012. **Tests** (SA): 15 (2003 to 2013-14); HS 84 v P (Cape Town) 2012-13; BB 5-33 v B (Chittagong) 2007-08. **LOI** (SA): 79 (2002-03 to 2014-15); HS 68 v I (Cardiff) 2013; BB 4-12 v B (Dhaka) 2010-11. **IT20** (SA): 21 (2005-06 to 2014-15); HS 34 v A (Centurion) 2008-09; BB 3-28 v A (Sydney) 2014-15. F-c Tours (SA): E 2003; A 2012-13; WI 2000-01 (SA A); P 2003-04; B 2003, 2007-08; UAE 2013-14 (v P). HS 130 EP v Gauteng (Johannesburg) 2002-03. CC HS 58 De v Northants (Chesterfield) 2010. 50 wkts (1): 51 (2010). BB 6-67 EP v Border (East London) 1999-00. CC BB 4-10 De v Sussex (Derby) 2010. LO HS 101 EP v Border (Pt Elizabeth) 2001-02. LO BB 7-24 Warriors v Eagles (East London) 2007-08. T20 HS 72*. T20 BB 3-19.

PIETERSEN, Kevin Peter (Maritzburg C; Natal U), b Pietermaritzburg, South Africa 27 Jun 1980. British passport (English mother) – qualified for England Oct 2004. 6'4". RHB, OB. Natal/KZN 1997-98 to 1999-00. Nottinghamshire 2001-04; cap 2002. Hampshire 2005-08; cap 2005 (no f-c appearances 2006-07, 2009-10). Surrey 2010-13. Dolphins 2010-11. MCC 2004. IPL: RCB 2009-10. DD 2012-14. Big Bash: MS 2014-15. MBE 2005. *Wisden* 2005. **Tests**: 104 (2005 to 2013-14, 3 as captain); HS 227 v A (Adelaide) 2010-11; BB 3-52 v SA (Leeds) 2012. **LOI**: 136 (2004-05 to 2013, 12 as captain); HS 130 v P (Dubai) 2011-12; BB 2-22 v SA (Leeds) 2008. **IT20**: 37 (2005 to 2013); HS 79 v Z (Cape Town) 2007-08; BB 1-27 v SA (Centurion) 2009-10. F-c Tours: A 2006-07, 2010-11, 2013-14; SA 2009-10; WI 2008-09; NZ 2007-08, 2012-13; I 2003-04 (Eng A), 2005-06, 2008-09 (Captain), 2012-13; P 2005-06; SL 2007-08, 2011-12; UAE 2011-12 (v P). 1000 runs (3); most – 1546 (2003). HS 254* Nt v Middx (Nottingham) 2002. Sy HS 234* v Lancs (Guildford) 2012. BB 4-31 Nt v Durham U (Nottingham) 2003. CC BB 3-72 Nt v Hants (Nottingham) 2004. Sy BB 2-24 v Notts (Oval) 2012. LO HS 147 Nt v Somerset (Taunton) 2002 (NL). LO BB 3-14 Nt v Middx (Lord's) 2004 (NL). T20 HS 103*. T20 BB 3-33.

NQ**SMITH, Graeme** Craig (K Edward VII S, Johannesburg), b Johannesburg, South Africa 1 Feb 1981. 6'3" LHB, OB. W Province 2000-01 to 2003-04. W Province Boland 2004-05. Somerset 2005. Cape Cobras 2010-11. Surrey 2013-14; cap 2013; captain 2013-14. *Wisden* 2003. **Tests** (SA): 117 (2001-02 to 2013-14, inc 1 for ICC; 109 as captain); HS 277 v E (Birmingham) 2003; BB 2-145 v WI (St John's) 2004-05. **LOI** (SA): 197 (2001-02 to 2013-14, inc 1 for Africa XI; 150 as captain); HS 141 v E (Centurion) 2009-10; BB 3-30 v SL (Perth) 2005-06. **IT20** (SA): 33 (2005-06 to 2011-12; 27 as captain); HS 89* v A (Johannesburg) 2005-06. F-c Tours (SA) (C=Captain): E 2003C, 2008C, 2012C; A 2005-06C, 2008-09C, 2012-13C; WI 2004-05C, 2010C; NZ 2003-04C, 2011-12C; I 2004-05C, 2007-08C, 2009-10C; P 2003-04C, 2007-08C; SL 2004C; B 2002-03C, 2007-08C; UAE (v P) 2010-11C, 2013-14C. HS 311 Sm v Leics (Taunton) 2005. Sy HS 103 v Glos (Oval) 2014. BB 2-145 (*see Tests*). CC BB 1-34 Sm v Durham (Taunton) 2005. LO HS 141 (*see LOI*). LO BB 3-30 (*see LOI*). T20 HS 105. T20 BB 3-23.

WINSLADE, Jack Robert (Whitgift S, Croydon), b Epsom 12 Apr 1995. Younger brother of T.S.Winslade (Loughborough MCCU 2010). 5'10". RHB, RMF. Surrey 2nd XI debut 2011, aged 16y 6d. LO HS – . LO BB 1-61 v Durham (Chester-le-St) 2014 (RLC).

T.M.Jewell left the staff without making a County 1st XI appearance in 2014.

SOMERSET RELEASED/RETIRED (continued from p 158)

KIRBY, Steven Paul (Elton HS; Bury C), b Ainsworth, nr Bolton, Lancs 4 Oct 1977. 6'3½". RHB, RFM. Leicestershire staff 1998 – no f-c appearances. Yorkshire 2001-04, debut as sub for M.J.Hoggard (England duty) taking 7-50; cap 2003. Gloucestershire 2005-10; cap 2005. Somerset 2011-13. MCC 2008, 2010-11, 2013. F-c Tour (Eng A): I 2003-04 (*part*). HS 57 Y v Hants (Leeds) 2002. Sm HS 19 v Durham (Taunton) 2011. 50 wkts (3); most – 67 (2003). BB 8-80 (13-154 match) Y v Somerset (Taunton) 2003. Sm BB 6-115 v Lancs (Liverpool) 2011. LO HS 15 Y v Leics (Leicester) 2003 (NL). LO BB 5-36 Gs v Middx (Lord's) 2007 (FPT). T20 HS 25. T20 BB 3-17.

MESCHEDE, C.A.J. – *see GLAMORGAN*.

NQ**NANNES, Dirk** Peter (Wesley C and Monash U, Melbourne), b Mount Waverley, Victoria, Australia 16 May 1976. 6'3". RHB, LFM. Victoria 2005-06 to 2009-10. Middlesex 2008; cap 2008. Dutch passport. Somerset T20 only in 2014. IPL: DD 2009-10. RCB 2011. CSK 2013. Big Bash: MR 2011-12. ST 2012-13 to date. **LOI** (A): 1 (2009); HS 1 and BB 1-20 v Scotland (Edinburgh) 2009. **IT20** (Neth/A): 17 (2 for Neth 2009; 15 for A 2009 to 2010-11); HS 12* A v P (Birmingham) 2010; BB 4-18 A v B (Bridgetown) 2010. HS 31* Vic v S Australia (Adelaide) 2007-08. CC HS 5 and CC BB 6-32 M v Worcs (Kidderminster) 2008. BB 7-50 (11-95 match) Vic v Q (Brisbane) 2008-09. LO HS 5* M v Somerset (Lord's) 2008. LO BB 4-38 M v Worcs (Kidderminster) 2008 (P40). T20 HS 12*. T20 BB 5-31.

PETERSEN, A.N. – *see LANCASHIRE*.

SURREY 2014

RESULTS SUMMARY

	Place	Won	Lost	Tied	Drew	NR
LV= County Championship (2nd Division)	5th	4	5		7	
All First-Class Matches		5	5		8	
Royal London One-Day Cup (Group B)	9th	1	5	1		1
NatWest t20 Blast (South Division)	SF	10	6			

LV= COUNTY CHAMPIONSHIP AVERAGES

BATTING AND FIELDING

Cap		M	I	NO	HS	Runs	Avge	100	50	Ct/St
2014	J.J.Roy	16	23	3	121*	1042	52.10	3	5	18
2014	Z.S.Ansari	16	26	7	112	913	48.05	2	5	6
2014	G.C.Wilson	15	20	4	160*	750	46.87	1	5	35/2
2011	S.M.Davies	16	23	–	174	937	40.73	2	5	9
2014	R.J.Burns	16	28	4	199	950	39.58	2	4	22
2014	V.S.Solanki	10	16	1	143	567	37.80	1	5	10
	T.M.Dilshan	3	5	–	69	185	37.00	–	2	1
2013	G.C.Smith	5	8	–	103	263	32.87	1	1	10
	A.Harinath	5	9	1	63	250	31.25	–	2	2
2014	C.T.Tremlett	10	11	2	90	273	30.33	–	2	2
	H.M.Amla	4	4	–	71	118	29.50	–	1	5
2012	S.C.Meaker	8	12	2	58	228	22.80	–	2	1
2011	G.J.Batty	11	14	3	29	175	15.90	–	–	5
	A.Kapil	2	4	–	38	60	15.00	–	–	1
	M.P.Dunn	12	10	5	31*	57	11.40	–	–	4
2011	J.W.Dernbach	9	10	3	24	76	10.85	–	–	2
	D.P.Sibley	5	8	–	34	79	9.87	–	–	5
	T.E.Linley	6	9	3	21*	41	6.83	–	–	1
	T.K.Curran	6	6	3	9*	16	5.33	–	–	1

Also played: K.J.O'Brien (1 match) 17.

BOWLING

	O	M	R	W	Avge	Best	5wI	10wM
G.J.Batty	400.3	113	915	39	23.46	8-68	1	–
T.K.Curran	143.4	25	477	16	29.81	5-51	1	–
S.C.Meaker	273.4	35	1028	32	32.12	7-90	1	1
C.T.Tremlett	260.1	48	811	25	32.44	6-59	2	–
T.E.Linley	177.4	36	558	16	34.87	4-79	–	–
Z.S.Ansari	294.5	51	884	24	36.83	5-93	1	–
M.P.Dunn	374.2	71	1444	39	37.02	5-48	2	–
J.W.Dernbach	256.3	49	900	23	39.13	4-72	–	–

Also bowled:

J.J.Roy	78	9	283	6	47.16	3- 9	–	–

H.M.Amla 1-0-2-0; R.J.Burns 6-1-18-1; T.M.Dilshan 15-3-29-2; A.Harinath 2-1-1-2;
A.Kapil 12.2-3-52-4; K.J.O'Brien 3-0-19-0; D.P.Sibley 16.4-2-60-1; V.S.Solanki 7.1-1-20-2.

The First-Class Averages (pp 217–233) give the records of Surrey players in all first-class
county matches (Surrey's other opponents being Cambridge MCCU and New Zealand A).

SURREY RECORDS

FIRST-CLASS CRICKET

Highest Total	For	811		v	Somerset	The Oval	1899
	V	863		by	Lancashire	The Oval	1990
Lowest Total	For	14		v	Essex	Chelmsford	1983
	V	16		by	MCC	Lord's	1872
Highest Innings	For	357*	R.Abel	v	Somerset	The Oval	1899
	V	366	N.H.Fairbrother	for	Lancashire	The Oval	1990

Highest Partnership for each Wicket

1st	428	J.B.Hobbs/A.Sandham	v	Oxford U	The Oval	1926
2nd	371	J.B.Hobbs/E.G.Hayes	v	Hampshire	The Oval	1909
3rd	413	D.J.Bicknell/D.M.Ward	v	Kent	Canterbury	1990
4th	448	R.Abel/T.W.Hayward	v	Yorkshire	The Oval	1899
5th	318	M.R.Ramprakash/Azhar Mahmood	v	Middlesex	The Oval	2005
6th	298	A.Sandham/H.S.Harrison	v	Sussex	The Oval	1913
7th	262	C.J.Richards/K.T.Medlycott	v	Kent	The Oval	1987
8th	205	I.A.Greig/M.P.Bicknell	v	Lancashire	The Oval	1990
9th	168	E.R.T.Holmes/E.W.J.Brooks	v	Hampshire	The Oval	1936
10th	173	A.Ducat/A.Sandham	v	Essex	Leyton	1921

Best Bowling	For	10-43	T.Rushby	v	Somerset	Taunton	1921
(Innings)	V	10-28	W.P.Howell	for	Australians	The Oval	1899
Best Bowling	For	16-83	G.A.R.Lock	v	Kent	Blackheath	1956
(Match)	V	15-57	W.P.Howell	for	Australians	The Oval	1899

Most Runs – Season	3246	T.W.Hayward	(av 72.13)	1906
Most Runs – Career	43554	J.B.Hobbs	(av 49.72)	1905-34
Most 100s – Season	13	T.W.Hayward		1906
	13	J.B.Hobbs		1925
Most 100s – Career	144	J.B.Hobbs		1905-34
Most Wkts – Season	252	T.Richardson	(av 13.94)	1895
Most Wkts – Career	1775	T.Richardson	(av 17.87)	1892-1904
Most Career W-K Dismissals	1221	H.Strudwick	(1035 ct; 186 st)	1902-27
Most Career Catches in the Field	605	M.J.Stewart		1954-72

LIMITED-OVERS CRICKET

Highest Total	50ov	496-4		v	Glos	The Oval	2007
	40ov	386-3		v	Glamorgan	The Oval	2010
	T20	224-5		v	Glos	Bristol	2006
Lowest Total	50ov	74		v	Kent	The Oval	1967
	40ov	64		v	Worcs	Worcester	1978
	T20	88		v	Kent	The Oval	2012
Highest Innings	50ov	268	A.D.Brown	v	Glamorgan	The Oval	2002
	40ov	203	A.D.Brown	v	Hampshire	Guildford	1997
	T20	101*	J.J.Roy	v	Kent	Beckenham	2010
Best Bowling	50ov	7-33	R.D.Jackman	v	Yorkshire	Harrogate	1970
	40ov	7-30	M.P.Bicknell	v	Glamorgan	The Oval	1999
	T20	6-24	T.J.Murtagh	v	Middlesex	Lord's	2005

SUSSEX

Formation of Present Club: 1 March 1839
Substantial Reorganisation: August 1857
Inaugural First-Class Match: 1864
Colours: Dark Blue, Light Blue and Gold
Badge: County Arms of Six Martlets
County Champions: (3) 2003, 2006, 2007
Gillette/NatWest/C&G Trophy Winners: (5) 1963, 1964, 1978, 1986, 2006
Pro 40/National League (Div 1) Winners: (2) 2008, 2009
Sunday League Winners: (1) 1982
Twenty20 Cup Winners: (1) 2009

Chief Executive: Zac Toumazi, The BrightonandHoveJobs.com County Ground, Eaton Road, Hove BN3 3AN • Tel: 0844 264 0202 • Fax: 01273 771549 • Email: info@sussexcricket.co.uk • Web: www.sussexcricket.co.uk • Twitter: @SussexCCC (19,564 followers)

Head Coach: Mark Robinson. **Club Coach**: Mark Davis. **Captains**: E.C.Joyce (f-c and l-o) and L.J.Wright (T20). **Vice-Captain**: C.D.Nash. **Overseas Players**: D.M.P.D.Jayawardena (T20 only) and S.J.Magoffin. **2015 Beneficiary**: L.J.Wright. **Head Groundsman**: Andy Mackay. **Scorer**: M.J. (Mike) Charman. ‡ New registration. NQ Not qualified for England.

ANYON, James Edward (Garstang HS; Preston C; Loughborough U), b Lancaster, Lancs 5 May 1983. 6'1". LHB, RFM. Squad No 30. Loughborough U 2003-04. Warwickshire 2005-09. Surrey 2009 (on loan). Sussex debut 2010; cap 2011. Cumberland 2003. HS 64* v Surrey (Horsham) 2012. 50 wkts (1): 55 (2011). BB 6-82 Wa v Glamorgan (Cardiff) 2008. Sx BB 5-14 v Loughborough MCCU (Hove) 2014. LO HS 12 Wa v Worcs (Birmingham) 2006 (CGT). LO BB 3-6 Wa v Notts (Nottingham) 2008 (FPT). T20 HS 8*. T20 BB 3-6.

Syed ASHAR Ahmed ZAIDI, b Karachi, Pakistan 13 Jul 1981. LHB, SLA. Squad No 1. UK citizen. Islamabad 1999-00 to 2009-10. PTC 2003-04 to 2005-06. Rawalpindi 2003-04 to 2004-05. Federal Areas 2007-08. Sussex debut 2013. HS 202 Islamabad v Sialkot (Sialkot) 2009-10. Sx HS 88 v Northants (Northampton) 2014. BB 4-50 Islamabad v Hyderabad (Islamabad) 2009-10. Sx BB 4-57 v Yorks (Hove) 2013. LO HS 141 Rupganj v Old DOHS (Mirpur) 2014-15. LO BB 4-39 Gazi Tank v PDSC (Mirpur) 2013-14. T20 HS 42*. T20 BB 3-32.

BEER, William Andrew Thomas (Reigate GS; Collyer's C, Horsham), b Crawley 8 Oct 1988. RHB, LB. Squad No 18. Debut (Sussex) 2008. No f-c appearances in 2009. HS 39 v Middx (Lord's) 2013. BB 3-31 v Worcs (Worcester) 2010. LO HS 45* v Durham (Hove) 2014 (RLC). LO BB 3-27 v Warwks (Hove) 2012 (CB40). T20 HS 37. T20 BB 3-14.

BROWN, Ben Christopher (Ardingly C), b Crawley 23 Nov 1988. RHB, WK. Squad No 26. Debut (Sussex) 2007; cap 2014. No f-c appearances in 2008 or 2009. HS 163 v Durham (Hove) 2014. BB – . LO HS 60 v Yorks (Scarborough) 2011 (CB40). T20 HS 68.

CACHOPA, Craig, b Welkom, OFS, South Africa 17 Jan 1992. Younger brother of Carl Cachopa (Auckland, C Districts 2004-05 to date) and B.Cachopa (Auckland, Canterbury 2010-11 to date). Portuguese passport holder. RHB, RM, occ WK. Squad No 12. Wellington 2011-12. Auckland 2012-13 to date. Sussex debut 2014. HS 203 Auckland v Wellington (Auckland) 2013-14. Sx HS 84 v Warwks (Horsham) 2014 – on Sx debut. BB – . LO HS 121 Auckland v Canterbury (Christchurch) 2012-13. T20 HS 79*.

FINCH, Harry Zachariah (St Richard's Catholic C, Bexhill; Eastbourne C), b Hastings 10 Feb 1995. RHB, RMF. Squad No 6. Debut (Sussex) 2013. Sussex 2nd XI debut 2011, aged 16y 69d. England U19 2012-13. HS 11 v Durham (Chester-le-St) 2013. BB – . LO HS 92* v Glamorgan (Hove) 2014 (RLC). LO BB – . T20 HS 22.

HATCHETT, Lewis James (Steyning GS), b Shoreham-by-Sea 21 Jan 1990. 6'3". LHB, LMF. Squad No 5. Debut (Sussex) 2010. HS 21 v Yorks (Hove) 2013. BB 5-47 v Leics (Leicester) 2010. LO HS 5 v Kent (Canterbury) 2014 (RLC). LO BB 3-44 v Surrey (Oval) 2014 (RLC). T20 HS 0*. T20 BB 3-23.

HOBDEN, Matthew Edward (Eastbourne C; UWIC), b Eastbourne 27 Mar 1993. RHB, RFM. Squad No 19. Cardiff MCCU 2012-13. Sussex debut 2011. Sussex 2nd XI debut 2011. HS 18 CfU v Glamorgan (Cardiff) 2013. Sx HS 4 and Sx BB 3-49 v Northants (Hove) 2014. BB 5-62 CfU v Warwks (Birmingham) 2012. LO HS 2 and LO BB 1-39 v Notts (Nottingham) 2013 (Y40). T20 BB – .

HUDSON-PRENTICE, Fynn Jake (Warden Park S, Cuckfield; Bede's S, Upper Dicker), b Haywards Heath 12 Jan 1996. RHB, RMF. Squad No 14. Sussex 2nd XI debut 2012. Awaiting f-c debut. LO BB – .

JACKSON, Callum Frederick (St Bede's S, Upper Dicker), b Eastbourne 7 Sep 1994. 5'11". RHB, WK. Squad No 16. Debut (Sussex) 2013. Sussex 2nd XI debut 2011, aged 16y 225d. England U19s 2012-13. No 1st XI appearances in 2014. HS 26 v Australians (Hove) 2013. LO HS – . T20 HS 3.

‡^{NQ}**JAYAWARDENA**, Denagamage Proboth **Mahela** De Silva (Nalanda C, Colombo), b Colombo, Sri Lanka 27 May 1977. 5'9". RHB, RM. Sinhalese SC 1996-97 to date. IPL: KXIP 2007-10. DD 2012-13. Joins Sussex for T20 only. *Wisden* 2006. **Tests** (SL): 149 (1997 to 2014, 38 as captain); HS 374 v SA (Colombo) 2006; BB 2-32 v P (Galle) 2000-01. **LOI** (SL): 447 (1997-98 to 2014-15, 129 as captain); HS 144 v E (Leeds) 2011; BB 2-56 v K (Southampton) 1999. **IT20** (SL): 55 (2006 to 2013-14); HS 100 v Z (Providence) 2010. F-c Tours (SL) (C=captain): E 1998, 2002, 2006C, 2011, 2014; A 2004, 2007-08C, 2012-13; SA 1997-98, 2000-01, 2002-03, 2011-12; WI 2003, 2007-08C; NZ 2004-05, 2006-07C; I 1997-98, 2005-06, 2009-10; P 1998-99, 1999-2000, 2001-02, 2004-05, 2008-09C; Z 1999-00, 2004; B 1998-99, 2005-06C, 2008-09C, 2013-14; UAE 2011-12 (v P), 2013-14 (v P). 1000 runs (0+2); most 1426 (2001-02). HS 374 (*see Tests*). BB 5-72 Sinhalese v Colts (Colombo) 1996-97. LO HS 163* Sinhalese v Bloomfield (Colombo) 2010-11. LO BB 3-25 Sinhalese v Sebastianites (Colombo) 1998-99. T20 HS 110*. T20 BB 2-22.

JORDAN, Christopher James (Comber Mere S, Barbados; Dulwich C), b Christ Church, Barbados 4 Oct 1988. 6'0". RHB, RFM. Squad No 8. Surrey 2007-12. Missed entire 2010 season with back injury. Barbados 2011-12 to 2012-13. Sussex debut 2013; cap 2014. **ECB central contract 2014-15. Tests**: 5 (2014); HS 35 v SL (Lord's) 2014; BB 4-18 v I (Oval) 2014. **LOI**: 22 (2013 to 2014-15); HS 38* v SL (Oval) 2014; BB 5-29 v SL (Manchester) 2014. **IT20**: 7 (2013-14 to 2014); HS 27* and BB 3-39 v WI (Bridgetown) 2013-14. HS 92 v Derbys (Derby) 2013. 50 wkts (1): 61 (2013). Barbados BB 7-43 Barbados v CC&C (Bridgetown) 2012-13. Sx BB 6-48 v Yorks (Leeds) 2013. LO HS 38* (*see LOI*). LO BB 5-29 (*see LOI*). T20 HS 37. T20 BB 3-39.

^{NQ}**JOYCE, Edmund** Christopher (Presentation C, Bray, Co Wicklow; Trinity C, Dublin), b Dublin, Ireland 22 Sep 1978. Brother of four Ireland cricketers: Augustine (2000), Dominick (2004-06), Cecilia (2001-07) and Isobel, her twin (1999-2007). 5'11". LHB, RM. Squad No 24. Ireland 1997-98. Middlesex 1999-2008; cap 2002. Sussex debut/cap 2009; captain 2013 to date. Qualified for England 2005. MCC 2006, 2008. **LOI** (E/Ire): 50 (17 for E 2006 to 2006-07; 33 for Ire 2010-11 to 2014-15); HS 116* Ire v P (Dublin) 2013. **IT20** (E/Ire): 18 (12 for E 2006 to 2006-07; 16 for Ire 2011-12 to 2013-14); HS 78* Ire v Scotland (Dubai, DSC) 2011-12. F-c Tour (Eng A): WI 2005-06. 1000 runs (8); most – 1668 (2005). HS 211 M v Warwks (Birmingham) 2006. Sx HS 204* v Notts (Nottingham) 2013. BB M 2-34 v Cambridge U (Cambridge) 2004. CC BB 1-4 M v Glamorgan (Cardiff) 2005. Sx BB 1-9 v Hants (Southampton) 2009. LO HS 146 v Glos (Hove) 2009 (FPT). LO BB 2-10 M v Notts (Nottingham) 2003 (NL). T20 HS 78*.

LIDDLE, Christopher John (Nunthorpe CS), b Middlesbrough, Yorks 1 Feb 1984. 6'5". RHB, LFM. Squad No 11. Leicestershire 2005-06. Sussex debut 2007. Missed entire 2009 season with a stress fracture of the right ankle. HS 53 v Worcs (Hove) 2007. BB 3-42 Le v Somerset (Leicester) 2006. Sx BB 2-24 v Middx (Lord's) 2013. LO HS 15 v Derbys (Derby) 2012 (CB40). LO BB 5-18 v Netherlands (Amstelveen) 2011 (CB40). T20 HS 16. T20 BB 5-17.

MACHAN, Matthew William (Brighton C), b Brighton 15 Feb 1991. 5'8". LHB, RM/OB. Squad No 15. Debut (Sussex) 2010. Sussex 2nd XI debut 2006, aged 15y 153d. Scotland 2012-13 to date. **LOI** (Scot): 22 (2012-13 to 2014-15); HS 114 and BB 3-31 v Kenya (Aberdeen) 2013. **IT20** (Scot): 6 (2012-13 to 2013-14); HS 67* v Netherlands (Dubai) 2013-14; BB 3-23 v Afghanistan (Sharjah) 2012-13. HS 119 v Loughborough MCCU (Hove) 2014. CC HS 103 v Somerset (Taunton) 2013. BB 1-36 Sc v Australia A (Edinburgh) 2013. LO HS 126* v Unicorns (Hove) 2012 (CB40). BB 3-31 (*see LOI*). T20 HS 90*. T20 BB 3-23.

NQ**MAGOFFIN, Stephen** James (Indooroopilly HS; Curtin U, Perth), b Corinda, Queensland, Australia 17 Dec 1979. 6'3". LHB, RFM. Squad No 64. W Australia 2004-05 to 2010-11. Surrey 2007 (one f-c match). Worcestershire 2008. Queensland 2011-12. Sussex debut 2012; cap 2013. HS 79 WA v Tas (Perth) 2008-09. UK HS 51 v Northants (Northampton) 2014. 50 wkts (3); most – 72 (2014). BB 8-20 (12-31 match) v Somerset (Horsham) 2013. LO HS 24* Wo v Hants (Southampton) 2008 (FPT). LO BB 4-58 Sy v Kent (Oval) 2007 (FPT). T20 HS 11*. T20 BB 2-15.

‡**MILLS, Tymal** Solomon (Mildenhall TC), b Dewsbury, Yorks 12 Aug 1992. 6'1". RHB, LF. Essex 2011-14. Essex 2nd XI debut 2010. England U19s 2010-11. F-c Tour (EL): SL 2013-14. HS 31* EL v Sri Lanka A (Colombo, RPS) 2013-14. CC HS 30 Ex v Kent (Canterbury) 2014. BB 4-25 Ex v Glamorgan (Cardiff) 2012. LO HS 2* Ex v Australians (Chelmsford) 2012. LO BB 3-23 Ex v Durham (Chelmsford) 2013 (Y40). T20 HS 8*. T20 BB 3-42.

NASH, Christopher David (Collyer's SFC; Loughborough U), b Cuckfield 19 May 1983. 5'11". RHB, OB. Squad No 23. Debut (Sussex) 2002 – no f-c appearances 2003-04; cap 2008. Loughborough UCCE 2003-04. British U 2004. 1000 runs (3); most – 1321 (2009). HS 184 v Leics (Leicester) 2010. BB 4-12 v Glamorgan (Cardiff) 2010. LO HS 124* v Kent (Canterbury) 2011 (CB40). LO BB 4-40 v Yorks (Hove) 2009 (FPT). T20 HS 80*. T20 BB 4-7.

PIOLET, Steffan Andrew (Warden Park S; Central Sussex C), b Redhill, Surrey 8 Aug 1988. 6'1". RHB, RM. Squad No 21. Warwickshire 2009-13. Sussex debut 2014. HS 103* v Loughborough MCCU (Hove) 2014 – on Sx debut. CC HS 32 v Yorks (Scarborough) 2014. BB 6-17 (10-43 match) Wa v Durham UCCE (Durham) 2009 – on debut. Sx BB 2-61 v Somerset (Taunton) 2014. LO HS 63* v Notts (Horsham) 2014 (RLC). LO BB 4-31 Wa v Derbys (Derby) 2012 (CB40). T20 HS 26*. T20 BB 3-14.

PRIOR, Matthew James (Brighton C), b Johannesburg, South Africa 26 Feb 1982. 5'11". RHB, WK. Squad No 13. Debut (Sussex) 2001; cap 2003; benefit 2012. MCC 2005. *Wisden* 2009. **Tests**: 79 (2007 to 2014); HS 131* v WI (Port of Spain) 2008-09 (scored 126* v WI on debut – first instance by England wicket keeper). **LOI**: 68 (2004-05 to 2010-11); HS 87 v WI (Birmingham) 2009. **IT20**: 10 (2007 to 2009-10); HS 32 v SA (Cape Town) 2007-08. F-c Tours: A 2010-11, 2013-14; SA 2009-10; WI 2008-09; NZ 2012-13; I 2003-04 (Eng A), 2008-09, 2012-13; SL 2004-05 (Eng A), 2007-08, 2011-12; B 2006-07 (Eng A), 2009-10; UAE 2011-12 (v P). 1000 runs (3); most – 1158 (2004). HS 201* v Loughborough U (Hove) 2004. CC HS 153* v Essex (Colchester) 2003. LO HS 144 v Warwks (Hove) 2005 (NL). T20 HS 117.

‡**SHAHZAD, Ajmal** (Woodhouse Grove S; Bradford U), b Huddersfield, Yorkshire 27 Jul 1985. 6'0". RHB, RFM. Yorkshire 2006-12 (first British-born Asian to play for Yorkshire); cap 2010. Lancashire 2012 (on loan). Nottinghamshire 2013-14. **Tests**: 1 (2010); HS 5 and BB 3-45 v B (Manchester) 2010. **LOI**: 11 (2009-10 to 2010-11); HS 9 v A (Brisbane) 2010-11; BB 3-41 v B (Bristol) 2010. **IT20**: 3 (2009-10 to 2010-11); HS 0*; BB 2-38 v P (Dubai) 2009-10. F-c Tours: A 2010-11; B 2009-10. HS 88 Y v Sussex (Hove) 2009. BB 5-51 Y v Durham (Chester-le-St) 2010. LO HS 59* Y v Kent (Leeds) 2011 (CB40). LO BB 5-51 Y v Sri Lanka A (Leeds) 2007. T20 HS 20. T20 BB 3-30.

WELLS, Luke William Peter (St Bede's S, Upper Dicker), b Eastbourne 29 Dec 1990. Son of A.P.Wells (Border, Kent, Sussex and England 1981-2000); nephew of C.M.Wells (Border, Derbyshire, Sussex and WP 1979-96). 6'4". LHB, OB. Squad No 31. Debut (Sussex) 2010. Colombo CC 2011-12. Sussex 2nd XI debut 2008. England U19s 2009 to 2010. 1000 runs (1): 1016 (2014). HS 208 v Surrey (Oval) 2013. BB 3-38 v Yorks (Scarborough) 2014. LO HS 23 v Notts (Horsham) 2014 (RLC). BB 3-19 v Netherlands (Amstelveen) 2011 (CB40). T20 HS 11.

WRIGHT, Luke James (Belvoir HS; Ratcliffe C; Loughborough U), b Grantham, Lincs 7 Mar 1985. Younger brother of A.S.Wright (Leicestershire 2001-02). 5'11". RHB, RMF. Squad No 10. Leicestershire 2003 (one f-c match). Sussex debut 2004; cap 2007; T20 captain 2015; benefit 2015. IPL: PW 2012-13. Big Bash: MS 2011-12 to date. **LOI**: 50 (2007 to 2013-14); HS 52 v NZ (Birmingham) 2008; BB 2-34 v NZ (Bristol) 2008 and 2-34 v A (Southampton) 2010. **IT20**: 51 (2007-08 to 2013-14); HS 99* v Afghanistan (Colombo, RPS) 2012-13; BB 2-24 v NZ (Hamilton) 2012-13. F-c Tour (EL): NZ 2008-09. HS 189 v Durham (Hove) 2014. BB 5-65 v Derbys (Derby) 2010. LO HS 143* EL v Bangladesh A (Bristol) 2013. LO BB 4-12 v Middx (Hove) 2004 (NL). T20 HS 153* v Essex (Chelmsford) 2014 – Sx record. T20 BB 3-17.

YARDY, Michael Howard (William Parker S, Hastings), b Pembury, Kent 27 Nov 1980. 6'0". LHB, LM/SLA. Squad No 20. Debut (Sussex) 2000; cap 2005; captain 2009-12; benefit 2014. **LOI**: 28 (2006 to 2010-11); HS 60* v A (Perth) 2010-11; BB 3-24 v P (Nottingham) 2006 – on debut. **IT20**: 14 (2006 to 2010-11); HS 35* v P (Cardiff) 2010; BB 2-19 v P (Bridgetown) 2009-10. F-c Tours (Eng A, C=Captain): WI 2005-06; I 2007-08C; B 2006-07C. 1000 runs (2); most – 1520 (2005). HS 257 (record Sx score v touring team) and BB 5-83 v Bangladeshis (Hove) 2005. CC HS 179 v Middx (Lord's) 2005. CC BB 3-15 v Yorks (Leeds) 2009. LO HS 98* v Surrey (Oval) 2006 (CGT). LO BB 6-27 v Warwks (Birmingham) 2005 (NL). T20 HS 76*. T20 BB 3-21.

RELEASED/RETIRED

(Having made a County 1st XI appearance in 2014)

HAMILTON-BROWN, Rory James (Millfield S), b St John's Wood, London 3 Sep 1987. 6'0". RHB, OB. Surrey 2005, 2010-12; captain 2010-12 (part); cap 2011. No f-c appearances 2006-07. Sussex 2008-14. 1000 runs (1): 1039 (2011). HS 171* v Yorks (Leeds) 2007. BB 2-5 v Somerset (Taunton) 2014. LO HS 115 Sy v Glamorgan (Oval) 2010 (CB40). LO BB 3-28 Sy v Leics (Leicester) 2007 (P40). T20 HS 87*. T20 BB 4-15.

LEWIS, Jonathan (Churchfields S, Swindon; Swindon C), b Aylesbury, Bucks 26 Aug 1975. 6'2". RHB, RMF. Gloucestershire 1995-2011; cap 1998; captain 2006-08; benefit 2007. Surrey 2012-13. Sussex 2014. MCC 2005, 2010. Wiltshire 1993, 1995. **Tests**: 1 (2006); HS 20 and BB 3-68 v SL (Nottingham) 2006. **LOI**: 13 (2005 to 2007); HS 17 v I (Leeds) 2007; BB 4-36 v A (Brisbane) 2006-07. **IT20**: 2 (2005 to 2006-07); HS 1 v A (Sydney) 2006-07; BB 4-24 v A (Southampton) 2005. F-c Tours (Eng A): WI 2000-01; SL 2004-05. HS 71 Gs v Middx (Uxbridge) 2011. Sx HS 61 v Yorks (Arundel) 2014. 50 wkts (9); most – 74 (2003). BB 8-95 Gs v Z (Gloucester) 2000. CC BB 7-38 (10-75 match) Gs v Somerset (Bristol) 2006. Sx BB 4-34 v Middx (Hove) 2014. Hat-trick Gs v Notts (Nottingham) 2000. LO HS 54 Gs v Durham (Cheltenham) 2009 (P40). LO BB 5-19 Gs v Hants (Southampton) 2005 (NL). T20 HS 43. T20 BB 4-24.

YASIR ARAFAT – see HAMPSHIRE.

SUSSEX 2014

RESULTS SUMMARY

	Place	Won	Lost	Aband	Drew	NR
LV= County Championship (1st Division)	3rd	6	4	1	5	
All First-Class Matches		6	4	1	6	
Royal London One-Day Cup (Group B)	8th	3	5			
NatWest t20 Blast (South Division)	7th	6	8			

LV= COUNTY CHAMPIONSHIP AVERAGES

BATTING AND FIELDING

Cap		M	I	NO	HS	Runs	Avge	100	50	Ct/St
2009	E.C.Joyce	14	23	2	164*	1398	66.57	7	3	11
2007	L.J.Wright	12	21	3	189	933	51.83	3	3	2
	Craig Cachopa	5	10	1	84	441	49.00	–	5	2
2008	C.D.Nash	12	22	–	178	867	39.40	1	6	6
	L.W.P.Wells	15	27	1	162	942	36.23	1	7	11
	J.C.Tredwell	5	8	1	50*	218	31.14	–	1	7
2005	M.H.Yardy	8	13	–	139	361	27.76	1	1	11
2014	B.C.Brown	15	23	2	163	579	27.57	1	–	49/4
	M.W.Machan	7	12	3	44*	218	24.22	–	–	3
	Ashar Zaidi	9	11	–	88	266	24.18	–	2	3
2013	S.J.Magoffin	15	21	10	51	245	22.27	–	1	–
	R.J.Hamilton-Brown	7	14	1	62	265	20.38	–	2	4
	J.Lewis	8	10	1	61	174	19.33	–	1	4
	S.A.Piolet	6	10	–	32	180	18.00	–	–	4
2011	J.E.Anyon	7	9	–	50	155	17.22	–	1	1
2014	C.J.Jordan	5	8	1	41	109	15.57	–	–	10
	L.J.Hatchett	8	11	5	20*	62	10.33	–	–	6
	M.E.Hobden	3	4	1	4	4	1.33	–	–	–

Also played: W.A.T.Beer (1 match) 8, 29; C.J.Liddle (1) 0, 0*; M.J.Prior (2 – cap 2003) 125, 30, 19* (5 ct).

BOWLING

	O	M	R	W	Avge	Best	5wI	10wM
S.J.Magoffin	539	144	1405	72	19.51	6- 60	4	–
C.J.Jordan	196	32	668	25	26.72	5- 76	1	–
M.E.Hobden	68	4	342	12	28.50	3- 49	–	–
Ashar Zaidi	189.2	24	579	19	30.47	3- 36	–	–
J.Lewis	204.5	58	546	17	32.11	4- 34	–	–
J.C.Tredwell	170	35	518	12	43.16	4- 7	–	–
J.E.Anyon	159.2	23	706	16	44.12	3- 67	–	–
L.J.Hatchett	246.5	32	974	22	44.27	5-113	1	–

Also bowled:
L.W.P.Wells	60.4	6	227	6	37.83	3- 38	–	–
S.A.Piolet	78.1	9	289	5	57.80	2- 61	–	–

W.A.T.Beer 13-1-76-0; B.C.Brown 4-1-14-0; R.J.Hamilton-Brown 6.5-0-30-2; C.J.Liddle 23-3-70-0; C.D.Nash 85.3-12-309-4; L.J.Wright 51-6-170-3.

The First-Class Averages (pp 217–233) give the records of Sussex players in all first-class county matches (Sussex's other opponents being Loughborough MCCU), with the exception of C.J.Jordan and J.C.Tredwell, whose first-class figures for Sussex are as above, and: M.J.Prior 3-5-1-125-217-54.25-1-0-5ct.

SUSSEX RECORDS

FIRST-CLASS CRICKET

Highest Total	For 742-5d		v	Somerset	Taunton	2009
	V 726		by	Notts	Nottingham	1895
Lowest Total	For 19		v	Surrey	Godalming	1830
	19		v	Notts	Hove	1873
	V 18		by	Kent	Gravesend	1867
Highest Innings	For 344*	M.W.Goodwin	v	Somerset	Taunton	2009
	V 322	E.Paynter	for	Lancashire	Hove	1937

Highest Partnership for each Wicket

1st	490	E.H.Bowley/J.G.Langridge	v	Middlesex	Hove	1933
2nd	385	E.H.Bowley/M.W.Tate	v	Northants	Hove	1921
3rd	385*	M.H.Yardy/M.W.Goodwin	v	Warwicks	Hove	2006
4th	363	M.W.Goodwin/C.D.Hopkinson	v	Somerset	Taunton	2009
5th	297	J.H.Parks/H.W.Parks	v	Hampshire	Portsmouth	1937
6th	335	L.J.Wright/B.C.Brown	v	Durham	Hove	2014
7th	344	K.S.Ranjitsinhji/W.Newham	v	Essex	Leyton	1902
8th	291	R.S.C.Martin-Jenkins/M.J.G.Davis	v	Somerset	Taunton	2002
9th	178	H.W.Parks/A.F.Wensley	v	Derbyshire	Horsham	1930
10th	156	G.R.Cox/H.R.Butt	v	Cambridge U	Cambridge	1908

Best Bowling	For 10- 48	C.H.G.Bland	v	Kent	Tonbridge	1899
(Innings)	V 9- 11	A.P.Freeman	for	Kent	Hove	1922
Best Bowling	For 17-106	G.R.Cox	v	Warwicks	Horsham	1926
(Match)	V 17- 67	A.P.Freeman	for	Kent	Hove	1922

Most Runs – Season	2850	J.G.Langridge	(av 64.77)	1949
Most Runs – Career	34150	J.G.Langridge	(av 37.69)	1928-55
Most 100s – Season	12	J.G.Langridge		1949
Most 100s – Career	76	J.G.Langridge		1928-55
Most Wkts – Season	198	M.W.Tate	(av 13.47)	1925
Most Wkts – Career	2211	M.W.Tate	(av 17.41)	1912-37
Most Career W-K Dismissals	1176	H R Butt	(911 ct; 265 st)	1890-1912
Most Career Catches in the Field	779	J.G.Langridge		1928-55

LIMITED-OVERS CRICKET

Highest Total	50ov	384-9		v	Ireland	Belfast	1996
	40ov	399-4		v	Worcs	Horsham	2011
	T20	239-5		v	Glamorgan	Hove	2010
Lowest Total	50ov	49		v	Derbyshire	Chesterfield	1969
	40ov	59		v	Glamorgan	Hove	1996
	T20	67		v	Hampshire	Hove	2004
Highest Innings	50ov	158*	M.W.Goodwin	v	Essex	Chelmsford	2006
	40ov	163	C.J.Adams	v	Middlesex	Arundel	1999
	T20	153*	L.J.Wright	v	Essex	Chelmsford	2014
Best Bowling	50ov	6- 9	A.I.C.Dodemaide	v	Ireland	Downpatrick	1990
	40ov	7-41	A.N.Jones	v	Notts	Nottingham	1986
	T20	5-11	Mushtaq Ahmed	v	Essex	Hove	2005

WARWICKSHIRE

Formation of Present Club: 8 April 1882
Substantial Reorganisation: 19 January 1884
Inaugural First-Class Match: 1894
Colours: Dark Blue, Gold and Silver
Badge: Bear and Ragged Staff
County Champions: (7) 1911, 1951, 1972, 1994, 1995, 2004, 2012
Gillette/NatWest Trophy Winners: (5) 1966, 1968, 1989, 1993, 1995
Benson and Hedges Cup Winners: (2) 1994, 2002
Sunday League Winners: (3) 1980, 1994, 1997
Clydesdale Bank 40 Winners: (1) 2010
Twenty20 Cup Winners: (1) 2014

Chief Executive: Colin Povey, County Ground, Edgbaston, Birmingham, B5 7QU • Tel: 0844 635 1902 • Fax: 0121 446 4544 • Email: info@edgbaston.com • Web: www.edgbaston.com • Twitter: @CricketingBears (19,292 followers)

Director of Cricket: Dougie Brown. **Batting Coach**: Tony Frost. **Bowling Coach**: Alan Richardson. **Fielding Coach**: Jim Troughton. **Captain**: V.Chopra. **Vice-Captain**: tba. **Overseas Player**: J.S.Patel. **2015 Beneficiary**: I.J.Westwood. **Head Groundsman**: Gary Barwell. **Scorer**: Mel Smith. New registration. ^{NQ} Not qualified for England.

ADAIR, Mark Richard (Sullivan Upper S, Hollywood), b Belfast, N Ireland 27 Mar 1996. RHB, RMF. Squad No 27. Warwickshire 2nd XI debut 2013. Awaiting 1st XI debut.

AMBROSE, Timothy Raymond (Merewether HS, NSW; TAFE C), b Newcastle, NSW, Australia 1 Dec 1982. ECB qualified – British/EU passport. 5'7". RHB, WK. Squad No 11. Sussex 2001-05; cap 2003. Warwickshire debut 2006; cap 2007. **Tests**: 11 (2007-08 to 2008-09); HS 102 v NZ (Wellington) 2007-08. **LOI**: 5 (2008); HS 6 v NZ (Oval) 2008. **IT20**: 1 (2008); HS – . F-c Tours: WI 2008-09; NZ 2007-08. HS 251* v Worcs (Worcester) 2007. LO HS 135 v Durham (Birmingham) 2007 (FPT). T20 HS 77.

BARKER, Keith Hubert Douglas (Moorhead HS; Fulwood C, Preston), b Manchester 21 Oct 1986. Son of K.H.Barker (British Guiana 1960-61 to 1963-64). Played football for Blackburn Rovers and Rochdale. 6'3". LHB, LM. Squad No 13. Debut (Warwickshire) 2009; cap 2013. HS 125 v Surrey (Guildford) 2013. 50 wkts (2); most – 56 (2012). BB 6-40 v Somerset (Taunton) 2012. LO HS 56 v Scotland (Birmingham) 2011 (CB40). LO BB 4-33 v Scotland (Birmingham) 2010 (CB40). T20 HS 46. T20 BB 4-19.

BELL, Ian Ronald (Princethorpe C), b Walsgrave-on-Sowe 11 Apr 1982. 5'9". RHB, RM. Squad No 4. Debut (Warwickshire) 1999; cap 2001; benefit 2011. MCC 2004. YC 2004. MBE 2005. *Wisden* 2007. **ECB central contract 2014-15**. **Tests**: 105 (2004 to 2014); HS 235 v I (Oval) 2011; BB 1-33 v P (Faisalabad) 2005-06. **LOI**: 161 (2004-05 to 2014-15); HS 141 v A (Hobart) 2014-15; BB 3-9 v Z (Bulawayo) 2004-05 – taking a wicket with his third ball in LOI. **IT20**: 8 (2006 to 2014); HS 60* v NZ (Manchester) 2008. F-c Tours: A 2006-07, 2010-11, 2013-14; SA 2009-10; WI 2000-01 (Eng A – *part*), 2008-09; NZ 2007-08, 2012-13; I 2005-06, 2008-09, 2012-13; P 2005-06; SL 2002-03 (ECB Acad), 2004-05, 2007-08, 2011-12; B 2009-10; UAE 2011-12 (v P). 1000 runs (4); most – 1714 (2004). HS 262* v Sussex (Horsham) 2004. BB 4-4 v Middx (Lord's) 2004. LO HS 158 EL v India A (Worcester) 2010. LO BB 5-41 v Essex (Chelmsford) 2003 (NL). T20 HS 85. T20 BB 1-12.

BEST, Paul Merwood (Bablake S, Coventry; Homerton C, Cambridge), b Nuneaton 8 Mar 1991. LHB, SLA. Squad No 15. Cambridge MCCU 2011-12 (blue 2011-12). Warwickshire debut 2011. Northamptonshire 2011. Warwickshire 2nd XI debut 2009. England U19s 2009-10 to 2010. HS 150 CU v Surrey (Cambridge) 2011. Wa HS 50* Oxford MCCU (Oxford) 2014. CC HS 31* Nh v Glamorgan (Swansea) 2011. BB 6-86 (9-131 match) CU v Oxford U (Cambridge) 2011. CC BB 2-69 v Durham (Chester-le-St) 2011. LO HS 16* and LO BB 3-43 v Yorks (Birmingham) 2012 (CB40). T20 HS – . T20 BB 3-19.

CHOPRA, Varun (Ilford County HS), b Barking, Essex 21 Jun 1987. 6'1''. RHB, LB. Squad No 3. Essex 2006-09, scoring 106 v Glos (Chelmsford) on CC debut. Warwickshire debut 2010; cap 2012; captain 2015. Tamil Union 2011-12. England U19s 2005 to 2006. F-c Tour (EL): SL 2013-14. 1000 runs (3); most – 1203 (2011). HS 233* TU v Sinhalese (Colombo, PSS) 2011-12. Wa HS 228 v Worcs (Worcester) 2011 (in 2nd CC game of season, having scored 210 v Somerset in 1st). BB – . LO HS 115 v Leics (Birmingham) 2011 (CB40). T20 HS 86*.

CLARKE, Rikki (Broadwater SS; Godalming C), b Orsett, Essex 29 Sep 1981. 6'4''. RHB, RFM. Squad No 81. Surrey 2002-07, scoring 107* v Cambridge U (Cambridge) on debut; cap 2005. Derbyshire cap/captain 2008. Warwickshire debut 2008; cap 2011. MCC 2006. YC 2002. **Tests**: 2 (2003-04); HS 55 and BB 2-7 v B (Chittagong) 2003-04. **LOI**: 20 (2003 to 2006); HS 39 v P (Lord's) 2006; BB 2-28 v B (Dhaka) 2003-04. F-c Tours: WI 2003-04, 2005-06; SL 2002-03 (ECB Acad), 2004-05; B 2003-04. 1000 runs (1): 1027 (2006). HS 214 Sy v Somerset (Guildford) 2006. Wa HS 140 v Lancs (Liverpool) 2012. BB 6-63 v Kent (Canterbury) 2010. Took seven catches in an innings v Lancs (Liverpool) 2011 to equal world record. LO HS 98* Sy v Derbys (Derby) 2002 (NL). LO BB 4-28 v Northants (Birmingham) 2011 (CB40). T20 HS 79*. T20 BB 3-11.

COLEMAN, Frederick Robert John (Strathallan S; Oxford Brookes U), b Edinburgh, Scotland 15 Dec 1991. RHB, WK, occ OB. Squad No 21. Scotland 2011-12 to date. Oxford MCCU 2012-13. Awaiting Warwickshire f-c debut. Warwickshire 2nd XI debut 2010. **LOI** (Scot): 16 (2013 to 2014-15); HS 70 v SL (Hobart) 2014-15. **IT20** (Scot): 1 (2013); HS 9 v Kenya (Aberdeen) 2013. HS 110 OU v Worcs (Oxford) 2012 – on UK debut. LO HS 70 (see *LOI*). T20 HS 20*.

EVANS, Laurie John (Whitgift S; The John Fisher S; St Mary's C, Durham U), b Lambeth, London 12 Oct 1987. 6'0''. RHB, RMF. Squad No 32. Durham UCCE 2007. MCC 2007. Surrey 2009-10. Warwickshire debut 2010. HS 178 v Notts (Birmingham) 2013. BB 1-30 Sy v Bangladeshis (Oval) 2010. LO HS 50 v Somerset (Birmingham) 2014 (RLC). LO BB 1-29. T20 HS 69*. T20 BB 1-5.

GORDON, Recordo Olton (Aston Manor S; Hamstead Hall SFC), b St Elizabeth, Jamaica 12 Oct 1991. RHB, RFM. Squad No 44. Debut (Warwickshire) 2013. Warwickshire 2nd XI debut 2011. HS 14* and BB 4-53 v Somerset (Taunton) 2014. LO HS 1 v Northants (Birmingham) 2013 (Y40). LO BB 3-25 v Surrey (Birmingham) 2014 (RLC). T20 HS – . T20 BB 3-18.

HAIN, Samuel Robert (Southport S, Gold Coast), b Hong Kong 16 July 1995. UK passport (British parents). RHB, OB. Squad No 16. Debut (Warwickshire) 2014. Warwickshire 2nd XI debut 2011. HS 208 v Northants (Birmingham) 2014. LO HS 1 v Worcs (Worcester) 2013 (Y40).

HANNON-DALBY, Oliver James (Brooksbank S, Leeds Met U), b Halifax, Yorkshire 20 Jun 1989. 6'7''. LHB, RMF. Squad No 20. Yorkshire 2008-12. No 1st XI appearances in 2009. Warwickshire debut 2013. HS 40 v Somerset (Taunton) 2014. BB 5-68 Y v Warwks (Birmingham) and 5-68 Y v Somerset (Leeds) 2010 – in consecutive matches. Wa BB 4-50 v Oxford MCCU (Oxford) 2013. LO HS 21* Y v Warwks (Scarborough) 2012 (CB40). LO BB 4-44 v Essex (Chelmsford) 2014 (RLC). T20 HS 2*. T20 BB 3-31.

JAVID, Ateeq (Aston Manor S), b Birmingham 15 Oct 1991. RHB, RM. Squad No 17. Debut (Warwickshire) 2009. Warwickshire 2nd XI debut 2008. England U19s 2010 to 2010-11. HS 133 v Somerset (Birmingham) 2013. BB 1-1 v Lancs (Manchester) 2014. LO HS 43 v Kent (Canterbury) 2013 (Y40). LO BB 3-48 v Glamorgan (Swansea) 2014 (RLC). T20 HS 41. T20 BB 4-17.

JONES, Richard Alan (Grange HS and King Edward VI C, Stourbridge; Loughborough U), b Wordsley, Stourbridge, Worcs 6 Nov 1986. 6'2". RHB, RMF. Squad No 25. Worcestershire 2007-13; cap 2007. Matabeleland Tuskers 2011-12. Warwickshire debut 2014. Leicestershire 2014 (on loan). HS 62 MT v SR (Bulawayo) 2011-12. UK HS 53* Wo v Durham (Worcester) 2009. Wa HS 35 and Wa BB 4-81 v Somerset (Taunton) 2014. BB 7-115 Wo v Sussex (Hove) 2010. LO HS 11* Wo v Sussex (Worcester) 2010 (CB40). LO BB 1-25 MT v ME (Bulawayo) 2011-12. T20 HS 9. T20 BB 5-34.

LEWIS, Thomas Peter (Princethorpe C, Rugby; Castle SFC, Kenilworth), b Coventry 7 Mar 1991. Younger brother of M.F.Lewis (Oxford UCCE 2009). LHB, RM. Squad No 7. Warwickshire 2nd XI debut 2008. MCC YC 2010-12. Awaiting 1st XI debut.

McKAY, Peter John (Polesworth Int Language C, Tamworth), b Staffs 12 Oct 1994. LHB, WK. Squad No 18. Debut (Warwickshire) 2013. Warwickshire 2nd XI debut 2012. HS 33 v Notts (Nottingham) 2013. LO HS 22* v Essex (Chelmsford) 2014 (RLC). T20 HS 2*.

MILNES, Thomas Patrick (Heart of England S, Coventry), b Stourbridge, Worcs 6 Oct 1992. RHB, RMF. Squad No 8. Debut (Warwickshire) 2011. Warwickshire 2nd XI debut 2009. England U19s 2010-11. No 1st XI appearances in 2014. HS 52* and BB 7-39 v Oxford MCCU (Oxford) 2013. CC HS 48 v Sussex (Birmingham) 2013. CC BB 2-64 v Somerset (Birmingham) 2013. LO HS 16 v Worcs (Birmingham) 2013 (Y40). LO BB 2-73 v Northants (Birmingham) 2013 (Y40).

NQ**PATEL, Jeetan** Shashi, b Wellington, New Zealand 7 May 1980. RHB, OB. Squad No 5. Wellington 1999-00 to date. Warwickshire debut 2009; cap 2012. **Tests** (NZ): 19 (2006-07 to 2012-13); HS 27* v SA (Cape Town) 2006-07; BB 5-110 v WI (Napier) 2008-09. **LOI** (NZ): 39 (2005 to 2009-10); HS 34 v SL (Kingston) 2006-07; BB 3-11 v SA (Mumbai, BS) 2006-07. **IT20** (NZ): 11 (2005-06 to 2008-09); HS 5 v E (Auckland) 2007-08; BB 3-20 v SA (Johannesburg) 2005-06. F-c Tours (NZ): E 2008; SA 2005-06, 2012-13; I 2010-11, 2012; SL 2009, 2012-13; Z 2010-11, 2011-12; B 2008-09. HS 120 v Yorks (Birmingham) 2009. 50 wkts (3); most – 59 (2014). BB 7-75 v Somerset (Taunton) 2012. LO HS 50 v Kent (Birmingham) 2013 (Y40). LO BB 4-16 NZ A v Aus A (Hyderabad) 2008-09. T20 HS 34*. T20 BB 4-11.

NQ**PORTERFIELD, William** Thomas Stuart (Strabane GS; Leeds Met U), b Londonderry, N.Ireland 6 Sep 1984. 5'11". LHB, OB. Squad No 10. Ireland 2006-07 to 2008-09. Gloucestershire 2008-10; cap 2008. Warwickshire debut 2011; cap 2011. MCC 2007. **LOI** (Ire): 78 (2006 to 2014-15, 55 as captain); HS 112* v Bermuda (Nairobi) 2006-07. **IT20** (Ire): 37 (2008 to 2013-14, 37 as captain); HS 56* v Kenya (Dubai, DSC) 2011-12. F-c Tours (Ire, C=Captain): WI 2009-10C; UAE 2013-14. HS 175 Gs v Worcs (Cheltenham) 2010. Wa HS 118 v Somerset (Birmingham) 2014. BB 1-29 Ire v Jamaica (Spanish Town) 2009-10. UK BB 1-57 Gs v Loughborough UCCE (Bristol) 2008. LO HS 112* (*see LOI*). T20 HS 127*.

POYSDEN, Joshua Edward (Cardinal Newman S, Hove; Anglia RU), b Shoreham-by-Sea, Sussex 8 Aug 1991. LHB, LB. Squad No 14. Cambridge MCCU 2011-13. Awaiting Warwickshire f-c debut. Hampshire 2nd XI 2010. Sussex 2nd XI 2011-13. Northants 2nd XI 2013. Unicorns (l-o) 2013. HS 47 and BB 3-20 CU v Surrey (Cambridge) 2011. LO HS 10* Unicorns v Glos (Wormsley) 2013 (Y40). LO BB 3-33 Unicorns v Middx (Lord's) 2013 (Y40). T20 BB – .

RANKIN, William Boyd (Strabane GS; Harper Adams UC), b Londonderry, Co Derry, N Ireland 5 Jul 1984. Brother of R.J.Rankin (Ireland U19 2003-04). 6'8". LHB, RFM. Squad No 30. Ireland 2006-07 to 2008. Derbyshire 2007. Warwickshire debut 2008; cap 2013. Middlesex summer contract 2004-05. Became available for England in 2012. **Tests**: 1 (2013-14); HS 13 and BB 1-47 v A (Sydney) 2013-14. **LOI** (E/Ire): 44 (37 for Ire 2006-07 to 2011-12, 7 for E 2013 to 2013-14); HS 7* Ire v SL (St George's) 2006-07; BB 4-46 E v Ire (Dublin) 2013. **IT20** (E/Ire): 17 (15 for Ire 2009 to 2012-13, 2 for E 2013); HS 7* Ire v Kenya (Mombasa) 2011-12; BB 3-20 Ire v Kenya (Dubai, DSC) 2011-12. F-c Tour: A 2013-14. HS 43 ICC Combined XI v England XI (Dubai) 2011-12. Wa HS 28 v Durham (Chester-le-St) 2011. 50 wkts (1): 55 (2011). BB 5-16 v Essex (Birmingham) 2010. LO HS 18* v Northants (Northampton) 2013 (Y40). LO BB 4-34 v Kent (Birmingham) 2010 (CB40). T20 HS 7*. T20 BB 4-9.

THOMASON, Aaron Dean (Barr Beacon S, Walsall), b Birmingham 26 Jun 1997. RHB, RMF. Squad No 26. Warwickshire 2nd XI debut 2014. Awaiting f-c debut. LO HS 0* and LO BB – v Middx (Lord's) 2014 (RLC) – only 1st XI appearance.

TROTT, Ian Jonathan Leonard (Rondebosch BHC; Stellenbosch U), b Cape Town, South Africa 22 Apr 1981. Stepbrother of K.C.Jackson (WP and Boland 1988-89 to 2001-02). 6'0". RHB, RM. Squad No 9. Boland 2000-01. W Province 2001-02. EU/British passport. Warwickshire debut 2003, scoring 134 v Sussex (Birmingham); cap 2005; benefit 2014. Otago 2005-06. *Wisden* 2010. **Tests**: 49 (2009 to 2013-14); HS 226 v B (Lord's) 2010; scored 119 v A (Oval) 2009 on debut. BB 1-5 v SL (Lord's) 2011. **LOI**: 68 (2009 to 2013); HS 137 v A (Sydney) 2010-11; BB 2-31 v A (Adelaide) 2010-11. **IT20**: 7 (2007 to 2009-10); HS 51 v SA (Centurion) 2009-10. F-c Tours: A 2010-11, 2013-14 (*part*); SA 2009-10, 2014-15 (EL); NZ 2008-09 (EL), 2012-13; I 2007-08 (EL), 2012-13; SL 2011-12; B 2009-10; UAE 2011-12 (v P). 1000 runs (6); most – 1400 (2009). HS 226 (*see Tests*). CC HS 210 v Sussex (Birmingham) 2005. BB 7-39 v Kent (Canterbury) 2003. LO HS 137 (*see LOI*). LO BB 4-55 v Hants (Lord's) 2005 (CGT). T20 HS 86*. T20 BB 2-19.

UMEED, Andrew Robert Isaac (High School of Glasgow), b Glasgow 19 Apr 1996. 6'1". RHB, LB. Squad No 23. Warwickshire 2nd XI debut 2014. Awaiting 1st XI debut.

WEBB, Jonathon Patrick (Bromsgrove S; Leeds U), b Solihull 12 Jan 1992. RHB, RM. Squad No 12. Leeds/Bradford MCCU 2012-13. Warwickshire 2nd XI debut 2008, aged 16y 200d. Awaiting Warwickshire f-c debut. HS 38 LBU v Surrey (Oval) 2012. T20 HS 50.

WESTWOOD, Ian James (Wheelers Lane S; Solihull SFC), b Birmingham 13 Jul 1982. 5'7½". LHB, OB. Squad No 22. Debut (Warwickshire) 2003; cap 2008; captain 2009-10; benefit 2015. HS 178 v West Indies A (Birmingham) 2006. CC HS 176 v Glamorgan (Cardiff) 2008. BB 2-39 v Hants (Southampton) 2009. LO HS 65 v Northants (Northampton) 2008 (FPT). BB 1-28 Wa CB v Cambs (March) 2001 (CGT). T20 HS 49*. T20 BB 3-29.

WOAKES, Christopher Roger (Barr Beacon Language S, Walsall), b Birmingham 2 March 1989. 6'2". RHB, RFM. Squad No 19. Debut (Warwickshire) 2006; cap 2009. MCC 2009. Herefordshire 2006-07. **ECB central contract 2014-15**. **Tests**: 4 (2013 to 2104); HS 26* v I (Manchester) 2014; BB 3-30 v I (Oval) 2014-15. **LOI**: 34 (2010-11 to 2014-15); HS 42* v B (Adelaide) 2014-15; BB 6-45 v A (Brisbane) 2010-11. **IT20**: 6 (2010-11 to 2014); HS 19* v A (Adelaide) 2010-11; BB 1-29 v A (Melbourne) 2010-11. F-c Tours (EL): WI 2010-11, SL 2013-14. HS 152* v Derbys (Derby) 2013. 50 wkts (2); most – 58 (2010). BB 7-20 (10-123 match) v Hants (Birmingham) 2011. LO HS 49* v Leics (Birmingham) 2010 (CB40). LO BB 6-45 (*see LOI*). T20 HS 55*. T20 BB 4-21.

WRIGHT, Christopher Julian Clement (Eggars S, Alton; Anglia Ruskin U), b Chipping Norton, Oxon 14 Jul 1985. 6'3". RHB, RFM. Squad No 31. Cambridge UCCE 2004-05. Middlesex 2004-07. Tamil Union 2005-06. Essex 2008-11. Warwickshire debut 2011; cap 2013. HS 77 Ex v Cambridge MCCU (Cambridge) 2011. CC HS 71* Ex v Middx (Chelmsford) 2008. Wa HS 65 v Notts (Birmingham) 2014. 50 wkts (1): 67 (2012). BB 6-22 Ex v Leics (Leicester) 2008. Wa BB 6-31 v Durham (Birmingham) 2013. LO HS 42 Ex v Glos (Cheltenham) 2011 (CB40). LO BB 4-20 Ex v Unicorns (Chelmsford) 2011 (CB40). T20 HS 6*. T20 BB 4-24.

RELEASED/RETIRED

(Having made a County 1st XI appearance in 2014)

[NO]**SHOAIB MALIK** (Government Arabic SS, Sialkot), b Sialko, Pakistan 1 Feb 1982. 5'6". RHB, OB. Debut (Pakistan A) 1997. Gujranwala 1997-98 to 1998-99. PIA 1998-99 to date. Pakistan Reserves 1999-00. Sialkot 2001-02 to 2012-13. Gloucestershire 2003-04. Warwickshire 2014 (T20 only). IPL: DD 2007-08. Big Bash: HH 20131-4 to date. **Tests** (P): 32 (2001 to 2010); HS 148* v SL (Colombo, SSC) 2005-06; BB 4-42 v SA (Lahore) 2003-04. **LOI** (P): 216 (1999-00 to 2013); HS 143 v I (Colombo, RPS) 2004; BB 4-19 v Hong Kong (Colombo, SSC) 2004. **IT20** (P): 59 (2006 to 2013-14); HS 57* v I (Bangalore) 2012-13; BB 2-7 v B (Dhaka) 2011-12. F-c Tours (P): E 1997 (Pak A), 2006, 2010; A 2004-05, 2009-10; WI 2005; NZ 2009-10; I 2007-08; SL 2005-06, 2009. HS 200 PIA v Faisalabad (Faisalabad) 2010-11. UK HS 110* P v Leics (Leicester) 2006. CC HS 63 Gs v Northants (Bristol) 2004. BB 7-81 PIA v WAPDA (Faisalabad) 2000-01. CC BB 3-76 Gs v Worcs (Cheltenham) 2003. LO HS 143 (*see LOI*). LO BB 5-35 PIA v Lahore Blues (Karachi) 2002-03. T20 HS 88*. T20 BB 5-13.

TROUGHTON, Jamie Oliver ('**Jim**') (Trinity S, Leamington Spa; Birmingham U), b Camden, London 2 Mar 1979. Great-grandson of H.T.Crichton (Warwicks 1908). 5'11". LHB, SLA. Warwickshire 2001-14; cap 2002; captain 2011 to date; benefit 2013. **LOI**: 6 (2003); HS 20 v P (Lord's) 2003. F-c Tour (ECB Acad): SL 2002-03. 1000 runs (1): 1067 (2002). HS 223 v Hants (Birmingham) 2009. BB 3-1 v Cambridge U (Cambridge) 2004. CC BB 2-26 v Lancs (Birmingham) 2006. LO HS 115* and BB 4-23 Wa CB v Cumberland (Millom) 2001 (CGT). T20 HS 68*. T20 BB 2-10.

WARWICKSHIRE 2014

RESULTS SUMMARY

	Place	Won	Lost	Tied	Drew	NR
LV= County Championship (1st Division)	2nd	8	4		4	
All First-Class Matches		8	4		5	
Royal London One-Day Cup (Group B)	Finalist	6	4			1
NatWest t20 Blast (North Division)	**Winners**	10	5			2

LV= COUNTY CHAMPIONSHIP AVERAGES
BATTING AND FIELDING

Cap		M	I	NO	HS	Runs	Avge	100	50	Ct/St
2001	I.R.Bell	4	8	1	189*	506	72.28	2	2	8
	S.R.Hain	12	18	2	208	823	51.43	4	1	6
2005	I.J.L.Trott	8	13	–	164	620	47.69	3	1	8
2014	W.T.S.Porterfield	14	23	1	118	778	35.36	1	5	18
2011	R.Clarke	12	18	2	94	550	34.37	–	5	18
2012	V.Chopra	16	25	2	160	785	34.13	2	4	17
2008	I.J.Westwood	8	11	–	129	370	33.63	1	1	3
2007	T.R.Ambrose	15	24	2	167	712	32.36	1	4	57/5
2012	J.S.Patel	16	20	3	105	510	30.00	1	2	9
2013	K.H.D.Barker	15	20	5	102*	444	29.60	1	1	5
2009	C.R.Woakes	9	16	2	91	317	22.64	–	1	4
2013	C.J.C.Wright	11	15	3	65	221	18.41	–	2	1
	O.J.Hannon-Dalby	8	9	4	40	73	14.60	–	–	2
	A.Javid	6	10	2	28	108	13.50	–	–	1
	R.A.Jones	3	5	–	35	57	11.40	–	–	
	L.J.Evans	7	12	–	24	127	10.58	–	–	6
2013	W.B.Rankin	7	8	3	12	35	7.00	–	–	1

Also played: R.O.Gordon (2 matches) 14* (1 ct); P.J.McKay (1) 28 (2 ct); J.O.Troughton (2 – cap 2002) 69, 23, 9 (2 ct).

BOWLING

	O	M	R	W	Avge	Best	5wI	10wM
W.B.Rankin	165.4	31	548	28	19.57	3-16	–	–
O.J.Hannon-Dalby	161.3	28	491	22	22.31	4-57	–	–
C.R.Woakes	283.1	68	912	40	22.80	5-35	2	–
J.S.Patel	536.2	136	1553	59	26.32	5-49	1	–
K.H.D.Barker	442.5	93	1377	50	27.54	6-46	2	–
C.J.C.Wright	291.1	47	1076	31	34.70	4-56	–	–
R.Clarke	249	46	743	19	39.10	3-54	–	–
Also bowled:								
R.O.Gordon	38.2	2	125	6	20.83	4-53	–	–
R.A.Jones	69	7	275	9	30.55	4-81	–	–

L.J.Evans 1-0-15-0; A.Javid 12-0-33-1; I.J.L.Trott 20-2-79-1.

The First-Class Averages (pp 217–233) give the records of Warwickshire players in all first-class county matches (Warwickshire's other opponents being Oxford MCCU), with the exception of I.R.Bell and C.R.Woakes, whose full first-class figures for Warwickshire are as above, and:

R.A.Jones 4-6-1-35-78-15.60-0-0-0ct. 80-13-288-11-26.18-4/81-0-0.

WARWICKSHIRE RECORDS

FIRST-CLASS CRICKET

Highest Total	For 810-4d		v	Durham	Birmingham	1994
	V 887		by	Yorkshire	Birmingham	1896
Lowest Total	For 16		v	Kent	Tonbridge	1913
	V 15		by	Hampshire	Birmingham	1922
Highest Innings	For 501*	B.C.Lara	v	Durham	Birmingham	1994
	V 322	I.V.A.Richards	for	Somerset	Taunton	1985

Highest Partnership for each Wicket

1st	377*	N.F.Horner/K.Ibadulla	v	Surrey	The Oval	1960
2nd	465*	J.A.Jameson/R.B.Kanhai	v	Glos	Birmingham	1974
3rd	327	S.P.Kinneir/W.G.Quaife	v	Lancashire	Birmingham	1901
4th	470	A.I.Kallicharran/G.W.Humpage	v	Lancashire	Southport	1982
5th	335	J.O.Troughton/T.R.Ambrose	v	Hampshire	Birmingham	2009
6th	226	T.R.Ambrose/H.H.Streak	v	Worcs	Worcester	2007
7th	289*	I.R.Bell/T.Frost	v	Sussex	Horsham	2004
8th	228	A.J.W.Croom/R.E.S.Wyatt	v	Worcs	Dudley	1925
9th	233	I.J.L.Trott/J.S.Patel	v	Yorkshire	Birmingham	2009
10th	214	N.V.Knight/A.Richardson	v	Hampshire	Birmingham	2002

Best Bowling	For	10-41	J.D.Bannister	v	Comb Servs	Birmingham	1959
(Innings)	V	10-36	H.Verity	for	Yorkshire	Leeds	1931
Best Bowling	For	15-76	S.Hargreave	v	Surrey	The Oval	1903
(Match)	V	17-92	A.P.Freeman	for	Kent	Folkestone	1932

Most Runs – Season	2417	M.J.K.Smith	(av 60.42)		1959
Most Runs – Career	35146	D.L.Amiss	(av 41.64)		1960-87
Most 100s – Season	9	A.I.Kallicharran			1984
	9	B.C.Lara			1994
Most 100s – Career	78	D.L.Amiss			1960-87
Most Wkts – Season	180	W.E.Hollies	(av 15.13)		1946
Most Wkts – Career	2201	W.E.Hollies	(av 20.45)		1932-57
Most Career W-K Dismissals	800	E.J.Smith	(662 ct; 138 st)		1904-30
Most Career Catches in the Field	422	M.J.K.Smith			1956-75

LIMITED-OVERS CRICKET

Highest Total	50ov	392-5		v	Oxfordshire	Birmingham	1984
	40ov	321-7		v	Leics	Birmingham	2010
	T20	205-2		v	Northants	Birmingham	2005
		205-7		v	Glamorgan	Swansea	2005
Lowest Total	50ov	94		v	Glos	Bristol	2000
	40ov	59		v	Yorkshire	Leeds	2001
	T20	73		v	Somerset	Taunton	2013
Highest Innings	50ov	206	A.I.Kallicharran	v	Oxfordshire	Birmingham	1984
	40ov	137	I.R.Bell	v	Yorkshire	Birmingham	2005
	T20	89	N.V.Knight	v	Worcs	Worcester	2003
Best Bowling	50ov	7-32	R.G.D.Willis	v	Yorkshire	Birmingham	1981
	40ov	6-15	A.A.Donald	v	Yorkshire	Birmingham	1995
	T20	5-19	N.M.Carter	v	Worcs	Birmingham	2005

WORCESTERSHIRE

Formation of Present Club: 11 March 1865
Inaugural First-Class Match: 1899
Colours: Dark Green and Black
Badge: Shield Argent a Fess between three Pears Sable
County Championships: (5) 1964, 1965, 1974, 1988, 1989
NatWest Trophy Winners: (1) 1994
Benson and Hedges Cup Winners: (1) 1991
Pro 40/National League (Div 1) Winners: (1) 2007
Sunday League Winners: (3) 1971, 1987, 1988
Twenty20 Cup Winners: (0); best – Quarter-Finalist 2004, 2007, 2012, 2014

Chief Executive: David Leatherdale, County Ground, New Road, Worcester, WR2 4QQ • Tel: 01905 748474 • Fax: 01905 748005 • Email: info@wccc.co.uk • Web: www.wccc.co.uk • Twitter : @WorcsCCC (18,089 followers)

Director of Cricket: Steve Rhodes. **Bowling/Assistant Coach**: Matt Mason. **Captain**: D.K.H.Mitchell. **Vice-Captain**: tba. **Overseas Players**: C.Munro and Saeed Ajmal. **2015 Beneficiary**: None. **Head Groundsman**: Tim Packwood. **Scorer**: Dawn Pugh. ‡ New registration. NQ Not qualified for England.

Worcestershire revised their capping policy in 2002 and now award players with their County Colours when they make their Championship debut.

ALI, Moeen Munir (Moseley S), b Birmingham, Warwks 18 Jun 1987. Brother of A.K.Ali (Worcestershire, Gloucestershire and Leicestershire 2000-12); cousin of Kabir Ali (*see LANCASHIRE*). 6'0". LHB, OB. Squad No 8. Warwickshire 2005-06. Worcestershire debut 2007. Moors SC 2011-12. MT 2012-13. MCC 2012. PCA 2013. **ECB Central Contract 2014-15. Tests**: 7 (2014); HS 108* v SL (Leeds) 2014; BB 6-67 v I (Southampton) 2014. **LOI**: 22 (2013-14 to 2014-15); HS 128 v Scotland (Christchurch) 2014-15; BB 2-34 v I (Leeds) 2014. **IT20**: 7 (2013-14 to 2014); HS 36 v NZ (Chittagong) 20131-4; BB 1-31 v I (Birmingham) 2014. F-c Tour (EL): SL 2013-14. 1000 runs (2); most – 1420 (2013). HS 250 v Glamorgan (Worcester) 2013. BB 6-29 (12-96 match) v Lancs (Manchester) 2012. LO HS 158 v Sussex (Horsham) 2011 (CB40). LO BB 3-28 v Notts (Nottingham) 2013 (Y40). T20 HS 85. T20 BB 5-34.

ANDREW, Gareth Mark (Ansford Community S; Richard Huish C), b Yeovil, Somerset 27 Dec 1983. 6'0". LHB, RMF. Squad No 14. Somerset 2003-05. Worcestershire debut 2008. Canterbury 2012-13. HS 180* v Auckland (Auckland) 2012-13. Wo HS 92* v Notts (Worcester) 2009. 50 wkts (1): 52 (2011). BB 5-40 v Glamorgan (Cardiff) 2014. LO HS 104 v Surrey (Oval) 2010 (CB40). LO BB 5-31 v Yorks (Worcester) 2009 (P40). T20 HS 65*. T20 BB 4-22.

BARNARD, Edward George (Shrewsbury S), b Shrewsbury, Shrops 20 Nov 1995. Younger brother of M.R.Barnard (Oxford MCCU 2010). 6'1". RHB, RMF. Squad No 30. Shropshire 2012. England U19s 2012-13 to 2014. Awaiting 1st XI debut.

CHOUDHRY, Shaaiq Hussain (Fir Vale S; Bradford U), b Rotherham, Yorkshire 3 Nov 1985. 5'10". RHB, SLA. Squad No 28. MCC 2007. Warwickshire 2009. Worcestershire debut 2010. Bradford/Leeds UCCE 2006-08 (not f-c). HS 75 Wa v Durham UCCE (Durham) 2009. CC HS 63 v Sussex (Hove) 2010. BB 4-38 v Lancs (Manchester) 2012. LO HS 44* v Essex (Worcester) 2014 (RLC). LO BB 4-54 v Surrey (Oval) 2010 (CB40). T20 HS 26*. T20 BB 2-21.

CLARKE, Joe Michael (Llanfyllin HS), b Shrewsbury, Shrops 26 May 1996. 5'11". RHB, WK. Squad No 33. Worcestershire 2nd XI debut 2013. Shropshire 2012-13. England U19s 2014. Awaiting 1st XI debut.

COX, Oliver Ben (Bromsgrove S), b Wordsley, Stourbridge 2 Feb 1992. 5'10". RHB, WK. Squad No 10. Debut (Worcestershire) 2009. Worcestershire 2nd XI debut 2009. HS 104 v Hants (Worcester) 2014. LO HS 39 v Derbys (Worcester) 2014 (RLC). T20 HS 46.

D'OLIVEIRA, Brett Louis (Worcester SFC), b Worcester 28 Feb 1992. Son of D.B.D'Oliveira (Worcs 1982-95), grandson of B.L.D'Oliveira (Worcs, EP and England 1964-80). 5'9". RHB, LB. Squad No 15. Debut (Worcestershire) 2012. Worcestershire 2nd XI debut 2010. HS 44 and BB 1-73 v Essex (Chelmsford) 2014. LO HS 28 v Kent (Worcester) 2013 (Y40). LO BB 3-35 v Warwks (Worcester) 2013 (Y40). T20 HS 15. T20 BB 3-20.

FELL, Thomas Charles (Oakham S; Oxford Brookes U), b Hillingdon, Middx 17 Oct 1993. 6'1". RHB, WK, occ OB. Squad No 29. Oxford MCCU 2013. Worcestershire debut 2013. Worcestershire 2nd XI debut 2010. HS 133 v Glamorgan (Worcester) 2014. LO HS 89 v Glos (Worcester) 2014 (RLC).

‡**GIDMAN, Alex** Peter Richard (Wycliffe C), b High Wycombe, Bucks 22 Jun 1981. Elder brother of W.R.S.Gidman (*see NOTTINGHAMSHIRE*). 6'3". RHB, RM. Gloucestershire 2002-14; cap 2004; captain 2009-12; benefit 2012. MCC YC 2001. MCC 2004, 2007, 2010. F-c Tour (Eng A): SL 2004-05. Appointed captain of Eng A tour to India 2003-04 but withdrew because of hand injury. 1000 runs (6); most – 1278 (2014). HS 264 Gs v Leics (Bristol) 2014, sharing Gs record 3nd wkt partnership of 392 with G.H.Roderick. BB 4-47 Gs v Glamorgan (Cardiff) 2005. LO HS 116 Gs v Sussex (Hove) 2009 (FPT). LO BB 5-42 Eng A v Bangladesh A (Mirpur) 2006-07. T20 HS 64. T20 BB 2-24.

HEPBURN, Alex, b Subiaco, WA, Australia 21 Dec 1995. RHB, RM. Squad No 26. Worcestershire 2nd XI debut 2013. Awaiting 1st XI debut.

KERVEZEE, Alexei Nicolaas (Duneside HS, Namibia; Grenoobi HS, SA; Segbroek C, Holland), b Walvis Bay, Namibia 11 Sep 1989. 5'8". RHB, OB. Squad No 5. Netherlands 2005 to 2009-10. Worcestershire debut 2008. Now qualified for England. **LOI** (Ne): 39 (2006 to 2011-12); HS 92 v Kenya (Voorburg) 2010; BB – . **IT20** (Ne): 10 (2009 to 2011-12); HS 58* v Afghanistan (Dubai, DSC) 2011-12. 1000 runs (1): 1190 (2010). HS 155 v Derbys (Derby) 2010. BB 1-14 Netherlands v Namibia (Windhoek) 2007-08. LO HS 121* Netherlands v Denmark (Potchefstroom) 2008-09. LO BB – . T20 HS 58*.

KOHLER-CADMORE, Tom (Malvern C), b Chatham, Kent 19 Aug 1994. 6'2". RHB, OB. Squad No 32. Debut (Worcestershire) 2014. Worcestershire 2nd XI debut 2010, aged 15y 342d. HS 99 v Leics (Worcester) 2014. LO HS 71 v Derbys (Worcester) 2014 (RLC). T20 HS 51.

LEACH, Joseph (Shrewsbury S; Leeds U), b Stafford 30 Oct 1990. 6'1". RHB, RMF. Squad No 23. Leeds/Bradford MCCU 2012. Worcestershire debut 2012. Worcestershire 2nd XI debut 2008. Staffordshire 2008-09. HS 114 v Glos (Cheltenham) 2013. BB 5-36 v Kent (Tunbridge W) 2014. LO HS 45* v Essex (Worcester) 2014 (RLC). LO BB 2-53 v Northants (Milton Keynes) 2014 (RLC). T20 HS 20. T20 BB 3-20.

MITCHELL, Daryl Keith Henry (Prince Henry's HS; University C, Worcester), b Badsey, near Evesham 25 Nov 1983. 5'10". RHB, RM. Squad No 27. Debut (Worcestershire) 2005; captain 2011 to date. Mountaineers 2011-12. 1000 runs (3); most – 1334 (2014). HS 298 v Somerset (Taunton) 2009. BB 4-49 v Yorks (Leeds) 2009. LO HS 107 v Sussex (Hove) 2013 (Y40). LO BB 4-19 v Northants (Milton Keynes) 2014 (RLC). T20 HS 68*. T20 BB 5-28 v Northants (Northampton) 2014 – Wo record.

MORRIS, Charles Andrew John (King's C, Taunton; Oxford Brookes U), b Hereford 6 Jul 1992. 6'0". RHB, RMF. Squad No 31. Oxford MCCU 2012-14. Worcestershire debut 2013. Worcestershire 2nd XI debut 2012. Kent 2nd XI 2012. MCC Univs 2012. Devon 2011-12. HS 33* OU v Warwks (Oxford) 2013. HS 24 v Glos (Worcester) 2014. 50 wkts (1): 56 (2014). BB 5-54 v Derbys (Derby) 2014. LO HS 16* v Northants (Milton Keynes) 2014 (RLC). LO BB 2-25 v Notts (Nottingham) 2013 (Y40). T20 HS 2*. T20 BB 2-44.

[NQ]**MUNRO, Colin**, b Durban, South Africa 11 Mar 1987. LHB, RM. Auckland 2006-07 to date. Worcestershire 2014 (L-o and T20 only). **Tests** (NZ): 1 (2012-13); HS 15 and BB 2-40 v SA (Port Elizabeth) 2012-13. **LOI** (NZ): 7 (2012-13 to 2013-14); HS 85 v B (Fatullah) 2013-14; BB – . **IT20** (NZ): 14 (2012-13 to 2013-14); HS 73* v B (Dhaka) 2013-14. F-c Tours (NZ): SA 2012-13; SL 2013-14. HS 269* Auckland v Wellington (Auckland) 2012-13, inc 27 fours and 14 sixes. BB 4-36 Auckland v CD (Auckland) 2010-11. LO HS 151 Auckland v Canterbury (Auckland) 2012-13. LO BB 3-45 Auckland v Otago (Oamaru) 2010-11. T20 HS 73*. T20 BB 2-26.

OLIVER, Richard Kenneth, b Stoke-on-Trent, Staffs 14 Nov 1989. LHB, RM. Squad No 43. Debut (Worcestershire) 2014. Shropshire 2008-14. HS 179 v Glos (Worcester) 2014. LO HS 14 v Northants (Milton Keynes) 2014 (RLC). T20 HS 77.

RHODES, George Harry (The Chase HS and SFC, Malvern), b 26 Oct 1993. Son of S.J.Rhodes (Worcestershire, Yorkshire and England 1981-2004); grandson of W.E.Rhodes (Nottinghamshire 1961-64). 5'11". RHB, OB. Squad No 34. Worcestershire 2nd XI debut 2012. Awaiting 1st XI debut.

RUSSELL, Christopher James (Medina HS), b Newport, IoW 16 Feb 1989. 6'1". RHB, RMF. Squad No 18. Debut (Worcestershire) 2012. HS 22 v Middx (Worcester) 2012. BB 4-43 v Warwks (Birmingham) 2012. LO HS 1* (twice). LO BB 4-32 v Netherlands (Rotterdam) 2013 (Y40). T20 HS 3*. T20 BB 4-40.

[NQ]**SAEED AJMAL**, b Faisalabad, Pakistan 14 Oct 1977. 5'4". RHB, OB. Squad No 50. Faisalabad 1996-97 to 2006-07. KRL 2000-01 to 2008-09. Islamabad 2001-02. Federal Areas 2007-08. ZTB 2009-10 to date. Worcestershire debut 2011. Big Bash: AS 2012-13. **Tests** (P): 35 (2009 to 2014); HS 50 v E (Birmingham) 2010; BB 7-55 (10-97 match) v E (Dubai) 2011-12. **LOI** (P): 111 (2008 to 2014); HS 33 v NZ (Abu Dhabi) 2009-10; BB 5-24 v I (Delhi) 2012-13. **IT20** (P): 63 (2009 to 2014); HS 21* v WI (Gros Islet) 2010-11; BB 4-19 v Ireland (Oval) 2009. F-c Tours (P): E 2010; A 2009-10; SA 2012-13; WI 2011; NZ 2009-10; SL 2009, 2012; Z 2011, 2013, 2014; B 2011-12; UAE 2010-11 (v SA), 2011-12 (v SL), 2011-12 (v E), 2013-14 (v SA), 2013-14 (v SL). HS 53* v Leics (Worcester) 2014. 50 wkts (1+1); most – 63 (2014). BB 7-19 (13-94 match) v Essex (Worcester) 2014. LO HS 33 (*see LOI*). LO BB 5-18 Faisalabad v Karachi (Karachi) 2003-04. T20 HS 21*. T20 BB 4-14.

SHANTRY, Jack David (Priory SS; Shrewsbury SFC; Liverpool U), b Shrewsbury, Shrops 29 Jan 1988. Son of B.K.Shantry (Gloucestershire 1978-79); brother of A.J.Shantry (Northants, Warwicks, Glamorgan 2003-11). 6'4". LHB, LM. Squad No 11. Debut (Worcestershire) 2009. Shropshire 2007-09. HS 101* v Surrey (Worcester) 2014. 50 wkts (1): 56 (2014). BB 7-60 v Oxford MCCU (Oxford) 2013. CC BB 7-69 v Essex (Worcester) 2013. LO HS 18 v Sussex (Hove) 2010 (CB40). LO BB 4-32 v Middx (Worcester) 2012 (CB40). T20 HS 12*. T20 BB 4-33.

WHILES, Graeme Philip (King James S, Knaresborough), b Harrogate, Yorks 14 Oct 1993. 6'3". LHB, RMF. Squad No 36. Yorkshire 2nd XI 2012-13. Worcestershire 2nd XI debut 2014. Awaiting 1st XI debut.

WHITELEY, Ross Andrew (Repton S), b Sheffield, Yorks 13 Sep 1988. 6'2". LHB, LM. Squad No 44. Derbyshire 2008-13. Worcestershire debut 2013. No f-c appearances in 2009-10. HS 130* De v Kent (Derby) 2011. Wo HS 56 v Northants (Worcester) 2013. BB 2-6 De v Hants (Derby) 2012. Wo BB 1-23 v Hants (Worcester) 2013. LO HS 53 v Derbys (Worcester) 2014 (RLC). LO BB 1-17 De v Unicorns (Wormsley) 2012 (CB40). T20 HS 84*. T20 BB 1-12.

RELEASED/RETIRED

(Having made a County 1st XI appearance in 2014)

[NO]**McCLENAGHAN, Mitchell** John, b Hastings, Hawke's Bay, New Zealand 11 Jun 1986. LHB, LMF. C Districts 2007-08 to 2010-11. Auckland 2011-12 to date. Worcestershire 2014. **LOI** (NZ): 35 (2012-13 to 2014-15); HS 34* v SA (Mt Maunganui) 2014-15; BB 5-58 v WI (Auckland) 2013-14. **IT20** (NZ): 16 (2012-13 to 2014-15); HS 6* v E (Auckland) 2012-13; BB 2-24 (three times). HS 34 v Auckland v CD (Napier) 2011-12. Wo HS 27 and Wo BB 5-78 v Derbys (Derby) 2014. BB 8-23 Auckland v Otago (Auckland) 2011-12. LO HS 34* (*see LOI*). LO BB 6-41 Auckland v Wellington (Auckland) 2011-12. T20 HS 13*. T20 BB 5-29.

PARDOE, Matthew Graham (Haybridge HS), b Stourbridge 5 Jan 1991. 6'1". LHB, LM. Worcestershire 2011-14. Southern Rocks 2012-13 to 2013-14. Worcestershire 2nd XI debut 2007. HS 102 v Glamorgan (Worcester) 2013. BB 2-34 SR v Mountaineers (Mutare) 2012-13. LO HS 42 SR v MT (Bulawayo) 2012-13. LO BB 1-9 SR v MT (Masvingo) 2013-14. T20 HS 1.

G.Cessford and N.L.Harrison left the staff without making a County 1st XI appearance in 2014.

WORCESTERSHIRE 2014

RESULTS SUMMARY

		Place	Won	Lost	Tied	Drew	NR
LV= County Championship	(2nd Division)	2nd	8	3		5	
All First-Class Matches			8	3		5	
Royal London One-Day Cup	(Group A)	7th	2	4			2
NatWest t20 Blast	(North Division)	QF	8	5			2

LV= COUNTY CHAMPIONSHIP AVERAGES

BATTING AND FIELDING

Cap		M	I	NO	HS	Runs	Avge	100	50	Ct/St
2008	M.M.Ali	8	11	–	162	676	61.45	1	6	6
2005	D.K.H.Mitchell	16	27	4	172*	1334	58.00	5	4	28
2014	R.K.Oliver	7	14	–	179	558	39.85	1	4	2
2009	A.N.Kervezee	16	26	1	110	829	33.16	2	5	8
2013	T.C.Fell	12	20	1	133	563	29.63	2	1	13
2009	J.D.Shantry	16	24	7	101*	481	28.29	1	–	7
2009	O.B.Cox	16	25	2	104	604	26.26	1	3	32/3
2011	M.G.Pardoe	9	13	1	52	284	23.66	–	1	6
2012	J.Leach	12	19	–	74	447	23.52	–	4	2
2010	S.H.Choudhry	6	10	1	44	209	23.22	–	2	2
2014	T.Kohler-Cadmore	13	23	–	99	516	22.43	–	4	15
2008	G.M.Andrew	4	6	1	71*	108	21.60	–	1	–
2011	Saeed Ajmal	9	10	2	53*	156	19.50	–	1	4
2013	R.A.Whiteley	9	12	–	43	214	17.83	–	–	3
2014	M.J.McClenaghan	4	7	1	27	86	14.33	–	–	–
2014	C.A.J.Morris	16	20	14	24	72	12.00	–	–	7

Also played (1 match each): B.L.D'Oliveira (cap 2012) 7, 44; A.D.Hales (cap 2014) 15, 63 (1 ct); C.J.Russell (cap 2012) did not bat.

BOWLING

	O	M	R	W	Avge	Best	5wI	10wM
G.M.Andrew	106	25	319	20	15.95	5-40	1	–
Saeed Ajmal	417.3	116	1038	63	16.47	7-19	6	2
J.D.Shantry	497	124	1336	56	23.85	6-53	2	1
C.A.J.Morris	499.4	135	1371	52	26.36	5-54	1	1
J.Leach	268.5	48	988	33	29.93	5-36	1	–
M.J.McClenaghan	120	27	466	13	35.84	5-78	1	–
M.M.Ali	190.5	36	552	15	36.80	3-43	–	–

Also bowled:
S.H.Choudhry 108.1 13 384 8 48.00 3-79

B.L.D'Oliveira 14-1-73-1; A.N.Kervezee 7.3-0-34-0; D.K.H.Mitchell 9-3-26-0; M.G.Pardoe 10-2-24-0; C.J.Russell 14-1-73-2; R.A.Whiteley 12-1-44-0.

Worcestershire played no first-class fixtures outside the County Championship in 2014. The First-Class Averages (pp 217–233) give the records of their players in all first-class county matches, with the exception of M.M.Ali, A.D.Hales and C.A.J.Morris, whose first-class figures for Worcestershire are as above.

† Worcestershire revised their capping policy in 2002 and now award players with their County Colours when they make their Championship debut.

WORCESTERSHIRE RECORDS

FIRST-CLASS CRICKET

Highest Total	For 701-6d		v	Surrey	Worcester	2007
	V 701-4d		by	Leics	Worcester	1906
Lowest Total	For 24		v	Yorkshire	Huddersfield	1903
	V 30		by	Hampshire	Worcester	1903
Highest Innings	For 405*	G.A.Hick	v	Somerset	Taunton	1988
	V 331*	J.D.B.Robertson	for	Middlesex	Worcester	1949

Highest Partnership for each Wicket

1st	309	H.K.Foster/F.L.Bowley	v	Derbyshire	Derby	1901
2nd	316	S.C.Moore/V.S.Solanki	v	Glos	Cheltenham	2008
3rd	438*	G.A.Hick/T.M.Moody	v	Hampshire	Southampton	1997
4th	330	B.F.Smith/G.A.Hick	v	Somerset	Taunton	2006
5th	393	E.G.Arnold/W.B.Burns	v	Warwicks	Birmingham	1909
6th	265	G.A.Hick/S.J.Rhodes	v	Somerset	Taunton	1988
7th	256	D.A.Leatherdale/S.J.Rhodes	v	Notts	Nottingham	2002
8th	184	S.J.Rhodes/S.R.Lampitt	v	Derbyshire	Kidderminster	1991
9th	181	J.A.Cuffe/R.D.Burrows	v	Glos	Worcester	1907
10th	119	W.B.Burns/G.A.Wilson	v	Somerset	Worcester	1906

Best Bowling	For	9- 23	C.F.Root	v	Lancashire	Worcester	1931
(Innings)	V	10- 51	J.Mercer	for	Glamorgan	Worcester	1936
Best Bowling	For	15- 87	A.J.Conway	v	Glos	Moreton-in-M	1914
(Match)	V	17-212	J.C.Clay	for	Glamorgan	Swansea	1937

Most Runs – Season	2654	H.H.I.H.Gibbons	(av 52.03)	1934
Most Runs – Career	34490	D.Kenyon	(av 34.18)	1946-67
Most 100s – Season	10	G.M.Turner		1970
	10	G.A.Hick		1988
Most 100s – Career	106	G.A.Hick		1984-2008
Most Wkts – Season	207	C.F.Root	(av 17.52)	1925
Most Wkts – Career	2143	R.T.D.Perks	(av 23.73)	1930-55
Most Career W-K Dismissals	1095	S.J.Rhodes	(991 ct; 104 st)	1985-2004
Most Career Catches in the Field	528	G.A.Hick		1984-2008

LIMITED-OVERS CRICKET

Highest Total	50ov	404-3		v	Devon	Worcester	1987
	40ov	376-6		v	Surrey	Oval	2010
	T20	227-6		v	Northants	Kidderminster	2007
Lowest Total	50ov	58		v	Ireland	Worcester	2009
	40ov	86		v	Yorkshire	Leeds	1969
	T20	86		v	Northants	Worcester	2006
Highest Innings	50ov	180*	T.M.Moody	v	Surrey	The Oval	1994
	40ov	160	T.M.Moody	v	Kent	Worcester	1991
	T20	116*	G.A.Hick	v	Northants	Luton	2004
Best Bowling	50ov	7-19	N.V.Radford	v	Beds	Bedford	1991
	40ov	6-16	Shoaib Akhtar	v	Glos	Worcester	2005
	T20	5-28	D.K.H.Mitchell	v	Northants	Northampton	2014

YORKSHIRE

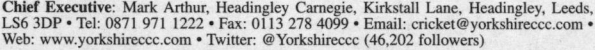

Formation of Present Club: 8 January 1863
Substantial Reorganisation: 10 December 1891
Inaugural First-Class Match: 1864
Colours: Dark Blue, Light Blue and Gold
Badge: White Rose
County Championships (since 1890): (31) 1893, 1896, 1898, 1900, 1901, 1902, 1905, 1908, 1912, 1919, 1922, 1923, 1924, 1925, 1931, 1932, 1933, 1935, 1937, 1938, 1939, 1946, 1959, 1960, 1962, 1963, 1966, 1967, 1968, 2001, 2014
Joint Champions: (1) 1949
Gillette/C&G Trophy Winners: (3) 1965, 1969, 2002
Benson and Hedges Cup Winners: (1) 1987
Sunday League Winners: (1) 1983
Twenty20 Cup Winners: (0); best – Finalist 2012

Chief Executive: Mark Arthur, Headingley Carnegie, Kirkstall Lane, Headingley, Leeds, LS6 3DP • Tel: 0871 971 1222 • Fax: 0113 278 4099 • Email: cricket@yorkshireccc.com • Web: www.yorkshireccc.com • Twitter: @Yorkshireccc (46,202 followers)

Director of Professional Cricket: Martyn Moxon. **Senior 1st XI Coach**: Jason Gillespie. **Captain**: A.W.Gale. **Overseas Players**: A.J.Finch (T20 only), G.J.Maxwell (T20 only), K.S.Williamson and Younus Khan. **2015 Beneficiary**: R.M.Pyrah. **Head Groundsman**: Andy Fogarty. **Scorer**: John Potter. ‡ New registration. ^{NQ} Not qualified for England.

ASHRAF, Moin Aqeeb (Dixons City Academy, Bradford), b Bradford 5 Jan 1992. 6'4". RHB, RMF. Squad No 23. Debut (Yorkshire) 2010. Yorkshire 2nd XI debut 2009. No 1st XI appearances in 2014. HS 10 and BB 5-32 v Kent (Leeds) 2010. LO HS 3* v Kent (Leeds) 2012 (CB40). LO BB 3-38 v Glamorgan (Leeds) 2013 (Y40). T20 HS 4. T20 BB 4-18.

BAIRSTOW, Jonathan Marc (St Peter's S, York; Leeds Met U), b Bradford 26 Sep 1989. Son of D.L.Bairstow (Yorkshire, GW and England 1970-90); brother of A.D.Bairstow (Derbyshire 1995). 6'0". RHB, WK, occ RM. Squad No 21. Debut (Yorkshire) 2009; cap 2011. Inaugural winner of Young Wisden Schools Cricketer of the Year 2008. YC 2011. **Tests**: 14 (2012 to 2013-14); HS 95 v SA (Lord's) 2012. **LOI**: 7 (2011 to 2012); HS 41* v I (Cardiff) 2011. **IT20**: 18 (2011 to 2012-13): HS 60* v P (Dubai) 2011-12. F-c Tours: A 2013-14; SA 2014-15 (EL); I 2012-13; WI 2010-11 (EL); SL 2013-14 (EL). 1000 runs (1): 1213 (2011). HS 205 v Notts (Nottingham) 2011. LO HS 123 EL v New Zealand A (Bristol) 2014. T20 HS 102*.

BALLANCE, Gary Simon (Peterhouse S, Marondera, Zimbabwe; Harrow S; Leeds Met U), b Harare, Zimbabwe 22 Nov 1989. Nephew of G.S.Ballance (Rhodesia B 1978-79) and D.L.Houghton (Rhodesia/Zimbabwe 1978-79 to 1997-98). 6'0". LHB, LB. Squad No 19. Debut (Yorkshire) 2008; cap 2012. MWR 2010-11 to 2011-12. Derbyshire (List A) 2006-07. **ECB central contract 2014-15. Tests**: 8 (2013-14 to 2014); HS 156 v I (Southampton) 2014; BB – . **LOI**: 16 (2013 to 2014-15); HS 79 v A (Melbourne) 2013-14. F-c Tour: A 2013-14. 1000 runs (1+1); most – 1363 (2013). HS 210 MWR v SR (Masvingo) 2011-12. Y HS 174 v Northants (Leeds) 2014. BB – . LO HS 139 v Unicorns (Leeds) 2013. T20 HS 68.

BRESNAN, Timothy Thomas (Castleford HS and TC; Pontefract New C), b Pontefract 28 Feb 1985. 6'0". RHB, RFM. Squad No 16. Debut (Yorkshire) 2003; cap 2006; benefit 2014. MCC 2006, 2009. Big Bash: HH 2014-15. *Wisden* 2011. **Tests**: 23 (2009 to 2013-14); HS 91 v B (Dhaka) 2009-10; BB 5-48 v I (Nottingham) 2011. **LOI**: 84 (2006 to 2013-14); HS 80 v SA (Centurion) 2009-10; BB 5-48 v I (Bangalore) 2010-11. **IT20**: 34 (2006 to 2013-14); HS 47* v WI (Bridgetown) 2013-14; BB 3-10 v P (Cardiff) 2010. F-c Tours: A 2010-11, 2013-14; I 2012-13; SL 2011-12; B 2006-07 (Eng A), 2009-10. HS 126* Eng A v Indians (Chelmsford) 2007. Y HS 116 v Surrey (Oval) 2007, sharing in Y record 9th wicket partnership of 246 with J.N.Gillespie. BB 5-42 v Worcs (Worcester) 2005. LO HS 80 (*see LOI*). BB 5-48 (*see LOI*). T20 HS 47*. T20 BB 3-10.

BROOKS, Jack Alexander (Wheatley Park S), b Oxford 4 Jun 1984. 6'2". RHB, RFM. Squad No 70. Northamptonshire 2009-12; cap 2012. Yorkshire debut 2013; cap 2013. Oxfordshire 2004-09. F-c Tour (EL): SA 2014-15. HS 53 Nh v Glos (Bristol) 2010. Y HS 37* and Y HS 5-36 v Northants (Leeds) 2014. 50 wkts (1): 71 (2014). BB 5-23 Nh v Leics (Leicester) 2011. LO HS 10 Nh v Middx (Uxbridge) 2009 (P40). LO BB 3-30 v Hants (Southampton) 2014 (RLC). T20 HS 33*. T20 BB 5-21.

CALLIS, Elliot (Worksop C), b Doncaster 8 Nov 1994. 6'2". RHB, LB. Yorkshire 2nd XI debut 2013. Awaiting f-c debut. LO HS 10 v Sri Lanka A (Leeds) 2014 – only 1st XI appearance.

CARVER, Karl (Thirsk S & SFC), b Northallerton 26 Mar 1996. 5'10". LHB, SLA. Squad No 29. Debut (Yorkshire) 2014. Yorkshire 2nd XI debut 2013. HS 2* and BB 2-27 v Warwks (Birmingham) 2014 – only 1st XI appearance.

COAD, Benjamin Oliver (Thirsk S & SFC), b Harrogate 10 Jan 1994. 6'2". RHB, RMF. Squad No 10. Yorkshire 2nd XI debut 2012. Awaiting f-c debut. LO HS 2* v Sri Lanka A (Leeds) 2014. LO BB 1-34 v Glos (Bristol) 2013 (Y40).

NQFINCH, Aaron James, b Colac, Victoria, Australia 17 Nov 1986. 5'9". RHB, LM. Victoria 2007-08 to date. IPL: RR: 2009-10. DD 2011-12. PW 2013. SH 2014. Big Bash: MR 2011-12 to date. **LOI** (A): 46 (2012-13 to 2014-15); HS 148 v Scotland (Edinburgh) 2013; BB 1-2 v I (Pune) 2013-14. **IT20** (A): 22 (2010-11 to 2014-15); HS 156 v E (Southampton) 2013 – world record IT20 score. F-c Tours (Aus A): SA/Z 2013; Z 2011. HS 122 Aus A v Zimbabwe XI (Harare) 2011. Y HS 110 v Warwks (Birmingham) 2014. BB 1-0 Vic v WA (Perth) 2013-14. Y BB 1-20 v Sussex (Arundel) 2014. LO HS 154 Vic v Q (Brisbane) 2012-13. LO BB 2-44 Aus A v EL (Hobart) 2012-13. T20 HS 156. T20 BB 1-11.

FISHER, Matthew David (Easingwold SS), b York 9 Nov 1997. 6'1". RHB, RFM. Squad No 7. Yorkshire 2nd XI debut 2013, aged 15y 201d. England U19s 2014. Awaiting f-c debut. LO HS 10 v Leics (Scarborough) 2013 (Y40). LO BB 1-29 v Worcs (Leeds) 2014 (RLC).

GALE, Andrew William (Whitcliffe Mount S; Heckmondwike GS), b Dewsbury 28 Nov 1983. 6'2". LHB, LB. Squad No 26. Debut (Yorkshire) 2004, 2006 to date; cap 2008; captain 2010 to date. F-c Tour (EL): WI 2010-11. 1000 runs (1): 1076 (2013). HS 272 v Notts (Scarborough) 2013. BB 1-33 v Loughborough UCCE (Leeds) 2007. LO HS 125* v Essex (Chelmsford) 2010 (CB40). T20 HS 91.

GIBSON, Barney Peter (Crawshaw HS, Pudsey), b Leeds 31 Mar 1996. 5'8½". RHB, WK. Debut (Yorkshire) 2011, aged 15y 27d, becoming youngest player to play f-c cricket, beating a record set in 1867. HS 1* v Durham MCCU (Durham) 2011.

GIBSON, Ryan (Fylinghall S), b Middlesbrough 22 Jan 1996. RHB, RM. 6'4". Yorkshire 2nd XI debut 2012. Awaiting f-c debut. LO HS 9 v Sri Lanka A (Leeds) 2014. LO BB 1-17 v Bangladesh A (Leeds) 2013.

HODD, Andrew John (Bexhill C; Loughborough U), b Chichester, Sussex 12 Jan 1984. 5'9". RHB, WK. Squad No 4. Sussex 2003-11. Surrey 2005 (1 match). Yorkshire debut 2012 (on loan). HS 123 Sx v Yorks (Hove) 2007. Y HS 68* v Somerset (Taunton) 2013. LO HS 91 Sx v Lancs (Hove) 2010 (CB40). T20 HS 26.

HODGSON, Daniel Mark (Richmond S; Leeds U), b Northallerton 26 Feb 1990. RHB, WK. Squad No 18. Leeds/Bradford MCCU 2012, scoring 64 v Surrey (Oval) on debut. Mountaineers 2012-13. Yorkshire debut 2014. Derbyshire 2014 (on loan). Yorkshire 2nd XI debut 2011. HS 94* Mountaineers v SR (Mutare) 2012-13. Y HS 18 v Leeds/Bradford MCCU (Leeds) 2014. CC HS 1 De v Worcs (Worcester) 2014. LO HS 90 v Glamorgan (Leeds) 2013 (Y40). T20 HS 52*.

LEANING, Jack Andrew (Archbishop Holgate's S, York; York C), b Bristol, Glos 18 Oct 1993. 5'10". RHB, RMF. Squad No 34. Debut (Yorkshire) 2013. Yorkshire 2nd XI debut 2011. HS 99 v Sussex (Arundel) 2014). BB – . LO HS 111* v Essex (Scarborough) 2014 (RLC). LO BB 5-22 v Unicorns (Leeds) 2013 (Y40). T20 HS 8. T20 BB – .

LEES, Alexander Zak (Holy Trinity SS, Halifax), b Halifax 14 Apr 1993. 6'3". LHB, LB. Squad No 14. Debut (Yorkshire) 2010; cap 2014. Yorkshire 2nd XI debut 2010. YC 2014. 1000 runs (1): 1018 (2014). HS 275* v Derbys (Chesterfield) 2013 (Y40). LO HS 102 v Northants (Northampton) 2014 (RLC). T20 HS 67*.

LYTH, Adam (Caedmon S, Whitby; Whitby Community C), b Whitby 25 Sep 1987. 5'8". LHB, RM. Squad No 9. Debut (Yorkshire) 2007; cap 2010. PCA 2014. F-c Tours (EL): SA 2014-15; WI 2010-11. 1000 runs (2); most – 1619 (2014). HS 251 v Lancs (Manchester) 2014, sharing in Y record 6th wicket partnership of 296 with A.U.Rashid. HS 2-15 v Somerset (Taunton) 2013. LO HS 109* v Sussex (Scarborough) 2009 (P40). LO BB 1-6 v Middx (Leeds) 2013 (Y40). T20 HS 78. T20 BB 2-5.

‡^{NO}**MAXWELL, Glenn** James, b Kew, Melbourne, Australia 14 Oct 1988. RHB, OB. Victoria 2010-11 to date. Hampshire 2014. Joins Yorkshire in 2015 for T20 only. IPL: DD 2012. MI 2013. KXIP 2014. Big Bash: MR 2011-12. MS 2012-13 to date. **Tests** (A): 3 (2012-13 to 2014-15); HS 37 v P (Abu Dhabi) 2014-15; BB 4-127 v I (Hyderabad) 2012-13. **LOI** (A): 46 (2012 to 2014-15); HS 102 v SL (Sydney) 2014-15; BB 4-46 v E (Perth) 2014-15. **IT20** (A): 24 (2012 to 2014-15); HS 74 v P (Dhaka) 2013-14; BB 3-13 v P (Dubai) 2014-15. F-c Tours (A): I 2012-13; SA/2 2013 (Aus A); UAE 2014-15 (v P). HS 155* Aus A v South Africa A (Pretoria) 2013. CC HS 85 and CC BB 2-33 H v Worcs (Worcester) 2014. BB 4-42 Vic v S Aus (Melbourne) 2012-13. LO HS 146 H v Lancs (Manchester) 2014 (RLC). LO BB 4-46 (see LOI). T20 HS 95. T20 BB 3-13.

PATTERSON, Steven Andrew (Malet Lambert CS; St Mary's SFC, Hull; Leeds U), b Hull 3 Oct 1983. 6'4". RHB, RMF. Squad No 17. Debut (Yorkshire) 2005; cap 2012. Bradford/Leeds UCCE 2003 (not f-c). HS 53 v Sussex (Hove) 2011. 50 wkts (2); most – 53 (2012). BB 5-43 v Notts (Nottingham) 2013. LO HS 25* v Worcs (Leeds) 2006 (P40). LO BB 6-32 v Derbys (Leeds) 2010. T20 HS 3*. T20 BB 4-30.

PLUNKETT, Liam Edward (Nunthorpe SS; Teesside Tertiary C), b Middlesbrough, Yorks 6 Apr 1985. 6'3". RHB, RFM. Squad No 28. Durham 2003-12. Dolphins 2007-08. Yorkshire debut 2013; cap 2013. **Tests**: 13 (2005-06 to 2014); HS 55* v I (Lord's) 2014; BB 5-64 v SL (Leeds) 2014. **LOI**: 29 (2005-06 to 2010-11); HS 56 v P (Lahore) 2005-06; BB 3-24 v A (Sydney) 2006-07. **IT20**: 1 (2006); HS – ; BB 1-37 v SL (Southampton) 2006. F-c Tours (EL): SA 2014-15; WI 2010-11; NZ 2008-09 (E), 2007-08; P 2005-06; SL 2013-14. HS 114 EL v Sri Lanka A (Colombo) 2013-14. CC HS 94* Du v Sussex (Hove) 2009. Y HS 86 v Warwks (Leeds) 2014. 50 wkts (3); most – 60 (2009). BB 6-33 v Leeds/Bradford MCCU (Leeds) 2013 on Y debut. CC BB 6-63 (11-119 match) Du v Worcs (Chester-le-St) 2009. LO HS 72 Du v Somerset (Chester-le-St) 2008 (P40). LO BB 4-15 Du v Essex (Chester-le-St) 2007 (FPT). T20 HS 41. T20 BB 5-31.

PYRAH, Richard Michael (Ossett S; Wakefield C), b Dewsbury 1 Nov 1982. 6'0''. RHB, RM. Squad No 27. Debut (Yorkshire) 2004; cap 2010; benefit 2015. HS 134* v Loughborough MCCU (Leeds) 2010. CC HS 117 v Lancs (Leeds) 2011. BB 5-58 v Notts (Leeds) 2011. LO HS 69 v Netherlands (Leeds) 2011 (CB40). LO BB 5-50 Yorks CB v Somerset (Scarborough) 2002 (CGT). T20 HS 42. T20 BB 5-16 v Durham (Scarborough) 2011 – Y record.

RASHID, Adil Usman (Belle Vue S, Bradford), b Bradford 17 Feb 1988. 5'8''. RHB, LBG. Squad No 3. Debut (Yorkshire) 2006; cap 2008. MCC 2007-09. YC 2007. Match double (114, 48, 8-157 and 2-45) for England U19 v India U19 (Taunton) 2006. **LOI**: 5 (2009 to 2009-10); HS 31* v A (Oval) 2009; BB 1-16 v Ireland (Belfast) 2009. **IT20**: 5 (2009 to 2009-10); HS 9* v SA (Nottingham) 2009; BB 1-11 v WI (Oval) 2009. F-c Tours (EL): WI 2010-11; I 2007-08; B 2006-07 (Eng A). HS 180 v Somerset (Leeds) 2013. 50 wkts (2); most – 65 (2008). BB 7-107 v Hants (Southampton) 2008. LO HS 71 v Glos (Leeds) 2014 (RLC). LO BB 5-33 v Hants (Southampton) 2014 (RLC). T20 HS 36*. T20 BB 4-20.

RHODES, William Michael Henry (Cottingham HS, Cottingham SFC, Hull), b Nottingham 2 Mar 1995. 6'2''. LHB, RMF. Squad No 35. Yorkshire 2nd XI debut 2012. Awaiting f-c debut. No 1st XI appearances in 2014. England U19s 2014. LO HS 19* v Glos (Leeds) 2013 (Y40). LO BB 2-26 v Leics (Scarborough) 2013 (Y40). T20 HS 13. T20 BB – .

ROOT, Joseph Edward (King Ecgbert S, Sheffield; Worksop C), b Sheffield 30 Dec 1990. 6'0''. RHB, OB. Squad No 5. Debut (Yorkshire) 2010; cap 2012. Yorkshire 2nd XI debut 2007. England U19s 2009-10 to 2010. YC 2012. **ECB central contract 2014-15. Tests**: 22 (2012-13 to 2014); HS 200* v SL (Lord's) 2014; BB 2-9 v A (Lord's) 2014. **LOI**: 54 (2012-13 to 2014-15); HS 121 v SL (Wellington) 2014-15; BB 2-15 v WI (North Sound) 2013-14. **IT20**: 9 (2012-13 to 2014); HS 90* v A (Southampton) 2014; BB 1-13 v A (Sydney) 2013-14. F-c Tours: A 2013-14; NZ 2012-13; I 2012-13. 1000 runs (3); most – 1228 (2013). HS 236 v Derbys (Leeds) 2013. BB 3-33 v Warwks (Leeds) 2011. LO HS 121 (*see LOI*). LO BB 2-10 EL v Bangladesh A (Sylhet) 2011-12. T20 HS 90*. T20 BB 1-12.

SHAW, Joshua (Crofton HS, Wakefield; Skills Exchange, Wakefield 3 Jan 1996. Son of C.Shaw (Yorkshire 1984-88). 6'1''. RHB, RMF. Squad No 25. Yorkshire 2nd XI debut 2102. England U19s 2012-13 to 2014. Awaiting 1st XI debut

SIDEBOTTOM, Ryan Jay (King James's GS, Almondbury), b Huddersfield 15 Jan 1978. Son of A.Sidebottom (Yorkshire, OFS and England 1973-91). 6'3''. LHB, LFM. Squad No 11. Debut (Yorkshire) 1997; cap 2000. Returned to Yorkshire in 2011. Nottinghamshire 2004-10; cap 2004; benefit 2010. *Wisden* 2007. **Tests**: 22 (2001 to 2009-10); HS 31 v SA (Kandy) 2007-08; BB 7-47 v NZ (Napier) 2007-08. Hat-trick v NZ (Hamilton) 2007-08. **LOI**: 25 (2001-02 to 2009-10); HS 24 v A (Southampton) 2009; BB 3-19 v SL (Dambulla) 2007-08. **IT20**: 18 (2007 to 2010); HS 5* and BB 3-16 v NZ (Auckland) 2007-08. F-c Tours: SA 2009-10; WI 2000-01 (Eng A), 2008-09; NZ 2007-08; SL 2007-08. HS 61 v Worcs (Worcester) 2011. 50 wkts (4); most – 62 (2011). BB 7-37 (11-98 match) v Somerset (Leeds) 2011. LO HS 32 Nt v Middx (Nottingham) 2005 (NL). LO BB 6-40 v Glamorgan (Cardiff) 1998 (SL). T20 HS 17*. T20 BB 4-25.

TATTERSALL, Jonathan Andrew (King James S, Knaresborough), b Harrogate 15 Dec 1994. 5'8''. RHB, LB. Squad No 12. Yorkshire 2nd XI debut 2012. Awaiting f-c debut. No 1st XI appearances in 2014. England U19s 2012-13 to 2014. LO HS 0.

WAINMAN, James Charles (Leeds GS), b Harrogate 25 Jan 1993. 6'4''. RHB, LMF. Squad No 15. Yorkshire 2nd XI debut 2010. Awaiting f-c debut. LO HS 33 and LO BB 3-51 v Sri Lanka A (Leeds) 2014 – only 1st XI appearance.

^{NO}**WILLIAMSON, Kane** Stuart (Tauranga Boys' C), b Tauranga, New Zealand 8 Aug 1990. Cousin of D.Cleaver (C Districts 2010-11 to date). 5'8". RHB, OB. N Districts 2007-08 to date. Gloucestershire 2011-12; cap 2011. Yorkshire debut 2013. **Tests** (NZ): 39 (2010-11 to 2014-15); HS 242* v SL (Wellington) 2014-15; scored 131 v I (Ahmedabad) 2010-11 on debut; BB 4-44 v E (Auckland) 2012-13. **LOI** (NZ): 71 (2010 to 2014-15); HS 145* v SA (Kimberley) 2012-13; BB 4-22 v SA (Paarl) 2012-13. **IT20** (NZ): 21 (2011-12 to 2014-15); HS 51 v SA (Chittagong) 2013-14; BB 1-6 v Z (Auckland) 2011-12. F-c Tours (NZ): E 2013; A 2011-12; SA 2012-13; WI 2012, 2014; I 2010-11, 2012; SL 2012-13; Z 2011-12; B 2013-14; UAE 2014-15 (v P). HS 284* ND v Wellington (Lincoln) 2011-12). UK HS 189 v Sussex (Scarborough) 2014. BB 5-75 ND v Canterbury (Christchurch) 2008-09. CC BB 3-58 Gs v Northants (Northampton) 2012. Y BB 2-44 v Sussex (Hove) 2013. LO HS 145* (*see LOI*). LO BB 5-51 ND v Auckland (Auckland) 2009-10. T20 HS 101*. T20 BB 3-33.

^{NO}**YOUNUS KHAN**, Mohammad (Shah Latif SS, Karachi; All Hadeed GHS, Karachi; b Mardan, North-West Frontier Province, Pakistan 29 Nov 1977. 5'11½". RHB, RM/LB. Peshawar 1998-99 to 2004-05. HB 1999-00 to date. Nottinghamshire 2005. Yorkshire debut 2007; cap 2007. NW Frontier Province 2007-08 to 2008-09. S Aus 2008-09. Surrey 2010. IPL: RR 2007-08. **Tests** (P): 96 (1999-00 to 2014-15, 9 as captain); HS 313 v SL (Karachi) 2008-09; BB 2-23 v SL (Galle) 2008. **LOI** (P): 264 (1999-00 to 2014-15, 21 as captain); HS 144 v Hong Kong (Colombo, SSC) 2004; BB 1-3 v Hong Kong (Karachi) 2008. **IT20** (P): 25 (2006 to 2010-11, 8 as captain); HS 51 v SL (Johannesburg) 2007-08; BB 3-18 v Kenya (Nairobi) 2007. F-c Tours (P) (C=Captain): E 2001, 2006; A 2004-05; SA 2002-03, 2006-07, 2012-13; WI 1999-00, 2004-05; NZ 2000-01, 2010-11; I 2004-05, 2007-08C; SL 2000, 2002-03 (v A), 2005-06, 2009C, 2012, 2014; Z 2002-03, 2011, 2013; B 2001-02; UAE 2001-02 (v WI), 2002-03 (v A), 2010-11 (v SA), 2011-12 (v SL), 2011-12 (v E), 2013-14 (v SA), 2013-14 (v SL), 2014-15 (v A), 2014-15 (v NZ). 1000 runs (0+1): 1315 (1999-00). HS 313 (*see Tests*). UK HS 217* v Kent (Scarborough) 2007. BB 4-52 v Hants (Southampton) 2007. LO HS 144 (*see LOI*). LO BB 3-5 Nt v Glos (Cheltenham) 2005 (NL). T20 HS 71*. T20 BB 3-18.

RELEASED/RETIRED

(Having made a County 1st XI appearance in 2014)

AZEEM Muhammad **RAFIQ** (Holgate S Sports C; Barnsley C), b Karachi, Pakistan 27 Feb 1991. 5'11". RHB, OB. Yorkshire 2009-14. Derbyshire (on loan) 2011. Yorkshire 2nd XI debut 2008. England U19s 2009 to 2010. HS 100 v Worcs (Worcester) 2009. BB 5-50 v Essex (Chelmsford) 2012. LO HS 34* v Unicorns (Leeds) 2012 (CB40). LO BB 5-30 v Bangladesh A (Leeds) 2013. T20 HS 21*. T20 BB 3-15.

ROBINSON, Oliver Edward (King's S, Canterbury), b Margate, Kent 1 Dec 1993. RHB, RM. Kent 2nd XI 2011-12. Leicestershire 2nd XI 2013. Yorkshire 2nd XI debut. Awaiting f-c debut. LO HS 12* v Leics (Leicester) 2013 (Y40). LO BB – . T20 HS 3. T20 BB 2-25.

YORKSHIRE 2014

RESULTS SUMMARY

	Place	Won	Lost	Tied	Drew	NR
LV= County Championship (1st Division)	**1st**	8	1		7	
All First-Class Matches		8	1		8	
Royal London One-Day Cup (Group A)	QF	6	3			
NatWest t20 Blast (North Division)	5th	6	5			3

LV= COUNTY CHAMPIONSHIP AVERAGES

BATTING AND FIELDING

Cap		M	I	NO	HS	Runs	Avge	100	50	Ct/St
2010	A.Lyth	16	23	1	251	1489	67.68	6	6	35
2012	G.S.Ballance	6	9	–	174	585	65.00	2	3	7
	K.S.Williamson	9	13	2	189	629	57.18	1	4	10
	A.J.Finch	5	6	–	110	291	48.50	1	1	8
2011	J.M.Bairstow	13	17	3	161*	647	46.21	1	4	38/4
2012	J.E.Root	4	6	–	97	275	45.83	–	3	1
2014	A.Z.Lees	15	22	–	138	971	44.13	2	5	10
2008	A.W.Gale	13	16	3	126*	562	43.23	2	1	2
2010	R.M.Pyrah	6	6	2	62	161	40.25	–	1	2
	J.A.Leaning	10	14	2	99	465	38.75	–	4	4
2008	A.U.Rashid	14	18	3	159*	577	38.46	2	1	9
2013	L.E.Plunkett	7	8	2	86	209	34.83	–	2	4
2006	T.T.Bresnan	10	10	–	95	338	33.80	–	4	5
	A.J.Hodd	5	6	1	55	144	28.80	–	1	18/1
2013	J.A.Brooks	16	14	8	37*	142	23.66	–	–	4
2012	S.A.Patterson	15	14	1	43	178	13.69	–	–	1
2000	R.J.Sidebottom	12	12	2	25	112	11.20	–	–	2

Also played (1 match each): Azeem Rafiq 14 (1 ct); K.Carver 2* (1 ct).

BOWLING

	O	M	R	W	Avge	Best	5wI	10wM
R.J.Sidebottom	351.1	84	881	48	18.35	7- 44	2	–
L.E.Plunkett	167	27	596	24	24.83	4- 42	–	–
A.U.Rashid	369.4	71	1199	46	26.06	5-117	1	–
S.A.Patterson	403.4	133	1001	36	27.80	4- 54	–	–
J.A.Brooks	523.2	105	1906	68	28.02	5- 36	2	–
T.T.Bresnan	331	76	947	30	31.56	4-112	–	–
Also bowled:								
A.Lyth	59.2	12	160	5	32.00	2- 18	–	–
K.S.Williamson	61.4	21	160	5	32.00	2- 45	–	–
R.M.Pyrah	99	26	309	6	51.50	3- 37	–	–

Azeem Rafiq 38-6-110-1; J.M.Bairstow 1-0-1-0; K.Carver 20-4-65-3; A.J.Finch 15-4-39-1; J.A.Leaning 6-1-13-0; J.E.Root 13-1-40-1.

The First-Class Averages (pp 217–233) give the records of Yorkshire players in all first-class county matches (Yorkshire's other opponents being Leeds/Bradford MCCU), with the exception of J.E.Root, whose first-class figures for Yorkshire are as above, and:
G.S.Ballance 7-10-0-174-686-68.60-3-3-8.
L.E.Plunkett 8-9-2-86-210-30.00-0-2-4ct. 186-28-663-26-25.50-4/42-0-0.

YORKSHIRE RECORDS

FIRST-CLASS CRICKET

Highest Total	For 887		v	Warwicks	Birmingham	1896
	V 681-7d		by	Leics	Bradford	1996
Lowest Total	For 23		v	Hampshire	Middlesbrough	1965
	V 13		by	Notts	Nottingham	1901
Highest Innings	For 341	G.H.Hirst	v	Leics	Leicester	1905
	V 318*	W.G.Grace	for	Glos	Cheltenham	1876

Highest Partnership for each Wicket

1st	555	P.Holmes/H.Sutcliffe	v	Essex	Leyton	1932
2nd	346	W.Barber/M.Leyland	v	Middlesex	Sheffield	1932
3rd	346	J.J.Sayers/A.McGrath	v	Warwicks	Birmingham	2009
4th	358	D.S.Lehmann/M.J.Lumb	v	Durham	Leeds	2006
5th	340	E.Wainwright/G.H.Hirst	v	Surrey	The Oval	1899
6th	296	A.Lyth/A.U.Rashid	v	Lancashire	Manchester	2014
7th	254	W.Rhodes/D.C.F.Burton	v	Hampshire	Dewsbury	1919
8th	292	R.Peel/Lord Hawke	v	Warwicks	Birmingham	1896
9th	246	T.T.Bresnan/J.N.Gillespie	v	Surrey	The Oval	2007
10th	149	G.Boycott/G.B.Stevenson	v	Warwicks	Birmingham	1982

Best Bowling	For	10-10	H.Verity	v	Notts	Leeds	1932
(Innings)	V	10-37	C.V.Grimmett	for	Australians	Sheffield	1930
Best Bowling	For	17-91	H.Verity	v	Essex	Leyton	1933
(Match)	V	17-91	H.Dean	for	Lancashire	Liverpool	1913

Most Runs – Season	2883	H.Sutcliffe	(av 80.08)		1932
Most Runs – Career	38558	H.Sutcliffe	(av 50.20)		1919-45
Most 100s – Season	12	H.Sutcliffe			1932
Most 100s – Career	112	H.Sutcliffe			1919-45
Most Wkts – Season	240	W.Rhodes	(av 12.72)		1900
Most Wkts – Career	3597	W.Rhodes	(av 16.02)		1898-1930
Most Career W-K Dismissals	1186	D.Hunter	(863 ct; 323 st)		1888-1909
Most Career Catches in the Field	665	J.Tunnicliffe			1891-1907

LIMITED-OVERS CRICKET

Highest Total	50ov	411-6		v	Devon	Exmouth	2004
	40ov	352-6		v	Notts	Scarborough	2001
	T20	213-7		v	Worcs	Leeds	2010
Lowest Total	50ov	76		v	Surrey	Harrogate	1970
	40ov	54		v	Essex	Leeds	2003
	T20	90-9		v	Durham	Chester-le-St[2]	2009
Highest Innings	50ov	160	M.J.Wood	v	Devon	Exmouth	2004
	40ov	191	D.S.Lehmann	v	Notts	Scarborough	2001
	T20	109	I.J.Harvey	v	Derbyshire	Leeds	2005
Best Bowling	50ov	7-27	D.Gough	v	Ireland	Leeds	1997
	40ov	7-15	R.A.Hutton	v	Worcs	Leeds	1969
	T20	5-16	R.M.Pyrah	v	Durham	Scarborough	2011

194

FIRST-CLASS UMPIRES 2015

† New appointment. See page 76 for key to abbreviations.

BAILEY, Robert John (Biddulph HS), b Biddulph, Staffs 28 Oct 1963. 6'3". RHB, OB. Northamptonshire 1982-99; cap 1985; benefit 1993; captain 1996-97. Derbyshire 2000-01; cap 2000. Staffordshire 1980. YC 1984. **Tests:** 4 (1988 to 1989-90); HS 43 v WI (Oval) 1988. **LOI:** 4 (1984-85 to 1989-90); HS 43* v SL (Oval) 1988. F-c Tours: SA 1991-92 (Nh); WI 1989-90; Z 1994-95 (Nh). 1000 runs (13); most – 1987 (1990). HS 224* Nh v Glamorgan (Swansea) 1986. BB 5-54 Nh v Notts (Northampton) 1993. F-c career: 374 matches; 21844 runs @ 40.52, 47 hundreds; 121 wickets @ 42.51; 272 ct. Appointed 2006. Umpired 9 LOI (2011 to 2014). **ICC International Panel 2011 to date.**

BAINTON, Neil Laurence, b Romford, Essex 2 October 1970. No f-c appearances. Appointed 2006.

†**BALDWIN, Paul** Kerr, b Epsom, Surrey 18 Jul 1973. No f-c appearances. Umpired 18 LOI (2006 to 2009). Reserve List 2010-14. Appointed 2015.

BENSON, Mark Richard (Sutton Valence S), b Shoreham, Sussex 6 Jul 1958. 5'10". LHB, OB. Kent 1980-95; cap 1981; captain 1991-96 (did not play in 1996); benefit 1991. **Tests:** 1 (1986); HS 30 v I (Birmingham) 1986. **LOI:** 1 (1986); HS 24 v NZ (Leeds) 1986. 1000 runs (11); most – 1725 (1987). HS 257 K v Hants (Southampton) 1991. BB 2-55 K v Surrey (Dartford) 1986. F-c career: 292 matches; 18387 runs @ 40.23, 48 hundreds; 5 wickets @ 98.60; 140 ct. Appointed 2000. Umpired 27 Tests (2004-05 to 2009-10) and 72 LOI (2004 to 2008-09). **ICC Elite Panel 2006-09.**

BODENHAM, Martin John Dale, b Brighton, Sussex 23 Apr 1950. No f-c appearances. Former football referee who officiated at the 1997 League Cup final and four internationals. Appointed 2009.

COOK, Nicholas Grant Billson (Lutterworth GS), b Leicester 17 Jun 1956. 6'0". RHB, SLA. Leicestershire 1978-85; cap 1982. Northamptonshire 1986-94; cap 1987; benefit 1995. **Tests:** 15 (1983 to 1989); HS 31 v A (Oval) 1989; BB 6-65 (11-83 match) v P (Karachi) 1983-84. **LOI:** 3 (1983-84 to 1989-90); HS – ; BB 2-18 v P (Peshawar) 1987-88. F-c Tours: NZ 1979-80 (DHR), 1983-84; P 1983-84, 1987-88; SL 1985-86 (Eng B); Z 1980-81 (Le), 1984-85 (EC). HS 75 Le v Somerset (Taunton) 1980. 50 wkts (8); most – 90 (1982). BB 7-34 (10-97 match) Nh v Essex (Chelmsford) 1992. F-c career: 356 matches; 3137 runs @ 11.66; 879 wickets @ 29.01; 197 ct. Appointed 2009.

COWLEY, Nigel Geoffrey Charles (Dutchy Manor SS, Mere), b Shaftesbury, Dorset 1 Mar 1953. 5'7". RHB, OB. Dorset 1972. Hampshire 1974-89; cap 1978; benefit 1988. Glamorgan 1990. 1000 runs (1): 1042 (1984). HS 109* H v Somerset (Taunton) 1977. BB 6-48 H v Leics (Southampton) 1982. F-c career: 271 matches; 7309 runs @ 23.35, 2 hundreds; 437 wickets @ 34.04; 105 ct. Appointed 2000.

EVANS, Jeffery Howard, b Llanelli, Carms 7 Aug 1954. No f-c appearances. Appointed 2001. Umpired in Indian Cricket League 2007-08.

†**EVANS, Russell** John (Colonel Frank Seely S), b Calverton, Notts 1 Oct 1965. Younger brother of K.P.Evans (Nottinghamshire 1984-99). 6'0". RHB, RM. Nottinghamshire 1987-90. Minor Cos 1994. Lincolnshire 1994-99. HS 59 MC v South Africans (Torquay) 1994. BB 3-40 Nt v OU (Oxford) 1988. F-c career: 7 matches; 201 runs @ 25.12; 3 wickets @ 32.33; 5 ct. Reserve List 2011-14. Appointed 2015.

GALE, Stephen Clifford, b Shrewsbury, Shropshire 3 Jun 1952. RHB, LB. No f-c appearances. Shropshire (list A only) 1976-85. Reserve List 2008-10. Appointed 2011.

GARRATT, Steven Arthur, b Nottingham 5 Jul 1953. No f-c appearances. Reserve List 2003-07. Appointed 2008.

GOUGH, Michael Andrew (English Martyrs RCS; Hartlepool SFC), b Hartlepool, Co Durham 18 Dec 1979. Son of M.P.Gough (Durham 1974-77). 6'5". RHB, OB. Durham 1998-2003. F-c Tours (Eng A): NZ 1999-00; B 1999-00. HS 123 Du v CU (Cambridge) 1998. CC HS 103 Du v Essex (Colchester) 2002. BB 5-56 Du v Middx (Chester-le-St) 2001. F-c career: 67 matches; 2952 runs @ 25.44, 2 hundreds; 30 wickets @ 45.00; 57 ct. Reserve List 2006-08. Appointed 2009. Umpired 14 LOI (2013 to 2014-15), including 2014-15 World Cup. **ICC International Panel 2012 to date.**

GOULD, Ian James (Westgate SS, Slough), b Taplow, Bucks 19 Aug 1957. 5'8". LHB, WK. Middlesex 1975 to 1980-81, 1996; cap 1977. Auckland 1979-80. Sussex 1981-90; cap 1981; captain 1987; benefit 1990. MCC YC. **LOI:** 18 (1982-83 to 1983); HS 42 v A (Sydney) 1982-83. F-c Tours: A 1982-83; P 1980-81 (Int); Z 1980-81 (M). HS 128 M v Worcs (Worcester) 1978. BB 3-10 Sx v Surrey (Oval) 1989. Middlesex coach 1991-2000. Reappeared in one match (v OU) 1996. F-c career: 298 matches; 8756 runs @ 26.05, 4 hundreds; 7 wickets @ 52.14; 603 dismissals (536 ct, 67 st). Appointed 2002. Umpired 43 Tests (2008-09 to 2014-15) and 101 LOI (2006 to 2014-15), including 2010-11 and 2014-15 World Cups. **ICC Elite Panel 2009 to date.**

HARTLEY, Peter John (Greenhead GS; Bradford C), b Keighley, Yorks 18 Apr 1960. 6'0". RHB, RMF. Warwickshire 1982. Yorkshire 1985-97; cap 1987; benefit 1996. Hampshire 1998-2000; cap 1998. F-c Tours (Y): SA 1991-92; WI 1986-87; Z 1995-96. HS 127* Y v Lancs (Manchester) 1988. 50 wkts (7); most – 81 (1995). BB 9-41 (inc hat-trick, 4 wkts in 5 balls and 5 in 9; 11-68 match) Y v Derbys (Chesterfield) 1995. Hat-trick 1995. F-c career: 232 matches; 4321 runs @ 19.91, 2 hundreds; 683 wickets @ 30.21; 68 ct. Appointed 2003. Umpired 6 LOI (2007 to 2009). **ICC International Panel 2006-09.**

ILLINGWORTH, Richard Keith (Salts GS), b Bradford, Yorks 23 Aug 1963. 5'11". RHB, SLA. Worcestershire 1982-2000; cap 1986; benefit 1997. Natal 1988-89. Derbyshire 2001. Wiltshire 2005. **Tests:** 9 (1991 to 1995-96); HS 28 v SA (Pt Elizabeth) 1995-96; BB 4-96 v WI (Nottingham) 1995. Took wicket of P.V.Simmons with his first ball in Tests – v WI (Nottingham) 1991. **LOI:** 25 (1991 to 1995-96); HS 14 v P (Melbourne) 1991-92; BB 3-33 v Z (Albury) 1991-92. F-c Tours: SA 1995-96; NZ 1991-92; P 1990-91 (Eng A); SL 1990-91 (Eng A); Z 1989-90 (Eng A), 1990-91 (Wo), 1993-94 (Wo), 1996-97 (Wo). HS 120* Wo v Warwks (Worcester) 1987 – as night-watchman. Scored 106 for England A v Z (Harare) 1989-90 – also as night-watchman. 50 wkts (5); most – 75 (1990). BB 7-50 Wo v OU (Oxford) 1985. F-c career: 376 matches; 7027 runs @ 22.45, 4 hundreds; 831 wickets @ 31.54; 161 ct. Appointed 2006. Umpired 14 Tests (2012-13 to 2014-15) and 38 LOI (2010 to 2014-15), including 2014-15 World Cup. **ICC Elite Panel 2013 to date.**

KETTLEBOROUGH, Richard Allan (Worksop C), b Sheffield, Yorks 15 Mar 1973. 6'0". LHB, RM. Yorkshire 1994-97. Middlesex 1998-99. F-c Tour (Y): Z 1995-96. HS 108 Y v Essex (Leeds) 1996. BB 2-26 Y v Notts (Scarborough) 1996. F-c career: 33 matches; 1258 runs @ 25.16, 1 hundred; 3 wickets @ 81.00; 20 ct. Appointed 2006. Umpired 26 Tests (2010-11 to 2014-15) and 54 LOI (2009 to 2014-15), including 2010-11 and 2014-15 World Cups. **ICC Elite Panel 2011 to date.**

LLONG, Nigel James (Ashford North S), b Ashford, Kent 11 Feb 1969. 6'0". LHB, OB. Kent 1990-98; cap 1993. F-c Tour (K): Z 1992-93. HS 130 K v Hants (Canterbury) 1996. BB 5-21 K v Middx (Canterbury) 1996. F-c career: 68 matches; 3024 runs @ 31.17, 6 hundreds; 35 wickets @ 35.97; 59 ct. Appointed 2002. Umpired 26 Tests (2007-08 to 2014-15) and 91 LOI (2006 to 2014-15), including 2010-11 and 2014-15 World Cups. **ICC Elite Panel 2012 to date.**

LLOYD, Graham David (Hollins County HS), b Accrington, Lancs 1 Jul 1969. Son of D.Lloyd (Lancs and England 1965-83). 5'9". RHB, RM. Lancashire 1988-2002; cap 1992; benefit 2001. **LOI:** 6 (1996 to 1998-99); HS 22 v A (Oval) 1997. F-c Tours: A 1992-93 (Eng A); WI 1995-96 (La). 1000 runs (5); most – 1389 (1992). HS 241 La v Essex (Chelmsford) 1996. BB 1-4. F-c career: 203 matches; 11279 runs @ 38.23, 24 hundreds; 2 wickets @ 220.00; 140 ct. Reserve List 2009-13. Appointed 2014.

LLOYDS, Jeremy William (Blundell's S), b Penang, Malaya 17 Nov 1954. 6'0". LHB, OB. Somerset 1979-84; cap 1982. Gloucestershire 1985-91; cap 1985. OFS 1983-84 to 1987-88. F-c Tour (Gl): SL 1986-87. 1000 runs (3); most – 1295 (1986). HS 132* Sm v Northants (Northampton) 1982. BB 7-88 Sm v Essex (Chelmsford) 1982. F-c career: 267 matches; 10679 runs @ 31.04, 10 hundreds; 333 wickets @ 38.86; 229 ct. Appointed 1998. Umpired 5 Tests (2003-04 to 2004-05) and 18 LOI (2000 to 2005-06). **ICC International Panel 2003-06.**

MALLENDER, Neil Alan (Beverley GS), b Kirk Sandall, Yorks 13 Aug 1961. 6'0". RHB, RFM. Northamptonshire 1980-86 and 1995-96; cap 1984. Somerset 1987-94; cap 1987; benefit 1994. Otago 1983-84 to 1992-93; captain 1990-91 to 1992-93. **Tests:** 2 (1992); HS 4 v P (Oval) 1992; BB 5-50 v P (Leeds) 1992 – on debut. F-c Tour (Nh): Z 1994-95. HS 100* Otago v CD (Palmerston N) 1991-92. UK HS 87* Sm v Sussex (Hove) 1990. 50 wkts (6); most – 56 (1983). BB 7-27 Otago v Auckland (Auckland) 1984-85. UK BB 7-41 Nh v Derbys (Northampton) 1982. F-c career: 345 matches; 4709 runs @ 17.18, 1 hundred; 937 wickets @ 26.31; 111 ct. Appointed 1999. Umpired 3 Tests (2003-04) and 22 LOI (2001 to 2003-04), including 2002-03 World Cup. **ICC Elite Panel 2004.**

MILLNS, David James (Garibaldi CS; N Notts C; Nottingham Trent U), b Clipstone, Notts 27 Feb 1965. 6'3". LHB, RF. Nottinghamshire 1988-89, 2000-01; cap 2000. Leicestershire 1990-99; cap 1991; benefit 1999. Tasmania 1994-95. Boland 1996-97. F-c Tours: A 1992-93 (Eng A); SA 1996-97 (Le). HS 121 Le v Northants (Northampton) 1997. 50 wkts (2); most – 76 (1994). BB 9-37 (12-91 match) Le v Derbys (Derby) 1991. F-c career: 171 matches; 3082 runs @ 22.01, 3 hundreds; 553 wickets @ 27.35; 76 ct. Reserve List 2007-08. Appointed 2009.

O'SHAUGHNESSY, Steven Joseph (Harper Green SS, Franworth), b Bury, Lancs 9 Sep 1961. 5'10½". RHB, RM. Lancashire 1980-87; cap 1985. Worcestershire 1988-89. Scored 100 in 35 min to equal world record for La v Leics (Manchester) 1983. 1000 runs (1): 1167 (1984). HS 159* La v Somerset (Bath) 1984. BB 4-66 La v Notts (Nottingham) 1982. F-c career: 112 matches; 3720 runs @ 24.31, 5 hundreds; 114 wickets @ 36.03; 57 ct. Reserve List 2009-10. Appointed 2011.

ROBINSON, Robert Timothy (Dunstable GS; High Pavement SFC; Sheffield U), b Sutton in Ashfield, Notts 21 Nov 1958. 6'0". RHB, RM. Nottinghamshire 1978-99; cap 1983; captain 1988-95; benefit 1992. *Wisden* 1985. **Tests:** 29 (1984-85 to 1989); HS 175 v A (Leeds) 1985. **LOI:** 26 (1984-85 to 1988); HS 83 v P (Sharjah) 1986-87. F-c Tours: A 1987-88; SA 1990-91 (Eng XI), 1996-97 (Nt); NZ 1987-88; WI 1985-86; I/SL 1984-85; P 1987-88. 1000 runs (14) inc 2000 (1): 2032 (1984). HS 220* Nt v Yorks (Nottingham) 1990. BB 1-22. F-c career: 425 matches; 27571 runs @ 42.15, 63 hundreds; 4 wickets @ 72.25; 257 ct. Appointed 2007. Umpired 4 LOI (2013 to 2014). **ICC International Panel (Third Umpire) 2012 to date.**

SAGGERS, Martin John (Springwood HS; King's Lynn; Huddersfield U), b King's Lynn, Norfolk 23 May 1972. 6'2". RHB, RMF. Durham 1996-98. Kent 1999-2009; cap 2001; benefit 2009. MCC 2004. Essex 2009 (on loan). Norfolk 1995-96. **Tests:** 3 (2003-04 to 2004); HS 1 and BB 2-29 v B (Chittagong) 2003-04 – on debut. F-c Tour: B 2003-04. HS 64 K v Worcs (Canterbury) 2004. 50 wkts (4); most – 83 (2002). BB 7-79 K v Durham (Chester-le-St) 2000. F-c career: 119 matches; 1165 runs @ 11.20; 415 wickets @ 25.33; 27 ct. Reserve List 2010-11. Appointed 2012.

WHARF, Alexander George (Buttershaw Upper S; Thomas Danby C), b Bradford, Yorks 4 Jun 1975. 6'5". RHB, RMF. Yorkshire 1994-97. Nottinghamshire 1998-99. Glamorgan 2000-08, scoring 100* v OU (Oxford) on debut; benefit 2009. **LOI:** 13 (2004 to 2004-05); HS 9 v India (Lord's) 2004; BB 4-24 v Z (Harare) 2004-05. F-c Tour (Eng A): WI 2005-06. HS 128* Gm v Glos (Bristol) 2007. 50 wkts (1): 52 (2003). BB 6-59 Gm v Glos (Bristol) 2005. F-c career: 121 matches; 3570 runs @ 23.03, 6 hundreds; 293 wickets @ 37.34; 63 ct. Reserve List 2011-13. Appointed 2014.

RESERVE FIRST-CLASS LIST: Ian D.Blackwell, Ben J.Debenham, Tom Lungley, Paul R.Pollard, Billy V.Taylor, Russell J.Warren, Christopher M.Watts.

Test Match and LOI statistics to 15 March 2015.

TOURING TEAMS REGISTER 2014

INDIA

Full Names	Birthdate	Birthplace	Team	Type	F-C Debut
AARON, Varun Raymond	29.10.89	Singhbhum	Jharkhand	RHB/RFM	2008-09
ASHWIN, Ravichandran	17.09.86	Madras	Tamil Nadu	RHB/OB	2006-07
BINNY, Stuart Terence Roger	03.06.84	Bangalore	Karnataka	RHB/RM	2003-04
DHAWAN, Shikhar	05.12.85	Delhi	Delhi	LHB/OB	2004-05
DHONI, Mahendra Singh	07.07.81	Ranchi	Chennai SK	RHB/WK	1999-00
GAMBHIR, Gautam	14.10.81	Delhi	Delhi	LHB/LB	1999-00
JADEJA, Ravindrasinh Anirudhsinh	06.12.88	Saurashtra	Saurashtra	LHB/SLA	2006-07
KOHLI, Virat	05.11.88	Delhi	Delhi	RHB/RM	2006-07
KUMAR, Bhuvneshwar	05.02.90	Meerut	Uttar Pradesh	RHB/RM	2007-08
MOHAMMED SHAMI Ahmed	09.03.90	Jonagar	Bengal	RHB/RFM	2010-11
PANKAJ SINGH	06.05.85	Sultanpur	Rajasthan	RHB/RMF	2004-05
PUJARA, Cheteshwar Arvind	25.01.88	Rajkot	Saurashtra	RHB/LB	2005-06
RAHANE, Ajinkya Madhukar	05.06.88	Ashwi Khurd	Mumbai	RHB/RM	2007-08
SHARMA, Ishant	02.09.88	Delhi	Delhi	RHB/RFM	2006-07
SHARMA, Rohit Gurunath	30.04.87	Nagpur	Mumbai	RHB/OB	2006
VIJAY, Murali	01.04.84	Madras	Tamil Nadu	RHB/OB	2006-07

NEW ZEALAND A

Full Names	Birthdate	Birthplace	Team	Type	F-C Debut
ASTLE, Todd Duncan	24.09.86	Palmerston North	Canterbury	RHB/LB	2005-06
BENNETT, Hamish Kyle	22.02.87	Timaru	Canterbury	LHB/RMF	2005-06
BRACEWELL, Michael Gordon	14.02.91	Masterton	Otago	LHB/WK	2010-11
BROWNLIE, Dean Graham	30.07.84	Perth, Australia	N Districts	RHB/RM	2009-10
CRAIG, Mark Donald	23.03.87	Auckland	Otago	RHB/OB	2010-11
De GRANDHOMME, Colin	22.07.86	Harare, Zim	Auckland	RHB/RFM	2005-06
HENRY, Matthew James	14.12.91	Christchurch	Canterbury	RHB/RM	2010-11
KUGGELEIJN, Scott Christopher	03.01.92	Hamilton	N Districts	RHB/RM	2011-12
LATHAM, Thomas William Maxwell	02.04.92	Christchurch	Canterbury	LHB/RM	2010-11
RUTHERFORD, Hamish Duncan	27.04.89	Dunedin	Otago	LHB	2008-09
WATLING, Bradley-John	09.07.85	Durban, SA	N Districts	RHB/WK	2004-05

SRI LANKA

Full Names	Birthdate	Birthplace	Team	Type	F-C Debut
CHANDIMAL, Lokuge Dinesh	18.11.89	Balapitiya	Nondescripts	RHB/WK	2009
ERANGA, R.M.Shaminda	23.06.86	Chilaw	Tamil Union	RHB/RFM	2006-07
FERNANDO, A.Nuwan Pradeep R.	19.10.86	Negombo	Bloomfield	RHB/RFM	2007-08
HERATH, H.M.Rangana K.B.	19.03.78	Kurunegala	Tamil Union	LHB/SLA	1996-97
JAYAWARDENA, D.P.Mahela D.	27.05.77	Colombo	Sinhalese	RHB/RM	1995-96
JAYAWARDENA, H.A.Prasanna W.	09.10.79	Colombo	Colombo	RHB/WK	1997-98
KARUNARATNE, F.Dimuth M.	21.04.88	Colombo	Sinhalese	LHB/RM	2008-09
KULASEKARA, K.M.D.Nuwan	22.07.82	Nittambuwa	Colts	RHB/RM	2002-03
MATHEWS, Angelo Davis	02.06.87	Colombo	Colts	RHB/RM	2006-07
PERERA, M.Dilruwan K.	22.07.89	Panadura	Colts	RHB/OB	2000-01
PRASAD, K.T.G.Dhammika	30.05.83	Ragama	Sinhalese	RHB/RFM	2001-02
SANGAKKARA, Kumar C.	27.10.77	Matale	Kandurata	LHB/OB	1997-98
SILVA, Jayan Kaushal	27.05.86	Colombo	Sinhalese	RHB/WK	2002-03
THIRIMANNE, H.D.R.Lahiru	08.09.89	Moratuwa	Ragama	LHB/RMF	2008-09
WELAGEDARA, U.W.M.B.Chanaka A.	20.03.81	Matale	Tamil Union	RHB/LFM	2002-03

NB: A.N.P.R.Fernando is also known as Nuwan Pradeep.

UNIVERSITIES REGISTER 2014

CAMBRIDGE († = Blue)

Full Names	Birthdate	Birthplace	College	Bat/Bowl	F-C Debut
†ABBOTT, James Barrington	25.05.94	Hammersmith	Magdalene	RHB/WK	2014
ARIF, Adil Tahir	08.11.94	Sharjah, UAE	Anglia RU	RHB/RM	2014
BARRETT, William John Michael	16.12.93	Hereford	Anglia RU	RHB/LMF	2014
BARTON, Adam Paul	05.95	Surrey	Anglia RU	LMF	2014
†BATH, Elliot Richard	10.02.92	Winchester	Trinity	LHB/SLA	2014
†DOWDALL, Thomas Robert	24.02.92	Cuckfield	Darwin	RHB/WK	2014
†ELLIOTT, Tom Christopher	21.11.91	Epsom	Sidney Sussex	RHB/RM	2012
ELLISON, Harry Richard Clive	22.02.93	Canterbury	Anglia RU	RHB/OB	2014
†HEARNE, Alexander Gordon	23.09.93	Kensington	St John's	RHB/LB	2013
JOHNSON, James Alexander Michael	25.11.91	Haywards Heath	Anglia RU	RHB/OB	2012
†KHAN, Izhan Saif	05.04.94	Nottingham	Pembroke	LHB/SLA	2014
MANSFIELD, Adam Peter	21.08.91	Bury St Edmunds	Anglia RU	LHB/WK	2014
†POLLOCK, Alasdair William	24.10.93	High Wycombe	Robinson	RHB/RMF	2013
†SADLER, Patrick Thomas	28.09.91	Waltham Forest	Churchill	RHB/RFM	2011
†SEARS, Alexander David	17.12.89	Grantham		RHB/RFM	2014
†SENARATNE, Nipuna Vikum S.	19.10.93	Leeds	Jesus	RHB/RM	2013
†WYLIE, Benjamin Alexander	24.04.94	Belfast	St Catharine's	LHB/SLA	2013
YATES, Chad Samuel Joseph	17.09.88	Leicester	Anglia RU	RHB/LB	2014
ZAIN SHAHZAD	20.09.91	Sialkot, Pakistan	Anglia RU	RHB/RMF	2014

CARDIFF

Full Names	Birthdate	Birthplace	College	Bat/Bowl	F-C Debut
ADAMS, Ryan James	11.03.94	Bristol	Cardiff Met	RHB/RM	2014
BRACEY, Samuel Nicholas	19.05.94	Bristol	Cardiff Met	RHB/WK	2014
GEORGE, Jacob	05.05.94	Ealing	Cardiff	RHB/OB	2014
GRIFFITHS, Sean William	16.05.95	Neath	Cardiff Met	RHB/RM	2014
HAMILTON, Thomas Stuart Ian	23.11.92	Derby	Cardiff	RHB/OB	2014
LIBBY, Jacob Daniel	03.01.93	Plymouth	Cardiff Met	RHB/OB	2014
MORGAN, Alun Owen	11.04.94	Swansea	Cardiff	RHB/SLA	2014
POWELL, Harrison William	01.06.95	Newport	Cardiff	RHB/RFM	2014
QURESHI, Uzair Asad	23.02.93	Lambeth	Cardiff Met	RHB/OB	2012
SALTER, Andrew Graham	01.06.93	Haverfordwest	Cardiff Met	RHB/OB	2012
SCRIVEN, Bradley	08.12.93	High Wycombe	Cardiff Met	RHB/RM	2014
THOMSON, Alexander Thomas	30.10.93	Stoke-on-Trent	Cardiff Met	RHB/OB	2014
WESTPHAL, Andrew Alexander	28.07.94	London	Cardiff Met	RHB/RMF	2014

DURHAM

Full Names	Birthdate	Birthplace	College	Bat/Bowl	F-C Debut
ALEXANDER, Timothy David	01.12.94	Norwich		RHB/RFM	2014
BISHNOI, Chaitanya	25.08.94	Delhi, India	Hatfield	LHB/SLA	2013
DARBY, Hugo Richard Hilton	05.10.93	Kensington		RHB/RM	2014
DIXON, Liam	26.04.93	Durham	Hild/Bede	RHB/RM	2014
JENKINS, William Henry	04.07.94	Yeovil		RHB/RM	2014
MILNES, Matthew Edward	29.07.94	Nottingham		RHB/RMF	2014
PARAAM, Anish Edward	19.07.90	Singapore		RHB/SLA	2014
PURSHOUSE, Christopher John	09.92	Rotherham		RHB/RM	2014
STEEL, Cameron Tate	13.09.95	California, USA		RHB/LB	2014
STEELE, Oliver James	15.10.93	Worcester	Collingwood	RHB/WK	2013
van den BERGH, Frederick Oliver Ed	14.06.92	Farnborough	Hatfield	RHB/SLA	2011

LEEDS/BRADFORD

Full Names	Birthdate	Birthplace	College	Bat/Bowl	F-C Debut
DAVIS, Christian Arthur Linghorne	11.10.92	Milton Keynes	Leeds	RHB/LFM	2014
GUBBINS, Nicholas Richard Trail	31.12.93	Richmond, Surrey	Leeds	LHB/LB	2012
LAWS, Andrew Robert	21.09.91	Reigate	Leeds Met	RHB/OB	2014
LILLEY, Alexander Edward	17.04.92	Halifax	Leeds	RHB/LM	2011
MacLEOD, Charles Alastair Roderick	31.10.92	Camden	Leeds	RHB/WK	2013
MacQUEEN, Alexander	12.01.93	Chertsey	Leeds	RHB/OB	2012
PATEL, Zafir Rashid	14.09.92	Kamboli, India	Bradford	RHB/RMF	2013
ROEBUCK, Charles George	14.08.91	Huddersfield	Bradford	RHB/RM	2010
ROSS, Peter Arthur	02.09.92	Aberdeen	Leeds Met	RHB/OB	2014
ROUSE, Harry Philip	20.10.93	Sheffield	Leeds	RHB/RFM	2013
THOMAS, Ivan Alfred Astley	25.09.91	Greenwich	Leeds	RHB/RMF	2012
VANDERSPAR, William Gordon Rufus	06.10.91	Camden	Leeds	RHB/RM	2013
YOUNG, Daniel Robert	03.10.90	Newcastle upon Tyne	Leeds Met	RHB/RM	2013

LOUGHBOROUGH

Full Names	Birthdate	Birthplace	College	Bat/Bowl	F-C Debut
AKRAM, Basil Mohammad R.	23.02.93	Waltham Forest	Loughborough	RHB/RMF	2014
BAKER, Gavin Charles	03.10.88	Edgware	Loughborough	RHB/RMF	2009
BEST, Mark Treloar	29.11.94	Nuneaton	Loughborough	LHB/RM	2014
BURGESS, Michael Gregory K.	08.07.94	Epsom	Loughborough	RHB/WK	2014
ENDERSBY, Devon Malcolm	12.05.92	East London, SA	Loughborough	RHB/RMF	2012
GRANT, Samuel Edward	30.08.95	Shoreham-by-Sea	Loughborough	LHB/LMF	2014
LESTER, Toby James	05.04.93	Blackpool	Loughborough	LHB/LFM	2012
MacVICAR, William Angus	16.01.92	Lambeth	Loughborough	RHB/RM	2013
PATEL, Anish Kirtesh	26.05.90	Manchester	Loughborough	RHB/OB	2013
RILEY, Adam Edward Nicholas	23.03.92	Sidcup	Loughborough	RHB/OB	2011
SOILLEUX, Adam Charles	29.11.91	Southend	Loughborough	RHB/RMF	2011
STERLAND, Jack Lee	07.01.93	Chelmsford	Loughborough	RHB/OB	2014

OXFORD († = Blue)

Full Names	Birthdate	Birthplace	College	Bat/Bowl	F-C Debut
†CATO, Samuel John	23.11.92	Chiswick	New	RHB/OB	2013
†DAVIES, Joseph Matthew	05.09.92	Salford	St Catherine's	RHB/WK	2012
DAVIES, Jasper William	03.10.92	Northampton	Brookes U	RHB/OB	2014
†FERRABY, Nicholas John	31.05.83	Mkt Harborough	Wycliffe	RHB/RM	2014
†FOGARTY, Ethan John	18.07.91	Canberra, Aus	St Catherine's	LHB/ON	2014
JEFFERY, Benjamin Anthony	31.07.91	Camden	St John's	RHB/LB	2011
†KENNEDY, Augustus Damian John	10.08.90	London	Wycliffe	RHB/RM	2010
KIDD, Matthew James Lewis	22.10.92	Cambridge	Brookes U	RHB/RM	2014
LEACH, Stephen Geoffrey	19.11.93	Stafford	Brookes U	LHB/LB	2014
MARRIOTT, Wilfred William John	11.04.94	Westminster	Brooks U	RHB/OB	2013
†MARSDEN, Jonathan	07.04.93	Sevenoaks	St Hilda's	RHB/RFM	2013
MARTIN, Alexander Thomas Ambrose	07.11.92	Huntingdon	Brookes U	RHB/WK	2014
MORRIS, James Edward	06.07.92	Hereford	Brookes U	RHB/RMF	2012
†O'GORMAN, Thomas Joseph James	10.09.90	Wandsworth	Wolfson	RHB/LB	2014
†O'GRADY, Richard James	21.01.95	Westminster	Merton	RHB/LB	2014
PATERNOTT, Lloyd Christopher	15.01.92	Watford	Brookes U	RHB/OB	2014
PENHALE, Karl William	03.02.92	Wycombe	Brookes U	RHB/RM	2014
POULSON, James Edward	20.02.95	Bury St Edmunds	Brookes U	LHB/RM	2014
SABIN, Lloyd Michael	22.06.94	Banbury	Brookes U	RHB/OB	2014
†SAKANDE, Abidine	22.09.94	Chester	St John's	RHB/RFM	2014
WELLER, Sam David	21.11.94	Chislehurst	Brookes U	RHB/RFM	2014
†WILLIAMS, Thomas James	04.05.94	Epsom	Balliol	RHB/RMF	2013
†WINTER, Matthew James	08.11.93	Crewe	Lady Margaret	RHB	2013

THE 2014 FIRST-CLASS SEASON STATISTICAL HIGHLIGHTS

FIRST TO INDIVIDUAL TARGETS

1000 RUNS	J.M.Vince	Hampshire	17 June
2000 RUNS	–	Most – 1619 A.Lyth (Yorkshire)	
50 WICKETS	Saeed Ajmal	Worcestershire	2 July
100 WICKETS	–	Most – 84 M.H.A.Footitt (Derbyshire)	

TEAM HIGHLIGHTS

HIGHEST INNINGS TOTALS

650-6d	Lancashire v Northamptonshire	Manchester
646	Gloucestershire v Leicestershire	Bristol
626-6d	Surrey v Gloucestershire	Bristol
615-7d	Glamorgan v Gloucestershire	Bristol
610-6d	Yorkshire v Lancashire	Manchester
602-9d	Warwickshire v Northamptonshire	Northampton

HIGHEST FOURTH INNINGS TOTAL

387-4	Nottinghamshire (set 385) v Middlesex	Nottingham

LOWEST INNINGS TOTALS († *One man short*)

54†	Cambridge MCCU v Surrey	Cambridge
67	Durham MCCU v Derbyshire	Derby
81	Surrey v Glamorgan	The Oval
83	Northamptonshire v Durham	Chester-le-Street
84	Worcestershire v Essex	Chelmsford
87	Warwickshire v Sussex	Birmingham
89	Warwickshire v Yorkshire	Leeds
90	Cambridge MCCU v Essex	Cambridge
90	Northamptonshire v Durham	Chester-le-Street
93	Loughborough MCCU v Sussex	Hove
94	Essex v Derbyshire	Chelmsford
94	India v England (*5th Test*)	The Oval
94	Northamptonshire v Yorkshire	Leeds
96	Leicestershire v Hampshire	Leicester
99	Warwickshire v Sussex	Horsham

MATCH AGGREGATES OF 1500 RUNS

1555-33	Middlesex (505 & 271-9d) v Nottinghamshire (392 & 387-4)	Nottingham
1517-29	Gloucestershire (646 & 306-9d) v Leicestershire (565)	Bristol

LARGE MARGINS OF VICTORY

470 runs	Hampshire (286 & 440-3d) beat Essex (121 & 135)	Southampton
408 runs	Derbyshire (289 & 372-3d) beat Leicestershire (141 & 112)	Derby
335 runs	Essex (300-9d & 250-9d) beat Cambridge MCCU (90 & 125)	Cambridge
309 runs	Durham (337 & 359-6d) beat Sussex (205 & 182)	Chester-le-Street
302 runs	Surrey (218 & 259-3d) beat Cambridge MCCU (54 & 121)	Cambridge
Inns & 244 runs	England (486) beat India (148 & 94) (*5th Test*)	The Oval
Inns & 219 runs	Durham (392) beat Northamptonshire (83 & 90)	Chester-le-Street
Inns & 200 runs	Lancashire (650-6d) beat Northamptonshire (180 & 270)	Manchester

NARROW MARGINS OF VICTORY

| 1 wkt | Nottinghamshire (261 & 170-9) beat Lancashire (225 & 205) | Liverpool |
| 1 wkt | Lancashire (421 & 107-9) beat Durham (340 & 187) | Manchester |

SIX FIFTIES IN AN INNINGS

Glamorgan (615-7d) v Gloucestershire	Bristol
Somerset (553) v Yorkshire	Taunton
Surrey (589-8d) v Glamorgan	Colwyn Bay

60 EXTRAS IN AN INNINGS

B	LB	W	NB			
71	26	11	12	22	Derbyshire (428) v Durham MCCU	Derby
68	12	10	2	44	Gloucestershire (646) v Leicestershire	Bristol

Under ECB regulations, Test matches excluded, two penalty extras were scored for each no-ball.

BATTING HIGHLIGHTS
DOUBLE HUNDREDS († *Team record*)

J.H.K.Adams	231	Hampshire v Leicestershire	Southampton
S.G.Borthwick	216	Durham v Middlesex	Chester-le-Street
C.D.J.Dent	203*	Gloucestershire v Cardiff MCCU	Bristol
A.P.R.Gidman	264	Gloucestershire v Leicestershire	Bristol
S.R.Hain	208	Warwickshire v Northamptonshire	Birmingham
A.Lyth (2)	230	Yorkshire v Northamptonshire	Northampton
	251	Yorkshire v Lancashire	Manchester
A.G.Prince	257*	Lancashire v Northamptonshire	Manchester
C.J.L.Rogers (2)	241*	Middlesex v Yorkshire	Lord's
	203*	Middlesex v Somerset	Taunton
J.E.Root	200*	England v Sri Lanka (*1st Test*)	Lord's
J.M.Vince	240	Hampshire v Essex	Southampton

HUNDRED IN EACH INNINGS OF A MATCH

N.L.J.Browne	132*	100*	Essex v Derbyshire	Chesterfield

His first two centuries in f-c cricket, carrying his bat in the first innings.

E.C.Joyce	117	151*	Sussex v Warwickshire	Birmingham
D.K.H.Mitchell	109	151*	Worcestershire v Glamorgan	Cardiff
B.T.Slater	104	119	Derbyshire v Leicestershire	Derby

His first two centuries in f-c cricket.

FASTEST HUNDRED AGAINST GENUINE BOWLING

J.J.Roy (121*)	55 balls Surrey v Gloucestershire	Bristol

MOST SIXES IN AN INNINGS

8	C.D.J.Dent (203*)	Gloucestershire v Cardiff MCCU	Bristol
8	J.J.Roy (121*)	Surrey v Gloucestershire	Bristol
8	M.H.Wessels (158)	Nottinghamshire v Northamptonshire	Nottingham

150 OR MORE RUNS FROM BOUNDARIES IN AN INNINGS

Runs 6s 4s
170	3	38	A.P.R.Gidman	Gloucestershire v Leicestershire	Bristol
154	3	34	J.H.K.Adams	Hampshire v Leicestershire	Southampton

HUNDRED ON FIRST-CLASS DEBUT IN BRITAIN

M.Vijay	146	India v England (*1st Test*)	Nottingham

CARRYING BAT THROUGH COMPLETED INNINGS

N.L.J.Browne	132*	Essex (277) v Derbyshire	Chesterfield
D.K.H.Mitchell	167*	Worcestershire (395) v Gloucestershire	Cheltenham
L.W.P.Wells	79*	Sussex (142) v Somerset	Hove

LONG INNINGS (Qualification 600 mins and/or 400 balls)

Mins Balls
525	421	I.A.Cockbain (151*)	Gloucestershire v Surrey	Bristol
589	446	A.Lyth (251)	Yorkshire v Lancashire	Manchester

BATTING FOR AN HOUR OR MORE WITHOUT SCORING

Mins Balls
81	55	J.M.Anderson	England v Sri Lanka (*2nd Test*)	Leeds

UNUSUAL DISMISSAL – HANDLED THE BALL

C.A.Pujara	Derbyshire v Leicestershire	Derby

NOTABLE PARTNERSHIPS († *Team record*)

Qualifications: 1st-4th wkts: 250 runs; 5th-6th: 225; 7th: 200; 8th: 175; 9th: 150; 10th: 100.

First Wicket
375	A.Lyth/A.Z.Lees	Yorkshire v Northamptonshire	Northampton
270	A.Lyth/A.Z.Lees	Yorkshire v Durham	Leeds
253	M.A.Carberry/J.H.K.Adams	Hampshire v Leicestershire	Southampton

Second Wicket
274†	M.D.Stoneman/S.G.Borthwick	Durham v Middlesex	Chester-le-Street

Third Wicket
392†	G.H.Roderick/A.P.R.Gidman	Gloucestershire v Leicestershire	Bristol
387	W.R.Smith/J.M.Vince	Hampshire v Essex	Southampton
272	C.J.L.Rogers/E.J.G.Morgan	Middlesex v Nottinghamshire	Nottingham

Fourth Wicket
360	I.J.L.Trott/S.R.Hain	Warwickshire v Northamptonshire	Birmingham
332	A.G.Prince/S.J.Croft	Lancashire v Northamptonshire	Manchester

Fifth Wicket
254*	C.D.J.Dent/C.L.Herring	Gloucestershire v Cardiff MCCU	Bristol

Sixth Wicket
335†	L.J.Wright/B.C.Brown	Sussex v Durham	Hove
296†	A.Lyth/A.U.Rashid	Yorkshire v Lancashire	Manchester
225	J.M.Vince/S.M.Ervine	Hampshire v Glamorgan	Cardiff

Eighth Wicket
192 G.C.Wilson/C.T.Tremlett Surrey v Leicestershire The Oval

Ninth Wicket
150† P.Mustard/P.Coughlin Durham v Lancashire Chester-le-Street

Tenth Wicket
198 J.E.Root/J.M.Anderson England v India (*1st Test*) Nottingham
This was a world record 10th-wkt Test partnership.
137† C.N.Miles/L.C.Norwell Gloucestershire v Worcestershire Cheltenham
115 D.J.Balcombe/J.A.Tomlinson Hampshire v Gloucestershire Southampton
111 B.Kumar/Mohammed Shami India v England (*1st Test*) Nottingham

BOWLING HIGHLIGHTS
EIGHT OR MORE WICKETS IN AN INNINGS

C.Rushworth 9-52 Durham v Northamptonshire Chester-le-Street
G.J.Batty 8-68 Surrey v Essex Chelmsford

TEN OR MORE WICKETS IN A MATCH

J.Allenby	10-128	Glamorgan v Hampshire	Cardiff
J.M.Anderson	10- 89	Lancashire v Northamptonshire	Northampton
Azhar Ullah	10-158	Northamptonshire v Sussex	Northampton
L.Gregory	11-122	Somerset v Northamptonshire	Northampton
M.G.Hogan	10-125	Glamorgan v Kent	Cardiff
S.C.Meaker	11-196	Surrey v Kent	Guildford
T.J.Murtagh	10-192	Middlesex v Durham	Lord's
M.S.Panesar	11-168	Essex v Glamorgan	Swansea
T.S.Roland-Jones	12-105	Middlesex v Northamptonshire	Northampton
C.Rushworth	15- 95	Durham v Northamptonshire	Chester-le-Street
J.D.Ryder	10-110	Essex v Kent	Canterbury
Saeed Ajmal (2)	13- 94	Worcestershire v Essex	Worcester
	12-140	Worcestershire v Glamorgan	Worcester
J.D.Shantry	10-131	Worcestershire v Surrey	Worcester
B.A.Stokes	10-121	Durham v Sussex	Chester-le-Street
R.J.W.Topley	10-108	Essex v Glamorgan	Chelmsford
P.D.Trego	11-153	Somerset v Yorkshire	Leeds

HAT-TRICKS

S.C.J.Broad England v Sri Lanka (*2nd Test*) Leeds
The first England bowler to take two hat-tricks in a Test career.
T.D.Groenewald Derbyshire v Essex Chelmsford
A.Sheikh Leicestershire v Gloucestershire Bristol
A.C.Thomas (4 in 4) Somerset v Sussex Taunton
The first Somerset bowler to achieve this feat in f-c cricket.

MOST RUNS CONCEDED IN AN INNINGS

T.M.J.Smith 52-6-183-3 Gloucestershire v Glamorgan Bristol

MOST OVERS BOWLED IN AN INNINGS

J.C.Tredwell 59-12-158-3 Sussex v Yorkshire Arundel

ALL-ROUND HIGHLIGHTS

MATCH DOUBLE (CENTURY AND TEN WICKETS IN MATCH)

J.D.Shantry (101* & 6-87, 4-44)   Worcestershire v Surrey   Worcester

MATCH DOUBLE (CENTURY AND FIVE WICKETS IN AN INNINGS)

A.U.Rashid (159* & 5-117)	Yorkshire v Lancashire	Manchester
J.D.Ryder (120* & 5-24)	Essex v Worcestershire	Chelmsford

WICKET-KEEPING HIGHLIGHTS

SIX OR MORE WICKET-KEEPING DISMISSALS IN AN INNINGS

H.R.Hosein	7ct	Derbyshire v Surrey	The Oval
T.R.Ambrose	6ct	Warwickshire v Lancashire	Manchester
J.M.Bairstow	6ct	Yorkshire v Sussex	Arundel
S.W.Billings	6ct	Kent v Hampshire	Canterbury
B.C.Brown	6ct	Sussex v Warwickshire	Horsham
J.S.Foster	6ct	Essex v Gloucestershire	Chelmsford

NINE OR MORE WICKET-KEEPING DISMISSALS IN A MATCH

H.R.Hosein	11ct	Derbyshire v Surrey	The Oval

Equalling the UK record for dismissals in a match, on his f-c debut.

T.R.Ambrose	8ct, 1st	Warwickshire v Lancashire	Manchester
B.C.Brown	9ct	Sussex v Warwickshire	Horsham
J.S.Foster	9ct	Essex v Gloucestershire	Chelmsford

FIELDING HIGHLIGHTS

SIX OR MORE CATCHES IN THE FIELD IN A MATCH

A.Lyth	7ct	Yorkshire v Middlesex	Scarborough
R.Clarke	6ct	Warwickshire v Durham	Birmingham
L.A.Dawson	6ct	Hampshire v Glamorgan	Southampton

COUNTY CHAMPIONSHIP 2014
LV= FINAL TABLES

DIVISION 1

	P	W	L	D	Bonus Points Bat	Bonus Points Bowl	Deduct Points	Total Points
1 YORKSHIRE (2)	16	8	1	7	48	44	–	255
2 Warwickshire (4)	16	8	4	4	47	43	–	238
3 Sussex (3)	16	6	4	6	44	40	–	210
4 Nottinghamshire (7)	16	6	6	4	50	40	–	206
5 Durham (1)	16	5	4	7	42	42	–	199
6 Somerset (6)	16	4	2	10	42	42	–	198
7 Middlesex (5)	16	4	5	7	35	38	2	170
8 Lancashire (-)	16	3	6	7	30	41	–	154
9 Northamptonshire (-)	16	–	12	4	27	32	–	79

DIVISION 2

	P	W	L	D	Bonus Points Bat	Bonus Points Bowl	Deduct Points	Total Points
1 Hampshire (4)	16	7	1	8	50	38	–	240
2 Worcestershire (5)	16	8	3	5	37	47	–	237
3 Essex (3)	16	7	2	7	37	45	–	229
4 Derbyshire (-)	16	6	5	5	26	41	–	188
5 Surrey (-)	16	4	5	7	43	44	3	183
6 Kent (7)	16	4	6	6	35	42	–	171
7 Gloucestershire (6)	16	4	5	7	28	36	–	163
8 Glamorgan (8)	16	3	6	7	29	41	–	153
9 Leicestershire (9)	16	–	10	6	36	42	–	108

Middlesex deducted 2 points for slow over rate.
Surrey deducted 3 points for slow over rate.

SCORING OF CHAMPIONSHIP POINTS 2014

(a) For a win, 16 points, plus any points scored in the first innings.

(b) In a tie, each side to score eight points, plus any points scored in the first innings.

(c) In a drawn match, each side to score five points, plus any points scored in the first innings (see also paragraph (f) below).

(d) If the scores are equal in a drawn match, the side batting in the fourth innings to score eight points plus any points scored in the first innings, and the opposing side to score three points plus any points scored in the first innings.

(e) **First Innings Points** (awarded only for performances **in the first 110 overs** of each first innings and retained whatever the result of the match).

    (i) A maximum of five batting points to be available as under:
        200 to 249 runs – 1 point; 250 to 299 runs – 2 points; 300 to 349 runs – 3 points; 350 to 399 runs – 4 points; 400 runs or over – 5 points.

    (ii) A maximum of three bowling points to be available as under:
        3 to 5 wickets taken – 1 point; 6 to 8 wickets taken – 2 points; 9 to 10 wickets taken – 3 points.

(f) If a match is abandoned without a ball being bowled, each side to score three points.

(g) The side which has the highest aggregate of points gained at the end of the season shall be the Champion County of their respective Division. Should any sides in the Championship table be equal on points, the following tie-breakers will be applied in the order stated: most wins, fewest losses, team achieving most points in contests between teams level on points, most wickets taken, most runs scored. At the end of the season, the top two teams from the Second Division will be promoted and the bottom two teams from the First Division will be relegated.

COUNTY CHAMPIONS

The English County Championship was not officially constituted until December 1889. Prior to that date there was no generally accepted method of awarding the title; although the 'least matches lost' method existed, it was not consistently applied. Rules governing playing qualifications were agreed in 1873 and the first unofficial points system 15 years later.

Research has produced a list of champions dating back to 1826, but at least seven different versions exist for the period from 1864 to 1889 (see *The Wisden Book of Cricket Records*). Only from 1890 can any authorised list of county champions commence.

That first official Championship was contested between eight counties: Gloucestershire, Kent, Lancashire, Middlesex, Nottinghamshire, Surrey, Sussex and Yorkshire. The remaining counties were admitted in the following seasons: 1891 – Somerset, 1895 – Derbyshire, Essex, Hampshire, Leicestershire and Warwickshire, 1899 – Worcestershire, 1905 – Northamptonshire, 1921 – Glamorgan, and 1992 – Durham.

The Championship pennant was introduced by the 1951 champions, Warwickshire, and the Lord's Taverners' Trophy was first presented in 1973. The first sponsors, Schweppes (1977-83), were succeeded by Britannic Assurance (1984-98), PPP Healthcare (1999-2000), CricInfo (2001), Frizzell (2002-05) and Liverpool Victoria (2006 to date). Based on their previous season's positions, the 18 counties were separated into two divisions in 2000. From 2000 to 2005 the bottom three Division 1 teams were relegated and the top three Division 2 sides promoted. This was reduced to two teams from the end of the 2006 season.

1890	Surrey	1935	Yorkshire	1979	Essex
1891	Surrey	1936	Derbyshire	1980	Middlesex
1892	Surrey	1937	Yorkshire	1981	Nottinghamshire
1893	Yorkshire	1938	Yorkshire	1982	Middlesex
1894	Surrey	1939	Yorkshire	1983	Essex
1895	Surrey	1946	Yorkshire	1984	Essex
1896	Yorkshire	1947	Middlesex	1985	Middlesex
1897	Lancashire	1948	Glamorgan	1986	Essex
1898	Yorkshire	1949	{ Middlesex	1987	Nottinghamshire
1899	Surrey		{ Yorkshire	1988	Worcestershire
1900	Yorkshire	1950	{ Lancashire	1989	Worcestershire
1901	Yorkshire		{ Surrey	1990	Middlesex
1902	Yorkshire	1951	Warwickshire	1991	Essex
1903	Middlesex	1952	Surrey	1992	Essex
1904	Lancashire	1953	Surrey	1993	Middlesex
1905	Yorkshire	1954	Surrey	1994	Warwickshire
1906	Kent	1955	Surrey	1995	Warwickshire
1907	Nottinghamshire	1956	Surrey	1996	Leicestershire
1908	Yorkshire	1957	Surrey	1997	Glamorgan
1909	Kent	1958	Surrey	1998	Leicestershire
1910	Kent	1959	Yorkshire	1999	Surrey
1911	Warwickshire	1960	Yorkshire	2000	Surrey
1912	Yorkshire	1961	Hampshire	2001	Yorkshire
1913	Kent	1962	Yorkshire	2002	Surrey
1914	Surrey	1963	Yorkshire	2003	Sussex
1919	Yorkshire	1964	Worcestershire	2004	Warwickshire
1920	Middlesex	1965	Worcestershire	2005	Nottinghamshire
1921	Middlesex	1966	Yorkshire	2006	Sussex
1922	Yorkshire	1967	Yorkshire	2007	Sussex
1923	Yorkshire	1968	Yorkshire	2008	Durham
1924	Yorkshire	1969	Glamorgan	2009	Durham
1925	Yorkshire	1970	Kent	2010	Nottinghamshire
1926	Lancashire	1971	Surrey	2011	Lancashire
1927	Lancashire	1972	Warwickshire	2012	Warwickshire
1928	Lancashire	1973	Hampshire	2013	Durham
1929	Nottinghamshire	1974	Worcestershire	2014	Yorkshire
1930	Lancashire	1975	Leicestershire		
1931	Yorkshire	1976	Middlesex		
1932	Yorkshire	1977	{ Kent		
1933	Yorkshire		{ Middlesex		
1934	Lancashire	1978	Kent		

COUNTY CHAMPIONSHIP RESULTS 2014

DIVISION 1

	DURHAM	LANCS	MIDDX	N'HANTS	NOTTS	SOM'T	SUSSEX	WARWKS	YORKS
DURHAM	–	C-le-St D 27	C-le-St Drawn	C-le-St D I/219	C-le-St D 54	C-le-St Drawn	C-le-St D 309	C-le-St W I/188	C-le-St Drawn
LANCS	Man L 1w	–	Man Drawn	Man L I/200	L'pool Nt 1w	Man Drawn	Man Drawn	Man Drawn	Man Y I/18
MIDDX	Lord's D 141	Lord's M 10w	–	Lord's Drawn	Lord's M 10w	Uxbridge Drawn	N'wood Aband	Lord's Drawn	Lord's M 6w
N'HANTS	No'ton Drawn	No'ton L 60	No'ton M I/84	–	No'ton Nt 5w	No'ton Sm 52	No'ton Drawn	No'ton W I/105	No'ton Y 271
NOTTS	N'ham Drawn	N'ham Nt 45	N'ham Nt 6w	N'ham Nt I/10	–	N'ham Nt 7w	N'ham Sx 191	N'ham W 98	N'ham Y I/152
SOM'T	Taunton Sm 7w	Taunton Drawn	Taunton Drawn	Taunton Drawn	Taunton Drawn	–	Taunton Sm 6w	Taunton W 215	Taunton Drawn
SUSSEX	Hove Drawn	Hove Sx 7w	Hove Sx I/127	Hove Sx I/85	Hove Drawn	Hove Sm I/11	–	Horsham Sx 226	Arundel Sx 9w
WARWKS	B'ham W I/13	B'ham Drawn	B'ham W I/47	B'ham W I/16	B'ham W 3w	B'ham Drawn	B'ham Sx 7w	–	B'ham Y I/8
YORKS	Leeds Drawn	Leeds Drawn	Scar Y 220	Leeds Y I/120	Leeds Drawn	Leeds Drawn	Scar Y 9w	Leeds Y I/155	–

DIVISION 2

	DERBYS	ESSEX	GLAM	GLOS	HANTS	KENT	LEICS	SURREY	WORCS
DERBYS	–	C'field Drawn	Derby D 6w	Derby Drawn	Derby Drawn	Derby Drawn	Derby D 408	Derby S 10w	Derby D 138
ESSEX	C'ford E 53	–	C'ford Drawn	C'ford E 10w	Colch'r E 2w	C'ford E 9w	C'ford Drawn	C'ford Drawn	C'ford E I/92
GLAM	Cardiff Gm 106	Swansea E 63	–	Cardiff Drawn	Cardiff H 291	Cardiff Gm I/11	Cardiff Drawn	Col B S 9w	Cardiff Drawn
GLOS	Chelt'm D 6w	Bristol Drawn	Bristol Drawn	–	Bristol H 8w	Bristol Gs 290	Bristol Drawn	Bristol Drawn	Chelt'm W 8w
HANTS	So'ton Drawn	So'ton H 470	So'ton H 6w	So'ton Drawn	–	So'ton H 196	So'ton H I/34	So'ton Drawn	So'ton Drawn
KENT	Cant K 10w	Cant Drawn	Cant Drawn	Cant Gs 244	Cant H 196	–	Cant Drawn	Cant K 8w	Tun W Drawn
LEICS	Leics D 9w	Leics E I/79	Leics Drawn	Leics Gs 9w	Leics H 278	Leics K 6w	–	Leics Drawn	Leics W 234
SURREY	Oval D 8w	Oval Drawn	Oval Gm 10w	Oval S 4w	Oval Drawn	Guildford K 89	Oval S 10w	–	Oval Drawn
WORCS	Worcs W I/64	Worcs W 72	Worcs W 249	Worcs Gs 7w	Worcs Drawn	Worcs W 125	Worcs W 204	Worcs W27	–

COUNTY CHAMPIONSHIP FIXTURES 2015

KEEP YOUR OWN RECORD (see page 208)

DIVISION 1

	DURHAM	HANTS	MIDDX	NOTTS	SOM'T	SUSSEX	WARWKS	WORCS	YORKS
DURHAM	–	C-le-St	C-le-St	C-le-St	C-le-St	C-le-St	C-le-St	C-le-St	C-le-St
HANTS	So'ton	–	So'ton	So'ton	So'ton	So'ton	So'ton	So'ton	So'ton
MIDDX	Lord's	Lord's	–	Lord's	N'wood	Lord's	Lord's	Uxbridge	Lord's
NOTTS	N'ham	N'ham	N'ham	–	N'ham	N'ham	N'ham	N'ham	N'ham
SOM'T	Taunton	Taunton	Taunton	Taunton	–	Taunton	Taunton	Taunton	Taunton
SUSSEX	Arundel	Hove	Hove	Horsham	Hove	–	Hove	Hove	Hove
WARWKS	B'ham	B'ham	B'ham	B'ham	B'ham	B'ham	–	B'ham	B'ham
WORCS	Worcs	Worcs	Worcs	Worcs	Worcs	Worcs	Worcs	–	Worcs
YORKS	Scar	Leeds	Leeds	Leeds	Leeds	Leeds	Leeds	Scar	–

DIVISION 2

	DERBYS	ESSEX	GLAM	GLOS	KENT	LANCS	LEICS	N'HANTS	SURREY
DERBYS	–	Derby	C'field	Derby	Derby	Derby	Derby	Derby	Derby
ESSEX	C'ford	–	C'ford	C'ford	C'ford	C'ford	C'ford	C'ford	Colch'r
GLAM	Cardiff	Cardiff	–	Swansea	Cardiff	Col B	Cardiff	Cardiff	Cardiff
GLOS	Bristol	Bristol	Bristol	–	Bristol	Bristol	Chelt'm	Chelt'm	Bristol
KENT	Cant	Tun W	Cant	Cant	–	Cant	Cant	Cant	Beck
LANCS	S'port	Man	Man	Man	Man	–	Man	Man	Man
LEICS	Leics	Leics	Leics	Leics	Leics	Leics	–	Leics	Leics
N'HANTS	No'ton	No'ton	No'ton	No'ton	No'ton	No'ton	No'ton	–	No'ton
SURREY	Oval	Oval	G'ford	Oval	Oval	Oval	Oval	Oval	–

ROYAL LONDON ONE-DAY CUP 2014

This latest format of limited-overs competition was launched in 2014, and is now the only List-A tournament played in the UK. The top four from each group went through to the quarter-finals, with the top team from each group having a home draw against the fourth team in the other group, and the second team in each group having a home draw against the third team in the other group. The winner is decided in the final at Lord's.

GROUP A	P	W	L	T	NR	Pts	Net RR
1 Yorkshire	8	6	2	–	–	12	+1.04
2 Essex	8	5	1	–	2	12	+0.38
3 Gloucestershire	8	4	2	–	2	10	−0.01
4 Derbyshire *	8	4	2	–	2	8	+0.04
5 Leicestershire	8	3	4	–	1	7	−0.39
6 Northamptonshire	8	2	4	–	2	6	−0.27
7 Worcestershire	8	2	4	–	2	6	−0.32
8 Lancashire	8	2	5	–	1	5	−0.27
9 Hampshire	8	1	5	–	2	4	−0.56

GROUP B	P	W	L	T	NR	Pts	Net RR
1 Nottinghamshire	8	4	1	1	2	11	+0.36
2 Kent	8	4	1	1	2	11	+0.24
3 Warwickshire	8	4	3	–	1	9	+0.34
4 Durham	8	4	3	–	1	9	+0.21
5 Glamorgan	8	4	4	–	–	8	+0.23
6 Somerset	8	3	4	1	–	7	+0.06
7 Middlesex	8	3	4	–	1	7	−0.28
8 Sussex	8	3	5	–	–	6	−0.50
9 Surrey	8	1	5	1	1	4	−0.64

Win = 2 points. Tie (T)/No Result (NR) = 1 point.

* Derbyshire were deducted 2 points for a poor pitch v Durham in the 2013 Yorkshire Bank 40.

Positions of counties finishing equal on points are decided by most wins or, if equal, the team with the higher net run rate (ie deducting from the average runs per over scored by that team in matches where a result was achieved, the average runs per over scored against that team); if still equal, the team that achieved the most points in the matches played between them. In the even teams still cannot be separated, the winner will be decided by drawing lots.

Statistical Highlights in 2014

Highest total	383-7	Kent v Somerset	Taunton
Biggest victory (runs)	148	Hampshire beat Lancashire	Manchester
Biggest victory (wkts)	10	Yorkshire beat Derbyshire	Scarborough
Most runs	575 (ave 82.14)	J.A.Rudolph (Glamorgan)	
Highest innings	169*	J.A.Rudolph	Glamorgan v Sussex	Hove
Highest partnership	222	W.J.Durston/W.L.Madsen	Derbyshire v Hampshire	Derby
Most wickets	23 (ave 17.00)	J.S.Patel (Warwickshire)	
Best bowling	5-33	A.U.Rashid	Yorkshire v Hampshire	Southampton
Most economical	10-4-16-2	D.D.Masters	Essex v Leicestershire	Chelmsford
Most expensive	10-0-96-1	M.E.Claydon	Kent v Somerset	Taunton
Most w/k dismissals	22	P.Mustard (Durham)	
Most catches	10	A.Lyth (Yorkshire)	

2014 ROYAL LONDON ONE-DAY CUP FINAL
DURHAM v WARWICKSHIRE

At Lord's, London, on 20 September.
Result: **DURHAM** won by three wickets.
Toss: Durham. Award: B.A.Stokes.

WARWICKSHIRE		Runs	Balls	4/6	Fall
* V.Chopra	b Rushworth	64	113	5	7-123
W.T.S.Porterfield	c Mustard b Rushworth	9	14	1	1- 16
I.J.L.Trott	lbw b Collingwood	2	15	–	2- 29
† T.R.Ambrose	c Breese b Collingwood	11	23	1	3- 63
L.J.Evans	c Breese b Stokes	0	5	–	4- 64
R.Clarke	b Stokes	2	9	–	5- 68
C.R.Woakes	c MacLeod b Breese	23	31	4	6-115
A.Javid	not out	22	28	–/1	
J.S.Patel	c Jennings b Breese	14	14	1/1	8-144
O.J.Hannon-Dalby	c Stokes b Breese	6	14	–	9-162
W.B.Rankin	run out	1	6	–	10-165
Extras	(LB 4, W 7)	11			
Total	**(47 overs)**	**165**			

DURHAM		Runs	Balls	4/6	Fall
* M.D.Stoneman	lbw b Patel	52	52	10	4- 74
† P.Mustard	b Clarke	0	2	–	1- 6
C.S.MacLeod	c Chopra b Clarke	0	7	–	2- 12
K.K.Jennings	lbw b Patel	8	27	1	3- 60
S.G.Borthwick	lbw b Patel	12	23	1	5- 86
P.D.Collingwood	c Porterfield b Hannon-Dalby	21	36	2	6-117
B.A.Stokes	not out	38	59	5	
G.J.Muchall	lbw b Patel	9	12	1	7-130
G.R.Breese	not out	15	24	3	
P.Coughlin					
C.Rushworth					
Extras	(LB 5, W 6)	11			
Total	**(7 wkts; 40.2 overs)**	**166**			

DURHAM	O	M	R	W	WARWICKSHIRE	O	M	R	W
Rushworth	10	2	24	2	Clarke	7	3	20	2
Coughlin	8	0	30	0	Woakes	7.2	0	50	0
Collingwood	10	0	36	2	Hannon-Dalby	7	2	22	1
Stokes	9	0	25	2	Patel	10	2	25	4
Breese	7	0	30	3	Rankin	9	0	44	0
Jennings	1	0	9	0					
Borthwick	2	0	7	0					

Umpires: M.A.Gough and P.J.Hartley

SEMI-FINALS

At Edgbaston, Birmingham, on 4 September. Toss: Kent. **WARWICKSHIRE** won by six wickets. Kent 215-8 (50; W.B.Rankin 3-34). Warwickshire 219-4 (46.3; I.J.L.Trott 58, T.R.Ambrose 51*, V.Chopra 50). Award: W.B.Rankin.

At Riverside Ground, Chester-le-Street, on 6 September. Toss: Nottinghamshire. **DURHAM** won by 83 runs. Durham 353-8 (50; B.A.Stokes 164, P.Mustard 89, A.Shahzad 3-73, L.J.Fletcher 3-82). Nottinghamshire 270 (46.1; J.W.A.Taylor 114, S.R.Patel 52, G.R.Breese 3-53, C.Rushworth 3-60). Award: B.A.Stokes.

PRINCIPAL LIST A RECORDS 1963-2014

These records cover all the major limited-overs tournaments played by the counties since the inauguration of the Gillette Cup in 1963.

Highest Totals		496-4	Surrey v Glos	The Oval	2007
		438-5	Surrey v Glamorgan	The Oval	2002
Highest Total Batting Second		429	Glamorgan v Surrey	The Oval	2002
Lowest Totals		23	Middlesex v Yorks	Leeds	1974
		36	Leics v Sussex	Leicester	1973
Largest Victory (Runs)		346	Somerset beat Devon	Torquay	1990
		304	Sussex beat Ireland	Belfast	1996
Highest Scores	268	A.D.Brown	Surrey v Glamorgan	The Oval	2002
	206	A.I.Kallicharran	Warwicks v Oxfords	Birmingham	1984
	203	A.D.Brown	Surrey v Hampshire	Guildford	1997
	201*	R.S.Bopara	Essex v Leics	Leicester	2008
	201	V.J.Wells	Leics v Berkshire	Leicester	1996
Fastest Hundred	36 balls	G.D.Rose	Somerset v Devon	Torquay	1990
	44 balls	M.A.Ealham	Kent v Derbyshire	Maidstone	1995
	44 balls	T.C.Smith	Lancashire v Worcs	Worcester	2012
	44 balls	D.I.Stevens	Kent v Sussex	Canterbury	2013
Most Sixes (Inns)	15	R.N.ten Doeschate	Essex v Scotland	Chelmsford	2013

Highest Partnership for each Wicket

1st	311	A.J.Wright/N.J.Trainor	Glos v Scotland	Bristol	1997
2nd	302	M.E.Trescothick/C.Kieswetter	Somerset v Glos	Taunton	2008
3rd	309*	T.S.Curtis/T.M.Moody	Worcs v Surrey	The Oval	1994
4th	234*	D.Lloyd/C.H.Lloyd	Lancashire v Glos	Manchester	1978
5th	221*	R.R.Sarwan/M.A.Hardinges	Glos v Lancashire	Manchester	2005
6th	226	N.J.Llong/M.V.Fleming	Kent v Cheshire	Bowdon	1999
7th	170	D.R.Brown/A.F.Giles	Warwicks v Essex	Birmingham	2003
8th	174	R.W.T.Key/J.C.Tredwell	Kent v Surrey	The Oval	2007
9th	155	C.M.W.Read/A.J.Harris	Notts v Durham	Nottingham	1984
10th	82	G.Chapple/P.J.Martin	Lancashire v Worcs	Manchester	1996

Best Bowling		8-21	M.A.Holding	Derbyshire v Sussex	Hove	1988
		8-26	K.D.Boyce	Essex v Lancashire	Manchester	1971
		8-31	D.L.Underwood	Kent v Scotland	Edinburgh	1987
		8-66	S.R.G.Francis	Somerset v Derbys	Derby	2004
Four Wkts in Four Balls			A.Ward	Derbyshire v Sussex	Derby	1970
			V.C.Drakes	Notts v Derbyshire	Nottingham	1999
			D.A.Payne	Gloucestershire v Essex	Chelmsford	2010
			G.R.Napier	Essex v Surrey	Chelmsford	2013

Most Economical Analyses

8-8-0-0	B.A.Langford	Somerset v Essex	Yeovil	1969
8-7-1-1	D.R.Doshi	Notts v Northants	Northampton	1977
12-9-3-1	J.Simmons	Lancashire v Suffolk	Bury St Eds	1985
8-6-2-3	F.J.Titmus	Middlesex v Northants	Northampton	1972

Most Expensive Analyses

9-0-108-3	S.D.Thomas	Glamorgan v Surrey	The Oval	2002
10-0-107-0	J.W.Dernbach	Surrey v Essex	The Oval	2008
11-0-103-0	G.Welch	Warwicks v Lancs	Birmingham	1995
8-0-100-0	D.S.Harrison	Glamorgan v Somerset	Taunton	2010

Century and Five Wickets in an Innings

154*, 5-26	M.J.Procter	Glos v Somerset	Taunton	1972
206, 6-32	A.I.Kallicharran	Warwicks v Oxfords	Birmingham	1984
103, 5-41	C.L.Hooper	Kent v Essex	Maidstone	1993
125, 5-41	I.R.Bell	Warwicks v Essex	Chelmsford	2003

Most Wicket-Keeping Dismissals in an Innings

8 (8 ct)	D.J.S.Taylor	Somerset v British Us	Taunton	1982
8 (8 ct)	D.J.Pipe	Worcs v Herts	Hertford	2001

Most Catches in an Innings by a Fielder

5	J.M.Rice	Hampshire v Warwicks	Southampton	1978
5	D.J.G.Sales	Northants v Essex	Northampton	2007

NATWEST t20 BLAST 2014

In 2014, the Twenty20 competition was sponsored by NatWest. Between 2003 and 2009, three regional leagues competed to qualify for the knockout stages, but this was reduced to two leagues in 2010, before returning to the three-division format in 2012. In 2014, the competition reverted to two regional leagues. (2013's positions in brackets.)

NORTH DIVISION

	P	W	L	T	NR	Pts	Net RR
Lancashire (2)	14	10	2	–	2	22	+0.84
Nottinghamshire (1)	14	9	3	–	2	20	+0.64
Worcestershire (5)	14	8	4	–	2	18	+0.48
Warwickshire (4)	14	7	5	–	2	16	+0.23
Yorkshire (6)	14	6	5	–	3	15	+0.58
Durham (3)	14	5	7	–	2	12	+0.10
Northamptonshire (1)	14	4	7	–	3	11	–0.89
Leicestershire (4)	14	4	9	–	1	9	–0.55
Derbyshire (5)	14	1	12	–	1	3	–1.40

SOUTH DIVISION

	P	W	L	T	NR	Pts	Net RR
Essex (3)	14	10	4	–	–	20	+0.40
Surrey (2)	14	9	5	–	–	18	+0.42
Hampshire (1)	14	9	5	–	–	18	+0.13
Glamorgan (3)	14	6	5	1	2	15	+0.14
Somerset (2)	14	6	7	–	1	13	–0.10
Kent (5)	14	6	7	1	–	13	–0.22
Sussex (6)	14	6	8	–	–	12	–0.02
Gloucestershire (6) *	14	5	7	–	2	10	–0.36
Middlesex (4)	14	2	11	–	1	5	–0.45

* Gloucestershire were deducted 2 points for a substandard pitch in 2013.

QUARTER-FINALS: LANCASHIRE beat Glamorgan by 1 run at Manchester.
SURREY beat Worcestershire by three wickets at The Oval.
WARWICKSHIRE beat Essex by 19 runs at Chelmsford.
HAMPSHIRE beat Nottinghamshire by five wickets at Nottingham.
SEMI-FINALS: WARWICKSHIRE beat Surrey by 16 runs at Birmingham.
LANCASHIRE beat Hampshire by 41 runs (D/L) at Birmingham.

LEADING AGGREGATES AND RECORDS 2014

BATTING (600 runs)		M	I	NO	HS	Runs	Avg	100	50	R/100b	Sixes
J.J.Roy (Surrey)		15	15	1	81*	677	48.35	–	9	157.0	27
L.J.Wright (Sussex)		14	14	2	153*	601	50.08	1	3	162.4	28

BOWLING (21 wkts)		O	M	R	W	Avge	BB	4w	R/Over	
J.S.Patel	(Warwicks)	53.0	–	324	25	12.96	4-19	1	6.11	
D.P.Nannes	(Somerset)	46.3	–	373	24	15.54	5-31	2	8.02	
M.G.Hogan	(Glamorgan)	51.0	–	410	21	19.52	3-30	–	8.03	
D.R.Briggs	(Hampshire)	59.0	–	435	21	20.71	4-28	1	7.37	

Highest total	229-4		Lancashire v Worcs	Worcester
Highest innings	153*	L.J.Wright	Sussex v Essex	Chelmsford
Best bowling	5-22	A.J.Ireland	Leicestershire v Derbys	Chesterfield
Most economical	4-0-8-1	R.Clarke	Warwickshire v Northants	Birmingham
Most expensive	3-0-62-1	B.W.Harmison	Kent v Essex	Colchester
Most w/k dismissals	13	G.C.Wilson (Surrey)		
Most catches	4	A.J.Finch	Yorkshire v Durham	Chester-le-Street
	4	D.K.H.Mitchell	Worcestershire v Northants	Northampton

2014 NATWEST t20 BLAST FINAL
WARWICKSHIRE v LANCASHIRE

At Edgbaston, Birmingham, on 23 August (floodlit).

Result: **WARWICKSHIRE** won by 4 runs.

Toss: Warwickshire. Award: L.J.Evans.

WARWICKSHIRE		Runs	Balls	4/6	Fall
I.R.Bell	c Brown b Flintoff	4	7	–	1- 19
* V.Chopra	b Croft	30	17	2/2	2- 64
W.T.S.Porterfield	b Parry	31	23	3/1	3- 84
R.Clarke	b Smith	27	27	1/1	4-107
L.J.Evans	c Prince b Smith	53	30	2/4	5-170
C.R.Woakes	not out	22	15	3	
A.Javid	not out	2	2	–	
† T.R.Ambrose					
J.S.Patel					
W.B.Rankin					
O.J.Hannon-Dalby					
Extras	(LB 7, W 3, NB 2)	12			
Total	**(5 wkts; 20 overs)**	**181**			

LANCASHIRE		Runs	Balls	4/6	Fall
T.C.Smith	c Evans b Woakes	19	16	–/2	1- 41
A.G.Prince	b Rankin	30	24	3	2- 62
U.T.Khawaja	c Evans b Rankin	16	17	2	3- 77
K.R.Brown	b Woakes	55	28	3/4	7-152
† J.C.Buttler	c Ambrose b Hannon-Dalby	11	8	1	4-102
S.J.Croft	b Hannon-Dalby	6	4	1	5-118
* P.J.Horton	c Ambrose b Patel	1	4	–	6-125
J.Clark	c Bell b Hannon-Dalby	10	8	–/1	8-154
A.Flintoff	not out	20	8	–/2	
S.D.Parry	not out	4	4	–	
J.M.Anderson					
Extras	(B 1, LB 1, W 1, NB 2)	5			
Total	**(8 wkts; 20 overs)**	**177**			

LANCASHIRE	O	M	R	W	WARWICKSHIRE	O	M	R	W
Croft	4	0	17	1	Javid	3	0	34	0
Anderson	4	0	52	0	Woakes	4	0	34	2
Flintoff	2	0	20	1	Clarke	2	0	21	0
Smith	3	0	30	2	Rankin	4	0	21	2
Parry	4	0	30	1	Patel	3	0	34	1
Clark	3	0	25	0	Hannon-Dalby	4	0	31	3

Umpires: R.J.Bailey and M.A.Gough

TWENTY20 CUP WINNERS

2003	Surrey	2007	Kent	2011	Leicestershire
2004	Leicestershire	2008	Middlesex	2012	Hampshire
2005	Somerset	2009	Sussex	2013	Northamptonshire
2006	Leicestershire	2010	Hampshire	2014	Warwickshire

PRINCIPAL TWENTY20 CUP RECORDS 2003-14

Highest Total	254-3		Gloucestershire v Middx	Uxbridge	2011
Highest Total Batting 2nd	226-3		Sussex v Essex	Chelmsford	2014
Lowest Total	47		Northants v Durham	Chester-le-St	2011
Largest Victory (Runs)	143		Somerset v Essex	Chelmsford	2011
Largest Victory (Balls)	75		Hampshire v Glos	Bristol	2010
Highest Scores	153*	L.J.Wright	Sussex v Essex	Chelmsford	2014
	152*	G.R.Napier	Essex v Sussex	Chelmsford	2008
	141*	C.L.White	Somerset v Worcs	Worcester	2006
	129	D.T.Christian	Middlesex v Kent	Canterbury	2014
Fastest Hundred	34 balls	A.Symonds	Kent v Middlesex	Maidstone	2004
Most Sixes (Innings)	16	G.R.Napier	Essex v Sussex	Chelmsford	2008
Most Runs in Career	2827	D.I.Stevens	Kent, Leicestershire		2003-14

Highest Partnership for each Wicket

1st	192	K.J.O'Brien/H.J.H.Marshall	Gloucestershire v Middx	Uxbridge	2011
2nd	186	J.L.Langer/C.L.White	Somerset v Glos	Taunton	2006
3rd	144*	J.H.K.Adams/S.M.Ervine	Hampshire v Surrey	Southampton	2010
4th	159*	L.J.Wright/M.W.Machan	Sussex v Essex	Chelmsford	2014
5th	117*	M.N.W.Spriegel/G.C.Wilson	Surrey v Middlesex	Lord's	2012
6th	126*	C.S.MacLeod/J.W.Hastings	Durham v Northants	Chester-le-St	2014
7th	80	D.T.Christian/T.S.Roland-Jones	Middlesex v Kent	Canterbury	2014
8th	68	M.W.Alleyne/J.Lewis	Glos v Glamorgan	Cardiff	2005
9th	59*	G.Chapple/P.J.Martin	Lancashire v Leics	Leicester	2003
9th	59*	D.J.Willey/J.A.Brooks	Northants v Warwickshire	Birmingham	2014
10th	59	H.H.Streak/J.E.Anyon	Warwickshire v Worcs	Birmingham	2005

Best Bowling	6-5	A.V.Suppiah	Somerset v Glamorgan	Cardiff	2011
	6-16	T.G.Southee	Essex v Glamorgan	Chelmsford	2011
	6-21	A.J.Hall	Northants v Worcs	Northampton	2008
	6-24	T.J.Murtagh	Surrey v Middlesex	Lord's	2005
Most Wkts in Career	136	Yasir Arafat	Kent, Lancashire, Somerset, Surrey, Sussex		2006-14
	136	Azhar Mahmood	Kent, Surrey		2006-14

Most Economical Innings Analyses (Qualification: 4 overs)

4-2-5-2	A.C.Thomas	Somerset v Hampshire	Southampton	2010
4-0-5-3	D.R.Briggs	Hampshire v Kent	Canterbury	2010
4-1-6-2	J.Louw	Northants v Warwicks	Birmingham	2004
4-0-6-1	M.W.Alleyne	Glos v Worcs	Worcester	2005

Most Maiden Overs in an Innings

4-2-9-1	M.Morkel	Kent v Surrey	Beckenham	2007
4-2-5-2	A.C.Thomas	Somerset v Hampshire	Southampton	2010

Most Expensive Innings Analyses

4-0-67-1	R.J.Kirtley	Sussex v Essex	Chelmsford	2008
4-0-65-2	M.J.Hoggard	Yorkshire v Lancs	Leeds	2005
4-0-64-0	Abdul Razzaq	Hampshire v Somerset	Taunton	2010
4-0-63-1	R.J.Kirtley	Sussex v Surrey	Hove	2004

Most Wicket-Keeping Dismissals in an Innings

5 (5 ct)	M.J.Prior	Sussex v Middlesex	Richmond	2006
5 (4 ct, 1 st)	G.L.Brophy	Yorkshire v Durham	Chester-le-St	2008
5 (3 ct, 2 st)	B.J.M.Scott	Worcs v Yorkshire	Worcester	2011
5 (4 ct, 1 st)	G.C.Wilson	Surrey v Hampshire	The Oval	2014
5 (5 ct)	N.J.O'Brien	Leics v Northants	Leicester	2014
5 (3 ct, 2 st)	J.A.Simpson	Middlesex v Surrey	Lord's	2014

Most Catches in an Innings by a Fielder

4	D.Pretorius	Warwicks v Glamorgan	Swansea	2005
4	W.R.Smith	Notts v Surrey	Nottingham	2006
4	D.J.G.Sales	Northants v Worcs	Northampton	2008
4	G.D.Elliott	Surrey v Kent	The Oval	2009
4	G.R.Breese	Durham v Yorkshire	Scarborough	2011
4	A.J.Finch	Yorkshire v Durham	Chester-le-St	2014
4	D.K.H.Mitchell	Worcs v Nothants	Northampton	2014

YOUNG CRICKETER OF THE YEAR

This annual award, made by The Cricket Writers' Club, is currently restricted to players qualified for England, Andrew Symonds meeting that requirement at the time of his award, and under the age of 23 on 1st May. In 1986 their ballot resulted in a dead heat. Up to 1 April 2015 their selections have gained a tally of 2,365 international Test match caps (shown in brackets).

1950	R.Tattersall (16)	1972	D.R.Owen-Thomas 1993	M.N.Lathwell (2)
1951	P.B.H.May (66)	1973	M.Hendrick (30)	1994	J.P.Crawley (37)
1952	F.S.Trueman (67)	1974	P.H.Edmonds (51)	1995	A.Symonds (26 – Australia)
1953	M.C.Cowdrey (114)	1975	A.Kennedy	1996	C.E.W.Silverwood (6)
1954	P.J.Loader (13)	1976	G.Miller (34)	1997	B.C.Hollioake (2)
1955	K.F.Barrington (82)	1977	I.T.Botham (102)	1998	A.Flintoff (79)
1956	B.Taylor	1978	D.I.Gower (117)	1999	A.J.Tudor (10)
1957	M.J.Stewart (8)	1979	P.W.G.Parker (1)	2000	P.J.Franks
1958	A.C.D.Ingleby-Mackenzie	1980	G.R.Dilley (41)	2001	O.A.Shah (6)
1959	G.Pullar (28)	1981	M.W.Gatting (79)	2002	R.Clarke (2)
1960	D.A.Allen (39)	1982	N.G.Cowans (19)	2003	J.M.Anderson (99)
1961	P.H.Parfitt (37)	1983	N.A.Foster (29)	2004	I.R.Bell (105)
1962	P.J.Sharpe (12)	1984	R.J.Bailey (4)	2005	A.N.Cook (109)
1963	G.Boycott (108)	1985	D.V.Lawrence (5)	2006	S.C.J.Broad (74)
1964	J.M.Brearley (39)	1986 {	A.A.Metcalfe	2007	A.U.Rashid
1965	A.P.E.Knott (95)	{	J.J.Whitaker (1)	2008	R.S.Bopara (13)
1966	D.L.Underwood (86)	1987	R.J.Blakey (2)	2009	J.W.A.Taylor (2)
1967	A.W.Greig (58)	1988	M.P.Maynard (4)	2010	S.T.Finn (23)
1968	R.M.H.Cottam (4)	1989	N.Hussain (96)	2011	J.M.Bairstow (14)
1969	A.Ward (5)	1990	M.A.Atherton (115)	2012	J.E.Root (22)
1970	C.M.Old (46)	1991	M.R.Ramprakash (52)	2013	B.A.Stokes (6)
1971	J.Whitehouse	1992	I.D.K.Salisbury (15)	2014	A.Z.Lees

THE PROFESSIONAL CRICKETERS' ASSOCIATION

PLAYER OF THE YEAR

Founded in 1967, the Professional Cricketers' Association introduced this award, decided by their membership, in 1970. The NatWest-sponsored award is presented at the PCA's Annual Awards Dinner in London.

1970 {	M.J.Procter	1985	N.V.Radford	2001	D.P.Fulton
{	J.D.Bond	1986	C.A.Walsh	2002	M.P.Vaughan
1971	L.R.Gibbs	1987	R.J.Hadlee	2003	Mushtaq Ahmed
1972	A.M.E.Roberts	1988	G.A.Hick	2004	A.Flintoff
1973	P.G.Lee	1989	S.J.Cook	2005	A.Flintoff
1974	B.Stead	1990	G.A.Gooch	2006	M.R.Ramprakash
1975	Zaheer Abbas	1991	Waqar Younis	2007	O.D.Gibson
1976	P.G.Lee	1992	C.A.Walsh	2008	M.van Jaarsveld
1977	M.J.Procter	1993	S.L.Watkin	2009	M.E.Trescothick
1978	J.K.Lever	1994	B.C.Lara	2010	N.M.Carter
1979	J.K.Lever	1995	D.G.Cork	2011	M.E.Trescothick
1980	R.D.Jackman	1996	P.V.Simmons	2012	N.R.D.Compton
1981	R.J.Hadlee	1997	S.P.James	2013	M.M.Ali
1982	M.D.Marshall	1998	M.B.Loye	2014	A.Lyth
1983	K.S.McEwan	1999	S.G.Law		
1984	R.J.Hadlee	2000	M.E.Trescothick		

2014 FIRST-CLASS AVERAGES

These averages involve the 489 players who appeared in the 165 first-class matches played by 27 teams in England and Wales during the 2014 season.

'Cap' denotes the season in which the player was awarded a 1st XI cap by the county he represented in 2014. If he played for more than one county in 2014, the county(ies) who awarded him his cap is (are) underlined. Durham abolished both their capping and 'awards' system after the 2005 season. Glamorgan's capping system is based on a player's number of appearances. Gloucestershire now cap players on first-class debut. Worcestershire now award county colours when players make their Championship debut.

Team abbreviations: CU – Cambridge University/Cambridge MCCU; CfU – Cardiff MCCU; De – Derbyshire; Du – Durham; DU – Durham MCCU; E – England; Ex – Essex; Gm – Glamorgan; Gs – Gloucestershire; H – Hampshire; I – India; K – Kent; La – Lancashire; LBU – Leeds/Bradford MCCU; Le – Leicestershire; LU – Loughborough MCCU; M – Middlesex; Nh – Northamptonshire; Nt – Nottinghamshire; NZA – New Zealand A; OU – Oxford University/Oxford MCCU; SL – Sri Lanka(ns); Sm – Somerset; Sy – Surrey; Sx – Sussex; Wa – Warwickshire; Wo – Worcestershire; Y – Yorkshire.

† Left-handed batsman. Cap: a dash (–) denotes a non-county player. A blank denotes uncapped by his current county.

BATTING AND FIELDING

	Cap	M	I	NO	HS	Runs	Avge	100	50	Ct/St
V.R.Aaron (Du/I)		4	7	2	13	31	6.20	–	–	1
J.B.Abbott (CU)	–	1	2	–	41	49	24.50	–	–	1
K.J.Abbott (H)		9	10	1	40	127	14.11	–	–	–
T.B.Abell (Sm)		4	7	–	95	292	41.71	–	3	4
A.R.Adams (Nt)	2007	9	11	–	19	61	5.54	–	–	9
† J.H.K.Adams (H)	2006	16	29	1	231	1215	43.39	1	8	7
R.Adams (CfU)	–	1	1	1	0*	0	–	–	–	2
A.P.Agathangelou (La)		6	12	1	48	185	16.8	–	–	7
B.M.R.Akram (LU)	–	1	2	–	36	37	18.50	–	–	–
T.D.Alexander (DU)	–	2	2	1	2	3	3.00	–	–	–
Kabir Ali (La)		7	11	3	26	134	16.75	–	–	–
† M.M.Ali (E/Wo)	2007	15	21	1	162	962	48.10	2	6	10
J.Allenby (Gm)	2010	17	29	2	100	969	35.88	1	5	15
† T.P.Alsop (H)		2	4	–	33	50	12.50	–	–	2
T.R.Ambrose (Wa)	2007	16	25	2	167	723	31.43	1	4	58/5
H.M.Amla (Sy)		4	4	–	71	118	29.50	–	1	5
† J.M.Anderson (E/La)	2003	11	16	4	81	214	17.83	–	1	5
† G.M.Andrew (Wo)	2008	4	6	1	71*	108	21.60	–	1	–
† Z.S.Ansari (Sy)	2014	18	30	7	112	1029	44.73	2	6	6
† J.E.Anyon (Sx)	2011	8	11	1	50	168	16.80	–	1	2
A.T.Arif (CU)	–	2	4	–	10	16	4.00	–	–	–
U.Arshad (Du)		5	6	1	38*	101	20.20	–	–	–
† Ashar Zaidi (Sx)		10	13	–	88	274	21.07	–	2	3
R.Ashwin (I)	–	2	4	1	46*	106	35.33	–	–	1
T.D.Astle (NZA)		1	1	–	5	5	5.00	–	–	–
Azeem Rafiq (Y)		1	1	–	14	14	14.00	–	–	1
Azhar Ullah (Nh)		14	25	15	28	137	13.70	–	–	–
T.E.Bailey (La)		3	5	3	25*	55	27.50	–	–	–
J.M.Bairstow (Y)	2011	14	18	3	161*	770	51.33	2	4	41/4
G.C.Baker (LU)	–	2	3	–	17	27	9.00	–	–	–
D.J.Balcombe (H)		4	4	2	65*	91	45.50	–	1	–
A.J.Ball (K)		9	10	2	50	268	33.50	–	1	5

217

	Cap	M	I	NO	HS	Runs	Avge	100	50	Ct/St
J.T.Ball (Nt)		5	8	–	31	87	10.87	–	–	–
† G.S.Ballance (E/Y)	2012	14	21	1	174	1390	69.50	6	6	15
† K.H.D.Barker (Wa)	2013	16	21	5	102*	448	28.00	1	1	6
C.A.Barrett (Nh)		1	1	1	20*	20	–	–	–	3
W.J.M.Barrett (CU)	–	1	–	–	–	–	–	–	–	–
A.W.R.Barrow (Sm)		4	7	2	88	218	43.60	–	1	14
A.P.Barton (CU)	–	1	2	1	1*	1	1.00	–	–	–
M.D.Bates (H)		7	10	3	50	181	25.85	–	1	16/2
† E.R.Bath (CU)	–	1	1	–	0	0	0.00	–	–	1
G.J.Batty (Sy)	2011	12	15	3	37	212	17.66	–	–	7
L.E.Beaven (Sy)		1	2	–	2	2	1.00	–	–	1
W.A.T.Beer (Sx)		1	2	–	29	37	18.50	–	–	–
I.R.Bell (E/Wa)	2001	11	19	1	189*	940	52.22	3	5	18
D.J.Bell-Drummond (K)		17	29	3	153	1058	40.69	3	6	5
† H.K.Bennett (NZA)	–	1	1	1	0*	0	–	–	–	–
G.K.Berg (M)	2010	1	–	–	–	–	–	–	–	–
† M.T.Best (LU)	–	2	3	–	50	51	17.00	–	1	1
† P.M.Best (Wa)		1	1	1	50*	50	–	–	1	–
S.W.Billings (K)		17	25	3	92	735	34.31	–	7	53/6
S.T.R.Binny (I)	–	3	6	1	78	118	23.60	–	1	1
† C.Bishnoi (DU)	–	2	3	–	65	89	29.66	–	1	1
† D.E.Bollinger (K)		8	9	5	33*	91	22.75	–	–	4
R.S.Bopara (Ex)	2005	13	20	1	162	863	45.42	2	2	2
P.M.Borrington (De)		7	13	2	86*	281	25.54	–	1	9
S.G.Borthwick (Du)		16	28	1	216	1187	43.96	3	5	30
† M.A.G.Boyce (Le)	2013	5	9	–	68	209	23.22	–	1	4
† M.G.Bracewell (NZA)	–	1	2	–	18	23	11.50	–	–	1
S.N.Bracey (CfU)	–	2	2	–	20	22	11.00	–	–	3
† W.D.Bragg (Gm)		17	31	3	100*	1008	36.00	1	6	6
G.R.Breese (Du)		5	7	–	62	182	26.00	–	1	8
T.T.Bresnan (Y)	2006	10	10	–	95	338	33.80	–	4	5
D.R.Briggs (H)	2012	8	10	4	38*	116	19.33	–	–	2
† S.C.J.Broad (E/Nt)	2008	9	11	1	47	191	19.10	–	–	1
J.A.Brooks (Y)	2013	17	15	8	37*	148	21.14	–	–	4
B.C.Brown (Sx)	2014	16	25	2	163	679	29.52	1	1	55/4
† K.R.Brown (La)		6	10	1	29	112	12.44	–	–	5
† N.L.J.Browne (Ex)		9	15	3	132*	650	54.16	3	2	9
D.G.Brownlie (NZA)	–	1	2	–	17	27	13.50	–	–	2
N.L.Buck (Le)	2011	9	15	6	29*	192	21.33	–	–	2
R.S.Buckley (Du)		1	2	1	9	11	11.00	–	–	–
K.A.Bull (Gm)		3	6	2	12	31	7.75	–	–	–
M.G.K.Burgess (LU)	–	2	3	–	49	91	30.33	–	–	1
† R.J.Burns (Sy)	2014	18	32	4	199	1055	37.67	2	5	24
I.G.Butler (Nh)		2	4	1	48*	76	25.33	–	–	–
J.C.Buttler (E/La)		13	21	1	100*	833	41.65	1	7	39
Craig Cachopa (Sx)		5	10	1	84	441	49.00	–	5	2
† M.A.Carberry (H)	2006	12	21	1	125	847	51.52	3	3	5
A.Carter (Nt)		6	8	1	11*	30	4.28	–	–	–
† K.Carver (Y)		1	1	1	2*	2	–	–	–	1
S.J.Cato (OU)	–	1	2	1	29	53	53.00	–	1	–
M.A.Chambers (Nh)		8	15	3	20	107	8.91	–	–	4
† S.Chanderpaul (De)	2014	8	13	2	92	587	53.36	–	7	–

	Cap	M	I	NO	HS	Runs	Avge	100	50	Ct/St
L.D.Chandimal (SL)	–	2	4	–	47	107	26.75	–	–	4
G.Chapple (La)	1994	15	23	4	45*	459	24.15	–	–	4
P.K.D.Chase (Du)		3	5	3	4*	7	3.50	–	–	1
V.Chopra (Wa)	2012	17	26	2	160	856	35.66	2	5	17
S.H.Choudhry (Wo)	2010	6	10	1	44	209	23.22	–	–	2
J.L.Clare (De)	2012	1	1	–	1	1	1.00	–	–	1
R.Clarke (Wa)	2011	13	19	2	94	574	33.76	–	5	18
† M.E.Claydon (K)		16	22	2	77	291	14.55	–	1	1
J.J.Cobb (Le)		14	26	3	137	803	34.91	1	7	8
I.A.Cockbain (Gs)	2011	9	16	1	151*	443	29.53	1	2	7
† K.J.Coetzer (Nh)	2013	10	18	–	54	350	19.44	–	2	5
M.T.Coles (H)		15	18	–	83	251	13.94	–	1	6
P.D.Collingwood (Du)	1998	17	29	5	102	966	40.25	3	5	9
N.R.D.Compton (Sm)	2011	17	27	3	156	1034	43.08	2	5	10
† A.N.Cook (E/Ex)	2005	11	18	1	181	861	50.64	2	4	18
C.B.Cooke (Gm)		13	21	1	171	870	43.50	1	8	4
D.A.Cosker (Gm)	2000	17	27	7	45	279	13.95	–	–	11
B.D.Cotton (De)		2	2	–	21	36	18.00	–	–	–
P.Coughlin (Du)		5	7	1	85	191	31.83	–	1	3
F.K.Cowdrey (K)		4	7	–	21	85	12.14	–	–	1
O.B.Cox (Wo)	2009	16	25	2	104	604	26.26	1	3	32/3
T.R.Craddock (Ex)		1	1	–	0	0	0.00	–	–	–
† M.D.Craig (Gs/NZA)	2014	2	3	–	28	47	15.66	–	–	2
S.J.Croft (La)	2010	12	20	1	156	786	46.23	2	4	16
S.P.Crook (Nh)	2013	9	16	1	131	378	25.20	1	1	5
G.D.Cross (De)		11	17	–	30	175	10.29	–	–	30/4
T.K.Curran (Sy)		7	7	3	9*	16	4.00	–	–	2
H.R.H.Darby (DU)	–	2	3	–	3	6	2.00	–	–	–
A.L.Davies (La)		10	17	–	62	469	27.58	–	3	16/1
J.M.Davies (OU)	–	1	2	–	7	7	3.50	–	–	4
J.W.Davies (OU)	–	1	1	–	5	5	5.00	–	–	1
† S.M.Davies (Sy)	2011	17	25	1	174	1040	43.33	3	5	9
C.A.L.Davis (LBU)	–	1	2	–	13	14	7.00	–	–	–
L.A.Dawson (H)	2013	10	18	1	64	354	20.82	–	1	15
C.de Grandhomme (NZA)	–	1	2	–	81	81	40.50	–	1	1
J.L.Denly (K)	2012	9	14	–	70	327	23.35	–	3	1
† C.D.J.Dent (Gs)	2010	14	23	1	203*	639	29.04	1	4	10
J.W.Dernbach (Sy)	2011	10	12	4	29	105	13.12	–	–	2
N.J.Dexter (M)	2010	13	22	3	163*	535	28.15	1	3	3
† S.Dhawan (I)	–	3	6	–	37	122	20.33	–	–	5
M.S.Dhoni (I)	–	5	10	–	82	349	34.90	–	4	17
T.M.Dilshan (Sy)		3	5	–	69	185	37.00	–	2	1
L.Dixon (DU)	–	2	2	–	1	1	0.50	–	–	–
G.H.Dockrell (Sm)		9	11	7	27	109	27.25	–	–	2
B.L.D'Oliveira (Wo)		1	2	–	44	51	25.50	–	–	–
A.H.T.Donald (Gm)		1	2	–	59	63	31.50	–	1	1
T.R.Dowdall (CU)	–	1	2	–	75	81	40.50	–	1	4/1
† B.M.Duckett (Nh)		14	24	1	144*	618	26.86	1	5	14/2
† M.P.Dunn (Sy)		14	13	6	31*	66	9.42	–	–	4
W.J.Durston (De)	2012	11	19	4	74*	533	35.53	–	5	14
E.J.H.Eckersley (Le)	2013	16	30	–	119	818	27.26	2	1	12
T.C.Elliott (CU)	–	3	6	–	27	49	8.16	–	–	4

219

	Cap	M	I	NO	HS	Runs	Avge	100	50	Ct/St
H.R.C.Ellison (CU)	–	1	2	–	32	32	16.00	–	–	–
S.L.Elstone (De)		6	9	–	63	199	22.11	–	1	2
D.M.Endersby (LU)	–	2	3	–	53	58	19.33	–	1	1
R.M.S.Eranga (SL)	–	2	4	3	20*	25	25.00	–	–	1
† S.M.Ervine (H)	2005	16	23	4	121	856	45.05	2	4	13
L.J.Evans (Wa)		8	13	–	98	225	17.30	–	1	7
T.C.Fell (Wo)	2013	12	20	1	133	563	29.63	2	1	13
A.N.P.R.Fernando (SL)	–	3	4	1	13	17	5.66	–	–	4
N.J.Ferraby (OU)	–	3	5	–	107	193	38.60	1	1	1
A.J.Finch (Y)		5	6	–	110	291	48.50	1	1	8
S.T.Finn (M)	2009	11	15	5	37*	125	12.50	–	–	6
L.J.Fletcher (Nt)	2014	12	21	–	49	286	13.61	–	–	4
B.T.Foakes (Ex)		11	18	3	132*	421	28.06	1	2	5
† E.J.Fogarty (OU)	–	1	2	–	37	45	22.50	–	–	1
M.H.A.Footitt (De)	2014	17	23	8	26*	156	10.40	–	–	4
J.S.Foster (Ex)	2001	17	25	3	132	976	44.36	2	5	57/3
† J.E.C.Franklin (Nt)		1	2	–	39	63	31.50	–	–	–
O.H.Freckingham (Le)		3	4	1	6	12	4.00	–	–	–
J.K.Fuller (Gs)	2011	7	7	1	28	88	14.66	–	–	1
† A.W.Gale (Y)	2008	13	16	3	126*	562	43.23	2	1	2
† G.Gambhir (I)	–	2	4	–	18	25	6.25	–	–	–
J.S.Gatting (H)		8	12	1	67	191	17.36	–	1	2
J.George (CfU)	–	2	3	–	9	16	5.33	–	–	1
A.P.R.Gidman (Gs)	2004	17	30	2	264	1278	45.64	4	3	14
† W.R.S.Gidman (Gs)	2011	14	21	5	125	852	53.25	3	2	5
J.C.Glover (Gm)		2	2	1	19*	25	25.00	–	–	–
† B.A.Godleman (De)		10	18	1	104*	485	28.52	1	4	7
M.W.Goodwin (Gm)		8	15	–	50	347	23.13	–	1	6
R.O.Gordon (Wa)		2	1	1	14*	14	–	–	–	1
† S.E.Grant (LU)	–	1	1	1	14*	14	–	–	–	–
L.Gregory (Sm)		10	12	1	69	311	28.27	–	1	5
P.J.Grieshaber (Gs)	2014	1	1	–	10	10	10.00	–	–	–
† D.A.Griffiths (K)		2	2	–	12	18	9.00	–	–	–
S.W.Griffiths (CfU)	–	2	2	–	40	61	30.50	–	–	–
T.D.Groenewald (De/Sm)	2011	9	13	3	56*	189	18.90	–	2	4
† N.R.T.Gubbins (LBU/M)		6	11	1	95	290	29.00	–	3	1
H.F.Gurney (Nt)		11	18	9	15	53	5.88	–	–	1
† C.J.Haggett (K)		4	7	–	44	119	17.00	–	–	–
S.R.Hain (Wa)		12	18	2	208	823	51.43	4	1	6
A.D.Hales (Nt/Wo)	2011/2014	12	22	1	183	1032	49.14	3	5	14
A.J.Hall (Nh)	2009	16	29	3	75	693	26.65	–	4	15
T.S.I.Hamilton (CfU)	–	1	1	–	38	38	38.00	–	–	–
R.J.Hamilton-Brown (Sx)		7	14	1	62	265	20.38	–	2	4
† O.J.Hannon-Dalby (Wa)		9	9	4	40	73	14.60	–	–	2
† A.Harinath (Sy)		6	11	1	63	303	30.30	–	2	2
† B.W.Harmison (K)		16	25	1	125	693	28.87	1	2	12
J.A.R.Harris (Gm/M)	2010	9	13	3	41*	156	15.60	–	–	5
J.Harrison (Du)		5	8	3	65	191	38.20	–	1	–
C.F.Hartley (K)		2	3	–	2	2	0.66	–	–	–
J.W.Hastings (Du)		8	14	1	83	337	25.92	–	3	2
† L.J.Hatchett (Sx)		9	13	5	20*	65	8.12	–	–	6
A.G.Hearne (CU)	–	2	4	1	88	127	42.33	–	1	–

	Cap	M	I	NO	HS	Runs	Avge	100	50	Ct/St
T.G.Helm (Gm/M)		5	7	3	17	36	9.00	–	–	2
M.J.Henry (NZA)	–	1	1	–	0	0	0.00	–	–	–
† H.M.R.K.B.Herath (SL)	–	2	4	1	48	65	21.66	–	–	2
C.L.Herring (Gs)	2013	5	7	1	114*	160	26.66	1	–	18/1
J.C.Hildreth (Sm)	2007	16	26	2	182	843	35.12	1	5	19
M F.Hobden (Sx)		3	4	1	4	4	1.33	–	–	–
A.J.Hodd (Y)		5	6	1	55	144	28.80	–	1	18/1
D.M.Hodgson (De/Y)		2	3	–	18	19	6.33	–	–	2
M.G.Hogan (Gm)	2013	13	21	7	36	183	13.07	–	–	6
† K.W.Hogg (La)	2010	8	10	1	47*	98	10.88	–	–	–
P.J.Horton (La)	2007	16	30	2	140	891	31.82	2	3	16
H.R.Hosein (De)		2	2	–	13	17	8.50	–	–	15
D.M.Housego (Gs)	2012	1	2	–	27	27	13.50	–	–	–
B.A.C.Howell (Gs)	2012	11	17	3	78*	360	25.71	–	2	8
A.L.Hughes (De)		13	21	4	82	448	26.35	–	3	5
† C.F.Hughes (De)		5	8	–	53	123	15.37	–	1	3
M.D.Hunn (K)		2	3	2	0*	0	0.00	–	–	1
Imran Tahir (H)		2	4	2	22*	44	22.00	–	–	3
† C.A.Ingram (Sm)		1	2	–	37	51	25.50	–	–	1
A.J.Ireland (Le)		6	10	2	52	111	13.87	–	1	–
† R.A.Jadeja (I)	–	4	8	–	68	177	22.12	–	1	2
P.A.Jaques (Nt)	2014	11	20	2	150*	894	49.66	2	6	3
K.M.Jarvis (La)		2	3	2	1*	1	1.00	–	–	–
A.Javid (Wa)		7	11	2	75	183	20.33	–	1	1
D.P.M.D.Jayawardena (SL)	–	3	6	–	79	220	36.66	–	2	3
H.A.P.W.Jayawardena (SL)	–	2	4	1	25	43	14.33	–	–	7/1
B.A.Jeffery (OU)	–	1	2	–	6	6	3.00	–	–	–
W.H.Jenkins (DU)	–	2	3	–	19	19	6.33	–	–	2
† K.K.Jennings (Du)		17	29	1	103	693	24.75	1	4	5
J.A.M.Johnson (CU)	–	2	4	–	5	14	3.50	–	–	2
R.M.Johnson (De)		3	4	–	21	30	7.50	–	–	8
C.R.Jones (Sm)		9	14	–	87	402	28.71	–	3	8
G.O.Jones (Gs)	2014	3	4	1	93	136	45.33	–	1	6
R.A.Jones (Le/Wa)		5	8	1	35	87	12.42	–	–	–
C.J.Jordan (E/Sx)	2014	10	14	1	41	234	18.00	–	–	18
R.H.Joseph (K)		7	7	2	29*	70	14.00	–	–	2
† E.C.Joyce (Sx)	2009	15	24	2	164*	1501	68.22	8	3	12
Junaid Khan (La)		1	–	–	–	–	–	–	–	–
A.Kapil (Sy)		3	6	1	104*	205	41.00	1	–	2
† F.D.M.Karunaratne (SL)	–	3	6	–	45	166	27.66	–	–	1
† G.Keedy (Nt)		3	6	3	15*	19	6.33	–	–	2
S.Kelsall (Nt)		1	2	–	57	62	31.00	–	1	1
A.D.J.Kennedy (OU)	–	1	2	1	91*	158	158.00	–	2	1
R.I.Keogh (Nh)		9	14	1	129	437	33.61	2	1	6
S.C.Kerrigan (La)	2013	16	24	6	33	156	8.66	–	–	5
A.N.Kervezee (Wo)	2009	16	26	1	110	829	33.16	2	5	8
J.M.Kettleborough (Nh)		9	16	–	73	398	24.87	–	3	4
R.W.T.Key (K)	2001	16	27	1	126	561	21.57	1	2	5
† I.S.Khan (CU)	–	1	1	–	6	6	6.00	–	–	–
† U.T.Khawaja (La)		7	13	–	117	413	31.76	1	3	8
M.J.L.Kidd (OU)	–	1	1	1	0*	0	–	–	–	–
C.Kieswetter (Sm)	2009	14	19	4	78*	509	33.93	–	5	39/4

221

	Cap	M	I	NO	HS	Runs	Avge	100	50	Ct/St
M.Klinger (Gs)	2013	10	18	1	129*	490	28.82	2	1	11
T.Kohler-Cadmore (Wo)	2014	13	23	–	99	516	22.43	–	4	15
V.Kohli (I)	–	5	10	–	39	134	13.40	–	–	1
S.C.Kuggeleijn (NZA)	–	1	2	1	16*	24	24.00	–	–	–
K.M.D.N.Kulasekara (SL)	–	1	2	–	9	10	5.00	–	–	–
B.Kumar (I)	–	5	10	1	63*	247	27.44	–	3	–
† T.J.Lancefield (Gm)		3	5	–	19	24	4.80	–	–	1
† T.W.M.Latham (NZA)	–	1	2	–	20	37	18.50	–	–	1
A.R.Laws (LBU)	–	2	2	–	7	12	6.00	–	–	2
J.Leach (Wo)	2012	12	19	–	74	447	23.52	–	4	2
† M.J.Leach (Sm)		3	3	1	43	59	29.50	–	–	–
† S.G.Leach (OU)	–	2	3	–	20	43	14.33	–	–	2
J.A.Leaning (Y)		11	15	2	99	478	36.76	–	4	4
† A.Z.Lees (Y)	2014	16	23	–	138	1018	44.26	2	5	10
† T.J.Lester (LU)	–	2	2	1	2*	4	4.00	–	–	–
R.E.Levi (Nh)		4	7	–	64	184	26.28	–	2	1
J.Lewis (Sx)		8	10	1	61	174	19.33	–	1	4
J.D.Libby (CfU/Nt)		3	5	1	108	201	50.25	1	1	3
C.J.Liddle (Sx)		2	4	3	0*	0	0.00	–	–	–
A.E.Lilley (LBU)	–	1	1	–	25	25	25.00	–	–	–
T.E.Linley (Sy)		8	12	3	21*	59	6.55	–	–	1
D.L.Lloyd (Gm)		4	6	–	41	82	13.66	–	–	2
† M.J.Lumb (Nt)	2012	14	26	–	99	740	28.46	–	3	4
† A.Lyth (Y)	2010	17	24	1	251	1619	70.39	7	6	36
G.J.McCarter (Gs)	2012	2	3	–	20	24	8.00	–	–	1
† M.J.McClenaghan (Wo)	2014	4	7	1	27	86	14.33	–	–	–
† P.J.McKay (Wa)		1	1	–	28	28	28.00	–	–	2
C.A.R.MacLeod (LBU)	–	2	2	–	4	7	3.50	–	–	3
C.S.MacLeod (Du)		3	5	–	84	142	28.40	–	1	4
A.MacQueen (LBU)	–	2	2	–	13	25	12.50	–	–	–
W.A.MacVicar (LU)	–	2	3	–	79	127	42.33	–	1	1
† M.W.Machan (Sx)		8	14	3	119	385	35.00	1	–	3
W.L.Madsen (De)	2011	17	30	2	111*	1088	38.85	1	8	21
† S.J.Magoffin (Sx)	2013	15	21	10	51	245	22.27	–	1	–
S.I.Mahmood (Ex)		2	4	1	17	30	10.00	–	–	1
G.T.Main (Du)		1	–	–	–	–	–	–	–	1
† D.J.Malan (M)	2010	15	26	1	154*	1137	45.48	2	4	21
† A.P.Mansfield (CU)	–	2	4	1	31*	38	12.66	–	–	6
W.W.J.Marriott (OU)	–	2	3	1	28	53	26.50	–	–	–
J.Marsden (OU)	–	3	4	2	0*	0	0.00	–	–	3
H.J.H.Marshall (Gs)	2006	17	28	3	118	821	32.84	2	3	2
A.T.A.Martin (OU)	–	1	2	–	3	4	2.00	–	–	1
D.D.Masters (Ex)	2008	10	13	–	26	106	8.15	–	–	2
A.D.Mathews (SL)	–	2	4	–	160	306	76.50	2	–	–
G.J.Maxwell (H)		1	2	–	85	109	54.50	–	1	–
S.C.Meaker (Sy)	2012	9	13	2	58	234	21.27	–	2	2
C.A.J.Meschede (Sm)		6	7	1	59*	144	24.00	–	1	2
J.C.Mickleburgh (Ex)	2013	10	16	1	67	374	24.93	–	1	9
J.D.Middlebrook (Nh)	2011	16	30	–	87	825	27.50	–	5	14
C.N.Miles (Gs)	2011	4	7	1	62*	170	28.33	–	1	1
T.S.Mills (Ex)		7	8	5	30	89	29.66	–	–	–
M.E.Milnes (DU)	–	2	2	–	9	9	4.50	–	–	2

222

	Cap	M	I	NO	HS	Runs	Avge	100	50	Ct/St
D.K.H.Mitchell (Wo)	2005	16	27	4	172*	1334	58.00	5	4	28
Mohammed Shami (I)	–	3	6	2	51*	79	19.75	–	1	–
S.C.Moore (De)		10	17	1	128	547	34.18	1	4	6
T.C.Moore (Ex)		4	4	2	17	27	13.50	–	–	1
† E.J.G.Morgan (M)	2008	11	20	1	191	871	45.84	2	4	7
A.O.Morgan (CfU)	–	1	1	1	28*	28	–	–	–	–
C.A.J.Morris (OU/Wo)	2014	17	22	14	24	78	9.75	–	–	7
G.J.Muchall (Du)		11	19	4	158*	550	36.66	1	2	11
S.J.Mullaney (Nt)	2013	12	23	–	91	433	18.82	–	4	10
D.Murphy (Nh)		5	10	3	23*	74	10.57	–	–	7/4
† T.J.Murtagh (M)	2008	14	17	3	42	231	16.50	–	–	3
† P.Mustard (Du)		14	22	2	91	503	25.15	–	4	46/1
J.G.Myburgh (Sm)		13	18	1	91	530	31.17	–	3	3
J.K.H.Naik (Le)	2013	13	22	6	59*	338	21.12	–	1	11
G.R.Napier (Ex)	2003	12	17	–	62	208	12.23	–	1	4
B.P.Nash (K)	2013	16	26	2	126	926	38.58	1	5	8
C.D.Nash (Sx)	2008	12	22	–	178	867	39.40	1	6	6
O.J.Newby (Ex)		2	3	1	4	4	2.00	–	–	1
R.I.Newton (Nh)		12	24	2	114	473	21.50	1	–	6
M.J.North (De)		5	8	–	44	148	18.50	–	–	3
S.A.Northeast (K)	2012	15	25	1	128	905	37.70	4	4	6
L.C.Norwell (Gs)	2011	10	12	5	78	173	24.71	–	1	1
K.J.O'Brien (Sy)		1	1	–	17	17	17.00	–	–	1
† N.J.O'Brien (Le)	2011	15	28	3	133	971	38.84	2	5	43/4
T.J.J.O'Gorman (OU)	–	1	1	1	1*	1	–	–	–	1
R.J.O'Grady (OU)	–	1	2	–	37	46	23.00	–	–	1
† R.K.Oliver (Wo)	2014	7	14	–	179	558	39.85	1	4	2
G.Onions (Du)		6	8	3	40*	111	22.20	–	–	–
C.Overton (Sm)		13	17	3	99	431	30.78	–	3	3
J.Overton (Sm)		8	9	3	56	166	27.66	–	2	–
W.T.Owen (Gm)		6	7	3	37*	93	23.25	–	–	1
A.P.Palladino (De)	2012	15	22	4	60*	342	19.00	–	1	4
† M.S.Panesar (Ex)		15	19	3	38	111	6.93	–	–	3
Pankaj Singh (I)	–	2	4	1	9	10	3.33	–	–	2
A.E.Paraam (DU)	–	2	3	1	22*	31	15.50	–	–	–
† M.G.Pardoe (Wo)	2011	9	13	1	52	284	23.66	–	1	6
S.D.Parry (La)		3	5	–	37	98	19.60	–	–	1
A.K.Patel (LU)	–	2	3	–	49	53	17.66	–	–	–
J.S.Patel (Wa)	2012	16	20	3	105	510	30.00	1	2	9
R.H.Patel (M)		7	6	4	18	27	13.50	–	–	2
S.R.Patel (Nt)	2008	17	32	–	156	1125	35.15	2	6	19
Z.R.Patel (LBU)	–	2	2	–	16	20	10.00	–	–	1
L.C.Paternott (OU)	–	2	3	–	50	68	22.66	–	1	1
S.A.Patterson (Y)	2012	16	15	2	43	183	14.07	–	–	1
D.A.Payne (Gs)	2011	8	11	5	54*	200	33.33	–	1	3
K.W.Penhale (OU)	–	1	2	–	21	26	13.00	–	–	2
M.D.K.Perera (SL)	–	1	2	1	59	59	59.00	–	1	–
S.D.Peters (Nh)	2007	14	26	1	88	599	23.96	–	3	4
A.N.Petersen (Sm)	2013	11	16	1	155	605	40.33	1	4	8
M.L.Pettini (Ex)	2006	4	7	–	71	181	25.85	–	2	6
† T.J.Phillips (Ex)	2006	2	3	–	12	17	5.66	–	–	3
S.A.Piolet (Sx)		7	12	1	103*	283	25.72	1	–	4

223

	Cap	M	I	NO	HS	Runs	Avge	100	50	Ct/St
L.E.Plunkett (E/Y)	2013	12	16	5	86	322	29.27	–	3	4
A.W.Pollock (CU)	–	3	5	1	45	90	22.50	–	–	–
J.A.Porter (Ex)		3	3	2	5	5	5.00	–	–	1
† W.T.S.Porterfield (Wa)	2014	14	23	1	118	778	35.36	1	5	18
J.E.Poulson (OU)	–	1	1	–	40	40	40.00	–	–	–
H.W.Powell (CfU)	–	2	1	1	16*	16	–	–	–	–
K.T.G.D.Prasad (SL)	–	2	3	–	27	27	9.00	–	–	1
† A.G.Prince (La)	2010	16	28	1	257*	1160	42.96	3	3	11
R.D.Pringle (Du)		2	4	1	63*	126	42.00	–	1	–
M.J.Prior (E/Sx)	2003	7	12	2	125	396	39.60	1	1	31
† L.A.Procter (La)		7	12	1	81*	273	24.81	–	1	2
C.A.Pujara (De/I)		8	16	2	100*	441	31.50	1	2	6
C.J.Purshouse (DU)	–	2	3	–	11	19	6.33	–	–	1
R.M.Pyrah (Y)	2010	6	6	2	62	161	40.25	–	1	2
U.A.Qureshi (CfU)	–	2	3	1	26	42	21.00	–	–	–
A.M.Rahane (I)	–	5	10	1	103	299	33.22	1	2	2
† B.A.Raine (Le)		7	13	1	55	239	19.91	–	1	2
† W.B.Rankin (Wa)	2013	7	8	3	12	35	7.00	–	–	1
A.U.Rashid (Y)	2008	15	19	3	159*	577	36.06	2	1	9
O.P.Rayner (M)		8	11	–	77	229	20.81	–	1	12
C.M.W.Read (Nt)	1999	17	27	5	96	952	43.27	–	6	57/1
† D.J.Redfern (Le)		9	17	1	64	463	28.93	–	5	2
† L.M.Reece (La)		9	17	1	53	262	16.37	–	1	4
† G.P.Rees (Gm)	2009	8	16	1	81	396	26.40	–	4	1
M.J.Richardson (Du)		17	29	–	148	1025	35.34	2	5	16
A.E.N.Riley (K/LU)		17	29	10	23*	160	12.30	–	–	12
N.J.Rimmington (H)		1	2	1	65*	65	65.00	–	1	–
A.J.Robson (Le)		16	30	–	115	1086	36.20	1	9	12
S.D.Robson (E/M)	2013	18	31	3	163	1010	36.07	2	5	17
G.H.Roderick (Gs)	2013	4	8	–	171	470	58.75	1	3	14
C.G.Roebuck (LBU)	–	1	2	1	27*	31	31.00	–	–	–
† C.J.L.Rogers (M)	2011	15	28	4	241*	1333	55.54	4	4	10
T.S.Roland-Jones (M)	2012	13	19	3	77	500	31.25	–	3	4
J.E.Root (E/Y)	2012	17	17	3	200*	1052	75.14	3	6	8
P.A.Ross (LBU)	–	2	3	1	16	17	8.50	–	–	2
A.M.Rossington (M/Nh)		9	15	–	103	465	31.00	1	2	14/3
A.P.Rouse (Gs)	2014	4	7	–	49	124	17.71	–	–	13/2
H.P.Rouse (LBU)	–	2	2	–	16	27	13.50	–	–	–
J.J.Roy (Sy)	2014	18	25	4	121*	1078	51.33	3	5	19
† J.A.Rudolph (Gm)	2014	15	27	–	139	857	31.74	2	5	13
C.Rushworth (Du)		17	23	5	46	246	13.66	–	–	4
C.J.Russell (Wo)	2012	1	–	–	–	–	–	–	–	–
† H.D.Rutherford (NZA)	–	1	2	–	5	5	2.50	–	–	–
J.D.Ryder (Ex)	2014	12	18	1	133	630	37.05	2	2	13
L.M.Sabin (OU)	–	2	3	–	29	42	14.00	–	–	1
P.T.Sadler (CU)	–	3	5	2	8	28	9.33	–	–	–
Saeed Ajmal (Wo)	2011	9	10	2	53*	156	19.50	–	1	4
A.Sakande (OU)	–	1	1	–	29	29	29.00	–	–	–
D.J.G.Sales (Nh)	1999	3	6	–	43	103	17.16	–	–	2
M.E.T.Salisbury (Ex)		4	6	1	19	50	10.00	–	–	–
A.G.Salter (CfU/Gm)		5	7	1	25*	75	12.50	–	–	2
G.S.Sandhu (M)		1	1	1	6*	6	–	–	–	–

224

	Cap	M	I	NO	HS	Runs	Avge	100	50	Ct/St
† K.C.Sangakkara (Du/SL)		5	9	–	159	588	65.33	2	3	5
R.R.Sarwan (Le)		5	10	–	60	184	18.40	–	1	3
I.D.Saxelby (Gs)	2008	2	3	–	20	24	8.00	–	–	–
B.Scriven (CfU)	–	2	2	1	44*	55	55.00	–	–	–
A.D.Sears (CU)		1	1	–	29	29	29.00	–	–	–
N.V.S.Senaratne (CU)	–	3	6	–	32	133	22.16	–	–	–
A.Shahzad (Nt)	2013	9	13	5	68*	238	29.75	–	1	2
† J.D.Shantry (Wo)	2009	16	24	7	101*	481	28.29	1	–	7
I.Sharma (I)	–	3	6	3	13	35	11.66	–	–	–
R.G.Sharma (I)	–	1	2	–	28	34	17.00	–	–	–
A.Sheikh (Le)		4	7	2	12	24	4.80	–	–	1
C.E.Shreck (Le)		15	23	6	56	332	19.52	–	1	4
D.P.Sibley (Sy)		6	10	–	61	156	15.60	–	1	5
P.M.Siddle (Nt)	2014	11	16	5	48*	250	22.72	–	–	5
† R.J.Sidebottom (Y)	2000	13	13	2	25	114	10.36	–	–	2
J.K.Silva (SL)	–	3	5	1	152*	298	74.50	1	2	3
J.A.Simpson (M)	2011	15	23	3	110	669	33.45	2	4	36/3
† B.T.Slater (De)		7	14	–	119	646	46.14	2	3	6
† G.C.Smith (Sy)	2013	5	8	–	103	263	32.87	1	1	10
G.M.Smith (Ex)		12	19	1	85	387	21.50	–	2	7
G.P.Smith (Le)		15	28	–	118	862	30.78	2	4	14
R.A.J.Smith (Gm)		8	11	1	57*	105	10.50	–	1	2
† T.C.Smith (La)	2010	15	27	4	79	773	33.60	–	7	10
T.M.J.Smith (Gs)	2013	14	20	4	80	496	31.00	–	1	5
W.R.Smith (H)		16	27	4	151*	1187	51.60	2	6	12
A.C.Soilleux (LU)	–	2	3	1	6*	6	3.00	–	–	1
V.S.Solanki (Sy)	2014	11	18	1	143	587	34.52	1	5	13
† M.N.W.Spriegel (Nh)		13	25	2	97	521	22.65	–	2	6
C.T.Steel (DU)	–	2	3	–	68	121	40.33	–	1	2
O.J.Steele (DU)	–	2	3	3	53*	69	–	–	1	1
J.L.Sterland (LU)	–	2	3	–	27	42	14.00	–	–	1
D.I.Stevens (K)	2005	17	27	2	105	904	36.16	1	4	16
P.R.Stirling (M)		6	10	2	66*	351	43.87	–	4	1
B.A.Stokes (Du/E)		9	14	–	85	314	22.42	–	2	2
O.P.Stone (Nh)		5	9	2	15	46	6.57	–	–	2
† M.D.Stoneman (Du)		17	29	–	187	1021	35.20	3	4	5
† J.S.Sykes (Le)		3	6	1	8*	35	7.00	–	–	2
Tanveer Sikandar (Ex)		2	2	–	5	5	2.50	–	–	–
W.A.Tavaré (Gs)	2014	16	28	2	139	1014	39.00	4	3	12
B.J.Taylor (H)		1	1	–	1	1	1.00	–	–	1
J.M.R.Taylor (Gs)	2010	3	5	–	40	76	15.20	–	–	–
J.W.A.Taylor (Nt)	2012	15	28	2	126	992	38.15	1	8	7
M.D.Taylor (Gs)	2013	10	12	5	32*	118	16.85	–	–	2
† R.M.L.Taylor (Le)		15	27	1	98	567	21.80	–	4	7
T.A.I.Taylor (De)		6	9	2	40	115	16.42	–	–	1
R.N.ten Doeschate (Ex)	2006	8	10	2	104*	283	35.37	1	1	3
† H.D.R.L.Thirimanne (SL)	–	3	5	–	156	160	32.00	1	–	3
A.C.Thomas (Sm)	2008	15	18	6	54	225	18.75	–	1	–
I.A.A.Thomas (LBU)	–	2	2	1	5*	8	8.00	–	–	1
A.T.Thomson (CfU)	–	2	2	–	25	25	12.50	–	–	–
M.A.Thornely (Le)		1	1	–	21	21	21.00	–	–	–
† J.A.Tomlinson (H)	2008	16	16	10	51	135	22.50	–	1	2

	Cap	M	I	NO	HS	Runs	Avge	100	50	Ct/St
R.J.W.Topley (Ex)	2013	4	5	3	12	18	9.00	–	–	–
† J.C.Tredwell (K/Sx)	2007	9	15	1	50*	299	21.35	–	1	16
P.D.Trego (Sm)	2007	15	20	1	107*	644	33.89	1	3	4
C.T.Tremlett (Sy)	2014	10	11	2	90	273	30.33	–	2	2
† M.E.Trescothick (Sm)	1999	17	27	–	133	1156	42.81	4	6	24
I.J.L.Trott (Wa)	2005	9	14	–	164	628	44.85	3	1	8
† J.O.Troughton (Wa)	2002	2	3	–	69	101	33.66	–	1	2
M.L.Turner (De)		2	3	–	6	6	2.00	–	–	1
F.O.E.van den Bergh (DU)	–	2	3	–	4	4	1.33	–	–	1
W.G.R.Vanderspar (LBU)	–	2	3	2	60*	85	85.00	–	1	1
K.S.Velani (Ex)		4	5	1	29	98	24.50	–	–	–
M.Vijay (I)	–	5	10	–	146	402	40.20	1	2	2
J.M.Vince (H)	2013	16	28	3	240	1525	61.00	4	7	22
G.G.Wagg (Gm)	2013	12	21	5	116*	572	35.75	1	5	4
† N.Wagner (Nh)		5	8	–	18	52	6.50	–	–	1
† D.J.Wainwright (De)	2012	14	22	5	109	467	27.47	1	3	4
† M.A.Wallace (Gm)	2003	17	29	3	82	669	25.73	–	4	68/3
S.J.Walters (Gm)		6	10	1	143	356	39.55	1	1	9
B.J.Watling (NZA)	–	1	2	1	55*	74	74.00	–	1	1
U.W.M.B.C.A.Welagedara (SL)	–	1	1	1	5*	5	–	–	–	–
S.D.Weller (OU)	–	2	3	1	18*	33	16.50	–	–	–
† L.W.P.Wells (Sx)		16	29	1	162	1016	36.28	1	7	11
T.J.Wells (Le)		1	2	–	15	28	14.00	–	–	1
M.H.Wessels (Nt)		17	31	4	158	1213	44.92	1	8	24
T.Westley (Ex)		17	29	3	116	744	28.61	1	4	21
A.A.Westphal (CfU)	–	2	1	–	4	4	4.00	–	–	–
† I.J.Westwood (Wa)	2008	8	11	–	129	370	33.63	1	1	3
A.J.A.Wheater (H)		12	20	1	107	610	32.10	1	3	19/2
G.G.White (Nh)		3	4	–	6	14	3.50	–	–	–
W.A.White (De/La)		8	12	1	38	93	8.45	–	–	2
R.A.Whiteley (Wo)	2013	9	12	–	43	214	17.83	–	–	3
D.J.Willey (Nh)	2013	9	16	–	53	289	18.06	–	2	1
T.J.Williams (OU)	–	1	1	–	29	29	29.00	–	–	–
K.S.Williamson (Y)		9	13	2	189	629	57.18	1	4	10
G.C.Wilson (Sy)	2014	17	24	5	160*	844	44.42	1	6	38/2
M.J.Winter (OU)	–	2	3	–	37	75	25.00	–	–	1
C.R.Woakes (E/Wa)	2009	12	19	4	91	350	23.33	–	1	6
C.P.Wood (H)		4	6	1	61	132	26.40	–	1	1
† L.Wood (Nt)		1	2	1	12	17	17.00	–	–	–
M.A.Wood (Du)		7	11	2	20*	127	14.11	–	–	1
† S.K.W.Wood (Nt)		1	2	1	24*	30	30.00	–	–	–
B.J.Wright (Gm)	2011	7	11	–	123	254	23.09	1	–	3
C.J.C.Wright (Wa)	2013	12	15	3	65	221	18.41	–	2	1
L.J.Wright (Sx)	2007	12	21	3	189	933	51.83	3	3	2
A.C.F.Wyatt (Le)		3	5	–	32	59	11.80	–	–	–
† B.A.Wylie (CU)	–	1	2	1	6	10	10.00	–	–	2
† M.H.Yardy (Sx)	2005	9	15	–	139	368	24.53	1	1	13
C.S.J.Yates (CU)	–	2	4	–	9	17	4.25	–	–	4
D.R.Young (LBU)	–	1	2	–	5	5	2.50	–	–	1
Zain Shahzad (CU)	–	2	4	–	16	44	11.00	–	–	–

BOWLING

See BATTING AND FIELDING section for details of matches and caps

	Cat	O	M	R	W	Avge	Best	5wI	10wM
V.R.Aaron (Du/I)	RFM	87.3	12	358	8	44.75	3- 97	–	–
K.J.Abbott (H)	RFM	251	77	732	36	20.33	5- 44	2	–
T.B.Abell (Sm)	RM	2	0	11	0			–	–
A.R.Adams (Nt)	RMF	294.5	47	1013	36	28.13	5- 65	1	–
R.Adams (CfU)	RM	20	1	78	0			–	–
B.M.R.Akram (LU)	RMF	17	3	88	2	44.00	2- 82	–	–
T.D.Alexander (DU)	RFM	34.5	3	148	5	29.60	4- 80	–	–
Kabir Ali (La)	RMF	146.4	31	517	17	30.41	3- 17	–	–
M.M.Ali (E/Wo)	OB	366.3	56	1170	37	31.62	6- 67	1	–
J.Allenby (Gm)	RM	451.4	123	1119	54	20.72	6- 54	2	1
H.M.Amla (Sy)	RM	1	0	2	0			–	–
J.M.Anderson (E/La)	RFM	460.4	135	1205	58	20.77	5- 41	4	1
G.M.Andrew (Wo)	RMF	106	25	319	20	15.95	5- 40	1	–
Z.S.Ansari (Sy)	SLA	303.5	51	914	25	36.56	5- 93	1	–
J.E.Anyon (Sx)	RFM	181.3	27	793	21	37.76	5- 14	1	–
A.T.Arif (CU)	RM	54.2	13	164	4	41.00	2- 29	–	–
U.Arshad (Du)	RMF	95.1	22	334	14	23.85	4- 78	–	–
Ashar Zaidi (Sx)	SLA	211.2	32	619	22	28.13	3- 36	–	–
R.Ashwin (I)	OB	35.3	3	101	3	33.66	3- 72	–	–
T.D.Astle (NZA)	LB	15	1	83	4	20.75	4- 83	–	–
Azeem Rafiq (Y)	OB	38	6	110	1	110.00	1- 79	–	–
Azhar Ullah (Nh)	RFM	462.1	92	1504	46	32.69	7- 76	1	1
T.E.Bailey (La)	RMF	85	19	272	6	45.33	2- 36	–	–
J.M.Bairstow (Y)	RM	1	0	1	0			–	–
G.C.Baker (LU)	RMF	40	3	212	1	212.00	1- 87	–	–
D.J.Balcombe (H)	RFM	63	10	244	5	48.80	3- 53	–	–
A.J.Ball (K)	LFM	95.2	11	364	7	52.00	2- 29	–	–
J.T.Ball (Nt)	RM	93	19	275	11	25.00	3- 60	–	–
G.S.Ballance (Y)	LB	2	1	5	0			–	–
K.H.D.Barker (Wa)	LM	456.5	96	1412	51	27.68	6- 46	2	–
C.A.Barnett (Nh)	RMF	27	2	109	0			–	–
W.J.M.Barrett (CU)	LMF	0.4	0	2	0			–	–
A.P.Barton (CU)	LMF	11	0	70	1	70.00	1- 25	–	–
E.R.Bath (CU)	SLA	39	7	103	2	51.50	1- 33	–	–
G.J.Batty (Sy)	OB	400.3	113	915	39	23.46	8- 68	1	–
L.E.Beaven (Sy)	SLA	23	6	86	2	43.00	1- 39	–	–
W.A.T.Beer (Sx)	LB	13	1	76	0			–	–
H.K.Bennett (NZA)	RMF	23	7	58	2	29.00	1- 25	–	–
G.K.Berg (M)	RMF	20	7	50	0			–	–
P.M.Best (Wa)	SLA	6	1	30	0			–	–
S.W.Billings (K)	(WK)	0.1	0	4	0			–	–
S.T.R.Binny (I)	RM	32	0	140	0			–	–
C.Bishnoi (DU)	SLA	24	2	89	4	22.25	3- 71	–	–
D.E.Bollinger (DU)	LFM	241.4	54	713	27	26.40	5- 29	2	–
R.S.Bopara (Ex)	RM	95	18	320	10	32.00	3- 14	–	–
S.G.Borthwick (Du)	LBG	183.2	13	762	13	58.61	3- 70	–	–
W.D.Bragg (Gm)	RM	19.3	2	76	0			–	–
G.R.Breese (Du)	OB	57	14	180	2	90.00	2- 39	–	–
T.T.Bresnan (Y)	RFM	331	76	947	30	31.56	4-112	–	–
D.R.Briggs (H)	SLA	250.1	73	705	27	26.11	5- 50	1	–

227

	Cat	O	M	R	W	Avge	Best	5wI	10wM
S.C.J.Broad (E/Nt)	RFM	320.5	92	856	31	27.61	6-25	1	–
J.A.Brooks (Y)	RFM	540.2	113	1941	71	27.33	5-36	2	–
B.C.Brown (Sx)	(WK)	4	1	14	0				
N.L.J.Browne (Ex)	LB	22	4	94	0				
N.L.Buck (Le)	RMF	327.1	54	1290	42	30.71	5-76	3	–
R.S.Buckley (Du)	OB	2	0	9	0				
K.A.Bull (Gm)	OB	44.3	6	168	7	24.00	4-62	–	–
R.J.Burns (Sy)	RM	6	1	18	1	18.00	1-18	–	–
I.G.Butler (Nh)	RFM	51	11	179	4	44.75	4-41	–	–
M.A.Carberry (H)	OB	5	0	31	0				
A.Carter (Nt)	RM	143.5	32	458	21	21.80	5-55	1	–
K.Carver (Y)	SLA	20	4	65	3	21.66	2-27	–	–
S.J.Cato (OU)	OB	49	18	69	1	69.00	1-31	–	–
M.A.Chambers (Nh)	RFM	222.3	37	814	13	62.61	2-23	–	–
G.Chapple (La)	RMF	500.4	99	1415	39	36.28	5-51	1	–
P.K.D.Chase (Du)	RMF	46.2	5	173	11	15.72	5-64	1	–
V.Chopra (Wa)	LB	1	0	1	0				
S.H.Choudhry (Wo)	SLA	108.1	13	384	8	48.00	3-79	–	–
J.L.Clare (De)	RMF	12.1	4	24	2	12.00	2- 6	–	–
R.Clarke (Wa)	RFM	261	46	771	20	38.55	3-54	–	–
M.E.Claydon (K)	RMF	525.1	93	1761	59	29.84	5-61	3	–
J.J.Cobb (Le)	LB	22	1	84	0				
K.J.Coetzer (Nh)	RM	41	2	155	2	77.50	1-26	–	–
M.T.Coles (H)	RMF	353.3	80	1165	41	28.41	4-84	–	–
P.D.Collingwood (Du)	RM	85	19	306	9	34.00	3-26	–	–
N.R.D.Compton (Sm)	OB	1	0	8	0				
A.N.Cook (E/Ex)	OB	2	0	6	1	6.00	1- 6	–	–
D.A.Cosker (Gm)	SLA	425.4	115	1183	42	28.16	5-39	3	–
B.D.Cotton (De)	RMF	39.1	10	111	8	13.87	4-20	–	–
P.Coughlin (Du)	RM	80	21	306	9	34.00	3-42	–	–
F.K.Cowdrey (K)	SLA	12.4	1	59	3	19.66	3-59	–	–
T.R.Craddock (Ex)	LB	11	1	53	1	53.00	1-30	–	–
M.D.Craig (Gs/NZA)	OB	34	4	132	3	44.00	2-85	–	–
S.J.Croft (La)	RMF	113	10	357	8	44.62	3-25	–	–
S.P.Crook (Nh)	RFM	244	25	963	16	60.18	3-26	–	–
T.K.Curran (Sy)	RFM	154.2	26	526	19	27.68	5-51	1	–
L.A.Dawson (H)	SLA	175.3	40	529	17	31.11	4-58	–	–
C.de Grandhomme (NZA)	RFM	10	2	29	2	14.50	2-16	–	–
J.L.Denly (M)	LB	43.2	7	157	4	39.25	2-31	–	–
C.D.J.Dent (Gs)	SLA	35.3	2	165	1	165.00	1-39	–	–
J.W.Dernbach (Sy)	RFM	275.3	55	949	28	33.89	4-72	–	–
N.J.Dexter (M)	RM	256	65	771	17	45.35	6-63	1	–
S.Dhawan (I)	OB	4	0	6	0				
T.M.Dilshan (Sy)	OB	15	3	29	2	14.50	2-29	–	–
L.Dixon (DU)	RM	32.5	3	183	5	36.60	3-92	–	–
G.H.Dockrell (Sm)	SLA	279.1	50	751	21	35.76	3-44	–	–
B.L.D'Oliveira (Wo)	LB	14	1	73	1	73.00	1-73	–	–
M.P.Dunn (Sy)	RFM	399.4	76	1547	47	32.91	5-48	2	–
W.J.Durston (De)	OB	180.5	20	600	21	28.57	5-19	1	–
E.J.H.Eckersley (Le)	OB	3.3	0	16	0				
S.L.Elstone (De)	OB	30.1	4	124	6	20.66	2- 8	–	–
D.M.Endersby (LU)	RMF	7	2	35	0				
R.M.S.Eranga (SL)	RFM	104.4	30	357	11	32.45	4-93	–	–

	Cat	O	M	R	W	Avge	Best	5wI	10wM
S.M.Ervine (H)	RM	217	43	686	19	36.10	3- 22	–	–
L.J.Evans (Wa)	RFM	1	0	15	0				
A.N.P.R.Fernando (SL)	RFM	94	11	378	7	54.00	4-123	–	–
N.J.Ferraby (OU)	RM	31	6	112	4	28.00	2- 19	–	–
A.J.Finch (Y)	LM	15	4	39	1	39.00	1- 20	–	–
S.T.Finn (M)	RF	393.1	58	1475	48	30.72	6- 80	2	–
L.J.Fletcher (Nt)	RMF	358.1	83	1103	41	26.90	4- 76	–	–
B.T.Foakes (Ex)	(WK)	1	0	6	0				
M.H.A.Footitt (De)	LFM	489.2	103	1612	84	19.19	6- 48	6	–
J.E.C.Franklin (Nt)	LM	9	1	36	1	36.00	1- 14	–	–
O.H.Freckingham (Le)	RMF	81.5	12	362	8	45.25	4-138	–	–
J.K.Fuller (Gs)	RFM	177.4	31	543	21	30.19	6- 47	1	–
J.S.Gatting (H)	OB	3	0	22	0				
W.R.S.Gidman (Gs)	RM	374.3	103	968	40	24.20	6- 50	2	–
J.C.Glover (Gm)	RMF	27	2	118	3	39.33	2- 36	–	–
R.O.Gordon (Wa)	RFM	38.2	2	125	6	20.83	4- 53	–	–
S.E.Grant (LU)	LMF	10	0	42	1	42.00	1- 42	–	–
L.Gregory (Sm)	RMF	342.5	75	1160	45	25.77	6- 47	3	1
D.A.Griffiths (K)	RFM	48.3	7	174	8	21.75	6- 63	1	–
S.W.Griffiths (CfU)	RM	45	8	180	1	180.00	1- 82	–	–
T.D.Groenewald (De/Sm)	RFM	238	57	718	24	29.91	5- 27	2	–
H.F.Gurney (Nt)	LFM	353.3	65	1277	41	31.14	4- 22	–	–
C.J.Haggett (K)	RMF	94	9	353	5	70.60	2- 48	–	–
A.D.Hales (Nt/Wo)	RM	2	0	4	0				
A.J.Hall (Nh)	RFM	451.1	83	1481	35	42.31	4- 77	–	–
T.S.I.Hamilton (CfU)	RM	4	0	26	0				
R.J.Hamilton-Brown (Sx)	OB	6.5	0	30	2	15.00	2- 5	–	–
O.J.Hannon-Dalby (Wa)	RMF	171.3	29	523	23	22.73	4- 57	–	–
A.Harinath (Sy)	OB	5	1	10	3	3.33	2- 1	–	–
B.W.Harmison (K)	RMF	35.1	3	141	3	47.00	2- 26	–	–
J.A.R.Harris (Gm/M)	RFM	245	59	804	17	47.29	4- 80	–	–
J.Harrison (Du)	LMF	116	20	412	11	37.45	3- 33	–	–
C.F.Hartley (K)	RMF	48	6	190	5	38.00	2- 40	–	–
J.W.Hastings (Du)	RFM	272	69	812	37	21.94	5- 94	1	–
L.J.Hatchett (Sx)	LMF	267.5	35	1038	30	34.60	5-113	1	–
T.G.Helm (Gm/M)	RMF	116	20	350	9	38.88	2- 9	–	–
M.J.Henry (NZA)	RFM	31.4	9	111	7	15.85	5- 18	1	–
H.M.R.K.B.Herath (SL)	SLA	127.3	23	351	8	43.87	4- 95	–	–
J.C.Hildreth (Sm)	RMF	14	1	48	1	48.00	1- 21	–	–
M.E.Hobden (Sx)	RM	68	4	342	12	28.50	3- 49	–	–
M.G.Hogan (Gm)	RFM	444.5	106	1232	63	19.55	5- 58	3	1
K.W.Hogg (La)	RFM	212.4	59	563	21	26.80	6- 70	1	–
D.M.Housego (Gs)	LB	6	0	25	0				
B.A.C.Howell (Gs)	RMF	250.2	59	714	23	31.04	4- 60	–	–
A.L.Hughes (De)	RM	144.4	33	440	10	44.00	4- 46	–	–
C.F.Hughes (De)	SLA	32.4	4	11	4	27.75	2- 37	–	–
M.D.Hunn (K)	RFM	36	6	155	3	51.66	1- 7	–	–
Imran Tahir (H)	LB	49.4	8	180	6	30.00	3-140	–	–
A.J.Ireland (Le)	RM	176.1	24	600	15	40.00	3- 81	–	–
R.A.Jadeja (I)	SLA	156	25	420	9	46.66	3- 52	–	–
K.M.Jarvis (La)	RFM	49	7	201	2	100.50	2- 88	–	–
A.Javid (Wa)	RM	12	0	33	1	33.00	1- 1	–	–
D.P.M.D.Jayawardena (SL)	RM	6	2	13	0				

	Cat	O	M	R	W	Avge	Best	5wI	10wM
W.H.Jenkins (DU)	RM	30	5	161	1	161.00	1- 89	–	–
K.K.Jennings (Du)	RMF	41	4	142	3	47.33	1- 4	–	–
R.A.Jones (Le/Wo)	RMF	108	19	381	13	29.30	4- 81	–	–
C.J.Jordan (E/Sx)	RFM	347	74	1164	40	29.10	5- 76	1	–
R.H.Joseph (K)	RFM	161	32	520	14	37.14	3- 43	–	–
Junaid Khan (La)	LMF	47	11	147	4	49.00	3- 84	–	–
A.Kapil (Sy)	RFM	12.2	3	52	4	13.00	2- 23	–	–
F.D.M.Karunaratne (SL)	RM	3	1	3	0				
G.Keedy (Nt)	SLA	127	12	465	13	35.76	5-163	–	–
R.I.Keogh (Nh)	OB	48	8	157	4	39.25	2- 46	–	–
S.C.Kerrigan (La)	SLA	530	99	1556	44	35.36	4- 38	–	–
A.N.Kervezee (Wo)	OB	7.3	0	34	0				
R.W.T.Key (K)	RM/OB	2	0	12	0				
I.S.Khan (CU)	SLA	22	5	67	0				
M.J.L.Kidd (OU)	RM	19	1	77	1	77.00	1- 77	–	–
S.C.Kuggeleijn (NZA)	RFM	25	1	103	2	51.50	1- 24	–	–
K.M.D.N.Kulasekara (SL)	RFM	37	5	148	2	74.00	1- 65	–	–
B.Kumar (I)	RM	172.5	45	506	19	26.63	6- 82	2	–
T.J.Lancefield (Gm)	LM	1	0	6	0				
A.R.Laws (LBU)	OB	7	0	24	1	24.00	1- 17	–	–
J.Leach (Wo)	RMF	268.5	48	988	33	29.93	5- 36	1	–
M.J.Leach (Sm)	SLA	121	34	286	8	35.75	3- 40	–	–
J.A.Leaning (Y)	RMF	6	1	13	0				
T.Lester (LU)	LFM	46.5	5	170	1	170.00	1- 59	–	–
J.Lewis (Sx)	RMF	204.5	58	546	17	32.11	4- 34	–	–
J.D.Libby (CfU/Nt)	OB	25.5	2	104	1	104.00	1- 18	–	–
C.J.Liddle (Sx)	LFM	37.5	5	123	0				
A.E.Lilley (LBU)	LM	31	4	102	6	17.00	5- 41	1	–
T.E.Linley (Sy)	RFM	214.4	48	658	21	31.33	4- 79	–	–
D.L.Lloyd (Gm)	OB	35	1	126	4	31.50	2- 22	–	–
A.Lyth (Y)	RM	59.2	12	160	5	32.00	2- 18	–	–
G.J.McCarter (Gs)	RFM	43.3	7	144	6	24.00	3- 64	–	–
M.J.McClenaghan (Wo)	LMF	120	27	466	13	35.84	5- 78	1	–
A.MacQueen (LBU)	OB	58	7	185	4	46.25	4-116	–	–
W.A.MacVicar (LU)	RM	27	3	78	1	78.00	1- 21	–	–
W.L.Madsen (De)	OB	9.5	2	36	0				
S.J.Magoffin (Sx)	RFM	539	144	1405	72	19.51	6- 60	4	–
S.I.Mahmood (Ex)	RF	17	0	76	3	25.33	3- 54	–	–
G.T.Main (Du)	RMF	13	2	72	3	24.00	3- 72	–	–
D.J.Malan (M)	LB	30.3	9	90	4	22.50	2- 16	–	–
W.W.J.Marriott (OU)	OB	8	0	34	0				
J.Marsden (OU)	RM	90	17	272	8	34.00	4- 65	–	–
H.J.H.Marshall (Gs)	RM	25	6	66	2	33.00	1- 21	–	–
D.D.Masters (Ex)	RMF	299.3	94	746	39	19.12	6- 46	2	–
A.D.Mathews (SL)	RMF	37	9	99	4	24.75	4- 44	–	–
G.J.Maxwell (H)	OB	6	0	33	2	16.50	2- 33	–	–
S.C.Meaker (Sy)	RMF	293.4	42	1072	41	26.14	7- 90	2	1
C.A.J.Meschede (Sm)	RMF	107	23	396	9	44.00	3-105	–	–
J.D.Middlebrook (Nh)	OB	414.3	93	1307	29	45.06	5- 62	2	–
C.N.Miles (Gs)	RMF	93	16	358	18	19.88	5- 90	1	–
T.S.Mills (Ex)	LFM	153	32	484	14	34.57	4- 45	–	–
M.E.Milnes (DU)	RMF	40	13	108	3	36.00	2- 37	–	–
D.K.H.Mitchell (Wo)	RM	9	3	26	0				

	Cat	O	M	R	W	Avge	Best	5wI	10wM
Mohammed Shami (I)	RFM	96	15	366	5	73.20	2-128	–	–
T.C.Moore (Ex)	RMF	98	19	328	8	41.00	4- 78	–	–
E.J.G.Morgan (M)	RM	0.5	0	7	0				
A.O.Morgan (CfU)	SLA	25	4	87	2	43.50	1- 19	–	–
C.A.J.Morris (OU/Wo)	RMF	528.4	141	1450	56	25.89	5- 54	1	–
S.J.Mullaney (Nt)	RM	108.2	20	312	12	26.00	2- 8	–	–
T.J.Murtagh (M)	RFM	527.4	116	1646	58	28.37	6- 60	5	1
J.G.Myburgh (Sm)	OB	212.1	39	581	11	52.81	2- 13	–	–
J.K.H.Naik (Le)	OB	445.2	81	1535	20	76.75	3- 76	–	–
G.R.Napier (Ex)	RM	252	49	813	52	15.63	7- 21	2	–
B.P.Nash (K)	LM	27	3	106	1	106.00	1- 15	–	–
C.D.Nash (Sx)	OB	85.3	12	309	4	77.25	2- 91	–	–
O.J.Newby (La)	RMF	52.1	18	179	3	59.66	2- 52	–	–
M.J.North (De)	OB	53.3	7	142	2	71.00	1- 25	–	–
S.A.Northeast (K)	OB	1	0	4	0				
L.C.Norwell (Gs)	RMF	304.4	51	1166	29	40.20	4- 69	–	–
K.J.O'Brien (Sy)	RMF	3	0	19	0				
T.J.J.O'Gorman (OU)	LB	25	4	73	1	73.00	1- 51	–	–
G.Onions (Du)	RFM	164.2	34	520	12	43.33	4- 65	–	–
C.Overton (Sm)	RMF	345.1	67	1198	42	28.52	5- 63	1	–
J.Overton (Sm)	RFM	174	16	748	11	68.00	2- 35	–	–
W.T.Owen (Gm)	RMF	128	24	523	10	52.30	3- 42	–	–
A.P.Palladino (De)	RMF	431.4	133	1032	42	24.57	5- 62	1	–
M.S.Panesar (Ex)	SLA	403.2	114	1144	46	24.86	6-111	4	1
Pankaj Singh (I)	RMF	75	17	292	2	146.00	2-113	–	–
A.E.Paraam (DU)	SLA	1	0	10	0				
M.G.Pardoe (Wo)	LM	10	2	24	0				
S.D.Parry (La)	SLA	60	5	197	4	49.25	3-109	–	–
J.S.Patel (Wa)	OB	536.2	136	1553	59	26.32	5- 49	1	–
R.H.Patel (M)	SLA	210.5	37	647	10	64.70	3- 49	–	–
S.R.Patel (Nt)	SLA	291	53	1015	23	44.13	3- 13	–	–
Z.R.Patel (LBU)	RMF	53	6	195	2	97.50	1- 56	–	–
S.A.Patterson (Y)	RMF	423.4	139	1041	39	26.69	4- 54	–	–
D.A.Payne (Gs)	LMF	199	46	631	11	57.36	3- 29	–	–
K.W.Penhale (OU)	RM	21.4	5	85	3	28.33	2- 69	–	–
M.D.K.Perera (SL)	OB	31	6	92	4	23.00	4- 92	–	–
A.N.Petersen (Sm)	RM/OB	32	5	78	1	78.00	1- 37	–	–
T.J.Phillips (Ex)	SLA	31	1	119	4	29.75	2- 59	–	–
S.A.Piolet (Sx)	RM	95.1	14	329	5	65.80	3- 82	–	–
L.E.Plunkett (E/Y)	RFM	372.5	59	1283	44	29.15	5- 64	1	–
A.W.Pollock (CU)	RMF	120	24	402	13	30.92	4- 60	–	–
J.A.Porter (Ex)	RMF	31.1	4	116	6	19.33	3- 26	–	–
J.E.Poulson (OU)	RM	22	0	81	2	40.50	2- 81	–	–
H.W.Powell (CfU)	RFM	28	4	147	1	147.00	1- 26	–	–
K.T.G.D.Prasad (SL)	RFM	57.1	9	193	10	19.30	5- 50	1	–
R.D.Pringle (Du)	OB	21.3	1	108	2	54.00	2- 94	–	–
L.A.Procter (La)	RM	59.3	10	205	5	41.00	4- 50	–	–
C.A.Pujara (DE/I)	LB	1	0	6	0				
R.M.Pyrah (Y)	RM	99	26	309	6	51.50	3- 37	–	–
B.A.Raine (Le)	RMF	196	45	656	18	36.44	3- 47	–	–
W.B.Rankin (Wa)	RFM	165.4	31	548	28	19.57	3- 16	–	–
A.U.Rashid (Y)	LB	379.4	73	1216	49	24.81	5-117	1	–
O.P.Rayner (M)	OB	219	36	596	5	119.20	2-101	–	–

	Cat	O	M	R	W	Avge	Best	5wI	10wM
D.J.Redfern (Le)	OB	62	10	251	8	31.37	2- 20	–	–
L.M.Reece (La)	LM	14	2	59	0			–	–
G.P.Rees (Gm)	LM	1	0	6	1	6.00	1- 6	–	–
A.E.N.Riley (K/LU)	OB	529.4	89	1755	57	30.78	5- 62	3	–
N.J.Rimmington (H)	RFM	16	4	51	2	25.50	2- 51	–	–
A.J.Robson (Le)	LB	16.3	1	84	0			–	–
S.D.Robson (E/M)	LB	1	0	6	0			–	–
C.G.Roebuck (LBU)	RM	1	0	3	0			–	–
C.J.L.Rogers (M)	LBG	1	0	2	0			–	–
T.S.Roland-Jones (M)	RMF	406.1	87	1337	43	31.09	6- 50	3	1
J.E.Root (E/Y)	OB	36	9	96	2	48.00	1- 5	–	–
H.P.Rouse (LBU)	RFM	55	7	215	1	215.00	1- 55	–	–
J.J.Roy (Sy)	RM	78	9	283	6	47.16	3- 9	–	–
J.A.Rudolph (Gm)	LBG	14.3	2	54	1	54.00	1- 25	–	–
C.Rushworth (Du)	RMF	501.1	105	1611	65	24.78	9- 52	3	1
C.J.Russell (Wo)	RMF	14	1	73	2	36.50	2- 73	–	–
J.D.Ryder (Ex)	RM	289.5	76	796	44	18.09	5- 24	4	1
L.M.Sabin (OU)	OB	1	0	5	0			–	–
P.T.Sadler (CU)	RFM	98	17	393	7	56.14	3- 50	–	–
Saeed Ajmal (Wo)	OB	417.3	116	1038	63	16.47	7- 19	6	2
A.Sakande (OU)	RFM	38	11	112	3	37.33	3- 71	–	–
M.E.T.Salisbury (Ex)	RMF	81	12	296	5	59.20	4- 50	–	–
A.G.Salter (CfU/Gm)	OB	117	19	438	5	87.60	2- 54	–	–
G.S.Sandhu (M)	LMF	30	3	118	1	118.00	1-118	–	–
K.C.Sangakkara (Du/SL)	OB	1	0	3	0			–	–
I.D.Saxelby (Gs)	RMF	20.1	5	71	3	23.66	3- 71	–	–
A.D.Sears (CU)	RFM	42.2	6	122	8	15.25	5- 73	1	–
A.Shahzad (Nt)	RFM	203.2	37	742	20	37.10	4- 46	–	–
J.D.Shantry (Wo)	LM	497	124	1336	56	23.85	6- 53	2	1
I.Sharma (I)	RFM	115	22	381	14	27.21	7- 74	1	–
R.G.Sharma (I)	OB	14	0	58	1	58.00	1- 26	–	–
A.Sheikh (Le)	LMF	98.5	16	444	9	49.33	4- 97	–	–
C.E.Shreck (Le)	RFM	560	135	1759	42	41.88	3- 44	–	–
D.P.Sibley (Sy)	LB	16.4	2	60	1	60.00	1- 41	–	–
P.M.Siddle (Nt)	RFM	351.5	80	1165	37	31.48	4- 61	–	–
R.J.Sidebottom (Y)	LFM	367.1	91	905	49	18.46	7- 44	2	–
G.M.Smith (Ex)	OB/RM	143.1	23	391	10	39.10	4- 46	–	–
R.A.J.Smith (Gm)	RM	167.4	21	666	12	55.50	3- 38	–	–
T.C.Smith (La)	RMF	365.3	83	1105	54	20.46	5- 42	4	–
T.M.J.Smith (Gs)	SLA	411.3	62	1358	33	41.15	4- 35	–	–
W.R.Smith (H)	OB	33.5	6	114	5	22.80	2- 27	–	–
A.C.Soilleux (LU)	RMF	45	8	135	5	27.00	3- 37	–	–
V.S.Solanki (Sy)	OB	7.1	1	20	2	10.00	2- 20	–	–
M.N.W.Spriegel (Nh)	OB	122	17	443	11	40.27	3- 26	–	–
C.T.Steel (DU)	LB	9	0	39	1	39.00	1- 39	–	–
J.L.Sterland (LU)	OB	1	0	5	0			–	–
D.I.Stevens (K)	RM	526.4	123	1553	56	27.73	6- 64	6	–
P.R.Stirling (M)	OB	14	2	49	1	49.00	1- 45	–	–
B.A.Stokes (Du/E)	RFM	275.3	39	988	37	26.70	7- 67	1	1
O.P.Stone (Nh)	RMF	154.3	36	503	19	26.47	5- 48	1	–
M.D.Stoneman (Du)	RM	23	0	85	0			–	–
J.S.Sykes (Le)	SLA	110	13	381	8	47.62	3- 72	–	–
Tanveer Sikandar (Ex)	RM	38	6	117	3	39.00	2- 90	–	–

	Cat	O	M	R	W	Avge	Best	5wI	10wM
B.J.Taylor (H)	OB	19	3	74	1	74.00	1- 64	–	–
J.M.R.Taylor (Gs)	OB	79.1	11	301	8	37.62	4-125	–	–
M.D.Taylor (Gs)	LMF	232.2	37	963	22	43.77	5- 75	1	–
R.M.L.Taylor (Le)	LM	349.3	66	1231	35	35.17	5- 55	2	–
T.A.I.Taylor (De)	RMF	142	31	451	15	30.06	5- 58	1	–
R.N.ten Doeschate (Ex)	RMF	33.2	1	176	4	44.00	2- 12	–	–
H.D.R.L.Thirimanne (SL)	RMF	1	0	7	0				
A.C.Thomas (Sm)	RFM	486.3	129	1365	57	23.94	5- 40	3	–
I.A.A.Thomas (LBU)	RMF	42	12	102	4	25.50	3- 39	–	–
A.T.Thomson (CfU)	OB	24	1	104	0				
M.A.Thornely (Le)	RM	2	0	6	0				
J.A.Tomlinson (H)	LMF	416.5	103	1215	47	25.85	6- 48	1	–
R.J.W.Topley (Ex)	LMF	150.2	30	502	25	20.08	6- 41	2	1
J.C.Tredwell (K/Sx)	OB	309	57	944	23	41.04	4- 7	–	–
P.D.Trego (Sm)	RMF	442.4	92	1391	49	28.38	7- 84	1	1
C.T.Tremlett (Sy)	RFM	260.1	48	811	25	32.44	6- 59	2	–
I.J.L.Trott (Wa)	RM	25	5	87	3	29.00	2- 8	–	–
M.L.Turner (De)	RMF	65	10	230	1	230.00	1- 80	–	–
F.O.E.van den Bergh (DU)	SLA	23	0	123	1	123.00	1- 92	–	–
W.G.R.Vanderspar (LBU)	RFM	14.5	2	53	3	17.66	2- 52	–	–
K.S.Velani (Ex)	RM	4.3	0	13	0				
M.Vijay (I)	OB	10	1	32	1	32.00	1- 10	–	–
J.M.Vince (H)	RM	57	7	190	2	95.00	1- 10	–	–
G.G.Wagg (Gm)	LM	367.4	77	1258	41	30.68	6- 29	1	–
N.Wagner (Nh)	LMF	182	26	728	10	72.80	5-104	1	–
D.J.Wainwright (De)	SLA	334.1	59	1119	27	41.44	5- 54	1	–
U.W.M.B.C.A.Welagedara (SL)	LMF	20	2	95	1	95.00	1- 95	–	–
S.D.Weller	RFM	46	15	126	6	21.00	3- 66	–	–
L.W.P.Wells (Sx)	OB	68.4	8	237	7	33.85	3- 38	–	–
T.J.Wells (Le)	RMF	5	1	34	0				
M.H.Wessels (Nt)	(WK)	5	0	19	0				
T.Westley (Ex)	OB	72.2	8	218	6	36.33	3- 35	–	–
A.A.Westphal (CfU)	RMF	30	5	116	5	23.20	3- 45	–	–
G.G.White (Nh)	SLA	56	6	261	2	130.50	2- 28	–	–
W.A.White (De/La)	RMF	166	29	560	19	29.47	4- 27	–	–
R.A.Whiteley (Wo)	LMF	12	1	44	0				
D.J.Willey (Nh)	LFM	183.1	40	577	20	28.85	4- 46	–	–
T.J.Williams (OU)	RMF	28.1	5	73	3	24.33	3- 52	–	–
K.S.Williamson (Y)	OB	61.4	21	160	5	32.00	2- 45	–	–
C.R.Woakes (E/Wa)	RFM	354.1	89	1129	45	25.08	5- 35	2	–
C.P.Wood (H)	LM	83	22	252	15	16.80	5- 39	1	–
L.Wood (Nt)	LM	39	4	180	3	60.00	2- 87	–	–
M.A.Wood (Du)	RMF	173.1	28	618	18	34.16	5- 37	2	–
C.J.C.Wright (Wa)	RFM	303.1	51	1107	33	33.54	4- 56	–	–
L.J.Wright (Sx)	RM	51	6	170	3	56.66	2- 31	–	–
A.C.F.Wyatt (Le)	RMF	60	14	214	4	53.50	3- 61	–	–
B.A.Wylie (CU)	SLA	7	0	28	0				
C.S.J.Yates (CU)	LB	5.3	0	32	0				
Zain Shahzad (CU)	RMF	82.3	21	225	11	20.45	4- 33	–	–

FIRST-CLASS CAREER RECORDS

Compiled by Philip Bailey

The following career records are for all players who appeared in first-class cricket during the 2014 season, and are complete to the end of that season. Some players who did not appear in 2014 but may do so in 2015 are included.

BATTING AND FIELDING

'1000' denotes instances of scoring 1000 runs in a season. Where these have been achieved outside the British Isles they are shown after a plus sign.

	M	I	NO	HS	Runs	Avge	100	50	1000	Ct/St
Aaron, V.R.	23	38	8	72	426	14.20	–	1	–	6
Abbott, J.B.	1	2	–	41	49	24.50	–	–	–	1
Abbott, K.J.	59	84	16	80	1243	18.27	–	4	–	13
Abdur Rehman	132	181	19	96	2721	16.79	–	13	–	57
Abell, T.B.	4	7	–	95	292	41.71	–	3	–	4
Adams, A.R.	170	232	23	124	4482	21.44	3	20	–	112
Adams, J.H.K.	175	308	27	262*	11025	39.23	20	57	5	142
Adams, R.J.	1	1	1	0*	0	–	–	–	–	2
Agathangelou, A.P.	47	84	5	158	2549	32.26	5	13	0+1	73
Akram, B.M.R.	1	2	–	36	37	18.50	–	–	–	–
Alexander, T.D.	2	2	1	2	3	3.00	–	–	–	–
Ali, K.	137	193	31	84*	2755	17.00	–	7	–	33
Ali, M.M.	124	211	18	250	7484	38.77	14	46	2	78
Allenby, J.	121	191	28	138*	6656	40.83	10	46	1	121
Alsop, T.P.	2	4	–	33	50	12.50	–	–	–	2
Ambrose, T.R.	181	274	26	251*	8438	34.02	12	52	–	464/28
Amla, H.M.	181	298	27	311*	13875	51.19	43	67	0+2	134
Anderson, C.J.	36	60	9	167	1846	36.19	3	7	–	22
Anderson, J.M.	174	217	79	81	1452	10.52	–	1	–	95
Andrew, G.M.	87	132	17	180*	2757	23.97	1	16	–	30
Ansari, Z.S.	41	67	12	112	1659	30.16	2	9	1	17
Anyon, J.E.	110	143	43	64*	1450	14.50	–	5	–	32
Arif, A.T.	2	4	–	10	16	4.00	–	–	–	–
Arshad, U.	11	14	1	83	318	24.46	–	1	–	2
Ashar Zaidi	100	162	12	202	5516	36.77	11	28	0+1	79
Ashwin, R.	56	75	19	124	2064	36.85	4	10	–	22
Astle, T.D.	79	128	12	101	2745	23.66	1	15	–	54
Azeem Rafiq	25	29	3	100	563	21.65	1	2	–	9
Azhar Mahmood	176	274	32	204*	7703	31.83	9	42	–	142
Azhar Ullah	76	105	59	41	634	13.78	–	–	–	16
Bailey, T.E.	4	5	3	25*	55	27.50	–	–	–	–
Bairstow, J.M.	101	163	23	205	6019	42.99	11	35	1	235/9
Baker, G.C.	9	13	1	66	354	29.50	–	3	–	1
Balbirnie, A.	9	13	1	38	181	15.08	–	–	–	6
Balcombe, D.J.	67	83	20	73	958	15.20	–	3	–	14
Ball, A.J.	20	28	3	69	560	22.40	–	2	–	10
Ball, J.T.	7	11	1	31	106	10.60	–	–	–	–
Ballance, G.S.	82	126	15	210	6162	55.51	24	28	2+1	77
Barker, K.H.D.	59	71	12	125	1660	28.13	4	3	–	21
Barrett, C.A.	1	1	1	20*	20	–	–	–	–	3
Barrett, W.J.M.	1	–	–	–	–	–	–	–	–	–
Barrow, A.W.R.	30	50	3	88	1000	21.27	–	4	–	44
Barton, A.P.	2	1	–	1*	1	1.00	–	–	–	–

F-C	M	I	NO	HS	Runs	Avge	100	50	1000	Ct/St
Bates, M.D.	46	60	7	103	1124	21.20	1	5	–	136/7
Bath, E.R.	1	1	–	0	0	0.00	–	–	–	1
Batty, G.J.	206	311	49	133	6202	23.67	2	28	–	152
Beaven, L.E.	1	2	–	2	2	1.00	–	–	–	1
Beer, W.A.T.	9	12	2	39	219	21.90	–	–	–	3
Bell, I.R.	246	415	46	262*	16938	45.90	48	87	4	188
Bell-Drummond, D.J.	38	63	5	153	1977	34.08	4	12	1	17
Bennett, H.K.	42	43	22	30*	177	8.42	–	–	–	11
Berg, G.K.	71	112	12	130*	2980	29.80	2	17	–	45
Best, M.T.	2	3	–	50	51	17.00	–	1	–	1
Best, P.M.	11	13	3	150	428	42.80	1	2	–	5
Billings, S.W.	25	37	3	131	1153	33.91	1	8	–	63/7
Binny, S.T.R.	58	90	5	189	3042	35.78	8	13	–	24
Bird, J.M.	24	23	12	26	112	10.18	–	–	–	10
Bishnoi, C.	4	7	–	65	228	32.57	–	3	–	3
Blake, A.J.	28	47	2	105*	993	22.06	1	4	–	17
Bollinger, D.E.	96	108	47	33*	490	8.03	–	–	–	36
Bopara, R.S.	151	249	29	229	9201	41.82	25	34	1	82
Borrington, P.M.	49	85	10	105	2034	27.12	2	9	–	33
Borthwick, S.G.	82	131	17	216	3902	34.22	7	21	2	113
Boyce, M.A.G.	98	172	9	135	4622	28.35	6	22	–	60
Bracewell, M.G.	32	58	7	190	2006	39.33	5	6	–	27
Bracey, S.N.	2	2	–	20	22	11.00	–	–	–	3
Bragg, W.D.	77	134	5	110	3823	29.63	2	25	2	31/1
Brathwaite, R.M.R.	26	28	10	76*	226	12.55	–	1	–	3
Breese, G.R.	125	200	22	165*	4693	26.36	4	28	–	114
Bresnan, T.T.	140	180	29	126*	4103	27.17	3	21	–	56
Briggs, D.R.	58	68	15	54	731	13.79	–	1	–	19
Broad, S.C.J.	131	176	28	169	3403	22.99	1	17	–	41
Brooks, J.A.	66	71	29	53	575	13.69	–	1	–	18
Brown, B.C.	67	104	15	163	2970	33.37	5	16	–	177/14
Brown, K.R.	61	102	6	114	2402	25.02	1	13	–	33
Browne, N.L.J.	12	20	4	132*	676	42.25	3	2	–	10
Brownlie, D.G.	58	105	11	171	3802	40.44	8	22	0+1	75
Buck, N.L.	60	82	24	29*	613	10.56	–	–	–	8
Buckley, R.S.	4	6	1	9	25	5.00	–	–	–	1
Bull, K.A.	3	6	2	12	31	7.75	–	–	–	–
Burgess, M.G.K.	2	3	–	49	91	30.33	–	–	–	1
Burke, J.E.	1	–	–	–	–	–	–	–	–	–
Burns, R.J.	45	78	7	199	2748	38.70	6	13	1	46
Butler, I.G.	72	95	28	73*	1261	18.82	–	5	–	16
Buttler, J.C.	61	91	7	144	2864	34.09	4	16	–	121/2
Cachopa, C.	26	44	2	203	2129	50.69	5	13	–	15
Carberry, M.A.	166	289	23	300*	11499	43.22	32	53	3	82
Carter, A.	24	27	9	17*	137	7.61	–	–	–	4
Carver, K.	1	1	1	2*	2	–	–	–	–	1
Cato, S.J.	2	3	1	33	86	43.00	–	–	–	1
Chambers, M.A.	58	77	24	58	388	7.32	–	1	–	18
Chanderpaul, S.	331	541	102	303*	24451	55.69	70	126	1+1	179
Chandimal, L.D.	58	95	11	244	4426	52.69	13	23	0+1	100/18
Chapple, G.	310	431	74	155	8674	24.29	6	37	–	102
Chase, P.K.D.	3	5	3	4*	7	3.50	–	–	–	1
Chopra, V.	136	224	16	233*	7815	37.57	16	39	3	152
Choudhry, S.H.	22	35	7	75	629	22.46	–	4	–	8
Christian, D.T.	44	78	8	131*	2027	28.95	3	8	–	45
Clare, J.L.	56	81	9	130	1721	23.90	2	8	–	28

235

F-C	M	I	NO	HS	Runs	Avge	100	50	1000	Ct/St
Clarke, R.	177	270	31	214	8454	35.37	16	42	1	269
Claydon, M.E.	69	89	16	77	1107	15.16	–	2	–	9
Cobb, J.J.	77	135	11	148*	3133	25.26	3	19	–	38
Cockbain, I.A.	37	63	4	151*	1751	29.67	3	10	–	30
Coetzer, K.J.	84	142	11	219	4183	31.93	8	18	–	41
Coleman, F.R.J.	7	12	–	110	219	18.25	1	–	–	4
Coles, M.T.	70	92	13	103*	1547	19.58	1	7	–	24
Collingwood, P.D.	250	429	39	206	14105	36.16	29	74	2	280
Compton, N.R.D.	139	240	31	254*	9163	43.84	22	44	5	71
Cook, A.N.	209	371	27	294	16262	47.27	47	79	5+1	205
Cooke, C.B.	26	43	3	171	1450	36.25	1	11	–	18/1
Cooper, T.L.W.	41	72	4	203*	2663	39.16	4	17	–	38
Cosker, D.A.	242	322	92	52	3296	14.33	–	1	–	144
Cotton, B.D.	2	2	–	21	36	18.00	–	–	–	–
Coughlin, P.	7	11	3	85	237	29.62	–	1	–	5
Cowdrey, F.K.	6	10	1	62	185	20.55	–	1	–	1
Cox, O.B.	41	69	13	104	1323	23.62	1	7	–	99/6
Craddock, T.R.	18	23	7	21	135	8.43	–	–	–	3
Craig, M.D.	27	38	5	93	802	24.30	–	4	–	24
Croft, S.J.	114	179	18	156	5293	32.87	8	31	–	104
Crook, S.P.	74	97	12	131	2470	29.05	1	17	–	26
Cross, G.D.	73	111	5	125	2371	22.36	3	11	–	185/27
Curran, T.K.	7	7	3	9*	16	4.00	–	–	–	2
Darby, H.R.H.	2	3	–	6	6	2.00	–	–	–	–
Davies, A.L.	14	20	1	62	527	27.73	–	3	–	21/1
Davies, J.M.	2	3	–	31	38	12.66	–	–	–	4
Davies, J.W.	1	1	–	5	5	5.00	–	–	–	1
Davies, S.M.	154	252	25	192	8912	39.25	16	43	5	393/20
Davis, C.A.L.	1	2	–	13	14	7.00	–	–	–	–
Dawson, L.A.	89	143	15	169	4243	33.14	6	23	1	111
de Grandhomme, C.	68	110	14	125	3444	35.87	8	18	–	71
Denly, J.L.	127	223	13	199	6952	33.10	15	35	2	51
Dent, C.D.J.	66	117	9	203*	3565	33.00	5	20	1	82
Dernbach, J.W.	93	119	43	56*	724	9.52	–	1	–	12
Dexter, N.J.	107	176	22	163*	5559	36.09	12	29	–	80
Dhawan, S.	92	151	9	224	6346	44.69	18	25	0+1	93
Dhoni, M.S.	129	206	18	224	6986	37.15	9	47	–	350/58
Dilshan, T.M.	230	378	22	200*	13910	39.07	38	59	0+2	352/27
Dixon, L.	2	2	–	1	1	0.50	–	–	–	–
Dockrell, G.H.	39	47	18	53	422	14.55	–	1	–	14
D'Oliveira, B.L.	4	8	–	44	113	14.12	–	–	–	–
Donald, A.H.T.	1	2	–	59	63	31.50	–	1	–	1
Dowdall, T.R.	1	2	–	75	81	40.50	–	1	–	4/1
Duckett, B.M.	18	30	2	144*	763	27.25	1	6	–	18/2
Dunn, M.P.	21	19	12	31*	69	9.85	–	–	–	4
Durston, W.J.	94	163	23	151	4832	34.51	6	30	1	98
Eckersley, E.J.H.	57	101	7	147	3313	35.24	8	11	1	92/3
Edwards, G.A.	4	5	1	19	56	14.00	–	–	–	1
Elliott, G.D.	83	134	7	196*	3883	30.57	8	20	–	46
Elliott, T.C.	8	14	1	101	306	23.53	1	–	–	4
Ellison, H.R.C.	1	2	–	32	32	16.00	–	–	–	–
Elstone, S.L.	6	9	–	63	199	22.11	–	1	–	2
Endersby, D.M.	6	9	–	53	107	11.88	–	1	–	6
Eranga, R.M.S.	61	82	30	100*	1065	20.48	1	4	–	29
Ervine, S.M.	184	285	33	237*	8995	35.69	16	47	–	154
Evans, L.J.	36	59	3	178	1927	34.41	4	10	–	23

236

F-C	M	I	NO	HS	Runs	Avge	100	50	1000	Ct/St
Fell, T.C.	22	36	3	133	1040	31.51	2	4	–	16
Fernando, A.N.P.R.	56	68	28	27*	226	5.65	–	–	–	25
Ferraby, N.J.	3	5	–	107	193	38.60	1	1	–	1
Finch, A.J.	44	76	1	122	2187	29.16	3	14	–	43
Finch, H.Z.	1	2	–	11	14	7.00	–	–	–	1
Finn, S.T.	104	127	39	56	692	7.86	–	1	–	35
Fletcher, L.J.	65	97	19	92	1176	15.07	–	3	–	16
Flintoff, A.	183	290	23	167	9027	33.80	15	53	–	185
Foakes, B.T.	32	45	6	132*	1223	31.35	3	6	–	23
Fogarty, E.J.	1	2	–	37	45	22.50	–	–	–	1
Footitt, M.H.A.	57	77	25	30	474	9.11	–	–	–	16
Foster, J.S.	240	361	47	212	11805	37.59	21	60	1	681/55
Franklin, J.E.C.	159	245	36	219	7615	36.43	18	31	–	66
Freckingham, O.H.	18	25	3	30	216	9.81	–	–	–	4
Fuller, J.K.	27	32	3	57	387	13.34	–	1	–	8
Gale, A.W.	124	190	16	272	6595	37.90	17	26	1	43
Gambhir, G.	158	268	22	233*	12281	49.92	36	53	–	95
Gatting, J.S.	43	62	5	152	1567	27.49	3	7	–	19
George, J.	2	3	–	9	16	5.33	–	–	–	1
Gidman, A.P.R.	191	328	26	264	11182	37.02	24	57	6	128
Gidman, W.R.S.	56	85	16	143	2752	39.88	5	14	1	14
Glover, J.C.	28	36	10	55	353	13.57	–	2	–	7
Godleman, B.A.	88	152	5	130	4207	28.61	6	22	–	62
Goodwin, M.W.	320	554	46	344*	23723	46.69	71	98	10+1	168
Gordon, R.O.	6	5	2	14*	52	17.33	–	–	–	3
Grant, S.E.	1	1	1	14*	14	–	–	–	–	–
Gregory, L.	26	34	4	69	593	19.76	–	2	–	8
Grieshaber, P.J.	1	1	–	10	10	10.00	–	–	–	–
Griffiths, D.A.	38	52	19	31*	220	6.66	–	–	–	4
Griffiths, S.W.	2	2	–	40	61	30.50	–	–	–	–
Groenewald, T.D.	91	126	34	78	1704	18.52	–	6	–	33
Gubbins, N.R.T.	8	15	1	95	330	23.57	–	3	–	2
Guptill, M.J.	81	147	9	195*	4972	36.02	9	28	–	78
Gurney, H.F.	54	65	30	24*	191	5.45	–	–	–	7
Haggett, C.J.	16	21	7	44*	368	26.28	–	–	–	3
Hain, S.R.	12	18	2	208	823	51.43	4	1	–	6
Hales, A.D.	73	126	6	184	4399	36.65	9	27	2	71
Hall, A.J.	242	361	47	163	11072	35.26	15	66	1	228
Hamilton, T.S.I.	1	1	–	38	38	38.00	–	–	–	–
Hamilton-Brown, R.J.	73	126	8	171*	3841	32.55	8	18	1	43
Hampton, T.R.G.	1	1	1	1*	1	–	–	–	–	–
Handscomb, P.S.P.	25	43	1	113	1260	30.00	1	9	–	37/4
Hannon-Dalby, O.J.	37	38	16	40	155	7.04	–	–	–	5
Harinath, A.	50	87	5	154	2384	29.07	3	14	–	13
Harmison, B.W.	78	123	10	125	3218	28.47	6	14	–	46
Harris, J.A.R.	85	115	24	87*	1877	20.62	–	7	–	24
Harrison, J.	13	20	5	65	337	22.46	–	1	–	–
Hartley, C.F.	2	3	–	2	2	0.66	–	–	–	–
Hastings, J.W.	47	68	5	93	1446	22.95	–	7	–	20
Hatchett, L.J.	22	29	9	21	169	8.45	–	–	–	8
Hearne, A.G.	4	7	1	88	174	29.00	–	1	–	–
Helm, T.G.	6	9	3	18	58	9.66	–	–	–	2
Henry, M.J.	15	19	3	51	263	16.43	–	1	–	5
Herath, H.M.R.K.B.	227	323	75	80*	3985	16.06	–	12	–	97
Herring, C.L.	11	14	1	114*	282	21.69	1	–	–	32/1
Higginbottom, M.	6	11	4	31*	108	15.42	–	–	–	–

F-C	M	I	NO	HS	Runs	Avge	100	50	1000	Ct/St
Hildreth, J.C.	184	300	24	303*	11723	42.47	30	55	4	164
Hilfenhaus, B.W.	95	132	35	56*	1170	12.06	–	2	–	28
Hobden, M.E.	7	6	2	18	37	9.25	–	–	–	–
Hodd, A.J.	75	104	18	123	2458	28.58	4	12	–	166/14
Hodgson, D.M.	12	22	2	94*	450	22.50	–	4	–	34/1
Hogan, M.G.	73	108	35	51	1165	15.95	–	1	–	36
Hogg, K.W.	114	143	27	88	2708	23.34	–	16	–	21
Horton, P.J.	152	257	21	209	8910	37.75	20	46	3	152/1
Hosein, H.R.	2	2	–	13	17	8.50	–	–	–	15
Housego, D.M.	39	67	6	217*	1948	31.93	4	7	–	21
Howell, B.A.C.	42	67	10	83*	1524	26.73	–	10	–	21
Hughes, A.L.	19	32	4	82	584	20.85	–	3	–	8
Hughes, C.F.	44	79	3	270*	2312	30.42	5	9	–	35
Hunn, M.D.	3	4	2	0*	0	0.00	–	–	–	2
Hussain, G.M.	34	53	20	42	319	9.66	–	–	–	5
Imran Tahir	172	215	54	77*	2308	14.33	–	4	–	74
Ingram, C.A.	66	116	9	190	3855	36.02	7	19	–	44
Ireland, A.J.	49	74	20	52	396	7.33	–	1	–	9
Jadeja, R.A.	55	83	7	331	3530	46.44	7	13	–	51
Jaques, P.A.	200	346	14	244	16035	48.29	44	76	4+2	149
Jarvis, K.M.	32	45	17	48	356	12.71	–	–	–	10
Javid, A.	27	43	6	133	1004	27.13	2	3	–	12
Jayawardena, D.P.M.D.	237	383	24	374	17843	49.70	51	80	0+2	308
Jayawardena, H.A.P.W.	238	368	45	229*	9738	30.14	15	43	–	543/119
Jeffery, B.A.	6	10	–	39	133	13.30	–	–	–	6
Jenkins, W.H.	2	3	–	19	19	6.33	–	–	–	2
Jennings, K.K.	44	77	3	127	2020	27.29	4	10	–	15
Johnson, J.A.M.	6	11	1	61	145	14.50	–	1	–	4
Johnson, R.M.	29	47	3	72	911	20.70	–	5	–	56/2
Jones, C.R.	37	60	2	130	1285	22.15	1	9	–	22
Jones, G.O.	193	293	28	178	8615	32.50	15	46	2	586/36
Jones, R.A.	49	75	13	62	720	11.61	–	2	–	18
Jordan, C.J.	69	92	13	92	1707	21.60	–	6	–	71
Joseph, R.H.	69	91	34	36*	605	10.61	–	–	–	14
Joyce, E.C.	215	356	32	211	15419	47.58	39	81	8	187
Junaid Khan	65	90	27	71	689	10.93	–	2	–	11
Kapil, A.	13	22	2	104*	445	22.25	1	1	–	4
Karunaratne, F.D.M.	82	132	11	210*	5621	46.45	17	25	0+1	92/1
Keedy, G.	226	262	128	64	1448	10.80	–	2	–	56
Kelsall, S.	3	6	–	57	112	18.66	–	1	–	2
Kennedy, A.D.J.	5	8	2	91*	341	56.83	–	3	–	12
Keogh, R.I.	18	27	3	221	901	37.54	3	2	–	1
Kerrigan, S.C.	71	82	28	62*	546	10.11	–	1	–	21
Kervezee, A.N.	87	147	8	155	4242	30.51	6	25	1	45
Kettleborough, J.M.	9	16	–	73	398	24.87	–	3	–	6
Key, R.W.T.	286	493	37	270*	18461	40.48	52	71	7	153
Khan, I.S.	1	1	–	6	6	6.00	–	–	–	–
Khawaja, U.T.	85	148	14	214	5392	40.23	13	29	–	58
Kidd, M.J.L.	1	1	1	0*	0	–	–	–	–	–
Kieswetter, C.	115	171	25	164	5728	39.23	11	31	1	331/12
Kleinveldt, R.K.	90	120	14	115*	2040	19.24	1	10	–	37
Klinger, M.	138	244	23	255	8169	36.96	19	35	1+1	130
Knight, T.C.	2	3	1	14	15	7.50	–	–	–	1
Kohler-Cadmore, T.	13	23	–	99	516	22.43	–	4	–	15
Kohli, V.	60	97	11	197	4043	47.01	13	17	–	56
Kuggeleijn, S.C.	27	35	4	142*	1037	33.45	1	7	–	6

F-C	M	I	NO	HS	Runs	Avge	100	50	1000	Ct/St
Kulasekara, K.M.D.N.	87	114	22	95	1684	18.30	–	5	–	35
Kumar, B.	57	84	9	128	2191	29.21	1	14	–	13
Lancefield, T.J.	14	23	1	74	488	22.18	–	2	–	6
Latham, T.W.M.	42	75	7	261	2956	43.47	4	20	–	56/1
Laws, A.R.	2	2	–	7	12	6.00	–	–	–	2
Leach, J.	26	42	3	114	921	23.61	1	7	–	5
Leach, M.J.	11	13	4	43	125	13.88	–	–	–	–
Leach, S.G.	2	3	–	20	43	14.33	–	–	–	2
Leaning, J.A.	12	16	2	99	478	34.14	–	4	–	4
Lees, A.Z.	31	48	4	275*	1881	42.75	6	6	1	12
Lester, T.J.	6	8	5	2*	5	1.66	–	–	–	–
Levi, R.E.	45	73	9	150*	2510	39.21	5	17	–	34
Lewis, J.	251	357	71	71	4693	16.40	–	14	–	65
Libby, J.D.	3	5	1	108	201	50.25	1	1	–	1
Liddle, C.J.	21	21	11	53	125	12.50	–	1	–	6
Lilley, A.E.	2	2	–	25	25	12.50	–	–	–	–
Lilley, A.M.	2	2	2	35*	39	–	–	–	–	–
Linley, T.E.	62	85	18	42	536	8.00	–	–	–	21
Lloyd, D.L.	7	11	1	41	109	10.90	–	–	–	2
Lumb, M.J.	180	303	18	221*	10114	35.48	19	54	3	107
Lyth, A.	99	157	7	251	6396	42.64	14	39	2	120
McCarter, G.J.	9	12	2	29*	121	12.10	–	–	–	2
McClenaghan, M.J.	32	39	13	34	273	10.50	–	–	–	6
McKay, C.J.	43	58	7	65	936	18.35	–	4	–	12
McKay, P.J.	3	5	1	33	73	18.25	–	–	–	2
MacLeod, C.A.R.	4	6	–	15	34	5.66	–	–	–	8
MacLeod, C.S.	14	20	3	84	419	24.64	–	3	–	9
MacQueen, A.	5	8	–	69	166	20.75	–	1	–	2
MacVicar, W.A.	4	6	–	79	188	31.33	–	1	–	3
Machan, M.W.	20	30	4	119	827	31.80	2	2	–	9
Madsen, W.L.	114	202	13	231*	7039	37.24	17	37	2	99
Magoffin, S.J.	119	165	45	79	2257	18.80	–	5	–	29
Mahmood, S.I.	121	158	20	94	2178	15.78	–	10	–	30
Main, G.T.	1	–	–	–	–	–	–	–	–	1
Malan, D.J.	110	187	13	156*	6322	36.33	12	31	2	138
Mansfield, A.P.	2	4	1	31*	38	12.66	–	–	–	6
Marriott, W.W.J.	3	5	1	81	139	34.75	–	1	–	–
Marsden, J.	4	4	2	0*	0	0.00	–	–	–	3
Marshall, H.J.H.	225	374	26	170	12652	36.35	26	61	2	112
Martin, A.T.	1	2	–	3	4	2.00	–	–	–	1
Masters, D.D.	186	226	32	119	2639	13.60	1	6	–	57
Mathews, A.D.	79	127	3	270	5729	55.08	13	29	0+1	47
Maxwell, G.J.	28	48	3	155*	1874	41.64	4	12	–	23
Meaker, S.C.	60	79	13	94	1091	16.53	–	6	–	8
Meschede, C.A.J.	28	37	4	62	657	19.90	–	4	–	11
Mickleburgh, J.C.	80	140	3	243	3897	28.44	6	18	–	56
Middlebrook, J.D.	220	320	43	127	7824	28.24	10	35	–	111
Miles, C.N.	18	22	2	62*	355	17.75	–	2	–	3
Mills, T.S.	29	34	15	31*	242	12.73	–	–	–	9
Milnes, M.E.	2	2	–	9	9	4.50	–	–	–	2
Mitchell, D.K.H.	131	238	29	298	8320	39.80	19	36	4	185
Mohammed Shami	27	40	10	51*	329	10.96	–	1	–	7
Moore, S.C.	155	279	20	246	9390	36.25	18	45	4	78
Moore, T.C.	4	4	2	17	27	13.50	–	–	–	1
Morgan, A.O.	1	1	1	28*	28	–	–	–	–	–
Morgan, E.J.G.	89	147	16	209*	4730	36.10	11	22	1	70/1

239

F-C	M	I	NO	HS	Runs	Avge	100	50	1000	Ct/St
Morris, C.A.J.	22	30	17	33*	157	12.07	–	–	–	9
Muchall, G.J.	149	258	15	219	7154	29.44	12	36	–	104
Mullaney, S.J.	66	110	6	165*	3207	30.83	5	20	–	48
Munro, C.	27	39	3	269*	1738	48.27	6	7	–	13
Murphy, D.	53	71	16	81	1425	25.90	–	10	–	146/13
Murtagh, T.J.	158	212	62	74*	3171	21.14	–	10	–	46
Mustard, P.	180	279	34	130	7467	30.47	6	46	–	601/19
Myburgh, J.G.	93	163	19	203	6039	41.93	13	35	–	55
Naik, J.K.H.	66	102	24	109*	1670	21.41	1	4	–	39
Nannes, D.P.	23	24	8	31*	108	6.75	–	–	–	7
Napier, G.R.	151	206	40	196	5072	30.55	6	29	–	55
Nash, B.P.	135	221	30	207	7523	39.38	18	32	1	50
Nash, C.D.	141	242	17	184	8724	38.77	17	44	3	67
Newby, O.J.	53	47	13	38*	327	9.61	–	–	–	9
Newton, R.I.	45	77	8	119*	2310	33.47	6	7	–	14
Noema-Barnett, K.	38	58	7	107	1533	30.05	2	9	–	17
North, M.J.	214	370	32	239*	13764	40.72	37	69	0+1	153
Northeast, S.A.	90	157	6	176	4905	32.48	10	28	–	48
Norwell, L.C.	28	37	17	78	294	14.70	–	1	–	5
O'Brien, K.J.	30	41	4	171*	1185	32.02	1	7	–	26
O'Brien, N.J.	141	223	23	182	7203	36.01	14	35	–	372/40
O'Gorman, T.J.J.	1	1	1	1*	1	–	–	–	–	1
O'Grady, R.J.	1	2	–	37	46	23.00	–	–	–	–
Oliver, R.K.	7	14	–	179	558	39.85	1	4	–	2
Onions, G.	127	162	59	41	1415	13.73	–	–	–	27
Overton, C.	21	26	4	99	514	23.36	–	4	–	7
Overton, J.	24	33	11	56	352	16.00	–	2	–	1
Owen, W.T.	24	28	9	69	363	19.10	–	1	–	6
Palladino, A.P.	105	145	31	106	1780	15.61	1	6	–	30
Panesar, M.S.	213	263	83	46*	1484	8.24	–	–	–	41
Pankaj Singh	79	109	22	74	1183	13.59	–	3	–	19
Param, A.E.	2	3	1	22*	31	15.50	–	–	–	–
Pardoe, M.G.	56	99	6	102	2291	24.63	1	14	–	27
Parry, S.D.	9	10	1	37	138	15.33	–	–	–	2
Patel, A.K.	4	6	–	49	114	19.00	–	–	–	1
Patel, J.S.	178	221	57	120	3770	22.98	2	19	–	85
Patel, R.H.	18	23	11	26*	162	13.50	–	–	–	5
Patel, S.R.	147	235	14	256	8610	38.95	20	42	3	98
Patel, Z.R.	3	4	–	16	20	5.00	–	–	–	1
Paternott, L.C.	2	3	–	50	68	22.66	–	1	–	1
Patterson, S.A.	89	97	30	53	990	14.77	–	1	–	14
Payne, D.A.	40	51	16	62	572	16.34	–	2	–	12
Penhale, K.W.	1	2	–	21	26	13.00	–	–	–	2
Perera, M.D.K.	154	246	15	134	5527	23.92	3	30	–	113
Peters, S.D.	250	423	32	222	13767	35.20	31	67	4	188
Petersen, A.N.	185	326	17	210	12105	39.17	35	50	1+2	143
Peterson, R.J.	136	205	26	130	4553	25.43	6	18	–	65
Pettini, M.L.	144	242	36	209	7230	35.09	9	44	1	105
Philander, V.D.	109	143	25	168	3085	26.14	2	10	–	29
Phillips, T.J.	78	109	17	89	1853	20.14	–	7	–	52
Pietersen, K.P.	213	352	23	254*	16053	48.79	49	70	3	151
Pinner, N.D.	13	19	–	82	397	20.89	–	3	–	12
Piolet, S.A.	11	19	2	103*	361	21.23	1	–	–	8
Plunkett, L.E.	136	185	36	114	3632	24.37	2	18	–	79
Pollock, A.W.	5	8	2	45	134	22.33	–	–	–	1
Porter, J.A.	3	3	2	5	5	5.00	–	–	–	1

F-C	M	I	NO	HS	Runs	Avge	100	50	1000	Ct/St
Porterfield, W.T.S.	107	176	7	175	5184	30.67	7	29	–	116
Poulson, J.E.	1	1	–	40	40	40.00	–	–	–	–
Powell, H.W.	2	1	1	16*	16	–	–	–	–	–
Poynter, S.W.	8	9	–	63	201	22.33	–	1	–	23/2
Poysden, J.E.	4	4	–	47	63	15.75	–	–	–	2
Prasad, K.T.G.D.	97	113	13	103*	2023	20.23	1	8	–	28
Prince, A.G.	272	442	48	257*	17006	43.16	40	85	3+1	208
Pringle, R.D.	2	4	1	63*	126	42.00	–	1	–	–
Prior, M.J.	249	381	44	201*	13228	39.25	28	75	3	642/41
Procter, L.A.	46	69	5	106	1977	30.89	1	11	–	9
Pujara, C.A.	101	167	26	352	8296	58.83	27	28	0+2	62/1
Purshouse, C.J.	2	3	–	11	19	6.33	–	–	–	1
Pyrah, R.M.	48	57	8	134*	1417	28.91	3	7	–	22
Qureshi, U.A.	6	9	1	47	134	16.75	–	–	–	–
Rahane, A.M.	74	126	14	265*	6495	57.99	22	28	0+3	60
Raine, B.A.	13	23	2	72	440	20.95	–	2	–	3
Rankin, W.B.	73	85	36	43	396	8.08	–	–	–	19
Rashid, A.U.	129	178	33	180	5111	35.24	9	27	–	63
Rayner, O.P.	88	113	20	143*	2268	24.38	2	11	–	106
Read, C.M.W.	307	462	76	240	14191	36.76	21	79	3	920/48
Redfern, D.J.	79	133	8	133	3676	29.40	2	28	–	39
Reece, L.M.	24	43	5	114*	1361	35.81	1	11	–	16
Rees, G.P.	109	191	10	154	5910	32.65	13	34	2	80
Richardson, M.J.	46	76	2	148	2332	31.51	4	12	1	77/1
Riley, A.E.N.	37	47	16	23*	278	8.96	–	–	–	20
Rimmington, N.J.	23	35	12	102*	530	23.04	1	1	–	8
Robson, A.J.	19	34	–	115	1145	33.67	1	9	1	12
Robson, S.D.	82	146	13	215*	5362	40.31	13	21	2	85
Roderick, G.H.	29	44	9	171	1587	45.34	3	8	–	67/1
Roebuck, C.G.	3	5	1	27*	54	13.50	–	–	–	–
Rogers, C.J.L.	275	492	36	319	22772	49.93	70	103	8+2	227
Roland-Jones, T.S.	53	74	15	77	1192	20.20	–	4	–	16
Root, J.E.	69	116	15	236	4903	48.54	12	20	3	39
Ross, P.A.	2	3	1	16	17	8.50	–	–	–	2
Rossington, A.M.	15	25	2	103*	692	30.08	2	3	–	30/4
Rouse, A.P.	5	8	–	49	133	16.62	–	–	–	13/2
Rouse, H.P.	3	4	–	16	56	14.00	–	–	–	–
Roy, J.J.	50	82	8	121*	2564	34.64	4	11	1	44
Rudolph, J.A.	250	429	26	228*	17502	43.42	48	82	4+1	218
Rushworth, C.	55	75	24	46	641	12.56	–	–	–	8
Russell, C.J.	18	22	4	22	129	7.16	–	–	–	4
Rutherford, H.D.	42	74	1	239	2600	35.61	7	9	0+1	31
Ryder, J.D.	91	151	9	236	6386	44.97	19	27	–	88
Sabin, L.M.	4	7	–	50	133	19.00	–	1	–	2
Sadler, P.T.	9	14	4	34	93	9.30	–	–	–	4
Saeed Ajmal	134	182	50	53*	1611	12.20	–	4	–	44
Sakande, A.	1	1	–	29	29	29.00	–	–	–	–
Sales, D.J.G.	249	395	35	303*	14140	39.27	29	64	6	221
Salisbury, M.E.T.	8	11	3	19	60	7.50	–	–	–	1
Salter, A.G.	12	17	4	25*	173	13.30	–	–	–	4
Sammy, D.J.G.	96	158	9	121	3549	23.81	2	22	–	137
Sandhu, G.S.	5	3	2	8	21	21.00	–	–	–	–
Sangakkara, K.C.	221	361	28	319	17099	51.34	49	75	0+1	343/33
Sarwan, R.R.	220	374	26	291	13405	38.52	33	71	–	155
Saxelby, I.D.	40	58	17	60*	650	15.85	–	1	–	12
Scriven, B.	2	2	1	44*	55	55.00	–	–	–	–

241

F-C	M	I	NO	HS	Runs	Avge	100	50	1000	Ct/St
Sears, A.D.	1	1	–	29	29	29.00	–	–	–	–
Senaratne, N.V.S.	6	12	–	82	251	20.91	–	1	–	–
Shah, O.A.	252	428	38	203	16357	41.94	45	79	8	200
Shahid Afridi	111	183	4	164	5631	31.45	12	30	–	75
Shahzad, A.	80	108	28	88	1940	24.25	–	6	–	12
Shantry, J.D.	57	75	20	101*	1070	19.45	1	2	–	19
Sharma, I.	85	113	43	31*	623	8.90	–	–	–	18
Sharma, R.G.	65	99	10	309*	5291	59.44	18	21	–	51
Sheikh, A.	5	9	2	12	30	4.28	–	–	–	2
Shoaib Malik	113	175	20	200	5626	36.29	15	25	–	58
Shreck, C.E.	143	167	90	56	683	8.87	–	1	–	38
Sibley, D.P.	9	14	–	242	420	30.00	1	1	–	6
Siddle, P.M.	104	141	25	103*	1963	16.92	1	4	–	39
Sidebottom, R.J.	202	249	69	61	2454	13.63	–	3	–	58
Silva, J.K.	147	230	28	193	9794	48.48	30	42	0+2	335/46
Simpson, J.A.	82	128	17	143	3356	30.23	4	19	–	248/16
Slater, B.T.	23	43	1	119	1230	29.28	2	7	–	9
Smith, G.C.	165	284	19	311	12916	48.73	37	51	–	241
Smith, G.M.	120	197	17	177	5559	30.88	7	33	–	40
Smith, G.P.	85	158	8	158*	4303	28.68	8	19	–	70
Smith, R.A.J.	11	15	2	57*	205	15.76	–	1	–	2
Smith, T.C.	98	145	25	128	3516	29.30	3	22	–	101
Smith, T.M.J.	36	51	9	80	926	22.04	–	2	–	11
Smith, W.R.	138	231	16	201*	7191	33.44	16	25	1	79
Sohail Tanvir	59	94	9	132	2389	28.10	4	12	–	24
Soilleux, A.C.	6	9	2	22	50	7.14	–	–	–	1
Solanki, V.S.	324	544	33	270	18325	35.86	34	98	6	348
Spriegel, M.N.W.	56	94	7	108*	1965	22.58	3	6	–	32
Steel, C.T.	2	3	–	68	121	40.33	–	1	–	2
Steele, O.J.	4	7	4	53*	91	30.33	–	1	–	2
Sterland, J.L.	2	3	–	27	42	14.00	–	–	–	1
Stevens, D.I.	235	376	23	208	12482	35.35	29	59	3	177
Stirling, P.R.	26	42	2	115	1282	32.05	3	9	–	13
Stokes, B.A.	72	118	7	185	3765	33.91	9	16	–	39
Stone, O.P.	8	12	3	26*	93	10.33	–	–	–	5
Stoneman, M.D.	101	175	5	187	5211	30.65	11	26	2	55
Styris, S.B.	128	213	20	212*	6048	31.33	10	30	–	103
Sykes, J.S.	10	18	3	34	174	11.60	–	–	–	5
Tait, S.W.	50	70	29	68	509	12.41	–	2	–	15
Tanveer Sikandar	3	3	–	5	10	3.33	–	–	–	–
Tavaré, W.A.	21	37	3	139	1276	37.52	4	6	1	12
Taylor, B.J.	2	3	1	20	21	10.50	–	–	–	2
Taylor, B.R.M.	83	152	9	217	6241	43.64	23	22	0+1	104/4
Taylor, J.M.R.	15	24	2	63	527	23.95	–	2	–	8
Taylor, J.W.A.	119	196	26	242*	7939	46.70	18	39	4	78
Taylor, M.D.	13	15	7	32*	149	18.62	–	–	–	2
Taylor, R.M.L.	31	53	3	101*	1055	21.10	1	5	–	15
Taylor, T.A.I.	6	9	2	40	115	16.42	–	–	–	1
ten Doeschate, R.N.	115	169	24	259*	6709	46.26	21	26	–	67
Terry, S.P.	6	7	1	59*	208	34.66	–	3	–	5
Thakor, S.J.	24	39	6	134	1288	39.03	2	9	–	6
Thirimanne, H.D.R.L.	65	113	13	156	4184	41.84	12	19	0+1	55
Thomas, A.C.	157	218	45	119*	4051	23.41	2	14	–	36
Thomas, I.A.A.	8	12	6	11	57	9.50	–	–	–	2
Thomson, A.T.	2	2	–	25	25	12.50	–	–	–	–
Thornely, M.A.	40	68	2	131	1455	22.04	2	6	–	32

F-C	M	I	NO	HS	Runs	Avge	100	50	1000	Ct/St
Tomlinson, J.A.	114	140	66	51	818	11.05	–	1	–	24
Topley, R.J.W.	29	34	16	12	52	2.88	–	–	–	7
Tredwell, J.C.	149	212	25	123*	4135	22.11	3	15	–	161
Trego, P.D.	172	251	32	141	7224	32.98	11	42	–	75
Tremlett, C.T.	143	178	44	90	2377	17.73	–	10	–	37
Trescothick, M.E.	327	561	30	284	22220	41.84	55	110	6	450
Trott, I.J.L.	218	364	39	226	14681	45.17	36	71	6	192
Troughton, J.O.	167	259	21	223	8491	35.67	19	44	1	88
Turner, M.L.	30	36	15	57	330	15.71	–	1	–	11
van den Bergh, F.O.E.	6	8	1	34	57	8.14	–	–	–	1
Vanderspar, W.G.R.	4	7	2	60*	163	32.60	–	1	–	2
Velani, K.S.	5	7	1	29	120	20.00	–	–	–	–
Vijay, M.	80	134	5	266	5724	44.37	14	22	0+1	74
Vince, J.M.	87	141	15	240	5235	41.54	14	20	2	76
Wagg, G.G.	113	163	18	116*	3613	24.91	2	22	–	36
Wagner, N.	89	117	28	70	1565	17.58	–	6	–	24
Wainwright, D.J.	77	108	25	109	2173	26.18	3	9	–	28
Wakely, A.G.	79	122	5	113*	3387	28.94	2	21	–	43
Wallace, M.A.	233	371	29	139	9968	29.14	15	46	1	611/52
Waller, M.T.C.	8	9	1	28	91	11.37	–	–	–	5
Walters, S.J.	71	118	8	188	3411	31.00	6	15	–	78
Watling, B.J.	90	159	20	164*	5340	38.41	11	32	–	175/3
Webb, J.P.	4	8	–	38	77	9.62	–	–	–	3
Welegadara, U.W.M.B.C.A.	107	130	44	76	925	10.75	–	1	–	23
Weller, S.D.	2	3	1	18*	33	16.50	–	–	–	–
Wells, L.W.P.	67	115	8	208	3674	34.33	8	16	1	38
Wells, T.J.	6	10	–	82	205	20.50	–	1	–	3
Wessels, M.H.	140	232	20	199	7534	35.53	15	38	1	233/14
Westley, T.	93	159	14	185	4521	31.17	8	22	–	64
Westphal, A.A.	2	1	–	4	4	4.00	–	–	–	–
Westwood, I.J.	130	217	20	178	6526	33.12	13	35	–	73
Wheater, A.J.A.	78	112	14	164	3760	38.36	7	21	–	113/5
White, G.G.	27	40	5	65	455	13.00	–	2	–	8
White, W.A.	76	121	17	101*	2511	24.14	1	13	–	24
Whiteley, R.A.	44	69	7	130*	1601	25.82	2	6	–	22
Willey, D.J.	52	72	9	81	1614	25.61	–	12	–	11
Williams, T.J.	2	2	1	29	38	38.00	–	–	–	–
Williamson, K.S.	92	159	10	284*	6670	44.76	17	35	–	88
Wilson, G.C.	61	88	13	160*	2553	34.04	3	14	–	103/3
Winter, M.J.	3	4	–	51	126	31.50	–	1	–	1
Woakes, C.R.	102	143	37	152*	4015	37.87	8	16	–	45
Wood, C.P.	34	48	4	105*	1039	23.61	1	5	–	12
Wood, L.	1	2	1	12	17	17.00	–	–	–	–
Wood, M.A.	21	32	6	58*	500	19.23	–	1	–	7
Wood, S.K.W.	3	4	1	45	77	25.66	–	–	–	–
Wright, B.J.	84	139	10	172	3506	27.17	6	14	–	44
Wright, C.J.C.	101	122	29	77	1609	17.30	–	7	–	16
Wright, L.J.	98	147	19	189	5069	39.60	14	23	–	39
Wyatt, A.C.F.	26	35	12	32	204	8.86	–	–	–	3
Wylie, B.A.	3	6	2	29*	45	11.25	–	–	–	2
Yardy, M.H.	182	302	27	257	9999	36.36	21	46	2	170
Yasir Arafat	197	287	41	170	6708	27.26	5	35	–	52
Yates, C.S.J.	2	4	–	9	17	4.25	–	–	–	4
Young, D.R.	3	6	–	14	31	5.16	–	–	–	4
Younus Khan	191	317	37	313	13868	49.52	44	54	0+1	195
Zain Shahzad	2	4	–	16	44	11.00	–	–	–	–

BOWLING

'50wS' denotes instances of taking 50 or more wickets in a season. Where these have been achieved outside the British Isles they are shown after a plus sign.

	Runs	Wkts	Avge	Best	5wI	10wM	50wS
Aaron, V.R.	2005	57	35.17	5- 17	1	–	–
Abbott, K.J.	4787	223	21.46	8- 45	13	2	0+1
Abdur Rehman	12826	488	26.28	9- 65	23	5	0+1
Abell, T.B.	11	0	–				
Adams, A.R.	16222	683	23.75	7- 32	32	6	3
Adams, J.H.K.	718	13	55.23	2- 16	–	–	–
Adams, R.J.	78	0	–				
Agathangelou, A.P.	436	9	48.44	2- 18	–	–	–
Akram, B.M.R.	88	2	44.00	2- 82	–	–	–
Alexander, T.D.	148	5	29.60	4- 80	–	–	–
Ali, K.	13731	500	27.46	8- 50	23	4	5
Ali, M.M.	6586	169	38.97	6- 29	5	1	–
Allenby, J.	6551	254	25.79	6- 54	5	1	1
Ambrose, T.R.	1	0	–				
Amla, H.M.	277	1	277.00	1- 10	–	–	–
Anderson, C.J.	1286	33	38.96	5- 22	1	–	–
Anderson, J.M.	18027	664	27.14	7- 43	32	5	3
Andrew, G.M.	7482	221	33.85	5- 40	5	–	1
Ansari, Z.S.	2068	54	38.29	5- 33	2	–	–
Anyon, J.E.	10954	311	35.22	6- 82	7	–	2
Arif, A.T.	164	4	41.00	2- 29	–	–	–
Arshad, U.	628	31	20.25	4- 78	–	–	–
Ashar Zaidi	2238	78	28.69	4- 50	–	–	–
Ashwin, R.	6835	241	28.36	7-103	20	5	–
Astle, T.D.	6792	188	36.12	8-148	7	1	–
Azeem Rafiq	2010	55	36.54	5- 50	1	–	–
Azhar Mahmood	15337	611	25.10	8- 61	27	3	0+1
Azhar Ullah	7278	261	27.88	7- 74	12	2	0+1
Bailey, T.E.	339	7	48.42	2- 36	–	–	–
Bairstow, J.M.	1	0	–				
Baker, G.C.	805	8	100.62	2- 35	–	–	–
Balbirnie, A.	95	2	47.50	1- 5	–	–	–
Balcombe, D.J.	6436	196	32.83	8- 71	9	2	1
Ball, A.J.	1094	25	43.76	3- 36	–	–	–
Ball, J.T.	420	17	24.70	3- 18	–	–	–
Ballance, G.S.	143	0	–				
Barker, K.H.D.	4746	181	26.22	6- 40	9	1	2
Barrett, C.A.	109	0	–				
Barrett, W.J.M.	2	0	–				
Barrow, A.W.R.	36	1	36.00	1- 4	–	–	–
Barton, A.P.	70	1	70.00	1- 25	–	–	–
Bath, E.R.	103	2	51.50	1- 33	–	–	–
Batty, G.J.	18186	544	33.43	8- 68	22	2	2
Beaven, L.E.	86	2	43.00	1- 39	–	–	–
Beer, W.A.T.	519	13	39.92	3- 31	–	–	–
Bell, I.R.	1598	47	34.00	4- 4	–	–	–
Bell-Drummond, D.J.	54	0	–				
Bennett, H.K.	4228	121	34.94	7- 50	2	–	–
Berg, G.K.	4504	140	32.17	6- 58	3	–	–
Best, P.M.	1445	32	45.15	6- 86	2	–	–
Billings, S.W.	4	0	–				
Binny, S.T.R.	2757	82	33.62	5- 49	3	1	–

F-C	Runs	Wkts	Avge	Best	5wI	10wM	50wS
Bird, J.M.	2356	115	20.48	6- 25	7	2	0+1
Bishnoi, C.	241	5	48.20	3- 71	–	–	–
Blake, A.J.	129	3	43.00	2- 9	–	–	–
Bollinger, D.E.	9174	331	27.71	6- 47	15	2	–
Bopara, R.S.	6583	160	41.14	5- 75	1	–	–
Borrington, P.M.	7	0	–				
Borthwick, S.G.	4813	140	34.37	6- 70	2	–	-
Boyce, M.A.G.	72	0	–				
Bracewell, M.G.	30	0	–				
Bragg, W.D.	344	4	86.00	2- 10	–	–	–
Brathwaite, R.M.R.	2309	71	32.52	5- 54	3	–	–
Breese, G.R.	8687	287	30.26	7- 60	12	3	–
Bresnan, T.T.	12448	398	31.27	5- 42	6	–	–
Briggs, D.R.	5416	170	31.85	6- 45	6	–	–
Broad, S.C.J.	13467	478	28.17	8- 52	22	3	–
Brooks, J.A.	6266	226	27.72	5- 23	7	–	1
Brown, B.C.	14	0	–				
Brown, K.R.	49	2	24.50	2- 30	–	–	–
Browne, N.L.J.	153	0	–				
Brownlie, D.G.	180	1	180.00	1- 13	–	–	–
Buck, N.L.	5667	150	37.78	5- 76	4	–	–
Buckley, R.S.	384	10	38.40	5- 86	1	–	–
Bull, K.A.	168	7	24.00	4- 62	–	–	–
Burke, J.E.	68	2	34.00	2- 51	–	–	–
Burns, R.J.	108	2	54.00	1- 18	–	–	–
Butler, I.G.	6315	204	30.95	6- 46	4	1	–
Buttler, J.C.	11	0	–				
Cachopa, C.	73	0	–				
Carberry, M.A.	1041	16	65.06	2- 85	–	–	–
Carter, A.	2080	70	29.71	5- 40	2	–	–
Carver, K.	65	3	21.66	2- 27	–	–	–
Cato, S.J.	69	1	69.00	1- 31	–	–	–
Chambers, M.A.	4968	141	35.23	6- 68	3	1	–
Chanderpaul, S.	2537	60	42.28	4- 48	–	–	–
Chandimal, L.D.	18	1	18.00	1- 13	–	–	–
Chapple, G.	25825	975	26.48	7- 53	39	3	7
Chase, P.K.D.	173	11	15.72	5- 64	1	–	–
Chopra, V.	116	0	–				
Choudhry, S.H.	1189	33	36.03	4- 38	–	–	–
Christian, D.T.	4011	109	36.79	5- 24	2	–	–
Clare, J.L.	4190	154	27.20	7- 74	6	1	–
Clarke, R.	9861	284	34.72	6- 63	2	–	–
Claydon, M.E.	5910	189	31.26	6-104	5	–	1
Cobb, J.J.	816	9	90.66	2- 11	–	–	–
Coetzer, K.J.	402	6	67.00	2- 16	–	–	–
Coles, M.T.	5749	195	29.48	6- 51	7	1	1
Collingwood, P.D.	5623	143	39.32	5- 52	1	–	–
Compton, N.R.D.	223	3	74.33	1- 1	–	–	–
Cook, A.N.	211	7	30.14	3- 13	–	–	–
Cooper, T.L.W.	643	10	64.30	2- 43	–	–	–
Cosker, D.A.	21032	589	35.70	6- 91	12	1	1
Cotton, B.D.	111	8	13.87	4- 20	–	–	–
Coughlin, P.	387	10	38.70	3- 42	–	–	–
Cowdrey, F.K.	129	3	43.00	3- 59	–	–	–
Craddock, T.R.	1251	41	30.51	5- 96	1	–	–
Craig, M.D.	2466	58	42.51	5- 56	2	–	–

245

F-C	Runs	Wkts	Avge	Best	5wI	10wM	50wS
Croft, S.J.	2404	59	40.74	6- 41	1	–	–
Crook, S.P.	6290	162	38.82	5- 48	3	–	–
Curran, T.K.	526	19	27.68	5- 51	1	–	–
Dawson, L.A.	3069	81	37.88	7- 51	2	–	–
de Grandhomme, C.	2977	97	30.69	6- 24	1	–	–
Denly, J.L.	1324	27	49.03	3- 43	–	–	–
Dent, C.D.J.	308	2	154.00	1- 12	–	–	–
Dernbach, J.W.	8530	265	32.18	6- 47	10	–	1
Dexter, N.J.	3126	84	37.21	6- 63	2	–	–
Dhawan, S.	133	3	44.33	2- 30	–	–	–
Dhoni, M.S.	87	0	–				
Dilshan, T.M.	3182	89	35.75	5- 49	1	–	–
Dixon, L.	183	5	36.60	3- 92	–	–	–
Dockrell, G.H.	3422	119	28.75	6- 27	6	–	–
D'Oliveira, B.L.	271	1	271.00	1- 73	–	–	–
Dunn, M.P.	2057	64	32.14	5- 48	3	–	–
Durston, W.J.	3601	86	41.87	5- 19	2	–	–
Eckersley, E.J.H.	58	2	29.00	2- 29	–	–	–
Edwards, G.A.	346	8	43.25	4- 44	–	–	–
Elliott, G.D.	3378	92	36.71	5- 33	1	–	–
Elstone, S.L.	124	6	20.66	2- 8	–	–	–
Endersby, D.M.	291	4	72.75	1- 38	–	–	–
Eranga, R.M.S.	4656	149	31.24	6- 21	2	–	–
Ervine, S.M.	10807	262	41.24	6- 82	5	–	–
Evans, L.J.	228	1	228.00	1- 30	–	–	–
Fernando, A.N.P.R.	4101	106	38.68	5- 36	2	–	–
Ferraby, N.J.	112	4	28.00	2- 19	–	–	–
Finch, A.J.	246	4	61.50	1- 0	–	–	–
Finch, H.Z.	15	0	–				
Finn, S.T.	11010	385	28.59	9- 37	11	1	2
Fletcher, L.J.	5910	202	29.25	5- 52	3	–	–
Flintoff, A.	11059	350	31.59	5- 24	4	–	–
Foakes, B.T.	6	0	–				
Footitt, M.H.A.	5223	198	26.37	6- 48	11	–	1
Foster, J.S.	128	1	128.00	1-122	–	–	–
Franklin, J.E.C.	12027	446	26.96	7- 14	14	1	–
Freckingham, O.H.	1946	44	44.22	6-125	1	–	–
Fuller, J.K.	2452	74	33.13	6- 24	4	1	–
Gale, A.W.	238	1	238.00	1- 33	–	–	–
Gambhir, G.	281	7	40.14	3- 12	–	–	–
Gatting, J.S.	152	2	76.00	1- 8	–	–	–
Gidman, A.P.R.	4521	102	44.32	4- 47	–	–	–
Gidman, W.R.S.	4294	194	22.13	6- 15	9	1	2
Glover, J.C.	2063	56	36.83	5- 38	1	–	–
Godleman, B.A.	35	0	–				
Goodwin, M.W.	376	7	53.71	2- 23	–	–	–
Gordon, R.O.	413	13	31.76	4- 53	–	–	–
Grant, S.E.	42	1	42.00	1- 42	–	–	–
Gregory, L.	1930	70	27.57	6- 47	4	1	–
Griffiths, D.A.	3828	113	33.87	6- 63	4	–	–
Griffiths, S.W.	180	1	180.00	1- 82	–	–	–
Groenewald, T.D.	7975	257	31.03	6- 50	11	–	–
Guptill, M.J.	542	7	77.42	3- 37	–	–	–
Gurney, H.F.	4914	145	33.88	5- 81	2	–	–
Haggett, C.J.	1260	31	40.64	4- 94	–	–	–
Hales, A.D.	171	3	57.00	2- 63	–	–	–

F-C	Runs	Wkts	Avge	Best	5wI	10wM	50wS
Hall, A.J.	17818	639	27.88	6- 77	17	1	–
Hamilton, T.S.I.	26	0	–				
Hamilton-Brown, R.J.	624	11	56.72	2- 5	–	–	–
Hampton, T.R.G.	42	1	42.00	1- 15	–	–	–
Hannon-Dalby, O.J.	2851	78	36.55	5- 68	2	–	–
Harinath, A.	46	4	11.50	2- 1	–	–	–
Harmison, B.W.	1512	37	40.86	4- 27	–	–	–
Harris, J.A.R.	8000	272	29.41	7- 66	9	1	1
Harrison, J.	1137	42	27.07	5- 31	2	–	–
Hartley, C.F.	190	5	38.00	2- 40	–	–	–
Hastings, J.W.	3903	156	25.01	5- 30	5	–	–
Hatchett, L.J.	2108	62	34.00	5- 47	2	–	–
Helm, T.G.	428	14	30.57	3- 46	–	–	–
Henry, M.J.	1360	62	21.93	5- 18	5	–	–
Herath, H.M.R.K.B.	22051	884	24.94	9-127	56	9	0+2
Higginbottom, M.	484	14	34.57	3- 59	–	–	–
Hildreth, J.C.	492	6	82.00	2- 39	–	–	–
Hilfenhaus, B.W.	10490	363	28.89	7- 58	12	1	0+1
Hobden, M.E.	775	25	31.00	5- 62	2	–	–
Hodd, A.J.	7	0	–				
Hogan, M.G.	7135	296	24.10	7- 92	13	1	2
Hogg, K.W.	7903	280	28.22	7- 27	8	1	2
Horton, P.J.	16	0	–				
Housego, D.M.	109	2	54.50	1- 5	–	–	–
Howell, B.A.C.	2009	59	34.05	5- 57	1	–	–
Hughes, A.L.	670	16	41.87	4- 46	–	–	–
Hughes, C.F.	581	15	38.73	2- 9	–	–	–
Hunn, M.D.	273	6	45.50	2- 51	–	–	–
Hussain, G.M.	3365	111	30.31	6- 33	4	–	1
Imran Tahir	18532	702	26.39	8- 76	48	10	2+2
Ingram, C.A.	1343	34	39.50	4- 16	–	–	–
Ireland, A.J.	4507	139	32.42	7- 36	4	1	–
Jadeja, R.A.	5231	189	27.67	7- 31	12	2	0+1
Jaques, P.A.	162	1	162.00	1- 75	–	–	–
Jarvis, K.M.	3281	129	25.43	7- 35	8	1	–
Javid, A.	266	3	88.66	1- 1	–	–	–
Jayawardena, D.P.M.D.	1629	52	31.32	5- 72	1	–	–
Jayawardena, H.A.P.W.	9	0	–				
Jenkins, W.H.	161	1	161.00	1- 89	–	–	–
Jennings, K.K.	240	7	34.28	2- 8	–	–	–
Jones, C.R.	17	1	17.00	1- 17	–	–	–
Jones, G.O.	26	0	–				
Jones, R.A.	4534	146	31.05	7-115	5	–	–
Jordan, C.J.	6358	201	31.63	7- 43	7	–	1
Joseph, R.H.	6092	188	32.40	6- 32	7	1	1
Joyce, E.C.	1025	11	93.18	2- 34	–	–	–
Junaid Khan	6637	287	23.12	7- 46	20	3	0+1
Kapil, A.	340	12	28.33	3- 17	–	–	–
Karunaratne, F.D.M.	134	0	–				
Keedy, G.	21744	691	31.46	7- 68	35	7	4
Keogh, R.I.	235	5	47.00	2- 46	–	–	–
Kerrigan, S.C.	6521	229	28.47	9- 51	11	2	2
Kervezee, A.N.	179	2	89.50	1- 14	–	–	–
Key, R.W.T.	331	3	110.33	2- 31	–	–	–
Khan, I.S.	67	0	–				
Khawaja, U.T.	98	1	98.00	1- 21	–	–	–

F-C	Runs	Wkts	Avge	Best	5wI	10wM	50wS
Kidd, M.J.L.	77	1	77.00	1- 77	–	–	–
Kieswetter, C.	29	2	14.50	2- 3	–	–	–
Kleinveldt, R.K.	7264	259	28.04	8- 47	10	1	–
Klinger, M.	3	0	–				
Knight, T.C.	143	2	71.50	2- 32	–	–	–
Kohli, V.	324	3	108.00	1- 19	–	–	–
Kuggeleijn, S.C.	2760	73	37.80	5- 63	2	–	–
Kulasekara, K.M.D.N.	6569	272	24.15	7- 27	9	1	0+1
Kumar, B.	4724	177	26.68	6- 77	10	–	–
Lancefield, T.J.	27	1	27.00	1- 12	–	–	–
Latham, T.W.M.	6	0	–				
Laws, A.R.	24	1	24.00	1- 17	–	–	–
Leach, J.	1520	51	29.80	5- 36	1	–	–
Leach, M.J.	804	23	34.95	5- 63	1	–	–
Leaning, J.A.	35	0	–				
Lees, A.Z.	14	0	–				
Lester, T.J.	530	6	88.33	2- 58	–	–	–
Lewis, J.	22303	849	26.26	8- 95	35	5	9
Libby, J.D.	104	1	104.00	1- 18	–	–	–
Liddle, C.J.	1345	24	56.04	3- 42	–	–	–
Lilley, A.E.	136	6	22.66	5- 41	1	–	–
Lilley, A.M.	212	2	106.00	1- 41	–	–	–
Linley, T.E.	5296	191	27.72	6- 57	5	1	1
Lloyd, D.L.	126	4	31.50	2- 22	–	–	–
Lumb, M.J.	255	6	42.50	2- 10	–	–	–
Lyth, A.	612	12	51.00	2- 15	–	–	–
McCarter, G.J.	762	21	36.28	4- 95	–	–	–
McClenaghan, M.J.	3722	95	39.17	8- 23	3	–	–
McKay, C.J.	4012	140	28.65	6- 40	3	–	–
MacLeod, C.S.	342	15	22.80	4- 66	–	–	–
MacQueen, A.	284	5	56.80	4-116	–	–	–
MacVicar, W.A.	231	3	77.00	2- 46	–	–	–
Machan, M.W.	72	1	72.00	1- 36	–	–	–
Madsen, W.L.	530	10	53.00	3- 45	–	–	–
Magoffin, S.J.	10503	441	23.81	8- 20	17	2	3
Mahmood, S.I.	10802	329	32.83	6- 30	9	2	–
Main, G.T.	72	3	24.00	3- 72	–	–	–
Malan, D.J.	1787	42	42.54	5- 61	1	–	–
Marriott, W.W.J.	40	0	–				
Marsden, J.	336	11	30.54	4- 65	–	–	–
Marshall, H.J.H.	1834	39	47.02	4- 24	–	–	–
Masters, D.D.	15475	612	25.28	8- 10	30	–	4
Mathews, A.D.	2337	49	47.69	5- 47	1	–	–
Maxwell, G.J.	1595	42	37.97	4- 42	–	–	–
Meaker, S.C.	5937	210	28.27	8- 52	11	2	1
Meschede, C.A.J.	1693	49	34.55	4- 43	–	–	–
Mickleburgh, J.C.	50	0	–				
Middlebrook, J.D.	17682	458	38.60	6- 78	14	1	1
Miles, C.N.	1753	63	27.82	6- 88	4	–	–
Mills, T.S.	1851	52	35.59	4- 25	–	–	–
Milnes, M.E.	108	3	36.00	2- 37	–	–	–
Mitchell, D.K.H.	840	19	44.21	4- 49	–	–	–
Mohammed Shami	3061	103	29.71	7- 79	4	2	–
Moore, S.C.	321	5	64.20	1- 13	–	–	–
Moore, T.C.	328	8	41.00	4- 78	–	–	–
Morgan, A.O.	87	2	43.50	1- 19	–	–	–

F-C	Runs	Wkts	Avge	Best	5wI	10wM	50wS
Morgan, E.J.G.	90	2	45.00	2- 24	–	–	–
Morris, C.A.J.	1945	66	29.46	5- 54	1	–	1
Muchall, G.J.	626	15	41.73	3- 26	–	–	–
Mullaney, S.J.	1458	34	42.88	4- 31	–	–	–
Munro, C.	1173	34	34.50	4- 36	–	–	–
Murphy, D.	3	0	–				
Murtagh, T.J.	14768	545	27.09	7- 82	26	4	6
Mustard, P.	9	1	9.00	1- 9	–	–	–
Myburgh, J.G.	1973	42	46.97	4- 56	–	–	–
Naik, J.K.H.	5820	150	38.80	7- 96	5	–	–
Nannes, D.P.	2327	93	25.02	7- 50	2	1	–
Napier, G.R.	12242	386	31.71	7- 21	12	–	2
Nash, B.P.	801	23	34.82	2- 7	–	–	–
Nash, C.D.	2826	74	38.18	4- 12	–	–	–
Newby, O.J.	4330	133	32.55	5- 69	1	–	–
Newton, R.I.	19	0	–				
Noema-Barnett, K.	1880	57	32.98	4- 20	–	–	–
North, M.J.	6175	158	39.08	6- 55	3	–	–
Northeast, S.A.	145	1	145.00	1- 60	–	–	–
Norwell, L.C.	2738	77	35.55	6- 46	2	–	–
O'Brien, K.J.	777	27	28.77	5- 39	1	–	–
O'Brien, N.J.	19	2	9.50	1- 4	–	–	–
O'Gorman, T.J.J.	73	1	73.00	1- 51	–	–	–
Onions, G.	12088	459	26.33	9- 67	21	3	5
Overton, C.	1628	55	29.60	5- 63	1	–	–
Overton, J.	2198	52	42.26	6- 95	1	–	–
Owen, W.T.	2241	51	43.94	5-124	1	–	–
Palladino, A.P.	8480	290	29.24	7- 53	11	–	2
Panesar, M.S.	21440	697	30.76	7- 60	39	6	6
Pankaj Singh	7949	302	26.32	8- 32	21	4	0+1
Param, A.E.	10	0	–				
Pardoe, M.G.	143	3	47.66	2- 34	–	–	–
Parry, S.D.	650	18	36.11	5- 23	1	–	–
Patel, J.S.	17378	470	36.97	7- 75	16	1	3
Patel, R.H.	1766	50	35.32	5- 69	1	–	–
Patel, S.R.	8579	208	41.24	7- 68	3	1	–
Patel, Z.R.	248	5	49.60	2- 32	–	–	–
Patterson, S.A.	6510	231	28.18	5- 43	3	–	2
Payne, D.A.	3350	93	36.02	6- 26	2	–	–
Penhale, K.W.	85	3	28.33	2- 69	–	–	–
Perera, M.D.K.	13286	524	25.35	7- 71	28	2	0+2
Peters, S.D.	31	1	31.00	1- 19	–	–	–
Petersen, A.N.	809	16	50.56	3- 58	–	–	–
Peterson, R.J.	12427	376	33.05	6- 67	15	1	1
Pettini, M.L.	263	1	263.00	1- 72	–	–	–
Philander, V.D.	8679	408	21.27	7- 61	20	2	0+2
Phillips, T.J.	6015	132	45.56	5- 41	1	–	–
Pietersen, K.P.	3752	73	51.39	4- 31	–	–	–
Pinner, N.D.	32	0	–				
Piolet, S.A.	570	19	30.00	6- 17	1	1	–
Plunkett, L.E.	12809	414	30.93	6- 33	11	1	3
Pollock, A.W.	620	17	36.47	4- 60	–	–	–
Porter, J.A.	116	6	19.33	3- 26	–	–	–
Porterfield, W.T.S.	138	2	69.00	1- 29	–	–	–
Poulson, J.E.	81	2	40.50	2- 81	–	–	–
Powell, H.W.	147	1	147.00	1- 26	–	–	–

F-C	Runs	Wkts	Avge	Best	5wI	10wM	50wS
Poysden, J.E.	264	5	52.80	3- 20	–	–	–
Prasad, K.T.G.D.	7675	268	28.63	6- 25	5	1	–
Prince, A.G.	179	4	44.75	2- 11	–	–	–
Pringle, R.D.	108	2	54.00	2- 94	–	–	–
Procter, L.A.	1883	58	32.46	7- 71	2	–	–
Pujara, C.A.	89	5	17.80	2- 4	–	–	–
Pyrah, R.M.	2454	55	44.61	5- 58	1	–	–
Rahane, A.M.	75	0	–				
Raine, B.A.	1012	27	37.48	4- 98	–	–	–
Rankin, W.B.	6481	242	26.78	5- 16	6	–	1
Rashid, A.U.	12880	374	34.43	7-107	18	1	2
Rayner, O.P.	6334	179	35.38	8- 46	7	1	–
Read, C.M.W.	90	0	–				
Redfern, D.J.	711	18	39.50	3- 33	–	–	–
Reece, L.M.	445	14	31.78	4- 28	–	–	–
Rees, G.P.	33	1	33.00	1- 6	–	–	–
Richardson, M.J.	13	0	–				
Riley, A.E.N.	3204	99	32.36	7-150	5	–	1
Rimmington, N.J.	1836	63	29.14	5- 46	1	–	–
Robson, A.J.	95	0	–				
Robson, S.D.	72	1	72.00	1- 4	–	–	–
Roebuck, C.G.	3	0	–				
Rogers, C.J.L.	133	1	133.00	1- 16	–	–	–
Roland-Jones, T.S.	4828	200	24.14	6- 50	11	2	1
Root, J.E.	914	16	57.12	3- 33	–	–	–
Rouse, H.P.	320	2	160.00	1- 55	–	–	–
Roy, J.J.	380	11	34.54	3- 9	–	–	–
Rudolph, J.A.	2626	59	44.50	5- 80	3	–	–
Rushworth, C.	4621	188	24.57	9- 52	9	2	2
Russell, C.J.	1566	38	41.21	4- 43	–	–	–
Ryder, J.D.	2803	99	28.31	5- 24	4	1	–
Sabin, L.M.	5	0	–				
Sadler, P.T.	885	11	80.45	3- 50	–	–	–
Saeed Ajmal	14147	546	25.91	7- 19	37	7	1+1
Sakande, A.	112	3	37.33	3- 71	–	–	–
Sales, D.J.G.	184	9	20.44	4- 25	–	–	–
Salisbury, M.E.T.	739	15	49.26	4- 50	–	–	–
Salter, A.G.	950	18	52.77	3- 66	–	–	–
Sammy, D.J.G.	6312	217	29.08	7- 66	10	–	–
Sandhu, G.S.	357	7	51.00	4- 49	–	–	–
Sangakkara, K.C.	150	1	150.00	1- 13	–	–	–
Sarwan, R.R.	2351	56	41.98	6- 62	1	–	–
Saxelby, I.D.	3335	109	30.59	6- 48	3	1	–
Sears, A.D.	122	8	15.25	5- 73	1	–	–
Shah, O.A.	1505	26	57.88	3- 33	–	–	–
Shahid Afridi	7023	258	27.22	6-101	8	–	–
Shahzad, A.	7140	201	35.52	5- 51	3	–	–
Shantry, J.D.	4903	165	29.71	7- 60	6	1	1
Sharma, I.	8934	281	31.79	7- 24	9	2	–
Sharma, R.G.	1021	23	44.39	4- 41	–	–	–
Sheikh, A.	596	14	42.57	4- 97	–	–	–
Shoaib Malik	6603	226	29.21	7- 81	8	1	–
Shreck, C.E.	15024	474	31.69	8- 31	21	2	3
Sibley, D.P.	64	1	64.00	1- 41	–	–	–
Siddle, P.M.	10218	363	28.14	6- 43	15	–	0+1
Sidebottom, R.J.	16185	663	24.41	7- 37	26	3	4

F-C	Runs	Wkts	Avge	Best	5wI	10wM	50wS
Silva, J.K.	33	1	33.00	1- 11	–	–	–
Slater, B.T.	28	0	–				
Smith, G.C.	1132	11	102.90	2-145	–	–	–
Smith, G.M.	6392	179	35.70	5- 42	4	–	–
Smith, G.P.	73	1	73.00	1- 64	–	–	–
Smith, R.A.J.	940	22	42.72	3- 38	–	–	–
Smith, T.C.	6433	226	28.46	6- 46	6	–	1
Smith, T.M.J.	3049	62	49.17	4- 35	–	–	–
Smith, W.R.	882	20	44.10	3- 34	–	–	–
Sohail Tanvir	6519	265	24.60	8- 54	17	3	0+1
Soilleux, A.C.	534	16	33.37	3- 37	–	–	–
Solanki, V.S.	4230	90	47.00	5- 40	4	1	–
Spriegel, M.N.W.	1485	35	42.42	3- 26	–	–	–
Steel, C.T.	39	1	39.00	1- 39	–	–	–
Sterland, J.L.	5	0	–				
Stevens, D.I.	7713	258	29.89	7- 21	10	1	1
Stirling, P.R.	394	7	56.28	2- 43	–	–	–
Stokes, B.A.	4587	162	28.31	7- 67	3	1	–
Stone, O.P.	705	24	29.37	5- 48	1	–	–
Stoneman, M.D.	85	0	–				
Styris, S.B.	6440	204	31.56	6- 32	9	1	–
Sykes, J.S.	1114	20	55.70	4-176	–	–	–
Tait, S.W.	5661	198	28.59	7- 29	7	1	0+1
Tanveer Sikandar	159	5	31.80	2- 90	–	–	–
Taylor, B.J.	180	5	36.00	4- 64	–	–	–
Taylor, B.R.M.	213	4	53.25	2- 36	–	–	–
Taylor, J.M.R.	1193	29	41.13	4-125	–	–	–
Taylor, J.W.A.	176	0	–				
Taylor, M.D.	1209	26	46.50	5- 75	1	–	–
Taylor, R.M.L.	2639	66	39.98	5- 55	3	–	–
Taylor, T.A.I.	451	15	30.06	5- 58	1	–	–
ten Doeschate, R.N.	6347	186	34.12	6- 20	7	–	–
Thakor, S.J.	796	16	49.75	3- 57	–	–	–
Thirimanne, H.D.R.L.	76	0	–				
Thomas, A.C.	13677	518	26.40	7- 54	24	2	1
Thomas, I.A.A.	467	16	29.18	3- 39	–	–	–
Thomson, A.T.	104	0	–				
Thornely, M.A.	533	10	53.30	2- 14	–	–	–
Tomlinson, J.A.	10935	348	31.42	8- 46	12	1	2
Topley, R.J.W.	3017	118	25.56	6- 29	7	2	–
Tredwell, J.C.	13529	375	36.07	8- 66	12	3	1
Trego, P.D.	12054	339	35.55	7- 84	4	1	1
Tremlett, C.T.	12939	453	28.56	8- 96	13	–	–
Trescothick, M.E.	1551	36	43.08	4- 36	–	–	–
Trott, I.J.L.	3040	64	47.50	7- 39	1	–	–
Troughton, J.O.	1416	22	64.36	3- 1	–	–	–
Turner, M.L.	2756	60	45.93	5- 32	1	–	–
van den Bergh, F.O.E.	522	11	47.45	4- 84	–	–	–
Vanderspar, W.G.R.	88	4	22.00	2- 52	–	–	–
Velani, K.S.	21	0	–				
Vijay, M.	256	4	64.00	1- 8	–	–	–
Vince, J.M.	737	17	43.35	5- 41	1	–	–
Wagg, G.G.	11402	340	33.53	6- 29	10	1	2
Wagner, N.	9818	372	26.39	7- 46	17	1	0+2
Wainwright, D.J.	6691	178	37.58	6- 33	6	–	1
Wakely, A.G.	322	6	53.66	2- 62	–	–	–

F-C	Runs	Wkts	Avge	Best	5wI	10wM	50wS
Wallace, M.A.	3	0	–				
Waller, M.T.C.	493	10	49.30	3- 33	–	–	–
Walters, S.J.	245	3	81.66	1- 4	–	–	–
Watling, B.J.	8	0	–				
Welagedara, U.W.M.B.C.A.	9034	290	31.15	5- 34	8	1	–
Weller, S.D.	126	6	21.00	3- 66	–	–	–
Wells, L.W.P.	733	14	52.35	3- 38	–	–	–
Wells, T.J.	163	1	163.00	1- 36	–	–	–
Wessels, M.H.	115	3	38.33	1- 10	–	–	–
Westley, T.	1633	37	44.13	4- 55	–	–	–
Westphal, A.A.	116	5	23.20	3- 45	–	–	–
Westwood, I.J.	300	7	42.85	2- 39	–	–	–
Wheater, A.J.A.	86	1	86.00	1- 86	–	–	–
White, G.G.	1868	39	47.89	4- 72	–	–	–
White, W.A.	6015	166	36.23	5- 54	4	–	–
Whiteley, R.A.	1392	28	49.71	2- 6	–	–	–
Willey, D.J.	3854	133	28.97	5- 29	5	1	–
Williams, T.J.	142	11	12.90	5- 34	1	–	–
Williamson, K.S.	3338	78	42.79	5- 75	1	–	–
Wilson, G.C.	89	0	–				
Woakes, C.R.	8836	346	25.53	7- 20	15	3	2
Wood, C.P.	2554	93	27.46	5- 39	3	–	–
Wood, L.	180	3	60.00	2- 87	–	–	–
Wood, M.A.	1723	70	24.61	5- 32	5	–	–
Wood, S.K.W.	92	3	30.66	3- 64	–	–	–
Wright, B.J.	174	2	87.00	1- 14	–	–	–
Wright, C.J.C.	9693	284	34.13	6- 22	8	–	1
Wright, L.J.	4823	120	40.19	5- 65	3	–	–
Wyatt, A.C.F.	2075	57	36.40	3- 35	–	–	–
Wylie, B.A.	210	1	210.00	1-111	–	–	–
Yardy, M.H.	2119	28	75.67	5- 83	1	–	–
Yasir Arafat	18480	767	24.09	9- 35	43	5	0+4
Yates, C.S.J.	32	0	–				
Young, D.R.	2	0	–				
Younus Khan	2033	44	46.20	4- 52			
Zain Shahzad	225	11	20.45	4- 33	–	–	–

LIMITED-OVERS CAREER RECORDS

Compiled by Philip Bailey

The following career records, to the end of the 2014 season, include all players currently registered with first-class counties. These records are restricted to performances in limited-overs matches of 'List A' status as defined by the Association of Cricket Statisticians and Historians now incorporated by ICC into their Classification of Cricket. The following matches qualify for List A status and are included in the figures that follow: Limited-Overs Internationals; Other International matches (e.g. Commonwealth Games, 'A' team internationals); Premier domestic limited-overs tournaments in Test status countries; Official tourist matches against the main first-class teams.

The following matches do NOT qualify for inclusion: World Cup warm-up games; Tourist matches against first-class teams outside the major domestic competitions (e.g. Universities, Minor Counties etc.); Festival, pre-season friendly games and Twenty20 Cup matches.

	M	Runs	Avge	HS	100	50	Wkts	Avge	Best	Econ
Abbott, K.J.	63	349	19.38	45*	–	–	79	28.60	4-36	5.07
Abdur Rehman	139	969	13.45	50	–	1	201	26.18	6-16	4.29
Adams, A.R.	165	1504	16.71	90*	–	1	209	28.50	5- 7	4.72
Adams, J.H.K.	91	2978	39.70	131	2	22	1	105.00	1-34	7.97
Akram, B.M.R.	1	1	1.00	1	–	–	0	–	–	12.00
Ali, M.M.	105	2979	30.39	158	7	14	56	39.37	3-28	5.69
Allenby, J.	95	2096	26.20	91*	–	10	80	31.83	5-43	4.93
Alsop, T.P.	1	0	0.00	0	–	–	–	–	–	–
Ambrose, T.R.	145	3074	30.43	135	3	15	–	–	–	139/28
Anderson, C.J.	35	907	33.59	131*	1	5	26	22.92	5-26	5.71
Anderson, J.M.	237	352	9.26	28	–	–	331	28.02	5-23	4.84
Andrew, G.M.	114	1175	18.07	104	1	2	104	35.25	5-31	6.24
Ansari, Z.S.	27	474	31.60	62	–	2	25	30.68	4-42	5.77
Anyon, J.E.	43	43	5.37	12	–	–	47	30.55	3- 6	5.53
Arshad, U.	1	–	–	–	–	–	0	–	–	4.33
Ashar Zaidi	65	1874	34.07	109	3	10	51	27.05	4-39	4.23
Azhar Mahmood	318	4550	22.08	101*	2	19	346	31.47	6-18	4.70
Azhar Ullah	41	57	8.14	9	–	–	63	26.42	5-38	5.42
Bailey, T.E.	4	4	–	4*	–	–	7	27.71	3-41	5.10
Bairstow, J.M.	58	1412	31.37	123	2	7	–	–	–	42/4
Balbirnie, A.	11	129	12.90	38	–	–	1	58.00	1-31	7.25
Balcombe, D.J.	14	10	2.00	6	–	–	18	27.33	4-38	5.68
Ball, A.J.	26	163	13.58	28	–	–	22	35.50	3-36	5.68
Ball, J.T.	33	86	10.75	19*	–	–	37	30.72	4-25	5.88
Ballance, G.S.	69	2791	51.68	139	6	17	–	–	–	–
Barber, T.E.	2	0	0.00	0	–	–	2	25.00	2-22	6.25
Barker, K.H.D.	43	397	17.26	56	–	1	48	30.58	4-33	5.87
Barrow, A.W.R.	17	276	27.60	72	–	2	–	–	–	14/1
Batty, G.J.	227	2230	16.04	83*	–	5	207	32.07	5-35	4.56
Beaven, L.E.	27	133	33.25	25*	–	–	20	44.50	3-35	5.84
Beer, W.A.T.	37	236	19.66	45*	–	–	35	37.77	3-27	5.22
Bell, I.R.	277	9561	39.67	158	10	68	33	34.48	5-41	5.29
Bell-Drummond, D.J.	13	352	27.07	83	–	3	0	–	–	7.50
Berg, G.K.	59	999	25.61	75	–	5	40	35.17	4-24	5.57
Best, P.M.	13	57	11.40	16*	–	–	11	42.09	3-43	6.27
Billings, S.W.	30	939	44.71	143	2	6	–	–	–	19/5

253

L-O	M	Runs	Avge	HS	100	50	Wkts	Avge	Best	Econ
Bird, J.M.	7	7	7.00	5*	–	–	8	34.62	3-39	4.35
Blake, A.J.	45	632	21.79	81*	–	3	3	24.66	2-13	5.28
Bollinger, D.E.	117	140	8.23	30	–	–	173	27.54	5-35	4.79
Bopara, R.S.	269	8174	40.26	201*	13	48	197	27.38	5-63	5.21
Borthwick, S.G.	63	520	15.75	80	–	2	46	37.63	4-51	5.82
Boyce, M.A.G.	67	1499	26.29	80	–	10	–	–	–	–
Bragg, W.D.	25	638	27.73	88	–	4	1	54.00	1-11	7.36
Bresnan, T.T.	233	2181	18.64	80	–	4	269	33.53	5-48	5.15
Briggs, D.R.	65	201	11.16	25	–	–	69	34.65	4-32	5.04
Broad, S.C.J.	126	516	12.00	45*	–	–	196	27.97	5-23	5.22
Brooks, J.A.	31	34	4.25	10	–	–	30	36.10	3-30	4.81
Brown, B.C.	46	513	20.52	60	–	3	–	–	–	43/9
Brown, K.R.	53	1656	40.39	129	2	9	0	–	–	17.00
Buck, N.L.	36	80	8.88	21	–	–	43	36.55	4-39	6.18
Burns, R.J.	15	387	27.64	87	–	1	–	–	–	–
Buttler, J.C.	98	2855	47.58	121	3	19	–	–	–	95/10
Cachopa, C.	31	733	24.43	121	1	3	–	–	–	–
Callis, E.	1	10	10.00	10	–	–	–	–	–	–
Carberry, M.A.	160	4470	33.11	150*	6	32	11	27.00	3-37	5.53
Carter, A.	20	35	5.83	12	–	–	26	27.00	4-45	6.41
Chambers, M.A.	12	6	2.00	2	–	–	14	33.21	3-29	6.72
Chanderpaul, S.	398	12727	42.14	150	12	93	56	24.78	4-22	4.95
Chapple, G.	284	2062	17.77	81*	–	9	320	28.55	6-18	4.50
Chase, P.K.D.	2	22	–	22*	–	–	1	131.00	1-60	8.73
Chopra, V.	85	3289	42.16	115	7	22	0	–	–	6.00
Choudhry, S.H.	29	246	20.50	44*	–	–	18	44.11	4-54	5.79
Christian, D.T.	82	1882	32.44	117	2	6	83	33.32	6-48	5.41
Clare, J.L.	41	321	11.46	57	–	1	30	40.13	3-39	5.59
Clark, J.	20	275	30.55	72	–	1	9	53.33	2-41	6.95
Clarke, R.	196	3653	25.72	98*	–	19	115	37.77	4-28	5.46
Claydon, M.E.	76	211	7.53	19	–	–	97	30.39	4-39	5.46
Coad, B.O.	7	3	–	2*	–	–	3	94.00	1-34	6.50
Cobb, J.J.	60	1921	36.94	137	5	9	22	49.68	3-34	5.84
Cockbain, I.A.	44	917	30.56	98*	–	7	–	–	–	–
Coetzer, K.J.	113	3272	33.38	133	5	20	4	93.25	1- 2	6.32
Coleman, F.R.J.	35	666	22.20	64*	–	4	–	–	–	–
Coles, M.T.	44	187	9.35	47	–	–	64	23.90	6-32	6.14
Collingwood, P.D.	405	10616	34.13	120*	9	60	256	33.50	6-31	4.81
Compton, N.R.D.	109	3016	37.70	131	6	19	1	53.00	1- 0	5.21
Cook, A.N.	143	5031	38.40	137	9	30	0	–	–	3.33
Cooke, C.B.	53	1535	35.69	137*	2	9	–	–	–	21/2
Cooper, T.L.W.	108	3624	40.26	126*	6	24	21	36.66	3-11	5.07
Cosker, D.A.	243	819	11.21	50*	–	1	254	32.34	5-54	4.80
Cotton, B.D.	4	28	28.00	18*	–	–	4	46.50	2-42	6.09
Coughlin, P.	8	2	1.00	2*	–	–	2	109.50	1-34	4.76
Cowdrey, F.K.	14	439	39.90	75	–	3	5	50.00	2-28	5.31
Cox, O.B.	34	266	14.77	39	–	–	–	–	–	–
Croft, S.J.	121	3074	34.93	107	1	24	54	37.07	4-24	5.43
Crook, S.P.	64	814	19.38	100	1	4	71	31.74	5-36	5.69
Curran, T.K.	5	3	1.00	1*	–	–	9	22.44	5-34	6.27

L-O	M	Runs	Avge	HS	100	50	Wkts	Avge	Best	Econ
Davies, A.L.	9	171	28.50	53	–	1				12/1
Davies, S.M.	150	4554	36.14	127*	6	30	–	–	–	126/41
Dawson, L.A.	92	1620	26.55	97	–	6	57	40.50	4-45	5.12
Denly, J.L.	104	3065	33.68	115	4	16	7	23.28	3-42	6.18
Dent, C.D.J.	32	723	30.12	151*	1	2	10	34.80	4-43	5.35
Dernbach, J.W.	115	197	7.29	31	–	–	173	28.63	5-31	6.09
Dexter, N.J.	92	1896	32.13	135*	2	8	31	59.32	3-17	5.58
Dockrell, G.H.	63	180	13.84	22*	–	–	63	32.46	4-24	4.44
D'Oliveira, B.L.	20	149	21.28	28	–	–	15	35.80	3-35	5.53
Duckett, B.M.	13	227	25.22	49	–	–	–	–	–	7/1
Dunn, M.P.	1	–	–	–	–	–	2	16.00	2-32	5.33
Durston, W.J.	109	2583	33.98	134	4	13	48	38.52	3- 7	5.66
Eckersley, E.J.H.	22	517	28.72	108	1	2	–	–	–	17/1
Edwards, G.A.	5	9	–	8*	–	–	2	100.50	1-29	7.44
Elliott, G.D.	171	3857	31.35	115	5	21	104	33.17	5-34	5.28
Elstone, S.L.	33	562	20.81	75*	–	1	1	58.00	1-22	6.00
Ervine, S.M.	225	5247	31.04	167*	7	24	203	33.85	5-50	5.60
Evans, L.J.	20	391	24.43	50	–	1	0	–	–	8.20
Fell, T.C.	14	483	37.15	89	–	5	–	–	–	–
Finch, A.J.	88	3366	40.55	154	8	18	7	29.85	2-44	5.20
Finch, H.Z.	2	92	–	92*	–	1	0	–	–	2.00
Finn, S.T.	95	237	11.28	42*	–	–	131	27.97	5-33	4.92
Fisher, M.D.	5	10	10.00	10	–	–	3	62.00	1-29	4.89
Fletcher, L.J.	40	142	10.92	40*	–	–	43	34.20	4-44	5.40
Flintoff, A.	282	6641	29.78	143	6	34	289	22.61	5-19	4.16
Foakes, B.T.	9	137	17.12	56	–	2	–	–	–	4/1
Foley, J.M.	1	–	–	–	–	–	–	–	–	–
Footitt, M.H.A.	28	24	6.00	11*	–	–	36	28.50	5-28	6.45
Foster, J.S.	202	3124	28.14	83*	–	15	–	–	–	223/59
Franklin, J.E.C.	253	4855	32.80	133*	3	27	209	34.52	5-42	4.94
Freckingham, O.H.	1	–	–	–	–	–	2	19.00	2-38	6.33
Fuller, J.K.	26	295	21.07	43	–	–	43	23.53	6-35	5.79
Gale, A.W.	132	3412	30.73	125*	2	18	–	–	–	–
Gatting, J.S.	45	988	27.44	122	1	4	0	–	–	6.60
Gibson, R.	5	19	6.33	9	–	–	5	31.60	1-17	5.44
Gidman, A.P.R.	194	4458	27.51	116	5	21	71	39.23	5-42	5.13
Gidman, W.R.S.	46	615	25.62	76	–	2	42	30.85	4-36	4.85
Godleman, B.A.	30	698	27.92	96	–	3	–	–	–	–
Gordon, R.O.	7	1	0.50	1	–	–	9	37.33	3-25	6.33
Gregory, L.	31	334	20.87	105*	1	–	39	26.56	4-27	6.32
Griffiths, D.A.	26	30	15.00	12*	–	–	34	28.88	4-29	6.00
Griffiths, G.T.	1	–	–	–	–	–	0	–	–	5.12
Groenewald, T.D.	77	550	17.74	57	–	2	82	32.21	4-22	5.50
Gubbins, N.R.T.	3	63	21.00	38	–	–	–	–	–	–
Guptill, M.J.	128	4545	40.58	189*	12	24	2	34.00	2- 7	5.16
Gurney, H.F.	53	33	4.12	13*	–	–	61	32.65	5-24	5.53
Haggett, C.J.	10	57	8.14	36	–	–	8	46.87	2-54	6.69
Hain, S.R.	1	1	1.00	1	–	–	–	–	–	–
Hales, A.D.	85	2907	35.88	150*	8	13	0	–	–	15.00
Handscomb, P.S.P.	22	545	36.33	67*	–	2	–	–	–	28/1

L-O	M	Runs	Avge	HS	100	50	Wkts	Avge	Best	Econ
Hannon-Dalby, O.J.	16	38	19.00	21*	–	–	20	33.90	4-44	6.16
Harinath, A.	6	105	26.25	52	–	1	0	–	–	5.33
Harmison, B.W.	69	1177	23.54	67	–	3	30	32.10	3-40	5.68
Harris, J.A.R.	47	227	10.31	29	–	–	62	29.62	4-48	5.79
Harrison, J.	2	7	–	7*	–	–	2	41.50	2-51	6.91
Hartley, C.F.	2	9	4.50	5	–	–	2	52.00	1-51	5.77
Hastings, J.W.	65	687	20.20	69*	–	1	97	27.73	5-46	4.84
Hatchett, L.J.	15	9	4.50	5_	–	–	19	33.15	3-44	5.64
Helm, T.G.	3	–	–	–	–	–	4	16.50	3-27	3.88
Higgins, R.F.	6	80	16.00	27	–	–	–	–	–	–
Hildreth, J.C.	168	4300	33.85	151	6	17	6	30.83	2-26	7.40
Hilfenhaus, B.W.	78	119	9.15	18*	–	–	89	35.95	5-33	4.60
Hill, L.J.	11	169	16.90	35	–	–	–	–	–	4/1
Hobden, M.E.	1	2	2.00	2	–	–	1	39.00	1-39	4.87
Hodd, A.J.	55	752	24.25	91	–	2	–	–	–	52/11
Hodgson, D.M.	14	296	29.60	90	–	3	–	–	–	14/3
Hogan, M.G.	44	99	12.37	27	–	–	77	24.46	5-44	4.89
Horton, P.J.	99	2463	31.57	111*	2	13	–	–	–	–
Howell, B.A.C.	44	1004	37.18	122	1	5	21	43.85	2-26	5.03
Hudson-Prentice, F.J.	1	–	–	–	–	–	0	–	–	8.50
Hughes, A.L.	24	273	24.81	59*	–	1	16	44.37	3-56	5.59
Hughes, C.F.	64	1435	24.74	81	–	12	22	34.27	5-29	5.15
Ingram, C.A.	122	4448	41.18	127	7	30	11	30.90	2-13	5.15
Jarvis, K.M.	39	67	5.15	13	–	–	45	38.64	4-35	5.79
Javid, A.	22	364	30.33	43	–	–	10	58.30	3-48	6.47
Jayawardena, D.P.M.D.	514	14305	33.19	163*	17	90	23	47.86	3-25	5.30
Jennings, K.K.	16	526	43.83	71*	–	6	1	109.00	1- 9	6.05
Jones, G.O.	200	3288	24.72	86	–	13	–	–	–	207/42
Jones, R.A.	12	23	7.66	11*	–	–	4	117.25	1-25	6.94
Jordan, C.J.	45	313	14.22	38*	–	–	69	27.24	5-29	5.58
Joseph, R.H.	38	46	9.20	15	–	–	43	30.06	5-13	5.28
Joyce, E.C.	258	8392	38.67	146	13	50	6	51.50	2-10	7.02
Kapil, A.	18	282	25.63	59	–	1	4	65.75	1-18	7.55
Keedy, G.	97	161	8.94	33	–	–	119	26.47	5-30	4.80
Keogh, R.I.	11	233	25.88	61	–	2	0	–	–	6.05
Kerrigan, S.C.	32	28	3.11	10	–	–	21	55.14	3-21	5.23
Kervezee, A.N.	99	2494	29.34	121*	2	12	0	–	–	9.00
Kettleborough, J.M.	1	26	26.00	26	–	–	–	–	–	–
Key, R.W.T.	225	6469	32.18	144*	8	37	–	–	–	–
Kieswetter, C.	134	4254	39.38	143	11	17	1	19.00	1-19	136/26
King, M.J.	2	8	8.00	8	–	–	0	–	–	3.50
Kleinveldt, R.K.	116	1042	17.36	55	–	2	135	29.86	4-22	4.72
Klinger, M.	129	5153	46.84	140*	11	34	–	–	–	–
Knight, T.C.	9	16	5.33	10	–	–	9	35.66	3-36	5.35
Kohler-Cadmore, T.	8	177	25.28	71	–	1	–	–	–	–
Leach, J.	10	178	89.00	45*	–	–	8	43.87	2-53	6.06
Leach, M.J.	9	20	6.66	18	–	–	9	39.11	3-53	4.95
Leaning, J.A.	14	342	38.00	111*	1	2	7	20.14	5-22	5.42
Leask, M.A.	21	223	13.11	50	–	1	8	53.50	2-42	6.72
Lees, A.Z.	17	651	43.40	102	1	6	–	–	–	–

L-O	M	Runs	Avge	HS	100	50	Wkts	Avge	Best	Econ
Levi, R.E.	81	2645	37.78	166	5	13	–	–	–	5.94
Liddle, C.J.	56	89	5.93	15	–	–	75	27.52	5-18	5.94
Lilley, A.M.	7	12	6.00	10	–	–	12	17.33	4-30	4.72
Linley, T.E.	25	84	21.00	20*	–	–	23	39.56	3-50	6.08
Lloyd, D.L.	7	53	10.60	32	–	–	8	18.62	4-10	4.80
Lumb, M.J.	200	5821	31.80	110	4	43	0	–	–	14.00
Lyth, A.	84	2245	31.61	109*	1	11	2	86.00	1- 6	6.37
McKay, C.J.	104	400	10.81	30	–	–	157	26.64	5-28	4.67
McKay, P.J.	6	48	24.00	22*	–	–	–	–	–	5/1
MacLeod, C.S.	80	1631	23.98	175	3	5	20	40.50	3-37	5.53
Machan, M.W.	39	1320	38.82	126*	2	6	11	43.09	3-31	5.53
Madsen, W.L.	65	1907	39.72	138	2	12	9	15.22	3-27	4.41
Magoffin, S.J.	52	227	22.70	24*	–	–	65	31.40	4-58	4.71
Malan, D.J.	93	2894	36.63	134	4	16	21	35.80	2- 4	5.82
Marshall, H.J.H.	286	6811	27.46	122	6	45	4	73.75	2-21	6.23
Masters, D.D.	161	542	11.78	39	–	–	162	31.72	5-17	4.53
Maxwell, G.J.	54	1531	37.34	146	2	11	29	43.96	4-63	5.20
Meaker, S.C.	48	82	5.46	21*	–	–	48	38.47	4-47	6.23
Meschede, C.A.J.	30	256	18.28	40*	–	–	37	24.27	4- 5	5.63
Mickleburgh, J.C.	20	400	30.76	73	–	2	–	–	–	–
Miles, C.N.	14	29	9.66	12	–	–	17	33.23	3-48	5.93
Mills, T.S.	21	4	1.33	2*	–	–	19	34.15	3-23	5.65
Mitchell, D.K.H.	100	2404	33.38	107	2	14	57	35.00	4-19	5.56
Moore, S.C.	141	3774	30.68	118	5	25	1	53.00	1- 1	7.75
Morgan, E.J.G.	229	6705	37.88	161	12	37	0	–	–	7.00
Morris, C.A.J.	11	31	10.33	16*	–	–	10	39.20	2-25	5.76
Muchall, G.J.	140	3294	33.61	101*	1	20	1	144.00	1-15	5.14
Mullaney, S.J.	69	877	21.39	63*	–	4	62	28.45	4-29	4.81
Munro, C.	51	1488	39.15	151	3	10	9	55.11	3-45	6.02
Murphy, D.	39	271	22.58	31*	–	–	–	–	–	23/11
Murtagh, T.J.	152	691	11.51	35*	–	–	195	29.51	4-14	5.22
Mustard, P.	176	4728	31.10	143	7	29	–	–	–	182/44
Myburgh, J.G.	100	2371	28.22	112	1	14	25	60.80	2-22	5.06
Naik, J.K.H.	37	192	11.29	36*	–	–	30	42.06	3-21	5.33
Napier, G.R.	236	2889	18.63	79	–	14	282	25.82	7-32	5.28
Nash, B.P.	88	1596	31.92	98*	–	8	16	35.12	4-20	4.22
Nash, C.D.	97	2737	31.45	124*	2	17	42	30.42	4-40	5.43
Newton, R.I.	25	616	28.00	88*	–	2	–	–	–	–
Noema-Barnett, K.	45	721	22.53	67	–	4	28	41.82	3-42	4.95
Northeast, S.A.	54	1479	32.86	132	2	8	–	–	–	–
Norwell, L.C.	4	1	–	1*	–	–	9	19.66	6-52	6.55
Nugent, T.M.	1	–	–	–	–	–	1	15.00	1-15	3.75
O'Brien, K.J.	140	3311	30.94	142	3	14	99	32.98	4-13	5.16
O'Brien, N.J.	175	4070	29.92	121	3	24	–	–	–	140/33
Oliver, R.K.	5	34	6.80	14	–	–	–	–	–	–
Onions, G.	85	130	5.90	19	–	–	98	30.44	4-45	5.10
Overton, C.	15	116	10.54	36	–	–	10	54.20	2-30	5.06
Overton, J.	14	47	15.66	14	–	–	20	27.00	4-42	6.27
Owen, W.T.	25	78	13.00	13*	–	–	37	21.13	5-49	6.08
Palladino, A.P.	52	251	10.91	31	–	–	54	33.35	5-49	5.31

L-O	M	Runs	Avge	HS	100	50	Wkts	Avge	Best	Econ
Panesar, M.S.	85	141	8.81	17*	–	–	83	34.84	5-20	4.65
Parry, S.D.	62	223	13.93	31	–	–	80	27.85	5-17	4.95
Patel, J.S.	163	578	9.96	50	–	1	191	31.13	4-16	4.60
Patel, R.H.	10	0	0.00	0*	–	–	11	44.45	3-71	5.62
Patel, S.R.	194	4724	33.26	99	3	26	179	30.54	6-13	5.26
Patterson, S.A.	59	137	19.57	25*	–	–	74	29.22	6-32	5.04
Payne, D.A.	44	70	14.00	18	–	–	81	20.50	7-29	5.68
Penrhyn Jones, D.	1	–	–	–	–	–	1	22.00	1-22	7.33
Peters, S.D.	177	3444	22.65	107	2	21	–	–	–	–
Petersen, A.N.	163	4859	33.51	145*	7	29	8	43.50	2-48	5.46
Peterson, R.J.	207	2902	25.45	101	1	16	226	29.79	7-24	4.67
Pettini, M.L.	161	3896	28.23	144	7	23	–	–	–	–
Philander, V.D.	105	1210	24.20	79*	–	4	99	34.10	4-12	4.68
Pietersen, K.P.	253	8112	40.76	147	15	46	41	51.75	3-14	5.32
Pinner, N.D.	17	227	14.18	37	–	–	0	–	–	6.75
Piolet, S.A.	41	328	17.26	63*	–	1	40	34.07	4-31	5.54
Plunkett, L.E.	124	1081	20.01	72	–	3	147	31.80	4-15	5.42
Podmore, H.W.	6	1	–	1*	–	–	4	68.00	2-46	6.91
Porter, M.J.	1	–	–	–	–	–	–	–	–	–
Porterfield, W.T.S.	174	5466	32.73	112*	7	33	–	–	–	–
Poynter, S.W.	7	160	32.00	109	1	–	–	–	–	–
Poysden, J.E.	10	15	7.50	10*	–	–	9	34.44	3-33	5.58
Prince, A.G.	255	6079	32.33	128	3	33	0	–	–	5.67
Pringle, R.D.	12	48	8.00	26	–	–	3	66.66	1-12	5.19
Prior, M.J.	222	5072	27.26	144	4	28	–	–	–	187/31
Procter, L.A.	20	252	28.00	97	–	2	12	37.58	3-29	6.26
Pyrah, R.M.	114	1077	19.23	69	–	2	140	25.65	5-50	5.68
Raine, B.A.	4	50	25.00	43	–	–	3	52.66	2-59	7.52
Rankin, W.B.	93	94	6.71	18*	–	–	112	28.24	4-34	4.86
Rashid, A.U.	92	889	19.75	71	–	1	106	30.25	5-33	5.14
Rayner, O.P.	43	402	28.71	61	–	1	30	41.96	3-31	5.40
Read, C.M.W.	308	5223	29.17	135	2	21	–	–	–	289/71
Redfern, D.J.	49	752	19.78	57*	–	3	9	39.00	2-10	4.96
Reece, L.M.	22	409	25.56	59	–	2	6	69.66	4-35	6.20
Richardson, M.J.	3	61	30.50	45	–	–	–	–	–	–
Riley, A.E.N.	23	11	5.50	5*	–	–	19	40.57	2-32	5.58
Robson, A.J.	6	92	15.33	28	–	–	–	–	–	–
Robson, S.D.	8	169	28.16	65	–	1	–	–	–	–
Roderick, G.H.	22	279	23.25	63	–	1	–	–	–	23/2
Rogers, C.J.L.	167	5345	36.86	140	5	36	2	13.00	2-22	6.50
Roland-Jones, T.S.	38	171	11.40	29*	–	–	64	23.92	4-42	5.52
Root, J.E.	64	1889	34.34	113	3	9	22	43.81	2-10	5.48
Rossington, A.M.	16	419	38.09	82	–	3	–	–	–	12/2
Rouse, A.P.	3	15	5.00	7	–	–	–	–	–	3/2
Roy, J.J.	55	1408	29.33	131	4	7	0	–	–	12.00
Rudolph, J.A.	232	9336	49.65	169*	16	64	13	33.84	4-40	5.73
Rushworth, C.	42	53	5.88	12*	–	–	72	20.54	5-31	5.26
Russell, C.J.	7	2	–	1*	–	–	5	41.00	4-32	6.21
Ryder, J.D.	129	3735	33.05	115	7	20	44	35.75	4-39	5.85
Saeed Ajmal	217	521	7.23	33	–	–	337	24.44	5-18	4.34

L-O	M	Runs	Avge	HS	100	50	Wkts	Avge	Best	Econ
Salisbury, M.E.T.	6	5	–	5*	–	–	5	33.60	4-55	6.46
Salter, A.G.	13	72	24.00	36*	–	–	9	44.44	2-41	4.83
Sammy, D.J.G.	171	2614	23.98	84	–	10	150	36.07	4-16	4.51
Sandhu, G.S.	2	0	0.00	0	–	–	4	12.00	3-28	3.69
Sangakkara, K.C.	480	16751	41.25	169	28	107				483/113
Saxelby, I.D.	17	30	6.00	7*	–	–	22	29.59	4-31	6.46
Shah, O.A.	360	10529	35.45	134	14	68	27	33.70	4-11	5.90
Shahid Afridi	482	10457	24.95	124	8	55	492	33.46	7-12	4.63
Shahzad, A.	76	449	13.60	59*	–	1	112	26.96	5-51	5.37
Shantry, J.D.	58	125	10.41	18	–	–	76	29.01	4-32	5.78
Shreck, C.E.	59	47	5.87	9*	–	–	71	31.18	5-19	5.17
Sibley, D.P.	3	43	43.00	37	–	–	–	–	–	–
Siddle, P.M.	42	96	7.38	25*	–	–	45	35.51	4-27	4.73
Sidebottom, R.J.	186	552	11.04	32	–	–	198	30.97	6-40	4.47
Simpson, J.A.	50	623	23.96	82	–	3	–	–	–	34/7
Slater, B.T.	7	109	18.16	46	–	–	–	–	–	–
Smith, G.C.	259	9331	39.20	141	14	67	47	38.21	3-30	5.47
Smith, G.M.	108	2342	24.65	89	–	11	72	36.87	4-53	5.61
Smith, G.P.	39	835	24.55	135*	1	4	–	–	–	–
Smith, R.A.J.	5	9	4.50	7	–	–	3	39.00	3-48	7.80
Smith, T.C.	67	1505	34.20	117	2	10	77	28.48	4-48	5.28
Smith, T.M.J.	43	204	15.69	65	–	1	33	40.57	3-26	5.63
Smith, W.R.	96	2108	28.10	120*	2	15	11	24.81	2-19	5.59
Sohail Tanvir	95	774	15.79	93	–	2	138	29.53	7-34	5.20
Solanki, V.S.	401	11041	32.47	164*	16	64	28	35.25	4-14	5.27
Stevens, D.I.	269	6673	30.05	133	5	43	106	32.33	5-32	4.95
Stirling, P.R.	107	3247	32.79	177	8	11	47	32.40	4-11	4.80
Stokes, B.A.	80	1838	29.17	164	3	7	68	25.66	5-61	5.38
Stone, O.P.	11	31	7.75	21	–	–	2	152.00	1-12	6.00
Stoneman, M.D.	44	1523	40.07	136*	4	9	–	–	–	–
Sykes, J.S.	17	41	8.20	15	–	–	15	36.00	3-34	5.40
Tait, S.W.	98	108	6.75	22*	–	–	178	23.43	8-43	5.10
Tanveer Sikandar	3	–	–	–	–	–	1	49.00	1-30	5.44
Tavaré, W.A.	3	100	33.33	77	–	1	–	–	–	–
Taylor, B.J.	2	2	–	2*	–	–	4	18.25	2-23	4.86
Taylor, B.R.M.	230	6709	32.72	145*	10	39	20	30.20	5-28	5.98
Taylor, J.M.R.	14	170	28.33	53	–	1	18	23.72	4-38	4.98
Taylor, J.W.A.	101	3987	53.16	146*	12	20	5	34.00	4 61	7.39
Taylor, M.D.	2	7	–	7*	–	–	4	22.25	2-43	6.43
Taylor, R.M.L.	35	421	18.30	48*	–	–	50	28.42	3-39	5.56
Taylor, T.A.I.	4	–	–	–	–	–	5	34.80	3-48	5.93
ten Doeschate, R.N.	175	4764	46.25	180	9	26	151	29.98	5-50	5.70
Terry, S.P.	8	161	32.20	63	–	2	–	–	–	–
Thakor, S.J.	24	356	18.73	83*	–	3	17	33.94	4-49	7.10
Thomas, A.C.	164	673	16.02	49*	–	–	216	27.96	6-18	5.20
Thomas, I.A.A.	1	1	1.00	1	–	–	0	–	–	5.22
Thomason, A.D.	1	0	–	0*	–	–	0	–	–	5.75
Tomlinson, J.A.	36	53	5.30	14	–	–	39	29.48	4-47	5.23
Topley, R.J.W.	21	25	6.25	19	–	–	30	27.66	4-26	5.80
Tredwell, J.C.	231	1661	17.30	88	–	4	248	30.52	6-27	4.69

L-O	M	Runs	Avge	HS	100	50	Wkts	Avge	Best	Econ
Trego, P.D.	153	3329	30.54	147	6	15	146	32.92	5-40	5.61
Tremlett, C.T.	133	563	10.05	38*	–	–	180	27.78	4-25	4.89
Trescothick, M.E.	372	12229	37.28	184	28	63	57	28.84	4-50	4.90
Trott, I.J.L.	244	8830	47.21	137	17	60	54	28.35	4-55	5.57
van den Bergh, F.O.E.	3	29	–	29*	–	–	0	–	–	4.69
Velani, K.S.	5	61	15.25	27	–	–	–	–	–	–
Vince, J.M.	75	2418	35.55	131	3	12	1	69.00	1-18	5.30
Wagg, G.G.	112	1411	17.86	54	–	1	125	33.84	4-35	5.92
Wainman, J.C.	1	33	33.00	33	–	–	3	17.00	3-51	6.37
Wainwright, D.J.	77	354	19.66	41	–	–	66	35.25	4-11	4.91
Waite, M.J.	1	12	12.00	12	–	–	0	–	–	6.50
Wakely, A.G.	52	1364	31.00	102	1	9	5	21.40	2-14	4.86
Wallace, M.A.	197	2684	20.80	118*	2	7	–	–	–	177/44
Waller, M.T.C.	39	71	17.75	25*	–	–	28	40.21	3-39	5.66
Wells, L.W.P.	13	80	8.88	23	–	–	3	20.33	3-19	4.75
Wells, T.J.	10	152	30.40	32*	–	–	0	–	–	6.50
Wessels, M.H.	133	3027	27.27	100	1	16	1	48.00	1- 0	5.87
Westley, T.	37	1093	35.25	111*	1	10	13	32.53	4-60	4.88
Westwood, I.J.	60	941	22.95	65	–	3	3	75.66	1-28	5.15
Wheater, A.J.A.	53	842	24.05	135	1	3	–	–	–	19/4
White, G.G.	49	214	13.37	39*	–	–	45	30.53	5-35	5.37
White, W.A.	68	755	18.87	46*	–	–	66	36.75	6-29	6.44
Whiteley, R.A.	33	473	18.92	53	–	2	6	56.66	1-17	6.60
Willey, D.J.	53	846	23.50	167	2	2	47	32.29	5-62	5.65
Williamson, K.S.	111	3725	41.85	145*	7	23	53	33.33	5-51	5.16
Wilson, G.C.	129	2391	22.99	113	1	15	–	–	–	85/22
Woakes, C.R.	85	707	18.12	49*	–	–	87	35.49	6-45	5.56
Wood, C.P.	54	245	11.13	41	–	–	79	25.10	5-22	5.52
Wood, M.A.	14	28	7.00	15*	–	–	17	25.82	3-23	5.28
Wood, S.K.W.	9	63	10.50	32	–	–	5	32.60	2-24	5.43
Wright, B.J.	73	1332	24.66	79	–	7	1	126.00	1-19	5.72
Wright, C.J.C.	90	219	10.42	42	–	–	91	35.35	4-20	5.58
Wright, L.J.	178	3768	30.63	143*	9	10	111	38.11	4-12	5.34
Wyatt, A.C.F.	14	13	3.25	9*	–	–	11	43.45	2-36	6.34
Yardy, M.H.	205	3639	25.27	98*	–	23	138	38.66	6-27	5.09
Yasir Arafat	245	2721	21.42	110*	1	9	393	24.44	6-24	4.97
Younus Khan	325	9311	33.73	144	11	61	28	38.64	3- 5	5.72
Zaib, S.A.	1	–	–	–	–	–	0	–	–	10.00

FIRST-CLASS CRICKET RECORDS

To the end of the 2014 season

TEAM RECORDS
HIGHEST INNINGS TOTALS

1107	Victoria v New South Wales	Melbourne	1926-27
1059	Victoria v Tasmania	Melbourne	1922-23
952-6d	Sri Lanka v India	Colombo	1997-98
951-7d	Sind v Baluchistan	Karachi	1973-74
944-6d	Hyderabad v Andhra	Secunderabad	1993-94
918	New South Wales v South Australia	Sydney	1900-01
912-8d	Holkar v Mysore	Indore	1945-46
910-6d	Railways v Dera Ismail Khan	Lahore	1964-65
903-7d	England v Australia	The Oval	1938
900-6d	Queensland v Victoria	Brisbane	2005-06
887	Yorkshire v Warwickshire	Birmingham	1896
863	Lancashire v Surrey	The Oval	1990
860-6d	Tamil Nadu v Goa	Panjim	1988-89
850-7d	Somerset v Middlesex	Taunton	2007

Excluding penalty runs in India, there have been 34 innings totals of 800 runs or more in first-class cricket. Tamil Nadu's total of 860-6d was boosted to 912 by 52 penalty runs.

HIGHEST SECOND INNINGS TOTAL

770	New South Wales v South Australia	Adelaide	1920-21

HIGHEST FOURTH INNINGS TOTAL

654-5	England (set 696 to win) v South Africa	Durban	1938-39

HIGHEST MATCH AGGREGATE

2376-37	Maharashtra v Bombay	Poona	1948-49

RECORD MARGIN OF VICTORY

Innings and 851 runs: Railways v Dera Ismail Khan	Lahore	1964-65

MOST RUNS IN A DAY

721	Australians v Essex	Southend	1948

MOST HUNDREDS IN AN INNINGS

6	Holkar v Mysore	Indore	1945-46

LOWEST INNINGS TOTALS

12	†Oxford University v MCC and Ground	Oxford	1877
12	Northamptonshire v Gloucestershire	Gloucester	1907
13	Auckland v Canterbury	Auckland	1877-78
13	Nottinghamshire v Yorkshire	Nottingham	1901
14	Surrey v Essex	Chelmsford	1983
15	MCC v Surrey	Lord's	1839
15	†Victoria v MCC	Melbourne	1903-04
15	†Northamptonshire v Yorkshire	Northampton	1908
15	Hampshire v Warwickshire	Birmingham	1922

† Batted one man short

There have been 28 instances of a team being dismissed for under 20.

LOWEST MATCH AGGREGATE BY ONE TEAM

34 (16 and 18)	Border v Natal	East London	1959-60

LOWEST COMPLETED MATCH AGGREGATE BY BOTH TEAMS

105	MCC v Australians	Lord's	1878

TIED MATCHES

Before 1949 a match was considered to be tied if the scores were level after the fourth innings, even if the side batting last had wickets in hand when play ended. Law 22 was amended in 1948 and since then a match has been tied only when the scores are level after the fourth innings has been completed. There have been 56 tied first-class matches, five of which would not have qualified under the current law. The most recent are:

Warwickshire (446-7d & forfeit) v Essex (66-0d & 380)	Birmingham	2003
Worcestershire (262 & 247) v Zimbabweans (334 & 175)	Worcester	2003
Habib Bank (245 & 178) v WAPDA (233 & 190)	Lahore	2011-12
Border (210 & 210) v Boland (219 & 201)	East London	2012-13

BATTING RECORDS
35,000 RUNS IN A CAREER

	Career	I	NO	HS	Runs	Avge	100
J.B.Hobbs	1905-34	1315	106	316*	**61237**	50.65	197
F.E.Woolley	1906-38	1532	85	305*	**58969**	40.75	145
E.H.Hendren	1907-38	1300	166	301*	**57611**	50.80	170
C.P.Mead	1905-36	1340	185	280*	**55061**	47.67	153
W.G.Grace	1865-1908	1493	105	344	**54896**	39.55	126
W.R.Hammond	1920-51	1005	104	336*	**50551**	56.10	167
H.Sutcliffe	1919-45	1088	123	313	**50138**	51.95	149
G.Boycott	1962-86	1014	162	261*	**48426**	56.83	151
T.W.Graveney	1948-71/72	1223	159	258	**47793**	44.91	122
G.A.Gooch	1973-2000	990	75	333	**44846**	49.01	128
T.W.Hayward	1893-1914	1138	96	315*	**43551**	41.79	104
D.L.Amiss	1960-87	1139	126	262*	**43423**	42.86	102
M.C.Cowdrey	1950-76	1130	134	307	**42719**	42.89	107
A.Sandham	1911-37/38	1000	79	325	**41284**	44.82	107
G.A.Hick	1983/84-2008	871	84	405*	**41112**	52.23	136
L.Hutton	1934-60	814	91	364	**40140**	55.51	129
M.J.K.Smith	1951-75	1091	139	204	**39832**	41.84	69
W.Rhodes	1898-1930	1528	237	267*	**39802**	30.83	58
J.H.Edrich	1956-78	979	104	310*	**39790**	45.47	103
R.E.S.Wyatt	1923-57	1141	157	232	**39405**	40.04	85
D.C.S.Compton	1936-64	839	88	300	**38942**	51.85	123
G.E.Tyldesley	1909-36	961	106	256*	**38874**	45.46	102
J.T.Tyldesley	1895-1923	994	62	295*	**37897**	40.60	86
K.W.R.Fletcher	1962-88	1167	170	228*	**37665**	37.77	63
C.G.Greenidge	1970-92	889	75	273*	**37354**	45.88	92
J.W.Hearne	1909-36	1025	116	285*	**37252**	40.98	96
L.E.G.Ames	1926-51	951	95	295	**37248**	43.51	102
D.Kenyon	1946-67	1159	59	259	**37002**	33.63	74
W.J.Edrich	1934-58	964	92	267*	**36965**	42.39	86
J.M.Parks	1949-76	1227	172	205*	**36673**	34.76	51
M.W.Gatting	1975-98	861	123	258	**36549**	49.52	94
D.Denton	1894-1920	1163	70	221	**36479**	33.37	69
G.H.Hirst	1891-1929	1215	151	341	**36323**	34.13	60
I.V.A.Richards	1971/72-93	796	63	322	**36212**	49.40	114
A.Jones	1957-83	1168	72	204*	**36049**	32.89	56
W.G.Quaife	1894-1928	1203	185	255*	**36012**	35.37	72
R.E.Marshall	1945/46-72	1053	59	228*	**35725**	35.94	68
M.R.Ramprakash	1987-2012	764	93	301*	**35659**	53.14	114
G.Gunn	1902-32	1061	82	220	**35208**	35.96	62

HIGHEST INDIVIDUAL INNINGS

501*	B.C.Lara	Warwickshire v Durham	Birmingham	1994
499	Hanif Mohammed	Karachi v Bahawalpur	Karachi	1958-59
452*	D.G.Bradman	New South Wales v Queensland	Sydney	1929-30
443*	B.B.Nimbalkar	Maharashtra v Kathiawar	Poona	1948-49
437	W.H.Ponsford	Victoria v Queensland	Melbourne	1927-28
429	W.H.Ponsford	Victoria v Tasmania	Melbourne	1922-23
428	Aftab Baloch	Sind v Baluchistan	Karachi	1973-74
424	A.C.MacLaren	Lancashire v Somerset	Taunton	1895
405*	G.A.Hick	Worcestershire v Somerset	Taunton	1988
400*	B.C.Lara	West Indies v England	St John's	2003-04
394	Naved Latif	Sargodha v Gujranwala	Gujranwala	2000-01
390	S.C.Cook	Lions v Warriors	East London	2009-10
385	B.Sutcliffe	Otago v Canterbury	Christchurch	1952-53
383	C.W.Gregory	New South Wales v Queensland	Brisbane	1906-07
380	M.L.Hayden	Australia v Zimbabwe	Perth	2003-04
377	S.V.Manjrekar	Bombay v Hyderabad	Bombay	1990-91
375	B.C.Lara	West Indies v England	St John's	1993-94
374	D.P.M.D.Jayawardena	Sri Lanka v South Africa	Colombo	2006
369	D.G.Bradman	South Australia v Tasmania	Adelaide	1935-36
366	N.H.Fairbrother	Lancashire v Surrey	The Oval	1990
366	M.V.Sridhar	Hyderabad v Andhra	Secunderabad	1993-94
365*	C.Hill	South Australia v NSW	Adelaide	1900-01
365*	G.St A.Sobers	West Indies v Pakistan	Kingston	1957-58
364	L.Hutton	England v Australia	The Oval	1938
359*	V.M.Merchant	Bombay v Maharashtra	Bombay	1943-44
359	R.B.Simpson	New South Wales v Queensland	Brisbane	1963-64
357*	R.Abel	Surrey v Somerset	The Oval	1899
357	D.G.Bradman	South Australia v Victoria	Melbourne	1935-36
356	B.A.Richards	South Australia v W Australia	Perth	1970-71
355*	G.R.Marsh	W Australia v S Australia	Perth	1989-90
355	B.Sutcliffe	Otago v Auckland	Dunedin	1949-50
353	V.V.S.Laxman	Hyderabad v Karnataka	Bangalore	1999-00
352	W.H.Ponsford	Victoria v New South Wales	Melbourne	1926-27
352	C.A.Pujara	Saurashtra v Karnataka	Rajkot	2012-13
350	Rashid Israr	Habib Bank v National Bank	Lahore	1976-77

There have been 196 triple hundreds in first-class cricket, W.V.Raman (313) and Arjan Kripal Singh (302*) for Tamil Nadu v Goa at Panjim in 1988-89 providing the only instance of two batsmen scoring 300 in the same innings.

MOST HUNDREDS IN SUCCESSIVE INNINGS

6	C.B.Fry	Sussex and Rest of England	1901
6	D.G.Bradman	South Australia and D.G.Bradman's XI	1938-39
6	M.J.Procter	Rhodesia	1970-71

TWO DOUBLE HUNDREDS IN A MATCH

244	202*	A.E.Fagg	Kent v Essex	Colchester	1938

TRIPLE HUNDRED AND HUNDRED IN A MATCH

333	123	G.A.Gooch	England v India	Lord's	1990
319	105	K.C.Sangakkara	Sri Lanka v Bangladesh	Chittagong	2013-14

DOUBLE HUNDRED AND HUNDRED IN A MATCH MOST TIMES

4	Zaheer Abbas	Gloucestershire	1976-81

TWO HUNDREDS IN A MATCH MOST TIMES

8	Zaheer Abbas	Gloucestershire and PIA	1976-82
8	R.T.Ponting	Tasmania, Australia and Australians	1992-2006
7	W.R.Hammond	Gloucestershire, England and MCC	1927-45
7	M.R.Ramprakash	Middlesex, Surrey	1990-2010

MOST HUNDREDS IN A SEASON

18	D.C.S.Compton	1947	16	J.B.Hobbs	1925

100 HUNDREDS IN A CAREER

	Total		100th Hundred	
	Hundreds	Inns	Season	Inns
J.B.Hobbs	197	1315	1923	821
E.H.Hendren	170	1300	1928-29	740
W.R.Hammond	167	1005	1935	679
C.P.Mead	153	1340	1927	892
G.Boycott	151	1014	1977	645
H.Sutcliffe	149	1088	1932	700
F.E.Woolley	145	1532	1929	1031
G.A.Hick	136	871	1998	574
L.Hutton	129	814	1951	619
G.A.Gooch	128	990	1992-93	820
W.G.Grace	126	1493	1895	1113
D.C.S.Compton	123	839	1952	552
T.W.Graveney	122	1223	1964	940
D.G.Bradman	117	338	1947-48	295
I.V.A.Richards	114	796	1988-89	658
M.R.Ramprakash	114	764	2008	676
Zaheer Abbas	108	768	1982-83	658
A.Sandham	107	1000	1935	871
M.C.Cowdrey	107	1130	1973	1035
T.W.Hayward	104	1138	1913	1076
G.M.Turner	103	792	1982	779
J.H.Edrich	103	979	1977	945
L.E.G.Ames	102	951	1950	915
G.E.Tyldesley	102	961	1934	919
D.L.Amiss	102	1139	1986	1081

MOST 400s: 2 – B.C.Lara, W.H.Ponsford

MOST 300s or more: 6 – D.G.Bradman; 4 – W.R.Hammond, W.H.Ponsford

MOST 200s or more: 37 – D.G.Bradman; 36 – W.R.Hammond; 22 – E.H.Hendren

MOST RUNS IN A MONTH

1294 (avge 92.42)	L.Hutton	Yorkshire	June 1949

MOST RUNS IN A SEASON

Runs			I	NO	HS	Avge	100	Season
3816	D.C.S.Compton	Middlesex	50	8	246	90.85	18	1947
3539	W.J.Edrich	Middlesex	52	8	267*	80.43	12	1947
3518	T.W.Hayward	Surrey	61	8	219	66.37	13	1906

The feat of scoring 3000 runs in a season has been achieved 28 times, the most recent instance being by W.E.Alley (3019) in 1961. The highest aggregate in a season since 1969 is 2755 by S.J.Cook in 1991.

1000 RUNS IN A SEASON MOST TIMES

28   W.G.Grace (Gloucestershire), F.E.Woolley (Kent)

HIGHEST BATTING AVERAGE IN A SEASON

(Qualification: 12 innings)

Avge			I	NO	HS	Runs	100	Season
115.66	D.G.Bradman	Australians	26	5	278	2429	13	1938
104.66	D.R.Martyn	Australians	14	5	176*	942	5	2001
103.54	M.R.Ramprakash	Surrey	24	2	301*	2278	8	2006
102.53	G.Boycott	Yorkshire	20	5	175*	1538	6	1979
102.00	W.A.Johnston	Australians	17	16	28*	102	–	1953
101.70	G.A.Gooch	Essex	30	3	333	2746	12	1990
101.30	M.R.Ramprakash	Surrey	25	5	266*	2026	10	2007
100.12	G.Boycott	Yorkshire	30	5	233	2503	13	1971

FASTEST HUNDRED AGAINST AUTHENTIC BOWLING

35 min	P.G.H.Fender	Surrey v Northamptonshire	Northampton	1920

FASTEST DOUBLE HUNDRED

113 min	R.J.Shastri	Bombay v Baroda	Bombay	1984-85

FASTEST TRIPLE HUNDRED

181 min	D.C.S.Compton	MCC v NE Transvaal	Benoni	1948-49

MOST SIXES IN AN INNINGS

16	A.Symonds	Gloucestershire v Glamorgan	Abergavenny	1995
16	G.R.Napier	Essex v Surrey	Croydon	2011
16	J.D.Ryder	New Zealanders v Australia A	Brisbane	2011-12
16	Mukhtar Ali	Rajshahi v Chittagong	Savar	2013-14

MOST SIXES IN A MATCH

20	A.Symonds	Gloucestershire v Glamorgan	Abergavenny	1995

MOST SIXES IN A SEASON

80	I.T.Botham	Somerset and England	1985

MOST FOURS IN AN INNINGS

72	B.C.Lara	Warwickshire v Durham	Birmingham	1994

MOST RUNS OFF ONE OVER

36	G.St A.Sobers	Nottinghamshire v Glamorgan	Swansea	1968
36	R.J.Shastri	Bombay v Baroda	Bombay	1984-85

Both batsmen hit for six all six balls of overs bowled by M.A.Nash and Tilak Raj respectively.

MOST RUNS IN A DAY

390*	B.C.Lara	Warwickshire v Durham	Birmingham	1994

There have been 19 instances of a batsman scoring 300 or more runs in a day.

LONGEST INNINGS

1015 min	R.Nayyar (271)	Himachal Pradesh v Jammu & Kashmir Chamba		1999-00

HIGHEST PARTNERSHIPS FOR EACH WICKET

First Wicket

561	Waheed Mirza/Mansoor Akhtar	Karachi W v Quetta	Karachi	1976-77
555	P.Holmes/H.Sutcliffe	Yorkshire v Essex	Leyton	1932
554	J.T.Brown/J.Tunnicliffe	Yorkshire v Derbys	Chesterfield	1898

Second Wicket

580	Rafatullah Mohmand/Aamer Sajjad	WAPDA v SSGC	Sheikhupura	2009-10
576	S.T.Jayasuriya/R.S.Mahanama	Sri Lanka v India	Colombo	1997-98
480	E.Elgar/R.R.Rossouw	Eagles v Titans	Centurion	2009-10
475	Zahir Alam/L.S.Rajput	Assam v Tripura	Gauhati	1991-92
465*	J.A.Jameson/R.B.Kanhai	Warwickshire v Glos	Birmingham	1974

Third Wicket

624	K.C.Sangakkara/D.P.M.D.Jayawardena	Sri Lanka v South Africa	Colombo	2006
539	S.D.Jogiyani/R.A.Jadeja	Saurashtra v Gujarat	Surat	2012-13
523	M.A.Carberry/N.D.McKenzie	Hampshire v Yorkshire	Southampton	2011

Fourth Wicket

577	V.S.Hazare/Gul Mahomed	Baroda v Holkar	Baroda	1946-47
574*	C.L.Walcott/F.M.M.Worrell	Barbados v Trinidad	Port-of-Spain	1945-46
502*	F.M.M.Worrell/J.D.C.Goddard	Barbados v Trinidad	Bridgetown	1943-44
470	A.I.Kallicharran/G.W.Humpage	Warwickshire v Lancs	Southport	1982

Fifth Wicket

520*	C.A.Pujara/R.A.Jadeja	Saurashtra v Orissa	Rajkot	2008-09
494	Marchall Ayub/Mehrab Hossain Jr	Central Zone v East Zone	Bogra	2012-13
479	Misbah-ul-Haq/Usman Arshad	Sui NGP v Lahore Shalimar	Lahore	2009-10
464*	M.E.Waugh/S.R.Waugh	NSW v W Australia	Perth	1990-91
420	Mohd. Ashraful/Marshall Ayub	Dhaka v Chittagong	Chittagong	2006-07
410*	A.S.Chopra/S.Badrinath	India A v South Africa A	Delhi	2007-08
405	S.G.Barnes/D.G.Bradman	Australia v England	Sydney	1946-47
401	M.B.Loye/D.Ripley	Northants v Glamorgan	Northampton	1998

Sixth Wicket

487*	G.A.Headley/C.C.Passailaigue	Jamaica v Tennyson's	Kingston	1931-32
428	W.W.Armstrong/M.A.Noble	Australians v Sussex	Hove	1902
417	W.P.Saha/L.R.Shukla	Bengal v Assam	Kolkata	2010-11
411	R.M.Poore/E.G.Wynyard	Hampshire v Somerset	Taunton	1899

Seventh Wicket

460	Bhupinder Singh jr/P.Dharmani	Punjab v Delhi	Delhi	1994-95
371	M.R.Marsh/S.M.Whiteman	Australia A v India A	Brisbane	2014
347	D.St E.Atkinson/C.C.Depeiza	W Indies v Australia	Bridgetown	1954-55
347	Farhad Reza/Sanjamul Islam	Rajshahi v Chittagong	Savar	2013-14
344	K.S.Ranjitsinhji/W.Newham	Sussex v Essex	Leyton	1902

Eighth Wicket

433	V.T.Trumper/A.Sims	Australians v C'bury	Christchurch	1913-14
392	A.Mishra/J.Yadav	Haryana v Karnataka	Hubli	2012-13
332	I.J.L.Trott/S.C.J.Broad	England v Pakistan	Lord's	2010

Ninth Wicket

283	J.Chapman/A.Warren	Derbys v Warwicks	Blackwell	1910
268	J.B.Commins/N.Boje	SA 'A' v Mashonaland	Harare	1994-95
261	W.L.Madsen/T.Poynton	Derbys v Northants	Northampton	2012
251	J.W.H.T.Douglas/S.N.Hare	Essex v Derbyshire	Leyton	1921

Tenth Wicket

307	A.F.Kippax/J.E.H.Hooker	NSW v Victoria	Melbourne	1928-29
249	C.T.Sarwate/S.N.Banerjee	Indians v Surrey	The Oval	1946
239	Aqil Arshad/Ali Raza	Lahore Whites v Hyderabad	Lahore	2004-05

BOWLING RECORDS
2000 WICKETS IN A CAREER

	Career	Runs	Wkts	Avge	100w
W.Rhodes	1898-1930	69993	**4187**	16.71	23
A.P.Freeman	1914-36	69577	**3776**	18.42	17
C.W.L.Parker	1903-35	63817	**3278**	19.46	16
J.T.Hearne	1888-1923	54352	**3061**	17.75	15
T.W.J.Goddard	1922-52	59116	**2979**	19.84	16
W.G.Grace	1865-1908	51545	**2876**	17.92	10
A.S.Kennedy	1907-36	61034	**2874**	21.23	15
D.Shackleton	1948-69	53303	**2857**	18.65	20
G.A.R.Lock	1946-70/71	54709	**2844**	19.23	14
F.J.Titmus	1949-82	63313	**2830**	22.37	16
M.W.Tate	1912-37	50571	**2784**	18.16	13+1
G.H.Hirst	1891-1929	51282	**2739**	18.72	15

	Career	Runs	Wkts	Avge	100w
C.Blythe	1899-1914	42136	**2506**	16.81	14
D.L.Underwood	1963-87	49993	**2465**	20.28	10
W.E.Astill	1906-39	57783	**2431**	23.76	9
J.C.White	1909-37	43759	**2356**	18.57	14
W.E.Hollies	1932-57	48656	**2323**	20.94	14
F.S.Trueman	1949-69	42154	**2304**	18.29	12
J.B.Statham	1950-68	36999	**2260**	16.37	13
R.T.D.Perks	1930-55	53771	**2233**	24.07	16
J.Briggs	1879-1900	35431	**2221**	15.95	12
D.J.Shepherd	1950-72	47302	**2218**	21.32	12
E.G.Dennett	1903-26	42571	**2147**	19.82	12
T.Richardson	1892-1905	38794	**2104**	18.43	10
T.E.Bailey	1945-67	48170	**2082**	23.13	9
R.Illingworth	1951-83	42023	**2072**	20.28	10
F.E.Woolley	1906-38	41066	**2068**	19.85	8
N.Gifford	1960-88	48731	**2068**	23.56	4
G.Geary	1912-38	41339	**2063**	20.03	11
D.V.P.Wright	1932-57	49307	**2056**	23.98	10
J.A.Newman	1906-30	51111	**2032**	25.15	9
A.Shaw	1864-97	24580	**2026+1**	12.12	9
S.Haigh	1895-1913	32091	**2012**	15.94	11

ALL TEN WICKETS IN AN INNINGS

This feat has been achieved 81 times in first-class matches (excluding 12-a-side fixtures).
Three Times: A.P.Freeman (1929, 1930, 1931)
Twice: V.E.Walker (1859, 1865); H.Verity (1931, 1932); J.C.Laker (1956)

Instances since 1945:

W.E.Hollies	Warwickshire v Notts	Birmingham	1946
J.M.Sims	East v West	Kingston on Thames	1948
J.K.R.Graveney	Gloucestershire v Derbyshire	Chesterfield	1949
T.E.Bailey	Essex v Lancashire	Clacton	1949
R.Berry	Lancashire v Worcestershire	Blackpool	1953
S.P.Gupte	President's XI v Combined XI	Bombay	1954-55
J.C.Laker	Surrey v Australians	The Oval	1956
K.Smales	Nottinghamshire v Glos	Stroud	1956
G.A.R.Lock	Surrey v Kent	Blackheath	1956
J.C.Laker	England v Australia	Manchester	1956
P.M.Chatterjee	Bengal v Assam	Jorhat	1956-57
J.D.Bannister	Warwicks v Combined Services	Birmingham (M & B)	1959
A.J.G.Pearson	Cambridge U v Leicestershire	Loughborough	1961
N.I.Thomson	Sussex v Warwickshire	Worthing	1964
P.J.Allan	Queensland v Victoria	Melbourne	1965-66
I.J.Brayshaw	Western Australia v Victoria	Perth	1967-68
Shahid Mahmood	Karachi Whites v Khairpur	Karachi	1969-70
E.E.Hemmings	International XI v W Indians	Kingston	1982-83
P.Sunderam	Rajasthan v Vidarbha	Jodhpur	1985-86
S.T.Jefferies	Western Province v OFS	Cape Town	1987-88
Imran Adil	Bahawalpur v Faisalabad	Faisalabad	1989-90
G.P.Wickremasinghe	Sinhalese v Kalutara	Colombo	1991-92
R.L.Johnson	Middlesex v Derbyshire	Derby	1994
Naeem Akhtar	Rawalpindi B v Peshawar	Peshawar	1995-96
A.Kumble	India v Pakistan	Delhi	1998-99
D.S.Mohanty	East Zone v South Zone	Agartala	2000-01
O.D.Gibson	Durham v Hampshire	Chester-le-Street	2007
M.W.Olivier	Warriors v Eagles	Bloemfontein	2007-08
Zulfiqar Babar	Multan v Islamabad	Multan	2009-10

MOST WICKETS IN A MATCH

19	J.C.Laker	England v Australia	Manchester	1956

MOST WICKETS IN A SEASON

Wkts		Season	Matches	Overs	Mdns	Runs	Avge
304	A.P.Freeman	1928	37	1976.1	423	5489	18.05
298	A.P.Freeman	1933	33	2039	651	4549	15.26

The feat of taking 250 wickets in a season has been achieved on 12 occasions, the last instance being by A.P.Freeman in 1933. 200 or more wickets in a season have been taken on 59 occasions, the last being by G.A.R.Lock (212 wickets, average 12.02) in 1957.

The highest aggregates of wickets taken in a season since the reduction of County Championship matches in 1969 are as follows:

Wkts		Season	Matches	Overs	Mdns	Runs	Avge
134	M.D.Marshall	1982	22	822	225	2108	15.73
131	L.R.Gibbs	1971	23	1024.1	295	2475	18.89
125	F.D.Stephenson	1988	22	819.1	196	2289	18.31
121	R.D.Jackman	1980	23	746.2	220	1864	15.40

Since 1969 there have been 50 instances of bowlers taking 100 wickets in a season.

MOST HAT-TRICKS IN A CAREER

7	D.V.P.Wright
6	T.W.J.Goddard, C.W.L.Parker
5	S.Haigh, V.W.C.Jupp, A.E.G.Rhodes, F.A.Tarrant

ALL-ROUND RECORDS
THE 'DOUBLE'

3000 runs and 100 wickets: J.H.Parks (1937)

2000 runs and 200 wickets: G.H.Hirst (1906)

2000 runs and 100 wickets: F.E.Woolley (4), J.W.Hearne (3), W.G.Grace (2), G.H.Hirst (2), W.Rhodes (2), T.E.Bailey, D.E.Davies, G.L.Jessop, V.W.C.Jupp, J.Langridge, F.A.Tarrant, C.L.Townsend, L.F.Townsend

1000 runs and 200 wickets: M.W.Tate (3), A.E.Trott (2), A.S.Kennedy

Most Doubles: 16 – W.Rhodes; 14 – G.H.Hirst; 10 – V.W.C.Jupp

Double in Debut Season: D.B.Close (1949) – aged 18, the youngest to achieve this feat.

The feat of scoring 1000 runs and taking 100 wickets in a season has been achieved on 305 occasions, R.J.Hadlee (1984) and F.D.Stephenson (1988) being the only players to complete the 'double' since the reduction of County Championship matches in 1969.

WICKET-KEEPING RECORDS
1000 DISMISSALS IN A CAREER

	Career	Dismissals	Ct	St
R.W.Taylor	1960-88	1649	1473	176
J.T.Murray	1952-75	1527	1270	257
H.Strudwick	1902-27	1497	1242	255
A.P.E.Knott	1964-85	1344	1211	133
R.C.Russell	1981-2004	1320	1192	128
F.H.Huish	1895-1914	1310	933	377
B.Taylor	1949-73	1294	1083	211
S.J.Rhodes	1981-2004	1263	1139	124
D.Hunter	1889-1909	1253	906	347
H.R.Butt	1890-1912	1228	953	275
J.H.Board	1891-1914/15	1207	852	355
H.Elliott	1920-47	1206	904	302
J.M.Parks	1949-76	1181	1088	93
R.Booth	1951-70	1126	948	178
L.E.G.Ames	1926-51	1121	703	418

	Career	Dismissals	Ct	St
D.L.Bairstow	1970-90	**1099**	961	138
G.Duckworth	1923-47	**1096**	753	343
H.W.Stephenson	1948-64	**1082**	748	334
J.G.Binks	1955-75	**1071**	895	176
T.G.Evans	1939-69	**1066**	816	250
A.Long	1960-80	**1046**	922	124
G.O.Dawkes	1937-61	**1043**	895	148
R.W.Tolchard	1965-83	**1037**	912	125
W.L.Cornford	1921-47	**1017**	675	342

By the end of the 2014 season, C.M.W.Read had 968 dismissals.

MOST DISMISSALS IN AN INNINGS

9	(8ct, 1st)	Tahir Rashid	Habib Bank v PACO	Gujranwala	1992-93
9	(7ct, 2st)	W.R.James	Matabeleland v Mashonaland CD	Bulawayo	1995-96
8	(8ct)	A.T.W.Grout	Queensland v W Australia	Brisbane	1959-60
8	(8ct)	D.E.East	Essex v Somerset	Taunton	1985
8	(8ct)	S.A.Marsh	Kent v Middlesex	Lord's	1991
8	(6ct, 2st)	T.J.Zoehrer	Australians v Surrey	The Oval	1993
8	(7ct, 1st)	D.S.Berry	Victoria v South Australia	Melbourne	1996-97
8	(7ct, 1st)	Y.S.S.Mendis	Bloomfield v Kurunegala Youth	Colombo	2000-01
8	(7ct, 1st)	S.Nath	Assam v Tripura (*on debut*)	Gauhati	2001-02
8	(8ct)	J.N.Batty	Surrey v Kent	The Oval	2004
8	(8ct)	Golam Mabud	Sylhet v Dhaka	Dhaka	2005-06
8	(8ct)	D.C.de Boorder	Otago v Wellington	Wellington	2009-10
8	(8ct)	R.S.Second	Free State v North West	Bloemfontein	2011-12
8	(8ct)	T.L.Tsolekile	South Africa A v Sri Lanka A	Durban	2012

MOST DISMISSALS IN A MATCH

14	(11ct, 3st)	I.Khaleel	Hyderabad v Assam	Guwahati	2011-12
13	(11ct, 2st)	W.R.James	Matabeleland v Mashonaland CD	Bulawayo	1995-96
12	(8ct, 4st)	E.Pooley	Surrey v Sussex	The Oval	1868
12	(9ct, 3st)	D.Tallon	Queensland v NSW	Sydney	1938-39
12	(9ct, 3st)	H.B.Taber	NSW v South Australia	Adelaide	1968-69
12	(12ct)	P.D.McGlashan	Northern Districts v Central Districts	Whangarei	2009-10
12	(11ct, 1st)	T.L.Tsolekile	Lions v Dolphins	Johannesburg	2010-11
12	(12ct)	Kashif Mahmood	Lahore Shalimar v Abbottabad	Abbottabad	2010-11
12	(12ct)	R.S.Second	Free State v North West	Bloemfontein	2011-12

MOST DISMISSALS IN A SEASON

128	(79ct, 49st)	L.E.G.Ames			1929

FIELDING RECORDS
750 CATCHES IN A CAREER

1018	F.E.Woolley	1906-38	784	J.G.Langridge	1928-55
887	W.G.Grace	1865-1908	764	W.Rhodes	1898-1930
830	G.A.R.Lock	1946-70/71	758	C.A.Milton	1948-74
819	W.R.Hammond	1920-51	754	E.H.Hendren	1907-38
813	D.B.Close	1949-86			

MOST CATCHES IN AN INNINGS

7	M.J.Stewart	Surrey v Northamptonshire	Northampton	1957
7	A.S.Brown	Gloucestershire v Nottinghamshire	Nottingham	1966
7	R.Clarke	Warwickshire v Lancashire	Liverpool	2011

MOST CATCHES IN A MATCH

10	W.R.Hammond	Gloucestershire v Surrey	Cheltenham	1928
9	R.Clarke	Warwickshire v Lancashire	Liverpool	2011

MOST CATCHES IN A SEASON

78	W.R.Hammond	1928	77	M.J.Stewart	1957

ENGLAND LIMITED-OVERS INTERNATIONALS 2014

AUSTRALIA v ENGLAND

LIMITED-OVERS INTERNATIONALS

Melbourne Cricket Ground, 12 January. Toss: England. **AUSTRALIA** won by six wickets. England 269-7 (50; G.S.Ballance 79, E.J.G.Morgan 50, C.J.McKay 3-44). Australia 270-4 (45.4; A.J.Finch 121, D.A.Warner 65). Award: A.J.Finch.

Woolloongabba, Brisbane, 17 January. Toss: England. **AUSTRALIA** won by one wicket. England 300-8 (50; E.J.G.Morgan 106, I.R.Bell 68). Australia 301-9 (49.3; J.P.Faulkner 69*, S.E.Marsh 55, G.J.Maxwell 54). Award: J.P.Faulkner.

Sydney Cricket Ground, 19 January. Toss: England. **AUSTRALIA** won by seven wickets. England 243-9 (50; E.J.G.Morgan 54, N.M.Coulter-Nile 3-47). Australia 244-3 (40; S.E.Marsh 71*, D.A.Warner 71). Award: D.A.Warner.

W.A.C.A.Ground, Perth, 24 January. Toss: Australia. **ENGLAND** won by 57 runs. England 316-8 (50; J.C.Buttler 71, B.A.Stokes 70, I.R.Bell 55, J.P.Faulkner 4-67). Australia 259 (47.4; G.J.Bailey 108, B.A.Stokes 4-38, T.T.Bresnan 3-45). Award: B.A.Stokes. *J.C.Buttler became the second England wicket-keeper (after G.O.Jones) to score a 50 and take five catches in an LOI.*

Adelaide Oval, 26 January. Toss: Australia. **AUSTRALIA** won by 5 runs. Australia 217-9 (50; G.J.Bailey 56, S.C.J.Broad 3-31, B.A.Stokes 3-43). England 212 (49.4; J.E.Root 55, N.M.Coulter-Nile 3-34, C.J.McKay 3-36). Award: J.P.Faulkner (27 and 2-37). Series award: A.J.Finch.

TWENTY20 INTERNATIONALS

Bellerive Oval, Hobart, 29 January. Toss: Australia. **AUSTRALIA** won by 13 runs. Australia 213-4 (20; C.L.White 75, A.J.Finch 52). England 200-9 (20; R.S.Bopara 65*, N.M.Coulter-Nile 4-30). Award: C.L.White.

Melbourne Cricket Ground, 31 January. Toss: England. **AUSTRALIA** won by eight wickets. England 130-9 (20; J.R.Hazlewood 4-30). Australia 131-2 (14.5; G.J.Bailey 60*, C.L.White 58*). Award: J.R.Hazlewood.

Sydney Cricket Ground, 2 February. Toss: Australia. **AUSTRALIA** won by 84 runs. Australia 195-6 (20; S.C.J.Broad 3-30). England 111 (17.2). Award: G.J.Bailey (49*). England debut : C.J.Jordan.

WEST INDIES v ENGLAND

LIMITED-OVERS INTERNATIONALS

Sir Vivian Richards Stadium, North Sound, Antigua, 28 February. Toss: England. **WEST INDIES** won by 15 runs. West Indies 269-6 (50; D.J.Bravo 87*, L.M.P.Simmons 65, D.J.G.Sammy 61, T.T.Bresnan 3-68). England 254-6 (50; M.J.Lumb 106). Award: D.J.Bravo. England debuts: M.M.Ali, M.J.Lumb. *M.J.Lumb became the second England batsman after D.L.Amiss to score a century on LOI debut.*

Sir Vivian Richards Stadium, North Sound, Antigua, 2 March. Toss: England. **ENGLAND** won by three wickets. West Indies 159 (44.2; L.M.P.Simmons 70, S.D.Parry 3-32). England 163-7 (44.5). Award: S.D.Parry. England debut: S.D.Parry.

Sir Vivian Richards Stadium, North Sound, Antigua, 5 March. Toss: West Indies. **ENGLAND** won by 25 runs. England 303-6 (50; J.E.Root 107, J.C.Buttler 99, M.M.Ali 55, D.J.Bravo 3-60). West Indies 278 (47.4; D.Ramdin 128, T.T.Bresnan 3-45). Award: J.E.Root. Series award: J.E.Root.

TWENTY20 INTERNATIONALS

Kensington Oval, Bridgetown, Barbados, 9 March. Toss: West Indies. **WEST INDIES** won by 27 runs. West Indies 170-3 (20; M.N.Samuels 69*). England 143-9 (20; S.Badree 3-17). Award: M.N.Samuels.

Kensington Oval, Bridgetown, Barbados, 11 March. Toss: England. **WEST INDIES** won by five wickets. England 152-7 (20; J.C.Buttler 67, K.Santokie 4-21). West Indies 155-5 (18.5). Award: K.Santokie. England debuts: M.M.Ali, S.D.Parry.

Kensington Oval, Bridgetown, Barbados, 13 March. Toss: England. **ENGLAND** won by 5 runs. England 165-6 (20; M.J.Lumb 63). West Indies 160-7 (20; L.M.P.Simmons 69, C.J.Jordan 3-39). Award: C.J.Jordan. Series award: D.J.G.Sammy.

ICC WORLD T20

See pages 274 for details of these matches.

SCOTLAND v ENGLAND

LIMITED-OVERS INTERNATIONAL

Mannofield Park, Aberdeen, 9 May. Toss: Scotland. **ENGLAND** won by 39 runs (D/L method). England 167-6 (20; I.R.Bell 50, J.H.Davey 3-28). Scotland 133-9 (20; J.C.Tredwell 4-41). Award: M.A.Leask (Scotland 42 in 16b). England debut: H.F.Gurney.

ENGLAND v SRI LANKA

NATWEST TWENTY20 INTERNATIONAL

The Oval, London, 20 May. Toss: England. **SRI LANKA** won by 9 runs. Sri Lanka 183-7 (20). England 174-7 (20; A.D.Hales 66, S.L.Malinga 3-28). Award: N.L.T.C.Perera (Sri Lanka 49 in 20b). England debuts: M.A.Carberry, H.F.Gurney.

ROYAL LONDON LIMITED-OVERS INTERNATIONALS

The Oval, London, 22 May. Toss: Sri Lanka. **ENGLAND** won by 81 runs (D/L method). England 247-6 (39; G.S.Ballance 64, I.R.Bell 50, S.M.S.M.Senanayake 3-30). Sri Lanka 144 (27.5/32; C.J.Jordan 3-25, J.C.Tredwell 3-28). Award: C.J.Jordan.

Riverside Ground, Chester-le-Street, 25 May. Toss: England. **SRI LANKA** won by 157 runs. Sri Lanka 256-8 (50; T.M.Dilshan 88, H.F.Gurney 3-59). England 99 (26.1; S.M.S.M.Senanayake 4-13, K.D.M.N.Kulasekara 3-15). Award: T.M.Dilshan.
This was England's worst LOI defeat on home soil.

Old Trafford, Manchester, 28 May. Toss: England. **ENGLAND** won by ten wickets. Sri Lanka 67 (24; C.J.Jordan 5-29). England 73-0 (12.1). Award: C.J.Jordan.
This was England's fifth ten-wicket victory in LOIs.

Lord's, London, 31 May. Toss: England. **SRI LANKA** won by 7 runs. Sri Lanka 300-9 (50; K.C.Sangakkara 112, T.M.Dilshan 71, H.F.Gurney 4-55). England 293-8 (50; J.C.Buttler 121, R.S.Bopara 51, S.L.Malinga 3-52). Award: J.C.Buttler.

Edgbaston, Birmingham, 3 June. Toss: England. **SRI LANKA** won by six wickets. England 219 (48.1; A.N.Cook 56, S.L.Malinga 3-50). Sri Lanka 222-4 (48.2; H.D.R.L.Thirimanne 60*, D.P.M.D.Jayawardena 53). Award: H.D.R.L.Thirimanne. Series award: S.L.Malinga.

ENGLAND v INDIA

ROYAL LONDON LIMITED-OVERS INTERNATIONALS

County Ground, Bristol, 25 August. MATCH ABANDONED.

Sophia Gardens, Cardiff, 27 August. Toss: England. **INDIA** won by 133 runs (D/L method). India 304-6 (50; S.K.Raina 100, R.G.Sharma 52, M.S.Dhoni 52, C.R.Woakes 4-52). England 161 (38.1/47; R.A.Jadeja 4-28). Award: S.K.Raina. England debut: A.D.Hales.

Trent Bridge, Nottingham, 30 August. Toss: India. **INDIA** won by six wickets. England 227 (50; R.Ashwin 3-39). India 228-4 (43; A.T.Rayudu 64*). Award: R.Ashwin.

Edgbaston, Birmingham, 2 September. Toss: India. **INDIA** won by nine wickets. England 206 (49.3; M.M.Ali 67, Mohammed Shami 3-28). India 212-1 (30.3; A.M.Rahane 106, S.Dhawan 97*). Award: A.M.Rahane.

Headingley, Leeds, 5 September. Toss: India. **ENGLAND** won by 41 runs. England 294-7 (50; J.E.Root 113). India 253 (48.4; R.A.Jadeja 87, A.T.Rayudu 53, B.A.Stokes 3-47). Award: J.E.Root. Series award: S.K.Raina.

NATWEST TWENTY20 INTERNATIONAL

Edgbaston, Birmingham, 7 September. Toss: England. **ENGLAND** won by 3 runs. England 180-7 (20; E.J.G.Morgan 71, Mohammed Shami 3-38). India 177-5 (20; V.Kohli 66). Award: E.J.G.Morgan. England debut: J.J.Roy.

SRI LANKA v ENGLAND

LIMITED-OVERS INTERNATIONALS

R.Premadasa Stadium, Colombo, 26 November. Toss: England. **SRI LANKA** won by 25 runs. Sri Lanka 317-6 (50; T.M.Dilshan 88, M.D.K.J.Perera 59, D.P.M.D.Jayawardena 55). England 292 (47.1; M.M.Ali 119, R.S.Bopara 65, N.L.T.C.Perera 3-44). Award: T.M.Dilshan.

R.Premadasa Stadium, Colombo, 29 November. Toss: England. **SRI LANKA** won by eight wickets. England 185 (43/45; R.S.Bopara 51, B.A.W.Mendis 3-33). Sri Lanka 186-2 (34.2/45; D.P.M.D.Jayawardena 77*, K.C.Sangakkara 67*). Award: D.P.M.D.Jayawardena.

Mahinda Rajapaksa International Cricket Stadium, Hambantota, 3 December. Toss: Sri Lanka. **ENGLAND** won by five wickets (D/L method). Sri Lanka 242-8 (35; K.C.Sangakkara 63, H.D.R.L.Thirimanne 62*, C.R.Woakes 3-41). England 236-5 (33.4/35; M.M.Ali 58, J.C.Buttler 55*). Award: J.C.Buttler.

R.Premadasa Stadium, Colombo, 7 December. Toss: England. **SRI LANKA** won by six wickets. England 265 (50; J.W.A.Taylor 90, E.J.G.Morgan 62, H.M.R.K.B.Herath 3-36, B.A.W.Mendis 3-56, T.M.Dilshan 3-64). Sri Lanka 267-4 (49.4; K.C.Sangakkara 86, A.D.Mathews 51*). Award: K.C.Sangakkara.

Pallekele International Cricket Stadium, 10, 11 December. Toss: England. **ENGLAND** won by five wickets. Sri Lanka 239 (49; K.C.Sangakkara 91, C.R.Woakes 6-47). England 240-5 (49.1; J.E.Root 104*, J.W.A.Taylor 68). Award: J.E.Root.

Pallekele International Cricket Stadium, 13 December. Toss: Sri Lanka. **SRI LANKA** won by 90 runs. Sri Lanka 292-7 (50; K.C.Sangakkara 112, T.M.Dilshan 68). England 202 (41.3; J.E.Root 55, R.A.S.Lakmal 4-30, S.M.S.M.Senanayake 3-33). Award: K.C.Sangakkara.

R.Premadasa Stadium, Colombo, 16 December. Toss: Sri Lanka. **SRI LANKA** won by 87 runs. Sri Lanka 302-6 (50; T.M.Dilshan 101, L.D.Chandimal 55*, N.L.T.C.Perera 54). England 215 (45.5; J.E.Root 80, S.Prasanna 3-35, T.M.Dilshan 3-37). Award: T.M.Dilshan. Series award: T.M.Dilshan.

ENGLAND'S RESULTS IN 2014

	P	W	L	T	NR
Limited Overs	25	9	16	–	–
Twenty20	12	3	9	–	–
Overall	37	12	25	–	–

600 RUNS IN LIMITED-OVERS INTERNATIONALS IN 2014

	M	I	NO	HS	Runs	Avge	100	50	S/Rate
J.E.Root	23	22	2	113	872	43.60	3	3	78.34
J.C.Buttler	25	24	4	121	704	35.20	1	3	112.46

20 WICKETS IN LIMITED-OVERS INTERNATIONALS IN 2014

	Pl	O	M	R	W	Avge	Best	4wI	Econ
C.J.Jordan	18	158	2	909	29	31.34	5-29	1	5.75
J.C.Tredwell	20	164.2	11	745	23	32.39	4-41	1	4.53

ICC WORLD T20 2013-14

The fifth ICC World T20 tournament took place in Bangladesh between 16 March and 6 April, beginning with a qualifying tournament from which Bangladesh and the Netherlands progressed to the Group stages.

GROUP 1	P	W	L	T	A	Pts	Net RR
Sri Lanka	4	3	1	–	–	6	+2.23
South Africa	4	3	1	–	–	6	+0.07
New Zealand	4	2	2	–	–	4	–0.67
England	4	1	3	–	–	2	–0.77
Netherlands	4	1	3	–	–	2	–0.86

Zahur Ahmed Chowdhury Stadium, Chittagong, 22 March. Toss: New Zealand. **NEW ZEALAND** won by 9 runs (D/L method). England 172-6 (20). New Zealand 52-1 (5.2). Award: C.J.Anderson (2-32).

Zahur Ahmed Chowdhury Stadium, Chittagong, 27 March. Toss: England. **ENGLAND** won by six wickets. Sri Lanka 189-4 (20; D.P.M.D.Jayawardena 89, T.M.Dilshan 55). England 190-4 (19.2; A.D.Hales 116*, E.J.G.Morgan 57, K.M.D.N.Kulasekara 4-32). Award: A.D.Hales.
A.D.Hales' score of 116 was the highest for England in all IT20s.*

Zahur Ahmed Chowdhury Stadium, Chittagong, 29 March. Toss: England. **SOUTH AFRICA** won by 3 runs. South Africa 196-5 (20; A.B.de Villiers 69*, H.M.Amla 56). England 193-7 (20; W.D.Parnell 3-31). Award: A.B.de Villiers.

Zahur Ahmed Chowdhury Stadium, Chittagong, 31 March. Toss: England. **NETHER-LANDS** won by 45 runs. Netherlands 133-5 (20; S.C.J.Broad 3-24). England 88 (17.4; L.V.van Beek 3-9, Mudassar Bukhari 3-12). Award: Mudassar Bukhari.
This was England's joint second lowest total in all IT20s.

GROUP 2	P	W	L	T	A	Pts	Net RR
India	4	4	–	–	–	8	+1.28
West Indies	4	3	1	–	–	6	+1.97
Pakistan	4	2	2	–	–	4	–0.38
Australia	4	1	3	–	–	2	–0.85
Bangladesh	4	–	4	–	–	0	–2.07

SEMI-FINALS

Shere Bangla National Stadium, Mirpur, 3 April. Toss: Sri Lanka. **SRI LANKA** won by 27 runs (D/L method). Sri Lanka 160-6 (20). West Indies 80-4 (13.5). Award: A.D.Mathews (SL, 40 in 23b).

Shere Bangla National Stadium, Mirpur, 4 April. Toss: South Africa. **INDIA** won by six wickets. South Africa 172-4 (20; F.du Plessis 58, R.Ashwin 3-22). India 176-4 (19.1; V.Kohli 72*). Award: V.Kohli.

FINAL

Shere Bangla National Stadium, Mirpur, 6 April. Toss: Sri Lanka. **SRI LANKA** won by six wickets. India 130-4 (20; V.Kohli 77). Sri Lanka 134-4 (17.5; K.C.Sangakkara 52*). Award: K.C.Sangakkara.

RECORDS

Highest score		196-5	South Africa v England Group 1 Chittagong
Lowest score		39 (10.3)	Netherlands v Sri Lanka Group 1 Chittagong
Highest innings	116*	A.D.Hales	England v Sri Lanka Group 1 Chittagong
Highest partnership	152	A.D.Hales/E.J.G.Morgan	England v Sri Lanka Group 1 Chittagong
Best analysis	5-3	H.M.R.K.B.Herath	Sri Lanka v New Zealand Group 1 Chittagong
Most runs	319	V.Kohli	India (ave 106.33, strike rate 129.1)
Most wickets	12	Imran Tahir	South Africa (ave 10.91, economy 6.55)
Man of the Series		V.Kohli	India (319 runs)

These records exclude any games played in the qualifying tournament.

LIMITED-OVERS INTERNATIONALS
CAREER RECORDS

These records, complete to 13 February 2015, include all players registered for county cricket for the 2015 season at the time of going to press, plus those who have appeared in LOI matches for ICC full member countries since 21 November 2013.

ENGLAND – BATTING AND FIELDING

	M	I	NO	HS	Runs	Avge	100	50	Ct/St
M.M.Ali	17	17	–	119	540	31.76	1	3	8
T.R.Ambrose	5	5	1	6	10	2.50	–	–	3
J.M.Anderson	188	76	42	28	264	7.76	–	–	57
J.M.Bairstow	7	6	1	41*	119	23.80	–	–	3
G.S.Ballance	12	11	1	79	261	26.10	–	2	7
G.J.Batty	10	8	2	17	30	5.00	–	–	4
I.R.Bell	155	151	13	141	5154	37.34	4	32	54
R.S.Bopara	119	109	21	101*	2695	30.62	1	14	34
S.G.Borthwick	2	2	–	15	18	9.00	–	–	–
T.T.Bresnan	84	64	20	80	871	19.79	–	1	20
D.R.Briggs	1	–	–	–	–	–	–	–	–
S.C.J.Broad	113	62	24	45*	497	13.07	–	–	25
J.C.Buttler	49	42	6	121	1139	31.63	1	6	66/8
M.A.Carberry	6	6	–	63	114	19.00	–	1	2
G.Chapple	1	1	–	14	14	14.00	–	–	–
R.Clarke	20	13	–	39	144	11.07	–	–	11
P.D.Collingwood	197	181	37	120*	5092	35.36	5	26	108
A.N.Cook	92	92	4	137	3204	36.40	5	19	36
S.M.Davies	8	8	–	87	244	30.50	–	1	8
J.L.Denly	9	9	–	67	268	29.77	–	2	5
J.W.Dernbach	24	8	1	5	19	2.71	–	–	5
S.T.Finn	52	20	8	35	112	9.33	–	–	11
A.Flintoff	138	119	16	123	3293	31.97	3	18	46
J.S.Foster	11	6	3	13	41	13.66	–	–	13/7
H.F.Gurney	10	6	4	6*	15	7.50	–	–	1
A.D.Hales	7	7	–	42	126	18.00	–	–	1
G.O.Jones †	49	41	8	80	815	24.69	–	4	68/4
C.J.Jordan	20	15	5	38*	132	13.20	–	–	11
E.C.Joyce †	17	17	–	107	471	27.70	1	3	6
R.W.T.Key	5	5	–	19	54	10.80	–	–	–
C.Kieswetter	46	40	5	107	1054	30.11	1	5	53/12
M.J.Lumb	3	3	–	106	165	55.00	1	–	1
S.C.Meaker	2	2	–	1	2	1.00	–	–	–
E.J.G.Morgan †	112	104	19	124*	3104	36.51	6	17	47
P.Mustard	10	10	–	83	233	23.30	–	1	9/2
G.Onions	4	1	–	1	1	1.00	–	–	–
M.S.Panesar	26	8	3	13	26	5.20	–	–	3
S.D.Parry	2	–	–	–	–	–	–	–	–
S.R.Patel	36	22	7	70*	482	32.13	–	1	7
K.P.Pietersen	136	125	16	130	4440	40.73	9	25	40
L.E.Plunkett	29	25	10	56	315	21.00	–	1	7
M.J.Prior	68	62	9	87	1282	24.18	–	3	71/8
W.B.Rankin †	7	2	1	4	5	2.50	–	–	–
A.U.Rashid	5	4	1	31*	60	20.00	–	–	2
C.M.W.Read	36	24	7	30*	300	17.64	–	–	41/2
J.E.Root	48	45	5	113	1600	40.00	3	8	18
O.A.Shah	71	66	6	107*	1834	30.56	1	12	21
A.Shahzad	11	8	2	9	39	6.50	–	–	4
R.J.Sidebottom	25	18	8	24	133	13.30	–	–	6

	M	I	NO	HS	Runs	Avge	100	50	Ct/St
V.S.Solanki	51	46	5	106	1097	26.75	2	5	16
B.A.Stokes	24	19	1	70	282	15.66	–	1	9
J.W.A.Taylor	11	11	1	90	343	34.30	–	4	5
J.C.Tredwell	44	25	11	30	163	11.64	–	–	13
C.T.Tremlett	15	11	4	19*	50	7.14	–	–	4
M.E.Trescothick	123	122	6	137	4335	37.37	12	21	49
I.J.L.Trott	68	65	10	137	2819	51.25	4	22	14
C.R.Woakes	29	23	5	41	310	17.22	–	–	15
L.J.Wright	50	39	4	52	707	20.20	–	2	18
M.H.Yardy	28	24	8	60*	326	20.37	–	2	10

ENGLAND – BOWLING

	O	M	R	W	Avge	Best	4wI	R/Over
M.M.Ali	135	1	634	17	37.29	2-34	–	4.69
J.M.Anderson	1551.2	124	7616	264	28.84	5-23	13	4.90
G.J.Batty	73.2	1	366	5	73.20	2-40	–	4.99
I.R.Bell	14.4	0	88	6	14.66	3- 9	–	6.00
R.S.Bopara	302	10	1492	38	39.26	4-38	1	4.94
S.G.Borthwick	9	0	72	0	–	–	–	8.00
T.T.Bresnan	697.3	33	3802	108	35.20	5-48	4	5.45
D.R.Briggs	10	0	39	2	19.50	2-39	–	3.90
S.C.J.Broad	954.5	53	5021	173	29.02	5-23	10	5.25
M.A.Carberry	1	0	12	0	–	–	–	12.00
G.Chapple	4	0	14	0	–	–	–	3.50
R.Clarke	78.1	3	415	11	37.72	2-28	–	5.30
P.D.Collingwood	864.2	14	4294	111	38.68	6-31	4	4.96
J.W.Dernbach	205.4	6	1308	31	42.19	4-45	1	6.35
S.T.Finn	454.4	26	2216	78	28.41	5-33	4	4.87
A.Flintoff	916	66	3968	168	23.61	5-19	8	4.33
H.F.Gurney	75.5	4	432	11	39.27	4-55	1	5.69
C.J.Jordan	174	2	993	33	30.09	5-29	1	5.70
S.C.Meaker	19	1	110	2	55.00	1-45	–	5.78
G.Onions	34	1	185	4	46.25	2-58	–	5.44
M.S.Panesar	218	10	980	24	40.83	3-25	–	4.49
S.D.Parry	19	2	92	4	23.00	3-32	–	4.84
S.R.Patel	197.5	4	1091	24	45.45	5-41	1	5.51
K.P.Pietersen	66.4	0	370	7	52.85	2-22	–	5.55
L.E.Plunkett	227.1	7	1321	39	33.87	3-24	–	5.81
W.B.Rankin	53.1	3	241	10	24.10	4-46	1	4.53
A.U.Rashid	34	0	191	3	63.66	1-16	–	5.61
J.E.Root	121	2	695	11	63.18	2-15	–	5.74
O.A.Shah	32.1	1	184	7	26.28	3-15	–	5.72
A.Shahzad	98	5	490	17	28.82	3-41	–	5.00
R.J.Sidebottom	212.5	12	1039	29	35.82	3-19	–	4.88
V.S.Solanki	18.3	0	105	1	105.00	1-17	–	5.67
B.A.Stokes	115	2	713	20	35.65	5-61	2	6.20
J.C.Tredwell	343.4	18	1641	59	27.81	4-41	3	4.77
C.T.Tremlett	130.4	2	705	15	47.00	4-32	1	5.39
M.E.Trescothick	38.4	0	219	4	54.75	2- 7	–	5.66
I.J.L.Trott	30.3	0	166	2	83.00	2-31	–	5.44
C.R.Woakes	232.2	8	1376	42	32.76	6-45	4	5.92
L.J.Wright	173	9	884	15	58.93	2-34	–	5.10
M.H.Yardy	222	7	1075	21	51.19	3-24	–	4.84

† G.O.Jones has also made 2 appearances for Papua New Guinea; E.C.Joyce has also made 28 appearances for Ireland; E.J.G.Morgan has also made 23 appearances for Ireland; and W.B.Rankin has also made 37 appearances for Ireland (see below).

AUSTRALIA – BATTING AND FIELDING

	M	I	NO	HS	Runs	Avge	100	50	Ct/St
S.A.Abbott	1	1	–	3	3	3.00	–	–	–
G.J.Bailey	56	53	6	156	1962	41.74	2	14	30
D.T.Christian	19	18	5	39	273	21.00	–	–	10
M.J.Clarke	238	217	44	130	7762	44.86	8	56	101
N.M.Coulter-Nile	10	7	3	16	60	15.00	–	–	1
P.J.Cummins	10	5	3	11*	22	11.00	–	–	2
B.C.J.Cutting	4	2	–	27	53	26.50	–	–	1
X.J.Doherty	59	22	15	15*	101	14.42	–	–	17
J.P.Faulkner	38	29	13	116	770	48.12	1	4	11
A.J.Finch	41	39	–	148	1447	37.10	5	6	20
B.J.Haddin	118	110	14	110	2996	31.20	2	16	154/11
J.W.Hastings	11	9	4	21*	82	16.40	–	–	2
J.R.Hazlewood	8	1	1	0*	0	–	–	–	–
M.C.Henriques	6	6	1	12	36	7.20	–	–	1
B.W.Hilfenhaus	25	11	8	16	29	9.66	–	–	10
P.J.Hughes	25	24	1	138*	826	35.91	2	4	5
M.G.Johnson	145	87	30	73*	920	16.14	–	2	31
N.M.Lyon	8	4	3	8*	12	12.00	–	–	1
C.J.McKay	59	31	10	30	190	9.04	–	–	7
M.R.Marsh	14	13	2	89	420	38.18	–	4	7
S.E.Marsh	46	45	2	151	1712	39.81	3	10	9
G.J.Maxwell	41	39	5	95	1043	30.67	–	9	24
J.L.Pattinson	13	7	3	13	40	10.00	–	–	2
K.W.Richardson	8	3	2	9*	11	11.00	–	–	–
G.S.Sandhu	2	–	–	–	–	–	–	–	–
P.M.Siddle	17	4	2	9*	21	10.50	–	–	1
S.P.D.Smith	50	38	6	104	1147	35.84	3	3	30
M.A.Starc	33	15	10	52*	162	32.40	–	1	6
A.C.Voges	31	28	9	112*	870	45.78	1	4	7
M.S.Wade	47	43	3	75	909	22.72	–	5	56/7
D.A.Warner	54	52	–	163	1702	32.73	3	10	19
S.R.Watson	180	159	24	185*	5478	40.57	9	31	62
C.L.White	88	74	15	105	2037	34.52	2	11	37

AUSTRALIA – BOWLING

	O	M	R	W	Avge	Best	4wI	R/Over
S.A.Abbott	5	0	25	1	25.00	1-25	–	5.00
D.T.Christian	121.1	4	595	20	29.75	5-31	1	4.91
M.J.Clarke	425.5	7	2132	56	38.07	5-35	2	5.00
N.M.Coulter-Nile	88	1	481	16	30.06	4-48	1	5.46
P.J.Cummins	84	2	497	14	35.50	3-28	–	5.91
B.C.J.Cutting	36	1	158	5	31.60	3-45	–	4.38
X.J.Doherty	458.2	17	2164	55	39.34	4-28	3	4.72
J.P.Faulkner	286.5	7	1618	50	32.36	4-48	2	5.64
A.J.Finch	9.1	0	48	2	24.00	1- 2	–	5.23
J.W.Hastings	91	1	410	8	51.25	2-35	–	4.50
J.R.Hazlewood	58.2	5	269	12	22.41	5-31	1	4.61
M.C.Henriques	34	1	157	5	31.40	3-32	–	4.61
B.W.Hilfenhaus	202.4	16	1075	29	37.06	5-33	1	5.30
M.G.Johnson	1184.4	72	5712	224	25.50	6-31	11	4.82
N.M.Lyon	73	7	330	11	30.00	4-44	1	4.52
C.J.McKay	494.1	38	2364	97	24.37	5-28	6	4.78
M.R.Marsh	57	1	290	6	48.33	2-23	–	5.08
G.J.Maxwell	196.4	5	1065	28	38.03	4-46	2	5.41
J.L.Pattinson	106.1	5	572	16	35.75	4-51	–	5.38
K.W.Richardson	63	6	299	8	37.37	2-36	–	4.74
G.S.Sandhu	20	0	107	3	35.66	2-49	–	5.35

AUSTRALIA – BOWLING (continued)

	O	M	R	W	Avge	Best	4wI	R/Over
P.M.Siddle	125.1	9	581	15	38.73	3-55	–	4.64
S.P.D.Smith	168.2	1	876	27	32.44	3-16	–	5.20
M.A.Starc	259.3	16	1298	61	21.27	6-43	9	5.00
A.C.Voges	50.1	1	276	6	46.00	1- 3	–	5.50
D.A.Warner	1	0	8	0	–	–	–	8.00
S.R.Watson	1041.4	35	5120	164	32.21	4-36	3	4.91
C.L.White	55.1	2	351	12	29.25	3- 5	–	6.36

SOUTH AFRICA – BATTING AND FIELDING

	M	I	NO	HS	Runs	Avge	100	50	Ct/St
K.J.Abbott	11	4	1	23	35	11.66	–	–	3
H.M.Amla	107	104	9	153*	5359	56.41	19	27	50
F.Behardien	21	18	3	63	318	21.20	–	2	8
H.Davids	2	2	–	7	8	4.00	–	–	–
Q.de Kock	36	36	1	135	1486	42.45	6	4	60/2
M.de Lange	3	–	–	–	–	–	–	–	–
A.B.de Villiers	174	167	29	149	7309	52.96	19	42	145/5
F.du Plessis	67	64	6	126	1963	33.84	3	12	39
J.P.Duminy	134	122	29	150*	3644	39.18	3	20	53
Imran Tahir	30	11	7	23*	52	13.00	–	–	7
C.A.Ingram	31	29	3	124	843	32.42	3	3	12
J.H.Kallis	323	309	53	139	11550	45.11	17	86	131
R.K.Kleinveldt	10	7	–	43	105	15.00	–	–	4
R.McLaren	54	41	15	71*	485	18.65	–	1	13
D.A.Miller	63	56	18	130*	1313	34.55	1	8	25
M.Morkel	88	34	12	23*	172	7.81	–	–	23
W.D.Parnell	45	24	8	56	356	22.25	–	1	5
A.N.Petersen	21	19	1	80	504	28.00	–	4	5
R.J.Peterson	79	41	14	68	556	20.59	–	1	28
A.M.Phangiso	14	8	2	18*	45	7.50	–	–	3
V.D.Philander	24	15	4	23	111	10.09	–	–	5
A.G.Prince	52	41	12	89*	1018	35.10	–	3	26
R.R.Rossouw	14	14	–	132	416	29.71	2	1	10
J.A.Rudolph	45	39	6	81	1174	35.57	–	7	11
M.Shezi	1	–	–	–	–	–	–	–	–
G.C.Smith	196	193	10	141	6989	38.19	10	47	105
D.W.Steyn	94	38	10	35	238	8.50	–	–	22
L.L.Tsotsobe	61	21	13	16*	56	7.00	–	–	9
M.N.van Wyk	14	14	1	82	349	26.84	–	3	8/1

SOUTH AFRICA – BOWLING

	O	M	R	W	Avge	Best	4wI	R/Over
K.J.Abbott	78.5	6	392	7	56.00	2-21	–	4.97
F.Behardien	67.4	1	346	12	28.83	3-19	–	5.11
M.de Lange	24.5	1	111	8	13.87	4-46	1	4.46
A.B.de Villiers	14	0	83	3	27.66	2-28	–	5.92
F.du Plessis	25	0	142	2	71.00	1- 8	–	5.68
J.P.Duminy	379.3	6	1917	47	40.78	3-31	–	5.05
Imran Tahir	253.2	10	1113	55	20.23	4-28	4	4.39
C.A.Ingram	1	0	17	0	–	–	–	17.00
J.H.Kallis	1773	77	8568	269	31.85	5-30	4	4.83
R.K.Kleinveldt	85.3	6	448	12	37.33	4-22	1	5.23
R.McLaren	400.3	13	2102	77	27.29	4-19	5	5.24
M.Morkel	727.3	36	3588	144	24.91	5-21	8	4.93
W.D.Parnell	342.1	16	1872	64	29.25	5-48	4	5.47
A.N.Petersen	1	0	7	0	–	–	–	7.00

	O	M	R	W	Avge	Best	4wI	R/Over
R.J.Peterson	546.2	15	2680	75	35.73	4-12	3	4.90
A.M.Phangiso	125.4	4	573	15	38.20	3-43	–	4.55
V.D.Philander	168.4	17	779	35	22.25	4-12	2	4.61
A.G.Prince	2	0	3	0	–	–	–	1.50
R.R.Rossouw	3	0	17	1	17.00	1-17	–	5.66
J.A.Rudolph	4	0	26	0	–	–	–	6.50
M.Shezi	6	2	8	1	8.00	1- 8	–	1.33
G.C.Smith	171	0	951	18	52.83	3-30	–	5.56
D.W.Steyn	780.5	58	3755	149	25.20	6-39	7	4.80
L.L.Tsotsobe	494	44	2347	94	24.96	4-22	7	4.75

WEST INDIES – BATTING AND FIELDING

	M	I	NO	HS	Runs	Avge	100	50	Ct/St
S.J.Benn	31	20	5	31	128	8.53	–	–	13
T.L.Best	26	16	8	24	76	9.50	–	–	4
C.R.Brathwaite	4	4	–	11	27	6.75	–	–	–
D.J.Bravo	164	141	24	112*	2968	25.36	2	10	73
D.M.Bravo	79	76	9	124	2171	32.40	2	16	25
J.L.Carter	5	5	–	40	80	16.00	–	–	3
J.Charles	30	39	–	130	869	28.96	2	2	19/1
S.S.Cottrell	2	2	2	2*	3	–	–	–	1
M.L.Cummins	1	–	–	–	–	–	–	–	–
N.Deonarine	31	29	3	65*	682	26.23	–	4	9
K.A.Edwards	16	16	2	123*	331	23.64	1	–	2
C.H.Gayle	260	255	17	153*	8826	37.08	21	45	108
J.O.Holder	26	17	6	22*	162	14.72	–	–	6
L.R.Johnson	6	6	–	51	98	16.33	–	1	2
N.O.Miller	45	26	12	51	264	18.85	–	1	17
S.P.Narine	52	35	9	36	282	10.84	–	–	12
B.P.Nash	9	7	3	39*	104	26.00	–	–	1
V.Permaul	6	3	1	10	11	5.50	–	–	–
K.A.Pollard	91	85	4	119	2042	25.20	3	7	50
K.O.A.Powell	28	28	–	83	772	27.57	–	7	8
D.Ramdin	120	92	20	169	1804	25.05	2	6	154/6
R.Rampaul	90	38	9	86*	359	12.37	–	1	14
K.A.J.Roach	64	41	25	34	216	13.50	–	–	16
A.D.Russell	43	36	7	92*	840	28.96	–	4	9
D.J.G.Sammy	119	100	30	84	1694	24.20	–	8	66
M.N.Samuels	167	157	24	126*	4401	33.09	7	25	44
L.M.P.Simmons	61	60	3	122	1785	31.31	1	15	26
D.R.Smith	99	83	5	97	1467	18.80	–	8	28
J.E.Taylor	72	34	7	43*	217	8.03	–	–	18
C.A.K.Walton	5	4	–	17	17	4.25	–	–	6/1

WEST INDIES – BOWLING

	O	M	R	W	Avge	Best	4wI	R/Over
S.J.Benn	253.5	13	1148	32	35.87	4-18	3	4.52
T.L.Best	216.4	9	1157	34	34.02	4-35	2	5.34
C.R.Brathwaite	24	1	116	0	–	–	–	4.83
D.J.Bravo	1085.1	38	5874	199	29.51	6-43	7	5.41
S.S.Cottrell	13	0	107	2	53.50	2-39	–	8.23
M.L.Cummins	6	1	42	1	42.00	1-42	–	7.00
N.Deonarine	83.3	2	475	6	79.16	2-18	–	5.68
C.H.Gayle	1177.5	38	5584	158	35.34	5-46	4	4.74
J.O.Holder	201.2	14	1118	37	30.21	4-13	2	5.55
N.O.Miller	317.4	16	1461	40	36.52	4-43	2	4.59

	O	M	R	W	Avge	Best	4wI	R/Over
S.P.Narine	470.4	31	1934	73	26.49	5-27	5	4.10
B.P.Nash	49	3	224	5	44.80	3-56	–	4.57
V.Permaul	51.1	0	240	8	30.00	3-40	–	4.69
K.A.Pollard	301	4	1677	44	38.11	3-27	–	5.57
R.Rampaul	661.1	33	3361	115	29.22	5-49	10	5.08
K.A.J.Roach	536.1	39	2632	98	26.85	6-27	5	4.90
A.D.Russell	298.5	8	1705	53	32.16	4-35	5	5.70
D.J.G.Sammy	798	41	3679	80	45.98	4-26	1	4.61
M.N.Samuels	776.1	18	3721	82	45.37	3-25	–	4.79
L.M.P.Simmons	25	0	160	1	160.00	1- 3	–	6.40
D.R.Smith	447.2	18	2258	60	37.63	5-45	4	5.04
J.E.Taylor	600	32	2983	106	28.14	5-48	4	4.97

NEW ZEALAND – BATTING AND FIELDING

	M	I	NO	HS	Runs	Avge	100	50	Ct/St
A.R.Adams	42	34	10	45	419	17.45	–	–	8
C.J.Anderson	26	23	4	131*	687	36.15	1	2	3
H.K.Bennett	14	7	5	4*	10	5.00	–	–	2
T.A.Boult	16	7	3	21*	52	13.00	–	–	4
D.G.Brownlie	10	9	1	47	203	25.37	–	–	4
A.P.Devcich	10	9	–	58	177	19.66	–	1	3
G.D.Elliott	58	47	9	115	1299	34.18	2	7	9
J.E.C.Franklin	110	80	27	98*	1270	23.96	–	4	26
M.J.Guptill	99	96	10	189*	3192	37.11	5	21	45
M.J.Henry	8	2	1	20*	21	21.00	–	–	1
T.W.M.Latham	26	25	4	86	502	23.90	–	1	13/1
M.J.McClenaghan	34	11	9	34*	59	29.50	–	–	3
B.B.McCullum	240	209	28	166	5480	30.27	5	27	253/15
N.L.McCullum	78	59	10	65	1030	21.02	–	4	37
H.J.H.Marshall	66	62	9	101*	1454	27.43	1	12	18
K.D.Mills	170	101	34	54	1047	15.62	–	2	42
A.F.Milne	16	3	2	19	38	38.00	–	–	8
C.Munro	7	6	–	85	167	27.83	–	2	–
J.D.S.Neesham	16	13	3	42*	146	14.60	–	–	5
J.S.Patel	39	13	7	34	88	14.66	–	–	12
L.Ronchi	40	32	6	170*	912	35.07	1	3	56/5
J.D.Ryder	48	42	1	107	1362	33.21	3	6	15
T.G.Southee	85	47	16	32	319	10.29	–	–	20
L.R.P.L.Taylor	150	138	21	131*	4913	41.99	12	29	98
D.L.Vettori	282	177	51	83	2151	17.07	–	4	80
K.S.Williamson	65	60	7	145*	2452	46.26	6	15	26

NEW ZEALAND – BOWLING

	O	M	R	W	Avge	Best	4wI	R/Over
A.R.Adams	314.1	15	1643	53	31.00	5-22	3	5.22
C.J.Anderson	160.2	6	1007	36	27.97	5-63	3	6.28
H.K.Bennett	100.2	3	543	23	23.60	4-16	2	5.41
T.A.Boult	133.4	9	629	18	34.94	4-44	1	4.70
A.P.Devcich	41	1	221	4	55.25	2-33	–	5.39
G.D.Elliott	132	7	668	25	26.72	4-31	1	5.06
J.E.C.Franklin	641.2	34	3354	81	41.40	5-42	1	5.22
M.J.Guptill	15.1	0	78	2	39.00	2- 7	–	5.14
M.J.Henry	65.4	3	324	21	15.42	5-30	3	4.93
M.J.McClenaghan	281.4	17	1639	66	24.83	5-58	7	5.81
N.L.McCullum	540.2	6	2628	55	47.78	3-24	–	4.86
K.D.Mills	1371.4	127	6485	240	27.02	5-25	9	4.72

	O	M	R	W	Avge	Best	4wI	R/Over
A.F.Milne	116.2	3	597	14	42.64	2-28	–	5.13
C.Munro	1	0	10	0	–	–	–	10.00
J.D.S.Neesham	90.2	0	580	18	32.22	4-42	2	6.42
J.S.Patel	300.4	9	1513	42	36.02	3-11	–	5.03
J.D.Ryder	67.5	0	412	12	34.33	3-29	–	6.07
T.G.Southee	689.2	44	3592	116	30.96	5-33	5	5.21
L.R.P.L.Taylor	7	0	35	0	–	–	–	5.00
D.L.Vettori	2227.3	93	9188	282	32.58	5- 7	8	4.12
K.S.Williamson	147.3	1	821	24	34.20	4-22	1	5.56

INDIA – BATTING AND FIELDING

	M	I	NO	HS	Runs	Avge	100	50	Ct/St
V.R.Aaron	9	3	2	6*	8	8.00	–	–	1
R.Ashwin	88	50	14	65	623	17.30	–	1	26
S.T.R.Binny	9	6	1	44	91	18.20	–	–	2
S.Dhawan	53	52	3	119	2095	42.75	6	11	22
M.S.Dhoni	251	219	63	183*	8088	51.84	8	56	226/82
R.A.Jadeja	111	76	26	87	1696	33.92	–	10	39
K.M.Jadhav	1	1	–	20	20	20.00	–	–	1
K.D.Karthik	71	60	13	79	1313	27.93	–	7	49/7
V.Kohli	150	142	21	183	6232	51.50	21	33	69
D.S.Kulkarni	4	–	–	–	–	–	–	–	1
B.Kumar	44	22	5	31	161	9.47	–	–	15
A.Mishra	27	7	2	9	24	4.80	–	–	4
Mohammed Shami	40	18	8	25	101	10.10	–	–	11
Parvez Rasool	1	–	–	–	–	–	–	–	–
A.R.Patel	13	7	2	17*	41	8.20	–	–	7
C.A.Pujara	5	5	–	27	51	10.20	–	–	–
A.M.Rahane	46	46	1	111	1376	30.57	2	8	22
S.K.Raina	207	178	34	116*	5104	35.44	4	33	90
A.T.Rayudu	27	24	6	121*	743	41.27	1	5	9
W.P.Saha	9	5	2	16	41	13.66	–	–	17/1
I.Sharma	76	27	13	13	72	5.14	–	–	17
K.V.Sharma	2	–	–	–	–	–	–	–	3
M.M.Sharma	12	5	3	8	20	10.00	–	–	2
R.G.Sharma	127	121	21	264	3890	38.90	6	23	43
M.K.Tiwary	9	9	1	104*	253	31.62	1	1	3
J.D.Unadkat	7	–	–	–	–	–	–	–	–
R.V.Uthappa	43	39	6	86	890	26.96	–	6	16/1
U.T.Yadav	40	14	11	17	44	14.66	–	–	7
Yuvraj Singh	290	265	38	139	8237	36.28	13	51	92

INDIA – BOWLING

	O	M	R	W	Avge	Best	4wI	R/Over
V.R.Aaron	63.2	1	419	11	38.09	3-24	–	6.61
R.Ashwin	797.5	25	3917	120	32.64	3-24	–	4.90
S.T.R.Binny	40.4	3	184	13	14.15	6- 4	1	4.52
M.S.Dhoni	6	0	31	1	31.00	1-14	–	5.16
R.A.Jadeja	912.4	44	4390	134	32.76	5-36	6	4.81
V.Kohli	93.3	0	582	4	145.50	1-15	–	6.22
D.S.Kulkarni	34.2	1	184	8	23.00	4-34	1	5.35
B.Kumar	361.1	38	1672	45	37.15	4- 8	1	4.62
A.Mishra	234.4	16	1078	45	23.95	6-48	3	4.59
Mohammed Shami	329.5	19	1872	70	26.74	4-36	4	5.67
Parvez Rasool	10	0	60	2	30.00	2-60	–	6.00
A.R.Patel	90.4	4	400	16	25.00	3-40	–	4.41

	O	M	R	W	Avge	Best	4wI	R/Over
S.K.Raina	298.2	3	1519	31	49.00	3-34	–	5.09
A.T.Rayudu	16	0	106	2	53.00	1- 8	–	6.62
I.Sharma	582.1	29	3313	106	31.25	4-34	5	5.69
K.V.Sharma	19	1	125	0	–	–	–	6.57
M.M.Sharma	81.1	8	405	10	40.50	4-22	1	4.98
R.G.Sharma	94.5	2	483	8	60.37	2-27	–	5.09
M.K.Tiwary	21	1	144	5	28.80	4-61	1	6.85
J.D.Unadkat	52	5	209	8	26.12	4-41	1	4.01
R.V.Uthappa	0.2	0	0	0	–	–	–	0.00
U.T.Yadav	302.4	13	1786	49	36.44	4-53	1	5.90
Yuvraj Singh	821.2	18	4171	110	37.91	5-31	3	5.07

PAKISTAN – BATTING AND FIELDING

	M	I	NO	HS	Runs	Avge	100	50	Ct/St
Abdur Rehman	31	23	6	31	142	8.35	–	–	7
Ahmed Shehzad	58	58	1	124	1985	34.82	6	10	22
Anwar Ali	9	9	3	43*	173	28.83	–	–	1
Asad Shafiq	53	52	3	84	1224	24.97	–	9	12
Azhar Mahmood	143	110	26	67	1521	18.10	–.	3	14
Bilawal Bhatti	10	7	1	39	89	14.83	–	–	2
Ehsan Adil	4	3	1	6	12	6.00	–	–	–
Fawad Alam	35	33	12	114*	948	45.14	1	6	9
Haris Sohail	11	10	1	85*	309	34.33	–	2	5
Junaid Khan	48	20	10	25	51	5.10	–	–	5
Misbah-ul-Haq	155	142	31	96*	4772	42.99	–	38	63
Mohammad Hafeez	155	155	9	140*	4542	31.10	9	23	54
Mohammad Irfan	40	24	15	12	40	4.44	–	–	8
Mohammad Talha	3	1	0	0	0	0.00	–	–	–
Nasir Jamshed	45	45	3	112	1413	33.64	3	8	12
Raza Hasan	1	1	–	0	0	0.00	–	–	–
Saeed Ajmal	111	69	24	33	324	7.20	–	–	25
Sarfraz Ahmed	36	25	5	65	473	23.65	–	1	30/10
Shahid Afridi	386	358	26	124	7911	23.82	6	39	124
Sharjeel Khan	11	11	–	61	194	17.63	–	1	2
Sohaib Maqsood	18	18	2	89*	572	35.75	–	4	7
Sohail Tanvir	62	40	11	59	399	13.75	–	1	15
Umar Akmal	104	93	15	102*	2749	35.24	2	19	65/13
Umar Amin	15	15	1	59	269	19.21	–	1	5
Umar Gul	125	63	17	39	451	9.80	–	–	15
Wahab Riaz	47	35	8	47*	326	12.07	–	–	14
Yasir Arafat	11	8	3	27	74	14.80	–	–	2
Younus Khan	261	251	23	144	7197	31.56	7	48	133
Zulfiqar Babar	4	4	2	14*	34	17.00	–	–	–

PAKISTAN – BOWLING

	O	M	R	W	Avge	Best	4wI	R/Over
Abdur Rehman	270.4	12	1142	30	38.06	4-48	1	4.21
Ahmed Shehzad	19.1	0	140	2	70.00	1-22	–	7.30
Anwar Ali	61.4	1	342	5	68.40	2-24	–	5.54
Asad Shafiq	2	0	18	0	–	–	–	9.00
Azhar Mahmood	1040.2	58	4813	123	39.13	6-18	5	4.62
Bilawal Bhatti	68.1	4	439	6	73.16	3-37	–	6.44
Ehsan Adil	25.3	0	161	2	80.50	1-32	–	6.31
Fawad Alam	66.2	1	377	5	75.40	1- 8	–	5.68
Haris Sohail	52	0	280	6	46.66	3-45	–	5.38
Junaid Khan	377.5	24	1943	75	25.90	4-12	3	5.14

PAKISTAN – BOWLING (continued)

	O	M	R	W	Avge	Best	4wI	R/Over
Misbah-ul-Haq	4	0	30	0	–	–	–	7.50
Mohammad Hafeez	1052.2	41	4273	122	35.02	3-17	–	4.06
Mohammad Irfan	348.1	20	1706	57	29.92	4-33	1	4.89
Mohammad Talha	20.2	1	146	4	36.50	2-22	–	7.18
Raza Hasan	10	0	68	1	68.00	1-68	–	6.80
Saeed Ajmal	980.5	49	4059	183	22.18	5-24	8	4.13
Shahid Afridi	2876.1	73	13290	391	33.98	7-12	13	4.62
Sohaib Maqsood	3	0	18	0	–	–	–	6.00
Sohail Tanvir	491.3	24	2566	71	36.14	5-48	4	5.22
Umar Amin	5	0	18	0	–	–	–	3.60
Umar Gul	972.4	67	5015	173	28.98	6-42	6	5.15
Wahab Riaz	346.4	13	1958	61	32.09	5-46	2	5.64
Yasir Arafat	69	2	373	4	93.25	1-28	–	5.40
Younus Khan	47.2	1	288	3	96.00	1- 3	–	6.08
Zulfiqar Babar	39	1	190	4	47.50	2-52	–	4.87

SRI LANKA – BATTING AND FIELDING

	M	I	NO	HS	Runs	Avge	100	50	Ct/St
P.V.D.Chameera	1	–	–	–	–	–	–	–	–
L.D.Chandimal	92	84	13	111	2066	29.09	2	12	33/2
P.C.de Silva	6	6	1	44	80	16.00	–	–	4
D.P.D.N.Dickwella	1	1	–	4	4	4.00	–	–	–
T.M.Dilshan	307	281	40	160*	9401	39.00	20	42	110/1
R.M.S.Eranga	17	10	7	12*	34	11.33	–	–	5
P.L.S.Gamage	4	2	1	0*	0	–	–	–	1
H.M.R.K.B.Herath	67	29	15	17*	127	9.07	–	–	11
D.P.M.D.Jayawardena	436	408	38	144	12256	33.12	17	75	211
H.K.S.R.Kaluhalamulla	30	17	1	56	254	15.87	–	1	7
S.H.T.Kandamby	39	36	6	93*	870	29.00	–	5	7
F.D.M.Karunaratne	13	11	1	60	153	15.30	–	1	3
K.M.D.N.Kulasekara	165	110	34	73	1152	15.15	–	3	40
R.A.S.Lakmal	31	14	8	4*	12	2.00	–	–	5
S.L.Malinga	177	87	26	56	442	7.24	–	1	25
A.D.Mathews	149	125	36	139*	3588	40.31	1	25	36
B.A.W.Mendis	83	40	18	19*	163	7.40	–	–	15
B.M.A.J.Mendis	52	38	9	72	591	20.37	–	1	10
A.K.Perera	3	1	–	1	1	1.00	–	–	1
M.D.K.Perera	5	4	–	30	44	11.00	–	–	–
M.D.K.J.Perera	41	39	3	106	839	23.30	1	4	14
N.L.T.C.Perera	98	73	12	80*	1073	17.59	–	5	40
K.T.G.D.Prasad	24	12	6	31*	129	21.50	–	–	1
S.Prasanna	22	19	2	42	181	10.64	–	–	2
S.M.A.Priyanjan	21	19	2	74	402	23.64	–	2	7
K.C.Sangakkara	390	366	38	169	13434	40.95	21	90	391/93
S.M.S.M.Senanayake	44	30	11	42	276	14.52	–	–	17
W.U.Tharanga	175	167	9	174*	5329	33.72	13	28	33
H.D.R.L.Thirimanne	87	68	9	102*	1871	31.71	3	10	29
K.D.K.Vithanage	6	6	1	27	75	15.00	–	–	2

SRI LANKA – BOWLING

	O	M	R	W	Avge	Best	4wI	R/Over
P.V.D.Chameera	8	0	60	2	30.00	2-60	–	7.50
P.C.de Silva	48.4	2	233	5	46.60	2-29	–	4.78
T.M.Dilshan	892.3	21	4308	97	44.41	4- 4	3	4.82
R.M.S.Eranga	112.2	4	652	20	32.60	3-46	–	5.80
P.L.S.Gamage	27	2	162	1	162.00	1-59	–	6.00

LOI   SRI LANKA – BOWLING (continued)

	O	M	R	W	Avge	Best	4wI	R/Over
H.M.R.K.B.Herath	505.3	18	2206	71	31.07	4-20	1	4.36
D.P.M.D.Jayawardena	96.3	1	544	8	68.00	2-56	–	5.63
H.K.S.R.Kaluhalamulla	231.3	5	1152	36	32.00	5-42	1	4.97
S.H.T.Kandamby	29	1	173	2	86.50	2-37	–	5.96
F.D.M.Karunaratne	1.4	0	11	0	–	–	–	6.60
K.M.D.N.Kulasekara	1264.4	103	6094	178	34.23	5-22	4	4.81
R.A.S.Lakmal	241.2	16	1323	44	30.06	4-30	1	5.48
S.L.Malinga	1413.1	84	7376	271	27.21	6-38	16	5.21
A.D.Mathews	699.5	45	3166	91	34.79	6-20	2	4.52
B.A.W.Mendis	668.2	34	3134	148	21.17	6-13	10	4.68
B.M.A.J.Mendis	217.5	2	1116	26	42.92	3-15	–	5.12
A.K.Perera	3	0	17	0	–	–	–	5.66
M.D.K.Perera	16	0	81	2	40.50	1-17	–	5.06
N.L.T.C.Perera	600.2	23	3403	113	30.11	6-44	6	5.66
K.T.G.D.Prasad	169.1	4	976	32	30.50	3-17	–	5.76
S.Prasanna	181.1	6	900	21	42.85	3-32	–	4.96
S.M.A.Priyanjan	44.1	1	233	5	46.60	2-11	–	5.27
S.M.S.M.Senanayake	362.4	10	1704	49	34.77	4-13	1	4.69
H.D.R.L.Thirimanne	17.2	0	94	3	31.33	2-36	–	5.42
K.D.K.Vithanane	2	0	17	0	–	–	–	8.50

H.K.S.R.Kaluhalamulla is also known as S.Randiv.

ZIMBABWE – BATTING AND FIELDING

	M	I	NO	HS	Runs	Avge	100	50	Ct/St
R.W.Chakabva	24	22	1	45	340	16.19	–	–	13
T.L.Chatara	21	13	8	23	76	15.20	–	–	3
E.Chigumbura	166	153	20	90	3339	25.10	–	18	58
S.M.Ervine	42	34	7	100	698	25.85	1	2	5
K.M.Jarvis	24	15	5	13	52	5.20	–	–	6
L.M.Jongwe	3	3	–	19	27	9.00	–	–	–
T.Kamungozi	11	9	4	12*	21	4.20	–	–	6
N.Madziva	5	5	1	25	44	11.00	–	–	1
T.Maruma	16	15	–	32	140	9.33	–	–	8
H.Masakadza	144	144	4	178*	3961	28.29	3	25	56
S.W.Masakadza	16	11	3	45*	170	21.25	–	–	7
T.M.K.Mawoyo	7	7	–	15	58	8.28	–	–	2
S.F.Mire	5	5	–	52	134	26.80	–	2	2
P.J.Moor	2	2	–	13	15	7.50	–	–	1
N.M'shangwe	6	6	1	16	38	7.60	–	–	1
R.Mutumbami	5	5	–	64	100	20.00	–	1	1
J.C.Nyumbu	10	9	1	18	31	3.87	–	–	4
T.Panyangara	38	31	8	16*	129	5.60	–	–	7
V.Sibanda	117	116	3	116	2812	24.45	2	20	41
Sikandar Raza	21	21	1	141	578	28.90	1	1	10
B.R.M.Taylor	161	160	15	145*	4825	33.27	6	31	94/20
D.T.Tiripano	4	2	–	3	4	2.00	–	–	–
P.Utseya	160	129	47	68*	1385	16.89	–	4	48
B.V.Vitori	15	9	2	20*	55	7.85	–	–	1
M.N.Waller	45	41	3	99*	818	21.52	–	4	13
S.C.Williams	69	68	11	78*	1782	31.26	–	17	24

ZIMBABWE – BOWLING

	O	M	R	W	Avge	Best	4wI	R/Over
T.L.Chatara	184.2	14	927	27	34.33	3-44	–	5.02
E.Chigumbura	657.1	23	3816	90	42.40	4-28	1	5.80
S.M.Ervine	274.5	10	1561	41	38.07	3-29	–	5.67

	O	M	R	W	Avge	Best	4wI	R/Over
K.M.Jarvis	202.5	9	1221	27	45.22	3-36	–	6.01
L.M.Jongwe	13	0	95	0	–	–	–	7.30
T.Kamungozi	85	1	424	11	38.54	2-36	–	4.98
N.Madziva	36	0	235	7	33.57	3-60	–	6.52
T.Maruma	37.3	1	230	4	57.50	2-50	–	6.13
H.Masakadza	259.3	5	1364	36	37.88	3-39	–	5.25
S.W.Masakadza	131.5	4	891	25	35.64	4-46	3	6.75
S.F.Mire	15.3	0	92	3	30.66	3-49	–	5.93
N.M'shangwe	56	4	260	3	86.66	2-50	–	4.64
J.C.Nyumbu	76.2	3	414	11	37.63	3-42	–	5.42
T.Panyangara	308.3	27	1750	41	42.68	3-28	–	5.67
V.Sibanda	36.3	0	204	3	68.00	1-12	–	5.58
Sikandar Raza	24	0	143	3	47.66	2-25	–	5.95
B.R.M.Taylor	66	0	406	9	45.11	3-54	–	6.15
D.T.Tiripano	31.1	4	188	9	20.88	5-63	1	6.03
P.Utseya	1391.3	65	6046	130	46.50	5-36	3	4.34
B.V.Vitori	126.2	3	707	24	29.45	5-20	2	5.59
M.N.Waller	68	0	355	5	71.00	1- 9	–	5.22
S.C.Williams	263.1	11	1253	22	56.95	3-23	–	4.76

BANGLADESH – BATTING AND FIELDING

	M	I	NO	HS	Runs	Avge	100	50	Ct/St
Abdur Razzak	153	97	39	53*	779	13.43	–	1	32
Abul Hasan	5	2	–	3	4	2.00	–	–	1
Al-Amin Hossain	11	5	3	2*	3	1.50	–	–	1
Anamul Haque	27	25	–	120	892	35.68	3	3	9
Arafat Sunny	8	6	4	5	10	5.00	–	–	4
Imrul Kayes	53	53	1	101	1390	26.73	1	10	16
Jubair Hossain	2	–	–	–	–	–	–	–	1
Mahmudullah	110	94	28	82*	2123	32.16	–	11	34
Mashrafe Mortaza	142	108	20	51*	1332	15.13	–	1	43
Mohammad Mithun	2	1	–	26	26	26.00	–	–	–
Mominul Haque	24	22	1	60	539	25.66	–	3	4
Mushfiqur Rahim	140	129	20	117	3153	28.92	2	18	104/36
Naeem Islam	59	51	15	84	975	27.08	–	5	19
Nasir Hossain	41	36	6	100	1044	34.80	1	6	19
Rubel Hossain	53	28	15	17	83	6.38	–	–	9
Sabbir Rahman	5	5	2	44*	83	27.66	–	–	1
Shafiul Islam	52	28	9	24*	124	6.52	–	–	8
Shakib Al Hasan	141	135	20	134*	3977	34.58	6	26	36
Shamsur Rahman	10	10	–	96	266	26.60	–	2	3
Sohag Gazi	20	16	4	30	184	15.33	–	–	7
Soumya Sarkar	1	1	–	20	20	20.00	–	–	–
Taijul Islam	1	–	–	–	–	–	–	–	–
Tamim Iqbal	135	134	1	154	3971	29.85	4	27	34
Taskin Ahmed	3	2	2	0*	0	–	–	–	–
Ziaur Rahman	13	11	–	41	124	11.27	–	–	5

BANGLADESH – BOWLING

	O	M	R	W	Avge	Best	4wI	R/Over
Abdur Razzak	1272.3	70	6065	207	29.29	5-29	9	4.56
Abul Hasan	27	1	177	0	–	–	–	6.55
Al-Amin Hossain	79.3	7	442	17	26.00	4-51	2	5.55
Arafat Sunny	68.5	5	285	16	17.81	4-27	2	4.14
Jubair Hossain	14	0	83	4	20.75	2-41	–	5.92
Mahmudullah	556	13	2824	67	42.14	3- 4	–	5.07
Mashrafe Mortaza	1178.2	101	5477	182	30.09	6-26	6	4.64

	O	M	R	W	Avge	Best	4wI	R/Over
Mominul Haque	36	1	175	7	25.00	2-13	–	4.86
Naeem Islam	290.3	9	1407	35	40.20	3-32	–	4.84
Nasir Hossain	60.1	2	301	3	100.33	2- 3	–	5.00
Rubel Hossain	399.5	14	2233	69	32.36	6-26	5	5.58
Sabbir Rahman	6	0	36	0	–	–	–	6.00
Shafiul Islam	357.4	24	2109	58	36.36	4-21	4	5.89
Shakib Al Hasan	1191.1	72	5082	182	27.92	4-16	5	4.26
Shamsur Rahman	1	0	13	0	–	–	–	13.00
Sohag Gazi	153.1	12	722	22	32.81	4-29	1	4.71
Taijul Islam	7	2	11	4	2.75	4-11	1	1.57
Tamim Iqbal	1	0	13	0	–	–	–	13.00
Taskin Ahmed	23	1	89	7	12.71	5-28	1	3.86
Ziaur Rahman	65	1	301	10	30.10	5-30	1	4.63

ASSOCIATES – BATTING AND FIELDING

	M	I	NO	HS	Runs	Avge	100	50	Ct/St
A.Balbirnie (Ireland)	11	10	1	38	157	17.44	–	–	1
P.K.D.Chase (Ireland)	1	–	–	–	–	–	–	–	–
K.J.Coetzer (Scotland)	20	19	1	133	718	39.88	1	5	8
F.R.J.Coleman (Scotland)	13	11	–	40	134	12.18	–	–	3
T.L.W.Cooper (Netherlands)	23	22	2	101	976	48.80	1	8	12
J.H.Davey (Scotland)	24	22	5	64	428	25.17	–	2	8
G.H.Dockrell (Ireland)	42	22	13	19	109	12.11	–	–	18
G.O.Jones (PNG)	2	2	–	25	47	23.50	–	–	–
E.C.Joyce (Ireland)	28	27	3	116*	883	36.79	1	6	8
A.N.Kervezee (Netherlands)	39	36	3	92	924	28.00	–	4	18
C.S.MacLeod (Scotland)	27	25	3	175	636	28.90	2	1	8
M.W.Machan (Scotland)	16	15	–	114	548	36.53	1	2	3
E.J.G.Morgan (Ireland)	23	23	2	115	744	35.42	1	5	9
D.Murphy (Scotland)	8	7	2	20*	58	11.60	–	–	8/3
T.J.Murtagh (Ireland)	10	6	2	23*	60	15.00	–	–	1
K.J.O'Brien (Ireland)	84	76	11	142	2178	33.50	2	10	39
N.J.O'Brien (Ireland)	64	63	7	80*	1649	29.44	–	12	41/7
W.T.S.Porterfield (Ireland)	73	72	3	112*	2137	30.97	6	10	35
W.B.Rankin (Ireland)	37	16	11	7*	35	7.00	–	–	6
P.R.Stirling (Ireland)	51	50	1	177	1726	35.22	5	6	23
R.N.ten Doeschate (Netherlands)	33	32	9	119	1541	67.00	5	9	13
R.M.L.Taylor (Scotland)	11	10	3	46*	129	18.42	–	–	5
G.C.Wilson (Ireland)	52	50	5	113	1129	25.08	1	7	42/9

ASSOCIATES – BOWLING

	O	M	R	W	Avge	Best	4wI	R/Over
A.Balbirnie	10	0	68	2	34.00	1-26	–	6.80
K.J.Coetzer	22	1	145	1	145.00	1-35	–	6.59
T.L.W.Cooper	92.1	5	438	13	33.69	3-11	–	4.75
J.H.Davey	160.5	14	842	43	19.58	6-28	3	5.23
G.H.Dockrell	334.3	20	1417	51	27.78	4-24	3	4.23
A.N.Kervezee	4	0	34	0	–	–	–	8.50
C.S.MacLeod	62	2	324	8	40.50	2-26	–	5.22
M.W.Machan	54	2	282	8	35.25	3-31	–	5.22
T.J.Murtagh	73	8	333	9	37.00	3-33	–	4.56
K.J.O'Brien	395.4	22	1925	68	28.30	4-13	2	4.86
W.B.Rankin	283.2	19	1391	43	32.34	3-32	–	4.90
P.R.Stirling	230.1	7	1005	27	37.22	4-11	1	4.36
R.M.L.Taylor	91.5	5	477	16	29.81	3-39	–	5.19
R.N.ten Doeschate	263.2	18	1327	55	24.12	4-31	3	5.03

LIMITED-OVERS INTERNATIONALS RESULTS

1970-71 to 13 February 2015

This chart excludes all matches involving multinational teams.

| | Opponents | Matches | Won | | | | | | | | | | | Tied | NR |
			E	A	SA	WI	NZ	I	P	SL	Z	B	Ass		
England	Australia	130	49	76	–	–	–	–	–	–	–	–	–	2	3
	South Africa	51	22	–	25	–	–	–	–	–	–	–	–	1	3
	West Indies	88	42	–	–	42	–	–	–	–	–	–	–	–	4
	New Zealand	77	33	–	–	–	38	–	–	–	–	–	–	2	4
	India	93	38	–	–	–	–	50	–	–	–	–	–	2	3
	Pakistan	72	42	–	–	–	–	–	28	–	–	–	–	–	2
	Sri Lanka	63	30	–	–	–	–	–	–	33	–	–	–	–	–
	Zimbabwe	30	21	–	–	–	–	–	–	–	8	–	–	–	1
	Bangladesh	15	13	–	–	–	–	–	–	–	–	2	–	–	–
	Associates	19	17	–	–	–	–	–	–	–	–	–	1	–	1
Australia	South Africa	88	–	46	39	–	–	–	–	–	–	–	–	3	–
	West Indies	135	–	70	–	59	–	–	–	–	–	–	–	3	3
	New Zealand	125	–	85	–	–	34	–	–	–	–	–	–	–	6
	India	117	–	67	–	–	–	40	–	–	–	–	–	–	10
	Pakistan	92	–	57	–	–	–	–	31	–	–	–	–	1	3
	Sri Lanka	90	–	55	–	–	–	–	–	31	–	–	–	–	4
	Zimbabwe	30	–	27	–	–	–	–	–	–	2	–	–	–	1
	Bangladesh	19	–	18	–	–	–	–	–	–	–	1	–	–	–
	Associates	19	–	18	–	–	–	–	–	–	–	–	0	–	1
S Africa	West Indies	57	–	–	42	13	–	–	–	–	–	–	–	1	1
	New Zealand	61	–	–	36	–	20	–	–	–	–	–	–	–	5
	India	70	–	–	42	–	–	25	–	–	–	–	–	–	3
	Pakistan	71	–	–	47	–	–	–	23	–	–	–	–	–	1
	Sri Lanka	59	–	–	28	–	–	–	–	29	–	–	–	1	1
	Zimbabwe	37	–	–	34	–	–	–	–	–	2	–	–	–	1
	Bangladesh	14	–	–	13	–	–	–	–	–	–	1	–	–	–
	Associates	20	–	–	20	–	–	–	–	–	–	–	0	–	–
W Indies	New Zealand	60	–	–	–	30	23	–	–	–	–	–	–	–	7
	India	115	–	–	–	60	–	52	–	–	–	–	–	1	2
	Pakistan	126	–	–	–	68	–	–	55	–	–	–	–	3	–
	Sri Lanka	51	–	–	–	27	–	–	–	21	–	–	–	–	3
	Zimbabwe	44	–	–	–	34	–	–	–	–	9	–	–	–	1
	Bangladesh	28	–	–	–	19	–	–	–	–	–	7	–	–	2
	Associates	20	–	–	–	18	–	–	–	–	–	–	1	–	1
N Zealand	India	93	–	–	–	–	41	46	–	–	–	–	–	1	5
	Pakistan	96	–	–	–	–	40	–	53	–	–	–	–	1	2
	Sri Lanka	89	–	–	–	–	41	–	–	40	–	–	–	1	7
	Zimbabwe	35	–	–	–	–	25	–	–	–	8	–	–	1	1
	Bangladesh	24	–	–	–	–	16	–	–	–	–	8	–	–	–
	Associates	13	–	–	–	–	13	–	–	–	–	–	0	–	–
India	Pakistan	126	–	–	–	–	–	50	72	–	–	–	–	–	4
	Sri Lanka	149	–	–	–	–	–	83	–	54	–	–	–	1	11
	Zimbabwe	56	–	–	–	–	–	44	–	–	10	–	–	2	–
	Bangladesh	28	–	–	–	–	–	24	–	–	–	3	–	–	1
	Associates	25	–	–	–	–	–	23	–	–	–	–	2	–	–
Pakistan	Sri Lanka	142	–	–	–	–	–	–	81	56	–	–	–	1	4
	Zimbabwe	47	–	–	–	–	–	–	42	–	3	–	–	1	1
	Bangladesh	32	–	–	–	–	–	–	31	–	–	1	–	–	–
	Associates	26	–	–	–	–	–	–	24	–	–	–	1	–	1
Sri Lanka	Zimbabwe	47	–	–	–	–	–	–	–	39	7	–	–	–	1
	Bangladesh	37	–	–	–	–	–	–	–	32	–	4	–	–	1
	Associates	18	–	–	–	–	–	–	–	17	–	–	1	–	–
Zimbabwe	Bangladesh	64	–	–	–	–	–	–	–	–	28	36	–	–	–
	Associates	47	–	–	–	–	–	–	–	–	36	–	8	1	2
Bangladesh	Associates	33	–	–	–	–	–	–	–	–	–	22	11	–	–
Associates	Associates	167	–	–	–	–	–	–	–	–	–	–	159	1	7
		3580	307	519	326	370	291	437	440	352	113	85	184	31	125

287

MERIT TABLE OF ALL L-O INTERNATIONALS

	Matches	Won	Lost	Tied	No Result	% Won (exc NR)
Australia	845	519	286	9	31	63.75
South Africa	528	326	181	6	15	63.54
Pakistan	830	440	365	8	17	54.12
West Indies	724	370	322	8	24	52.85
India	872	437	389	7	39	52.46
England	638	307	303	7	21	49.75
Sri Lanka	745	352	357	4	32	49.36
New Zealand	673	291	339	6	37	45.75
Bangladesh	294	85	205	–	4	29.31
Zimbabwe	437	113	310	5	9	26.40
Associate Members (v Full*)	240	25	208	1	6	10.68

* Results of games between two Associate Members and those involving multi-national sides are excluded from this list; Associate Members have participated in 407 LOIs, 167 LOIs being between Associate Members.

TEAM RECORDS
HIGHEST TOTALS

† Batting Second

443-9	(50 overs)	Sri Lanka v Netherlands	Amstelveen	2006
439-2	(50 overs)	South Africa v West Indies	Johannesburg	2014-15
438-9†	(49.5 overs)	South Africa v Australia	Johannesburg	2005-06
434-4	(50 overs)	Australia v South Africa	Johannesburg	2005-06
418-5	(50 overs)	South Africa v Zimbabwe	Potchefstroom	2006-07
418-5	(50 overs)	India v West Indies	Indore	2011-12
414-7	(50 overs)	India v Sri Lanka	Rajkot	2009-10
413-5	(50 overs)	India v Bermuda	Port of Spain	2006-07
411-8†	(50 overs)	Sri Lanka v India	Rajkot	2009-10
404-5	(50 overs)	India v Sri Lanka	Kolkata	2014-15
402-2	(50 overs)	New Zealand v Ireland	Aberdeen	2008
401-3	(50 overs)	India v South Africa	Gwalior	2009-10
399-6	(50 overs)	South Africa v Zimbabwe	Benoni	2010-11
398-5	(50 overs)	Sri Lanka v Kenya	Kandy	1995-96
397-5	(44 overs)	New Zealand v Zimbabwe	Bulawayo	2005
392-4	(50 overs)	India v New Zealand	Christchurch	2008-09
392-6	(50 overs)	South Africa v Pakistan	Pretoria	2006-07
391-4	(50 overs)	England v Bangladesh	Nottingham	2005
387-5	(50 overs)	India v England	Rajkot	2008-09
385-7	(50 overs)	Pakistan v Bangladesh	Dambulla	2010
383-6	(50 overs)	India v Australia	Bangalore	2013-14
377-6	(50 overs)	Australia v South Africa	Basseterre	2006-07
376-2	(50 overs)	India v New Zealand	Hyderabad, India	1999-00
374-4	(50 overs)	India v Hong Kong	Karachi	2008
373-6	(50 overs)	India v Sri Lanka	Taunton	1999
373-8	(50 overs)	New Zealand v Zimbabwe	Napier	2011-12
372-6	(50 overs)	New Zealand v Zimbabwe	Whangarei	2011-12
371-9	(50 overs)	Pakistan v Sri Lanka	Nairobi	1996-97
370-4	(50 overs)	India v Bangladesh	Dhaka	2010-11
369-5	(50 overs)	New Zealand v Pakistan	Napier	2014-15
368-5	(50 overs)	Australia v Sri Lanka	Sydney	2005-06
365-2	(50 overs)	South Africa v India	Ahmedabad	2009-10
364-7	(50 overs)	Pakistan v New Zealand	Sharjah	2014-15
363-3	(50 overs)	South Africa v Zimbabwe	Bulawayo	2001-02
363-4	(50 overs)	West Indies v New Zealand	Hamilton	2013-14
363-5	(50 overs)	New Zealand v Canada	Gros Islet	2006-07
363-5	(50 overs)	India v Sri Lanka	Colombo (RPS)	2008-09
363-5	(50 overs)	India v Sri Lanka	Cuttack	2014-15
363-7	(55 overs)	England v Pakistan	Nottingham	1992

362-1†	(43.3 overs)	India v Australia	Jaipur	2013-14
362-3	(50 overs)	Australia v Scotland	Edinburgh	2013
361-5	(42 overs)	South Africa v West Indies	Centurion	2014-15
361-8	(50 overs)	Australia v Bangladesh	Dhaka	2010-11
360-4	(50 overs)	West Indies v Sri Lanka	Karachi	1987-88
360-5	(50 overs)	New Zealand v Sri Lanka	Dunedin	2014-15
359-2	(50 overs)	Australia v India	Johannesburg	2002-03
359-3	(50 overs)	New Zealand v England	Southampton	2013
359-5	(50 overs)	Australia v India	Sydney	2003-04
359-5	(50 overs)	Australia v India	Jaipur	2013-14
358-4	(50 overs)	South Africa v Bangladesh	Benoni	2008-09
358-4	(50 overs)	South Africa v India	Johannesburg	2013-14
358-5	(50 overs)	Australia v Netherlands	Basseterre	2006-07
358-6	(50 overs)	New Zealand v Canada	Mumbai	2010-11
357-9	(50 overs)	Sri Lanka v Bangladesh	Lahore	2008
356-4	(50 overs)	South Africa v West Indies	St George's	2006-07
356-9	(50 overs)	India v Pakistan	Vishakhapatnam	2004-05
354-3	(50 overs)	South Africa v Kenya	Cape Town	2001-02
354-6	(50 overs)	South Africa v England	Cape Town	2009-10
354-7	(50 overs)	India v Australia	Nagpur	2009-10
353-3	(40 overs)	South Africa v Netherlands	Basseterre	2006-07
353-5	(50 overs)	India v New Zealand	Hyderabad, India	2003-04
353-6	(50 overs)	Pakistan v England	Karachi	2005-06
351-3	(50 overs)	India v Kenya	Paarl	2001-02
351-4	(50 overs)	Pakistan v South Africa	Durban	2006-07
351-4†	(49.3 overs)	India v Australia	Nagpur	2013-14
351-5	(50 overs)	South Africa v Netherlands	Mohali	2010-11
351-6	(50 overs)	South Africa v Zimbabwe	Bloemfontein	2010-11
351-7	(50 overs)	Zimbabwe v Kenya	Mombasa	2008-09
350-4	(50 overs)	Australia v India	Hyderabad, India	2009-10
350-6	(50 overs)	India v Sri Lanka	Nagpur	2005-06
350-6	(50 overs)	Australia v India	Nagpur	2013-14
350-6	(50 overs)	Australia v Zimbabwe	Harare	2014
350-9†	(49.3 overs)	New Zealand v Australia	Hamilton	2006-07

The highest for Bangladesh is 326-3 (v Pakistan, Dhaka, 2013-14).

HIGHEST TOTALS BATTING SECOND

WINNING:	438-9	(49.5 overs)	South Africa v Australia	Johannesburg	2005-06
LOSING:	411-8	(50.0 overs)	Sri Lanka v India	Rajkot	2009-10

HIGHEST MATCH AGGREGATES

872-13	(99.5 overs)	South Africa v Australia	Johannesburg	2005-06
825-15	(100 overs)	India v Sri Lanka	Rajkot	2009-10

LARGEST RUNS MARGINS OF VICTORY

290 runs	New Zealand beat Ireland	Aberdeen	2008
272 runs	South Africa beat Zimbabwe	Benoni	2010-11
258 runs	South Africa beat Sri Lanka	Paarl	2011-12
257 runs	India beat Bermuda	Port of Spain	2006-07
256 runs	Australia beat Namibia	Potchefstroom	2002-03
256 runs	India beat Hong Kong	Karachi	2008
245 runs	Sri Lanka beat India	Sharjah	2000-01
243 runs	Sri Lanka beat Bermuda	Port of Spain	2006-07
234 runs	Sri Lanka beat Pakistan	Lahore	2008-09
233 runs	Pakistan beat Bangladesh	Dhaka	1999-00
232 runs	Australia beat Sri Lanka	Adelaide	1984-85
231 runs	South Africa beat Netherlands	Mohali	2010-11
229 runs	Australia beat Netherlands	Basseterre	2006-07
224 runs	Australia beat Pakistan	Nairobi	2002
221 runs	South Africa beat Netherlands	Basseterre	2006-07
217 runs	Pakistan beat Sri Lanka	Sharjah	2001-02

215 runs	Australia beat New Zealand	St George's	2006-07
215 runs	West Indies beat Netherlands	Delhhi	2010-11
212 runs	South Africa beat Zimbabwe	Centurion	2009-10
210 runs	New Zealand beat USA	The Oval	2004
210 runs	Sri Lanka beat Canada	Hambantota	2010-11
209 runs	South Africa beat West Indies	Cape Town	2003-04
208 runs	South Africa beat Kenya	Cape Town	2001-02
208 runs	Australia beat India	Sydney	2003-04
208 runs	West Indies beat Canada	Kingston	2009-10
206 runs	New Zealand beat Australia	Adelaide	1985-86
206 runs	Sri Lanka beat Netherlands	Colombo (RPS)	2002-03
206 runs	South Africa beat Bangladesh	Dhaka	2010-11
205 runs	Pakistan beat Kenya	Hambantota	2010-11
203 runs	Australia beat Scotland	Basseterre	2006-07
203 runs	West Indies beat New Zealand	Hamilton	2013-14
202 runs	England beat India	Lord's	1975
202 runs	South Africa beat Kenya	Nairobi	1996-97
202 runs	Zimbabwe beat Kenya	Dhaka	1998-99
202 runs	New Zealand beat Zimbabwe	Napier	2011-12
200 runs	India beat Bangladesh	Dhaka	2002-03
200 runs	New Zealand beat India	Dambulla	2010
200 runs	Australia beat Scotland	Edinburgh	2013

LOWEST TOTALS (Excluding reduced innings)

35	(18.0 overs)	Zimbabwe v Sri Lanka	Harare	2003-04
36	(18.4 overs)	Canada v Sri Lanka	Paarl	2002-03
38	(15.4 overs)	Zimbabwe v Sri Lanka	Colombo (SSC)	2001-02
43	(19.5 overs)	Pakistan v West Indies	Cape Town	1992-93
43	(20.1 overs)	Sri Lanka v South Africa	Paarl	2011-12
44	(24.5 overs)	Zimbabwe v Bangladesh	Chittagong	2009-10
45	(40.3 overs)	Canada v England	Manchester	1979
45	(14.0 overs)	Namibia v Australia	Potschefstroom	2002-03
54	(26.3 overs)	India v Sri Lanka	Sharjah	2000-01
54	(23.2 overs)	West Indies v South Africa	Cape Town	2003-04
55	(28.3 overs)	Sri Lanka v West Indies	Sharjah	1986-87
58	(18.5 overs)	Bangladesh v West Indies	Dhaka	2010-11
58	(17.4 overs)	Bangladesh v India	Dhaka	2014
61	(22.0 overs)	West Indies v Bangladesh	Chittagong	2011-12
63	(25.5 overs)	India v Australia	Sydney	1980-81
63	(18.3 overs)	Afghanistan v Scotland	Abu Dhabi	2014-15
64	(35.5 overs)	New Zealand v Pakistan	Sharjah	1985-86
65	(24.0 overs)	USA v Australia	Southampton	2004
65	(24.3 overs)	Zimbabwe v India	Harare	2005
67	(31.0 overs)	Zimbabwe v Sri Lanka	Harare	2008-09
67	(24.4 overs)	Canada v Netherlands	King City	2013
67	(24.0 overs)	Sri Lanka v England	Manchester	2014
68	(31.3 overs)	Scotland v West Indies	Leicester	1999
69	(28.0 overs)	South Africa v Australia	Sydney	1993-94
69	(22.5 overs)	Zimbabwe v Kenya	Harare	2005-06
69	(23.5 overs)	Kenya v New Zealand	Chennai	2010-11
70	(25.2 overs)	Australia v England	Birmingham	1977
70	(26.3 overs)	Australia v New Zealand	Adelaide	1985-86
70	(23.5 overs)	West Indies v Australia	Perth	2012-13
70	(24.4 overs)	Bangladesh v West Indies	St George's	2014

The lowest for England is 86 (v A, Manchester, 2001).

LOWEST MATCH AGGREGATES

73-11	(23.2 overs)	Canada (36) v Sri Lanka (37-1)	Paarl	2002-03
75-11	(27.2 overs)	Zimbabwe (35) v Sri Lanka (40-1)	Harare	2003-04
78-11	(20.0 overs)	Zimbabwe (38) v Sri Lanka (40-1)	Colombo (SSC)	2001-02

BATTING RECORDS
5000 RUNS IN A CAREER

		LOI	I	NO	HS	Runs	Avge	100	50
S.R.Tendulkar	I	463	452	41	200*	18426	44.83	49	96
R.T.Ponting	A/ICC	375	365	39	164	13704	42.03	30	82
K.C.Sangakkara	SL/Asia/ICC	397	373	39	169	13693	40.99	21	93
S.T.Jayasuriya	SL/Asia	445	433	18	189	13430	32.36	28	68
D.P.M.D.Jayawardena	SI/Asia	441	413	39	144	12525	33.48	18	77
Inzamam-ul-Haq	P/Asia	378	350	53	137*	11739	39.52	10	83
J.H.Kallis	SA/Afr/ICC	328	314	53	139	11579	44.36	17	86
S.C.Ganguly	I/Asia	311	300	23	183	11363	41.02	22	72
R.S.Dravid	I/Asia/ICC	344	318	40	153	10889	39.16	12	83
B.C.Lara	WI/ICC	299	289	32	169	10405	40.48	19	63
Mohammad Yousuf	P/Asia	288	272	40	141*	9720	41.71	15	64
A.C.Gilchrist	A/ICC	287	279	11	172	9619	35.89	16	55
T.M.Dilshan	SL	307	281	40	160*	9401	39.00	20	42
M.Azharuddin	I	334	308	54	153*	9378	36.92	7	58
P.A.de Silva	SL	308	296	30	145	9284	34.90	11	64
C.H.Gayle	WI/ICC	263	258	17	153*	8881	36.85	21	46
Saeed Anwar	P	247	244	19	194	8824	39.21	20	43
S.Chanderpaul	WI	268	251	40	150	8778	41.60	11	59
D.L.Haynes	WI	238	237	28	152*	8648	41.37	17	57
M.S.Atapattu	SL	268	259	32	132*	8529	37.57	11	59
M.E.Waugh	A	244	236	20	173	8500	39.35	18	50
Yuvraj Singh	I/Asia	293	268	39	139	8329	36.37	13	51
V.Sehwag	I/Asia/ICC	251	245	9	219	8273	35.05	15	38
M.S.Dhoni	I/Asia	254	222	64	183*	8262	52.29	9	56
H.H.Gibbs	SA	248	240	16	175	8094	36.13	21	37
S.P.Fleming	NZ/ICC	280	269	21	134*	8037	32.40	8	49
Shahid Afridi	P/Asia/ICC	391	363	26	124	7948	23.58	6	39
M.J.Clarke	A	238	217	44	130	7762	44.86	8	56
S.R.Waugh	A	325	288	58	120*	7569	32.90	3	45
A.B.de Villiers	SA/Afr	179	172	29	149	7459	52.16	19	43
A.Ranatunga	SL	269	255	47	131*	7456	35.84	4	49
Javed Miandad	P	233	218	41	119*	7381	41.70	8	50
Younus Khan	P	261	251	23	144	7197	31.56	7	48
Salim Malik	P	283	256	38	102	7170	32.88	5	47
N.J.Astle	NZ	223	217	14	145*	7090	34.92	16	41
G.C.Smith	SA/Afr	197	194	10	141	6989	37.98	10	47
M.G.Bevan	A	232	196	67	108*	6912	53.58	6	46
G.Kirsten	SA	185	185	19	188*	6798	40.95	13	45
A.Flower	Z	213	208	16	145	6786	35.34	4	55
I.V.A.Richards	WI	187	167	24	189*	6721	47.00	11	45
G.W.Flower	Z	221	214	18	142*	6571	33.52	6	40
Ijaz Ahmed	P	250	232	29	139*	6564	32.33	10	37
A.R.Border	A	273	252	39	127*	6524	30.62	3	39
R.B.Richardson	WI	224	217	30	122	6248	33.41	5	44
V.Kohli	I	150	142	21	183	6232	51.50	21	33
M.L.Hayden	A/ICC	161	155	15	181*	6133	43.80	10	36
D.M.Jones	A	164	161	25	145	6068	44.61	7	46
D.C.Boon	A	181	177	16	122	5964	37.04	5	37
J.N.Rhodes	SA	245	220	51	121	5935	35.11	2	33
Ramiz Raja	P	198	197	15	119*	5841	32.09	9	31
R.R.Sarwan	WI	181	169	33	120*	5804	42.67	5	38
C.L.Hooper	WI	227	206	43	113*	5761	35.34	7	29
W.J.Cronje	SA	188	175	31	112	5565	38.64	2	39
Shoaib Malik	P	216	193	25	143	5490	32.67	7	31
B.B.McCullum	NZ	240	209	28	166	5480	30.27	5	32
S.R.Watson	A	180	159	24	185*	5478	40.57	9	31
M.E.K.Hussey	A	185	157	44	109*	5442	48.15	3	39
H.M.Amla	SA	107	104	9	153*	5359	56.41	19	27
A.Jadeja	I	196	179	36	119	5359	37.47	6	30

		LOI	I	NO	HS	Runs	Avge	100	50
D.R.Martyn	A	208	182	51	144*	**5346**	40.80	5	37
W.U.Tharanga	SL/Asia	176	168	9	174*	**5339**	33.57	13	28
G.Gambhir	I	147	143	11	150*	**5238**	39.68	11	34
A.D.R.Campbell	Z	188	184	14	131*	**5185**	30.50	7	30
R.S.Mahanama	SL	213	198	23	119*	**5162**	29.49	4	35
I.R.Bell	E	155	151	13	141	**5154**	37.34	4	32
C.G.Greenidge	WI	128	127	13	133*	**5134**	45.03	11	31
S.K.Raina	I	207	178	34	116*	**5104**	35.44	4	33
P.D.Collingwood	E	197	181	37	120*	**5092**	35.36	5	26
A.Symonds	A	198	161	33	156	**5088**	39.75	6	30
Abdul Razzaq	P/Asia	265	228	57	112	**5080**	29.70	3	23

The most for Bangladesh is 3977 in 135 innings by Shakib Al Hasan.

HIGHEST INDIVIDUAL INNINGS

264	R.G.Sharma	India v Sri Lanka	Kolkata	2014-15
219	V.Sehwag	India v West Indies	Indore	2011-12
209	R.G.Sharma	India v Australia	Bangalore	2013-14
200*	S.R.Tendulkar	India v South Africa	Gwalior	2009-10
194*	C.K.Coventry	Zimbabwe v Bangladesh	Bulawayo	2009
194	Saeed Anwar	Pakistan v India	Madras	1996-97
189*	I.V.A.Richards	West Indies v England	Manchester	1984
189*	M.J.Guptill	New Zealand v England	Southampton	2013
189	S.T.Jayasuriya	Sri Lanka v India	Sharjah	2000-01
188*	G.Kirsten	South Africa v UAE	Rawalpindi	1995-96
186*	S.R.Tendulkar	India v New Zealand	Hyderabad	1999-00
185*	S.R.Watson	Australia v Bangladesh	Dhaka	2010-11
183*	M.S.Dhoni	India v Sri Lanka	Jaipur	2005-06
183	S.C.Ganguly	India v Sri Lanka	Taunton	1999
183	V.Kohli	India v Pakistan	Dhaka	2011-12
181*	M.L.Hayden	Australia v New Zealand	Hamilton	2006-07
181	I.V.A.Richards	West Indies v Sri Lanka	Karachi	1987-88
178*	H.Masakadza	Zimbabwe v Kenya	Harare	2009-10
177	P.R.Stirling	Ireland v Canada	Toronto	2010
175*	Kapil Dev	India v Zimbabwe	Tunbridge Wells	1983
175	H.H.Gibbs	South Africa v Australia	Johannesburg	2005-06
175	S.R.Tendulkar	India v Australia	Hyderabad, India	2009-10
175	V.Sehwag	India v Bangladesh	Dhaka	2010-11
175	C.S.MacLeod	Scotland v Canada	Christchurch	2013-14
174*	W.U.Tharanga	Sri Lanka v India	Kingston	2013
173	M.E.Waugh	Australia v West Indies	Melbourne	2000-01
172*	C.B.Wishart	Zimbabwe v Namibia	Harare	2002-03
172	A.C.Gilchrist	Australia v Zimbabwe	Hobart	2003-04
172	L.Vincent	New Zealand v Zimbabwe	Bulawayo	2005
171*	G.M.Turner	New Zealand v East Africa	Birmingham	1975
170*	L.Ronchi	New Zealand v Sri Lanka	Dunedin	2014-15
169*	D.J.Callaghan	South Africa v New Zealand	Pretoria	1994-95
169	B.C.Lara	West Indies v Sri Lanka	Sharjah	1995-96
169	K.C.Sangakkara	Sri Lanka v South Africa	Colombo (RPS)	2013
167*	R.A.Smith	England v Australia	Birmingham	1993
166	B.B.McCullum	New Zealand v Ireland	Aberdeen	2008
164	R.T.Ponting	Australia v South Africa	Johannesburg	2005-06
163*	S.R.Tendulkar	India v New Zealand	Christchurch	2008-09
163	D.A.Warner	Australia v Sri Lanka	Brisbane	2011-12
161*	S.R.Watson	Australia v England	Melbourne	2010-11
161	A.C.Hudson	South Africa v Netherlands	Rawalpindi	1995-96
161	J.A.H.Marshall	New Zealand v Ireland	Aberdeen	2008
160*	T.M.Dilshan	Sri Lanka v India	Hobart	2011-12
160	Imran Nazir	Pakistan v Zimbabwe	Kingston	2006-07
160	T.M.Dilshan	Sri Lanka v India	Rajkot	2009-10
159*	D.Mongia	India v Zimbabwe	Gauhati	2001-02
158	D.I.Gower	England v New Zealand	Brisbane	1982-83

158	M.L.Hayden	Australia v West Indies	North Sound	2006-07
158	A.J.Strauss	England v India	Bangalore	2010-11
157*	X.M.Marshall	West Indies v Canada	King City (NW)	2008
157	S.T.Jayasuriya	Sri Lanka v Netherlands	Amstelveen	2006
156	B.C.Lara	West Indies v Pakistan	Adelaide	2004-05
156	A.Symonds	Australia v New Zealand	Wellington	2005-06
156	H.Masakadza	Zimbabwe v Kenya	Harare	2009-10
156	G.J.Bailey	Australia v India	Nagpur	2013-14
154	A.C.Gilchrist	Australia v Sri Lanka	Melbourne	1998-99
154	Tamim Iqbal	Bangladesh v Zimbabwe	Bulawayo	2009
154	A.J.Strauss	England v Bangladesh	Birmingham	2010
153*	I.V.A.Richards	West Indies v Australia	Melbourne	1979-80
153*	M.Azharuddin	India v Zimbabwe	Cuttack	1997-98
153*	S.C.Ganguly	India v New Zealand	Gwalior	1999-00
153*	C.H.Gayle	West Indies v Zimbabwe	Bulawayo	2003-04
153*	H.M.Amla	South Africa v West Indies	Johannesburg	2014-15
153	B.C.Lara	West Indies v Pakistan	Sharjah	1993-94
153	R.S.Dravid	India v New Zealand	Hyderabad	1999-00
153	H.H.Gibbs	South Africa v Bangladesh	Potchefstroom	2002-03
152*	D.L.Haynes	West Indies v India	Georgetown	1988-89
152*	C.H.Gayle	West Indies v South Africa	Johannesburg	2003-04
152	C.H.Gayle	West Indies v Kenya	Nairobi	2001-02
152	S.R.Tendulkar	India v Namibia	Pietermaritzburg	2002-03
152	A.J.Strauss	England v Bangladesh	Nottingham	2005
152	S.T.Jayasuriya	Sri Lanka v England	Leeds	2006
151*	S.T.Jayasuriya	Sri Lanka v India	Bombay	1996-97
151	A.Symonds	Australia v Sri Lanka	Sydney	2005-06
151	S.E.Marsh	Australia v Scotland	Edinburgh	2013
150*	G.Gambhir	India v Sri Lanka	Kolkata	2009-10
150*	J.P.Duminy	South Africa v Netherlands	Amstelveen	2013
150	S.Chanderpaul	West Indies v South Africa	East London	1998-99
150	G.Gambhir	India v Sri Lanka	Colombo (RPS)	2008-09
150	H.M.Amla	South Africa v England	Southampton	2012

HUNDRED ON DEBUT

D.L.Amiss	103	England v Australia	Manchester	1972
D.L.Haynes	148	West Indies v Australia	St John's	1977-78
A.Flower	115*	Zimbabwe v Sri Lanka	New Plymouth	1991-92
Salim Elahi	102*	Pakistan v Sri Lanka	Gujranwala	1995-96
M.J.Guptill	122*	New Zealand v West Indies	Auckland	2008-09
C.A.Ingram	124	South Africa v Zimbabwe	Bloemfontein	2010-11
R.J.Nicol	108*	New Zealand v Zimbabwe	Harare	2011-12
P.J.Hughes	112	Australia v Sri Lanka	Melbourne	2012-13
M.J.Lumb	106	England v West Indies	North Sound	2013-14

Shahid Afridi scored 102 for P v SL, Nairobi, 1996-97, in his second match having not batted in his first.

Fastest 100	31 balls	A.B.de Villiers (149)	SA v WI	Johannesburg	2014-15
Fastest 50	16 balls	A.B.de Villiers (149)	SA v WI	Johannesburg	2014-15

15 HUNDREDS

		Inns	100	E	A	SA	WI	NZ	I	P	SL	Z	B	Ass
S.R.Tendulkar	I	452	**49**	2	9	5	4	5	–	5	8	5	1	5
R.T.Ponting	A	365	**30***	5	–	2	2	6	6	1	4	1	1	1
S.T.Jayasuriya	SL	433	**28**	4	2	–	1	5	7	3	–	1	4	1
S.C.Ganguly	I	300	**22**	1	1	3	–	3	–	2	4	3	1	4
V.Kohli	I	142	**21**	2	3	–	3	2	–	1	6	1	3	–
H.H.Gibbs	SA	240	**21**	2	3	–	5	2	2	2	1	2	1	1
C.H.Gayle	WI	258	**21**	2	–	3	–	2	4	3	1	2	1	3
K.C.Sangakkara	SL	373	**21**	3	1	2	–	2	6	2	–	–	4	1

		Inns	100	E	A	SA	WI	NZ	I	P	SL	Z	B	Ass
Saeed Anwar	P	244	20	–	1	–	2	4	4	–	7	2	–	–
T.M.Dilshan	SL	281	20	–	1	2	–	3	4	2	–	2	3	1
H.M.Amla	SA	104	19	1	1	–	4	1	2	2	3	3	1	1
A.B.de Villiers	SA	172	19	1	1	–	4	1	3	3	2	3	1	
B.C.Lara	WI	289	19	1	3	3	–	2	–	5	2	1	1	1
M.E.Waugh	A	236	19	1	–	2	3	3	3	1	1	3	–	1
D.P.M.D.Jayawardena	SL	413	18*	5	–	–	1	3	4	2	–	–	1	1
D.L.Haynes	WI	237	17	2	6	–	–	2	2	4	1	–	–	
J.H.Kallis	SA	314	17	1	1	–	4	3	2	1	3	1	–	1
N.J.Astle	NZ	217	16	2	1	1	1	–	5	2	–	3	–	1
A.C.Gilchrist	A	279	16*	2	–	2	–	2	1	1	6	1	–	–
V.Sehwag	I	245	15	1	–	–	2	6	–	2	2	–	1	1
Mohammad Yousuf	P	273	15	–	1	2	1	–	2	3	3	1		

* = Includes hundred scored against multi-national side. The most for England is 12 by M.E.Trescothick (in 122 innings), for Zimbabwe 7 by A.D.R.Campbell (184), and for Bangladesh 6 by Shakib Al Hasan (135).

HIGHEST PARTNERSHIP FOR EACH WICKET

1st	286	W.U.Tharanga/S.T.Jayasuriya	Sri Lanka v England	Leeds	2006
2nd	331	S.R.Tendulkar/R.S.Dravid	India v New Zealand	Hyderabad (Ind)	1999-00
3rd	258	D.M.Bravo/D.Ramdin	West Indies v Bangladesh	Basseterre	2014
4th	275*	M.Azharuddin/A.Jadeja	India v Zimbabwe	Cuttack	1997-98
5th	226*	E.J.G.Morgan/R.S.Bopara	England v Ireland	Dublin	2013
6th	267*	G.D.Elliott/L.Ronchi	New Zealand v Sri Lanka	Dunedin	2014-15
7th	130	A.Flower/H.H.Streak	Zimbabwe v England	Harare	2001-02
8th	138*	J.M.Kemp/A.J.Hall	South Africa v India	Cape Town	2006-07
9th	132	A.D.Mathews/S.L.Malinga	Sri Lanka v Australia	Melbourne	2010-11
10th	106*	I.V.A.Richards/M.A.Holding	West Indies v England	Manchester	1984

BOWLING RECORDS
200 WICKETS IN A CAREER

		LOI	Balls	R	W	Avge	Best	5w	R/Over
M.Muralitharan	SL/Asia/ICC	350	18811	12326	534	23.08	7-30	10	3.93
Wasim Akram	P	356	18186	11812	502	23.52	5-15	6	3.89
Waqar Younis	P	262	12698	9919	416	23.84	7-36	13	4.68
W.P.J.U.C.Vaas	SL/Asia	322	15775	11014	400	27.53	8-19	4	4.18
S.M.Pollock	SA/Afr/ICC	303	15712	9631	393	24.50	6-35	5	3.67
Shahid Afridi	P/Asia/ICC	391	17328	13350	393	33.96	7-12	9	4.62
G.D.McGrath	A/ICC	250	12970	8391	381	22.02	7-15	7	3.88
B.Lee	A	221	11185	8877	380	23.36	5-22	9	4.76
A.Kumble	I/Asia	271	14496	10412	337	30.89	6-12	2	4.30
S.T.Jayasuriya	SL	445	14874	11871	323	36.75	6-29	4	4.78
J.Srinath	I	229	11935	8847	315	28.08	5-23	3	4.44
S.K.Warne	A/ICC	194	10642	7541	293	25.73	5-33	1	4.25
D.L.Vettori	NZ/ICC	286	13605	9367	290	32.30	5- 7	2	4.13
Saqlain Mushtaq	P	169	8770	6275	288	21.78	5-20	6	4.29
A.B.Agarkar	I	191	9484	8021	288	27.85	6-42	2	5.07
Z.Khan	I/Asia	200	10097	8301	282	29.43	5-42	1	4.93
J.H.Kallis	SA/Afr/ICC	328	10750	8680	273	31.79	5-30	2	4.84
A.A.Donald	SA	164	8561	5926	272	21.78	6-23	2	4.15
S.L.Malinga	SL	177	8479	7376	271	27.21	6-38	7	5.21
Abdul Razzaq	P/Asia	265	10941	8564	269	31.83	6-35	3	4.69
M.Ntini	SA/ICC	173	8687	6559	266	24.65	6-22	4	4.53
J.M.Anderson	E	188	9308	7616	264	28.84	5-23	2	4.90
Harbhajan Singh	I/Asia	229	12059	8651	259	33.40	5-31	3	4.30
Kapil Dev	I	225	11202	6945	253	27.45	5-43	1	3.72
Shoaib Akhtar	P/Asia/ICC	157	7764	6169	247	24.97	6-16	4	4.76
K.D.Mills	NZ	170	8230	6485	240	27.02	5-25	1	4.72
H.H.Streak	Z/Afr	189	9468	7129	239	29.82	5-32	1	4.51
D.Gough	E/ICC	159	8470	6209	235	26.42	5-44	2	4.39

		LOI	Balls	R	W	Avge	Best	5w	R/Over
C.A.Walsh	WI	205	10822	6918	**227**	30.47	5- 1	1	3.83
C.E.L.Ambrose	WI	176	9353	5429	**225**	24.12	5-17	4	3.48
M.G.Johnson	A	145	7108	5712	**224**	25.50	6-31	3	4.82
Abdur Razzak	B	153	7965	6065	**207**	29.29	5-29	4	4.56
C.J.McDermott	A	138	7460	5018	**203**	24.71	5-44	1	4.03
C.Z.Harris	NZ	250	10667	7613	**203**	37.50	5-42	1	4.28
C.L.Cairns	NZ/ICC	215	8168	6594	**201**	32.80	5-42	1	4.84

SIX WICKETS IN AN INNINGS

8-19	W.P.J.U.C.Vaas	Sri Lanka v Zimbabwe	Colombo (SSC)	2001-02
7-12	Shahid Afridi	Pakistan v West Indies	Providence	2013
7-15	G.D.McGrath	Australia v Namibia	Potschefstroom	2002-03
7-20	A.J.Bichel	Australia v England	Port Elizabeth	2002-03
7-30	M.Muralitharan	Sri Lanka v India	Sharjah	2000-01
7-36	Waqar Younis	Pakistan v England	Leeds	2001
7-37	Aqib Javed	Pakistan v India	Sharjah	1991-92
7-51	W.W.Davis	West Indies v Australia	Leeds	1983
6- 4	S.T.R.Binny	India v Bangladesh	Dhaka	2014
6-12	A.Kumble	India v West Indies	Calcutta	1993-94
6-13	B.A.W.Mendis	Sri Lanka v India	Karachi	2008
6-14	G.J.Gilmour	Australia v England	Leeds	1975
6-14	Imran Khan	Pakistan v India	Sharjah	1984-85
6-14	M.F.Maharoof	Sri Lanka v West Indies	Mumbai	2006-07
6-15	C.E.H.Croft	West Indies v England	Kingstown	1980-81
6-16	Shoaib Akhtar	Pakistan v New Zealand	Karachi	2001-02
6-18	Azhar Mahmood	Pakistan v West Indies	Sharjah	1999-00
6-19	H.K.Olonga	Zimbabwe v England	Cape Town	1999-00
6-19	S.E.Bond	New Zealand v Zimbabwe	Harare	2005
6-20	B.C.Strang	Zimbabwe v Bangladesh	Nairobi	1997-98
6-20	A.D.Mathews	Sri Lanka v India	Colombo (RPS)	2009-10
6-22	F.H.Edwards	West Indies v Zimbabwe	Harare	2003-04
6-22	M.Ntini	South Africa v Australia	Cape Town	2005-06
6-23	A.A.Donald	South Africa v Kenya	Nairobi	1996-97
6-23	A.Nehra	India v England	Durban	2002-03
6-23	S.E.Bond	New Zealand v Australia	Port Elizabeth	2002-03
6-25	S.B.Styris	New Zealand v West Indies	Port of Spain	2002
6-25	W.P.J.U.C.Vaas	Sri Lanka v Bangladesh	Pietermaritzburg	2002-03
6-26	Waqar Younis	Pakistan v Sri Lanka	Sharjah	1989-90
6-26	Mashrafe Mortaza	Bangladesh v Kenya	Nairobi	2006
6-26	Rubel Hossain	Bangladesh v New Zealand	Dhaka	2013-14
6-27	Naved-ul-Hasan	Pakistan v India	Jamshedpur	2004-05
6-27	C.R.D.Fernando	Sri Lanka v England	Colombo (RPS)	2007-08
6-27	M.Kartik	India v Australia	Mumbai	2007-08
6-27	K.A.J.Roach	West Indies v Netherlands	Delhi	2010-11
6-28	H.K.Olonga	Zimbabwe v Kenya	Bulawayo	2002-03
6-28	J.H.Davey	Scotland v Afghanistan	Abu Dhabi	2014-15
6-29	B.P.Patterson	West Indies v India	Nagpur	1987-88
6-29	S.T.Jayasuriya	Sri Lanka v England	Moratuwa	1992-93
6-29	B.A.W.Mendis	Sri Lanka v Zimbabwe	Harare	2008-09
6-30	Waqar Younis	Pakistan v New Zealand	Auckland	1993-94
6-31	P.D.Collingwood	England v Bangladesh	Nottingham	2005
6-31	M.G.Johnson	Australia v Sri Lanka	Pallekele	2011
6-35	S.M.Pollock	South Africa v West Indies	East London	1998-99
6-35	Abdul Razzaq	Pakistan v Bangladesh	Dhaka	2001-02
6-38	Shahid Afridi	Pakistan v Australia	Dubai	2009
6-38	S.L.Malinga	Sri Lanka v Kenya	Colombo (RPS)	2010-11
6-39	K.H.MacLeay	Australia v India	Nottingham	1983
6-39	D.W.Steyn	South Africa v Pakistan	Port Elizabeth	2013-14
6-41	I.V.A.Richards	West Indies v India	Delhi	1989-90
6-42	A.B.Agarkar	India v Australia	Melbourne	2003-04
6-42	Umar Gul	Pakistan v England	The Oval	2010
6-43	D.J.Bravo	West Indies v Zimbabwe	St George's	2012-13
6-43	M.A.Starc	Australia v India	Melbourne	2014-15

6-44	Waqar Younis	Pakistan v New Zealand	Sharjah	1996-97
6-44	N.L.T.C.Perera	Sri Lanka v Pakistan	Pallekele	2012
6-45	C.R.Woakes	England v Australia	Brisbane	2010-11
6-46	A.G.Cremer	Zimbabwe v Kenya	Harare	2009-10
6-47	C.R.Woakes	England v Sri Lanka	Pallekele	2014-15
6-48	A.Mishra	India v Zimbabwe	Bulawayo	2013
6-49	L.Klusener	South Africa v Sri Lanka	Lahore	1997-98
6-50	A.H.Gray	West Indies v Australia	Port of Spain	1990-91
6-52	C.B.Mpofu	Zimbabwe v Kenya	Nairobi (Gym)	2008-09
6-55	S.Sreesanth	India v England	Indore	2005-06
6-59	Waqar Younis	Pakistan v Australia	Nottingham	2001
6-59	A.Nehra	India v Sri Lanka	Colombo (RPS)	2005

HAT-TRICKS

Jalaluddin	Pakistan v Australia	Hyderabad	1982-83
B.A.Reid	Australia v New Zealand	Sydney	1985-86
C.Sharma	India v New Zealand	Nagpur	1987-88
Wasim Akram	Pakistan v West Indies	Sharjah	1989-90
Wasim Akram	Pakistan v Australia	Sharjah	1989-90
Kapil Dev	India v Sri Lanka	Calcutta	1990-91
Aqib Javed	Pakistan v India	Sharjah	1991-92
D.K.Morrison	New Zealand v India	Napier	1993-94
Waqar Younis	Pakistan v New Zealand	East London	1994-95
Saqlain Mushtaq	Pakistan v Zimbabwe	Peshawar	1996-97
E.A.Brandes	Zimbabwe v England	Harare	1996-97
A.M.Stuart	Australia v Pakistan	Melbourne	1996-97
Saqlain Mushtaq	Pakistan v Zimbabwe	The Oval	1999
W.P.J.U.C.Vaas	Sri Lanka v Zimbabwe	Colombo (SSC)	2001-02
Mohammad Sami	Pakistan v West Indies	Sharjah	2001-02
W.P.J.U.C.Vaas[1]	Sri Lanka v Bangladesh	Pietermaritzburg	2002-03
B.Lee	Australia v Kenya	Durban	2002-03
J.M.Anderson	England v Pakistan	The Oval	2003
S.J.Harmison	England v India	Nottingham	2004
C.K.Langeveldt	South Africa v West Indies	Bridgetown	2004-05
Shahadat Hossain	Bangladesh v Zimbabwe	Harare	2006
J.E.Taylor	West Indies v Australia	Mumbai	2006-07
S.E.Bond	New Zealand v Australia	Hobart	2006-07
S.L.Malinga[2]	Sri Lanka v South Africa	Providence	2006-07
A.Flintoff	England v West Indies	St Lucia	2008-09
M.F.Maharoof	Sri Lanka v India	Dambulla	2010
Abdur Razzak	Bangladesh v Zimbabwe	Dhaka	2010-11
K.A.J.Roach	West Indies v Netherlands	Delhi	2010-11
S.L.Malinga	Sri Lanka v Kenya	Colombo (RPS)	2010-11
S.L.Malinga	Sri Lanka v Australia	Colombo (RPS)	2011
D.T.Christian	Australia v Sri Lanka	Melbourne	2011-12
N.L.T.C.Perera	Sri Lanka v Pakistan	Colombo (RPS)	2012
C.J.McKay	Australia v England	Cardiff	2013
Rubel Hossain	Bangladesh v New Zealand	Dhaka	2013-14
P.Utseya	Zimbabwe v South Africa	Harare	2014
Taijul Islam	Bangladesh v Zimbabwe	Dhaka	2014-15

[1] The first three balls of the match. Took four wickets in opening over (W W W 4 wide W 0).
[2] Four wickets in four balls.

WICKET-KEEPING RECORDS
100 DISMISSALS IN A CAREER

Total			LOI	Ct	St
474†‡	K.C.Sangakkara	Sri Lanka/Asia/ICC	353	379	95
472‡	A.C.Gilchrist	Australia/ICC	287	417	55
424	M.V.Boucher	South Africa/Africa	295	402	22
314	M.S.Dhoni	India/Asia	254	229	85
287‡	Moin Khan	Pakistan	219	214	73
242†‡	B.B.McCullum	New Zealand	185	227	15
233	I.A.Healy	Australia	168	194	39
220‡	Rashid Latif	Pakistan	166	182	38
206‡	R.S.Kaluwitharana	Sri Lanka	187	131	75
204‡	P.J.L.Dujon	West Indies	169	183	21
189	R.D.Jacobs	West Indies	147	160	29
187	Kamran Akmal	Pakistan	154	156	31
165	B.J.Haddin	Australia	118	154	11
165	D.J.Richardson	South Africa	122	148	17
165†‡	A.Flower	Zimbabwe	213	133	32
163†‡	A.J.Stewart	England	170	148	15
160	D.Ramdin	West Indies	120	154	6
154‡	N.R.Mongia	India	140	110	44
145	T.Taibu	Zimbabwe/Africa	150	112	33
138	Mushfiqur Rahim	Bangladesh	140	102	36
136†‡	A.C.Parore	New Zealand	179	111	25
126	Khaled Masud	Bangladesh	126	91	35
124	R.W.Marsh	Australia	92	120	4
103	Salim Yousuf	Pakistan	86	81	22

† *Excluding catches taken in the field.* ‡ *Excluding matches when not wicket-keeper.*

SIX DISMISSALS IN AN INNINGS

6	(6ct)	A.C.Gilchrist	Australia v South Africa	Cape Town	1999-00
6	(6ct)	A.J.Stewart	England v Zimbabwe	Manchester	2000
6	(5ct/1st)	R.D.Jacobs	West Indies v Sri Lanka	Colombo (RPS)	2001-02
6	(5ct/1st)	A.C.Gilchrist	Australia v England	Sydney	2002-03
6	(6ct)	A.C.Gilchrist	Australia v Namibia	Potchefstroom	2002-03
6	(6ct)	A.C.Gilchrist	Australia v Sri Lanka	Colombo (RPS)	2003-04
6	(6ct)	M.V.Boucher	South Africa v Pakistan	Cape Town	2006-07
6	(5ct/1st)	M.S.Dhoni	India v England	Leeds	2007
6	(6ct)	A.C.Gilchrist	Australia v India	Baroda	2007-08
6	(5ct/1st)	A.C.Gilchrist	Australia v India	Sydney	2007-08
6	(6ct)	M.J.Prior	England v South Africa	Nottingham	2008
6	(6ct)	J.C.Buttler	England v South Africa	The Oval	2013
6	(6ct)	M.H.Cross	Scotland v Canada	Christchurch	2013-14
6	(5ct/1st)	Q.de Kock	South Africa v New Zealand	Mt Maunganui	2014-15

FIELDING RECORDS
100 CATCHES IN A CAREER

Total			LOI
217	D.P.M.D.Jayawardena	Sri Lanka/Asia	441
160	R.T.Ponting	Australia/ICC	375
156	M.Azharuddin	India	334
140	S.R.Tendulkar	India	463
133	S.P.Fleming	New Zealand/ICC	280
131	J.H.Kallis	South Africa/Africa/ICC	328
130	M.Muralitharan	Sri Lanka/Asia/ICC	350
128	Younus Khan	Pakistan	261
127	A.R.Border	Australia	273
124	R.S.Dravid	India/Asia/ICC	344
124	Shahid Afridi	Pakistan/Asia/ICC	391
123	S.T.Jayasuriya	Sri Lanka/Asia	445

Total			LOI
120	C.L.Hooper	West Indies	227
120	B.C.Lara	West Indies/ICC	299
113	Inzamam-ul-Haq	Pakistan/Asia	378
111	S.R.Waugh	Australia	325
109	R.S.Mahanama	Sri Lanka	213
109	C.H.Gayle	West Indies/ICC	263
108	P.D.Collingwood	England	197
108	M.E.Waugh	Australia	244
108	H.H.Gibbs	South Africa	248
108	S.M.Pollock	South Africa/Africa/ICC	303
105	M.E.K.Hussey	Australia	185
105	G.C.Smith	South Africa/Africa	197
105	J.N.Rhodes	South Africa	245
105	T.M.Dilshan	Sri Lanka	307
101	M.J.Clarke	Australia	238
100	I.V.A.Richards	West Indies	187
100	S.C.Ganguly	India/Asia	311

The most for Zimbabwe is 86 by G.W.Flower (221), and for Bangladesh 43 by Mashrafe Mortaza (142).

FIVE CATCHES IN AN INNINGS

5	J.N.Rhodes	South Africa v West Indies	Bombay (BS)	1993-94

APPEARANCE RECORDS

250 MATCHES

463	S.R.Tendulkar	India	293	Yuvraj Singh	India/Asia
445	S.T.Jayasuriya	Sri Lanka/Asia	288	Mohammad Yousuf	Pakistan/Asia
441	D.P.M.D.Jayawardena	Sri Lanka/Asia	287	A.C.Gilchrist	Australia/ICC
397	K.C.Sangakkara	Sri Lanka/Asia/ICC	286	D.L.Vettori	New Zealand/ICC
391	Shahid Afridi	Pakistan/Asia/ICC	283	Salim Malik	Pakistan
378	Inzamam-ul-Haq	Pakistan/Asia	280	S.P.Fleming	New Zealand/ICC
375	R.T.Ponting	Australia/ICC	273	A.R.Border	Australia
356	Wasim Akram	Pakistan	271	A.Kumble	India/Asia
350	M.Muralitharan	Sri Lanka/Asia/ICC	269	A.Ranatunga	Sri Lanka
344	R.S.Dravid	India/Asia/ICC	268	M.S.Atapattu	Sri Lanka
334	M.Azharuddin	India	268	S.Chanderpaul	West Indies
328	J.H.Kallis	South Africa/Africa/ICC	265	Abdul Razzaq	Pakistan/Asia
325	S.R.Waugh	Australia	263	C.H.Gayle	West Indies/ICC
322	W.P.J.U.C.Vaas	Sri Lanka/Asia	262	Waqar Younis	Pakistan
311	S.C.Ganguly	India/Asia	261	Younus Khan	Pakistan
308	P.A.de Silva	Sri Lanka	254	M.S.Dhoni	India/Asia
307	T.M.Dilshan	Sri Lanka	251	V.Sehwag	India/Asia/ICC
303	S.M.Pollock	South Africa/Africa	250	C.Z.Harris	New Zealand
299	B.C.Lara	West Indies/ICC	250	Ijaz Ahmed	Pakistan
295	M.V.Boucher	South Africa/Africa	250	G.D.McGrath	Australia/ICC

The most for England is 197 by P.D.Collingwood, for Zimbabwe 221 by G.W.Flower, and for Bangladesh 175 by Mohammad Ashraful.

The most consecutive appearances is 185 by S.R.Tendulkar for India (Apr 1990-Apr 1998).

100 MATCHES AS CAPTAIN

LOI			W	L	T	NR	% Won (exc NR)
230	R.T.Ponting	Australia/ICC	165	51	2	12	75.68
218	S.P.Fleming	New Zealand	98	106	1	13	47.80
193	A.Ranatunga	Sri Lanka	89	95	1	8	48.10
178	A.R.Border	Australia	107	67	1	3	61.14
174	M.Azharuddin	India	90	76	2	6	53.57
170	M.S.Dhoni	India	93	62	4	11	58.49
150	G.C.Smith	South Africa/Africa	92	51	1	6	63.88
147	S.C.Ganguly	India/Asia	76	66	–	5	53.52
139	Imran Khan	Pakistan	75	59	1	4	55.55
138	W.J.Cronje	South Africa	99	35	1	3	73.33
129	D.P.M.D.Jayawardena	Sri Lanka	71	49	1	8	58.67
125	B.C.Lara	West Indies	59	59	–	7	50.42
118	S.T.Jayasuriya	Sri Lanka	66	47	2	3	57.39
109	Wasim Akram	Pakistan	66	41	2	–	60.55
106	S.R.Waugh	Australia	67	35	3	1	63.80
105	I.V.A.Richards	West Indies	67	36	–	2	65.04

The most for England is 69 by A.N.Cook, for Zimbabwe 86 by A.D.R.Campbell, and for Bangladesh 69 by Habibul Bashar.

100 LOI UMPIRING APPEARANCES

209	R.E.Koertzen	South Africa	09.12.1992	to	09.06.2010
192	B.F.Bowden	New Zealand	23.03.1995	to	17.01.2015
181	S.A.Bucknor	West Indies	18.03.1989	to	29.03.2009
174	D.J.Harper	Australia	14.01.1994	to	19.03.2011
174	S.J.A.Taufel	Australia	13.01.1999	to	02.09.2012
172	D.R.Shepherd	England	09.06.1983	to	12.07.2005
165	Alim Dar	Pakistan	16.02.2000	to	08.12.2014
139	D.B.Hair	Australia	14.12.1991	to	24.08.2008
136	R.B.Tiffin	Zimbabwe	25.10.1992	to	06.09.2014
130	S.J.Davis	Australia	12.12.1992	to	25.01.2015
122	E.A.R.de Silva	Sri Lanka	22.08.1999	to	13.06.2012
112	B.R.Doctrove	West Indies	04.04.1998	to	20.01.2012
107	D.L.Orchard	South Africa	02.12.1994	to	07.12.2003
100	R.S.Dunne	New Zealand	06.02.1989	to	26.02.2002

INTERNATIONAL TWENTY20 RECORDS

MATCH RESULTS
2004–05 to 12 April 2015

Team	Opponents	Matches	Won											Tied	NR
			E	A	SA	WI	NZ	I	P	SL	Z	B	Ass		
England	Australia	12	4	7	–	–	–	–	–	–	–	–	–	–	1
	South Africa	9	3	–	5	–	–	–	–	–	–	–	–	–	1
	West Indies	12	4	–	–	8	–	–	–	–	–	–	–	–	–
	New Zealand	12	7	–	–	–	4	–	–	–	–	–	–	–	1
	India	8	5	–	–	–	–	3	–	–	–	–	–	–	–
	Pakistan	10	7	–	–	–	–	–	3	–	–	–	–	–	–
	Sri Lanka	6	2	–	–	–	–	–	–	4	–	–	–	–	–
	Zimbabwe	1	1	–	–	–	–	–	–	–	–	–	–	–	–
	Bangladesh	0	–	–	–	–	–	–	–	–	–	0	–	–	–
	Associates	4	1	–	–	–	–	–	–	–	–	–	2	–	1
Australia	South Africa	14	–	9	5	–	–	–	–	–	–	–	–	–	1
	West Indies	11	–	5	–	6	–	–	–	–	–	–	–	–	–
	New Zealand	5	–	4	–	–	0	–	–	–	–	–	–	1	–
	India	9	–	4	–	–	–	5	–	–	–	–	–	–	–
	Pakistan	13	–	5	–	–	–	–	7	–	–	–	–	1	–
	Sri Lanka	8	–	2	–	–	–	–	–	6	–	–	–	–	–
	Zimbabwe	1	–	0	–	–	–	–	–	–	1	–	–	–	–
	Bangladesh	3	–	3	–	–	–	–	–	–	–	0	–	–	–
	Associates	1	–	1	–	–	–	–	–	–	–	–	0	–	–
S Africa	West Indies	9	–	–	6	3	–	–	–	–	–	–	–	–	–
	New Zealand	12	–	–	9	–	3	–	–	–	–	–	–	–	–
	India	8	–	–	2	–	–	6	–	–	–	–	–	–	–
	Pakistan	11	–	–	6	–	–	–	5	–	–	–	–	–	–
	Sri Lanka	5	–	–	3	–	–	–	–	2	–	–	–	–	–
	Zimbabwe	3	–	–	3	–	–	–	–	–	0	–	–	–	–
	Bangladesh	2	–	–	2	–	–	–	–	–	–	0	–	–	–
	Associates	3	–	–	3	–	–	–	–	–	–	–	0	–	–
W Indies	New Zealand	10	–	–	–	3	4	–	–	–	–	–	–	3	–
	India	4	–	–	–	2	–	2	–	–	–	–	–	–	–
	Pakistan	4	–	–	–	2	–	–	2	–	–	–	–	–	–
	Sri Lanka	6	–	–	–	1	–	–	–	5	–	–	–	–	–
	Zimbabwe	3	–	–	–	2	–	–	–	–	1	–	–	–	–
	Bangladesh	6	–	–	–	3	–	–	–	–	–	2	–	–	1
	Associates	4	–	–	–	2	–	–	–	–	–	–	1	–	1
N Zealand	India	4	–	–	–	–	4	0	–	–	–	–	–	–	–
	Pakistan	11	–	–	–	–	4	–	7	–	–	–	–	–	–
	Sri Lanka	13	–	–	–	–	5	–	–	6	–	–	–	1	1
	Zimbabwe	5	–	–	–	–	5	–	–	–	0	–	–	–	–
	Bangladesh	3	–	–	–	–	3	–	–	–	–	0	–	–	–
	Associates	4	–	–	–	–	4	–	–	–	–	–	0	–	–
India	Pakistan	6	–	–	–	–	–	4	1	–	–	–	–	1	–
	Sri Lanka	6	–	–	–	–	–	3	–	3	–	–	–	–	–
	Zimbabwe	2	–	–	–	–	–	2	–	–	0	–	–	–	–
	Bangladesh	2	–	–	–	–	–	2	–	–	–	0	–	–	–
	Associates	4	–	–	–	–	–	3	–	–	–	–	0	–	1
Pakistan	Sri Lanka	12	–	–	–	–	–	–	7	5	–	–	–	–	–
	Zimbabwe	5	–	–	–	–	–	–	5	–	0	–	–	–	–
	Bangladesh	7	–	–	–	–	–	–	7	–	–	0	–	–	–
	Associates	6	–	–	–	–	–	–	6	–	–	–	0	–	–
Sri Lanka	Zimbabwe	3	–	–	–	–	–	–	–	3	0	–	–	–	–
	Bangladesh	4	–	–	–	–	–	–	–	4	–	0	–	–	–
	Associates	4	–	–	–	–	–	–	–	4	–	–	0	–	–
Zimbabwe	Bangladesh	3	–	–	–	–	–	–	–	–	1	2	–	–	–
	Associates	5	–	–	–	–	–	–	–	–	3	–	1	1	–
Bangladesh	Associates	11	–	–	–	–	–	–	–	–	–	7	4	–	–
Associates	Associates	59	–	–	–	–	–	–	–	–	–	–	65	–	1
		415	34	40	44	32	36	30	50	42	6	11	73	8	9

MATCH RESULTS SUMMARY

	Matches	Won	Lost	Tied	NR	Win %
Sri Lanka	67	42	23	1	1	63.63
Pakistan	85	50	33	2	0	58.82
Ireland	37	20	14	0	3	58.82
South Africa	76	44	31	0	1	58.66
India	53	30	21	1	1	57.69
Netherlands	29	15	13	0	1	53.57
Australia	77	40	34	2	1	52.63
Hong Kong	4	2	2	0	0	50.00
Nepal	4	2	2	0	0	50.00
England	74	34	36	0	4	48.57
Afghanistan	25	12	13	0	0	48.00
West Indies	69	32	32	3	2	47.76
New Zealand	79	36	36	5	2	46.75
Kenya	29	10	19	0	0	34.48
Scotland	25	8	16	0	1	33.33
Bangladesh	41	11	29	0	1	27.50
Canada	19	4	14	1	0	21.05
Zimbabwe	31	6	24	1	0	19.35
Bermuda	3	0	3	0	0	0.00
United Arab Emirates	3	0	3	0	0	0.00

INTERNATIONAL TWENTY20 RECORDS
(To 12 April 2015)

TEAM RECORDS
HIGHEST INNINGS TOTALS
† Batting Second

260-6	Sri Lanka v Kenya	Johannesburg	2007-08
248-6	Australia v England	Southampton	2013
241-6	South Africa v England	Centurion	2009-10
236-6†	West Indies v South Africa	Johannesburg	2014-15
231-7	South Africa v West Indies	Johannesburg	2014-15
225-7	Ireland v Afghanistan	Abu Dhabi	2013-14
221-5	Australia v England	Sydney	2006-07
219-4	South Africa v India	Johannesburg	2011-12
218-4	India v England	Durban	2007-08
215-5	Sri Lanka v India	Nagpur	2009-10
214-5	Australia v New Zealand	Auckland	2004-05
214-6	New Zealand v Australia	Christchurch	2009-10
214-4†	Australia v New Zealand	Christchurch	2009-10
214-7	England v New Zealand	Auckland	2012-13
213-4	Australia v England	Hobart	2013-14
211-5	South Africa v Scotland	The Oval	2009
211-4†	India v Sri Lanka	Mohali	2009-10
211-3	Sri Lanka v Pakistan	Dubai	2013-14
209-3	Australia v South Africa	Brisbane	2005-06
209-2	West Indies v New Zealand	Lauderhill	2012
209-6†	England v Australia	Southampton	2013
208-8	West Indies v England	The Oval	2007
208-2†	South Africa v West Indies	Johannesburg	2007-08
206-7	Sri Lanka v India	Mohali	2009-10
205-6	West Indies v South Africa	Johannesburg	2007-08
205-4	West Indies v Australia	Colombo (RPS)	2012-13
204-5	New Zealand v Bangladesh	Dhaka	2013-14
203-5	Pakistan v Bangladesh	Karachi	2007-08

The highest total for Zimbabwe is 200-2 (v New Zealand, Hamilton, 2011-12) and for
Bangladesh is 190-5 (v Ireland, Belfast, 2012).

LOWEST COMPLETED INNINGS TOTALS

† Batting Second

39 (10.3)	Netherlands v Sri Lanka	Chittagong	2013-14
56† (18.4)	Kenya v Afghanistan	Sharjah	2013-14
60† (15.3)	New Zealand v Sri Lanka	Chittagong	2013-14
67 (17.2)	Kenya v Ireland	Belfast	2008
68† (16.4)	Ireland v West Indies	Providence	2009-10
69† (17.0)	Hong Kong v Nepal	Chittagong	2013-14
70	Bermuda v Canada	Belfast	2008
71 (19.0)	Kenya v Ireland	Dubai	2011-12
72 (17.1)	Afghanistan v Bangladesh	Dhaka	2013-14
72	Nepal v Hong Kong	Colombo (PSS)	2014-15
73 (16.5)	Kenya v New Zealand	Durban	2007-08
74 (17.3)	India v Australia	Melbourne	2007-08
74† (19.1)	Pakistan v Australia	Dubai	2012
75† (19.2)	Canada v Zimbabwe	King City (NW)	2008-09
78 (17.3)	Bangladesh v New Zealand	Hamilton	2009-10
78† (18.5)	Kenya v Scotland	Aberdeen	2013
79† (14.3)	Australia v England	Southampton	2005
79-7†	West Indies v Zimbabwe	Port of Spain	2009-10
80† (16.0)	Afghanistan v South Africa	Bridgetown	2009-10
80† (15.5)	New Zealand v Pakistan	Christchurch	2010-11
80† (17.2)	Afghanistan v England	Colombo (RPS)	2012-13
80† (14.4)	England v India	Colombo (RPS)	2012-13
81† (15.4)	Scotland v South Africa	The Oval	2009
81 (17.3)	New Zealand v Sri Lanka	Lauderhill	2010
82† (17.5)	Pakistan v West Indies	Dhaka	2013-14
83† (15.5)	Bangladesh v Sri Lanka	Johannesburg	2007-08
84 (15.1)	Zimbabwe v New Zealand	Providence	2009-10
85-9†	Bangladesh v Pakistan	Dhaka	2011-12
85-8†	Ireland v West Indies	Kingston	2013-14

The lowest total for South Africa is 100 (v Pakistan, Centurion, 2012-13) and for Sri Lanka 87 (v Australia, Bridgetown, 2009-10).

BATTING RECORDS
1000 RUNS IN A CAREER

Runs			M	I	NO	HS	Avge	50	R/100B
2105	B.B.McCullum	NZ	70	69	10	123	35.67	15	135.2
1493	D.P.M.D.Jayawardena	SL	55	55	8	100	31.76	10	133.1
1466	T.M.Dilshan	SL	62	61	10	104*	28.74	10	119.5
1444	D.A.Warner	A	52	52	3	90*	29.46	11	138.8
1406	J.P.Duminy	SA	59	54	16	96*	37.00	7	122.4
1406	C.H.Gayle	WI	45	43	3	117	35.15	14	142.5
1382	K.C.Sangakkara	SL	56	53	9	78	31.40	8	119.5
1316	Mohammad Hafeez	P	60	58	3	86	23.92	7	115.1
1273	M.J.Guptill	NZ	48	46	6	101*	31.82	6	121.5
1259	Umar Akmal	P	59	56	10	94	27.36	6	121.8
1176	K.P.Pietersen	E	37	36	5	79	37.93	7	141.5
1156	S.R.Watson	A	48	46	3	81	26.88	10	143.9
1147	E.J.G.Morgan	E	50	49	10	85*	29.41	6	131.9
1142	Shahid Afridi	P	77	71	11	54*	19.03	4	145.2
1120	L.R.P.L.Taylor	NZ	63	57	10	63	23.82	5	119.1
1062	A.D.Hales	E	33	33	5	116*	37.92	8	138.4
1007	A.B.de Villiers	SA	57	54	9	79*	22.37	5	125.2

HIGHEST INDIVIDUAL INNINGS

Score	Balls				
156	63	A.J.Finch	A v E	Southampton	2013
123	58	B.B.McCullum	NZ v B	Pallekele	2012-13
119	56	F.du Plessis	SA v WI	Johannesburg	2014-15
117*	51	R.E.Levi	SA v NZ	Hamilton	2011-12
117	57	C.H.Gayle	WI v SA	Johannesburg	2007-08
116*	56	B.B.McCullum	NZ v A	Christchurch	2009-10
116*	64	A.D.Hales	E v SL	Chittagong	2013-14
114*	70	M.van Wyk	SA v WI	Durban	2014-15
111*	62	Ahmed Shehzad	P v B	Dhaka	2013-14
104*	57	T.M.Dilshan	SL v A	Pallekele	2011
101*	69	M.J.Guptill	NZ v SA	East London	2012-13
101	60	S.K.Raina	I v SA	Gros Islet	2009-10
100	64	D.P.M.D.Jayawardena	SL v Z	Providence	2009-10
100	58	R.D.Berrington	Sc v B	The Hague	2012
99*	55	L.J.Wright	E v Af	Colombo (RPS)	2012-13
99	68	A.D.Hales	E v WI	Nottingham	2012
98*	55	R.T.Ponting	A v NZ	Auckland	2004-05
98*	56	D.P.M.D.Jayawardena	SL v WI	Bridgetown	2009-10
98*	64	Ahmed Shehzad	P v Z	Harare	2013
98	66	C.H.Gayle	WI v I	Bridgetown	2009-10
96*	57	T.M.Dilshan	SL v WI	The Oval	2009
96*	54	J.P.Duminy	SA v Z	Kimberley	2010-11
96	56	D.R.Martyn	A v SA	Brisbane	2005-06

The highest score for Zimbabwe is 79 by H.Masakadza (v Can, King City, 2008-09) and for Bangladesh 88* by Tamim Iqbal (v West Indies, Dhaka, 2012-13).

HIGHEST PARTNERSHIP FOR EACH WICKET

1st	170	G.C.Smith/L.E.Bosman	SA v E	Centurion	2009-10
2nd	166	D.P.M.D.Jayawardena/K.C.Sangakkara	SL v WI	Bridgetown	2009-10
3rd	152	A.D.Hales/E.J.G.Morgan	E v SL	Chittagong	2013-14
4th	112*	K.P.Pietersen/E.J.G.Morgan	E v P	Dubai	2009-10
5th	119*	Shoaib Malik/Misbah-ul-Haq	P v A	Johannesburg	2007-08
6th	101*	C.L.White/M.E.K.Hussey	A v SL	Bridgetown	2009-10
7th	91	P.D.Collingwood/M.H.Yardy	E v WI	The Oval	2007
8th	64*	W.D.Parnell/J.Theron	SA v A	Johannesburg	2011-12
9th	63	Sohail Tanvir/Saeed Ajmal	P v SL	Dubai	2013-14
10th	31*	Wahab Riaz/Shoaib Akhtar	P v NZ	Auckland	2010-11

BOWLING RECORDS

40 WICKETS IN A CAREER

Wkts			Matches	Overs	Mdns	Runs	Avge	Best	R/Over
85	Saeed Ajmal	P	63	235.0	2	1491	17.54	4-19	6.34
82	Umar Gul	P	57	192.3	2	1364	16.63	5- 6	7.08
81	Shahid Afridi	P	77	280.2	3	1181	22.44	4-11	6.48
68	S.L.Malinga	SL	57	197.5	–	1435	21.10	5-31	7.25
66	B.A.W.Mendis	SL	39	147.3	5	952	14.42	6- 8	6.45
65	S.C.J.Broad	E	56	195.3	2	1491	22.93	4-24	7.62
55	D.W.Steyn	SA	38	136.1	2	879	15.98	4- 9	6.45
52	N.L.McCullum	NZ	57	166.1	–	1121	21.55	4-16	6.74
51	G.P.Swann	E	39	135.0	4	859	16.84	3-13	6.36
46	K.M.D.N.Kulasekara	SL	41	143.1	5	1040	22.60	4-32	7.26
46	Mohammad Hafeez	P	60	166.2	1	1106	24.04	4-10	6.64
45	M.Morkel	SA	38	134.4	3	985	21.88	4-17	7.31
45	T.G.Southee	NZ	37	133.0	2	1137	25.26	5-18	8.54

Wkts			Matches	Overs	Mdns	Runs	Avge	Best	R/Over
44	Shakib Al Hasan	B	35	128.1	1	832	18.90	4-21	6.49
44	Abdur Razzak	B	34	121.4	4	838	19.04	4-16	6.88
43	D.J.G.Sammy	WI	58	139.4	–	994	23.11	5-26	7.11
43	K.D.Mills	NZ	42	149.3	1	1228	28.55	3-26	8.21

BEST FIGURES IN AN INNINGS

6- 8	B.A.W.Mendis	SL v Z	Hambantota	2012-13
6-16	B.A.W.Mendis	SL v A	Pallekele	2011
5- 3	H.M.R.K.B.Herath	SL v NZ	Chittagong	2013-14
5- 6	Umar Gul	P v NZ	The Oval	2009
5- 6	Umar Gul	P v SA	Centurion	2012-13
5-13	Elias Sunny	B v Ire	Belfast	2012
5-13	Samiullah Shenwari	Af v K	Sharjah	2013-14
5-18	T.G.Southee	NZ v P	Auckland	2010-11
5-19	R.McLaren	SA v WI	North Sound	2009-10
5-19	M.A.A.Jamil	Neth v SA	Chittagong	2013-14
5-20	N.Odhiambo	K v Sc	Nairobi (Gym)	2009-10
5-23	D.Wiese	SA v WI	Durban	2014-15
5-26	D.J.G.Sammy	WI v Z	Port of Spain	2009-10
5-31	S.L.Malinga	SL v E	Pallekele	2012-13
4- 2	S.O.Tikolo	K v Sc	Dubai	2013-14
4- 6	S.J.Benn	WI v Z	Port of Spain	2009-10
4- 7	M.R.Gillespie	NZ v K	Durban	2007-08
4- 8	Umar Gul	P v A	Dubai	2009
4- 9	D.W.Steyn	SA v WI	Port Elizabeth	2007-08
4-10	Mohammad Hafeez	P v Z	Harare	2011
4-10	R.S.Bopara	E v WI	The Oval	2011

HAT-TRICKS

B.Lee	Australia v Bangladesh	Melbourne	2007-08
J.D.P.Oram	New Zealand v Sri Lanka	Colombo (RPS)	2009
T.G.Southee	New Zealand v Pakistan	Auckland	2010-11

WICKET-KEEPING RECORDS
20 DISMISSALS IN A CAREER

Dis			Matches	Ct	St
60	Kamran Akmal	Pakistan	54	28	32
47	D.Ramdin	West Indies	51	30	17
45	K.C.Sangakkara	Sri Lanka	56	25	20
36	M.S.Dhoni	India	50	25	11
34	Mushfiqur Rahim	Bangladesh	38	14	20
32†	B.B.McCullum	New Zealand	70	24	8
26†	A.B.de Villiers	South Africa	57	20	6
24	Q.de Kock	South Africa	20	18	6
23	B.J.Haddin	Australia	34	17	6
20	C.Kieswetter	England	25	17	3

† *Excluding catches taken in the field.*

MOST DISMISSALS IN AN INNINGS

4 (4 ct)	A.C.Gilchrist	Australia v Zimbabwe	Cape Town	2007-08
4 (4 ct)	M.J.Prior	England v South Africa	Cape Town	2007-08
4 (4 ct)	A.C.Gilchrist	Australia v New Zealand	Perth	2007-08
4 (4 st)	Kamran Akmal	Pakistan v Netherlands	Lord's	2009
4 (3 ct, 1 st)	N.J.O'Brien	Ireland v Sri Lanka	Lord's	2009
4 (4 ct)	M.S.Dhoni	India v Afghanistan	Gros Islet	2009-10

4 (2 ct, 2 st) A.B.de Villiers	South Africa v West Indies	North Sound	2009-10
4 (3 ct, 1 st) G.C.Wilson	Ireland v Kenya	Dubai	2011-12
4 (4 ct) A.B.de Villiers	South Africa v Zimbabwe	Hambantota	2012-13
4 (4 ct) M.S.Dhoni	India v Pakistan	Colombo (RPS)	2012-13
4 (2 ct, 2 st) Q.de Kock	South Africa v Pakistan	Dubai	2013-14
4 (4 ct) W.Barresi	Netherlands v Kenya	Dubai	2013-14
4 (4 st) D.Ramdin	West Indies v Pakistan	Dhaka	2013-14

FIELDING RECORDS
20 CATCHES IN A CAREER

Total			Matches	Total			Matches
38	L.R.P.L.Taylor	New Zealand	63	24	M.J.Guptill	New Zealand	48
32	A.B.de Villiers	South Africa	57	23	C.L.White	Australia	47
29	D.A.Warner	Australia	52	21	E.J.G.Morgan	England	50
29	D.J.Bravo	West Indies	53	21	S.C.J.Broad	England	56
27	D.J.G.Sammy	West Indies	58	21	N.L.McCullum	New Zealand	57
27	Umar Akmal	Pakistan	59	20	J.M.Bairstow	England	18
26	J.P.Duminy	South Africa	59	20	M.E.K.Hussey	Australia	38
26	Shoaib Malik	Pakistan	59	20	K.A.Pollard	West Indies	43
25	T.M.Dilshan	Sri Lanka	62	20	S.K.Raina	India	44
24	D.J.Hussey	Australia	39	20	Shahid Afridi	Pakistan	77

MOST CATCHES IN AN INNINGS

4	D.J.G.Sammy	West Indies v Ireland	Providence	2009-10
4	P.W.Borren	Netherlands v Bangladesh	The Hague	2012
4	C.J.Anderson	New Zealand v South Africa	Port Elizabeth	2012-13
4	L.D.Chandimal	Sri Lanka v Bangladesh	Chittagong	2013-14
4	A.M.Rahane	India v England	Birmingham	2014

APPEARANCE RECORDS
55 APPEARANCES

77	Shahid Afridi	Pakistan	58	D.J.G.Sammy	West Indies
70	B.B.McCullum	New Zealand	57	A.B.de Villiers	South Africa
63	Saeed Ajmal	Pakistan	57	N.L.McCullum	New Zealand
63	L.R.P.L.Taylor	New Zealand	57	S.L.Malinga	Sri Lanka
62	T.M.Dilshan	Sri Lanka	57	Umar Gul	Pakistan
60	Mohammad Hafeez	Pakistan	56	S.C.J.Broad	England
59	J.P.Duminy	South Africa	56	K.C.Sangakkara	Sri Lanka
59	Shoaib Malik	Pakistan	55	D.M.P.D.Jayawardena	Sri Lanka
59	Umar Akmal	Pakistan			

25 MATCHES AS CAPTAIN

			W	L	T	NR	%age wins
49	M.S.Dhoni	India	26	21	1	1	54.16
39	D.J.G.Sammy	West Indies	21	15	1	2	56.75
37	W.T.S.Porterfield	Ireland	20	14	–	3	58.82
30	P.D.Collingwood	England	17	11	–	2	60.71
29	Mohammad Hafeez	Pakistan	17	11	1	–	58.62
28	G.J.Bailey	Australia	14	13	1	–	50.00
28	D.L.Vettori	New Zealand	13	13	2	–	46.42
27	G.C.Smith	South Africa	18	9	–	–	66.66
27	B.B.McCullum	New Zealand	13	13	–	1	50.00
27	S.C.J.Broad	England	11	15	–	1	42.30

UNIVERSITY MATCH RESULTS

Played: 169. Wins: Cambridge 58; Oxford 55. Drawn: 56. Abandoned: 1

In 2001, for the very first time, Cambridge hosted the University Match, cricket's oldest surviving first-class fixture, after the ECB's re-organisation of university cricket around six centres of excellence had removed it from Lord's. Dating from 1827 it has, wartime interruptions apart, been played annually since 1838. With the exception of five matches played in the area of Oxford (1829, 1843, 1846, 1848 and 1850), all the previous fixtures had been staged at Lord's. Since 2001 it has been played over four days rather than three.

In 2003, Oxford (with Brookes), Cambridge (with Anglia) and Durham were joined by Loughborough in playing three first-class matches against counties. In 2012, two other centres – Cardiff (with UWIC and Glamorgan), and Leeds (with Bradford and Leeds Metropolitan) – were also granted first-class status. All six university sides now play two games each against the counties.

1827	Drawn	1878	Cambridge	1925	Drawn	1974	Drawn
1829	Oxford	1879	Cambridge	1926	Cambridge	1975	Drawn
1836	Oxford	1880	Cambridge	1927	Cambridge	1976	Oxford
1838	Oxford	1881	Oxford	1928	Drawn	1977	Drawn
1839	Cambridge	1882	Cambridge	1929	Drawn	1978	Drawn
1840	Cambridge	1883	Cambridge	1930	Cambridge	1979	Cambridge
1841	Cambridge	1884	Oxford	1931	Oxford	1980	Drawn
1842	Cambridge	1885	Cambridge	1932	Drawn	1981	Drawn
1843	Cambridge	1886	Oxford	1933	Drawn	1982	Cambridge
1844	Drawn	1887	Oxford	1934	Drawn	1983	Drawn
1845	Oxford	1888	Drawn	1935	Cambridge	1984	Oxford
1846	Oxford	1889	Cambridge	1936	Cambridge	1985	Drawn
1847	Cambridge	1890	Cambridge	1937	Oxford	1986	Cambridge
1848	Oxford	1891	Cambridge	1938	Drawn	1987	Drawn
1849	Cambridge	1892	Oxford	1939	Oxford	1988	Abandoned
1850	Oxford	1893	Cambridge	1946	Oxford	1989	Drawn
1851	Cambridge	1894	Oxford	1947	Drawn	1990	Drawn
1852	Oxford	1895	Cambridge	1948	Oxford	1991	Drawn
1853	Oxford	1896	Oxford	1949	Cambridge	1992	Cambridge
1854	Oxford	1897	Cambridge	1950	Drawn	1993	Oxford
1855	Oxford	1898	Oxford	1951	Oxford	1994	Drawn
1856	Cambridge	1899	Drawn	1952	Drawn	1995	Oxford
1857	Oxford	1900	Drawn	1953	Cambridge	1996	Drawn
1858	Oxford	1901	Drawn	1954	Drawn	1997	Drawn
1859	Cambridge	1902	Cambridge	1955	Drawn	1998	Cambridge
1860	Cambridge	1903	Oxford	1956	Drawn	1999	Drawn
1861	Cambridge	1904	Drawn	1957	Cambridge	2000	Drawn
1862	Cambridge	1905	Cambridge	1958	Cambridge	2001	Oxford
1863	Oxford	1906	Cambridge	1959	Oxford	2002	Oxford
1864	Oxford	1907	Cambridge	1960	Drawn	2003	Oxford
1865	Oxford	1908	Oxford	1961	Drawn	2004	Oxford
1866	Oxford	1909	Drawn	1962	Drawn	2005	Oxford
1867	Cambridge	1910	Oxford	1963	Drawn	2006	Oxford
1868	Cambridge	1911	Oxford	1964	Drawn	2007	Drawn
1869	Cambridge	1912	Cambridge	1965	Drawn	2008	Drawn
1870	Cambridge	1913	Cambridge	1966	Oxford	2009	Cambridge
1871	Oxford	1914	Oxford	1967	Drawn	2010	Oxford
1872	Cambridge	1919	Oxford	1968	Drawn	2011	Cambridge
1873	Oxford	1920	Drawn	1969	Drawn	2012	Drawn
1874	Oxford	1921	Cambridge	1970	Drawn	2013	Oxford
1875	Oxford	1922	Cambridge	1971	Drawn	2014	Drawn
1876	Cambridge	1923	Oxford	1972	Cambridge		
1877	Oxford	1924	Cambridge	1973	Drawn		

CAMBRIDGE UNIVERSITY RECORDS
ALL FIRST-CLASS MATCHES

Highest Total	For 703-9d		v	Sussex	Hove	1890
	V 730-3		by	W Indians	Cambridge	1950
Lowest Total	For 30		v	Yorkshire	Cambridge	1928
	V 32		by	Oxford U	Lord's	1878
Highest Innings	For 254*	K.S.Duleepsinhji	v	Middlesex	Cambridge	1927
	V 313*	S.S.Agarwal	for	Oxford U	Cambridge	2013

Highest Partnership					
(2nd wicket)	429*	J.G.Dewes/G.H.G.Doggart	v	Essex	Cambridge	1949
Best Innings Bowling	10-69	S.M.J.Woods	v	Thornton's XI	Cambridge	1890
Best Match Bowling	15-88	S.M.J.Woods	v	Thornton's XI	Cambridge	1890
Most Runs – Season	1581	D.S.Sheppard		(av 79.05)	1952
Most Runs – Career	4310	J.M.Brearley		(av 38.48)	1961-68
Most 100s – Season	7	D.S.Sheppard			1952
Most 100s – Career	14	D.S.Sheppard			1950-52
Most Wkts – Season	80	O.S.Wheatley		(av 17.63)	1958
Most Wkts – Career	208	G.Goonesena		(av 21.82)	1954-57

UNIVERSITY MATCH RECORDS

Highest Total	604		Oxford	2002
Lowest Total	39		Lord's	1858
Highest Innings	211	G.Goonesena	Lord's	1957
Best Innings Bowling	8-44	G.E.Jeffery	Lord's	1873
Best Match Bowling	13-73	A.G.Steel	Lord's	1878

Hat-Tricks: F.C.Cobden (1870), A.G.Steel (1879), P.H.Morton (1880), J.F.Ireland (1911), R.G.H.Lowe (1926)

OXFORD UNIVERSITY RECORDS
ALL FIRST-CLASS MATCHES

Highest Total	For 651		v	Sussex	Hove	1895
	V 679-7d		by	Australians	Oxford	1938
Lowest Total	For 12		v	MCC	Oxford	1877
	V 24		by	MCC	Oxford	1846
Highest Innings	For 313*	S.S.Agarwal	v	Cambridge U	Cambridge	2013
	V 338	W.W.Read	for	Surrey	The Oval	1888

Highest Partnership					
(3rd wicket)	408	S.Oberoi/D.R.Fox	v	Cambridge U	Cambridge	2005
Best Innings Bowling	10-38	S.E.Butler	v	Cambridge U	Lord's	1871
Best Match Bowling	15-65	B.J.T.Bosanquet	v	Sussex	Oxford	1900
Most Runs – Season	1307	Nawab of Pataudi sr	(av 93.35)	1931
Most Runs – Career	3319	N.S.Mitchell-Innes	(av 47.41)	1934-37
Most 100s – Season	6	Nawab of Pataudi sr		1931
	6	M.P.Donnelly		1946
Most 100s – Career	9	A.M.Crawley		1927-30
	9	Nawab of Pataudi sr		1928-31
	9	N.S.Mitchell-Innes		1934-37
	9	M.P.Donnelly		1946-47
Most Wkts – Season	70	I.A.R.Peebles	(av 18.15)	1930
Most Wkts – Career	182	R.H.B.Bettington	(av 19.38)	1920-23

UNIVERSITY MATCH RECORDS

Highest Total	611-5d		Oxford	2010
Lowest Total	32		Lord's	1878
Highest Innings	313*	S.S.Agarwal	Cambridge	2013
Best Innings Bowling	10-38	S.E.Butler	Lord's	1871
Best Match Bowling	15-95	S.E.Butler	Lord's	1871

Match Doubles: P.R.le Couteur (160 and 11-66 in 1910); G.J.Toogood (149 and 10-93 in 1985)

INDIAN PREMIER LEAGUE 2014

The seventh IPL tournament was held in India between 16 April and 1 June.

Team	P	W	L	T	NR	Pts	Net RR
1 Kings XI Punjab (6)	14	11	3	–	–	22	+0.96
2 Kolkata Knight Riders (7)	14	9	5	–	–	18	+0.41
3 Chennai Super Kings (1)	14	9	5	–	–	18	+0.38
4 Mumbai Indians (2)	14	7	7	–	–	14	+0.09
5 Rajasthan Royals (3)	14	7	7	–	–	14	+0.06
6 Sunrisers Hyderabad (4)	14	6	8	–	–	12	–0.39
7 Royal Challengers Bangalore (5)	14	5	9	–	–	10	–0.42
8 Delhi Daredevils (9)	14	2	12	–	–	4	–1.18

1st Qualifying Match: At Eden Gardens, Kolkata, 27, 28 May (floodlit). Toss: Kings XI Punjab. **KOLKATA KNIGHT RIDERS** won by 28 runs. Kolkata Knight Riders 163-8 (20; Karanveer Singh 3-40). Kings XI Punjab 135-8 (20; U.T.Yadav 3-23). Award: U.T.Yadav.

Elimination Final: At Brabourne Stadium, Mumbai, 28 May (floodlit). Toss: Chennai Super Kings. **CHENNAI SUPER KINGS** won by seven wickets. Mumbai Indians 173-8 (20; L.M.P.Simmons 67, M.M.Sharma 3-42). Chennai Super Kings 176-3 (18.4; S.K.Raina 54*). Award: S.K.Raina.

2nd Qualifying Match: At Wankhede Stadium, Mumbai, 30 May (floodlit). Toss: Chennai Super Kings. **KINGS XI PUNJAB** won by 24 runs. Kings XI Punjab 226-6 (20; V.Sehwag 122). Chennai Super Kings 202-7 (20; S.K.Raina 87). Award: V.Sehwag.

FINAL: At M.Chinnaswamy Stadium, Bangalore, 1 June (floodlit). Toss: Kolkata Knight Riders. **KOLKATA KNIGHT RIDERS** won by three wickets. Kings XI Punjab 199-4 (20; W.P.Saha 115*, M.Vohra 67). Kolkata Knight Riders 200-7 (19.3; M.K.Pandey 94, Karanveer Singh 4-54). Award: M.K.Pandey. Series award: G.J.Maxwell (Kings XI Punjab).

IPL winners:	2008	Rajasthan Royals	2009	Deccan Chargers
	2010	Chennai Super Kings	2011	Chennai Super Kings
	2012	Kolkata Knight Riders	2013	Mumbai Indians

TEAM RECORDS
HIGHEST TOTALS

263-5 (20)	Bangalore v Pune	Bangalore	2013
246-5 (20)	Chennai v Rajasthan	Chennai	2010

LOWEST TOTALS

58 (15.1)	Rajasthan v Bangalore	Cape Town	2009
67 (15.2)	Kolkata v Mumbai	Mumbai	2008

LARGEST MARGINS OF VICTORY

140 runs	Kolkata (222-3) v Bangalore (82)	Bangalore	2008
10 wickets	Mumbai (154-7) v Deccan (155-0)	Mumbai	2008
10 wickets	Rajasthan (92) v Bangalore (93-0)	Bangalore	2010
10 wickets	Mumbai (133-5) v Rajasthan (134-0)	Mumbai	2011
10 wickets	Rajasthan (162-6) v Mumbai (163-0)	Jaipur	2012
10 wickets	Punjab (138) v Chennai (139-0)	Mohali	2013

Delhi beat Punjab by ten wickets in a reduced game in 2009.

BATTING RECORDS
700 RUNS IN A SEASON

Runs			Year	M	I	NO	HS	Ave	100	50	6s	4s	R/100B
733	C.H.Gayle	Bangalore	2012	15	14	2	128*	61.08	1	7	59	46	160.7
733	M.E.K.Hussey	Chennai	2013	17	17	3	95	52.35	–	6	17	81	129.5
708	C.H.Gayle	Bangalore	2013	16	16	4	175*	59.00	1	4	51	57	156.2

HIGHEST SCORES

Score	Balls				
175*	66	C.H.Gayle	Bangalore v Pune	Bangalore	2013
158*	73	B.B.McCullum	Kolkata v Bangalore	Bangalore	2008
128*	62	C.H.Gayle	Bangalore v Delhi	Delhi	2012
127	56	M.Vijay	Chennai v Rajasthan	Chennai	2010
122	58	V.Sehwag	Punjab v Chennai	Mumbai	2014

FASTEST HUNDRED

30 balls	C.H.Gayle (175*)	Bangalore v Pune	Bangalore	2013

MOST SIXES IN AN INNINGS

17	C.H.Gayle	Bangalore v Pune	Bangalore	2013

HIGHEST STRIKE RATE IN A SEASON (Qualification: 100 runs or more)

R/100B	Score	Balls			
204.34	188	92	B.B.McCullum	Kolkata	2008

HIGHEST STRIKE RATE IN AN INNINGS (Qualification: 25 runs, 300+ strike rate)

R/100B	Score	Balls			
400.0	28	7	J.A.Morkel	Chennai v Bangalore	Chennai	2012
387.5	31	8	A.B.de Villiers	Bangalore v Pune	Bangalore	2013
385.7	27*	7	B.Akhil	Bangalore v Deccan	Hyderabad	2008
348.0	87	25	S.K.Raina	Chennai v Punjab	Mumbai	2014
346.1	45*	13	K.A.Pollard	Mumbai v Delhi	Mumbai (BS)	2010
340.0	34	10	L.J.Wright	Pune v Punjab	Mohali	2013
327.2	72	22	Y.K.Pathan	Kolkata v Hyderabad	Kolkata	2014

BOWLING RECORDS
25 WICKETS IN A SEASON

Wkts			Year	P	O	M	Runs	Avge	Best	4w	R/Over
32	D.J.Bravo	Chennai	2013	18	62.3	–	497	15.53	4-42	1	7.95
28	S.L.Malinga	Mumbai	2011	16	63.0	2	375	13.39	5-13	1	5.95
28	J.P.Faulkner	Rajasthan	2013	16	63.1	2	427	15.25	5-16	2	6.75
25	M.Morkel	Delhi	2012	16	63.0	1	453	18.12	4-20	1	7.19

BEST BOWLING FIGURES IN AN INNINGS

6-14	Sohail Tanvir	Rajasthan v Chennai	Jaipur	2008
5- 5	A.Kumble	Bangalore v Rajasthan	Cape Town	2009
5-12	I.Sharma	Deccan v Kochi	Kochi	2011
5-13	S.L.Malinga	Mumbai v Delhi	Delhi	2011

MOST ECONOMICAL BOWLING ANALYSIS

O	M	R	W				
4	1	6	0	F.H.Edwards	Deccan v Kolkata	Cape Town	2009
4	1	6	1	A.Nehra	Delhi v Punjab	Bloemfontein	2009

MOST EXPENSIVE BOWLING ANALYSIS

O	M	R	W				
4	0	66	0	I.Sharma	Hyderabad v Chennai	Hyderabad	2013
4	0	65	0	U.T.Yadav	Delhi v Bangalore	Delhi	2013
4	0	65	1	Sandeep Sharma	Punjab v Hyderabad	Hyderabad	2014
4	0	63	2	V.R.Aaron	Delhi v Chennai	Chennai	2012
4	0	63	0	A.B.Dinda	Pune v Mumbai	Mumbai	2013
4	0	62	0	M.G.Neser	Punjab v Bangalore	Mohali	2013
4	0	60	2	R.McLaren	Kolkata v Mumbai	Mumbai	2013

CHAMPIONS LEAGUE TWENTY20 2014

The sixth Champions League Twenty20 tournament took place in India between 13 September and 4 October. Twelve teams took part, having qualified from their domestic Twenty20 competitions: four from India's IPL, two each from Australia and South Africa, and one each from New Zealand, Pakistan, Sri Lanka and West Indies. Mumbai Indians and Southern Express were eliminated in a qualifying round.

GROUP A

Team	P	W	L	T	NR	Pts	Net RR
1 Kolkata Knight Riders	4	4	–	–	–	16	+0.71
2 Chennai Super Kings	4	2	1	–	1	10	+0.94
3 Perth Scorchers	4	2	2	–	–	8	–0.03
4 Lahore Lions	4	1	2	–	1	6	–0.05
5 Dolphins	4	–	4	–	–	0	–1.33

GROUP B

Team	P	W	L	T	NR	Pts	Net RR
1 Kings XI Punjab	4	4	–	–	–	16	+2.13
2 Hobart Hurricanes	4	3	1	–	–	12	+1.19
3 Barbados Tridents	4	1	3	–	–	4	–0.25
4 Cape Cobras	4	1	3	–	–	4	–0.95
5 Northern Districts	4	1	3	–	–	4	–2.66

1st Semi-Final: At Rajiv Gandhi International Stadium, Hyderabad, 2 October (floodlit). Toss: Hobart Hurricanes. **KOLKATA KNIGHT RIDERS** won by seven wickets. Hobart Hurricanes 140-6 (20; Shoaib Malik 66*). Kolkata Knight Riders 141-3 (19.1; J.H.Kallis 54*). Award: J.H.Kallis.

2nd Semi-Final: At Rajiv Gandhi International Stadium, Hyderabad, 2 October (floodlit). Toss: Kings XI Punjab. **CHENNAI SUPER KINGS** won by 65 runs. Chennai Super Kings 182-7 (20; D.J.Bravo 67, P.Awana 4-30). Kings XI Punjab 117 (18.2). Award: D.J.Bravo.

FINAL: At M.Chinnaswamy Stadium, Bangalore, 4 October (floodlit). Toss: Chennai Super Kings. **CHENNAI SUPER KINGS** won by eight wickets. Kolkata Knight Riders 180-6 (20; G.Gambhir 80, P.Negi 5-22). Chennai Super Kings 185-2 (18.3; S.K.Raina 109*). Award: P.Negi. Series award: S.K.Raina.

Champions League Winners:	2009	New South Wales	2010	Chennai Super Kings
	2011	Mumbai Indians	2012	Sydney Sixers
	2013	Mumbai Indians		

TOURNAMENT RECORDS 2009-14

Highest total	242-4		Otago v Perth Scorchers	Jaipur	2013
	242-6		Chennai v Dolphins	Bangalore	2014
Lowest total	70		Central Districts v Wayamba	Port Elizabeth	2010
Largest victory	120 runs		Punjab (215-5) v N Dists (95)	Chandigarh	2014
	10 wkts		Sydney (124-0) v Lions (121)	Johannesburg	2012
Highest score	135*	D.A.Warner	New South Wales v Chennai	Chennai	2011
Most runs overall	842	S.K.Raina (ave 38.27) Chennai			2010-14
Most runs in season	328	D.A.Warner (ave 109.33) New South Wales			2011
Highest partnership	153*	R.V.Uthappa/M.K.Pandey KKR v Dolphins		Hyderabad	2014
Best bowling	5-22	P.Negi	Chennai v KKR	Bangalore	2014
Most wickets overall	39	S.P.Narine (ave 9.20) KKR, T&T			2011-14
Most wickets in season	14	M.A.Starc (ave 12.35) Sydney Sixers			2012
Most economical	4-1-6-2	K.D.Mills	Auckland v Sialkot	Johannesburg	2012
Most expensive	4-0-69-0	S.Aravind	Bangalore v S.Australia	Bangalore	2011
Most catches in field	4	O.A.Shah	Cape Cobras v Mumbai	Bangalore	2011

ENGLAND WOMEN'S
INTERNATIONAL REGISTER

The following players have played for England since the start of the 2013-14 Ashes series.

BEAUMONT, Tamsin (**'Tammy'**) Tilley, b Dover, Kent 11 Mar 1991. RHB, WK. Kent 2007 to date. Diamonds 2007-12. Sapphires 2008. Emeralds 2011-13. **Tests**: 2 (2013 to 2014); HS 12 v I (Wormsley) 2014. **LOI**: 23 (2009-10 to 2014); HS 44 v I (Taunton) 2012. **IT20**: 33 (2009-10 to 2013-14); HS 29* v NZ (Bridgetown) 2013-14.

BRINDLE, Arran (née Thompson), b Steeton, Yorks 23 Nov 1981. RHB, RM. Lancashire 1998-2011. Emeralds 2006-13. Sussex 2011 to date. Sapphires 2012. **Tests**: 11 (2001 to 2013-14); HS 101* v A (Hove) 2005; BB – . **LOI**: 88 (1999 to 2013-14, 3 as captain); HS 107* v SA (Potchefstroom) 2011-12; BB 3-0 v WI (Mumbai) 2012-13. **IT20**: 35 (2005 to 2013-14); HS 42* v WI (Manchester) 2012; BB 3-11 v NZ (Chelmsford) 2011.

BRUNT, Katherine Helen, b Barnsley, Yorks 2 Jul 1985. RHB, RMF. Yorkshire 2004 to date. Sapphires 2006-08. Diamonds 2011-12. **Tests**: 9 (2004 to 2013-14); HS 52 v A (Worcester) 2005; BB 6-69 v A (Worcester) 2009. **LOI**: 79 (2004-05 to 2014-15); HS 26 v NZ (Mt Maunganui) 2014-15; BB 5-18 v A (Wormsley) 2011. **IT20**: 47 (2005 to 2014-15); HS 35 v WI (Arundel) 2012; BB 3-6 v NZ (Lord's) 2009.

CROSS, Kathryn ('Kate') Laura, b Manchester, Lancs 3 Oct 1991. RHB, RMF. Lancashire 2005 to date. Sapphires 2007-08. Emeralds 2012. **Tests**: 2 (2013-14 to 2014); HS 4 and BB 3-29 v I (Wormsley) 2014. **LOI**: 9 (2013-14 to 2014-15); HS 4* v I (Scarborough) 2014; BB 5-24 v NZ (Lincoln) 2014-15. **IT20**: 4 (2013-14 to 2014-15); HS – ; BB 2-27 v NZ (Whangarei) 2014-15.

DIBBLE, Jodie Marie, b Exeter, Devon 17 Sep 1994. RHB, LFM. Devon 2008 to date. Berkshire 2011. Emeralds 2012. **IT20**: 1 (2013-14); HS 0 and BB – v WI (Sylhet) 2013-14.

EDWARDS, Charlotte Marie, b Huntingdon, Cambs 17 Dec 1979. RHB, LB. East Anglia 1994-99. Kent 2000 to date. N Districts 2000-01 to 2002-03. Diamonds 2006-12. Sapphires 2013. W Australia 2014-15. MBE 2009. CBE 2014. *Wisden* 2013. **Tests**: 22 (1996 to 2014, 9 as captain); HS 117 v NZ (Scarborough) 2004; BB 2-28 v A (Harrogate) 1998. **LOI**: 185 (1997 to 2014-15, 111 as captain); HS 173* v Ire (Pune) 1997-98; BB 4-30 v SL (Colombo, PSS) 2010-11. **IT20**: 84 (2004 to 2014-15, 82 as captain); HS 92* v A (Hobart) 2013-14; BB 3-21 v SL (Colombo, NCC) 2010-11.

ELWISS, Georgia Amanda, b Wolverhampton, Staffs 31 May 1991. RHB, RMF. Staffordshire 2004-10. Sapphires 2006-12. Diamonds 2008. Australia CT 2009-10 to 2010-11. Emeralds 2011. Sussex 2011 to date. Rubies 2013. **LOI**: 10 (2011-12 to 2012-13); HS 10 v I (Taunton) 2012; BB 3-17 v I (Wormsley) 2012. **IT20**: 8 (2011-12 to 2013-14); HS – ; BB 2-30 v NZ (Invercargill) 2011-12.

FARRANT, Natasha (**'Tash'**) Eleni (Sevenoaks S), b Athens, Greece 29 May 1996. LHB, LM. Kent 2012 to date. Sapphires 2013. **LOI**: 1 (2013-14); HS 1* and BB 1-14 v WI (Port of Spain) 2013-14. **IT20**: 7 (2013 to 2013-14); HS 1* and BB 2-15 v P (Loughborough) 2013.

GREENWAY, Lydia Sophie, b Farnborough, Kent 6 Aug 1985. LHB, OB. Kent 2000 to date. Rubies 2006-13. Diamonds 2008. **Tests**: 13 (2002-03 to 2014); HS 70 v SA (Shenley) 2003. **LOI**: 121 (2003 to 2014-15); 125* v SA (Potchefstroom) 2011-12. **IT20**: 77 (2004 to 2014-15); HS 80* v A (Southampton) 2013.

GRUNDY, Rebecca Louise, b Solihull, Warwicks 12 Jul 1990. LHB, SLA. Warwickshire 2007 to date. Rubies 2013. **LOI**: 4 (2014-15); HS 1* v NZ (Mt Maunganui) 2014-15 – twice; BB 3-36 v NZ (Lincoln) 2014-15 – twice. **IT20**: 6 (2013-14); HS 1* v WI (Sylhet) 2013-14; BB 2-13 v SL (Sylhet) 2013-14.

GUNN, Jennifer ('Jenny') Louise, b Nottingham 9 May 1986. RHB, RMF. Nottinghamshire 2001 to date. Emeralds 2006-08. S Australia 2006-07 to 2007-08. Diamonds 2007. W Australia 2008-09. Yorkshire 2011. Rubies 2012-13. MBE 2014. **Tests:** 11 (2004 to 2014); HS 62* and BB 5-19 v I (Wormsley) 2014. **LOI:** 125 (2003-04 to 2014-15); HS 73 v NZ (Taunton) 2007; BB 5-22 v P (Louth) 2013. **IT20:** 83 (2004 to 2014-15, 3 as captain); HS 69 v SL (Colombo, NCC) 2010-11; BB 5-18 v NZ (Bridgetown) 2013-14.

HAZELL, Danielle ('Danni'), b Durham 13 May 1988. RHB, OB. Durham 2002-04. Sapphires 2006-13. Emeralds 2007. Yorkshire 2008 to date. **Tests:** 3 (2010-11 to 2013-14); HS 15 v A (Perth) 2013-14; BB 2-32 v A (Sydney) 2010-11. **LOI:** 39 (2009-10 to 2014-15); HS 24* v Ire (Kibworth) 2010; BB 3-22 v SL (Colombo, NCC) 2010-11. **IT20:** 60 (2009-10 to 2014-15); HS 18* v WI (Arundel) 2012; BB 4-12 v WI (Hove) 2012.

JONES, Amy Ellen, b Solihull, Warwicks 13 Jun 1993. RHB, WK. Warwickshire 2008 to date. Diamonds 2011. Emeralds 2012. Rubies 2013. **LOI:** 4 (2012-13 to 2014-15); HS 41 v SL (Mumbai, BS) 2012-13. **IT20:** 9 (2013 to 2014-15); HS 14 v A (Melbourne) 2013-14.

KNIGHT, Heather Clare, b Rochdale, Lancs 26 Dec 1990. RHB, OB. Devon 2008-09. Emeralds 2008-13. Berkshire 2010 to date. Sapphires 2011-12. Tasmania 2014-15. **Tests:** 4 (2010-11 to 2014); HS 157 v A (Wormsley) 2013; BB 1-7 v I (Wormsley) 2014. **LOI:** 49 (2009-10 to 2014-15); HS 79 v NZ (Mt Maunganui) 2014-15; BB 4-47 v NZ (Mt Maunganui) 2014-15 – separate matches. **IT20:** 23 (2010-11 to 2014-15); HS 30 v NZ (Whangarei) 2014-15; BB 3-10 v NZ (Whangarei) 2014-15 – separate matches.

MARSH, Laura Alexandra, b Pembury, Kent 5 Dec 1986. RHB, RMF/OB. Sussex 2003-10. Rubies 2006-07. Emeralds 2008. Sapphires 2011. Kent 2011 to date. **Tests:** 6 (2006 to 2013); HS 55 v A (Wormsley) 2013; BB 3-44 v I (Leicester) 2006. **LOI:** 71 (2006 to 2014-15); HS 67 v Ire (Kibworth) 2010; BB 5-15 v P (Sydney) 2008-09. **IT20:** 58 (2007 to 2014-15); HS 54 v P (Galle) 2012-13; BB 3-17 v WI (Basseterre) 2010.

ODEDRA, Sonia Balu, b Isleworth, Middx 3 Jun 1988. RHB, RMF. Leicestershire 2008. Nottinghamshire 2009 to date. Rubies 2011-13. Sapphires 2012-13. **Tests:** 1 (2014); HS 1 and BB 1-25 v I (Wormsley) 2014.

SCIVER, Natalie Ruth, b Tokyo, Japan 20 Aug 1992. RHB, RM. Surrey 2010 to date. Rubies 2011. Emeralds 2012-13. **Tests:** 2 (2013-14 to 2014); HS 49 and BB 1-30 v A (Perth) 2013-14. **LOI:** 17 (2013 to 2014-15); HS 65* v NZ (Lincoln) 2014-15; BB 3-19 v WI (Port of Spain) 2013-14. **IT20:** 25 (2013 to 2014-15); HS 37* v A (Chester-le-St) 2013; BB 4-21 v NZ (Bridgetown) 2013-14.

SHRUBSOLE, Anya, b Bath, Somerset 7 Dec 1991. RHB, RM. Somerset 2004 to date. Rubies 2006-12. Emeralds 2006-13. **Tests:** 3 (2013 to 2014); HS 14 v I (Wormsley) 2014; BB 4-51 v A (Perth) 2013-14. **LOI:** 28 (2008 to 2014-15); HS 29 v NZ (Mt Maunganui) 2014-15; BB 5-17 v SA (Cuttack) 2012-13. **IT20:** 36 (2008 to 2014-15); HS 10 v WI (Sylhet) 2013-14; BB 5-11 v NZ (Wellington) 2011-12.

TAYLOR, Sarah Jane, b Whitechapel, London 20 May 1989. RHB, WK. Sussex 2004 to date. Rubies 2006-12. Emeralds 2008-13. Wellington 2010-11 to 2011-12. S Australia 2014-15. **Tests:** 7 (2006 to 2014); HS 40 v I (Wormsley) 2014. **LOI:** 95 (2006 to 2014-15); HS 129 v SA (Lord's) 2008. **IT20:** 70 (2006 to 2014-15); HS 77 v A (Chelmsford) 2013.

WINFIELD, Lauren, b York 16 Aug 1990. RHB, WK. Yorkshire 2007 to date. Diamonds 2011. Sapphires 2012. Rubies 2012. **Tests:** 1 (2014); HS 35 v I (Wormsley) 2014. **LOI:** 10 (2013 to 2014-15); HS 31 v WI (Port of Spain) 2013-14. **IT20:** 13 (2013 to 2014-15); HS 74 v SA (Birmingham) 2014.

WYATT, Danielle ('Danni') Nicole, b Stoke-on-Trent, Staffs 22 Apr 1991. RHB, OB. Staffordshire 2005-12. Emeralds 2006-08. Sapphires 2011-13. Victoria 2011-12. Nottinghamshire 2013 to date. **LOI:** 33 (2009-10 to 2014-15); HS 40 v WI (Mumbai) 2012-13; BB 3-7 v SA (Cuttack) 2012-13. **IT20:** 56 (2009-10 to 2014-15); HS 41 v P (Loughborough) 2012; BB 4-11 v SA (Basseterre) 2010.

WOMEN'S TEST CRICKET RECORDS

1934-35 to 1 April 2015

RESULTS SUMMARY

	Opponents	Tests	E	A	NZ	SA	WI	I	P	SL	Ire	H	Drawn
							Won by						Drawn
England	Australia	47	9	11	–	–	–	–	–	–	–	–	27
	New Zealand	23	6	–	0	–	–	–	–	–	–	–	17
	South Africa	6	2	–	–	0	–	–	–	–	–	–	4
	West Indies	3	2	–	–	–	0	–	–	–	–	–	1
	India	13	1	–	–	–	–	2	–	–	–	–	10
Australia	New Zealand	13	–	4	1	–	–	–	–	–	–	–	8
	West Indies	2	–	0	–	–	0	–	–	–	–	–	2
	India	9	–	4	–	–	–	0	–	–	–	–	5
New Zealand	South Africa	3	–	–	1	0	–	–	–	–	–	–	2
	India	6	–	–	0	–	–	0	–	–	–	–	6
South Africa	India	2	–	–	–	0	–	2	–	–	–	–	–
	Netherlands	1	–	–	–	1	–	–	–	–	–	0	–
West Indies	India	6	–	–	–	–	1	1	–	–	–	–	4
	Pakistan	1	–	–	–	–	0	–	0	–	–	–	1
Pakistan	Sri Lanka	1	–	–	–	–	–	–	0	1	–	–	–
	Ireland	1	–	–	–	–	–	–	0	–	1	–	–
		137	20	19	2	1	1	5	0	1	1	0	87

	Tests	Won	Lost	Drawn	Toss Won
England	92	20	13	59	54
Australia	71	19	10	42	24
New Zealand	45	2	10	33	21
South Africa	12	1	5	6	6
West Indies	12	1	3	8	6†
India	36	5	6	25	18†
Pakistan	3	–	2	1	1
Sri Lanka	1	1	–	–	1
Ireland	1	1	–	–	–
Netherlands	1	–	1	–	1

† *Results of tosses in five of the six India v West Indies Tests in 1976-77 are not known*

TEAM RECORDS
HIGHEST INNINGS TOTALS

569-6d	Australia v England	Guildford	1998
525	Australia v India	Ahmedabad	1983-84
517-8	New Zealand v England	Scarborough	1996
503-5d	England v New Zealand	Christchurch	1934-35
497	England v South Africa	Shenley	2003
467	India v England	Taunton	2002
455	England v South Africa	Taunton	2003
440	West Indies v Pakistan	Karachi	2003-04
427-4d	Australia v England	Worcester	1998
426-7d	Pakistan v West Indies	Karachi	2003-04
426-9d	India v England	Blackpool	1986
414	England v New Zealand	Scarborough	1996
414	England v Australia	Guildford	1998
404-9d	India v South Africa	Paarl	2001-02
403-8d	New Zealand v India	Nelson	1994-95

| 400-6d | India v South Africa | Mysore | 2014-15 |

The highest totals for countries not included above are:

316	South Africa v England	Shenley	2003
193-3d	Ireland v Pakistan	Dublin	2000
108	Netherlands v South Africa	Rotterdam	2007

LOWEST INNINGS TOTALS

35	England v Australia	Melbourne	1957-58
38	Australia v England	Melbourne	1957-58
44	New Zealand v England	Christchurch	1934-35
47	Australia v England	Brisbane	1934-35
50	Netherlands v South Africa	Rotterdam	2007
53	Pakistan v Ireland	Dublin	2000

The lowest innings totals for countries not included above are:

65	India v West Indies	Jammu	1976-77
67	West Indies v England	Canterbury	1979
89	South Africa v New Zealand	Durban	1971-72

BATTING RECORDS
1000 RUNS IN TESTS

		Career	M	I	NO	HS	Avge	100	50
1935	J.A.Brittin (E)	1979-98	27	44	5	167	49.61	5	11
1645	C.M.Edwards (E)	1996-2014	22	41	5	117	45.69	4	9
1594	R.Heyhoe-Flint (E)	1960-79	22	38	3	179	45.54	3	10
1301	D.A.Hockley (NZ)	1979-96	19	29	4	126*	52.04	4	7
1164	C.A.Hodges (E)	1984-92	18	31	2	158*	40.13	2	6
1110	S.Agarwal (I)	1984-95	13	23	1	190	50.45	4	4
1078	E.Bakewell (E)	1968-79	12	22	4	124	59.88	4	7
1030	S.C.Taylor (E)	1999-2009	15	27	2	177	41.20	4	2
1007	M.E.Maclagan (E)	1934-51	14	25	1	119	41.95	2	6
1002	K.L.Rolton (A)	1995-2009	14	22	4	209*	55.66	2	5

HIGHEST INDIVIDUAL INNINGS

242	Kiran Baluch	P v WI	Karachi	2003-04
214	M.Raj	I v E	Taunton	2002
209*	K.L.Rolton	A v E	Leeds	2001
204	K.E.Flavell	NZ v E	Scarborough	1996
204‡	M.A.J.Goszko	A v E	Shenley	2001
200	J.Broadbent	A v E	Guildford	1998
193	D.A.Annetts	A v E	Collingham	1987
192	M.D.T.Kamini	I v SA	Mysore	2014-15
190	S.Agarwal	I v E	Worcester	1986
189	E.A.Snowball	E v NZ	Christchurch	1934-35
179	R.Heyhoe-Flint	E v A	The Oval	1976
177	S.C.Taylor	E v SA	Shenley	2003
176*	K.L.Rolton	A v E	Worcester	1998
167	J.A.Brittin	E v A	Harrogate	1998
161*	E.C.Drumm	E v A	Christchurch	1994-95
160	B.A.Daniels	E v NZ	Scarborough	1996
158*	C.A.Hodges	E v NZ	Canterbury	1984
157	H.C.Knight	E v A	Wormsley	2013
155*	P.F.McKelvey	NZ v E	Wellington	1968-69

‡ *On debut*

FIVE HUNDREDS

			Opponents								
		M	*I*	*E*	*A*	*NZ*	*SA*	*WI*	*IND*	*P*	*SL*	*IRE*
5	J.A.Brittin (E)	27	44	–	3	1	–	–	1	–	–	–

HIGHEST PARTNERSHIP FOR EACH WICKET

1st	241	Kiran Baluch/Sajjida Shah	P v WI	Karachi	2003-04
2nd	275	M.D.T.Kamini/P.G.Raut	I v SA	Mysore	2014-15
3rd	309	L.A.Reeler/D.A.Annetts	A v E	Collingham	1987
4th	253	K.L.Rolton/L.C.Broadfoot	A v E	Leeds	2001
5th	138	J.Logtenberg/C.van der Westhuizen	SA v E	Shenley	2003
6th	229	J.M.Fields/R.L.Haynes	A v E	Worcester	2009
7th	157	M.Raj/J.Goswami	I v E	Taunton	2002
8th	181	S.J.Griffiths/D.L.Wilson	A v NZ	Auckland	1989-90
9th	107	B.Botha/M.Payne	SA v NZ	Cape Town	1971-72
10th	119	S.Nitschke/C.R.Smith	A v E	Hove	2005

BOWLING RECORDS

50 WICKETS IN TESTS

Wkts		*Career*	*M*	*Balls*	*Runs*	*Avge*	*Best*	*5wI*	*10wM*
77	M.B.Duggan (E)	1949-63	17	3734	1039	13.49	7- 6	5	–
68	E.R.Wilson (A)	1948-58	11	2885	803	11.80	7- 7	4	2
63	D.F.Edulji (I)	1976-91	20	5098†	1624	25.77	6- 64	1	–
60	M.E.Maclagan (E)	1934-51	14	3432	935	15.58	7- 10	3	–
60	C.L.Fitzpatrick (A)	1991-2006	13	3603	1147	19.11	5- 29	2	–
60	S.Kulkarni (I)	1976-91	19	3320†	1647	27.45	6- 99	5	–
57	R.H.Thompson (A)	1972-85	16	4304	1040	18.24	5- 33	1	–
55	J.Lord (NZ)	1966-79	15	3108	1049	19.07	6-119	4	1
50	E.Bakewell (E)	1968-79	12	2697	831	16.62	7- 61	3	1

† *Excludes balls bowled in Sixth Test v West Indies 1976-77*

TEN WICKETS IN A TEST

13-226	Shaiza Khan	P v WI	Karachi	2003-04
11- 16	E.R.Wilson	A v E	Melbourne	1957-58
11- 63	J.M.Greenwood	E v WI	Canterbury	1979
11-107	L.C.Pearson	E v A	Sydney	2002-03
10- 65	E.R.Wilson	A v NZ	Wellington	1947-48
10- 75	E.Bakewell	E v WI	Birmingham	1979
10- 78	J.Goswami	I v E	Taunton	2006
10-107	K.Price	A v I	Lucknow	1983-84
10-118	D.A.Gordon	A v E	Melbourne	1968-69
10-137	J.Lord	NZ v A	Melbourne	1978-79

SEVEN WICKETS IN AN INNINGS

8-53	N.David	I v E	Jamshedpur	1995-96
7- 6	M.B.Duggan	E v A	Melbourne	1957-58
7- 7	E.R.Wilson	A v E	Melbourne	1957-58
7-10	M.E.Maclagan	E v A	Brisbane	1934-35
7-18	A.Palmer	A v E	Brisbane	1934-35
7-24	L.Johnston	A v NZ	Melbourne	1971-72
7-34	G.E.McConway	E v I	Worcester	1986
7-41	J.A.Burley	NZ v E	The Oval	1966
7-51	L.C.Pearson	E v A	Sydney	2002-03
7-59	Shaiza Khan	P v WI	Karachi	2003-04
7-61	E.Bakewell	E v WI	Birmingham	1979

HAT-TRICKS

E.R.Wilson	Australia v England	Melbourne	1957-58
Shaiza Khan	Pakistan v West Indies	Karachi	2003-04
R.M.Farrell	Australia v England	Sydney	2010-11

WICKET-KEEPING AND FIELDING RECORDS
25 DISMISSALS IN TESTS

Total			Tests	Ct	St	
58	C.Matthews	Australia	20	46	12	1984-95
43	J.Smit	England	21	39	4	1992-2006
36	S.A.Hodges	England	11	19	17	1969-79
28	B.A.Brentnall	New Zealand	10	16	12	1966-72

EIGHT DISMISSALS IN A TEST

9 (8ct, 1st)	C.Matthews	A v I	Adelaide	1990-91
8 (6ct, 2st)	L.Nye	E v NZ	New Plymouth	1991-92

SIX DISMISSALS IN AN INNINGS

8 (6ct, 2st)	L.Nye	E v NZ	New Plymouth	1991-92
6 (2ct, 4st)	B.A.Brentnall	NZ v SA	Johannesburg	1971-72

20 CATCHES IN THE FIELD IN TESTS

Total			Tests	
25	C.A.Hodges	England	18	1984-92
21	S.Shah	India	20	1976-91
20	L.A.Fullston	Australia	12	1984-87

APPEARANCE RECORDS
25 TEST MATCH APPEARANCES

27	J.A.Brittin	England	1979-98

12 MATCHES AS CAPTAIN

			Won	Lost	Drawn	
14	P.F.McKelvey	New Zealand	2	3	9	1966-79
12	R.Heyhoe-Flint	England	2	–	10	1966-76
12	S.Rangaswamy	India	1	2	9	1976-84

ENGLAND WOMEN'S TEST MATCH RESULTS IN 2014

At W.A.C.A.Ground, Perth, on 10, 11, 12, 13 January 2014. Toss: England. Result: **ENGLAND** won by 61 runs. England 201 (A.Brindle 68, R.M.Farrell 4-68) and 190 (C.M.Edwards 56, E.A.Perry 5-38). Australia 207 (E.A.Perry 71, A.Shrubsole 4-51) and 123. Award: E.A.Perry.

At Sir Paul Getty's Ground, Wormsley, on 13, 14, 15, 16 August 2014. Toss: India. Result: **INDIA** won by six wickets. England 92 (N.Niranjana 4-19) and 202 (J.L.Gunn 62*, J.Goswani 4-48). India 114 (J.L.Gunn 5-19) and 183-4 (S.Mandhana 51, M.Raj 50*). Award: J.L.Gunn.

WOMEN'S LIMITED-OVERS RECORDS

1973 to 12 March 2015

RESULTS SUMMARY

	Matches	Won	Lost	Tied	NR	% Won (exc NR)
Australia	279	216	56	1	6	79.12
England	294	168	114	2	10	59.15
India	214	110	99	1	4	52.38
South Africa	122	58	56	1	7	50.43
New Zealand	283	138	137	2	6	49.81
West Indies	130	62	63	1	4	49.20
Sri Lanka	117	50	62	–	5	44.64
Trinidad & Tobago	6	2	4	–	–	33.33
Ireland	130	38	87	–	5	30.40
Pakistan	115	34	79	–	2	30.08
Bangladesh	16	4	11	–	1	26.66
Jamaica	5	1	4	–	–	20.00
Netherlands	101	19	81	–	1	19.00
Denmark	33	6	27	–	–	18.18
International XI	18	3	14	–	1	17.64
Young England	6	1	5	–	–	16.66
Scotland	8	1	7	–	–	12.50
Japan	5	–	5	–	–	0.00

TEAM RECORDS
HIGHEST INNINGS TOTALS

455-5 (50 overs)	New Zealand v Pakistan	Christchurch	1996-97
412-3 (50 overs)	Australia v Denmark	Mumbai	1997-98
397-4 (50 overs)	Australia v Pakistan	Melbourne	1996-97
376-2 (50 overs)	England v Pakistan	Vijayawada	1997-98

HIGHEST MATCH AGGREGATES

577-12 (96.4 overs)	Australia v New Zealand	Sydney	2012-13
570-14 (98 overs)	New Zealand v Australia	Hamilton	2008-09
563-16 (98.2 overs)	England v New Zealand	Chennai	2006-07

LARGEST RUNS MARGIN OF VICTORY

408 runs	New Zealand beat Pakistan	Christchurch	1996-97
374 runs	Australia beat Pakistan	Melbourne	1996-97

LOWEST INNINGS TOTALS

22 (23.4 overs)	Netherlands v West Indies	Deventer	2008
23 (24.1 overs)	Pakistan v Australia	Melbourne	1996-97
24 (21.3 overs)	Scotland v England	Reading	2001

BATTING RECORDS
2000 RUNS IN A CAREER

Runs		Career	M	I	NO	HS	Avge	100	50
5812	C.M.Edwards (E)	1997-2015	185	174	23	173*	38.49	9	45
4888	M.Raj (I)	1999-2014	153	140	40	114*	48.88	5	36
4844	B.J.Clark (A)	1991-2005	118	114	12	229*	47.49	5	30
4814	K.L.Rolton (A)	1995-2009	141	132	32	154*	48.14	8	33
4101	S.C.Taylor (E)	1998-2011	126	120	18	156*	40.20	8	23

Runs		Career	M	I	NO	HS	Avge	100	50
4064	D.A.Hockley (NZ)	1982-2000	118	115	18	117	41.89	4	34
3144	S.J.Taylor (E)	2006-2015	95	88	11	129	40.83	5	16
2977	S.R.Taylor (WI)	2008-2014	80	79	10	171	43.14	5	19
2919	H.M.Tiffen (NZ)	1999-2009	117	111	16	100	30.72	1	18
2856	A.Chopra (I)	1995-2012	127	112	21	100	31.38	1	18
2844	E.C.Drumm (NZ)	1992-2006	101	94	13	116	35.11	2	19
2728	L.C.Sthalekar (A)	2001-2013	125	111	22	104*	30.65	2	16
2630	L.M.Keightley (A)	1995-2005	82	78	12	156*	39.84	4	21
2620	A.J.Blackwell (A)	2003-2014	113	100	21	106*	33.16	2	18
2413	L.S.Greenway (E)	2003-2015	121	107	26	125*	29.79	1	11
2328	S.W.Bates (NZ)	2006-2015	71	69	6	168	36.95	6	11
2272	S.J.McGlashan (NZ)	2002-2015	126	119	16	97*	22.05	–	11
2201	R.J.Rolls (NZ)	1997-2007	104	91	3	114	25.01	2	12
2121	J.A.Brittin (E)	1979-1998	63	59	9	138*	42.42	5	8
2091	J.Sharma (I)	2002-2008	77	75	7	138*	30.75	2	14
2047	S.Nitschke (A)	2004-2011	80	69	9	113*	34.11	1	14
2002	N.J.Browne (NZ)	2002-2014	125	102	28	63	27.05	–	10

HIGHEST INDIVIDUAL INNINGS

229*	B.J.Clark	Australia v Denmark	Mumbai	1997-98
173*	C.M.Edwards	England v Ireland	Pune	1997-98
171	S.R.Taylor	West Indies v Sri Lanka	Mumbai	2012-13
168	S.W.Bates	New Zealand v Pakistan	Sydney	2008-09
156*	L.M.Keightley	Australia v Pakistan	Melbourne	1996-97
156*	S.C.Taylor	England v India	Lord's	2006
154*	K.L.Rolton	Australia v Sri Lanka	Christchurch	2000-01
153*	J.Logtenberg	South Africa v Netherlands	Deventer	2007
151	K.L.Rolton	Australia v Ireland	Dublin	2005

HIGHEST PARTNERSHIP FOR EACH WICKET

1st	268	S.J.Taylor/C.M.G.Atkins	England v South Africa	Lord's	2008
2nd	262	H.M.Tiffen/S.W.Bates	New Zealand v Pakistan	Sydney	2008-09
3rd	244	K.L.Rolton/L.C.Sthalekar	Australia v Ireland	Dublin	2005
4th	224*	J.Logtenberg/M.du Preez	South Africa v Netherlands	Deventer	2007
5th	188*	S.C.Taylor/J.Cassar	England v Sri Lanka	Lincoln	2000-01
6th	139*	S.J.McGlashan/N.J.Browne	New Zealand v South Africa	Bowral	2008-09
7th	104*	J.Tsukigawa/N.J.Browne	New Zealand v England	Chennai	2006-07
8th	85*	S.L.Clarke/N.J.Shaw	England v Scotland	Reading	2001
9th	73	L.R.F.Askew/I.T.Guha	England v New Zealand	Chennai	2006-07
10th	58	A.Sharma/G.Sultana	India v England	Taunton	2012

BOWLING RECORDS
100 WICKETS IN A CAREER

		LOI	Balls	R	W	Avge	Best	4w	R/Over
C.L.Fitzpatrick (A)	1993-2007	109	6017	3023	180	16.79	5-14	11	3.01
J.Goswami (I)	2002-2014	138	6601	3516	167	21.05	6-31	6	3.19
L.C.Sthalekar (A)	2001-2013	125	5964	3646	146	24.97	5-35	2	3.66
N.David (I)	1995-2008	97	4892	2305	141	16.34	5-20	6	2.82
A.Mohammed (WI)	2003-2014	82	3709	2027	115	17.62	7-14	11	3.27
J.L.Gunn (E)	2004-2015	125	5082	3181	115	27.66	5-22	5	3.75
S.R.Taylor (WI)	2008-2014	80	3516	1793	102	17.57	4-17	5	3.05
C.E.Taylor (E)	1988-2005	105	5140	2443	102	23.95	4-13	2	2.85
I.T.Guha (E)	2001-2011	83	3767	2345	101	23.21	5-14	4	3.73
N.Al Khadeer (I)	2002-2012	78	4036	2402	100	24.02	5-14	5	3.57

SIX OR MORE WICKETS IN AN INNINGS

7- 4	Sajjida Shah	Pakistan v Japan	Amsterdam	2003
7- 8	J.M.Chamberlain	England v Denmark	Haarlem	1991
7-14	A.Mohammed	West Indies v Pakistan	Dhaka	2011-12
7-24	S.Nitschke	Australia v England	Kidderminster	2005
6-10	J.Lord	New Zealand v India	Auckland	1981-82
6-10	M.Maben	India v Sri Lanka	Kandy	2003-04
6-10	S.Ismail	South Africa v Netherlands	Savar	2011-12
6-20	G.L.Page	New Zealand v Trinidad & T	St Albans	1973
6-31	J.Goswami	India v New Zealand	Southgate	2011
6-32	B.H.McNeill	New Zealand v England	Lincoln, NZ	2007-08

WICKET-KEEPING AND FIELDING RECORDS
100 DISMISSALS IN A CAREER

Total			LOI	Ct	St
133	R.J.Rolls	New Zealand	104	89	44
114	J.Smit	England	109	69	45
108	S.J.Taylor	England	95	70	38
103	T.Chetty	South Africa	67	74	29

SIX DISMISSALS IN AN INNINGS

6 (4ct, 2st)	S.L.Illingworth	New Zealand v Australia	Beckenham	1993
6 (1ct, 5st)	V.Kalpana	India v Denmark	Slough	1993
6 (2ct, 4st)	Batool Fatima	Pakistan v West Indies	Karachi	2003-04
6 (4ct, 2st)	Batool Fatima	Pakistan v Sri Lanka	Colombo (PSS)	2011

50 CATCHES IN THE FIELD IN A CAREER

Total			LOI	Career
51	L.S.Greenway	England	121	2003-2015
50	J.Goswani	India	133	2002-2014
50	C.M.Edwards	England	185	1997-2015

FOUR CATCHES IN THE FIELD IN AN INNINGS

4	Z.J.Goss	Australia v New Zealand	Adelaide	1995-96
4	J.L.Gunn	England v New Zealand	Lincoln	2014-15

APPEARANCE RECORDS
125 APPEARANCES

185	C.M.Edwards	England	1997-2015
153	M.Raj	India	1999-2014
141	K.L.Rolton	Australia	1995-2009
138	J.Goswani	India	2002-2014
127	A.Chopra	India	1995-2012
126	S.J.McGlashan	New Zealand	2002 2015
126	S.C.Taylor	England	1998-2011
125	N.J.Browne	New Zealand	2002-2014
125	J.L.Gunn	England	2004-2015
125	L.C.Sthalekar	Australia	2001-2013

MOST CONSECUTIVE APPEARANCES

109	M.Raj	India	17.04.2004 to 07.02.2013

100 MATCHES AS CAPTAIN

			Won	Lost	No Result	
111	C.M.Edwards	England	69	35	7	2005-2015
101	B.J.Clark	Australia	83	17	1	1994-2005

WOMEN'S INTERNATIONAL TWENTY20 RECORDS

2004 to 18 March 2015

MATCH RESULTS SUMMARY

	Matches	Won	Lost	Tied	NR	Win %
England	88	62	23	2	1	71.26
Australia	76	47	27	2	–	61.84
West Indies	78	43	30	3	2	56.57
New Zealand	74	39	32	2	1	53.42
India	53	26	27	–	–	49.05
South Africa	56	23	32	–	1	41.81
Pakistan	57	23	32	1	1	41.07
Sri Lanka	51	15	33	–	3	31.25
Bangladesh	23	5	18	–	–	21.73
Ireland	33	7	26	–	–	21.21
Netherlands	11	–	10	–	1	0.00

WOMEN'S INTERNATIONAL TWENTY20 RECORDS
(To 18 March 2015)

TEAM RECORDS
HIGHEST INNINGS TOTALS

205-1	South Africa v Netherlands	Potchefstroom	2010-11
191-4	West Indies v Netherlands	Potchefstroom	2010-11
191-4	Australia v Ireland	Sylhet	2013-14
186-7	New Zealand v South Africa	Taunton	2007
185-2	Australia v Pakistan	Sylhet	2013-14
184-4	West Indies v Ireland	Dublin	2008
180-5	England v South Africa	Taunton	2007
180-5	New Zealand v West Indies	Gros Islet	2010

HIGHEST INNINGS TOTAL BATTING SECOND

165-2	England (set 164) v Australia	The Oval	2009

LOWEST COMPLETED INNINGS TOTALS † Batting Second

57†	(19.4)	Sri Lanka v Bangladesh	Guangzhou	2012-13
58-9†		Bangladesh v England	Sylhet	2013-14
60†	(16.5)	Pakistan v England	Taunton	2009
60	(19.4)	New Zealand v England	Whangarei	2014-15

BATTING RECORDS
1000 RUNS IN A CAREER

Runs			M	I	NO	HS	Avge	50	R/100B
2299	C.M.Edwards	E	84	82	13	92*	33.31	10	106.6
1744	S.J.Taylor	E	70	68	10	77	30.06	11	108.1
1677	S.R.Taylor	WI	59	58	10	90	34.93	15	101.2†
1664	S.W.Bates	NZ	70	69	3	94*	25.11	9	105.0
1421	D.J.S.Dottin	WI	73	72	14	112*	24.50	6	127.6†
1411	M.M.Lanning	A	49	49	6	126	32.81	7	120.2
1267	M.Raj	I	47	46	12	67	37.26	7	94.5†
1141	L.S.Greenway	E	77	67	21	80*	24.80	2	97.6
1027	A.J.Blackwell	A	73	62	10	61	19.75	1	93.5

† No information on balls faced for games at Roseau on 22 and 23 February 2012.

HIGHEST INDIVIDUAL INNINGS

Score	Balls				
126	65	M.M.Lanning	A v Ire	Sylhet	2013-14
116*	71	S.A.Fritz	SA v Neth	Potchefstroom	2010-11
112*	45	D.J.S.Dottin	WI v SA	Basseterre	2010
96*	53	K.L.Rolton	A v E	Taunton	2005
94*	61	S.W.Bates	NZ v P	Sylhet	2013-14
92*	59	C.M.Edwards	E v A	Hobart	2013-14

HIGHEST PARTNERSHIP FOR EACH WICKET

1st	170	S.A.Fritz/T.Chetty	SA v Neth	Potchefstroom	2010-11
2nd	118*	S.W.Bates/A.L.Watkins	NZ v A	Taunton	2009
3rd	124	T.D.Smartt/S.A.C.A.King	WI v Neth	Potchefstroom	2010-11
4th	147*	K.L.Rolton/K.A.Blackwell	A v E	Taunton	2005
5th	118	S.F.Daley/D.J.S.Dottin	WI v SA	Basseterre	2010
6th	68	K.L.Rolton/A.J.Blackwell	A v SA	Taunton	2009
7th	51	S.R.Taylor/M.R.Aguilleira	WI v SL	Cayon	2010
8th	32*	M.A.D.D.Surangika/S.S.Weerakkody	SL v WI	Port of Spain	2012
9th	33*	D.Hazell/H.L.Colvin	E v WI	Bridgetown	2013-14
10th	23*	L.N.McCarthy/E.J.Tice	Ire v SL	Dublin	2013

BOWLING RECORDS

50 WICKETS IN A CAREER

Wkts			Matches	Overs	Mdns	Runs	Avge	Best	R/Over
85	A.Mohammed	WI	71	239.3	3	1281	15.07	5-10	5.34
72	S.F.Daley	WI	68	227.1	8	1113	15.45	5-15	4.89
65	D.Hazell	E	60	228.0	6	1170	18.00	4-12	5.13
63	H.L.Colvin	E	50	186.5	4	971	15.41	4- 9	5.19
62	E.A.Perry	A	63	205.1	4	1215	19.59	4-20	5.92
60	L.C.Sthalekar	A	54	199.2	1	1161	19.35	4-18	5.82
56	L.A.Marsh	E	58	216.3	4	1139	20.33	3-17	5.26
55	J.L.Gunn	E	83	160.5	–	1010	18.36	5-18	6.27
54	S.R.Taylor	WI	59	162.1	4	868	16.07	3-10	5.35

FIVE OR MORE WICKETS IN AN INNINGS

6-17	A.E.Satterthwaite	NZ v E	Taunton	2007
5-10	A.Mohammed	WI v SA	Cape Town	2009-10
5-11	A.Shrubsole	E v NZ	Wellington	2011-12
5-11	J.Goswami	I v A	Visakhapatnam	2011-12
5-12	A.Mohammed	WI v NZ	Bridgetown	2013-14
5-15	S.F.Daley	WI v SL	Colombo (RPS)	2012-13
5-16	P.Roy	I v P	Taunton	2009
5-16	S.L.Quintyne	WI v E	Bridgetown	2013-14
5-18	J.L.Gunn	E v NZ	Bridgetown	2013-14
5-22	J.L.Hunter	A v WI	Colombo (RPS)	2012-13

HAT-TRICKS

Asmavia Iqbal	Pakistan v England	Loughborough	2012
Ekta Bisht	Sri Lanka v India	Colombo (NCC)	2012-13
M.Kapp	South Africa v Bangladesh	Potchefstroom	2013-14
N.R.Sciver	England v New Zealand	Bridgetown	2013-14
Sana Mir	Pakistan v Sri Lanka	Sharjah	2014-15

WICKET-KEEPING RECORDS
25 DISMISSALS IN A CAREER

Dis			Matches	Ct	St
62	S.J.Taylor	England	70	20	42
50	Batool Fatima	Pakistan	45	11	39
45	R.H.Priest	New Zealand	50	24	21
45	T.Chetty	South Africa	54	24	21
40	J.M.Fields	Australia	37	25	15
38	M.R.Aguilleira	West Indies	68	19	19
31	S.Naik	India	31	10	21

FIVE DISMISSALS IN AN INNINGS

5 (1ct, 4st)	Kycia A.Knight	West Indies v Sri Lanka	Colombo (RPS)	2012-13
5 (1ct, 4st)	Batool Fatima	Pakistan v Ireland	Dublin	2013
5 (1ct, 4st)	Batool Fatima	Pakistan v Ireland	Dublin	2013

FIELDING RECORDS
25 CATCHES IN A CAREER

Total			Matches	Total			Matches
50	J.L.Gunn	England	83	32	S.W.Bates	New Zealand	70
47	L.S.Greenway	England	77	27	S.J.McGlashan	New Zealand	65
33	J.E.Cameron	Australia	58	27	A.J.Blackwell	Australia	73

FOUR CATCHES IN AN INNINGS

4	L.S.Greenway	England v New Zealand	Chelmsford	2010

APPEARANCE RECORDS
60 APPEARANCES

84	C.M.Edwards	England		68	M.R.Aguilleira	West Indies
83	J.L.Gunn	England		68	S.F.Daley	West Indies
77	L.S.Greenway	England		67	S.A.Campbelle	West Indies
73	A.J.Blackwell	Australia		65	S.J.McGlashan	New Zealand
73	D.J.S.Dottin	West Indies		63	E.A.Perry	Australia
71	A.Mohammed	West Indies		61	S.A.C.A.King	West Indies
70	S.W.Bates	New Zealand		60	D.Hazell	England
70	S.J.Taylor	England				

25 MATCHES AS CAPTAIN

			W	L	T	NR	%age wins
82	C.M.Edwards	England	60	20	1	1	74.07
67	M.R.Aguilleira	West Indies	36	27	2	2	55.38
53	Sana Mir	Pakistan	20	31	1	1	38.46
37	M.du Preez	South Africa	19	17	–	1	52.77
35	S.W.Bates	New Zealand	16	18	1	–	45.71
31	H.A.S.D.Siriwardene	Sri Lanka	9	20	–	2	31.03
29	A.L.Watkins	New Zealand	19	10	–	–	65.51
26	J.M.Fields	Australia	16	10	–	–	61.53

UNICORNS MINOR COUNTIES
FIXTURES 2015

Sun 19 April
Dean Park
Newport
Manor Park
Grantham
Shrewsbury
High Wycombe
Colwall

KNOCK-OUT TROPHY
Dorset v Cornwall (1)
Wales MC v Wiltshire (1)
Norfolk v Hertfordshire (2)
Lincolnshire v Cheshire (3)
Shropshire v Cumberland (3)
Buckinghamshire v Staffordshire (4)
Herefordshire v Berkshire (4)

Sun 26 April
North Devon
Warminster
Hertford
Ipswich School
Nantwich
Swalwell
Henley
Wormsley

KNOCK-OUT TROPHY
Devon v Wales MC (1)
Wiltshire v Dorset (1)
Hertfordshire v Bedfordshire (2)
Suffolk v Norfolk (2)
Cheshire v Shropshire (3)
Northumberland v Lincolnshire (3)
Berkshire v Buckinghamshire (4)
Oxfordshire v Herefordshire (4)

Sun 3 May
St Austell
Dean Park
Dunstable
Clare College
Kendal
Oswestry
Wormsley
Stone

KNOCK-OUT TROPHY
Cornwall v Wiltshire (1)
Dorset v Devon (1)
Bedfordshire v Suffolk (2)
Cambridgeshire v Hertfordshire (2)
Cumberland v Cheshire (3)
Shropshire v Northumberland (3)
Buckinghamshire v Oxfordshire (4)
Staffordshire v Berkshire (4)

Mon 4 May
Luton

KNOCK-OUT TROPHY
Bedfordshire v Cambridgeshire (2)

Sun 10 May
Sidmouth
Brymbo
Manor Park
Bury St Edmunds
Bracebridge Heath
Jesmond
Brockhampton
Bicester & N Oxford

KNOCK-OUT TROPHY
Devon v Cornwall (1)
Wales MC v Dorset (1)
Norfolk v Bedfordshire (2)
Suffolk v Cambridgeshire (2)
Lincolnshire v Shropshire (3)
Northumberland v Cumberland (3)
Herefordshire v Buckinghamshire (4)
Oxfordshire v Staffordshire (4)

Sun 17 May
Werrington
Warminster
Leys School
Harpenden
Hyde
Cockermouth
Wokingham
Himley

KNOCK-OUT TROPHY
Cornwall v Wales MC (1)
Wiltshire v Devon (1)
Cambridgeshire v Norfolk (2)
Hertfordshire v Suffolk (2)
Cheshire v Northumberland (3)
Cumberland v Lincolnshire (3)
Berkshire v Oxfordshire (4)
Staffordshire v Herefordshire (4)

Sun 24 – Tue 26 May
Luton

MCCA CHAMPIONSHIP
Bedfordshire v Norfolk

Sun 31 May	**TWENTY20 KNOCK-OUT**
Chester B Hall	Cumberland v Cheshire
Chester B Hall	Staffordshire v Northumberland
Eastnor	Herefordshire v Wales MC
Eastnor	Oxfordshire v Shropshire
Exmouth	Cornwall v Dorset
Exmouth	Devon v Wiltshire
Sawston	Cambridgeshire v Norfolk
Sawston	Suffolk v Lincolnshire
Harpenden	Berkshire v Buckinghamshire
Harpenden	Hertfordshire v Bedfordshire

Sun 7 – Tue 9 June	**MCCA CHAMPIONSHIP**
Henley	Berkshire v Oxfordshire
High Wycombe	Buckinghamshire v Hertfordshire
Sandford	Devon v Wales MC
Dean Park	Dorset v Wiltshire
Colwall	Herefordshire v Cornwall
S Northumberland	Northumberland v Cumberland
Whitchurch	Shropshire v Cheshire
West Bromwich D	Staffordshire v Cambridgeshire
Bury St Edmunds	Suffolk v Lincolnshire

Sun 14 June	**KNOCK-OUT TROPHY – Quarter-finals**
Match 1	Winner Gp 2 v Runner-up Gp 1
Match 2	Winner Gp 1 v Runner-up Gp 4
Match 3	Winner Gp 3 v Runner-up Gp 2
Match 4	Winner Gp 4 v Runner-up Gp 3

Sun 21 – Tue 23 June	**MCCA CHAMPIONSHIP**
Wisbech	Cambridgeshire v Buckinghamshire
Truro	Cornwall v Devon
Netherfield	Cumberland v Staffordshire
Eastnor	Herefordshire v Shropshire
Hertford	Hertfordshire v Bedfordshire
Sleaford	Lincolnshire v Northumberland
Aston Rowant	Oxfordshire v Dorset
Copdock	Suffolk v Norfolk
Newport	Wales MC v Cheshire
Corsham	Wiltshire v Berkshire

Sun 28 June	**TWENTY20 KNOCK-OUT**
Harpenden winner	Harpenden v Sawston

Sun 5 – Tue 7 July	**MCCA CHAMPIONSHIP**
Falkland	Berkshire v Shropshire
Burnham	Buckinghamshire v Bedfordshire
March	Cambridgeshire v Suffolk
Grappenhall	Cheshire v Dorset
Grampound Road	Cornwall v Wiltshire
Sedbergh School	Cumberland v Lincolnshire
Sidmouth	Devon v Herefordshire
Harpenden	Hertfordshire v Northumberland
Gt & Little Tew	Oxfordshire v Wales MC

Sun 12 July	**TWENTY20 KNOCK-OUT**
Banbury	Finals day

Sun 19 – Tue 21 July	**MCCA CHAMPIONSHIP**
Bedford School	Bedfordshire v Cumberland
Finchampstead	Berkshire v Devon
St Austell	Cornwall v Cheshire
Dean Park	Dorset v Shropshire
Brockhampton	Herefordshire v Oxfordshire
Grantham	Lincolnshire v Cambridgeshire
Manor Park	Norfolk v Hertfordshire
Jesmond	Northumberland v Buckinghamshire
Longton	Staffordshire v Suffolk
Pontarddulais	Wales MC v Wiltshire
Sun 26 July	**KNOCK-OUT TROPHY – Semi-finals**
tbc	Winner match 1 v Winner match 2
tbc	Winner match 4 v Winner match 3
Sun 26 – Tue 28 July	**MCCA CHAMPIONSHIP**
Manor Park	Norfolk v Staffordshire
Thu 30 – Fri 31 July	
Loughborough	Unicorns v England Under-19
Sun 2 – Tue 4 August	**MCCA CHAMPIONSHIP**
Tring Park	Buckinghamshire v Lincolnshire
Alderley Edge	Cheshire v Berkshire
Carlisle	Cumberland v Hertfordshire
Exmouth	Devon v Dorset
Manor Park	Norfolk v Cambridgeshire
Jesmond	Northumberland v Staffordshire
Banbury	Oxfordshire v Cornwall
Bridgnorth	Shropshire v Wales MC
Ipswich School	Suffolk v Bedfordshire
South Wilts	Wiltshire v Herefordshire
Sun 16 – Tue 18 August	**MCCA CHAMPIONSHIP**
Luton	Bedfordshire v Northumberland
Saffron Walden	Cambridgeshire v Cumberland
Chester B Hall	Cheshire v Herefordshire
Dean Park	Dorset v Berkshire
Long Marston	Hertfordshire v Suffolk
Cleethorpes	Lincolnshire v Norfolk
Shifnal	Shropshire v Devon
Knypersley	Staffordshire v Buckinghamshire
Usk	Wales MC v Cornwall
Devizes	Wiltshire v Oxfordshire
Wed 26 August	**KNOCK-OUT TROPHY Final**
Wormsley	Final
Sun 6 – Wed 9 September	**MCCA CHAMPIONSHIP**
Winners of East	Championship Final

MCCA KNOCK-OUT TROPHY GROUPS

Group 1	*Group 2*	*Group 3*	*Group 4*
Cornwall	Bedfordshire	Cheshire	Berkshire
Devon	Cambridgeshire	Cumberland	Buckinghamshire
Dorset	Hertfordshire	Lincolnshire	Herefordshire
Wales MC	Norfolk	Northumberland	Oxfordshire
Wiltshire	Suffolk	Shropshire	Staffordshire

SECOND XI CHAMPIONSHIP FIXTURES 2015

THREE-DAY MATCHES

APRIL

Mon 27	Moseley	Warwicks v Northants
Tue 28	Hinckley	Leics v Yorkshire
	Cheam	Surrey v MCC YC

MAY

Mon 4	Richmond	Durham v Notts
	Mumbles	Glamorgan v Essex
Tue 5	Bristol	Glos v Middlesex
	Leicester	Leics v Derbyshire
Mon 11	tbc	Glos v Hampshire
Tue 12	Brandon	Durham v Leics
	H Wycombe	MCC YC v Sussex
	Milton Keynes	Northants v Worcs
Mon 18	Southampton	Hampshire v Middlesex
Tue 19	Chester-le-St	Durham v Warwicks
	B Stortford	Essex v Glos
	Blackstone	Sussex v Somerset
Wed 20	Maidstone	Kent v Surrey
Mon 25	Cov'try/N Wk	Warwicks v Lancashire
Wed 27	Stowe S	Northants v Notts
	Taunton Vale	Somerset v Glamorgan

JUNE

Mon 1	tbc	Derbyshire v Lancashire
	Darlington	Durham v Worcs
	Bristol	Glos v Somerset
	Shenley	MCC YC v Glamorgan
	Notts SC	Notts v Warwicks
	Wimbledon	Surrey v Hampshire
Tue 2	Billericay	Essex v Middlesex
Mon 8	Radlett	Middlesex v Glamorgan
	Notts SC	Notts v Lancashire
	Kidderminster	Worcs v Leics
	York	Yorkshire v Northants
Tue 9	Maidstone	Kent v Essex
	Horsham	Sussex v Surrey
Mon 15	Hinckley	Leics v Northants
Tue 16	Southend	Essex v Sussex
	tbc	Glos v Kent
	Northwood	Middlesex v Somerset
	Scarborough	Yorkshire v Derbyshire
Mon 22	Todmorden	Lancashire v Northants
	Moseley	Warwicks v Leics
	Barnt Green	Worcs v Yorkshire
Tue 23	Belper Meadows	Derbyshire v Durham
	Cardiff CC	Glamorgan v Surrey
	Eastbourne	Sussex v Glos
Wed 24	H Wycombe	MCC YC v Kent
Mon 29	Derby	Derbyshire v Notts
Tue 30	Neath	Glamorgan v Kent

	Liverpool	Lancashire v MCC Univs
	Taunton Vale	Surrey v Somerset

JULY

Mon 6	Oxford	MCC Univs v Warwicks
	Notts SC	Notts v Worcs
	Leeds	Yorkshire v Lancashire
Tue 7	Southampton	Hampshire v Sussex
	Taunton Vale	Somerset v MCC YC
Wed 8	Northampton	Northants v Durham
Mon 13	Preston Nom	Sussex v Glamorgan
	Worcester RGS	Worcs v MCC Univs
Mon 20	Panteg	Glamorgan v Glos
	Crosby	Lancashire v Durham
	Desborough	MCC Univs v Leics
	Worcester RGS	Worcs v Derbyshire
Tue 21	Coggleshall	Essex v Surrey
	Radlett	Middlesex v Kent
	Harrogate	Yorkshire v Warwicks
Wed 22	Newclose IoW	MCC YC v Hampshire
Mon 27	Swarkestone	Derbyshire v Northants
	Bath	Glos v MCC YC
	Cambridge	MCC Univs v Notts
Tue 28	Richmond	Middlesex v Sussex
	Taunton Vale	Somerset v Kent
Wed 29	Southampton	Hampshire v Glamorgan
	Ashby Hastings	Leics v Lancashire

AUGUST

Mon 3	Denby	Derbyshire v MCC Univs
	Polo Farm	Kent v Hampshire
	Southport & B	Lancashire v Worcs
Tue 4	Cheam	Surrey v Glos
Wed 5	Radlett	MCC YC v Middlesex
	Taunton Vale	Somerset v Essex
Mon 10	Milton Keynes	Northants v MCC Univs
	Wimbledon	Surrey v Middlesex
Tue 11	Chester-le-St	Durham v Yorkshire
	Halstead	Essex v MCC YC
Wed 12	Beckenham	Kent v Sussex
	Notts SC	Notts v Leics
	Worcester RGS	Worcs v Warwicks
Mon 17	Leeds Wwood	MCC Univs v Yorkshire
	Taunton Vale	Somerset v Hampshire
Mon 24	Basingstoke	Hampshire v Essex
	S North'land	MCC Univs v Durham
	Coventry/N Wk	Warwicks v Derbys
	Stamford Bg	Yorkshire v Notts

SEPTEMBER

Mon 7	tbc	FINAL (Four days)

SECOND XI TROPHY FIXTURES 2015

ONE DAY

APRIL
Mon 27 Leicester Ivanhoe Leics v Yorkshire

MAY
Thu 7 Richmond Durham v Notts

JUNE
Thu 4 tbc Derbyshire v Lancashire
    Guildford Surrey v Sussex
Tue 9 Knowle & D Warwicks v Derbyshire
Mon 15 Southend Essex v Sussex
    Marske Yorkshire v Derbyshire
Tue 16 Burnopfield Durham v Unicorns
Fri 19 Cov'try/N Wk Warwicks v Notts
Thu 25 Westhoughton Lancashire v Northants
Fri 26 Southampton Hampshire v Essex
Mon 29 Dunstable Northants v Leics
    Taunton Vale Surrey v Somerset

JULY
Wed 1 Finedon Dol Northants v Durham
    Kidderminster Worcs v Unicorns
Thu 2 Derby Derbyshire v Notts
    Gt & Lit Tew Unicorns v Warwicks
    Kidderminster Worcs v Durham
Fri 3 Newport Glamorgan v Kent
    Desborough Northants v Unicorns
Mon 6 tbc Glos v Middlesex
    Southampton Hampshire v Sussex
    Taunton Vale Somerset v MCC YC
Wed 8 Uxbridge Middlesex v Essex
Thu 9 Trent Coll Notts v Worcs
    Pudsey Congs Yorkshire v Lancashire
Fri 10 Sunbury Surrey v Middlesex
Mon 13 Southampton Hampshire v Surrey
    Canterbury Kent v Glos
Tue 14 Long Marston Unicorns v Leics

Wed 15 Long Marston Unicorns v Yorkshire
Thu 16 Preston Nom Sussex v Glamorgan
Fri 17 Leicester Leics v Warwicks
Mon 20 Radlett Middlesex v Kent
    York Yorkshire v Warwicks
Tue 21 Newclose IoW MCC YC v Hampshire
Thu 23 Cardiff CC Glamorgan v Glos
    Middlewich Lancashire v Durham
    Notts SC Notts v Northants
    Worcester RGS Worcs v Derbyshire
Fri 24 Coggleshall Essex v Surrey
    Cardiff CC Glamorgan v Somerset
Mon 27 Richmond Middlesex v Somerset
    Taunton Vale Somerset v Kent
Tue 28 Southampton Hampshire v Glamorgan
    Leicester Leics v Lancashire
Thu 30 tbc Derbyshire v Northants
    Bath Glos v MCC YC

AUGUST
Mon 3 Guildford Surrey v Glos
Tue 4 Radlett MCC YC v Middlesex
    Taunton Vale Somerset v Essex
Thu 6 Polo Farm Kent v Hampshire
    Manchester Lancashire v Worcs
Mon 10 Chester-le-St Durham v Yorkshire
    Halstead Essex v MCC YC
    tbc Glos v Somerset
Tue 11 Beckenham Kent v Sussex
    Notts SC Notts v Leics
    Olton & W Wk Warwicks v Worcs
Fri 14 St Fagan's MCC YC v Glamorgan
Fri 21 tbc Semi-finals
Thu 27 tbc **FINAL**

SECOND XI TWENTY20 CUP FIXTURES 2015

APRIL

Mon 27	Notts SC	Notts v Derbyshire
Thu 30	Birmingham	Warwicks v Northants

MAY

Fri 1	tbc	Glos v Glamorgan
Tue 5	Hove	Sussex v Hampshire
Thu 7	Cardiff	Glamorgan v Essex
Fri 8	Northop Hall	Lancashire v Yorkshire
	tbc	Leics v Derbyshire
	Purley	Surrey v MCC YC
Mon 11	Brandon	Durham v Leics
	H Wycombe	MCC YC v Sussex
	Milton Keynes	Northants v Worcs
Tue 12	Neston	Lancashire v Derbyshire
Thu 14	tbc	Glos v Hampshire
Mon 18	Benwell Hill	Durham v Warwicks
	B Stortford	Essex v Glos
	Maidstone	Kent v Surrey
	Horsham	Sussex v Somerset
	Knypersley	Unicorns v Worcs
Tue 19	Glossop	Derbyshire v Yorkshire
Wed 20	Liverpool	Lancashire v Unicorns
Thu 21	Derby	Derbyshire v Unicorns
	Southampton	Hampshire v Middlesex
	Harrogate	Yorkshire v Notts
Fri 22	Oundle S	Northants v Lancashire
Tue 26	Southampton	Hampshire v MCC YC
	Northampton	Northants v Notts
	Taunton Vale	Somerset v Glamorgan
	Horsham	Sussex v Kent
	York	Yorkshire v Durham
Wed 27	Shenley	MCC YC v Essex
Thu 28	Walmley	Warwicks v Lancashire

Fri 29	Sunbury	Middlesex v Surrey

JUNE

Mon 1	Billericay	Essex v Middlesex
Thu 4	Chester-le-St CC	Durham v Worcs
	Shenley	Glamorgan v MCC YC
	tbc	Leics v Unicorns
	Trent Coll	Notts v Warwicks
	Taunton Vale	Somerset v Glos
Mon 8	Horsham	Sussex v Surrey
Thu 11	Radlett	Middlesex v Glamorgan
	Worksop Coll	Notts v Lancashire
	Kidderminster	Worcs v Leics
	Barnsley	Yorkshire v Northants
Fri 12	Maidstone	Kent v Essex
Mon 15	tbc	Glos v Kent
	Northwood	Middlesex v Somerset
Tue 16	Purley	Surrey v Hampshire
	Kidderminster	Worcs v Warwicks
Wed 17	Burnopfield	Unicorns v Durham
Thu 18	Leicester	Leics v Northants
Mon 22	Leek	Derbyshire v Durham
	Chelmsford	Essex v Somerset
	Cardiff CC	Glamorgan v Surrey
	Beckenham	Kent v Middlesex
	Eastbourne	Sussex v Glos
Tue 23	H Wycombe	MCC YC v Kent
Wed 24	Taunton Vale	Somerset v Hampshire
Thu 25	Challow & Ch	Unicorns v Notts
	Birmingham	Warwicks v Leics
	Barnt Green	Worcs v Yorkshire

JULY

Thu 16	Arundel	FINALS DAY

WOMEN'S INTERNATIONAL FIXTURES 2015

Tue 21 July
LOI Taunton England v Australia

Thu 23 July
LOI Bristol England v Australia

Sun 26 July
LOI Worcester England v Australia

Tue 11 – Fri 14 August
TM Canterbury England v Australia

Wed 26 August
IT20 F Chelmsford England v Australia

Fri 28 August
IT20 F Hove England v Australia

Mon 31 August
IT20 Cardiff England v Australia

ENGLAND UNDER-19 FIXTURES 2015

Tue 4 – Fri 7 August
TM Chester-le-St England v Australia

Tue 11 August
LOI S N'humberland England v Australia

Fri 14 August
LOI Chesterfield England v Australia

Mon 17 August
LOI F Derby England v Australia

Thu 20 August
LOI Leicester England v Australia

Sat 22 August
LOI Worcester England v Australia

MCC UNIVERSITIES CHALLENGE 2015

Tue 21 – Wed 22 April
Cambridge Fenners Cambridge v Durham
Leeds Weetwood Leeds/Bradford v Oxford
Loughborough Loughborough v Cardiff

Tue 28 – Wed 29 April
Usk Cardiff v Oxford
Durham Racecourse Durham v Loughborough
Leeds Weetwood Leeds/Bradford v Cambridge

Wed 6 – Thu 7 May
Usk Cardiff v Leeds/Bradford

Thu 7 – Fri 8 May
Oxford Parks Oxford v Durham

Tue 12 – Wed 13 May
Cambridge Fenners Cambridge v Oxford

Leeds Weetwood Leeds/Bradford v Loughborough

Wed 20 – Thu 21 May
Loughborough Loughborough v Cambridge

Wed 27 – Thu 28 May
Oxford Parks Oxford v Loughborough

Tue 2 – Wed 3 June
Durham Racecourse Durham v Cardiff

Tue 9 – Wed 10 June
Cambridge Fenners Cambridge v Cardiff
Durham Racecourse Durham v Leeds/Bradford

Tue 23 June
Lord's MCCU Challenge

PRINCIPAL FIXTURES 2015

CC1	LV= County Championship Division 1	
CC2	LV= County Championship Division 2	
F	Floodlit	
FCF	First-Class Friendly	
LOI	Royal London One-Day Series	
50L	Royal London One-Day Cup	

T20	NatWest T20 Blast
IT20	NatWest Twenty20 International
TM	Investec Test Match
MCCU	MCC University
Uni	University match

Sun 22 – Wed 25 March

FCF	Abu Dhabi	MCC v Yorkshire

Thu 2 – Sat 4 April

Uni	Cambridge	Cambridge MCCU v Northants
Uni	Cardiff	Glamorgan v Cardiff MCCU
Uni	Southampton	Hampshire v Loughboro MCCU
Uni	Oxford	Oxford MCCU v Worcs
Uni	Taunton Vale	Somerset v Durham MCCU
Uni	Hove	Sussex v Leeds/Brad MCCU

Tue 7 – Thu 9 April

Uni	Cambridge	Cambridge MCCU v Leics
Uni	Chester-le-St	Durham v Durham MCCU
Uni	Bristol	Glos v Cardiff MCCU
Uni	Nottingham	Notts v Loughboro MCCU
Uni	Oxford	Oxford MCCU v Middlesex
Uni	Leeds	Yorkshire v Leeds/Brad MCCU

Sun 12 – Wed 15 April

CC1	Southampton	Hampshire v Sussex
CC1	Lord's	Middlesex v Notts
CC1	Taunton	Somerset v Durham
CC1	Worcester	Worcs v Yorkshire
CC2	Leicester	Leics v Glamorgan
CC2	Northampton	Northants v Glos

Sun 12 – Tue 14 April

Uni	Cambridge	Cambridge MCCU v Derbyshire
Uni	Chelmsford	Essex v Cardiff MCCU
Uni	Canterbury	Kent v Loughboro MCCU
Uni	Manchester	Lancashire v Leeds/Brad MCCU
Uni	Oxford	Oxford MCCU v Surrey
Uni	Birmingham	Warwicks v Durham MCCU

Sun 19 – Wed 22 April

CC1	Nottingham	Notts v Yorkshire
CC1	Hove	Sussex v Worcs
CC1	Birmingham	Warwicks v Hampshire
CC2	Derby	Derbyshire v Lancashire
CC2	Chelmsford	Essex v Kent
CC2	Cardiff	Glamorgan v Surrey

Sun 26 – Wed 29 April

CC1	Chester-le-St	Durham v Sussex
CC1	Southampton	Hampshire v Notts
CC1	Taunton	Somerset v Middlesex
CC1	Leeds	Yorkshire v Warwicks

CC2	Bristol	Glos v Derbyshire
CC2	Manchester	Lancashire v Kent
CC2	Leicester	Leics v Northants
CC2	The Oval	Surrey v Essex

Sat 2 – Tue 5 May

CC1	Lord's	Middlesex v Durham

Sun 3 – Wed 6 May

CC1	Worcester	Worcs v Somerset
CC2	Chelmsford	Essex v Glos
CC2	Cardiff	Glamorgan v Derbyshire
CC2	Canterbury	Kent v Lancashire
CC2	Northampton	Northants v Lancashire

Fri 8 – Mon 11 May

FCF	Taunton	Somerset v New Zealanders

Fri 8 May

LOI	Dublin	Ireland v England

Sat 9 – Tue 12 May

CC1	Birmingham	Warwicks v Worcs

Sun 10 – Wed 13 May

CC1	Chester-le-St	Durham v Notts
CC1	Hove	Sussex v Middlesex
CC1	Leeds	Yorkshire v Hampshire
CC2	Derby	Derbyshire v Northants
CC2	Canterbury	Kent v Glamorgan
CC2	Manchester	Lancashire v Glos
CC2	The Oval	Surrey v Leics

Thu 14 – Sun 17 May

FCF	Worcester	Worcs v New Zealanders

Fri 15 May

T20	Chester-le-St	Durham v Northants
T20	Bristol	Glos v Middlesex
T20 F	Southampton	Hampshire v Essex
T20 F	Canterbury	Kent v Sussex
T20 F	Manchester	Lancashire v Leics
T20 F	Nottingham	Notts v Warwicks
T20 F	The Oval	Surrey v Glamorgan
T20 F	Leeds	Yorkshire v Derbyshire

Sat 16 May

T20	Chelmsford	Essex v Surrey

Sun 17 – Wed 20 May
CC1 Southampton Hampshire v Middlesex
CC1 Nottingham Notts v Somerset
CC1 Birmingham Warwicks v Durham
CC2 Leicester Leics v Lancashire

Sun 17 May
T20 Hove Sussex v Glos

Mon 18 – Thu 21 May
CC2 Cardiff Glamorgan v Essex
CC2 Bristol Glos v Kent
CC2 Northampton Northants v Surrey

Thu 21 – Mon 25 May
TM1 Lord's ENGLAND v NEW ZEALAND

Fri 22 May
T20 F Cardiff Glamorgan v Essex
T20 F Southampton Hampshire v Kent
T20 F Manchester Lancashire v Durham
T20 Leicester Leics v Derbyshire
T20 F Nottingham Notts v Yorkshire
T20 Taunton Somerset v Sussex
T20 F Birmingham Warwicks v Worcs

Sun 24 – Wed 27 May
CC1 Taunton Somerset v Yorkshire
CC1 Hove Sussex v Warwicks
CC1 Worcester Worcs v Durham
CC2 Beckenham Kent v Surrey
CC2 Southport Lancashire v Derbyshire

Sun 24 May
T20 Bristol Glos v Essex

Thu 28 May
T20 Leicester Leics v Durham
T20 F Lord's Middlesex v Kent

Fri 29 May – Tue 2 June
TM2 Leeds ENGLAND v NEW ZEALAND

Fri 29 May
T20 F Derby Derbyshire v Lancashire
T20 Chester-le-St Durham v Yorkshire
T20 F Chelmsford Essex v Somerset
T20 F Cardiff Glamorgan v Hampshire
T20 Beckenham Kent v Surrey
T20 F Northampton Northants v Warwicks
T20 F Hove Sussex v Middlesex
T20 Worcester Worcs v Leics

Sun 31 May – Wed 3 June
CC1 Southampton Hampshire v Worcs
CC1 Lord's Middlesex v Warwicks
CC2 Derby Derbyshire v Glos
CC2 Chelmsford Essex v Leics
CC2 Cardiff Glamorgan v Northants

CC2 The Oval Surrey v Lancashire

Sun 31 May
T20 Nottingham Notts v Durham
T20 Taunton Somerset v Kent

Mon 1 – Thu 4 June
CC1 Nottingham Notts v Sussex

Thu 4 June
T20 F Southampton Hampshire v Middlesex

Fri 5 June
T20 F Derby Derbyshire v Durham
T20 F Cardiff Glamorgan v Middlesex
T20 Beckenham Kent v Glos
T20 F Northampton Northants v Worcs
T20 F Nottingham Notts v Leics
T20 Taunton Somerset v Hampshire
T20 F The Oval Surrey v Essex
T20 F Leeds Yorkshire v Lancashire

Sat 6 June
 Leicester Leics v New Zealanders
T20 Chester-le-St Durham v Warwicks

Sun 7 – Wed 10 June
CC1 Chester-le-St Durham v Somerset
CC1 Hove Sussex v Hampshire
CC1 Leeds Yorkshire v Middlesex
CC2 Bristol Glos v Lancashire
CC2 Canterbury Kent v Derbyshire
CC2 Leicester Leics v Surrey
CC2 Northampton Northants v Essex

Sun 7 June
T20 Worcester Worcs v Notts

Tue 9 June
LOI F Birmingham England v New Zealand

Thu 11 June
T20 F Northampton Northants v Derbyshire
T20 F Chelmsford Essex v Glos

Fri 12 June
LOI F The Oval England v New Zealand
T20 Chester-le-St Durham v Worcs
T20 Bristol Glos v Glamorgan
T20 F Canterbury Kent v Hampshire
T20 F Manchester Lancashire v Derbyshire
T20 Leicester Leics v Northants
T20 Taunton Somerset v Surrey
T20 F Hove Sussex v Essex
T20 F Birmingham Warwicks v Notts

Sat 13 June
T20 Cardiff Glamorgan v Somerset

331

Sun 14 – Wed 17 June

CC1	Taunton	Somerset v Notts
CC1	Worcester	Worcs v Warwicks
CC2	Chelmsford	Essex v Derbyshire
CC2	Manchester	Lancashire v Leics

Sun 14 June

LOI	Southampton	England v New Zealand
T20	Richmond	Middlesex v Glos
T20	Arundel	Sussex v Surrey
T20	Leeds	Yorkshire v Northants

Mon 15 – Thu 18 June

CC1	Arundel	Sussex v Durham
CC2	Guildford	Surrey v Glamorgan

Wed 17 June

LOI	Nottingham	England v New Zealand

Thu 18 June

T20 [F]	Derby	Derbyshire v Leics
T20 [F]	Canterbury	Kent v Essex
T20 [F]	Manchester	Lancashire v Worcs
T20 [F]	Lord's	Middlesex v Hampshire

Fri 19 June

T20 [F]	Chelmsford	Essex v Glamorgan
T20	Bristol	Glos v Somerset
T20 [F]	Southampton	Hampshire v Sussex
T20 [F]	Northampton	Northants v Lancashire
T20 [F]	The Oval	Surrey v Kent
T20 [F]	Birmingham	Warwicks v Leics
T20	Worcester	Worcs v Derbyshire
T20 [F]	Leeds	Yorkshire v Notts

Sat 20 – Tue 23 June

CC2	Northampton	Northants v Kent

Sat 20 June

LOI	Chester-le-St	England v New Zealand

Sun 21 – Wed 24 June

CC1	Southampton	Hampshire v Somerset
CC1	Uxbridge	Middlesex v Worcs
CC2	Derby	Derbyshire v Surrey
CC2	Bristol	Glos v Essex

Sun 21 June

T20	Birmingham	Warwicks v Yorkshire
T20	Cardiff	Glamorgan v Sussex

Mon 22 – Thu 25 June

CC1	Leeds	Yorkshire v Notts
CC2	Cardiff	Glamorgan v Leics

Tue 23 June

IT20 [F]	Manchester	England v New Zealand

Thu 25 – Sun 28 June

FCF	Canterbury	Kent v Australians

Thu 25 June

T20	Chester-le-St	Durham v Lancashire

Fri 26 June

T20	Derby	Derbyshire v Notts
T20 [F]	Chelmsford	Essex v Hampshire
T20 [F]	Cardiff	Glamorgan v Surrey
T20	Bristol	Glos v Sussex
T20 [F]	Manchester	Lancashire v Warwicks
T20,	Leicester	Leics v Yorkshire
T20	Uxbridge	Middlesex v Somerset
T20	Worcester	Worcs v Northants

Sat 27 – Tue 30 June

CC2	The Oval	Surrey v Glos

Sat 27 June

T20	Lord's	Oxford U v Cambridge U
T20	Nottingham	Notts v Northants

Sun 28 June – Wed 1 July

CC1	Chester-le-St	Durham v Yorkshire
CC1	Lord's	Middlesex v Hampshire
CC1	Birmingham	Warwicks v Sussex

Sun 28 June

T20	Taunton	Somerset v Glamorgan

Mon 29 June – Thu 2 July

CC1	Nottingham	Notts v Worcs
CC2	Manchester	Lancashire v Northants

Tue 30 June – Fri 3 July

FCF	Cambridge	Cambridge U v Oxford U

Wed 1 – Sat 4 July

FCF	Chelmsford	Essex v Australians

Wed 1 July

T20 [F]	The Oval	Surrey v Glos

Thu 2 July

T20 [F]	Lord's	Middlesex v Sussex

Fri 3 July

T20	Chester-le-St	Durham v Leics
T20 [F]	Southampton	Hampshire v Glamorgan
T20 [F]	Manchester	Lancashire v Yorkshire
T20 [F]	Nottingham	Notts v Worcs
T20	Taunton	Somerset v Glos
T20 [F]	The Oval	Surrey v Middlesex
T20 [F]	Hove	Sussex v Kent
T20 [F]	Birmingham	Warwicks v Derbyshire

Sat 4 July

T20	Leicester	Leics v Warwicks

Sun 5 – Wed 8 July

CC1	Nottingham	Notts v Middlesex
CC1	Taunton	Somerset v Sussex

CC1	Birmingham	Warwicks v Yorkshire
CC2	Leicester	Leics v Kent

Sun 5 July

T20	Chesterfield	Derbyshire v Northants
T20	Worcester	Worcs v Durham

Mon 6 – Thu 9 July

CC1	Worcester	Worcs v Hampshire
CC2	Chesterfield	Derbyshire v Glamorgan
CC2	Manchester	Lancashire v Essex

Wed 8 – Sun 12 July

TM1	Cardiff	ENGLAND v AUSTRALIA

Wed 8 – Sat 11 July

CC2	Cheltenham	Glos v Northants

Fri 10 July

T20 [F]	Southampton	Hampshire v Surrey
T20 [F]	Canterbury	Kent v Somerset
T20	Leicester	Leics v Lancashire
T20	Richmond	Middlesex v Essex
T20 [F]	Nottingham	Notts v Derbyshire
T20 [F]	Hove	Sussex v Glamorgan
T20	Worcester	Worcs v Warwicks
T20 [F]	Leeds	Yorkshire v Durham

Sat 11 – Tue 14 July

CC1	Northwood	Middlesex v Somerset

Sun 12 – Wed 15 July

CC1	Chester-le-St	Durham v Warwicks
CC2	Chelmsford	Essex v Glamorgan

Sun 12 July

T20	Chesterfield	Derbyshire v Yorkshire
T20	Cheltenham	Glos v Kent
T20	Northampton	Northants v Leics

Mon 13 – Thu 16 July

CC2	The Oval	Surrey v Kent

Tue 14 July

T20	Cheltenham	Glos v Hampshire
T20 [F]	Leeds	Yorkshire v Worcs

Wed 15 – Sat 18 July

CC2	Cheltenham	Glos v Leics

Wed 15 July

T20 [F]	Manchester	Lancashire v Notts

Thu 16 – Mon 20 July

TM2	Lord's	ENGLAND v AUSTRALIA

Fri 17 July

T20 [F]	Derby	Derbyshire v Worcs
T20	Chester-le-St	Durham v Notts
T20 [F]	Chelmsford	Essex v Middlesex
T20	Tunbridge W	Kent v Glamorgan

T20 [F]	Northampton	Northants v Yorkshire
T20 [F]	The Oval	Surrey v Somerset
T20 [F]	Hove	Sussex v Hampshire
T20 [F]	Birmingham	Warwicks v Lancashire

Sat 18 – Tue 21 July

CC1	Birmingham	Warwicks v Somerset
CC2	Northampton	Northants v Derbyshire

Sun 19 – Wed 22 July

CC1	Southampton	Hampshire v Durham
CC1	Horsham	Sussex v Notts
CC1	Scarborough	Yorkshire v Worcs
CC2	Colwyn Bay	Glamorgan v Lancashire
CC2	Tunbridge W	Kent v Essex

Wed 22 July

T20 [F]	Birmingham	Warwicks v Northants

Thu 23 – Sat 25 July

FCF	Derby	Derbyshire v Australians

Thu 23 July

T20 [F]	Southampton	Hampshire v Somerset
T20 [F]	Lord's	Middlesex v Surrey

Fri 24 July

T20 [F]	Chelmsford	Essex v Kent
T20 [F]	Cardiff	Glamorgan v Glos
T20	Leicester	Leics v Notts
T20 [F]	Northampton	Northants v Durham
T20	Taunton	Somerset v Middlesex
T20 [F]	The Oval	Surrey v Sussex
T20	Worcester	Worcs v Lancashire
T20 [F]	Leeds	Yorkshire v Warwicks

Sat 25 July

50L	Northampton	Northants v Durham
50L	Welbeck Coll	Notts v Warwicks

Sun 26 July

50L	Tunbridge W	Kent v Essex
50L	Leicester	Leics v Surrey
50L	Lord's	Middlesex v Warwicks
50L	Welbeck Coll	Notts v Glamorgan
50L	Taunton	Somerset v Derbyshire
50L	Horsham	Sussex v Lancashire
50L	Scarborough	Yorkshire v Glos

Mon 27 July

50L [F]	Derby	Derbyshire v Yorkshire
50L	Chester-le-St	Durham v Worcs
50L [F]	Chelmsford	Essex v Lancashire
50L [F]	Southampton	Hampshire v Sussex
50L [F]	The Oval	Surrey v Northants

Tue 28 July

50L [F]	Cardiff	Glamorgan v Kent

Wed 29 July – Sun 2 August
TM3 Birmingham ENGLAND v AUSTRALIA

Wed 29 July
50L F	Chelmsford	Essex v Warwicks
50L	Bristol	Glos v Derbyshire
50L	Blackpool	Lancashire v Middlesex
50L F	Northampton	Northants v Leics
50L	Taunton	Somerset v Durham
50L	The Oval	Surrey v Yorkshire

Thu 30 July
50L F	Canterbury	Kent v Hampshire
50L F	Hove	Sussex v Notts
50L	Worcester	Worcs v Yorkshire

Fri 31 July
50L F	Derby	Derbyshire v Northants
50L	Chester-le-St	Durham v Surrey
50L F	Cardiff	Glamorgan v Essex
50L	Leicester	Leics v Glos
50L	Radlett	Middlesex v Kent
50L	Taunton	Somerset v Worcs

Sat 1 August
| 50L | Southampton | Hampshire v Middlesex |

Sun 2 August
50L	Chester-le-St	Durham v Yorkshire
50L	Chelmsford	Essex v Notts
50L	Cardiff	Glamorgan v Hampshire
50L	Bristol	Glos v Somerset
50L	Canterbury	Kent v Sussex
50L	Manchester	Lancashire v Warwicks
50L	Guildford	Surrey v Derbyshire
50L	Worcester	Worcs v Northants

Mon 3 August
50L F	Northampton	Northants v Somerset
50L F	Hove	Sussex v Middlesex
50L F	Birmingham	Warwicks v Glamorgan
50L	Leeds	Yorkshire v Leics

Tue 4 – Fri 7 August
CC2 Canterbury Kent v Northants

Tue 4 August
50L F	Derby	Derbyshire v Leics
50L	Bristol	Glos v Durham
50L F	Southampton	Hampshire v Essex
50L	Liverpool	Lancashire v Notts
50L F	The Oval	Surrey v Worcs

Wed 5 August
50L	Colchester	Essex v Middlesex
50L	Swansea	Glamorgan v Sussex
50L F	Birmingham	Warwicks v Hampshire
50L	Worcester	Worcs v Glos
50L	Scarborough	Yorkshire v Somerset

Thu 6 – Mon 10 August
TM4 Nottingham ENGLAND v AUSTRALIA

Thu 6 – Sun 9 August
CC2 Swansea Glamorgan v Glos

Thu 6 August
| 50L | Leicester | Leics v Durham |
| 50L | Lord's | Middlesex v Notts |

Fri 7 – Mon 10 August
CC1	Southampton	Hampshire v Warwicks
CC1	Lord's	Middlesex v Sussex
CC1	Worcester	Worcs v Notts
CC1	Scarborough	Yorkshire v Durham
CC2	Colchester	Essex v Surrey
CC2	Leicester	Leics v Derbyshire

Sat 8 August
| 50L | Canterbury | Kent v Lancashire |

Wed 12 August
| T20 F | tbc | Quarter-final 1 |

Thu 13 August
| T20 F | tbc | Quarter-final 2 |

Fri 14 – Sun 16 August
FCF Northampton Northants v Australians

Fri 14 August
| T20 F | tbc | Quarter-final 3 |

Sat 15 August
| T20 | tbc | Quarter-final 4 |

Mon 17 August
50L	Chester-le-St	Durham v Derbyshire
50L F	Southampton	Hampshire v Lancashire
50L	Lord's	Middlesex v Glamorgan
50L	Northampton	Northants v Glos
50L F	Nottingham	Notts v Kent
50L	Taunton	Somerset v Surrey
50L	Rugby S	Warwicks v Sussex
50L	Worcester	Worcs v Leics

Tue 18 August
50L	Derby	Derbyshire v Worcs
50L	Bristol	Glos v Surrey
50L	Leicester	Leics v Somerset
50L	Leeds	Yorkshire v Northants

Wed 19 August
50L F	Manchester	Lancashire v Glamorgan
50L F	Nottingham	Notts v Hampshire
50L F	Hove	Sussex v Essex
50L F	Birmingham	Warwicks v Kent

Thu 20 – Mon 24 August
TM5 The Oval ENGLAND v AUSTRALIA

Fri 21 – Mon 24 August

CC1	Chester-le-St	Durham v Middlesex
CC1	Nottingham	Notts v Warwicks
CC1	Taunton	Somerset v Worcs
CC1	Hove	Sussex v Yorkshire
CC2	Derby	Derbyshire v Kent
CC2	Bristol	Glos v Surrey
CC2	Manchester	Lancashire v Glamorgan
CC2	Northampton	Northants v Leics

Tue 25 August

| 50L [F] | tbc | Quarter-final 1 & 2 |

Wed 26 August

| 50L | tbc | Quarter-final 3 |

Thu 27 August

| LOI | Belfast | **Ireland v Australia** |
| 50L [F] | tbc | Quarter-final 4 |

Sat 29 August

| T20 [F] | Birmingham | Semi-finals and FINAL |

Mon 31 August

| IT20 | Cardiff | **England v Australia** |

Tue 1 – Fri 4 September

CC1	Chester-le-St	Durham v Hampshire
CC1	Birmingham	Warwicks v Middlesex
CC1	Worcester	Worcs v Sussex
CC1	Leeds	Yorkshire v Somerset
CC2	Chelmsford	Essex v Northants
CC2	Canterbury	Kent v Lancashire
CC2	Leicester	Leics v Glos
CC2	The Oval	Surrey v Derbyshire

Thu 3 September

| LOI [F] | Southampton | **England v Australia** |

Sat 5 September

| LOI | Lord's | **England v Australia** |

Sun 6 September

| 50L | tbc | Semi-final 1 |

Mon 7 September

| 50L [F] | tbc | Semi-final 2 |

Tue 8 September

| LOI [F] | Manchester | **England v Australia** |

Wed 9 – Sat 12 September

CC1	Lord's	Middlesex v Yorkshire
CC1	Nottingham	Notts v Durham
CC1	Taunton	Somerset v Hampshire
CC2	Derby	Derbyshire v Essex
CC2	Cardiff	Glamorgan v Kent

Fri 11 September

| LOI | Leeds | **England v Australia** |

Sun 13 September

| LOI | Manchester | **England v Australia** |

Mon 14 – Thu 17 September

CC1	Chester-le-St	Durham v Worcs
CC1	Southampton	Hampshire v Yorkshire
CC1	Hove	Sussex v Somerset
CC1	Birmingham	Warwicks v Notts
CC2	Canterbury	Kent v Glos
CC2	Manchester	Lancashire v Surrey
CC2	Leicester	Leics v Essex
CC2	Northampton	Northants v Glamorgan

Sat 19 September

| 50L | Lord's | FINAL |

Tue 22 – Fri 25 September

CC1	Nottingham	Notts v Hampshire
CC1	Taunton	Somerset v Warwicks
CC1	Worcester	Worcs v Middlesex
CC1	Leeds	Yorkshire v Sussex
CC2	Derby	Derbyshire v Leics
CC2	Chelmsford	Essex v Lancashire
CC2	Bristol	Glos v Glamorgan
CC2	The Oval	Surrey v Northants

First published in 2015
by HEADLINE PUBLISHING GROUP

Front cover photograph Joe Root (England and Yorkshire)
© REUTERS/Philip Brown/Action Images

Back cover photograph Michael Clarke (Australia)
© Scott Barbour/Getty Images Sport

1

Cataloguing in Publication Data is available from the British Library

ISBN 978 1 4722 1218 4

Typeset in Times by
Letterpart Limited, Caterham on the Hill, Surrey

Printed and bound in Great Britain by
Clays Ltd St Ives plc

HEADLINE PUBLISHING GROUP
An Hachette UK Company
338 Euston Road
London NW1 3BH

www.headline.co.uk
www.hachette.co.uk